Human Sexuality in Nursing Process

Edited by

Elizabeth M. Lion, R.N., M.S.Hyg.P.H.N.

Associate Professor
Indiana University School of Nursing
Indianapolis, Indiana

175 YEARS OF PUBLISHING

1807 1982

A WILEY MEDICAL PUBLICATION
JOHN WILEY & SONS
New York · Chichester · Brisbane · Toronto · Singapore

Production Editor: Rosalind Straley
Cover design: Wanda Lubelska

Chapter Opening Photo Credits:
Chapters 1, 4, 7, 9, 10, 12, and 15: Courtesy of Suzanne Coles-Ketcham and Beverly Kelly.
Chapters 2, 3, 5, 8, 11, 13, and 14: Courtesy of Suzanne Coles-Ketcham.
Chapter 6: Courtesy of Suzanne Coles-Ketcham and Ric Cradick.
Chapters 16 and 17: Courtesy of Jeffrey Hamish.

Many of the interventions used in the nursing process sections throughout the book are from
Nursing Diagnosis and Intervention in Nursing Practice by Claire Campbell (John Wiley &
Sons, Inc., 1978). Copyright © 1978 by Claire Campbell. Used with permission.

Library of Congress Cataloging in Publication Data:

Main entry under title:

Human sexuality in nursing process.

  (A Wiley medical publication)
  Includes index.
  1. Sex. 2. Nursing. 3. Sexual disorders—Nursing. 4. Sick—Sexual behavior.
I. Lion, Elizabeth M. II. Series. [DNLM: 1. Sex—Nursing texts. 2. Sex behavior—
Nursing texts. 3. Sex education—Nursing texts. WY 150 H918]
RT87.S49H85   613.9′5′024613   81-16201
ISBN 0-471-03869-5   AACR2

Printed in the United States of America

10 9 8 7 6 5 4 3 2 1

To:
My family, who nourish me,
My friends, who support me,
My colleagues, from whom I learn,
My students, who teach me, and
My clients, with whom I grow.

E.M.L.

Contributors

Marguerite Supko Casey, R.N., M.S.N.
Assistant Professor
Indiana University School of Nursing
Indianapolis, Indiana

Jane M. Egan, R.N., M.S.N.
Clinical Nurse Specialist, Rehabilitation
SCI Nurse Practitioner
Veterans Administration Hospital
Indianapolis, Indiana

Alice A. Fleming, M.S.Ed., Ed.S.
Formerly of Indiana University School of Education,
    Counseling and Guidance
Bloomington, Indiana

Marianna B. Heister, R.N., P.N.A., M.Ed.
Pediatric Nurse Practitioner
Bloomington, Indiana

Elizabeth M. Lion, R.N., M.S.Hyg.P.H.N.
Associate Professor
Indiana University School of Nursing
Indianapolis, Indiana

Valerie Jackson Markley, R.N., M.S.N.
Assistant Professor
Indiana University School of Nursing
Indianapolis, Indiana

Caroline M. Myer, R.N., M.S.
Assistant Professor
Indiana University School of Nursing
Indianapolis, Indiana

Josephine Novo Osborne, R.N., M.S.N.
Assistant Professor
Indiana University School of Nursing
Indianapolis, Indiana

Roselle Vlcek Partridge, R.N., M.S.
Assistant Professor
Indiana University School of Nursing
Indianapolis, Indiana

Collin C. Schwoyer, Ed.D.
Formerly of Indiana University School of Education,
    Adult Education
Bloomington, Indiana

Penelope L. Wadleigh, R.N., M.S.
Head Nurse
Westview Osteopathic Hospital
Indianapolis, Indiana

Preface

Students and practitioners of nursing have the responsibility to understand, educate, and counsel about human sexuality. The purpose of this book is to integrate sexual health into total health. The intent is to enable the nurse to examine the sexual self, develop a human sexuality knowledge base, sensitize and refine communication skills, and place sexual health care within the nursing process.

This book provides structured learning experiences about sexual health care for nurses as health professionals. Each chapter presents and connects affective learning, cognitive knowledge, and communication skills needed to assess, diagnose, plan, implement, and evaluate sexual health care as part of total health care.

Each chapter begins with a values clarification exercise. The goal of these exercises is to facilitate self-understanding through the examination of the sexual self. The exercises are designed to provide students and faculty with a variety of individual and group discussion activities that will enable them to acknowledge their feelings and thoughts, audit their attitudes and beliefs, consider their convictions and behaviors, and recognize the content and power of their sexual value systems. Learning that includes struggling with one's own sexuality and confronting the sexuality of others is growth producing. The acceptance of one's own sexuality and the sexuality of others as a positive and real part of oneself and others is essential to effective nurse-client interaction about sexual health care.

In this book, sex and sexuality are presented as behaviors that are molded and influenced by physiosexual and psychosocial experiences. Each chapter presents a sexual health knowledge base for the development of attitudes and behaviors based on factual and current information about human sexuality. When the nurse's attitudes and behaviors are based on knowledge, as opposed to myths and misconceptions, the rationale for nursing process addresses the sexual health needs of the client, is supported by theory and reasoning, and can facilitate change.

Each chapter deals with the pivotal skill of communication. In sexual health care, the initial stages of nurse-client interaction are crucial, and the collection of subjective or objective data may be facilitated or hindered by the words used, attitudes expressed, and behaviors demonstrated by the nurse. Nurses who are comfortable with their own sexuality and the sexuality of others, who have a sexual health knowledge base, and who cultivate perceptive communication skills effectively integrate sexuality into nursing process.

The development of a vocabulary about sexuality and sexual health care is significant and important to all the steps of the nursing process. In this book, the five principles of talking about sex and sexuality with clients are presented and explained.

Each chapter ends with a nursing process that demonstrates the use of affective, cognitive, and communication knowledge and skills in nurse-client interactions about sexual health care. The nursing process demonstrates also how the nurse who is prepared in sexual health care can make a positive difference in the ability of clients to meet their sexual health care needs.

In this book, the role of the nurse in sexual health care is that of educator-counselor. As educator, the nurse provides reliable information that removes or reduces uncertainties about present or potential problems and enables clients to make responsible decisions about sex and sexuality for themselves and in their relationships with others. As counselor, the nurse listens attentively, encourages expression of feelings, demonstrates acceptance, and provides support as clients sift through and sort their sexual concerns, expectations, and anxieties. The nurse's goal is to assist clients as they seek their own solutions of their own problems using their own sexual value systems.

E.M.L.

Acknowledgments

I acknowledge the many students, colleagues, and clients whose direct and indirect association and collaboration brought this book into being.

As editor, I acknowledge the contributors who gave their knowledge, shared their skills, and invested their time and energy in the preparation of this book.

Sincere appreciation is extended to former nursing editor Cathy Somer, who provided the initial impetus, and to Linda Turner, assistant editor, whose sustained efforts and sensitive editing moved the book toward completion.

Special acknowledgment is made to Jeanne Pontious, Martha Sparks, Susie Cerkamis, and Anna Mecca for their continued encouragement and interest; to Marilyn Major for her significant support and consultation; and to Ann J. Van Camp and Joan Scherer Brewer for their consistently effective guidance and counsel in library work.

Special thanks to Judy Pett Kinzie and Cindy Holmes for their expert secretarial and proofreading skills.

I am deeply grateful to my sister, Margaret E. Meehan, who persistently urged endurance, and to my daughter, Margaret Lion, who laughed when it was needed most.

E.M.L.

Contents

Human Sexuality
in Nursing Process

Introduction:
Chapter Format

Elizabeth M. Lion

Each of the chapters in this book has values clarification exercises, illustrations, behavioral objectives, content, and an example of a nursing process involving sexual health care.

VALUES CLARIFICATION EXERCISES

The study of human sexuality involves cognitive and affective learning. Values clarification deals with affective learning and is based on the recognition that affective teaching–learning about sexuality and sexual issues is as important as cognitive teaching–learning. The goal of values clarification is to facilitate self-understanding through the examination of the sexual self. The plan is to provide students and faculty with a variety of individual and group exercises and discussion activities that will enable them to acknowledge their feelings and thoughts, examine their attitudes and beliefs, consider their convictions and behaviors, and clarify the content and power of their sexual value system. Learning that includes reflecting on and taking stock of one's own knowledge, attitudes, beliefs, and values with another person and other people is personally and professionally growth producing. Often, understanding the experiences and confronting the principles and beliefs that determine behavior in other people help one to understand one's own values and to see how they influence decisions, judgments, and behavior. The process of values clarification has the additional benefit of serving as a guide to the nurse in assessing client values and of providing direction for nursing intervention.

The individual exercises can be accomplished before discussion period begins, or time can be allowed before selected group activities begin. The activities are best held in a room large enough to permit small-group (4, 6, or 8 persons) discussion before the larger class group interacts. The supplies or equipment needed are paper, pencils, blackboard and chalk, or an easel with butcher paper and pen markers.

ILLUSTRATIONS

The illustrations are a visual means of facilitating self-understanding through the examination of the sexual self. The illustrations in this book show people being and relating. They were selected to encourage students and faculty to become aware of and examine the thoughts and feeling elicited. The intent is to provide a way of ackowledging and dealing with discomfort in ourselves and others. Feelings, thoughts, and behavior are related. Recognition of how feelings affect behavior enables nurses to assume responsibility for their behavior. They can select the behaviors that contribute to the dignity and worth of their clients and facilitate positive nurse–client interactions in assessing and planning for sexual health care.

As you encounter the illustrations, react and respond to these questions:

What do I see?
What feelings do I have? (Pleasure, fear, joy, jealousy, etc.)
What are my thoughts?
What is the source of these feelings and thoughts? (Parental teaching, religious standards, peer information, etc.)
How is my behavior affected by these feelings and thoughts?
Have I made any judgments? Drawn any conclusions? Come to a decision?
How could my behavior affect a nurse–client interaction?

Share your reactions and responses with others. Note the similarities and discuss the differences. Discuss how feelings and thoughts affect behavior. Identify behaviors that could contribute to the self-esteem of clients and to positive nurse–client interaction involving sexual health care.

BEHAVIORAL OBJECTIVES

Each chapter has a list of behavioral objectives. They are statements of instructional intent. Each objective delineates and describes behavior the learner is expected to exhibit at the completion of the teaching–learning experience structured within the chapter. Behavioral objectives offer students an opportunity to direct their own learning and teachers an opportunity to select priorities for effective teaching.

CONTENT

The content portion of each chapter is concerned with cognitive learning—the building of a knowledge base about human sexuality. What is considered basic, essential, current, and relevant information for each topic has been selected and presented. What is known and understood through agreement, custom, and practice, what has been learned, and what is yet to be learned through study and inquiry are included. A growing and expanding sexuality knowledge base is required for the nurse to interact competently and responsibly with a client who has questions and concerns about human sexuality.

NURSING PROCESS

The nursing process is the means through which the nurse provides sexual health care for clients—individuals, groups, families, or communities. The nursing process is a tool for effecting change. Assessing, diagnosing, planning, implementing, and evaluating make up a logical process based on information, knowledge, and experience. Carrying out this process generates new patterns of thought and behavior that aid in the formulation of alternative courses of action. The nursing process at the end of each chapter is a demonstration of how nurses can make a positive difference in the ability of clients to meet their sexual health-care needs.

1. Human Sexuality: A Concept Basic to Nursing

Elizabeth M. Lion

VALUES CLARIFICATION EXERCISE

Exercise A

In our society it is not unusual for a person to feel discomfort and anxiety when sex and sexuality are discussed. As a child you may have learned that society placed restrictions and prohibitions on the discussion of sex and sexuality. It might be helpful, as you begin your study of human sexuality, to explore your own levels of comfort and discomfort when sexual phenomena are being discussed. This exercise is designed to help you and your study group discover some of the circumstances that hinder and facilitate discussion of sex and sexuality.

Read, consider, and complete the following sentences. The purpose is to help you remember some of the circumstances and feelings involved in your experiences with the discussion of sex and sexuality.

1. As a child, I remember sex being talked about when———.
2. The first question I remember asking about sex was———.
3. In high school, my teachers discussed sex when———.
4. When my mother told me about sex I———.
5. What my father said about sex was———.
6. My friends explained that sex was———.
7. My religion taught me that sex was———.
8. My best discussions about sex and sexuality happen when———.
9. I am most comfortable with the topic of sex when———.
10. I am most uncomfortable with the topic of sex when———.
11. When a child asks me about sex now, I———.

Divide into groups of four to six persons. Share your answers with the group. Were there any experiences that were common to most of the group members? What circumstances hindered the discussion of sex? What circumstances facilitated the discussion of sex? In general, what were the individual and social messages the members of the group received about the discussion of sex and sexuality?

Select a recorder. Divide a large sheet of paper in half. On the left hand side, list the circumstances and the associated feelings that hinder the discussion of sex; on the right hand side, list the circumstances and associated feelings that facilitate the discussion of sex. Post the list.

After all the participants have read the lists and returned to their seats, the participant to the left of the recorder in each group should read the lists out loud. Members of the group can make additional comments and all participants can ask for clarification.

A recorder from one of the groups should underline, in each of the columns, the two to three circumstances and feelings that appeared most frequently. All of the participants should discuss what generalizations might be made or conclusions drawn about the circumstances and feelings that hinder a discussion of sex and sexuality. Also discuss circumstances and feelings that facilitate the discussion of sex and sexuality.

Exercise B

In our society, it is not unusual to find that such words as *sexuality, sex,* and *sexy* have different meanings and arouse different emotions in different people. It might be helpful to learn and understand how you and other members of your study group define, describe and feel about the words and phrases in this exercise.

Read, respond, and react to the following statements and questions. Write your answers and note your initial feelings. Save your answers. When you have read the chapter, look at your answers and consider whether or how you would change your answers.

1. What do the words *human sexuality* and *human sex* mean to you? How are the words the same and how are they different? Does the meaning of words change when the word *human* is omitted and you read just *sexuality* and *sex*?
2. What do the words a *sexual being* and *sexy person* mean to you? Describe a sexual being. Describe a sexy man, a sexy woman, a sexy person.
3. How would you describe a *sexually healthy person*? What kinds of behavior would you expect to observe in a sexually healthy person?
4. What does the term *sexual health* mean to you? Have you ever been involved in planning for sexual health? Give an example of a nurse–client situation that you think involves sexual health.

Discuss your answers and share your feelings with another person and in a group. During the discussion, consider the following questions: What are the similarities in the answers? Are there any significant differences? Are the feelings shared similar in nature and intensity?

BEHAVIORAL OBJECTIVES

After completing this chapter, you will be able to

- Discuss the concept of human sexuality.
- Define sexual health care.
- Discuss the three elements of sexual health care.
- Describe the characteristics of sexually healthy people.
- Justify the three objectives of education for sexual health care.
- Illustrate the role of the nurse in sexual health care.

HUMAN SEXUALITY AND HEALTH PROFESSIONALS

The last two decades have brought remarkable advances in our knowledge of human sexuality and an escalation of public interest in sexuality. Self-instruction books are on bestseller lists. Major films with sexual themes are produced and widely attended. Premarital sex, orgasm, impotency, homosexuality, teenage pregnancy, male and female sexual fantasies, sex reassignment, and incest are just some of the topics presented on television documentaries and talk shows.

Along with the escalation in public interest has come an escalation in public demands for reliable information about sexual concerns and issues. Health professionals—counselors, nurses, physicians, psychologists, and social workers—are the group from which information and counseling about sexual health are primarily expected.

This public expectation has compelled nurses to prepare themselves to place human sexuality within the nursing process. By tradition and education the focus of nursing is on the client as a whole person. This makes the nurse an appropriate person to deal with the sexual aspects of the client's health concerns.

THE CONCEPT OF SEXUALITY

Definitions and descriptions of the concepts of human sexuality are complex and elusive. Sexuality is described as an important dimension of being a person, a powerful and purposeful aspect of human nature, and a quality of being human (Fonseca, 1970). It is also described as a celebration of living, a voyage into one's body, mind, and spirit that has a revivifying effect that adds to the enjoyment of many other areas of life as well (Adams, 1976; Otto, 1971).

Sexuality is present from birth through death. It is an inseparable part of building an identity, of the maturational process of learning to be a person, and of the acceptance of self at all levels (Sutterley & Donnelly, 1973). Sexuality includes a person's cognitive, affective, and psychomotor abilities and values. It is an integration of idea, emotion, and act, and it is inherent in the process of self-actualization (Otto, 1971; Stephens, 1970).

Sexuality involves physical release of sexual tensions and the giving and receiving of sensual pleasure, and it is part of the desire for intimacy and closeness (Miller, 1975). Sexuality is involved in all human relationships. It is involved when humans express the subtle feelings of tenderness and the intense feelings of passion. It is present in the binding together of two people for a long or short period of time, as well as the merging with another being to reach ecstatic heights and spiritual dimensions (Miller, 1975).

The concept of sexuality

refers to the totality of being a person. It includes all of those aspects of the human being that relate specifically to being boy or girl, woman or man, and is an entity subject to life-long dynamic change. Sexuality reflects our human character, not solely our genital nature. As a function of the total personality it is concerned with the biological, psychological, sociological, spiritual, and cultural variables of life which, by their effects on personality development and interpersonal relations, can in turn affect social structure. [SIECUS, 1980, p. 8]

THE CONCEPT OF SEXUAL HEALTH

Early in 1974, a task force of the World Organization met to discuss education and treatment in human sexuality and the training of health professionals for sexual health care. The report defines sexual health care as "the integration of the somatic, emotional, intellectual, and social aspects of sexual being, in ways that are positively enriching and that enhance personality, communication, and love" (WHO, 1975, p. 6).

The definition recognizes the biological, psychological, sociocultural, and spiritual dimensions of sexual health. It addresses itself to the continuity and wholeness of a person, the incorporation of sexual health and total health, and the integration of sex and love as an optimum goal. Definitions contain value-laden terms subject to different interpretations. If love and communication are interpreted as an agreeable consistency of thoughts and feelings and a matching of expectations and behaviors, the definition becomes broad enough to include persons for whom sexual relationships do not include physical love but do include caring, respect, consideration, and individual responsibility for pleasure.

The concept of sexual health has three basic and interrelated elements. The first is the capacity to enjoy and control sexual and reproductive behavior in accord with social and personal ethics. The second is freedom from fear, shame, guilt, misconceptions, and other psychological factors that inhibit sexual response and impair sexual relationships. The third is freedom from organic disorders, diseases, and deficiencies that may interfere with either sexual or reproductive functions or both (WHO, 1975).

The concept of sexual health implies a positive and holistic approach to human sexuality. This concept views the right to sexual information and pleasure as fundamental and sees the purpose of sexual health care as the enhancement of life and personal relationships.

CHARACTERISTICS OF SEXUALLY HEALTHY PEOPLE

The characteristics identified as typifying sexually healthy people should fit people at various ages and stages of life, people involved in varied life styles, people living in other cultures, and the androgynous, celibate, transsexual, mentally retarded, and physically disabled. Although it is difficult to arrive at universally acceptable and applicable traits, sexually healthy people have certain characteristics.

Sexually healthy people have a positive *body image*—their mental–emotional picture of themselves being, functioning, and relating is approved, appreciated, and affirmed. Sexual organs and bodily functions are accepted as normal and natural. Sexually healthy people enjoy themselves and their bodies, not because their bodies are beautiful or whole, but because they function—think, cough, sleep, sweat, eat, excrete, and feel (Read, 1979). For sexually healthy people, sex is a function of sexuality and not an objective to be gained. Sex is not something one does but rather an expression of oneself through the body. Sex is a component of life-style and of total interpersonal relationships.

Sexually healthy people have cognitive knowledge about human sexuality. The knowledge is factual and free from myths and misconceptions, and it grows and changes as information becomes available and is processed. Sexually healthy people are able to differentiate between what they know and what they believe about sexuality; they are able to make discoveries about their own sexuality and the sexuality of others and maintain their balance (Read, 1979).

Sexually healthy people experience a congruence with the biologic manifestations of male or female, the psychosexual identity of boy or girl, man or woman, and society's expectations of sex-role behaviors (Maddock, 1975). Sexually healthy people act in ways consistent with their own concept of who they are, and experience harmony in their physiological, psychological, and sociological lives.

Sexually healthy people are aware of and appreciate their own feelings and attitudes about sexuality. They have the physical and psychosexual capacity to initiate and respond to erotic stimuli in ways that enhance themselves and others (Maddock, 1975). They are comfortable with a range of sexual behavior and life-styles in which they and others engage and accept individual responsibility for pleasure and reproduction (Maddock, 1975).

Sexually healthy people have the ability to create effective interpersonal relationships with members of both sexes, in which length, quality, meaning, intensity, and pleasures are delineated by the people involved. They prize the essential open-endedness of a relationship that allows for change, adventure, growth, and expression of sexuality in sharing, enhancing, respectful, and responsible ways.

Sexually healthy people have a developing and usable value system that enables them to measure the merits to be gained against the hazards to be faced and encourages acceptance of mistakes without blame for others or excuses for self. A developing and usable value system evolves by means of physical, mental, and emotional growth, and it is of service as the person weathers and endures the inevitable stresses, strains, pleasures, and joys of living.

EDUCATION FOR SEXUAL HEALTH CARE

Knowledge of genital anatomy alone does not prepare the nurse to help an adolescent manage sexual feelings and desires. Knowledge of surgical dressing techniques for mastectomy does not prepare the nurse to help a woman whose breast has been removed cope with an altered body image. Knowledge of the pathogenesis of diabetes does not prepare the nurse to help a middle-aged man who is panicky about the loss of sexual functioning.

Nurse educators have the responsibility to improve the quality of nursing practice by including human sexuality content in their offerings. Core content about human sexuality must be identified and built into curricula, programs, and courses in the same manner as other concepts basic to nursing. The selecting and placing of sexual health-care concepts within the nursing process of laboratory experiences involves a planned series of actions. Laboratory objectives and evaluations, guides for nursing assessment, nursing-care plans, and recording must be reviewed and revised to include sexual health care (Hanson, 1978). Along with content presentation and laboratory experience, students need to participate in the affective learning involved in planned and scheduled one- to three-day sexual-attitude assessment (Hanson, 1978). Elective courses that allow further study of and experience with selected aspects of sexual health care can be structured for those students who are interested in this aspect of nursing care. An interdisciplinary approach facilitating an understanding and appreciation of the actual and potential contributions of other health professionals can be used.

The three objectives in educating nurses in sexual health care involve attitude, knowledge, and skills (Mims, 1975; WHO, 1975). The first objective is to examine the sexual self. Because sexuality entails emotionally laden attitudes and powerful value systems, affective learning must be connected to cognitive learning. Examining the sexual self involves the hard work of taking stock of one's own sexuality and confronting the sexuality of others. The process of self-examination enables the nurse to become aware of and recognize intensity, confront content, determine meaning, and accept his or her own feelings, thoughts, behaviors, and values about sexuality. The process of sharing feelings, thoughts, opinions, and attitudes in group discussions is vital to growth. Discussions provide practice, build a basis of understanding, and establish a pattern of process that enables nurses to interact with their peers and colleagues of both sexes and with clients in a manner that will be of lasting value in their interpersonal relationships throughout their lives (Calderwood, 1971). Examining the sexual self does not require changing personal values or behavior, but it does require developing a clear concept of their content and power. The work of coming to grips with one's own sexuality is the beginning of and gives impetus to becoming aware of and being comfortable with a wide range of variations in the sexual values and behavior of others. Acceptance of the sexuality of others is essential for the care of clients whose sexual life-styles are different from those of the nurse.

Full acceptance of one's sexuality and the sexuality of others means approving the negative as well as the positive aspects of sexuality. Only by acknowledging both the negative and the positive can one be comfortable with and accept sexuality as a normal and integral part of every person's life. An attitude of acceptance of sexuality as a positive and real part of oneself and others enables effective nurse–client interaction about sexuality.

To develop a sexual-health knowledge base is the second objective. The nurse needs to have accurate and scientific knowledge about sexual anatomy, psychosexual development throughout the life span, sexual functioning, response, and reproduction, sexual health and gender issues, implications of the cultural, religious, ethical, and legal views of sexual health, and the range of human sexual expression and behaviors. The more knowledge nurses have of sexuality and sexual health, the more positive will be their attitudes and the more comfortable and competent they will be in nurse–client interactions with sexual content (Payne, 1976).

A sexual-health knowledge base is the foundation for the development of attitudes and behavior based on factual and current information rather than on myths or misconceptions. When attitudes and behaviors are based on knowledge as opposed to myths, nursing process is supported by reasoning and theory and addresses the individual sexual health-care needs of the client. Nursing process based on myth will perpetuate an unvarying pattern. Nursing process based on knowledge will be informative and usable and will facilitate change.

The pivotal skill in sexual health care is communication. Thus the third objective is to cultivate—to sensitize and to refine—communication skills. Nurses learn and practice communication skills in each nurse—client interactions. The social prohibition regarding the discussion of sex and sexuality make the giving and receiving of sexual data difficult, however. Sensitive and perceptive practice of communication skills in sexual health care requires the integration of cognitive and affective learning about sexuality (Mims & Swenson, 1980).

In sexual health care, the initial stages of nurse—client interaction are crucial and the data collected may not be as important as the words used and attitudes expressed in its collection. Planned teaching–learning opportunities are needed to cultivate sexual health-care communication skill. Role playing with students participating as client and nurse, teacher–student evaluation of audio tapes, and the use of programmed clients with videotapes are effective teaching strategies (Engel, Resnick, & Levine, 1976).

Nurses who are comfortable with their own sexuality and the sexuality of others, who have a sexual-health knowledge base, and who cultivate sensitive and perceptive communication skills can effectively integrate sexuality into the nursing process.

THE ROLE OF THE NURSE IN SEXUAL HEALTH CARE

In sexual health care, the roles of the nurse are educator and counselor. When the nurse deliberately and consciously responds to a client's need to know about the cognitive or affective aspects of sexuality, the nurse is an educator. Sexual-health knowledge and information are provided in such a way that the client not only will know but also will contribute to his or her sexual well-being (Narrow, 1979).

As an educator about sexuality, the nurse provides accurate information, clarifying personal attitudes and values, increasing comfort in discussing sexual topics, and increasing acceptance of sexual values and behaviors in self and others. The goal is to provide reliable information that will enable clients to make responsible decisions about sexuality for themselves and in their relationships with others.

The role of counselor is activated when clients need someone to whom they can express their feelings, someone who can offer understanding and support and who can provide reliable information and direction in the sifting and sorting of sexual concerns and anxieties. Using the nursing process, the nurse and client can uncover what has been, assess what is, move toward the resolution of doubts, and formulate alternatives for action.

In dealing with both personal and social issues of sexuality, the nurse is alert to the client's need to make up his or her own mind. The nurse does not offer personal experiences or beliefs as guidelines, and expresses personal feelings cautiously. The nurse avoids standard solutions to difficult problems and does not insist on conformity to a social norm. The nurse knows that the responsibility for decisions belongs to the client. The nurse recognizes that the goal of counseling is to guide clients to their own solutions of their own problems using their own sexual value systems (Wilson, 1974).

Referral to appropriate community resources is used when the client's sexual concerns, anxieties, and conflicts involve disorders and dysfunctions beyond the knowledge and skills of the nurse educator-counselor and require specialized care or sex therapy (see Chapter 8). The nurse is not a sex therapist. Therapists require specialized training after completion of their basic professional education, supervision in sex therapy, clinical work in an approved training program, and skills in both individual and marital therapy. When a referral for sex therapy is made, the nurse as educator-counselor can provide information about what sex therapy is and what it is not, what the therapist's preparation and qualifications are, and a list of therapists and clinics in the community. The nurse and the client may discuss why sexual counseling and therapy might be helpful, what kinds of results other people have obtained, and the amount of time counseling might involve.

The nurse is educated to view the whole client and knows that the client cannot be separated into biological, psychological, sociocultural, spiritual, and sexual components. The nurse educated in sexual health care is the member of the health team who can ensure that no part of the client is lost.

NURSING PROCESS

Client: Roberta Benson—at the conclusion of a physical examination for life insurance.

Nurse: Alice Matthews—reviewing the data collected during the physical examination.

Assessment

Subjective Data

"Jim, my husband, has taken up jogging seriously and has entered next
    month's marathon.
"He says we have to cut down on sex during these next couple of weeks of
    training, and cut it out altogether the week before the marathon
    because sex is too physically draining before big athletic events.
"I feel just awful to have lovemaking—you know, sexual intercourse—
    with me seem as using up or wasting his strength.
"Do you know anything about what he's saying?"

Objective Data

Age 25 years
Married, one child, age 2 years
First-grade teacher
Husband training for marathon
Restrictions on intercourse imposed by husband
Lowered self-esteem
Anger
Seeks current information about effect of intercourse on athletic perfor-
    mance

Nursing Diagnosis

Anger related to husband-imposed restrictions on intercourse
Lowered self-esteem related to husband-imposed restrictions on inter-
    course
Lack of knowledge about intercourse and athletic performance related to
    husband-imposed restrictions on intercourse

Planning

Express warmth and friendliness
Provide an atmosphere of acceptance

Encourage expression of feelings

Offer feedback of client's expressed feelings

Explain that the client's emotional response is appropriate and commonly experienced

Advise that significant persons express love and acceptance of one another

Advise against causing defensive responses about preparation for marathon in husband

Encourage expression of feelings about restriction of intercourse with husband

Explain the importance of offering emotional support to one another

Provide information about effect of intercourse on athletic performance (Psychologically the achievement of orgasm is rarely more demanding than most activities of daily living. Orgasm may bring relief of sexual tension with a feeling of relaxation and readiness for sleep, but a sense of weariness is more likely the result of improper eating, sleeping, and drinking and feelings of guilt. After a sexual experience, athletes should be able to perform at maximum ability if they are allowed a recuperation period of one to five minutes [McCary, 1977].)

Encourage mutual decision making

Indicate availability of further information and counseling.

Implementation

Initiate unhurried discussion of thoughts and feelings related to restrictions placed on intercourse

Share feelings of love and acceptance

Discuss current information about athletic performance not being diminished by sexual intercourse

Initiate mutual decision-making process about restrictions on sexual intercourse

Evaluation

Reports satisfactory communication.

Reports information about sexual intercourse and athletic performance useful for mutual decision-making.

Reports enhancement of relationship.

BIBLIOGRAPHY

Adams, G. Reorganizing the range of human sexual needs and behavior. *American Journal of Maternal and Child Nursing,* 1976, *1,* 166–169.

Calderwood, D. *About your sexuality: About the program.* Boston: Beacon Press, 1971.

Campbell, C. *Nursing diagnosis and intervention in nursing practice.* New York: Wiley, 1978.

Carrera, M. A., & Calderone, M. S. Training of health professionals in education for sexual health. *SIECUS Report,* 1976, *4,* 1–2.

Chilgren, R. A., & Briggs, M. M. On being explicit: Sex education for professionals. *SIECUS Report,* 1973, *1,* 1–2.

Elder, M. S. Nurse counseling on sexuality: An unmet challenge. *Nursing Outlook,* 1970, *18,* 38–40.

Engel, E. M., Resnick, P. H., & Levine, S. B. The use of programmed patients and videotapes in teaching medical students to take a sexual history. *Journal of Medical Education,* 1976, *51,* 245–247.

Fonseca, J. D. Sexuality—a quality of being human. *Nursing Outlook,* 1970, *18,* 25.

Fontaine, K. L. Human sexuality: Faculty knowledge and attitudes. *Nursing Outlook,* 1976, *24,* 174–176.

Hanson, E. U. Sexuality curriculum and the nurse. In N. Rosenzweig & F. P. Pearsall (Eds.), *Sex education for the health professional: A curriculum guide.* New York: Grune & Stratton, 1978.

Jacobson, L. Illness and human sexuality. *Nursing Outlook,* 1974, *22,* 50–53.

Krizenofski, M. T. Human sexuality and nursing practice. *Nursing Clinics of North America,* 1973, *8,* 673–679.

Lief, H. P. Why sex education for health practitioner? In R. Green (Ed.), *Human Sexuality: A health practitioner's text* (2nd ed.). Baltimore: Williams & Wilkins, 1979.

Lief, H. I., & Payne, T. Sexuality—knowledge and attitudes. *American Journal of Nursing,* 1975, *75,* 2026–2029.

Long, R. C. Sexual health care. *SIECUS Report,* 1974, *3,* 1–14.

McCary, J. L. *Sexual myths and fallacies.* New York: Schocken Books, 1977.

Maddock, J. W. Sexual health and sexual health care. *Postgraduate Medicine,* 1975, *58,* 52–58.

Mandetta, A. F., & Woods, N. G. Learning about human sexuality. *Nursing Outlook,* 1974, *22,* 525–527.

Megenity, J. A plea for sex education in nursing curriculum. *American Journal of Nursing,* 1975, *75,* 1171.

Miller, D. (Executive Producer). *Human sexuality and nursing practice: An instructor's manual.* Costa Mesa, Cal.: Concept Media, 1975.

Mims, F. H. Sexual health education and counseling. *Nursing Clinics of North America,* 1975, *10,* 519–528.

Mims, F. H. Sexuality in nursing curriculum. *Nurse Educator,* 1977, *2,* 20–23.

Mims, F. H., & Swenson, M. *Sexuality: A nursing perspective.* New York: McGraw-Hill, 1980.

Mims, F., Yeaworth, R., & Horstein, S. Effectiveness of an interdisciplinary course in human sexuality. *Nursing Research,* 1974, *23,* 248–253.

Morrison, E. S., & Price, M. U. *Values in sexuality: A new approach to sex education.* New York: Hart Publishing, 1974.

Narrow, B. W. *Patient teaching in nursing practice: A patient and family-centered approach.* New York: John Wiley & Sons, 1979.

Otto, H. A. *The new sexuality.* Palo Alto, Cal.: Science and Behavior Books, 1971.

Payne, T. Sexuality for nurses: Correlations of knowledge, attitudes, and behavior. *Nursing Research,* 1976, *25,* 286–292.

Picconi, J. Human sexuality: A nursing challenge. *Nursing 77,* 1977, *5,* 720–727.

Read, D. A. *Healthy sexuality: The key to a rich and rewarding sex life.* New York: Macmillan, 1979.

Sex Information and Education Council of the United States. The SIECUS/New York University/Uppsala principles basic to education for sexuality. *SIECUS Report,* 1980, *8,* 8–9.

Steele, S. M., & Harmon, V. M. *Values clarification in nursing.* New York: Appleton-Century-Crofts, 1979.

Stephens, G. F. Man body continuum in human sexuality. *American Journal of Nursing,* 1970, *70,* 1468–1471.

Sutterley, D. C., & Donnelly, G. F. *Perspectives in human development.* Philadelphia: Lippincott, 1973.

Wilson, R. R. *Introduction to sexual counseling.* Chapel Hill, N. C.: Carolina Population Center, 1974.

Woods, N. F. *Human sexuality in health and illness* (2nd ed.). St. Louis: 1979.

Woods, N. F., & Mandetta, A. Changes in students' knowledge and attitudes following a course in human sexuality. *Nursing Research,* 1975, *24,* 10–15.

World Health Organization. *Education and treatment in human sexuality: The training of health professionals* (Report of a WHO Meeting, Technical Report Series No. 572). Geneva: Author, 1975.

Zalar, M. Sex education for nurses. In H. A. Otto (Ed.), *The new sex education: The sex educator's resource book.* Chicago: Follett, 1978.

2. Assessment for Sexual Health

Elizabeth Lion

The client's comfort level during the taking of a sexual-health history and the physical examination of the genitalia is directly proportional to the comfort level of the nurse. This exercise is meant to have you examine your own feelngs, thoughts, and behaviors about asking for and receiving sexual information and taking part in the physical examination of the male or female genitalia.

For this exercise it might be well to remember that there are no right or wrong feelings. Feelings just happen, and we have no control over them. Neither are there right or wrong answers to the questions, for the responses come from your thoughts and your life experiences. It is important, however, to pay attention to your feelings and thoughts, for they influence behavior and you are responsible for your behavior.

Respond to the following questions. Write your answers and make note of the feelings you have.

1. If you were a member of a group and the topic of sex was unexpectedly introduced, would you feel your sense of privacy had been invaded? Would you worry about the feelings of other people in the group?
2. Would what you could say about sex be different if you were talking to a man than if you were talking to a woman? A boy? A girl?
3. Would what you could ask about sex be different if you were asking a man than if you were asking a woman? A boy? A girl?
4. Some people enjoy sexual humor. Do you? Do you feel it is appropriate to express sexual humor in mixed company? Do you have a favorite "dirty" joke?
5. There is street language for terms related to sex and sexuality. Are you familiar with any street-language words for intercourse? Penis? Vagina? Breasts? Menstruation? Masturbation? Do you remember when you first became aware of these words? Are some words more difficult to say than others? Which ones? Are there circumstances when it is appropriate to use street language?

6. Think about a recent interaction you had with a client. Was touch part of the interaction? What are some of the nonverbal techniques you use to show comfort with and acceptance of the client as a person?
7. In a client interaction, would you feel more comfortable touching a man or a woman? A boy or a girl? Would where you feel comfortable touching a woman be different than where you would feel comfortable touching a man? A boy? A girl? How do you think you learned your touching behavior?
8. Imagine examining your own genitalia with a hand mirror. What kinds of feelings might you have? Anxious? Embarrassed? Ashamed? Childlike? Happy? Pleased? Interested? Disgusted? Turned on? Turned off? Have you ever thought about examining your genitalia? What did you do about that thought? Did what you have been taught influence what you did about that thought?

Discuss your answers and share your feelings with another person and in a group of your peers or colleagues. How were the feelings and reactions of the group similar? Dissimilar? Discuss what nurse behaviors might increase the comfort level of the client during sexual history taking and physical examination of the genitalia.

BEHAVIORAL OBJECTIVES

After completing this chapter, you will be able to

- State the purpose and use of the sexual health history.
- Identify the factors that influence taking a sexual health history.
- Illustrate the principles of talking about sexuality.
- Identify the sequence and categories of questions on a sexual health history form for an adult.
- Describe the use of the sexual health history form with an adult.
- Describe the use of a child's sexual health history as education for the parent.
- Describe the physical examination of the male and female genitalia as a sexual health teaching experience.
- Describe the role of the nurse as educator-counselor in assessment of sexual health.

THE PROCESS OF ASSESSMENT OF SEXUAL HEALTH

Assessment begins with the collection and analysis of subjective and objective data, ends with a nursing diagnosis, and is the base from which the nurse plans, implements, and evaluates nursing care (Yura & Walsh,

1978). Taking a sexual health history and performing or assisting with a pelvic and breast examination of women and a genitorectal examination of men are means of collecting data for the nursing process. Incorporating a sexual health history into a total nursing history and making the physical examination of the breasts and genitalia a time for sexual health teaching are skills to be learned and practiced by the nurse.

PURPOSE OF THE SEXUAL HEALTH HISTORY

Elder (1970) recommends that a sexual health history be obtained from any man or woman from puberty through old age. Adams (1966a, 1966b) makes it clear that the sexual health history uncovers information about the relationship of the present state of health or illness to the client's sexuality, the status of relationships and living arrangements with support systems, and the need for sexual information, counseling, or referral. Mims and Swenson (1980) maintain that a sexual health history is necessary, that it increases the nurse's understanding of the psychological and physical needs of the client, and that it gives the client permission to discuss sexual concerns either at present or in future. For Green (1979), the inclusion of sexual health in the total history communicates to the client that the nurse appreciates the importance of sexual health and is comfortable with and ready to attend to sexual health needs.

Sexual health is part of total health, and a sexual health history is an integral part of a nursing history. The nursing history is an essential tool, and the taking of a nursing history is an essential event in planned data gathering (Little & Carnevali, 1976). The taking of a nursing history is a purposeful conversation between the nurse and the client that involves a formal exchange of information and feelings relevant to nursing. It is a systematic and planned process during which the nurse listens, questions, and gathers needed data about the client's needs, problems, and coping patterns (Bower, 1977). The taking of a nursing history is the initial contact between the nurse and the client. It establishes the range of nursing care, the fullness of the client's participation, and the depth and scope of the nurse–client relationship. The nursing history is used by all team members and is the foundation upon which all data are built (Little & Carnevali, 1976).

The sexual health history, as part of the nursing history, focuses on needs, expectations, and behavior and identifies concerns, misconceptions, and issues for education, counseling, and referral in relation to sexuality. It is the client's story of past and present events that may affect present and future sexual health, and it centers on the client's knowledge of himself or herself as a physical, emotional, social, and sexual being (Mahoney, Verdisco, & Shortridge, 1976). The sexual health history, as part of the nursing history, enables the nurse to understand, appreciate, and value the totality of the client's life experiences and to plan, implement, and evaluate comprehensive nursing care.

FACTORS THAT INFLUENCE TAKING A SEXUAL HEALTH HISTORY

Multiple and varied factors make each client different and distinct from every other client. There are immeasurable differences in personal, social, and sexual expectations and behaviors between cultures and subcultures of the same society. Each client enters the health-care system with his or her own unique sexual development, personal and interpersonal sexual experiences, sexual self-concept, sexual value system, and pattern of communication about sex and sexuality.

Sexual history taking is not as objective as physical assessment, and the information sought may be perceived by the client as personal, private, and even secret. Relatively few clients have openly discussed or examined their sexual self-concept, roles, or relationships, and sexual history taking may precipitate feelings of being judged or criticized. Clients may be reluctant to give information about sex and sexuality and may be anxious that such information be discovered or disclosed. Unless the nurse is capable of interacting with each client as a unique person with individual, personal, and genuine sexual needs, wants, concerns, and expectations, the data collected will be inaccurate and scant.

The Nurse

All nurses who work with clients should have the attitudes, knowledge, and skills that allow clients to have, express, and inquire about their sexual feelings and concerns. These same knowledge, attitudes, and skills should be helpful to clients as they examine and explore their sexual expectations and behaviors. Nurses must have grappled with the personal struggle of auditing their own sexual experiences, knowledge, and values before they can be helpful to others with sexual concerns and anxieties. No amount of knowledge and no communication skills with individuals or groups can make up for this necessary prerequisite (Carrera & Calderone, 1976).

Nurses with heightened self-awareness and acceptance of their own sexuality avoid imposing their own sexual value system on clients. Self-awareness and acceptance also help in the collection of data from clients and their significant others. Nurses with such qualities find themselves able to ask questions and receive accurate and useful information.

Sexual history taking provides an opportunity for nurses to feel and to convey high levels of empathy, respect, and sincerity. Nurses are more likely to accept their clients and significant others as real people if they are able to be genuine and forthright in their interactions with them.

Trust, Acceptance, and Critical Listening

Trust, acceptance, and critical listening are interrelated, interdependent factors that affect sexual history taking. Trust is fundamental to a nurse–client interaction. If clients do not perceive nurses as trustworthy, they may withhold information or request assurance that the information not be used to hurt them. Clients may need assurance that the information is secure and that it will be used only for and within the participatory decisions of the nursing process.

Clients need to feel known, understood, and accepted. This requires that nurses develop nonjudgmental and nonevaluative attitudes and communicate these attitudes to clients and their significant others. Nurses must express verbally and nonverbally that clients are viewed as valued people. Touch is the most basic nonverbal communication, and it is a way of conveying unconditional interest, concern, assurance, and acceptance.

Critical listening—listening to the words, hearing how they are spoken, and knowing who is speaking them—influences the amount and the kind of data gathered. Clients and their significant others will hold back information if they feel the nurse is not really hearing them. The nurse who fails to listen critically misses valuable information and loses the opportunity for full participation with clients and their significant others.

Physical Setting

A physical setting that is conducive to sharing information is needed for sexual history taking. Most clients appreciate the nurse's effort to arrange for a suitable environment. The place selected should be well lighted, well ventilated, and equipped with a comfortable chair for the nurse and a comfortable chair or bed for the client. It is preferable for the nurse and client to sit and face each other about an arm's length away. Looking down at the client is to be avoided; sitting tells the client the nurse is interested, will listen, and plans to stay.

Privacy is essential. Clients may not disclose personal information if there is the likelihood that they may be overheard by others. An office or room is desirable. A screen or curtain may be what is available, but even with low-pitched voices the giving and receiving of sexual information can be severely hampered in such a setting.

The setting should be free of unpredictable and unexplained noises, for such distracting noises can interfere with the hearing and listening of both the client and the nurse. The setting should be free of interruptions, so that significant information is not missed or continuity lost. The nurse has the responsibility for controlling interruptions. The client's visitors are asked to wait. The nurse requests that he or she not be called away. Neither the nurse nor the client answers or uses the telephone.

Subjective and Objective Data Collected

The information collected from and about the client is separated into subjective and objective data. Subjective data are units of information concerning the client's view of what he or she is experiencing. Subjective data are what the client has decided the nurse is to know about himself or herself, his or her environment, support systems, desires, expectations, and perceived needs (Little & Carnevali, 1976; Walter, Pardee, & Malbo, 1976). The client is the only source of subjective data. These units of information, about which the client alone is the true expert, are often written or stated as quotations.

Objective data are observable phenomena and conditions about the responses and health status of the client that can be qualitatively and quantitatively described and verified by others. Objective data may come from vital signs, physical examination, laboratory tests, or verbal and nonverbal behavior and may consist of any observable clues and cues from or about the client (Little & Carnevali, 1976; Walter, Pardee, & Malbo, 1976). These units of information include anything the nurse sees, touches, smells, hears, or reads about the client.

In the collection of objective data, the nurse may move from the primary source—the client—to secondary sources—parents, siblings, friends, or persons who are resources or support systems for the client. Collecting data from secondary sources must be as systematic and thorough as that from the primary source. The secondary sources provide objective data about the client and subjective data about themselves. Nurses need to identify secondary sources of data about the client and to distinguish objective and subjective data obtained from those sources.

Recording the Data Collected

The recording of data, as the nursing history is being taken, can present a problem. Recording data as it is given is an acceptable and appropriate practice for nurses and other health professionals. However, record keeping increases the client's concern about confidentiality, it may mean the nurse misses some facial expressions and body language, and it is time consuming.

Little and Carnevali (1976) suggest that the nurse encourage clients to see what is being written. When clients see what the nurse is writing, they feel free to participate fully. Another way the feeling against record keeping may be decreased is for the nurse to state out loud what he or she is writing.

Recording while collecting data is an acquired skill. The nurse selects the length or brevity of the notation, the abbreviations used, and the method of recording. Recording can be used to enhance the clients participation, ensure the accuracy of the notations, and make economical use of time.

Nursing Diagnosis and Planning, Implementing, and Evaluating

Making a nursing diagnosis is the final and critical step in assessment. The nursing diagnosis is the conclusion reached by means of the analysis, appraisal, and interpretation of the meaning and importance of the data obtained (Yura & Walsh, 1978). It is the nurses statement of a present or potential sexual health problem of a client that falls within the competence of the nurse as educator-counselor, and it is the springboard for planning, implementing, and evaluating nursing care.

Planning involves informed and responsible decision making about options, priorities, goals, and actions. *Planning* is stated in terms of what the nurse does in order to facilitate the behaviors selected by the client to reduce or alleviate the sexual health problem identified in the nursing diagnosis. *Implementation* is stated in terms of what the client does with the selected tasks and activities formulated to accomplish the plans made. *Evaluation* is the process of deciding if the planned-for goals have been met. It is the start of the data base for reassessment.

PRINCIPLES OF TALKING ABOUT SEXUALITY

Sex and sexuality are emotionally laden topics. What to say about sex, how to say it, and when to say it can be a problem. Initiating a discussion and responding to and hearing the sexual implications of a question are the nurse's responsibilities. Easing the emotional load and enabling open and clear discussions of sex and sexuality can be achieved by learning and applying six basic principles (Wahl, 1967; Pomeroy, 1974; Cashman, 1980).

1. Progress from the topics that are easy to discuss to those that are difficult to discuss. Approach emotionally charged areas gradually. If the nurse–client interaction makes it appropriate, before collecting data about intercourse gather information about menstruation from women and information about nocturnal emissions from men.

Whether the client is a man or woman, his or her socioeconomic status can make a difference in the sequence of the data collected. Upper-class men tend to be more comfortable if the sequence of data gathering is masturbation, petting, intercourse, homosexual behavior. For upper-class women, the more comfortable sequence tends to be petting, intercourse, masturbation, homosexuality (Pomeroy, 1974). With lower-class men and women, data about intercourse can be discussed before masturbation and petting (Hammond & Ladner, 1969).

2. Discuss how the client acquired sexual information and current attitudes toward sex before discussing sexual experience. In collecting data about sexual experience, begin with data usually less sensitive and threatening. If the nurse–client interaction involves concerns or anxieties about homosexuality, inquire first how the client learned about the sexual behavior, move to questions about current feelings and attitudes, and then approach the actual sexual behavior. First, "At what age did you first learn some people are physically attracted to people of the same sex?" then "What were your early attitudes about that?" followed by "What are your current attitudes?" and then "What kinds of homosexual experiences have you had?"

3. Initiate discussions or precede questions about emotionally charged sexual experiences with an informational statement about the universality or normality of the topic. Such statements reflect current knowledge and contain information about the natural, common, and general occurrence of the sexual experience. For example, "As you know, people find out about masturbation in many ways—from friends, family members, books, or in other ways. How did you become aware of this activity?" and "There are older people who are involved in close and sexual relationships, and there are others who wonder if such relationships are perfectly normal. How do you feel?" Note these statements are open-ended and contain alternatives. The nurse is saying that there are many ways to learn and behave sexually. Open-ended questions require more than a "yes" or "no" answer and give the client permission to talk about sexual concerns.

4. Assume the full range of sexual experience. Thus, do not ask "Did you ever masturbate?" but "How old were you when you first began to masturbate?" Ask: "When did you first have intercourse?" not "Have you ever had intercourse?"

When the nurse assumes the sexual activity is part of the client's experience, it decreases the client's anxiety and reduces misinformation and falsehood. If what the nurse assumes is in direct violation of the client's value system, if the client is unready to discuss the issue, or if it is not part of the client's experience, he or she will deny it.

5. Keep your sense of humor about sexual words. "What the heck does that mean?" may be an acceptable response to a word about which you are uncertain. Requesting clarification with humor decreases tension, maintains contact, and may add a new word or a different meaning of a word to your vocabulary (Cashman, 1980).

6. Use the sexual words and phrases known by, understood by, and comfortable for the client. Sexual words, in addition to describing a phenomenon, are likely to arouse such emotions as embarrassment, revulsion, guilt, defiance, and hostility and such behaviors as blushing, leering, frowning, coughing, stuttering, smiling, and giggling. The nurse's emotional response to an explicit sexual phrase used by a client can block the nurse from hearing anything else the client is saying. The nurse must assume responsibility for becoming desensitized to sexually explicit words and phrases and thus to eliminate the power of words to hurt, accuse, demean, and stigmatize (Cashman, 1980).

Annon (1976) suggests a method of dealing with the cultural phenomenon of *logophobia*—the phobic reaction to and the attribution of power to words. The nurse can prepare a written list of sexually explicit words and phrases and practice saying them out loud, clearly and distinctly, over and over again. Or the nurse can select a cooperative colleague, and they can practice saying the words out loud to each other. The important point is to become used to seeing, saying, and hearing the words until they cease to elicit any emotional response.

There are standard terms like *sexual satisfaction, sexual outlet, making love,* and *climax* that occur in polite conversation and are read in the newspaper. *Conjugation, copulation,* and *sexual intercourse* are synonymous standard terms for the sex act. *Cohabitation, sexual relations,* and *adultery* are also synonymous with the sex act but carry with them legal and moral implications (Berne, 1970). Standard terms are intended to communicate information nonoffensively. Scientific terms like *penis, vagina, coitus,* and *orgasm* have Greek or Latin origins. These words are objective, select, and specific but tend to depersonalize and dehumanize sexuality. Childhood terms, such as *weewee, number 2,* and *making babies,* are intended to diminish embarrassment and avoid confrontation (Morrison & Price, 1974). There are street language words, such as *fuck* and *cock.* These words can be powerful, graphic, and humorous, but they can also be hostile, demeaning, biased, and narrow and their erotic component often blocks understanding of what is being described. Most of our modern so-called dirty words were once perfectly clean, and even today many people find nothing wrong with them and use them regularly in private interactions and public settings (Haeberle, 1978).

The nurse must avoid the use of euphemisms such as "sleeping together," "privates," "down there," and "having sex." These terms may be less offensive to hear and say, but they are less direct and have different meanings for different people. Depending on the client, the experience, and the circumstances, "having sex" may mean vagina-penis intercourse, oral sex, or mutual masturbation. Clarification of an indirect or nonspecific term is needed so that the client and the nurse are clear about the sexual phenomenon being discussed.

Nurses need to know the street language equivalent to standard scientific terms. The words *fellatio* (the act of taking a penis into the mouth and sucking it for erotic pleasure) and *cunnilingus* (the act of licking or sucking a woman's sex organ for erotic pleasure) may be used by some clients; however, "mouth-genital sex," "sucking," "blowing," and "going down" may be used by others. The nurse is responsible for understanding the client's words and meanings; if not, he or she must ask for a clarification.

The words "promiscuous" and "unfaithful" have an emotional impact; make a judgment, and can hurt and stigmatize. The nurse's language must be nonjudgmental (Green, 1979). The word *promiscuous* is meant to describe repetitive sexual experiences with varied or transient partners. *Unfaithful* refers to a married person who engages in a sexual interaction outside of che marriage (Chapter 8). It is the nurse's responsibility to describe behaviors and not use words that carry with them judgments or accusations.

It is useful for the nurse to know and use a full sexual vocabulary—the standard, scientific, childhood, and street words and phrases. Such a vocabulary can help bridge the communication gap between the client and the nurse. It is important for the client to know that the nurse is able to talk directly, plainly, and specifically about sex and sexuality.

USE OF THE SEXUAL HEALTH HISTORY FORM

The sexual health history form, like the nursing history, consists of an organized and predetermined sequence of topics and questions relevant to nursing that serves as guide and reminder to the nurse (Bower, 1977; Lief, 1976). Generally the progression of questions follows the growth-and-development patterns of the life cycle—childhood, adolescence, adulthood—and proceeds from less sensitive to more threatening topics—knowledge, feelings and attitudes, and behavior. The content varies with agencies and care settings. The selection of topics and questions is best developed from goals and objectives of the nursing practice.

The history form is not a series of questions to which the client is subjected. The outline is a guide for data gathering and recording and is part of the nurse's learning process. The nurse should know the questions without referring to the form. The phrasing of the questions, the nuances of voice, gesture, and touch are learned and practiced in every nurse–client interaction. The nurse will develop a format and process comfortable to him or her and adaptable to clients with a variety of concerns and in a variety of settings.

The nurse may want to prepare statements to open and conclude sexual history taking. Mims and Swenson (1980) suggest the use of universal statements that request information and collaboration. "As a nurse I'm interested in your total health, and sexual health is an important part.

Sometimes it is helpful to pay attention—to better understand what you might think is an important part of your life. I'm going to ask you some questions about your sexual health." The nurse might be ready to add "As you know, what we discuss is confidential in the same way as the rest of the nursing history." If the client is hesitant or reluctant to answer some of the questions, the nurse can say "I understand how you feel, and the questions can be put aside. If you change your mind, I'll be available to go over them with you." A general closing statement showing readiness to return upon request is helpful. "I hope that if you think of any other questions you'll contact me. I can make the time to talk with you."

The intent of taking a sexual history is to gather information from the client. If nurses find they are doing most of the talking, they can ask themselves these questions (Calderwood, 1971).

1. Am I allowing time for the client to respond? The client may be new at discussing his or her sexual health. Allow time for responses to form and avoid filling up moments of silence.

2. Am I nervous or apprehensive over my presentation of my knowledge of sexual health? It is quite natural to feel uncertain as you present what you are now learning about sexual health. With time the knowledge will increase, and with practice and experience the nervousness will diminish.

3. Am I working too hard at getting the questions asked? Do not rush the questions or shut off the answer. Allow time for thinking and answering, even if the next question has to wait or not be asked at all. Give the question asked and the answer being considered and spoken adequate time.

4. Am I afraid the client will question me about something I do not know? You do not need to know all the answers. You can admit to your apprehension and lack of information. Such openness, coupled with a readiness to obtain the information, will be accepted and appreciated by the client.

5. Do I really know what the client knows about sexual health? Do not assume you know more than the client does or that the client knows more than you. The nursing history and sexual health history will help you identify what the client knows and you will be able to make use of it and build upon it within the nursing process.

6. Am I talking about my experiences? My opinions? my solutions? Some clients will ask you to talk about your own personal experiences or to tell them what you would do or have done in similar situations. Remember, the responsibility for decision making belongs to the client. Discuss with the client that sexual health is a personal and individual matter and that you do not want the decisions you made or what you think is appropriate for yourself to influence his or her choices or decisions.

The following form can be part of a nursing history for adolescents and adults (Table 2.1). The data gathered connects the client's presenting health problems—symptoms, condition, illness, or disease—with sexuality. The first two questions gather data on the acquisition of sexual information and past and present attitudes. Questions 3, 4, and 5 deal with sexual role, sexual being, and sexual functioning. The last question provides an opportunity for exploration and clarification. The form is a guide. It is the nurse's decision to use all the questions or leave some out and add others.

Sexual health is part of the total health of a child, and a sexual health history provides information about the growth and development of the whole child (Table 2.2). Mims and Swenson (1980) state:

> One of the greatest benefits . . . may be the education of the parent which can take place during the interview. Subtle messages are conveyed which include that (1) children are sexual, (2) children normally ask questions about sex, (3) children need to know about reproduction, masturbation, menstruation, and nocturnal emissions (taking into consideration the child's age and developmental level), and (4) parents sometimes have difficulty coping with the sexuality of the children. [p. 131]

Most parents are interested in getting information about growth and development and are concerned about their children's sex education. As

Table 2.1.   Sexual Health History (Adult)

1. As a child, how did you learn about sex? Who were the people to whom you turned for answers? When you were a teenager, how did you get your sexual information?
2. What were your early beliefs and attitudes about sex? In what way are your beliefs and attitudes different now?
3. Has your health problem made any difference in your being a (wife, mother, husband, father, sexual partner)? What is it like for you? How did you become aware of the difference?
4. Has your health problem changed the way you feel about yourself as a man/woman? How does this affect you? At the present time, how important is a sexual relationship to you?
5. Has your health problem changed your ability to function sexually? How does this affect you? How does this affect your relationship with your partner? Have you tried to change or make some adjustment to the situation? Have you discussed this with your partner? How would you like your situation to be different? Are you taking any medicine that you think affects your sexual functioning?
6. Is there anything about these questions you would like to go over again or talk about further?

SOURCE: Adapted from F.H. Mims & M. Swenson *Sexuality: A nursing perspective,* New York: McGraw-Hill 1980, p. 130. Items 3, 4, 5 adapted from N.F. Woods, *Human sexuality in health and illness,* 2nd ed. St. Louis: Mosby, 1979, p. 79.

Table 2.2.   **Sexual Health History (Child)**[a]

1. How have you answered your child's questions about sex?
2. Who else does your child ask about sex?
3. How old was your child when you first talked about reproduction (intercourse, how babies are made)? Does your child know about menstruation? Erection? Wet dreams?
4. Describe your child's sexual activity
   a. when he or she was younger
   b. now
   c. What changes do you expect in the next year?
5. Is there anything you would change about your child's sexual activity?
6. Do you have any concerns about your child's relationship with friends or with family members?
7. Is there anything you think your child needs to or wants to know that you are unable to discuss with him or her?
8. Would you like help from someone in discussing that difficult area?
9. Do you have any questions about your own sexuality, sexual activity, or sexual health?

SOURCE: F.H. Mims & M. Swenson, *Sexuality: A nursing perspective*, New York: McGraw-Hill, 1980, p. 132.
[a]Developed by M. Swenson

before, if the parent chooses not to respond or is selective in responding to the questions on the sexual health history, the nurse accepts the behavior and indicates that he or she is available for questions in the future. The nurse can make an introductory statement requesting the parent's assistance and participation: "Many parents feel that providing sex education is an important part of being a parent. Share with me some of your child's sexual history so I can better understand what you have done or might be thinking of doing" (Mims & Swenson, 1980).

The form can be used to question the child directly. The questions need to be adjusted to the developmental level of each child. The nurse is responsible for using sensitive phrasing and words understood by the child.

INTERPERSONAL ASPECTS OF PHYSICAL EXAMINATION

At some time in their lives, most men and women will experience a physical examination of their genitalia. These men and women have been socially conditioned to consider the genitalia as private, somehow un-

clean, beyond explanation, requiring concealment; self-touching is discouraged, and touching by others is sanctioned only during lovemaking.
The rectal area is thought of as dirty, associated with feelings of embarrassment, humiliation, and shame, and ridiculed, scorned, and excluded
from lovemaking. Genitalia are subjects of pornography, and the rectal
area is the subject of scatologic humor.

As women claim the right to know about their bodies and to assume
responsibility for their own bodies and health, the character of the pelvic
and breast examination is changing. Women's health centers have demonstrated to nurse and physician examiners that acquiring the technical
skill can be accompanied by developing awareness of the client's concerns
and learning to communicate information and to demonstrate caring behaviors in the conduct of the examination. Men have derived benefits
from this new awareness, too. The examiner's attitudes and techniques of
gathering data during the genitorectal examination of men are being
modified through the recognition of men's need for information and dignity. The physical assessment of sexuality can be an information-sharing
experience and a time of affirmation of sexuality as a wholesome phenomenon and validation of the person's sexuality.

BREAST AND PELVIC EXAMINATION OF WOMEN

Physical examination of the breast and pelvis of women begins with the
lower abdomen, moves to the breasts, and involves inspection and palpation of the external genitalia, speculum inspection of the vagina and
cervix, manual manipulation of the ovaries and uterus, and evaluation of
the integrity of the muscles of the perineum and pelvic flow.

Preferably, history taking precedes the physical examination so that
the client and the examiner have established a relationship. If this is not
possible, the client is disrobed, gowned, and sitting on the examining
table before the examiner enters. It is helpful, in dealing with a woman's
feelings of intrusion, for the client and the examiner to be at the same eye
level when communication begins. The examiner introduces himself or
herself, discusses the purposes of the examination, describes the procedure, and solicits questions from the client. A woman may intellectually
consent to being examined before she emotionally consents (Merrill,
1968).

Some women object to the use of a drape because it prevents them from
seeing what is happening and thus suggests to them that the examination is shameful. Other women want the cover the drape provides and feel
it adds to their dignity. The examiner who places the sheet on the client's

lap and says, "May I help you with this?" allows the client to choose. The examiner moves to the head of the table to help the client lie down and assume the lithotomy position. Helping from the head of the table assures the client the examiner is looking at her and not her genitalia. The examiner who leaves during positioning and reappears at the pelvic end of the table loses the continuity of eye contact and breaks the continuity of personal concern.

The examination begins with the palpation of the abdomen, which establishes physical contact in a relatively nonthreatening area. Examination of the breasts can provoke anxiety and is best begun with one hand resting on the abdomen. Establishing touch and maintaining an uninterrupted pattern of touch throughout the examination reduces startle responses and conveys acceptance, concern, and comfort (Fordney-Settlage, 1979). The breast examination is the ideal time to teach self-examination for breast lumps or disease. The client can be instructed to follow the hand of the examiner with her own hand and then repeat the technique herself.

When the examination of the pelvis begins, the pattern of touch is from knee to thigh to external genitalia (Fordney-Settlage, 1979). Elevating the head of the table to about seventy-five degrees, or elevating it to about thirty degrees and providing a pillow allows eye contact with the client when the examiner is seated. An explanation that gloves are worn to prevent transmission of infection communicates to the client that she is not abnormal or unclean. Showing and demonstrating the speculum should be routine, and only a warm speculum should be used. Holding a speculum under a stream of warm water for a few seconds renders it a comfortable temperature and moistens it sufficiently for insertion. The examiner can offer a mirror and even use a lighted speculum so that the client can view her own anatomy. Instruction is given to the client for visual and tactile self-examination of the external genitalia and for self-exploration and palpation of the vagina and cervix. Teaching and encouraging self-examination counteracts old prohibitions and restrictions and gives permission for the client to look, touch, feel, learn, and know.

Throughout the examination the examiner explains and describes what he or she is doing, such as palpating more deeply, moving to another area, or inserting an instrument. The examiner explains what the client may feel and encourages the client to report and describe any discomfort. The examiner listens for and elicits questions, concerns, and complaints. The examiner can begin with, "I understand you are probably nervous. I find that most clients are. So let me tell you what I am doing." Examples of explanation and information are: "Now I am going to examine your pubic hair"; "The outer lips are called the labia"; and "I'm making sure your glands are not swollen." When inserting the speculum the examiner could say, "Now I'm going to put two fingers in your vagina and then insert the speculum. Now I am opening the speculum and am looking at your cervix and checking it for irritation and infection. I don't see any. Your cervix looks very healthy. Can you see your cervix?" Explanations of what is being done and observed enables communication, allows questions and participation, and involves the client in her own sexual health care. Familiarity with her own body is every woman's right and is often the first step toward sexual health.

GENITORECTAL EXAMINATION OF MEN

The examiner must not assume that men have little or no emotional reaction to genitorectal examination. Fordney-Settledge (1979) states, "Men may even have more problems than women because the examination requires both passive yielding of control and allowance of bodily penetration. Both experiences are rarely experienced by men" (p. 34). As in the examination of women, the examiner maintains physical contact through touch, maintains eye contact, explains techniques and sensations, and encourages involvement in self-examination.

The examination of the male genitalia includes inspection and palpation of the lower abdomen and external genitalia and palpation of the prostate gland by rectal examination. The examination of the male breast is brief but should not be overlooked. The nipple and areola are inspected and palpated for nodules, swelling, or ulceration.

As with the woman client, the physical examination of the man should be done after the history is taken so that the examiner and the client have had an opportunity to establish a relationship. When the examination is part of a general physical, the client is disrobed and gowned; otherwise it is sufficient for the client to have removed his clothing from the waist to the knees. Before the examination begins, the examiner introduces himself or herself, establishes eye contact, explains the purpose of the examination, describes the process, indicates a readiness to respond to concerns and complaints, and demonstrates caring behavior about anxiety or embarrassment observed in the client. If the examiner is a woman, she wears gloves to decrease the tactile stimulation and discusses with the client the possibility of him having an erection. This is spoken of and described as a normal but somewhat embarrassing occurrence (Mims & Swenson, 1980).

The examination of the lower abdomen for hernia and inspection and palpation of the external genitalia can be done in either of two positions. In the first position, the client lies on the examination table with his head elevated on a small pillow. An abdominal and leg drape is used and the client is asked to spread his legs slightly. Physical touch is easily maintained as groin, scrotum, testes, and penis are examined. In the second position that can be used, the client stands and the examiner sits on a low stool. The second position is better for hernia evaluation but is not as satisfactory for examination of external genitalia. In the second position it is difficult to use drapes, and the eye-level used to examine the client's genitalia can be anxiety-producing.

There are two positions for inspecting the perineum and the posterior scrotal wall and palpating the prostate and seminal vesicles. In the first position, the client is asked to stand spread-legged and bend his upper body onto his forearms on the examination table. In the second position, the client is asked to lie on his left side (on the examination table) with his left leg slightly flexed, his right leg markedly flexed, and his legs draped. Each position is satisfactory for data gathering. Clients, however, find that the eye contact and less exposure provided by the second position make it more acceptable than the first position described.

Throughout the examination, the examiner explains and describes what he or she is doing and observing. For example, "I'm looking at the distribution of your hair, and looking at the skin for lesions or changes"; "The scrotum is a muscular pouch of skin that contains two testes, the epididymis, the beginnings of the spermatic cord, and the vas deferens"; "I'm going to examine each of the testes. They are sensitive to pressure, so tell me if you feel any discomfort"; "Now I would like to show you how you can examine yourself." The client is encouraged to assist and learn during the examination by retracting his penile foreskin, palpating his epididymis, testes, and vas, and squeezing his glans penis to check for discharge. The client may choose to use a hand mirror for self-examination.

For both men and women clients, self-examination is not a substitute for medical examination but a supplement to it (Fordney-Settlage, 1979). Education does away with the obscurity and confusion of the examination and can affirm wholesome sexuality. Education provides a verbal, tactile, and visual information for responsible decision-making about seeking professional knowledge, skill, evaluation, and treatment.

NURSING PROCESS

Client: Elaine Richards—requested help for a personal problem about sex at a gynecological clinic in a large metropolitan hospital

Nurse: Joan Bundy—nursing student assigned to sexual health assessment of the client

Assessment

Subjective Data

"I've never had an orgasm during intercourse."
"I've never had an orgasm. Some of my girlfriends say they help them-
   selves, but I've never masturbated."
"I've had intercourse with two other men, and I faked orgasm."
"I've known Sam for a year and have been living with him for four
   months."
"I love him and he loves me—we're committed to each other."
"I thought it would be different—that with him I'd have an orgasm."
"I love him and I won't fake it."
"He tells me I'm tense—that I won't let it happen no matter what he
   does."
"We are arguing a whole lot about everything."
"I want him to enjoy making love to me, and I like loving him, but I want
   something more."
"I don't think there is anything wrong with me, but I want to make sure."
"There must be something I can do, some way I can help myself."

Objective Data

24 years old
Employed—bank teller
Pelvic examination reveals normal vagina and internal organs.
Uses diaphragm and reports satisfaction with method.
Somewhat anxious but able to respond well to questions.
Denies masturbation.
Reports absence of orgasm in intercourse.
Faked orgasm with previous sexual partners.
Has lived with present sexual partner (4 months) and refuses to fake
   orgasm.
Thought loving, committed relationship would ensure sexual fulfillment.
Partner attributes her lack of orgasm to tension during intercourse.
Anger in relationship.
Seeks confirmation of normalcy.
Wants personal fulfillment of sexuality.
Seeks help in achieving orgasm in intercourse.

Nursing Diagnosis

Inadequate information about achieving sexual fulfillment related to absence of orgasmic experience.

Conflict in present relationship due to absence of orgasmic experience of female sexual partner during intercourse.

Planning

Express warmth and friendliness.

Provide atmosphere of acceptance.

Encourage expression of feelings.

Offer feedback of client's expressed feelings.

Explain that client's emotional response is appropriate and commonly experienced.

Advise against causing defensive reactions in sexual partner.

Advise that significant persons express love and acceptance of one another.

Encourage expression of feelings with sexual partner about absence of orgasm during intercourse.

Explain the importance of offering emotional support to one another.

Provide information about normalcy of pelvic organs.

Provide information about male and female sexual response cycle (Chapter 5).

Provide information about female orgasm. (Most health professionals believe that numerous and interdependent psychological factors are largely responsible for the absence of orgasms. Physiologically the female orgasm is triggered by stimulation of the clitoris and expressed by vaginal contractions. Whether the friction is applied by the woman's finger, by her partner's finger, or by vaginal/penile intercourse, the female orgasm is almost always evoked by clitoral stimulation [Kaplan, 1974].)

Provide information about preorgasmic work groups for women. (These work groups are usually designed to provide physiological information and psychological support and exercises to enable each woman in the group to learn more about her own body and its needs and to realize her own sexual potential. In order to enhance understanding of one's own responsiveness, the exercises begin with self-discovery and move to pleasuring and sharing with the partner. It is essential for a woman to get in touch with her own body before she can effectively communicate her needs to her partner. The easiest, most effective way of getting in touch with one's sexual responses is masturbating. It turns out to be one of the most important stepping stones to a healthier, happier self and more satisfying and fulfilling relationship [Barbach, 1975].)

Provide information about content, approach, and time involved in sexual growth program for women offered at local community health center.

Suggest attendance in program if congruent with personal values and expectations.
Suggest reading books if congruent with personal values and expectations.

1. Barbach, L.G. *For yourself: The fulfillment of female sexuality*. New York: New American Library, 1975.
2. Hite, S. *The Hite report*. New York: MacMillan, 1976.
3. Kaplan, H. S. *The new sex therapy*. New York: Bruner/Mazel, 1974.

Encourage recognition of feelings.
Encourage expression of thoughts and feelings to partner about attending sexual growth program for women.
Encourage mutual decision making.
Indicate availability for further information and counseling.

Implementation

Get verbal and written information about sexual growth program for women.
Buy Barbach book (paperback), borrow Hite book from friend, and get Kaplan book from library.
Share feelings about lack of sexual fulfillment with partner.
Share information about male and female sexual response cycle.
Share information about female orgasm.
Discuss attending sexual growth program.
Ask partner to be part of a learning experience.
Arrange time to attend ten sessions over a five-week period with one hour of homework each day.
Make commitment to attend program.

Evaluation

Reports completion of program.
Reports more comfort with and awareness of own body.
Reports achievement of orgasm during intercourse and greater fulfillment of personal sexuality.
Reports closer and more fulfilling relationship with sexual partner.

BIBLIOGRAPHY

Adams, G. Recognizing the range of human sexual needs and behavior. *American Journal of Maternal Child Nursing*, 1976, *1*, 166–179. (a)

Adams, G. The sexual history as an integral part of the patient history. *American Journal of Maternal Child Nursing*, 1976, *1*, 170–175. (b)

Annon, J. S. *Behavioral treatment of sexual problems: Brief therapy*. Hagerstown, Maryland: Harper & Row, 1976.

Barbach, L. G. *For Yourself: The fulfillment of female sexuality*. New York: New American Library, 1975.

Bates, B. A guide to physical examination (2nd ed.). Philadelphia: Lippincott, 1979.

Berne, E. *Sex in human loving*. New York: Simon and Schuster, 1970.

Billinger, J. A., & Stoeckle, J. D. Pelvic examination instruction and the doctor–patient relationship. *Journal of Medical Education*, 1977, *52*, 834–839.

Bogen, I. Logophobia—some hypotheses and implications. *Journal of Sex Education and Therapy*, 1978, *4*, 47–53.

The Boston Women's Health Book Collective. *Our bodies, ourselves* (2nd ed.). New York: Simon and Schuster, 1976.

Bower, F. L. *Nursing assessment*. New York: Wiley, 1977.

Brown, M. A. Human sexuality. In D. C. Longo & R. A. Williams (Eds.), *Clinical practice in psychosocial nursing: Assessment and intervention*. New York: Appleton-Century-Crofts, 1978.

Calderwood, D. *About your sexuality: About the program*. Boston: Beacon Press, 1971.

Campbell, C. *Nursing diagnosis and intervention in nursing practice*. New York: Wiley 1978.

Carrera, M. A., & Calderone, M. S. Training of health professionals in education for sexual health. *SIECUS Report*, 1976, *4*, 1–2.

Cashman, P. H. Learning to talk about sex. *SIECUS Report*, 1980, *9*, 1; 4; 14.

Chez, R. The female patient's sexual history. In C. W. Wahl (Ed.), *Sexual problems: Diagnosis and treatment in medical problems*. New York: Free Press, 1967.

Debroriner, C. H. Psychological aspects of vaginal examination. *Medical Aspects of Human Sexuality*, 1975, *9*, 163–164.

Diagram Group. *Man's body: An owner's manual*. New York: Bantam, 1977.

Elder, M. S. The unmet challenge: Nurse counseling on sexuality. *Nursing Outlook*, 1970, *18*, 38–40.

Fordney-Settlage, D. S. Pelvic examination of women; genitorectal examination of men. In R. Green (Ed.), *Human sexuality: A health practitioner's text* (2nd ed.). Baltimore: Williams & Wilkins, 1979.

Francis, G. M., & Munjas, B. A. *Manual of socialpsychologic assessment*. New York: Appleton-Century-Crofts, 1976.

Green, R. (Ed.). *Human sexuality: A health practitioner's text* (2nd ed.). Baltimore: Williams & Wilkins, 1979.

Group for the Advancement of Psychiatry. *Assessment of sexual function: A guide to interviewing (Vol. 3, Report No. 88)*. *New York:* Author, 1973.

Haeberle, E. J. *The sex atlas: A new illustrated guide.* New York: Seabury Press, 1978.

Hammond, E., & Ladner, J. Socialization in a Negro ghetto. In C. Broderick & J. Bernard (Eds.), *The individual, sex, and society.* Baltimore: Johns Hopkins University Press, 1969.

Hite, S. *The Hite report.* New York: Macmillan, 1976.

Hogan, R. *Human sexuality: A nursing perspective.* New York: Appleton-Century-Crofts, 1980.

Julty, S. *Men's bodies; men's selves.* New York: Delta, 1979.

Kaplan, J. S. *The new sex therapy.* New York: Bruner/Mazel, 1974.

Krozy, R. Becoming comfortable with sexual assessment. *American Journal of Nursing,* 1978, *78,* 1036–1038.

Lief, H. I., & Berman, E. M. Sexual interviewing of the individual patient through the life cycle. In W. W. Oaks, G. A. Melchiode, & I. Ficher, (Eds.), *Sex and the life cycle.* New York: Grune & Stratton, 1976.

Levitt, E. E. Sexual counseling: What the busy physician can and cannot do. *Postgraduate Medicine,* 1975, *58,* 91–97.

Little, E. D., & Carnevali, D. L. *Nursing care planning* (2nd ed.). Philadelphia: Lippincott, 1976.

Mahoney, E. A., Verdisco, L., & Shortridge, L. *How to collect and record a health history.* Philadelphia: Lippincott, 1976.

Marbach, A. H., Mead, B. T., Rutherford, R. N., Wahl, C. W., Holmes, D. J., & Fink, P. J. In what types of presenting complaints should physicians inquire about sexual practices or take a sexual history? *Medical Aspects of Human Sexuality,* 1973, *7,* 34–44.

Mayers, M. G. *A systematic approach to the nursing care plan* (2nd ed.). New York: Appleton-Century-Crofts, 1978.

Mims, F. H., & Swenson, M. *Sexuality: A nursing perspective.* New York: McGraw-Hill, 1980.

Mirrell, J. A. Examining the young girl and the virgin woman. *Medical Aspects of Human Sexuality,* 1968, *2,* 37–42.

Morrison, E. S., & Price, M. U. *Values in sexuality: A new approach to sex education.* New York: Hart Publishing, 1974.

O'Connor, J. F. When your patient's problem is sexual. *Medical Times,* 1973, *101,* 65–72.

Peddicora, M. P., & Willingham, D. Adding a sexual assessment to the health interview. *Journal of Public Health Nursing and Mental Health Services,* 1978, *16,* 17–22; 27.

Pomeroy, W. B. The sex interview in counseling. In M. S. Calderone (Ed.), *Sexuality and human values.* New York: Association Press, 1974.

Roznoy, M. S. How to take a sexual history. *American Journal of Nursing,* 1976, *76,* 1279–1282.

Schwartz, R. M. Sexual history taking. *Journal of the American College Health Association,* 1974, *22,* 405–408.

Tunnadine, P. Psychological aspects of the vaginal examination. *Medical Aspects of Human Sexuality,* 1973, *7,* 1973.

Wahl, C. W. Psychiatric techniques in the taking of a sexual history. In C. W. Wahl (Ed.), *Sexual problems: Diagnosis and treatment in medical problems.* New York: The Free Press, 1967.

Walter, J. B., Pardee, G. P., & Malbo, D. M. *Dynamics of problem oriented approaches: Patient care and documentation.* Philadelphia: Lippincott, 1976.

Watts, R. J. Dimensions of sexual health. *American Journal of Nursing,* 1979, *79,* 1568–1572.

Woods, N. F. *Human sexuality in health and illness* (2nd ed.). St. Louis: Mosby, 1979.

Yura, H., & Walsh, M. B. *The nursing process: Assessing, planning, implementing, evaluating* (3rd ed.). New York: Appleton-Century-Crofts, 1978.

Zalar, M. Human sexuality: A component of total patient care. *Nursing Digest,* 1975, *3,* 40–43.

3. Sexuality in Infancy and Childhood

Marianna B. Heister

VALUES CLARIFICATION EXERCISE

Growth and development proceed along a continuum. The person you are now contains elements of the child you were. It would be helpful for you to try to remember and examine what you learned and felt about sex and sexuality as a child. The following questions are meant to help you examine the early influences on your sexual beliefs and behavior and decide what is now appropriate and functional for you.

Read and react to these questions. Write your answers, and try to distinguish your thoughts from your feelings as you do so.

1. Can you remember the first time you were aware of being a boy or a girl? What was the occasion? What were your feelings?
2. Did your parents expect different things from the boys and girls in your family? Do you remember ever being told, "No, boys don't do that" or "No, girls don't do that"? How did you feel about the negative injunctions?
3. What do you remember about your first sexual experience as a child? What were your feelings then? What are your feelings now about that first experience?
4. Were you and your family comfortable with household nudity?
5. What do you remember about your childhood sex play?
6. What was the first sex information you received from your parents? How comfortable were your parents with sex questions? What was the overriding message you received about sex from your family? From your peers?
7. What experiences in your childhood are a significant part of your attitudes and behavior about your present sexuality?

Now share your responses with a group of your peers and colleagues. How were your experiences similar? Different? Unique? What have you learned about the significance of early childhood experiences? How do you think family teaching and learning about sexuality affects childhood and later development?

BEHAVIORAL OBJECTIVES

At the completion of this chapter you will be able to:

- Explain the genetic factors involved in conception, gender decision, and fetal development.
- Identify the most frequently encountered chromosomal and hormonal sex abnormalities.
- Identify three theories of gender identity development and state the differences among them.
- Describe behavior in infancy that is conducive to optimal sexual adaptation.
- Explain the relationship between toilet training and sexuality.
- Discuss the possible effects of household nudity on children.
- Discuss genital self-stimulation as normal developmental behavior.
- Explain the significance of childhood sex play.
- Assess cross-gender behavior.
- Illustrate the role of the nurse as educator-counselor for childhood sex questions.

BIOLOGIC BEGINNINGS

Twenty-two of the twenty-three pairs of human chromosomes are called *autosomes*; the twenty-third pair is called the *sex chromosomes*. This twenty-third pair is of primary importance in sex determination. The female ovum carries an X chromosome and the male sperm either an X or a Y chromosome. Hence, normal females are designated as 46, XX and normal males are 46, XY. It is the Y-carrying sperm that carries the genes for maleness—the differentiation of the embryonic sex gonad into testes rather than ovaries.

The genetic decision is made at conception, but the resultant embryonic gonad is neutral and undifferentiated for six weeks. This primordial gonad consists of the *cortex*, or outer cells, which appear to be ovarian cells, and the *medulla*, or center layer, whose appearance is similar to the cells of the male testes. At six to eight weeks, if the embryo has a Y chromosome, the instructions from the Y call for the medulla cells to become primitive testes that will subsequently secrete male hormone and trigger further male development. With two X chromosomes, the cortex of the primitive gonad becomes an ovary. This feminine differentiation does not occur until approximately 12 weeks after conception.

By the seventh week of embryonic development, the primitive forms of both male and female reproductive duct systems are present. The male duct system is called the Wolffian, which eventually becomes the epididymus, vas deferens, and seminal vesicle. The Müllerian (female) duct forms the fallopian tubes, uterus, and upper two-thirds of the vagina (see Figure 3.1). In males, the embryonic testes produces fetal *androgens* (male hormones) to promote the differentiation of the Wolffian system and the MIS or Müllerian-inhibiting substance, to halt development of the Müllerian ducts.

As outlined above, female development is not dependent on ovarian secretion. It appears that intrinsically the embryo is female. A gamete (fertilized egg) with only one chromosome, an X chromosome (normally written as Xo), will develop as female. A gamete with only a single Y chromosome will die. Genetically, the addition of the Y chromosome is vital for male gender; on the hormonal level the added MIS and androgen are necessary for maleness to occur. In a genetically female embryo no additional hormone is needed for the Wolffian duct to degenerate and the Müllerian duct to produce the internal female reproductive structures (Figure 3.2).

During the third and fourth months of gestation, testicular androgens convert the undifferentiated external genitalia to male genitalia. At this time, the absence of androgens or the inability of the target site to use them will result in the appearance of external female genitalia. This is known as *male androgen-insensitivity syndrome*. During late pregnancy the testes descend from the abdomen into the scrotal sac, completing the prenatal physical sex differentiation.

Research dealing with biologic sex determinants has tended to cluster around two principal themes. Money (1972) and Sherfey (1972) believe that Wolffian and Müllerian duct systems develop in both XX and XY embryos. The growth of one and repression of the other is dependent on the presence or absence of sex hormones. In contrast, Jost (1973) maintains that maleness is imposed on basically female structures and hence that maleness is a deviation from intrinsic femaleness. The primary gonad is an ovary and only with the Y chromosome is testicular growth initiated.

What is clear is the critical timing of hormone release in fetal development. If all the programming is correct, 280 days after conception, an infant will be born whose genetic sex is correctly expressed: in other words, the outward visible manifestation of gender match will match the internal gender programming.

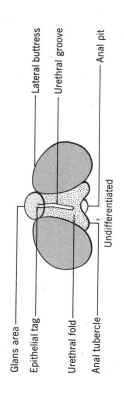

Glans area —
Epithelial tag —
Urethral fold —
Anal tubercle —

— Lateral buttress
— Urethral groove
— Anal pit

Undifferentiated

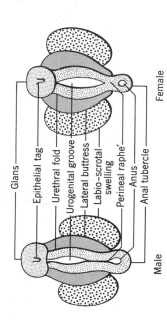

Glans —
Epithelial tag —
Urethral fold —
Urogenital groove —
Lateral buttress —
Labio–scrotal swelling —
Perineal raphé —
Anus —
Anal tubercle —

Female

Male

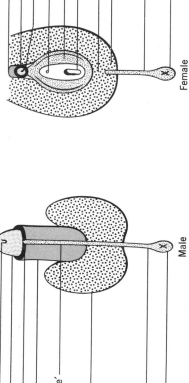

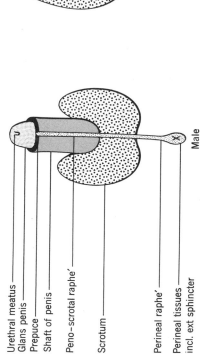

Corpus clitoridis —
Prepuce —
Glans clitoris —
Urethral meatus —
Labium minus —
Vagina —
Post. commissure —
Labium majus —

Perineal raphé —
Perineal tissues incl. ext. sphincter —

Female

Urethral meatus —
Glans penis —
Prepuce —
Shaft of penis —
Peno–scrotal raphé —

Scrotum —

Perineal raphé —
Perineal tissues incl. ext. sphincter —

Male

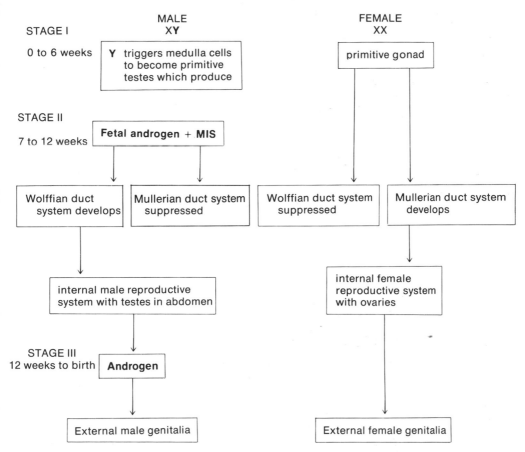

STAGE I
0 to 6 weeks

MALE
XY

FEMALE
XX

Y triggers medulla cells to become primitive testes which produce

primitive gonad

STAGE II
7 to 12 weeks

Fetal androgen + MIS

Wolffian duct system develops

Mullerian duct system suppressed

Wolffian duct system suppressed

Mullerian duct system develops

internal male reproductive system with testes in abdomen

internal female reproductive system with ovaries

STAGE III
12 weeks to birth

Androgen

External male genitalia

External female genitalia

Figure 3.2. Schemata of prenatal hormonal influences in gender differentiation. Source: M. Heister.

Figure 3.1. Differentiation of the external genital organs. Males and females start out the same, but areas that are equivalent for the two sexes in the undifferentiated state will become different organs by the time of birth. You can see this by tracing the fates of the various stippled areas in male development (on the left) and in female development (on the right). Top: undifferentiated state of early fetal development. Middle: differentiation begins at the third to fourth month of pregnancy. In this depiction of early differentiation, the most noticeable difference is the greater degree of fusion of the urethral fold in the male. Bottom: completed differentiation of the external genitals at birth. Reprinted with permission from Z. Luria, & M. D. Rose. *Psychology of human sexuality*. New York: John Wiley & Sons, 1979.

BIOLOGIC-GENDER PROBLEMS

Problems in *homologous* (matching in structure, position, and origin) prenatal sexual development can arise in chromosomal and hormonal areas. Chromosomal abnormalities include:

1. Turner's syndrome (45, X0), in which the genetic constitution (*genotype*) and observable constitution (*phenotype*) are female but the infant is without either ovaries or testes. External genitalia is female and the uterus is developed. These girls are usually short and have widely spaced nipples, webbing of the neck, and a low posterior hair line. Hormone replacement at the time of expected puberty will induce the development of secondary sexual characteristics; breast development and menstruation will occur, and female body contours will develop. These females typically exhibit strong psychological feminine behavior and interest patterns.
2. Klinefelter's syndrome (44, XXY). These infants are phenotypically male and the syndrome is often not recognized until puberty, when feminine secondary sex characteristics appear. Adults are usually tall and gangling with small testes and prostate gland and underdeveloped facial and body hair. Their sex drive is often reduced and they have a higher incidence than the general populace of behavioral disturbances. Money and Ehrhardt (1972) conjecture that the extra X chromosome introduces an element of vulnerability to psychological impairment. Klinefelter's syndrome, like Turner's syndrome, results in sterility.
3. 47, XXX. This syndrome produces phenotypical females, most of whom suffer some degree of mental retardation. These persons are usually fertile.
4. 47, XYY. These phenotypical males, although able to reproduce, often have reduced sperm count. They show an intellectual impairment on intelligence tests and have a substantially lower mean educational level attained than the general population. Elevated crime rates have been reported in the XYY group (Witkin et al., 1976), but these data may reflect a high detection rate rather than a high rate of commission of crimes, as was previously reported.

Hormonal sex abnormalities include:

1. The feminine androgenital syndrome. These are females with internal female sex organs who mature with external male sexual characteristics. There is excessive androgen production, usually resulting from a malfunctioning adrenal gland. If this condition is discovered shortly after birth, these children are treated with cortisone and surgically

feminized. Although puberty may be delayed, they are able to reproduce.

2. The male androgen insensitivity (testicular feminization). This condition results from a lack of sensitivity to androgen in genetic males. The fetus produces normal amounts of androgen and estrogen, but the target sites respond only to estrogen. These males have a feminine appearance and abdominal testes. They are sterile but psychologically normally feminine.

GENDER IDENTITY

Social gender differentiation begins at birth when the infant is labeled male or female. This sex-linked identification is critical for the awaiting family. It is at this point that indoctrination begins and that parental and social pressures and reinforcements begin to provide messages about appropriate role behavior. The optimum outcome of this patterning is a strong and positive gender identity for the child and a firm grasp of the behaviors that will provoke the desired response and confirm the child's gender identity.

Gender identity is the personal sense of one's own integral maleness or femaleness. It is emeshed with our gender role, or sex role, which is the public expression of that gender identity. The traditional belief that people are born male or female and simply grow up naturally as either men or women has been replaced with a recognition of the complexities of that maturation and an appreciation of the synergism of biologic input, social learning theory, and cognitive data. There is much theoretical discussion and debate about how we arrive at our gender identity, but these theories have yet to be proved.

Biologic Theories

The biologic viewpoint proposes that the physiologic differences between the sexes produce the inevitable realization of our gender. Our behavior, these theories argue, unfolds in a fixed and specific manner; our differences are gene-specific and unyielding.

Proponents of the biologic school include as evidence the physical differences between the species: Men are, in general, taller and heavier, have more physical energy, and have shorter life expectancies than women. They also propose that the observed behavior differences between the sexes are the effect of a biologically based gender state.

Current biology-based research is focused in two areas: the effect of hormones on sex typing, and the development and lateralization of brain function (Hetherington & Parke, 1979). Hormones are specialized and powerful chemical substances that interact with predisposed or precoded cells. Male and female hormones are found in varying amounts in persons of both sexes at every age. The biologic and psychologic predisposition to maleness or femaleness are affected by these hormones. Reports of current research suggest that hormonal differences experienced prenatally or during later development may contribute to differences in social behavior between sexes and within the same sex. Young, Goy, and Phoenix (1964) found that after prenatal injection of testosterone, a pregnant monkey gave birth to a pseudohermaphroditic female that exhibited both genital alterations and the social behavior characteristics of a male monkey. These behaviors included mounting behavior, threatening gestures, and rough play.

Sex behavior is thought to be determined to some extent by the manner in which the two cerebral hemispheres are organized, and it has been suggested that at a critical period in prenatal development sex hormones may determine potentials for hemispheric lateralization and brain organization. Prenatal hormone may in fact sensitize the brains of females to be more effective processors of verbal information and males of spatial information (Fennema, 1974).

Cognitive Theory

Kohlberg (1966) describes the development of sex typing in a Piaget-based cognitive framework. He maintains that children differentiate their gender roles and identify themselves as more similar to the same-sexed model before their gender identification is solidified. On the basis of sex-role differences and physical differences such as clothing, hair styles, and body types, children categorize themselves as male or female. It then becomes rewarding to behave in a like manner and imitate the chosen same-sex model. Kohlberg's 1966 framework presents three stages that all children pass through:

1. Basic gender identity: the child recognizes the self as a boy or a girl.
2. Gender stability: The child accepts that boys remain boys and girls remain girls.
3. Gender constancy: The child recognizes that superficial changes in appearance or activities do not alter gender.

Gender labels are understood by children as early as age three

(Thompson, 1975), but gender constancy does not develop fully until five to seven years of age (Emmerich & Goldman, 1972).

Social Learning Theory

Social learning theorists argue that gender identity is a consequence of socialization. Our culture has certain expectations regarding the abilities, interests, and values each sex should espouse. Parents and peers influence children to fulfill those expectations. The evidence for this view is impressive, especially the research with children whose external genitalia is either opposite to their chromosomal sex, or ambiguous. Money and Ehrhardt (1972) have a well-documented case of a seven-month-old twin boy whose penis was accidentally damaged beyond medical intervention at circumcision. His parents subsequently decided to raise him as a girl, and plastic surgery physically feminized him. The parents viewed the child as a girl and expected her to show feminine behavior. The child seemed normally feminine, but some ambiguity arose near puberty. In this situation, environmental expectations appear to have strongly influenced outcomes.

Social learning advocates believe that differential treatment of boys and girls begins early; mothers and fathers rough and tumble with male infants more than with females, and they engage more frequently in face-to-face talking with females (Moss, 1967). Schools perpetuate social learning factors. Girls are expected to be more proficient in English, boys in math and science (Dwerk, 1975). The media also reinforce social learning (Weitzman et al., 1972). Textbooks and reading books still often portray women as passive and supportive and men as intelligent and active, although this has changed somewhat in recent years.

There are unresolved questions concerning the role of these approaches in explaining gender identification. Two points can be made, however, First, most theorists agree to a basic premise of acquisition: Children learn to name their gender early and then to attach value to that gender. At that point they mark people around them as the same or different and will imitate those of their own gender most frequently. Second, theorists are aware of the strong interactional factor in gender identity. Biologic, social learning, and cognitive factors all play a role in determining a child's self-concept of gender, and the proportion of each influence may differ with cultures, ethnic groups, and even with individual children. Psychosocial-cognitive gender identity may be best envisaged as developing in the manner of infant bilingualism. Infants who learn two native languages must somehow code all that confront them in one language or the other. The young child must confront male and female role stimuli, decode them, internalize some, and inhibit others correctly to achieve homeostatic sexual identity.

Social Disruptions

Current research has looked at the effect of family disharmony on sex-role identification. Father unavailability from disinterest, divorce, or death has been shown to interfere with sex-typing in preadolescent boys, especially if the separation has occurred before age five (Drake & McDougall, 1977). For girls, the effects of father absence are largely relegated to adolescence, when significant deviations in heterosexual relationships appear (Hetherington, 1972). Maternal behavior can modify these results.

In families without a permanent male parent, both positive mothering from psychologically sound women who are able to utilize their own and outside resources and effective role modeling from other male figures can provide positive reinforcement for masculine identity and the development of masculine traits (Turnbull, 1980).

THE PSYCHOSEXUAL CONTINUUM

Nursing literature has long been congnizant of the psychosexual development theory proposed by Freud and developed by Erikson—that sexuality progresses along a continuum; it does not simply appear, full-blown, during adolescence. Infants and young children have the potential for a broad range of sexual expression, but the behaviors they exhibit and practice do not carry adult sexual significance. Simon and Gagnon (1971) believe that sexual behavior in childhood is learned, patterned behavior and, as such, is not the masked expression of a primordial drive. It is, instead, behavior with content that over time and with input from others becomes erotic in intent and outcome. This premise is the base that is used to discuss age-related sexual development and the problems that may occur in it.

Psychosexual development is continuous; however, continuity is not causality. Infant experiences defined as sexual are influential, not in a fixed cause-and-effect way but because of their pervasive character. An isolated sexual experience may affect many areas of a child's development, particularly if parental feedback occurs. The quality and intensity of the family's response to a child's sexual experiences programs the child for self-acceptance or guilt, trust in the self and in others or fear of intimacy. Society's acceptance of the child's right to grow sexually as well as cognitively and emotionally is critical.

INFANT SEXUALITY

Infancy, defined for our purposes as the age period ranging from 0 to 18 months, is marked by infants' needs to develop trust in their surroundings—trust that their caretakers will handle them frequently and gently, that they will be kept free of hunger and cold, and that they will be responded to with a sense of joy and acceptance. This sense of trust is predominantly a preverbal experience; it is a kinesthetic learning. Infants are stroked, massaged, fondled, and patted. They learn to distinguish between discomfort and comfort and to connect their sensations with the world around them and with the people who care for their needs.

The infants' first introduction to their sensuality occurs at birth when their mother greets them with her touch. Klaus and Kennell (1976) observed that when nude infants are placed next to their mothers shortly after birth, most mothers pattern their touch progressively. Fingertip touching of the infant's extremities was succeeded in four to eight minutes by massaging and stroking and by palm contact with the trunk. This attachment behavior bonds the maternal–child dyad and validates the infant. The body is caressed. The infant is accepted.

Breast feeding is now increasing in frequency and duration. The acceptance of the child's body is promoted by childbirth educators and the La Leche League. Both groups frequently advocate the family bed and increased skin-to-skin contact between infants and parents. This sensuality is the best possible foundation for healthy adult sexuality. In the context of warmth and gentleness children learn to feel good about their bodies and the pleasurable sensations they can experience.

Imbued in the developmental process is the ability to learn an overtly sexual sensual response. Children feel pleasure at the touch of others and at their own touch. With self-stimulation infant girls will lubricate, boys will have erections, and both will masturbate. Infants will repeat the self-stimulating behaviors that result in the feeling of pleasure. However, only in that pleasure-seeking dimension are these acts similar to adult sexual acts. The implications of infants' and children's masturbation are unlike those of adolescents and adults, who invest psychic and emotional qualities in the act. Infants may masturbate to orgasm. Leis and Kagen (1965) described pelvic thrust movements seen in male and female infants at eight to ten months. These appear to occur as part of an expression of affection in which the baby holds on to the parent, nuzzles her, and then rapidly thrusts and rotates the pelvis for a few seconds. This seems to be more an evidence of pleasure—an ecstatic rather than erotic mood—and it decreases with age as the close holding of the infant gives way to ambulation.

It is impossible to know what such experiences mean to children, but we do know that they almost uniformly alarm parents, who confuse infant sensuousness with adult eroticism. Sensitive counseling can inform and reassure parents about childhood sexual development and behaviors. Nothing in child development is lost. The pattern of healthy sensuality imprinted with care and tenderness in infancy will predispose children and their parents to accept the continued unfolding of their sexuality.

CHILDHOOD SEXUALITY

Sexual concerns in childhood are most often parental concerns about children. Children are not anxious about their sexual development as much as they are interested and curious. In dealing with children and their sexual development, practitioners often do not have direct access to the child. Information must filter through the parents and may be altered by the parents' biases and fears. A slow, gradual approach is vital. The parents must feel that their position on sexuality is respected. Nowhere in parent teaching is the nurse treading on as sensitive a ground as when she is counseling on sexuality. The topic should be approached gradually and sensitively. Parents must sense that their beliefs and values are respected by the nurse so that they become open to incorporating new information and different approaches.

For purposes of discussion in this portion of the chapter, *"childhood"* will refer to the age group from 18 months to 11 years. In American society today, children in the sixth grade are socially, if not physically, considered preadolescents, and their concerns are discussed in Chapter 4. There is obviously an overlap in age-demarcated sexual development. Some five-year-olds may request information that other eight-year-olds seek, and rigid age lines are not useful. Guidance must be geared to the age of the child in question, his or her emotional and intellectual readiness, and the parents' attitudes about the issue being discussed.

Toilet Training

Toilet training can be considered a sexual as well a a developmental milestone, for mastering self-control over the excretory processes in a socially acceptable manner should build on the self-acceptance of the body begun in infancy. Children may have occasional accidents, but they are not bad because of them. An accident should be viewed by parents as the accident that it is, not as an enduring blemish. In teaching parents about toilet training, it may be necessary for the nurse to specifically discuss the long-term sexual implications of labeling bowel movements as dirty and the less-than-tender touch of the parent when cleaning the child.

The toilet-training period often marks the beginning of the division of parental labor; both sexes tend to view this as mother's job, not father's. If father does get involved, he is much more likely to work with his son and leave his daughter to his wife. If this occurs, an unfortunate message is sent—little girls shouldn't let a man (even a daddy) see their genitalia. A far healthier precedent could be set if toilet training were viewed as a developmental milestone to be supported by the family rather than a mysterious, somewhat unclean hurdle for the child to scale.

Household Nudity

Anxiety about household nudity is primarily the parent's; the child may be uninterested or curious, but not worried. There is no research to support the Freudian view that household nudity is "overstimulating" to the child, with a consequent overloading of erotic sexualized stimuli (Green, 1976). Absence of parental nudity may involve the absence in the child of the appropriate cues for sex-typed self-labeling.

Certainly, negative messages concerning the child's body, particularly the genitalia, may translate into negative sexual inhibitions (Masters & Johnson, 1972). Deliberate household nudity, when practiced by sensitive parents, may promote children's positive self-acceptance of bodies in general and their own in particular. Nudity gives children a physical demonstration of their own gender identity classification, invites them to ask questions and draw conclusions about differences and sameness, and provides a nonthreatening framework for learning what they might look like when they are grown. It provides information as well as good feelings.

Children signal when they are no longer comfortable with household nudity. They close their bedroom doors, for example (Pogrebin, 1980). The need for privacy and modesty is tied to children's growing need to identify with their peers and to define their boundaries of self. They will stay fully clothed around the family and insist that the family does the same.

With parents who are not comfortable with intentional nudity, counseling about their reactions to accidental nudity is vital. A child who walks in on a parent in the bath may be gently shooed and the issue of privacy made paramount, not anger and embarrassment.

Genital Self-Stimulation

We know that children begin to masturbate in infancy and continue to do so in childhood. They discover by chance and then by conditional response that tactually stimulating themselves is pleasurable. Self-stimulation is obviously pleasurable for the child, does not harm another (specifically the parent), and there is no research to indicate present or potential harm for the child (Pogrebin, 1980).

In a study of 432 white adolescents, 56% of the boys and 30% of the girls reported masturbation before puberty (Elias & Gebhard, 1969). Manual stimulation is the most-practiced technique, but children also use forms of rhythmic rocking and press objects between their thighs.

For some parents, the realization that their child is masturbating is anxiety provoking if not alarming. Concerns about frequency may be brought up as well as ways to restrict the setting for the activity: "How often is too often?" "What if she does it in public?" Masturbation must be evaluated in terms of the child's activities in general. If a six-year-old elects to stay indoors and masturbate rather than interact socially with his or her friends, then masturbation is a psychosocial problem that must be addressed, not a sexual problem. When masturbation becomes compulsive or is used to ward off anxiety that is not primarily sexual in nature, it is excessive and symptomatic. The practitioner must help parents cut through their own sexual anxiety to the real issue of the child's use of sexual behavior.

The problem of the child selecting a poor setting for self-stimulation is more fiction than fact. Children have an acute awareness of society's restrictions on masturbation. If slip-ups do occur, a gentle "Not here" will suffice.

Elementary-school-age girls are frequent targets for teacher concerns about masturbation. The child may squirm, scratch, and pull at her pants. Urinary tract infections and pinworms should be ruled out before a decision is made that she is masturbating. The question of general school and home adjustment must be evaluated and the probability of sexual activity because of nonsexual problems kept in mind.

The ideal is to give children permission to experience delight in their bodies. This permission may range from nonintervention to explicit instructions depending on the parent's degree of comfort. The message "That's okay with us" is essential. Acceptance of the wonder of one's own body and its sexuality is probably the best precursor to successful adult sexual fulfillment.

Childhood Sex Play

Curiosity over genital difference will persist even if family nudity is permitted, although to a lesser degree. This curiosity will expand to available and equally curious collaborators, the child's peers. For the children, this is rarely a problem. Trouble comes when the parent becomes aware of sex play, expresses alarm, and transmits this anxiety to the child. Parents generally express two fears about mutual childhood exploration: homosexuality and exploitation of the child.

Current theories about the cause of homosexuality include the genetic theory: Homosexuals are born, not made. How then to explain that fact that exclusive heterosexuals will parent homosexuals? The hormone theory (too much testosterone or too little) is challenged by the ambiguous results of experiments attempting to link testosterone levels and homesexual orientation (Pogrebin, 1980). Also, increased testosterone, when given exogenously increases the amount of the sex drive; it does not alter its direction (Teitelbaum, 1976).

Psychoanalytic theory blames homosexuality on the family, especially the mother. Unresolved Oedipal and Electra complexes (the child loves, then rejects the opposite-sex parent, choosing instead the same-sex parent as a model) are crucial to this theory. Current evidence points to the fact that sex roles do not determine sexual orientation (Pogrebin, 1980). "Feminine" women may choose to be lesbians. The bottom line for parents is that no one knows why a child chooses heterosexuality or homosexuality. Preschoolers playing doctor with same-sex friends are not generally programming themselves for adult sexual orientation but exploring and learning. Parents can use the occasion to explain anatomical differences, to answer or raise questions, and to relieve anxiety.

There is rarely an exploitive element in sex play when the children are close in age. The potential is present, however, when one child is older, bigger, and coercive and the younger child is a passive, reluctant participant. The critical issues here are the intent of the older child (to bully or to harm) and the inappropriateness of a much older child choosing to play with a developmentally younger child. The nurse can help parents to react to the behavioral rather than the sexual nature of the incident. The younger child needs to be reassured that he or she need not submit to coercive sex play. The nurse can also suggest that the parents of the younger child discuss with the older child's parents the coercive aspect of the behavior. This older child and his or her family are also in need of supportive counseling.

Cross-Gender Behavior

A problem that may be classified as either parent activated or child activated is *cross-gender behavior*. Cross-gender behavior occurs when a child persistently chooses play partners, dress preferences and interest patterns stereotypically associated with the opposite sex. This behavior is parent activated when the child is satisfied with his or her core sexual identity of being anatomically male or female but expresses play activity preferences that do not fit parental expectations. Children, particularly boys, may experience social conflict and isolation from their peers because of the androgenous choice. Parents need to be encouraged to accept the child's play preferences and to be guided to help the child find other children whose interests also do not fit the cultural stereotype.

Cross-gender behavior may be child activated when the child is anatomically normal but wishes to belong to the opposite sex. These children believe that modifying their dress or hair length is sufficient to change their sex, and the determination to belong to the other sex will persist over time. Practitioners may be called on to help parents evaluate cross-gender behavior to determine its classification, its management, and the possible need for referral. Ask both the child and the parents:

Is the child happy?
To what degree is the cross-gender behavior causing the child and his or her parents distress?
How long have these behaviors been evident?
What secondary gain, if any, is the child receiving from these actions?

Ideally, children should be able to rise above gender-role limitations and develop psychological harmony with their inner needs and temperaments. But this transcendence must follow the stage of conformity in which children are motivated to comply with the rules of sex-role differentiation. If either the parent or the child perceives a problem in the conformist stage, there is a problem. The nurse must help the family determine the origin of the problem by evaluating the child's behavior and motives as well as the parent's expectations and biases.

THE ROLE OF THE NURSE AS EDUCATOR-COUNSELOR

A universal concern for American parents is the timing, approach, and quality of sex education for their children. It is important that basic sex information be without sex-role distortion, be anatomically correct, and begin early. Sex is not just for procreation, as children will learn from movies and friends, but parents may need encouragement and support to deal constructively with presenting sexuality in more than one dimension.

The nurse needs to help parents avoid the double message, "Sex is dirty—save it for someone you love" (Bernstein, 1978), and to help them appreciate the value of showing gestures of affection to each other as lovers; children learn how sexual intimates relate by observation. The warmth and communion of physical love may be expressed without the clinical details but with elements of supportive, tender caring visible to the child.

Parts of the body should be given their anatomical name as well as their street names. A second grader may know sexual words but may rarely know the anatomical term or its definition. The nurse should encourage parents to start with open-ended questions: "What have you heard this called?" "What do you think happens when a baby is made?" These questions can be asked at varying ages and appropriate details supplied for the childs age-level readiness. It is not necessary for parents to understand all the complexities of sexual reproduction to teach children what they want to know. Learning will continue throughout life. If there is a relaxed aura of acceptance of sexuality, children will question the parent. If, because of past reticence, the questions don't come, the parents must initiate the discussion and should recognize the need for reinforcement. Discussing sexual intercourse once and expecting total understanding and acceptance is as foolish as explaining the concept of time to a six-year-old only once.

What and When To Teach

Bernstein (1978) has classified children's questions about sex and their readiness for explanations in line with Piaget's stages of development. As in all development, the stages are overlapping and sequential.

Level-one children range in age from three to seven. When asked, "Where do babies come from:" they answer as geographers, generally choosing stores, hospitals, "God's place," or mommies' bodies. When talking with level-one children, the nurse should use this interest in places to teach, giving them the language of sex: womb, vagina, penis. By four years of age, children should know:

1. The names of the body's sexual parts
2. The socially shared words for elimination
3. The basic fact that babies grow in mother's bodies
4. Enough anatomy, by direct observation, to understand the difference between boys and girls even if they cannot explain how they know
5. That babies are made by men and women together.

Level-two children are four to eight years old. Children at this stage understand that babies have not always existed, they must be manufactured. These children are familiar with the notion of a seed in conception but are puzzled about how the seeds get from point of origin to their destination, and they tend to view sex for procreation only. In talking with level-two children, who are magical thinkers, language is vital. For them, each word conjures up a concrete image. An egg, for example, is white, cold, and from a refrigerator or a chicken. The terms "ovum" and "sperm" should be used to avoid confusion.

Level-three children are the in-betweens, ages five to ten. They are preoperational and concrete-operational thinkers. They know the parts of the reproductive system, social relationships, sexual intercourse, and the union of the sperm and the egg, but they do not connect these ideas into a coherent whole. These children will explain parenthood as a matter of legality or biology and often still find the process of sexual intercourse mysterious. This is the age when earlier teachings need to be reinforced, misunderstandings corrected, and the idea stressed that sexual intercourse is pleasurable and valued for itself.

Children between seven and twelve years old are level four, the reporters. They are concerned about accuracy and engrossed by social rules and societal prescriptions of reproduction. Laws are important at this age, and these children have acquired an understanding of conservation: things can be equal even though they appear different. Children at this level can reverse the direction of their thinking and consider past and future. This is the time to help children sort out feelings and social arrangements in sexuality and to deal expressly with values.

Level five, the theoreticians, begins at 10 years of age, and level six as early as 11 or 12 years of age. In these stages, children speculate on the principle of conception and assimilate the various elements of reproduction into a unified whole. By now they need to understand the biologic and social implications of their sexual behavior.

The nurse may need to remind parents that knowing more about sex does not lead to doing more; information is not permission. Failure to provide information about sexual behavior, physical changes during puberty, and contraception leaves children unprotected and lacking knowledge that is vital to their personal comfort, safety and growth. The defense that "my child is not into that yet" is no defense. By the time children are "into it," it will be too late. Sex information should be anticipatory, given before the need for it arises; often it is the parent's level of comfort and need to give information that provides the timing, not the child's readiness to learn. Children need correct information to make intelligent choices. To surround sexuality with mystery and guilt is to invite misunderstanding, frustration, and very possibly tragedy. Gadpaille (1975) advises "that nothing be taught to a child that must be subsequently unlearned for successful adulthood." That overriding concept is the guide for parents and their children in every area of sexuality.

NURSING PROCESS

Client: Lynn Oldhouse—mother of three-year-old child attending a day care center

Nurse: Ellen Dryden—school nurse and mother of child attending same day-care center. The women often meet as they come for their children at the end of their work day.

Assessment

Subjective Data

"I know you are a nurse and I want to ask you something."
"My boy, Todd, he's the same age as yours, I think—three years old."
"I've been married for six months to Tom."
"He—Tom—goes around the house with no clothes on."
"He says it was that way with his family."
"It wasn't that way in my house—we weren't that free."
"Before we were married, and we were at his place, it was okay with me."
"But now—with Todd—I can't be comfortable without clothes when Todd
    is around."
"Tom can, but I just can't."
"And I worry what it will do to Todd. He never saw me without clothes
    before—and now he sees both of us."
"I worry. There never was a man around the house before Tom and I got
    married."
"Should I ask Tom to wear clothes when Todd is around?"

Objective Data

27 years old
Mother of three-year-old child.
Married to Tom six months.
First marriage for both partners.
Both partners employed—legal secretary and credit manager.
Worried about effect of household nudity on three-year-old child.
Seeks opinion about strategy for coping with new experience of household
    nudity.

Nursing Diagnosis

Inadequate information related to coping with different patterns of
    household nudity within new family unit.

Planning

Provide atmosphere of acceptance.

Reassure verbally.

Explain that client's emotional response is appropriate and commonly experienced by others.

Encourage expression of feelings about household nudity for self, within sexual relationship, with children, and particularly with Todd.

Offer feedback of client's expressed feelings.

Explore fears of possible consequences of household nudity on child.

Explain that household nudity for three-year-old child can provide information and clarification for the process of acquiring a positive body image.

Explain that a variety of family experiences—dressing and bathing together, "skinny dipping" together—can be helpful for the process of acquiring a positive body image.

Explain that growing up in a family comfortable with household nudity can contribute to a positive sexual awareness.

Explain the difference between secrecy and privacy.

Explain that acceptance of household nudity does not necessarily mean open display.

Explain that acceptance of household nudity is an individual and family choice.

Explain that comfort with and acceptance of household nudity by a child in the family is directly proportional to the comfort with and acceptance of household nudity by the adults in the family.

Advise that significant others express love and acceptance of one another.

Explain the importance of offering emotional support to one another.

Encourage discussion of feelings and concerns with Tom about household nudity for self, within sexual relationship, and within family unit.

Recommend that patterns of household nudity be set by the family.

Advise observation of Todd for negative reaction to household nudity (withdrawal, acting out).

Encourage limitation of nudity to sexual relationship if negative reaction occurs in Todd.

Emphasize that major task of new family grouping is the establishment of family relationships.

Explain that patterns of family interactions need attention.

Indicate availability for more information and further counseling.

Implementation

Initiate discussion about household nudity with Tom.

Share feelings of love and acceptance with Tom.

Share feelings of comfort and acceptance of household nudity for self and
within sexual relationship.
Share feelings and concerns about effects of household nudity on Todd.
Discuss readiness to continue dressing and bathing together as family.
Discuss significance of task of establishing family relationship.
Discuss ways of strengthening or building interactions.
Encourage Tom to continue to develop relationship with Todd.
Give Todd permission not to follow patterns of household nudity.
Give Todd permission to express feeling about new person (Tom) in his
day-to-day life.

Evaluation (three months later)

Reports acceptance of pattern of household nudity for self.
Reports acceptance of patterns of household nudity for Todd.
Reports Todd seeking out Tom.

BIBLIOGRAPHY

Bell, A. P., & Weinberg, M. S. *Homosexualities*. New York: Simon and Schuster,
1978.
Bernstein, A. *The flight of the stork*. New York: Delacorte Press, 1978.
Burgess, J. K. Children in one parent families. *Sexual Behavior*, 1973, *3*, 9–13.
Campbell, C. *Nursing diagnosis and intervention in nursing practice*. New York:
Wiley, 1979.
Crooks, R., & Baur, K. *Our sexuality*. Menlo Park, Cal.: Benjamin/Cummings,
1980.
Drake, C. T., & McDougall, D. Effects of the absence of a father and other male
models on the development of a boy's sex role. *Developmental Psychology*,
1977, *13*, 537–538.
Dwerk, C. S. Sex differences in the meaning of negative evaluations in achieve-
ment situations: Determinants and consequences. Paper presented at the
meeting of the Society for Research in Child Development. Denver, April,
1975.
Erhardt, A., Greenberg, N., & Mahoney, J. Female gender identity and absence of
fetal hormones: Turner's syndrome. *Johns Hopkins Medical Journal*, 1970,
125, 234, 248.
Elias, J. E., & Gebhard, P. H. Sexuality and sexual learning in childhood. *Phi
Delta Kappan*, 1969, *5*, 401–405.
Emmerich, W., & Goldman, K. S. Boy and girl identify task (technical report). In
V. Shipman (Ed.), *Disadvantaged children and their first school experience*.

Technical report PR-72-20, Princeton, N.J.: Educational Testing Service, 1972.

Fennema, E. *Mathematics, spatial ability, and the sexes.* Paper presented at the American Education Research Association Annual Meeting, Chicago, 1974.

Flaste, R. Is it harmful for children to see parents in the nude? *Medical Aspects of Sexuality,* April 1971, *5,* 35–41.

Gadpaille, W. J. *The cycles of sex.* New York: Scribner, 1975.

Goy, R. W. Organizing effects of androgen on the behavior of rhesus monkeys. In R. P. Michael (Ed.), *Endocrinology and human behavior.* New York: Oxford University Press, 1968.

Green, R. (Ed.). *Human sexuality: A health practitioner's guide.* Baltimore: Williams & Wilkins, 1975.

Green, R. *Sexual identity conflicts in children and adults.* New York: Basic Books, 1974.

Green, R. The sexual problems of children. In W. W. Oaks (Ed.), *Sex and the life cycle,* New York: Grune & Stratton, 1976.

Hetherington, E. M. Effects of father absence on personality development in adolescent daughters. *Developmental Psychology,* 1972, *7,* 313–326.

Hetherington, E. M., & Parke, R. D. *Child psychology, a contemporary viewpoint* (2nd ed.). New York: McGraw-Hill, 1979.

Hyde, J. S. *Understanding human sexuality.* New York: McGraw-Hill, 1979.

Janda, L. H., & Klenke-Hamel, K. E. *Human sexuality.* New York: Van Nostrand, 1980.

Jost, A. 'Maleness' is imposed on a basically feminine fetus. *Science Digest,* 1973, *73,* 4.

Klaus, M. H., & Kennell, J. H. *Maternal-infant bonding.* St. Louis: Mosby, 1976.

Kohlberg, L. A. cognitive-developmental analysis of children's sex-role concepts and attitudes. In E. E. Maccoby (Ed.), *The development of sex differences.* Stanford, Cal.: Stanford University Press, 1966.

Kolodny, R. C., Masters, W., Johnson, V. E., & Biggs, M. A. *Textbook of human sexuality for nurses.* Boston: Little, Brown, 1979.

Lewis, M., & Kagan, J. Studies in attention. *Merrill-Palmer Quarterly,* 1965, *11,* 95–127.

Luria, Z., & Rose, M. D. *Psychology of human sexuality.* New York: Wiley, 1979.

Martinson, F. M. *Infant and child sexuality: A sociological perspective.* St. Peter, Minn.: The Book Mark, GAC, 1973.

Masters, W., & Johnson, V. E. *Human sexual inadequacy.* Boston: Little, Brown, 1970.

Mertens, T. R. *Human genetics.* New York: Wiley, 1975.

Mims, F. H., & Swenson, M. *Sexuality: A Nursing perspective.* New York: McGraw-Hill, 1980.

Money, J. *Determinants of human sexual identity and behavior.* In C. Sager & H. Singer Kaplan (Eds.), *Progress in group and family therapy.* New York: Bruner-Mazel, 1972.

Money, J. Fatherhood behavior and gender identity. *Medical Aspects of Human Sexuality,* 1972, *3,* 67–80.

Money, J., Ehrhardt, A. A. *Man, woman, boy, and girl.* Baltimore: Johns Hopkins University Press, 1972.

Money, J., & Tucker, P. *Sexual signatures.* Boston: Little, Brown, 1975.

Moss, H. A. Sex age and state as determination of mother–infant interaction. *Merrill-Palmer Quarterly,* 1967, *13*, 19–36.

Pogrebin, L. C. *Growing up free.* New York: McGraw-Hill, 1980.

Roberts, E. J. *Family life and sexual learning: A study of the role of parents in the social learning of children.* New York: Population Education, Inc., 1978.

Sears, R., Maccoby, E. C., & Levin, H. *Patterns of child rearing.* Evanston, Ill.: Dow, Peterson, 1957.

Sherfey, J. *The nature and evolution of female sexuality.* New York: Random House, 1972.

Simon, W., & Gagnon, J. On psychosexual development. In D. L. Grummon & A. M. Barclay (Eds.), *Sexuality, Search for Perspective.* New York: Van Nostrand, 1971.

Teitelbaum, M. A. (Ed.). *Sex differences: Social and biological perspectives.* New York: Anchor Press, 1976.

Thompson, S. K. Gender labels and early sex role development. *Child Development,* 1975, *46*, 339–347.

Turnbull, J. M. Masculinity of father absent boys. *Medical Aspects of Human Sexuality,* 1980, *14*, 149–163.

Weitzman, L. J., Eifler, D., Hodada, E., & Ross, C. Sex role socialization in picture books for pre-school children. *American Journal for Socialization.* 1972, *77*, 1125–1150.

Witkin, H. A., Mednick, S. A., Schulsinger, F., Bakkestrom, E., Christiansen, K. O., Goodenough, D. R., Hirschhorn, K., Lundsteen, C., Owen, D. R., Philip, J., Rubin, D. B., & Stocking, M. Criminality in XYY and XXY men. *Science,* 1976, *193* 547–555.

Witters, W. L., & Jones-Witters, P. *Human sexuality: A biological perspective.* New York: Van Nostrand, 1980.

Woods, N. F., & Mandetta, A. F. Sexuality throughout the life cycle: Prenatal life through adolescence. *In Human sexuality in health and illness* (2nd ed.). St. Louis: Mosby, 1979.

Young, W. C., Goy, R. W., & Phoenix, C. H. Hormones and sexual behavior. *Science,* 1964, *143*, 212–218.

4. Sexuality in Adolescence

Alice A. Fleming

VALUES CLARIFICATION EXERCISE

The sexual learning and experiences that occurred during your adolescence are significant to the person you are now. The following questions concern your feelings and thoughts about your body image, how you obtained information about sex, your early explorations of sexual activities, and your sexual decision-making history. Read these questions, react to them, and write down your reactions.

Try to recall your own experience of puberty. Describe, through your own recollections, the changes that occurred. How did you feel about these changes? Good? Curious? Anxious? Enticing to others? Sexy? Vulnerable? Awkward? Pleased? Secretive? Proud? Dirty? Relieved? Scared?

Were you pleased with your body? Did you want to change part or all of it? How?

How did your body compare with others of the same gender?

Did you feel your body was attractive to others who were the gender of your sexual preference?

From what sources did you acquire information about sex? From peers of the same or other gender? Parent or siblings of the same or other gender? Teachers? Clergy? Relatives?

What was the atmosphere in which you acquired this information? Open? Secretive? Embarrassed? Factual?

What were the underlying messages? Virginity is prized? Sex is for procreation only? Love is good; lust is bad? Sex is for fun? "Good girls" versus "bad girls"? Did these differ from "good boys" and "bad boys"? If so, how?

Was the information you received concerning sex and sexuality the information you wanted? Explain.

When and under what circumstances did you first experience feelings of love or being in love? What was that like for you?

When and under what circumstances did you first experience sexual arousal? Were these feelings for the same or opposite gender or both? What reactions did you have to these feelings?

When did you first experience kissing, holding, or touching? What were the circumstances? Were these activities with a person of the same or opposite gender or both? How did you feel about these experiences?

Do you recall being unsure of your preference for gender of sexual partners? How did you feel about this ambiguity? How did you feel about your sexual orientation once the ambiguity began to lessen?

When did you first become interested in becoming sexually active? Was a particular person involved? Were peers experimenting with sexual activity? What was the connotation of this activity? Taboo? Healthy? Dirty? Normal? Rebelling? Exciting? Fun?

What factors were important in your decision to become sexually active? Peer pressure? Partner pressure? Family teachings? Personal convictions? Religious views? Fear of pregnancy?

A popular theme today is that the availability of contraceptives increases the likelihood of a teenager becoming sexually active. From your own experience and the experience of your friends, what is your opinion of that statement?

Can you recall a process of making the decision to become sexually active, or did you find yourself sexually active before you acknowledged that the decision had been made? Can you recall an active decision to use or not use contraceptives once you became sexually involved?

How did you feel about yourself when you first became sexually active? How did you feel about your partner?

What feelings have you had while going through the exercise above? Embarrassed? Anxious? Joyous? Confused? Excited? Exposed? Vulnerable?

Share your answers with a group of four or five of your peers or colleagues. Note the similarities and the differences. Were there strong opinions and feelings? Were the differences accepted, and were the strong feelings tolerated? How do you think your opinions and feelings might influence your interaction with a client? How do you think the opinions and feelings of the group members would affect the nursing plan for the sexual health of an adolescent client?

After you have read this chapter, review what you wrote about the process of sexual decision-making. Does the material in the chapter affect how you see the process? If so, in what ways? You may choose to discuss these reactions and responses with a group of peers or colleagues, as well.

BEHAVIORAL OBJECTIVES

After completing this chapter, you will be able to

- Identify the major anatomical and physiological changes that occur during puberty.
- Identify and define the major components of sexuality during adolescence.
- Discuss the major components of sexuality in terms of adolescent psychosexual development.
- Discuss research findings on masturbation, heterosexual, and homosexual behaviors in adolescents.
- Identify changes in attitudes about sex and sexuality that have occurred in this country in recent decades.
- Identify the common misconceptions and misinformation that exist among adolescents.
- Identify some of the factors that correlate with adolescent failure to use contraceptives.
- Describe the special concerns of the sexually active adolescent girl (aged 11 to 13).
- Outline the decision-making process and the special considerations for adolescents learning this process.
- Discuss the role of the nurse as educator-counselor of adolescents.

HEALTH CARE AND ADOLESCENT SEXUALITY

To give effective health care to adolescents, the health professional must understand the extent to which the development of adolescents' sexuality affects and is affected by virtually every aspect of their overall development. The definition of human sexuality this text has used as its foundation clearly states the pervasiveness of a person's sexuality throughout her or his life:

> The SIECUS concept of *sexuality* refers to the totality of being a person. It includes all of those aspects of the human being that relate specifically to being boy or girl, woman or man, and is an entity subject to life-long dynamic change. Sexuality reflects our human character, not solely our genital nature. As a function of the total personality it is concerned with the biological, psychological, sociological, spiritual, and cultural variables of life which, by their effects on personality development and interpersonal relations, can in turn affect social structure. [SIECUS/UPPSALA, 1980, p. 8]

In light of the inseparability of sexuality from the whole person, and in consideration of the extensive formative development an adolescent undergoes, the rationale for consistently addressing adolescent sexual health as integral to comprehensive health care becomes quite clear.

Although the nurse who works with adolescents will need to have extensive knowledge of all aspects of typical and atypical adolescent development, the focus of this chapter is to provide a perspective that will help the nurse view adolescents as sexual beings whose development during this life phase is specifically sexual in nature and significance.

PUBERTY

Puberty refers to the second stage of physiological and anatomical sexual development (the first stage is prenatal). *Adolescence* is a sociological term used in reference to the period of transition from childhood to adulthood, and its study includes consideration of the psychological, social, moral, emotional, and cognitive aspects of development during that transitional phase. Adolescence is somewhat vaguely demarcated by the onset of puberty, as its beginning, and by the start of young adulthood—usually cited as age 19 in this society—as its end point. In this chapter, the terms "girls" and "boys" refer to adolescents through age 16, and the terms "young women" and "young men" refer to adolescents aged 17 through 19. Puberty comprises a series of bodily changes that are predictable in nature and sequence. Adolescence is much less predictable, and is as unique as the person and the society in which that person grows up.

The many bodily changes of puberty culminate midway through adolescence in full sexual functionality and fecundity. Strong emotional demands are placed on an adolescent by this process of change. Even with adequate foreknowledge of the events of puberty—which a majority of adolescents still do not receive from any quarter—and an accepting environment in which to grow, an adolescent will feel apprehension in response to this process; the body from which he or she had, in part, derived self-definition suddenly undergoes change. These changes can be particularly troublesome in that they follow genetic rather than personally chosen guidelines, and yet they have far-reaching social and sexual ramifications. Clearly, there are also psychological, cognitive, social, and moral issues raised for the adolescent, who is now obtaining the sexual appearance and capacities of an adult. These issues are especially poignant in this society where sex and sexuality are at once strongly idolized and idealized and taboo. The specific events of puberty are briefly reviewed below. The experience and meaning of these events for the adolescent can only be understood, however, if these occurrences are seen in the context described above and in ensuing portions of this chapter.

In girls, puberty is instigated (and subsequently regulated) by a sudden rise in the production and release of sex hormones. Its onset first becomes visible with breast budding, although renewed ovarian growth begins one to two years before this time. Growth of the hips and buttocks begins at approximately the same time as breast budding. Within a year, pubic hair will begin to grow, and the growth spurt will have begun. In girls, the growth spurt entails broadening of the pelvic girdle and an increase in height. Slightly past the peak of the growth spurt, at an average age of 12.5 years in this country at this time, menarche will occur. Ovulation will begin within two years after menarche. The adolescent girl is now capable of conceiving and bearing children.

Puberty in boys is similarly instigated by a sharp rise in sex hormones. The first changes in boys are enlargement of both the testes and scrotum. The growth of pubic hair may begin shortly after. Organs that will contribute to the production of semen, including the seminal vesicles, epididymis, and prostate, begin to mature. The penis now begins to enlarge, as does the larynx (causing the voice to begin deepening). At about this same time, a boy's growth spurt starts, and involves an increase in shoulder breadth, musculature, and height. Erections will begin increasing in frequency. Just before the peak of the growth spurt, at an average age of about 14, the first ejaculation will occur. Within a year, the ejaculate will contain viable sperm. The adolescent boy can now father children.

Adolescents experience an increase in their level of energy and strong feelings of sexual arousal, often before the first physical changes of puberty become visible. Many sex researchers postulate that learning and culturalization combine with endocrinological factors to form the sex drive that emerges so strongly in adolescence (Chilman, 1978; Simon & Gagnon, 1971). Testosterone, one of the primary sex hormones responsible for pubertal development in both girls and boys, is probably involved in this increased sex drive in both genders (Kolodny, Masters, Johnson, & Biggs, 1979).

Side effects of the increased level of another sex hormone, estrogen, frequently occur in adolescent girls and boys. Estrogen may cause temporary weight gain and acne in both genders. In almost 80% of adolescent boys, temporary breast enlargement occurs. Estrogen often causes irritability, depression, and sudden shifts in mood. This is particularly true for girls, in whom the amount of estrogen is much greater and the fluctuation of the hormone's level much more marked.

The onset and subsequent developmental rate of puberty vary widely. Girls begin puberty at an average age of 8 to 12, reach their maximum growth rate at about age 12.14 (±.88) years, and attain their maximum height at an average age of 16. Boys are, on an average, about two years behind girls in each of these developmental stages (Hyde, 1979; Kolodny et al., 1979). This difference between genders frequently causes adolescents to feel anxious about their body image and interpersonal, other-sex relationships (see the section in this chapter on body image). Actual ages for the onset, spurt, and cessation of pubertal development varies much more from one adolescent to the next than the averages above indicate. Puberty may begin any time between ages 8 and 16 and usually proceeds without any physiological or anatomical difficulty; problems resulting from early or late development are more likely to be psychological, emotional, and social in nature. Cases of true precocious and delayed puberty do occur, however, and may require medical attention. A final aspect of variance in the timing of puberty is that over recorded history, the average age of onset has steadily declined. In 1930, the average age of menarche in the United States was 13.5 years; in 1960, 13.0; in 1975, 12.5. The rate of this decline seems to be slowing, however (Hyde, 1979).

Once puberty has begun, the specific anatomical and physiological changes almost always progress in the order described above. Very rarely, for example, does menarche occur before breast budding, or penile growth before scrotal growth.

All aspects of puberty have sexual significance for both girls and boys. Adolescents become fully sexual in appearance and in physiological terms, and they experience sharply increased sexual arousal. These pubertal changes play a significant role in an adolescent's psychosexual development.

PSYCHOSEXUAL DEVELOPMENT

The primary developmental task for adolescents is to redefine themselves in an independent identity within a sexual and social context predictive of adulthood. Pressure for growth and reintegration are placed on adolescents by both parental and societal demands and the physiological factors of puberty. These pressures to change may cause an adolescent to feel vulnerable and to vacillate frequently in behavior and attitude. Questions such as "Am I normal?" and "How do I compare?" or "Am I good enough?" become central to all aspects of early adolescent development, but most particularly in relation to the adolescent's developing sexuality. Psychosexual development is inextricably mixed with development of the psychological, social, moral, cognitive, and emotional aspects of personality. Adolescents' developing sexuality affects and is affected by their self-esteem, the formation of all relationships, the ability to attain intimacy within relationships, and their life and work goals.

An overview of the major components of sexuality shows the importance of the adolescent phase of psychosexual development. Biological gender, body image, gender identity, preference for gender of partner, a sexual value system, sexual identity, and sexual self-concept together make up a person's sexuality. What does each of these components entail for the adolescent?

Biologic Gender

The *biologic gender* of a person has been described by Money and Ehrhardt (1972) as consisting of five variables: chromosomes, gonadal and hormonal gender, internal accessory organs, and external genitalia. With the exception of surgery, severe injury, or diseases that may affect the pubertal portion of biologic gender development, all of these variables are determined at conception or during prenatal development. Usually, the assignment of biologic gender is the aspect of sexuality with which the adolescent is least concerned.

Body Image

Body image, a significant component of a person's sexuality, is the way in which a person perceives her or his physical appearance and presence. Physical appearance includes consideration of a person's specific features and general attractiveness, which involves the person's affect. It also entails how the person wears clothes, particularly in terms of fashion. A person's physical presence involves the sense of the way he or she moves (gracefully? clumsily?) and fills space. To illustrate, each of us is aware of how we must move, given our size and coordination, in order to avoid bumping into things. This sense becomes part of our body image. These types of perceptions, both of physical appearance and presence, are significant not only in terms of how people view themselves but also of the way people believe others view them. As such, body image lies at the crux of a person's overall concept of self and, more specifically, of sexuality. This last point becomes particularly poignant in light of the fact that there is relatively little people can do, barring surgery, to change the actual facts of their physical appearance. A person's body image begins forming during the first three years of life. Throughout life, this image is continually being modified through feedback—or presumed feedback— from others, as well as through comparisons of self with others and with the cultural ideal.

During adolescence a critical reassessment of this body image occurs as puberty changes an adolescent's physical appearance and function, often quite dramatically. Puberty also changes the context in which adolescents view themselves and are viewed by others. All of the changes of puberty have sexual meaning. The shape of a young woman's hips, the size of her breasts, her height (especially as compared to that of male peers), her increased sexual drive, menarche, and her developing genitalia have a strong sexual impact on her body image. A young man's height, musculature, deepening voice, penis size, increased sexual drive, frequency of erections (often awkwardly timed), and his newly acquired ejaculatory function will similarly have a sexually significant impact on his body image. Weight gain, acne, clumsiness, moodiness, or gynecomastia (breast enlargement in boys) also affect the adolescent's body image in a sexual context.

Adjusting to a changing body image is especially difficult for adolescents in that this change echoes and compounds other feelings caused by the many other changes of adolescence. They feel vulnerable and caught in the double bind of wanting both to conform to their peers and to be unique. Many questions emerge for the adolescent in response to these feelings. "Am I normal?" is a question often asked in relation to the ways in which an adolescent's appearance is changing, her or his awkwardness, and so on. Wide discrepancies in the age of puberty's onset, as described earlier, may also cause anxiety in this regard. This is most true for boys who begin pubertal development late and for girls who begin very early or late. "Am I good enough?" is another common question. Breast size and penis size are two issues frequently examined from this judgmental perspective. Such questions are complicated by the media, which promulgate so-called ideal bodies and ideal ways of looking and acting, often with strong sexual overtones.

Body image strongly influences other aspects of sexual development, particularly gender identity and sexual self-concept. Hence it affects virtually all aspects of a person's life. In this light, the importance of helping adolescents toward the formation of a positive and accepting body image becomes clear.

Gender Identity

Gender identity is described by Hyde (1979) as "the person's private, internal sense of maleness or femaleness—which is expressed in personality and behavior—and the integration of this sense with the rest of the personality and with the gender roles prescribed by society" (p. 57).

A person's gender identity is central to the way in which that person formulates life and work goals. For example, a woman whose sense of being female precludes looking for life satisfaction in a competitive career that challenges her (and her male counterparts') capacities of thought and judgment will formulate other types of life and work goals more commensurate with her gender identity. Adolescence is a critical period for both girls and boys in that both gender identity and the foundation of life and work goals are explored and largely integrated during this time.

A person's gender identity is perhaps even more fundamental to the way in which he or she forms and maintains interpersonal relationships. A person's sense of femaleness or maleness strongly affects such issues within a relationship as dominance and responsibility: Who is in control? Who is responsible to whom in what ways and to what extent? Patterns of relating in these and similar terms are established during adolescence through a process of experimenting with various peer interactions, using adults—particularly parents—as primary role models until personalized modes of interaction emerge. The interpersonal issues of dominance and responsibility have ramifications of particular concern within early adolescent heterosexual relationships. The responsibility for the decision to become sexually active, and to use contraceptives, is frequently sublimated (hence the decision becomes a passive one) or given over to the partner because of constraints imposed by gender identity. The young adolescent girl often gives her partner the responsibility of deciding whether or not she will become sexually active and in so doing denies her own responsibility for contraception. The young adolescent boy often views his partner as responsible for avoiding pregnancy, and likewise does not use contraceptives. In this light, some aspects of female and male gender identity that are still quite prevalent can be seen as contributing to the continued increase in teenage pregnancies (see the section in this chapter on heterosexual behaviors).

Gender identity may play an important role in the development of adult preference for the gender of partners. Gender conformity or nonconformity is a measure of whether the femaleness or maleness of persons' gender identities agrees with their biological genders, and it is correlated to adult heterosexual or homosexual orientation. Bell, Weinberg, and Hammersmith (1981) found childhood gender nonconformity—a considerable and consistent identification with and interest in the activities of parents and others of the other gender—to be highly predictive of adult homosexual preference (see the section in this chapter on preference for gender of partner). Adolescence is a time of realizing the short- and long-term significance of gender identity and sexual preference and of striving to integrate these with all other aspects of sexuality and self-concept.

Preference for Gender of Partner

Preference for gender of partner is another critical component of a person's sexuality. Kinsey, Pomeroy and Martin (1948) define sexual preference as existing along a continuum that ranges from full homosexuality, through various combinations of homosexuality–heterosexuality, to full heterosexuality, according to behaviors. Although speculation is plentiful on the topic, the exact mechanisms that guide people into these preferences are not yet clear. Several important factors consistently and conspicuously emerge, however. First, societal guidelines determine the relative acceptability of various partner preferences. For example, attitudes toward homosexuality range from restrictive to accepting across societies. Second, people are "born with a potential for both homosexual and heterosexual responses" (Bell, 1979, p. 17). Given this context, it is not surprising to find that many people, if not most, experience a sense of sexual ambiguity, particularly during childhood and adolescence. Third, preference for gender of partner is probably determined by the end of childhood (if not at conception). In reference to extensive survey data gathered in 1970–1971 by the Institute for Sex Research, Bell (1980) states that "the impression one gets from these data is that sexual preference is established early in life and is so deep-seated that it may not be susceptible to dramatic modification in a person's later years" (p. 13). Adolescence, then, is a time of searching to discover what preference is already established and of determining what this new awareness will mean in terms of self-definition and the way in which life will be played out. Last, relatively few adolescents are fully heterosexual or homosexual in their behaviors, feelings of arousal, or fantasies. Health professionals working with adolescents cannot realistically assume a heterosexual orientation in any person or group with whom they speak.

Adolescent sociosexual development typically has three stages for persons of predominantly heterosexual preference. Early adolescent behavior involves primarily same-gender, often best-friend, relationships. During this period, many adolescents (primarily boys) engage in specific same-gender sexual activities. These activities vary in nature across the whole range of same-gender possibilities. They may stem from curiosity, close friendship, increasing sexual arousal, and fear of the unknown—persons of the other gender. Same-gender contacts often take place before cultural taboos are fully realized. Subsequent self-condemnation may well occur, often accompanied with harsh judgment by others if these behaviors become known. Conflict with the sexual self-concept may occur and may have important ramifications throughout adulthood.

During the second adolescent phase of sociosexual, heterosexual development, girls and boys begin socializing more together, initially in mixed groups. This is seen as a tentative but relatively safe step toward demystifying the other gender. Adolescents at this stage often develop crushes on peers and on celebrity idols, and they may drop these associations as quickly as they are formed. All of these efforts help adolescents try on different personas. In essence, this process is a rudimentary way of beginning to sort through alternative solutions to the problems of "What do I want to be like? What kind of person do I want for a partner? What kind of relationship do I want with an intimate? How do I want to act with an intimate?"

The third adolescent stage of development toward formalizing a heterosexual partner preference is that of dating. Dating provides a forum for experimentation with other-gender sexual contact, as well as for learning about personal commitment and intimacy within the context of a couple.

This description of adolescent sociosexual, heterosexual development is clearly oversimplified. It does not reflect the intense insecurity, the feelings of isolation and vulnerability, the confusion and worry over the possibility of being different that most adolescents feel at least occasionally while attempting to navigate these passages of sociosexual change.

The sociosexual developmental pattern for adolescents of predominantly homosexual orientation often does not differ markedly—in terms of behaviors—from that described above. Most homosexually oriented girls and boys have social and sexual contacts with people of the other as well as the same gender during adolescence that appear quite comparable to those of their heterosexually oriented peers.

How does the psychosexual development of homosexually oriented adolescents differ? Adolescence for them, though it may contain many positive experiences, will usually entail keeping a significant portion of their thoughts and feelings closed off from general—even personal—view, because being different is so troublesome for adolescents. As Bell et al. (1981) poi.at out, this may apply particularly to homosexually oriented adolescents' arousal patterns, fantasies, and level of interest in heterosexual activities (even though they engage in such activities), all of which will probably differ from those of their heterosexually oriented peers. Most homosexually oriented adolescents begin feeling that they are sexually different from their peers about two years before the label "homosexual" is applied by themselves or others. When the full realization of this label's significance occurs, the experience is usually a negative one. Many homosexually oriented adolescents then have the difficult task of trying to resolve an internal conflict between condemning homosexuality—which they have learned to do while growing up—and wanting to value themselves, homosexuals, as sexual and social beings. One adolescent recalls his feelings at that time: " 'It made me feel inadequate with everyone, the fact that I couldn't respond in the same way others did, that I was a part of a fantastic minority. I couldn't relate to anyone, couldn't talk to anyone about it' " (Bell, 1979, p. 13).

In addition, homosexually oriented adolescents do not have the opportunity to experience the trying on of personas and preferred-gender relationships, as described above for heterosexually oriented adolescents. They may envision their future lives as devoid of alternatives, in terms both of choosing a lifestyle and a partner.

Whether adolescents are heterosexually or homosexually oriented, they need opportunities to explore what their preference means within their own lives and their own sexualities.

Sexual Value System

A person's *sexual value system* is integral to his or her sexuality. This system includes values that define sexual activity as good or bad or both; as intended primarily for procreation or recreation or both; as appropriate only for a married, heterosexual couple or for any committed couple or for any two consenting people or for the gratification of one desirous person. A sexual value system is reflected in a person's gender identity. Issues within a relationship, such as dominance and responsibility are heavily value-laden. One's sexual value system is closely intertwined with one's sexual self-concept: the amount of congruence between a person's sexual value system on the one hand and sexual behaviors on the other affects, positively or negatively, the person's sexual self-concept. The sexual value system will also have an impact on life and work goals.

The task for adolescents in this regard is to decipher and integrate personal value systems that actively incorporate the sexual components described above and that are independent of—though evolved from—those of their parents. Accomplishment of this task by adolescents (if, indeed, it is ever fully accomplished) typically occurs during the process of trying on personas through crushes, best friends, idols, peer-group identification, and comparisons with peers. Although it may appear to adults that adolescents reject parental values outright, this is rarely, if ever, the case. Parents do gradually lose the power to influence an adolescent's values directly. In time, however, adolescents acknowledge and adhere to many of the values they learned from their parents regardless of the exact nature of those values. If, for example, an adolescent girl grows up in a household where fertility is valued—often the case in minority and low socioeconomic settings (Butts, 1979)—she may well espouse this value and choose to become pregnant while still quite young. Another girl might be taught to value pursuit of a career and defer child bearing until much later.

The consistency of adolescents' value systems depends in large part on the consistency of their parents' sexual value systems, as they have modeled these both directly and indirectly. Adolescents also compare this parental model to that of peers and of the larger community. This process has been especially confusing for adolescents growing up in the 1970s and 1980s, as sexual value systems within and between each of these levels—societal, peer, and parental—have become decidedly less consistent than in times past (see the section in this chapter on values and attitudes among adolescents today). Just as consistency within an adolescent's developing sexual value system is a possible outcome of socialization, so is inconsistency and conflict.

Sexual Identity

Sexual identity is closely tied to the other components of sexuality, particularly sexual value system and sexual self-concept. It is, however, emerging in contemporary literature as a factor of such significance that a separate category seems appropriate. Sexual identity refers to a person's definition and acceptance of self as a sexually active person.

People face two specific developmental steps in the formation of their sexual identities (Van Arsdale, personal communication, 1980). The first is to acknowledge themselves as sexual beings. Some adolescents, for a variety of reasons, will withdraw in the face of this task altogether. "Asexual" adolescents, defined by Bell (1978) as appearing "bereft of sexual feelings and interests of any kind" (p. 333), may involve themselves in activities that do not require much social interaction. Most adolescents, however, eventually acknowledge themselves as sexual beings, but not without mixed emotional reactions.

The second developmental step toward forming a sexual identity entails acknowledging oneself as a sexually active person. For adolescents who do become sexually active, this is a critical and usually much more difficult step than the first. Adolescence is traditionally a time of strong peer influence, risk taking and experimentation, changing self-image, vulnerability, and vacillation, along with great sexual interest and arousal. This combination of factors typically tempts the adolescent to become sexually active. For adolescents today, the confusion in the sexual value systems they must model after creates yet another pressure for considering early sexual activity. On the other hand, becoming sexually active in response to the sum of all these pressures may leave adolescent girls and boys in still more conflict with their own sexual value systems. This conflict has a direct bearing on adolescents' sexual identity and may lead to an inability to accept themselves as the sexually active persons they actually are. This is most often true of girls, in whom denial may take the form of "I didn't really intend to have sex" or "I don't have sex often, so I'm not really doing it."

This denial of sexual activity has particularly troublesome ramifications for heterosexual relationships. Adolescents will not acknowledge the risk of pregnancy as long as they do not acknowledge sexual involvement. And the issue of contraception, if it arises at all, will only follow acceptance of the existence of a pregnancy risk (Van Arsdale, personal communication, 1980). Denial of sexual activity is a primary reason for failure to use contraceptives (Chilman, 1978; Zelnik & Kantner, 1977).

Sexual Self-concept

Sexual self-concept is a measure of how people value themselves as sexual beings. It is also a measure of the relative compatibility of all other components of their sexuality. As one's sexual self-concept develops, it will in turn affect continued development of the other components of one's sexuality. If a young woman's body image conflicts with that portion of her gender identity that defines the so-called ideal feminine body, her sexual self-concept will be negatively affected; she will value herself less as a sexual being. Her diminished sexual self-concept will then become an underlying source of continued conflict throughout all aspects of her psychosexual development.

Adolescence is a critical time in the continued formation of one's sexual self-concept. All aspects of an adolescent's sexuality change and grow rapidly, and peer interaction provides an active forum for this development. Conflicts that may negatively affect an adolescent's sexual self-concept frequently arise within the context of the all-important peer interaction. The adolescent girl who is looking for popularity and acceptance among her peers may become sexually active before her sexual identity and value system have matured to the point of sanctioning this behavior. The adolescent boy may similarly compromise his sexual identity and value system by becoming sexually active in order to decrease self-doubts or fears of inadequacy (Hogan, 1980). In both cases, sexual self-concept is impaired. Note that the examples just cited were selected to reflect the double standard that is still prevalent and commanding in its effects on the sexualities of both women and men.

The sexual self-concept formed during adolescence has far-reaching significance. If negative, it may prevent or markedly tarnish the formation of all relationships. If positive—a state not easily acquired—it will provide a good foundation for the formation of intimacy within relationships throughout life.

Significant Factors Affecting Psychosexual Development

The development of the components of sexuality described above is affected by a number of factors. Perhaps the most critical of these is the amount of self-esteem a person has acquired before adolescence, which is in large part determined by the nature and outcomes of childhood interpersonal interactions. The level of self-esteem profoundly affects an adolescent's ability to grow, work through conflicts, and change.

Adolescents' physical capacities and appearances, as dictated by genetics and nutrition, may positively or negatively affect psychosexual development. The preference for gender of partner brought into adolescence from early childhood has far-reaching effects. Cultural and family backgrounds are also strong determinants of sexuality. Although adolescence is typically a time for gaining independence from parents and rebelling against societal norms, the values and expectancies of parents and society remain a significant force. Socioeconomic status, religious beliefs, value systems, and effectiveness of parental modeling have an impact on all aspects of an adolescent's psychosexual development. Additionally, the strength of parental control is important; a compromise between permissiveness and unyielding control allows the adolescent room for self-exploration while it provides fundamental guidelines for responsible growth (Waechter & Blake, 1976).

Finally, the way in which parents react to their adolescent's developing sexuality is critical. Often, at least part of this response is negative. These negative feelings have several causes: parents may sense their loss of control over their children at a time when they still feel responsible for their welfare; the adolescent's sexuality may unearth old, unresolved difficulties the parents had in their own sexual growth; or, not infrequently, parents may feel sexually attracted to their adolescent children and be alarmed at that response. Negative parental reactions, from any source, can give the adolescent the message that sexuality is undesirable.

When rapid development of sexuality begins, the adolescent's concurrent level of cognitive development becomes critical. Piaget (1972) defines adolescence as the time when the cognitive process shifts from the concrete to the formal operations level, although the timing of this transition is highly individual (indeed, many people never fully attain formal operations level). Adolescents who are still at the concrete operations level and are thus unable to view their actions in terms of possible risks and future repercussions have added difficulty in dealing with sexual development. Of particular concern in this light are the issues of pregnancy and contraception, which cognitively less mature adolescents give little consideration. Parents and other adults who view the adolescent's "It can't happen to me" attitude as irresponsible will be highly frustrated by their own efforts to change the situation. Unfortunately, as the age of menarche continues to fall, increasing numbers of adolescents are becoming fecund while they are still cognitively immature.

The degree of synchronization of all other areas of adolescent development—including psychological, emotional, social, and moral—is individual and clearly affects development of sexuality. No two adolescents have the same profile when all of these facets are considered. This individuality creates a problem both for adolescents, who expend great energy in comparing themselves with others and trying to conform to peer norms, and for parents and professionals, who are involved in helping this age group.

It should be evident that, although this chapter has emphasized a psychosexual perspective of adolescent development, the sexuality of adolescents—or of persons of any age group—is not a separate entity. It is, as reflected in the definition given by SIECUS, very much a part of their whole being and affects their overall self-concept, ability to form intimate relationships, and the nature of their life and work goals.

ADOLESCENT SEXUALITY TODAY

In the last decade, considerable concern has been voiced in this country about the so-called sexual revolution, especially among adolescents. Of persistent and well-founded concern is the steady increase in adolescent heterosexual coital activity, the continued failure to use contraceptives, and the rise in incidence of adolescent pregnancies and sexually transmitted diseases.

The magnitude of public concern has lessened somewhat regarding a second area of current adolescent sexuality—the moral and attitudinal aspect. Contrary to initial fears, it has become apparent that adolescents do not advocate sexual activity free of affection, commitment or responsibility; they have not rejected the society's moral foundation. Modified interpretations of fundamental morals have emerged in this society, however, and they are, in some cases, a source of significant difficulty for the many adolescents who espouse them.

A third area of concern about adolescents today is that they are often misinformed and lacking in critical knowledge about human sexuality. This is reflected in the increasing numbers of teenage pregnancies. Often, even when contraception is attempted by sexually active adolescents, ineffective methods are used or effective methods are incorrectly used. A less visible, yet very important, ramification of the dearth of information is the many adolescents who, for lack of reliable information and appropriate counseling, continue to worry about various aspects of their own developing sexuality.

Many studies about adolescent sexual behavior have been done. There are problems with much of this research, however: most studies are local, involving an isolated population, and carried out on a one-time basis rather than repeated over time for trends in that population; studies have been conducted so variously that comparisons are not clear-cut; statistical analyses are typically not provided; and very few studies consider sexual behaviors or attitudes of adolescent males or of homosexuals of either gender. What follows is an attempt to extract from this body of research some salient facts about contemporary adolescent sexual behavior.

Adolescent Sexual Behaviors

Masturbation

Noncoital sexual behaviors of adolescents have not received the same research attention as have coital. It seems, however, that masturbation
practices probably begin somewhat earlier today for both girls and boys
and that more adolescent girls are masturbating than were several decades ago (Chilman, 1978). Approximately 30% of girls and 50% of boys
masturbate by age 15. By age 20, about 60% of women and 85% of men
have begun masturbating (Hunt, 1974; Sorensen, 1973). There is a discrepancy between girls and boys not only in the numbers who masturbate
but also in the stimuli that increase the desire to masturbate and the
fantasies that accompany masturbation. Girls tend to respond to interpersonal issues, such as feeling lonely, and to fantasize about participating in nonsexual activities with their boyfriends. Boys tend to masturbate in order to relieve sexual tension—sometimes heightened by nonorgasmic sexual encounters with their girlfriends—and to fantasize about
specific sexual encounters with one partner or a group. These fantasies
often involve submission of the partner or partners to the boys' wishes
(Bell, 1974).

Heterosexual Behaviors

A discussion of heterosexual behaviors does not assume anything about
sexual preference of those participating. Most homosexually oriented
adolescents engage in heterosexual activities at least some time during
adolescence. In an in-depth survey of about 1,000 male and female, black
and white, young and old homosexual adults, three-quarters recalled dating other-sex peers during adolescence. Seventy-five percent of the men
and more than that percentage of the women remembered necking with
members of the other gender. Most engaged in petting, and about one-
quarter of all the homosexuals interviewed had had heterosexual intercourse, primarily with peers. Only 25% of the men and less than 10% of
the women engaged exclusively in homosexual behaviors during adolescence (Bell et al., 1981). References to heterosexual behaviors in this
section do not distinguish between the homosexual or heterosexual preferences of those involved, because the preponderance of research cited
has not made this distinction.

Chilman (1978), in reviewing the available research, finds that petting
has not increased as rapidly as has sexual intercourse for teenage girls.
Similarly, Walsh (1978) states there has been an "evolutionary" rather
than revolutionary increase in the incidence of petting by adolescent

boys. Chilman states that especially for 18- and 19-year-old women, the rate of physical intimacy (in a more general sense) has not increased as significantly as the data might indicate, but more women are not stopping with petting to orgasm. Moreover, once sexual activity has been initiated, especially within a couple relationship, preintercourse activity declines sharply. That is, there is a strong emphasis on intercourse itself.

It now appears that an upward trend in the number of sexually active adolescents began to occur during the late 1960s, and has continued to the present time. This is true of both boys and girls, but the rate of increase among girls has been much greater, resulting in a convergence of sexual participation between genders. The ratio of adolescent men to women involved in premarital sexual activity in 1940 was almost three to one (Diepold, 1976). Although there is still a clear discrepancy among younger adolescents, the ratio has become almost one to one by age 16 or 17 (Miller & Simon, 1974; Vener & Stewart, 1974). In the years between 1925 and 1965, approximately 20% of white adolescent girls and 50% of white boys (statistics are not available for blacks) had had sexual intercourse by the end of their teens (Chilman, 1978; Kinsey et al., 1948; Kinsey et al., 1953). In 1971, the proportion of 19-year-old adolescent women, black and white combined, in the urban United States having had premarital sexual experience was 46%. In 1976 it was 60%; in 1979, 69%. In the same years, sexual participation by 15-year-olds was 14, 19, and 23%, respectively. Trends were similar for nonurban adolescent women (surveyed in 1971 and 1976 only). The marked increases in the numbers of sexually active adolescent women seen in the data from 1965 to the present is only in part due to inclusion of the black population within the 1970s data. In fact, although more black adolescent women than white are sexually active, the increase in sexual activity of the total population of adolescent women between 1976 and 1979 is almost entirely due to an increase in sexual participation by white women (Zelnik & Kantner, 1980).

Survey information on premarital sexual participation of adolescent men is less available. There has been an increase in male sexual activity since the 1925–1965 period, although the rate of increase is much slower than for women. Studies in the early 1970s of largely white samplings found that 50 to 60% of the men were sexually active by age 18 to 19 (Finkel & Finkel, 1975; Hunt, 1973; Sorensen, 1973). A more recent study shows 66% premarital involvement by age 18 for men (black and white combined) and 78% by age 19 (Zelnik & Kantner, 1980). In several studies the percentage of sexually active black adolescent men is significantly higher than white (Finkel & Finkel, 1975; Zelnik & Kantner, 1980).

The average age at which adolescents are becoming sexually active is declining, but it is still somewhat higher for women than for men (Jessor & Jessor, 1975; Vener & Stewart, 1974; Zelnik & Kantner, 1977). A 1976 report from the Planned Parenthood Federation found that approximately one-fifth of the 13- to 14-year age group had experienced intercourse. In their study, Vener and Stewart (1974) found that 10% of the girls and 28% of the boys in the 13-and-younger category had become sexually active. Sorensen (1973) found that 7% of the girls and 17% of the boys in his study had begun sexual activity by age 12 or under.

Among adolescent women, the frequency of intercourse, once initiated, has not been very high and has not apparently increased in the past decade. Zelnik and Kantner (1977) found that fewer than one-third of the women in their 15- to 19-year-old sexually active group had had intercourse as much as three times during the month before the survey. Frequency increases with age for both women and men, and it nearly doubles for both genders between ages 17 and 18 (Diepold & Young, 1976).

There is an apparent increase in the number of sexual partners both adolescent women and men have had (Vener & Stewart, 1974). Zelnik and Kantner (1977) found that for white and black women aged 15 to 19, the number of sexually active women having had more than one partner had increased from 39% of the total sexually active group in 1971 to 50% in 1976. Those having had six or more partners had increased most strikingly for 18- to 19-year-old whites to include 15% of that group in 1976; almost 10% of the total 15- to 19-year-old white and black population had had six or more partners. Some, but not all, of the increase in multiple partnering may be explained by an earlier onset of sexual activity and a deferring of marriage by the 1976 study group. Adolescents who have had more than one sexual partner have typically done so in succession rather than concurrently. Serial monogamy was a pattern followed by twice as many women as men in the Sorensen (1973) study, however.

Adolescent women, especially those who are 17 to 19 years old, typically date men two to three years older than themselves (Zelnik & Kantner, 1980). A majority of adolescent sexual activity occurs in the home of the man partner, the woman partner, or a friend or relative, in descending order of preference. Less than 20% of sexual activity occurs any place other than these (Sorensen, 1973; Zelnik & Kantner, 1977).

There has been a steady increase in the premarital adolescent pregnancy rate over the past decade. This has been well documented throughout that period and is most recently corroborated by the 1979 Zelnik and Kantner survey. In that study, 16% of all women aged 15 to 19 (including those who were sexually active and those who were not, from both black and white populations) had been pregnant premaritally, as compared to 13% in 1976 and 9% in 1971. Among the faction of 15- to 19-year-old women who were sexually active, the 1979 premarital pregnancy rate was 33%. The comparable figure in 1976 was 30%; in 1971 it was 28% (Zelnik & Kantner, 1980).

Fewer premaritally pregnant adolescent women are getting married before the resolution (live birth, still birth, or abortion) of the pregnancy.

This is true for both blacks and whites. A combined figure shows 16% married before the resolution of pregnancy in 1979, compared to 33% in 1971. The number of live births out of wedlock for black and white adolescent women combined decreased from 67% in 1971 to 50% in 1979. The number of induced abortions increased within that same period from 23 to 37%. The years from 1976 to 1979, however, showed a slight but notable reversal in these two trends among white women in the study (Zelnik & Kantner, 1980).

There has been an increase in the use of contraception by adolescent women. Of all premaritally sexually active women aged 15 to 19, blacks and whites combined, those who report always using contraceptives rose from 29% in 1976 to 34% in 1979; those using contraceptives at least some of the time also increased in number. Additionally, more sexually active adolescent women are using contraception earlier, at least on a sometime basis. Although the number of women who never use contraceptives had fallen from the 36% figure of 1976, 27% of the sexually active 15- to 19-year-old adolescent women surveyed in 1979 still did not ever use contraceptives (Zelnik & Kantner, 1980).

There has been a continued increase in the number of premaritally pregnant adolescents who say they had not wanted to become pregnant and who had been using contraception when conception occurred. Among those saying they had not wanted the pregnancy, however, 64% of whites and 78% of blacks were still not using contraception (Zelnik & Kantner, 1980).

With the apparent increases in contraceptive use, why is the pregnancy rate still climbing? Zelnik and Kantner (1980) suggest that increased frequency of intercourse may account for the higher pregnancy rate among those not using contraception. (An analysis of the frequency data from their study has yet to be completed, however.) Those who are practicing contraception may be using less effective methods. The 1979 study indicates a decline in the use of the pill and IUD and an increase in the use of other methods, particularly withdrawal.

Very few studies concerning adolescent contraceptive use have looked at participation by men. Finkel and Finkel (1975), in studying adolescent men in a localized urban area, found the majority of blacks to be ineffective users of contraceptives. That is, they either used no method or a relatively ineffective one. A majority of whites tended to be effective users of contraceptives. Ineffective use of contraception generally declined for both groups with increasing age. Blacks declined from 94% ineffective at age 15 to 21% at age 18 to 19. Whites decreased from 28 to 11% ineffective at comparable ages.

Scales (1977) reviewed the literature on teenage men and their part in contraception and, in so doing, added some valuable insight. Referring to the data of Kantner and Zelnik (1972) and Sorensen (1973), he pointed out that (a) 70% of adolescent women do not always use contraception; (b)

70% of women who do not use contraceptives think they cannot get pregnant; and (c) one-half of the contraception now practiced by adolescents involves methods which rely on the man—condoms and withdrawal. These data appear to place a considerable amount of the existing responsibility for contraception on men, a fact that is not recognized by adolescent men or women. As Scales further notes, Sorensen's data indicate that 60% of the men in his sample entrusted contraception to luck.

Cvetkovich (1980) found that of those men in his study who had discussed contraception with their partners before intercourse, virtually all were protected for their first sexual encounter, and most continued to use contraception. Unfortunately, 40% of the men in that study did not discuss contraception with their partners, either before or after intercourse, and 51% never discussed the possibility of pregnancy.

Homosexual Behaviors

As with heterosexual behaviors, a discussion of homosexual behaviors does not assume anything about the sexual preferences of those participating. Same-gender sexual activities are common among both heterosexually and homosexually oriented adolescents. In this section, a distinction is made between the homosexual behaviors of homosexually oriented adolescents and those of their heterosexually oriented peers, in that the primary study cited here, that of Bell, Weinberg and Hammersmith (1981), has considered this difference. In that study, self-identified homosexual and heterosexual adults were asked to recall in-depth information about their adolescent experiences.

During adolescence, almost all homosexually oriented women and 9% of heterosexually oriented women had homosexual experiences of one sort or another. Generally, same-sex activities included visual examination, caressing of each other's genitals, and mutual masturbation. None of the heterosexual women engaged in cunnilingus during adolescence.

Among the men, almost all homosexually oriented and more than a third of heterosexually oriented adolescents participated in sexual experiences with other men. For most homosexuals and for 23% of heterosexuals, these experiences involved physical contact. Forty to 80% of homosexual and 2 to 19% of heterosexual adolescent men engaged in being masturbated or masturbating someone else, practicing fellatio, or rubbing bodies together to achieve orgasm, in descending order of frequency (Bell, Weinberg, & Hammersmith, 1981).

Homosexual contacts are, almost always, between peers. Sorensen (1973) found that, of all adolescents who had same-sex experiences, only 8% had done so with adults.

Although the Bell, Weinberg, and Hammersmith study cited above was large and comprehensive, it is the only such study that considers homosexual behaviors, as compared to numerous surveys of heterosexual behaviors. Clearly there is a need for continuing study in this area.

Values and Attitudes among Adolescents

Adolescent values and attitudes about sex and sexuality have changed noticeably in this country in recent decades. Although honesty, love, respect, and commitment remain important and fundamental morals, adolescents' interpretations of these morals have altered. What is the context of this change?

The 1960s perception of our national possibilities, riding on the crest of industrialization's greatest moment, was almost one of an aristocracy for all. Greater sexual freedom had grown in part out of increased leisure time and the freedom to search for what was meaningful in life. The perception of that period gave way—with much resentment—to the realities of economic and political uncertainty brought by the 1970s. An inward turning to self-actualization, then to "me first," has been apparent through this last decade to the present time. In addition, the depersonalization of our society, as underwritten by industrialization, still exists. These large shifts in our national self-concept have occurred within a very short span of time, leaving the values of this country fragmented (Chilman, 1978).

Today's adolescents, who have first-hand knowledge only of the 1960s and 1970s, are faced with the challenge of integrating fragmented national and parental values into personal value systems. For many, this remains at best a confusing task. But new attitudes and modified values are emerging as common adolescent themes, and they are quite evident in adolescents' views of sexuality.

Increasingly, adolescents interpret decisions regarding one's sexuality as a matter of self-determination rather than societal or parental dictate (Sorensen, 1973; Yankelovich, 1974). This attitude applies to the decision to become sexually active as well as to the way in which adolescents choose to express their sexuality; however, some distinction is made between what is acceptable for oneself and what is acceptable for others. For example, masturbation and interpersonal sexual activity—both heterosexual and homosexual—are increasingly accepted by adolescents today—for others. Adolescents often do not afford themselves the same degree of tolerance for these behaviors. Guilt and worry after participation in sexual experiences are less pervasive today but are still present, especially among girls. These reactions lessen considerably with experience and age, however (Lieberman, Mahoney, & Poppen, 1977; Vener & Stewart, 1974).

There is an increased emphasis among adolescents (as well as among adults) on nonprocreative sexuality. This broader interpretation of sexuality among adolescents does not, however, imply disregard of all traditional mores. Reiss (1960) identified four standards regarding premarital sex: abstinence, double standard (premarital sex is accepted for men but not for women), permissiveness without affection, and permissiveness with affection. Until recently, abstinence and the double standard have been the accepted norms. Today, although many adults fear that permissiveness without affection is the standard for the majority of adolescents, results of surveys indicate this is not the case. Rather, permissiveness with affection seems to be the pervasive attitude about premarital sexual activity (Jessor & Jessor, 1975; Sorensen, 1973; Vener & Stewart, 1974).

The standard of permissiveness with affection is evidenced in the Jessor & Jessor (1975) study, wherein the positive function of sexual activity most often cited by adolescents was "It's a way of expressing love for someone one is close to" (p. 483). The negative function most frequently cited after fear of pregnancy was "Not caring enough about someone to want to." Sorensen (1973) found that "the majority of adolescents have some affection for their sex partners, and most guard against using a person or being used sexually" (p. 117).

Permissiveness with affection is a more important standard than permissiveness without affection or sex for recreation. There has been only a slight increase in the casualness with which teenagers view their sexual activity. A majority of adolescents do not place the physical enjoyment of sex foremost; relatively few adolescents view sex primarily as a recreational activity, even with a partner for whom there is affection (Hunt, 1973; Sorensen, 1973).

Permissiveness with affection is also evidenced in the pattern of sexual involvement among adolescents. Most teens limit their sexual activity to one partner, at least at any given time, within the context of a "steady, committed relationship" (Chilman, 1978, p. 122).

The double-standard norm cited by Reiss, although still present, appears to be decreasing somewhat among adolescents. For example, in this society women have traditionally linked sex with love far more than have men. Men, on the other hand, have emphasized performance. Today, adolescent boys are feeling freer to want affection before and with sex (Sorensen, 1973). Adolescent girls are more accepting of their own sexuality outside the context of a committed relationship and are more desirous of orgasmic sexual satisfaction (Walsh, 1978). Both boys and girls still approve of premarital sex more for men than women, but the strength of this attitude is lessening (Sorensen, 1973).

Several current adolescent standards for premarital sexual activity were not identified in Reiss's scheme: sex as a means for gaining popularity (especially among girls); sex as a way of avoiding sexual self-doubt (especially among boys); sex as a means to becoming pregnant; and sex as acting out. These standards and that of permissiveness with affection are not mutually exclusive; however, each of the standards just cited clearly has negative connotations for adolescents who espouse them, whether or not affection is present. The last two in particular warrant additional comment.

Sex as a means to becoming pregnant is a standard ascribed to by some adolescent girls. The latest Zelnik and Kantner (1980) survey indicates that 18% of the 15- to 19-year-olds who had become pregnant premaritally had wanted to do so. Reasons for wanting pregnancy include valuing fertility (this is especially true for minorities and those of low socioeconomic background [Butts, 1979]); wanting to be loved and needed by a child or its father; and wanting to be married in order to be independent and happy. Clearly, there are pitfalls in this reasoning that have serious ramifications for the adolescent.

Sex as a way of acting out is a standard probably used by many adolescents today. Indications of this become apparent when factors correlated with adolescent premarital sexual activity are studied (see Table 4.1). Note that many of these factors also correlate with adolescent rebellion or with the conventional construct of adolescent delinquency. Indeed, Jessor and Jessor (1975) found that adolescents in their study still viewed sexual intercourse as a rite of passage to independence. To the adolescent in rebellion, this independence, and sexual activity, may represent an attempt to reject parental and societal values. In light of the current confusion in value systems in our country, as well as the distrust, disillusionment, and growing feelings of self-determination among adolescents, this rebellious group may well be large. For these adolescents, parental and societal anxiety about the so-called teenage sexual revolution may act as a self-fulfilling prophecy. To other adolescents, the sense of independence gained by means of becoming sexually active may represent a more permanent life script associated with poverty or racism. In a sense, these adolescents are actually conforming to the problem-filled backgrounds in which they grew up rather than rebelling against them.

The factors in Table 4.1 are strongly correlated to sexual activity. Jessor and Jessor (1975) found they could reliably predict, as much as one year in advance, the onset of sexual activity, according to the emergence of factors such as these in a given adolescent. These findings become troublesome when compared to correlates of contraceptive behaviors among adolescents. Many of the factors that are positively correlated with sexual activity are negatively related to contraception. The adolescents who are most likely to begin sexual activity, particularly at a young age, are least likely to practice contraception. Table 4.2 summarizes factors that are associated with adolescents—particularly girls—who do not practice contraception. Because women are still assumed to have primary responsibility for contraception, the implications of these findings are bleak indeed.

Table 4.1. Summary of Major Factors Apparently Associated with Nonmarital Intercourse Among Adolescents

Factors	Males	Females
Social Situation		
Father having less than a college education	unknown	yes, for blacks
Low level of religiousness	yes	yes
Norms favoring equality between the sexes	probably	yes
Permissive sexual norms of the larger society	yes	yes
Racism and poverty	yes	yes
Migration from rural to urban areas	unknown	yes
Peer-group pressure	yes	not clear
Lower social class	yes (probably)	yes (probably)
Sexually permissive friends	unknown	unknown
Single-parent (probably low-income) family	unknown	yes
Psychological		
Use of drugs and alcohol	yes	no
Low self-esteem	no[a]	yes[a]
Desire for affection	no[a]	yes[a]
Low education goals and poor educational achievement	yes	yes
Alienation	no[a]	yes[a]
Deviant attitudes	yes	yes
High social criticism	no[a]	yes[a]
Permissive attitudes of parents	yes[a]	yes[a]
Strained parent-child relationships and little parent-child communication	yes	yes
Going steady, being in love	yes[a]	yes[a]
Risk-taking attitudes	yes[a]	yes[a]
Passivity and dependence	no[a]	yes[a]
Aggression; high levels of activity	yes	no[a]
High degree of interpersonal skills with opposite sex	yes[a]	no[a]
Lack of self-assessment of psychological readiness	no[a]	yes[a]
Biological		
Older than 16	yes	yes
Early puberty	yes	yes (probably for blacks)

SOURCE: Chilman, C. S. Social and psychological research concerning adolescent childbearing: 1970–1980. *Journal of Marriage and the Family*, 1980, *42*, 796. Copyrighted 1980 by the National Council on Family Relations. Reprinted by permission.

*Variables supported by only one or two small studies. Other variables are supported by a number of investigations.

Table 4.2.   Variables Associated with the Failure of Adolescents to Use
Contraceptives at All or to Use Effective Contraceptives Consistently

Demographic variables

   Age lower than 18

   Single status

   Lower socioeconomic status

   Minority group membership

   Nonattendance at college

   Fundamentalist Protestant affiliation

Situational variables

   Not being in a steady, committed relationship

   Not having experienced a pregnancy

   Having intercourse sporadically and without prior planning

   Contraceptives not available at the moment of need

   Being in a high stress situation

   Not having ready access to a free, confidential family planning service that
      does not require parental consent

   Lack of communication with parents regarding contraceptives

Psychological variables

   Desiring a pregnancy—high fertility values

   Ignorance of pregnancy risks, of family planning services

   Attitudes of fatalism, powerlessness, alienation, incompetence, trusting to luck

   Passive, dependent, traditional female role attitudes

   High levels of anxiety—low ego strength

   Lack of acceptance of the reality of one's own sex behavior—thinking coitus
      won't occur

   Risk-taking, pleasure-oriented attitudes

   Fear of contraceptive side effects and possible infertility

   Wrong assumptions about the "safe time" of the menstrual cycle

SOURCE: Chilman, C. S. Social and psychological research concerning adolescent childbearing: 1970–1980. *Journal of Marriage and the Family*, 1980, *42*, 797. Copyrighted 1980 by the National Council on Family Relations. Reprinted by permission.

Adolescent Knowledge about Sex and Sexuality

Of particular concern today, especially in light of the increasing incidence of adolescent sexual activity and pregnancy, is adolescents' critical lack of knowledge about sex, sexuality, conception, and contraception. Because of the sophistication adolescents project by means of their manner of dress and speech, adults often assume, erroneously, that adolescents know quite a lot about sex-related topics. Unfortunately, much sex education is still acquired from peers rather than from well-informed adults. And all too often, adolescents avoid asking questions of adults for fear of appearing stupid, especially in front of peers. Regretfully, the "most sexually active adolescents also tend to be the most ignorant and misinformed regarding the basic facts of human sexuality" (Langdell, 1980, p. 96). As noted earlier, those girls who do not have good communication with their parents, are not active decision-makers, and who espouse the traditional female role of passivity and dependence tend to begin sexual activity earlier and to fail to use contraceptives when they do become active (Tables 4.1 and 4.2). These girls are also not apt to take responsibility for obtaining correct information about sex and sexuality.

Table 4.3 illustrates the type of misconceptions and ignorance of fact prevalent among today's adolescents. Note that the misconceptions arise not only from poor information but also from immature—or concrete operational—levels of cognition. "It can't happen to me" is an example of this kind of reasoning. This misinformation may lead to pregnancy. Additionally, several of the misconceptions in Table 4.3 might lead to a poor sense of one's own sexuality. The denial evidenced in many of the misconceptions affects an adolescent's sexual identity and sexual self-concept. And where the assumption of homosexuality or heterosexuality is made in a negative context and without adequate personal exploration, the development of a person's gender preference and sexual self-concept is compromised.

Table 4.3. Common Adolescent Misconceptions about Sex and Sexuality

It can't happen to me.

I can't get pregnant if:

>   I am at the midpoint ("safe" time) in my menstrual cycle.
>
>   I just started having periods.
>
>   I really don't want to.
>
>   I didn't get pregnant the first time (I'm sterile).
>
>   I douche afterward (using Coke, vinegar, aspirins, etc.).
>
>   I use vaginal deodorants or suppositories.
>
>   I don't have sex very often.
>
>   he uses plastic wrap (for a condom).
>
>   he takes his penis out in time.
>
>   he doesn't really put it in all the way.

If I didn't plan to do it ahead of time, it doesn't really count.

I can't get V.D. if I'm on the pill.

Masturbation is perverted; it will damage me if I do it.

If I messed around with (same gender peer) I must be "queer."

If I have sex with him, he'll like me.

If I get pregnant, we'll get married and I'll be happy.

Sexual concerns that adolescents frequently express reflect a similar lack of knowledge. Table 4.4 lists several of these concerns. Notice that many of the concerns reflect questions of "Am I normal?" and "Am I good enough?" that are so much a part of the adolescent stage of psychosexual development.

Given this extreme lack of knowledge and prevalence of misinformation among adolescents, combined with their 60-to-70% involvement in sexual activity by age 18, it becomes difficult to understand the resistance of many adults, parents and professionals alike, to providing adequate sex education and counseling through every available channel.

A Scenario

The following scenario focuses on a sector of the adolescent population of particular concern today, the 10- to 14-year-old adolescent girl. It is included both to tie together information presented throughout this chapter and to highlight important implications for that group.

The adolescent girl who becomes sexually active in her early teens is likely to have come from a lower socioeconomic background. Being young, she may be cognitively immature and therefore unable to understand the possible consequences of her behaviors. She will probably not take responsibility for obtaining appropriate contraception, because she is likely to deny being sexually active. Nor are the parents of this girl likely to establish good communication with her about topics related to sexuality.

Table 4.4.   Questions about Sex and Sexuality Commonly Raised by Adolescents

Why haven't I started menstruating?

Is my penis big enough?

Are my breasts too small?

Do they like me because my breasts are so big?

Why am I having erections so often, and at such embarrassing times?

Why do I have wet dreams?

Do I get cramps because I masturbate?

I don't want to go out on dates—what's wrong with me?

Can I get pregnant if I stand up while we have sex?

How many times do we have to have sex before I could get pregnant?

Am I a fag?

What do other people look like naked? Should I be thinking about such things? Am I perverted?

What do other people think about sex?

This adolescent is a very probable candidate for pregnancy. She may, in fact, want to become pregnant for reasons that include valuing fertility, wanting affection from a child or its father, or wanting independence from an unhappy parental situation. The girl who wants to become pregnant or who does not want to abort an unwanted pregnancy—these factors are also highly correlated (Rosen & Martindale, 1976)—is least likely to have the self-esteem and sense of competence needed to be an effective parent (see the sections on psychosexual development and on values and attitudes among adolescents).

The adolescent mother is two times more likely to be a high-school dropout and six times less likely to have any job skills than a woman who waits until her early twenties to have a child. An adolescent mother is thus much more likely to be unemployed and welfare dependent. A girl who has her first child when between the ages of 13 and 15 is almost three times more likely to be below poverty level than one who waits to bear children (Planned Parenthood Federation, 1976). Considering the high statistical probability that the very young mother will have come from a background of poverty or racism, it can be convincingly argued that she would likely not have achieved well academically or financially even if she had not become a mother. Certainly, however, early parenting increases this likelihood. And negative implications for children born of this young adolescent are also quite far-reaching, as is indicated by the lower cognitive development these children attain as they grow, probably due to the immaturity of their parental care. Thus the scenario perpetuates itself (Baldwin & Cain, 1980; Chilman, 1980).

There are medical, as well as social and developmental, concerns for the sexually active young adolescent girl. Sexually transmitted diseases, particularly gonorrhea, are widespread. And there is increasing indication that cervical cancer is correlated to early sexual activity; women who began sexual activity at young ages are now showing greater incidence of this disease. The two most effective methods of contraception, the pill and the IUD, are not recommended for young adolescents who have not finished their growth spurt. Additionally, in the event of pregnancy, there are critical problems for both the young mother and the fetus or infant. The risk of an adolescent dying from complications of early pregnancy and delivery is 60% higher if she is under 15 years old. The fetal death rate is also higher, as is the number of low-birth-weight babies. And approximately 6% of first-born children of girls under the age of 15 die within the first year of life (Planned Parenthood Federation, 1976). Results of recent research indicate that these risks, both to the fetus or infant and to the adolescent mother, are probably due not to the biological immaturity of the mother but rather to insufficient prenatal care (Baldwin & Cain, 1980; Chilman, 1980). The young adolescent girl of disadvantaged background is not only more likely to become pregnant, she is also less likely to receive adequate prenatal care if she does. Again, the twin effects of poverty and racism have serious ramifications for the young adolescent girl.

The scenario above does not take into account the fact that most adolescents, including those young girls just described, value such norms as sex with affection and commitment within a relationship. The scenario also does not imply a need to return to rigid family and societal structures. As noted elsewhere in the chapter, too firm a hand is as potentially harmful as too loose a hand and often will lead to stronger adolescent rebellion. Neither approach provides the developing adolescent with the self-esteem, skills, or the sense of personal control needed to understand, manage, and integrate developing sexuality. Specifically, in the context of the scenario above, adolescent girls are more likely to delay initiation of sexual activity and to use contraceptives upon becoming active if they have:

- high self-esteem
- high perceived competence
- high personal aspirations
- good communication with parents, including communication about sex and sexuality
- active decision-making skills
- low traditional woman's role espousal
- lack of racism
- lack of poverty

If these criteria are to be met, more and improved communication with adolescents is needed, both from parents and from helping professionals. This communication should provide guidelines, reliable information, empathy, and support while allowing adolescents room to explore and undertake their own integration of sexuality. Furthermore, resolution of the problems outlined in the scenario are not likely until societal problems of poverty and racism are effectively addressed. Clearly, helping adolescents steer away from the problems posed in the scenario and toward a more positive sexuality must be a broad-based and multipronged process.

THE NURSE AS EDUCATOR-COUNSELOR

A prerequisite for the nurse who wants to work effectively with adolescents is the ability to accept adolescents as sexual beings. Nurses must be knowledgeable about all aspects of adolescents' developing sexuality and overall maturation. Above all, nurses must continue to explore their own sexuality, their own biases and blind spots, and their own values about sex and adolescents.

The nurse must have both teaching and counseling skills to work with adolescents as they explore their developing sexuality. Adolescents need reliable information about sex and sexuality. They need specific skills, such as communication, values clarification, and decision-making skills, with which to explore their sexual concerns and conflicts. They need to learn to distinguish facts, feelings, and values regarding sexual issues. They need a caring and accepting environment that gives them the freedom to explore, learn about, and integrate all that is happening to them. To help adolescents with each of these needs, the nurse must be an effective teacher and counselor.

Much of the nurse's work may be outreach, because adolescents, as a population, need relatively little traditional medical care and often do not present problems related to sexuality. The nurse must make an effort to build and spread his or her reputation as a well-informed professional who is concerned about and accepting of adolescents' sexual health needs. In addition, nurses should include questions about adolescents' sexual health as a regular part of taking a medical history.

Nurses working with adolescents must take the initiative in disseminating reliable information and in dispelling myths. Most adolescents, and especially young boys and girls, need to hear these facts a number of times before they begin to integrate them. There are many reasons for this apparent inability to learn: the adolescent is not yet sexually involved and this information seems unimportant; the adolescent denies his or her sexual activity and therefore does not want to listen; the adolescent is unable—because of immature cognitive levels—to comprehend the future ramifications of today's actions. Difficulty in learning and retaining information about sex and sexuality does not necessarily imply irresponsibility on the adolescent's part or a lack of need for the information. Repetition of facts and repeated efforts to dispel misconceptions should follow each person throughout adolescence.

Dissemination of reliable information should address the following issues in detail:

- the changes that occur during puberty
- such questions as "Am I normal?" and "Am I good enough?"
- gender preference and the need for personal exploration
- sexual behaviors, including masturbation, petting, and intercourse, and the importance of each in a person's sexual life
- how and when a woman can get pregnant
- contraception—a description of the various methods, their effectiveness, risks, and availability
- adolescent parenting—freedoms that are relinquished versus rewards that may be gained
- abortion—procedures and risks involved, various moral views, availability

- sexually transmitted diseases—their prevalence, effects, symptoms; methods of and places for treatment
- the confusion, ambivalence, and anxiousness most adolescents feel, at least occasionally, about their sexuality

The nurse must try to dispel misconceptions as this information is presented. This process can be problematic, in that it is difficult to unearth misconceptions when the adolescent has accepted them as fact or is too embarrassed to ask questions. The nurse will find McCary (1978, pp. 21–26) and Gordon, Scales, and Everly (1979, pp. 35–44) helpful in identifying many adolescent misconceptions about sex and sexuality. Individual and small-group work, using discussions, movies, books, and guest speakers, are all effective methods of disseminating information.

Finally, reliable information must be given so that both girls and boys know exactly what they have been told. This may help open the doors of communication among adolescents and rout out attitudes like "He probably knows more than I do, so it must be okay if he says it is."

The nurse can help adolescents begin to recognize their feelings and to distinguish these from facts and values about sex and sexuality. Nurses' training programs should provide them with basic initial intervention counseling skills appropriate for any setting or population of people. Skills and approaches that are particularly important in talking with adolescents about their sexual concerns include (Meeks, 1971; Weiner, 1970):

- being caring and genuine
- being accepting, nonjudgmental, and nonmoralizing
- being active and taking some initiative
- being accessible
- assuring the maintenance of confidentiality unless life-threatening circumstances arise
- being concrete and helping adolescents be the same
- clarifying all ambiguous terminology
- using adolescents' terminology, once clarified
- giving assurance, when appropriate, that many other adolescents have similar concerns
- being prepared to hear about a wide variety of sexual behaviors and concerns
- being prepared for day-to-day vacillations in an adolescent's feelings and thoughts
- encouraging adolescents to go to a professional counselor when appropriate.

Individual and small-group counseling are both useful formats for helping adolescents identify and begin integrating their feelings and concerns about their sexual health.

Adolescents today need extra help in clarifying their value systems. The only values that should selectively be encouraged are those of responsibility to oneself and to others and of tolerance for the broad range of sexual behaviors and life-styles that exist between consenting participants (assuming maturity enough to make a realistic decision about involvement). Beyond these, adolescents must come to understand their own values and the ways in which these values affect their attitudes and behaviors toward others. Several excellent sources of values clarification exercises are available (see Simon & Clark, 1975; Simon, Howe, & Kirschenbaum, 1972).

Adolescents need assistance in learning and practice in using decision-making skills. Significant, life-influencing decisions about sexuality are made during adolescence. These include decisions about when and under what circumstances to become sexually active. If an adolescent decides to become heterosexually active, then a decision regarding contraception becomes critical. Decisions about pregnancy and abortion may also have to be reached. All too often, these decisions are made passively rather than actively.

The decision-making process in the context of sexual issues is largely the same as in any other setting. There are special considerations, however. Because the adolescent is just learning to make active decisions, the nurse will need to take extra care in soliciting adolescents' own views of the facts as well as their feelings and values. If the "facts" are actually misconceptions, they must be corrected and pertinent information supplied. The adolescent must be allowed and encouraged to be an active participant in this process. The nurse must be patient and supportive throughout the process and prepared for vacillation. Steps in the decision-making process are:

1. Establish that there is a problem or a need to make a decision. This is not always easily done; a comprehensive program of education about sex and sexuality and the nurse's good reputation among adolescents will help facilitate this step.
2. Define the problem, including
   - facts involved in the problem
   - feelings and values the adolescent has about the problem
   - feelings and values of significant others (boyfriend or girlfriend, parents)
   - identifying the ways in which relationships with significant others will be affected by this decision
   - identifying any other factors that the adolescent or nurse thinks might affect or be affected by the decision.
3. Identify alternative solutions. The nurse should first identify alternatives the adolescent has thought of, then offer any additional possibilities.

4. Determine the adolescent's preferred alternative.
5. Discuss that alternative in terms of
   • factual background
   • significant others that would be pleased or displeased with that alternative, and how important these reactions are to the adolescent
   • responsibilities involved in carrying out that alternative
   • needs and goals that would or would not be addressed by that alternative
   • immediate and long-term difficulties that might be involved in implementing that alternative.

   Again, the adolescent should be allowed to take the lead in this discussion.

6. Review the acceptability of the alternative in light of the discussion in number 5 above. If it is no longer acceptable to the adolescent, return to the alternatives identified in number 3 and follow through the subsequent steps. If, on the other hand, the alternative is still acceptable, go on to step number 7.
7. Discuss ways to enact the chosen alternative; include a review of the facts and responsibilities involved (e.g. contraception, if the decision is about becoming sexually active).
8. Encourage the adolescent to make a return visit; schedule a follow-up appointment.

In the case of making decisions about becoming sexually active and about becoming pregnant, adolescents should be encouraged to take time in making their decision. Problems involved in each, particularly for young adolescents, decrease markedly in later adolescence and young adulthood. Decisions about contraception and abortion must obviously be given shorter deliberation times.

For adolescents having difficulty coming to terms with their preference for gender of partner, a combination of information giving, counseling, and decision-making is appropriate. As discussed earlier in this chapter, sexual preferences are probably already well engrained by the end of childhood. Realization of the significance that a given preference will have throughout life is a task left for adolescence, however. The nurse's role therefore is not simply one of helping adolescents decide whether they will call themselves homosexual or heterosexual. Adolescents need acceptance, support, and encouragement so that they may better explore their own sexual whereabouts and find individualized ways to integrate these into a healthy self-concept (see the nursing process section in this chapter).

Parents must be encouraged to become involved in their adolescents' sexual health needs. Many schools, agencies, and health-care centers sponsor groups for parents that provide the same information their adolescent children are receiving. In addition, these groups provide a forum for parents to discuss their concerns and questions and to share their feelings about their children's rapidly developing sexuality. Any help the nurse can provide toward increasing the quantity and quality of communication between parents and adolescents will be a direct and vital investment in the sexual health of those adolescents.

Finally, nurses must support, in whatever ways they can, community efforts to alter the apathy, racism, and poverty that continue to fuel the cycle of early adolescent sexual activity, pregnancy, and parenting.

Nurses are in an excellent position to provide the services described above and they can be the source of nonparental authority adolescents need and want. Nurses can do much to help an adolescent move toward a healthy sexuality that includes a sense of self-worth, responsibility to self and others, personal control of his or her own life, effective interpersonal communication skills, and respect for the sexuality of others.

NURSING PROCESS

Client: William (Bill) Streeter, undergoing the physical examination required for participation on high-school football team
Nurse: Ralph Rodriguez, nurse at Creighton Adolescent Health Center

Assessment

Subjective Data

"I'm just as healthy as I was last year."
"All the guys on the team will pass again."
"Owen would too—except he graduated last year."
"He was a great quarterback and he said he would come and see the team and me play every Saturday."
"He'll probably be able to come and see the team after the game and help us celebrate when we win."
"He's training to be an electrical technician, but he said he would come to see the games on Saturday anyway."
"Yes, it's important for me to have him come to the games."
"Owen and me—we're—we're really—very tight."
"I've never wanted to have a girlfriend."
"Last year—this summer too—Owen and me—we fooled around—we . . . we grabbed and sucked."
"My hands are sweaty."
"My God—I think I'm—do you think I'm queer?"

Objective Data

Age 15, 5'10", 165 pounds.

Sophomore in high school.

Student Council representative, member freshman football team.

High-school counselor reports he is well-liked by peers and has good academic standing.

Parents—father foreman at Bates Foundry; mother chief cashier at Andersen's Supermarket.

Siblings—four; third child, second-oldest boy.

Infrequent eye contact.

Speech hesitant, blurts out emotion-laden phrases.

Clenches and unclenches hands.

Palms of hands moist.

Twists and turns in chair.

Anxious about sexual experiences with partner of same gender.

Confused about meaning of sexual experience with partner of same gender.

Planning

Provide atmosphere of acceptance.

Touch judiciously.

Explain that emotional response is appropriate and commonly experienced.

Encourage expression of feelings.

Rephrase and repeat expressed feelings.

Give permission to discuss sex and sexuality.

Ask for clarification of words and phrases "really tight," "fooled around," "grabbed and sucked," and "queer."

Rephrase and repeat content and affective responses.

Explain the need to recognize a highly stressful situation.

Explain the importance of maintaining a positive self-image.

Support realistic assessment of situation.

Explain that people are born with the potential for both homosexual and heterosexual response.

Explain that different cultures place different values on homosexual and heterosexual behaviors.

Explain that sexual ambiguity and exploration are not uncommon in adolescence.

Encourage self-examination and evaluation of
  • content of sexual fantasies, impulses, and behaviors
  • advantages and disadvantages of homosexual and heterosexual relationships

- personal needs fulfilled by homosexual or heterosexual relationships
- personal goals about roles and relationships
- risks involved in obtaining personal goals
- strategies involved in obtaining personal goals (Bell, 1978).

Emphasize the client's value as an individual.

Encourage continued examination of feelings, concerns, experiences, and outcomes.

Encourage examination of feelings and concerns with selected significant others of same and other sex.

Encourage examination of feelings and concerns about projected responses of significant others to knowledge of sexual relationship with Owen.

Encourage increasing social interactions and relationships with people of same and other sex.

Encourage participation in support groups that foster growth and enhance the esteem of self and others.

Encourage exploration of behaviors that contribute to worth and esteem of self and others.

Encourage exploration of sexual roles and relationships meaningful to personal needs and goals.

Indicate availability for more information and further counseling.

Suggest use of counseling staff at adolescent health center for individual and group counseling.

Implementation

Initiate discussion with Owen about significance of relationship.

Make a list of personal needs and goals.

Make a list of personal concerns about sexual roles and relationships.

Keep personal records, draw pictures when appropriate, of content of sexual fantasies.

Begin keeping diary of feelings about interactions with people of same and other sex.

Discuss with parents possibility of attending discussion group at Creighton Adolescent Health Center.

Arrange personal time.

Make appointment with counselor.

Evaluation (three months later)

Reports satisfaction with individual and group counseling efforts at adolescent health center.

Reports that examination of sexual self continues although it is often turbulent.

BIBLIOGRAPHY

Baldwin, W., & Cain, V. S. The children of teenage parents. *Family Planning Perspectives*, 1980, *12*, 34–43.

Bell, A. P. Childhood and adolescent sexuality. Paper presented at the Institute for Sex Research, Indiana University, Summer 1974.

Bell, A. P. The homosexual as patient. In R. Green (Ed.), *Human sexuality: A health practitioner's text*. Baltimore: Williams & Wilkins, 1975.

Bell, A. P. The new sex education and homosexuality. In H. A. Otto (Ed.), *The new sex education*. Chicago: Follett, 1978.

Bell, A. P. Homosexuality and the schools. Unpublished paper, Institute for Sex Research, Indiana University, 1979.

Bell, A. P. Sexual preference: Its development among men and women. Unpublished paper, Institute for Sex Research, Indiana University, 1980.

Bell, A. P., Weinberg, M. S., & Hammersmith, S. K. Sexual preference: Its development among men and women. Bloomington: Indiana University Press, 1981.

Butts, J. D. *Adolescent sexuality and the impact of teenage pregnancy from a black perspective*. Washington, D.C.: Family Impact Seminar, 1979.

Chilman, C. S. Some policy and program implications of an overview of research concerning adolescent sexuality. Paper presented at the Annual Meeting of the National Council on Family Relations, San Diego, 1977.

Chilman, C. S. *Adolescent sexuality in a changing American society* (DHEW Publication No. NIH 79-1426). Washington, D.C.: U.S. Government Printing Office, 1978.

Chilman, C. S. Social and psychological research concerning adolescent childbearing: 1970–1980. *Journal of Marriage and the Family*, 1980, *42*, 793–805.

Crist, R., Hickenlooper, G. Problems in adolescent sexuality. In M. N. Bernard, B. J. Clancy, & K. E. Krantz (Eds.), *Human sexuality for health professionals*. Philadelphia: Saunders, 1978.

Cvetkovich, G. T. Male teenagers—sexual debut, psychosocial development and contraceptive use. Unpublished paper, Institute for Sex Research, Indiana University, 1980.

Cvetkovich, G., Grote, B., Bjorseth, A., & Sarkissian, J. On the psychology of adolescents' use of contraceptives. *Journal of Sex Research*, 1975, *11*, 256–270.

DeLora, J. S., Warren, C. A. B., & Ellison, C. R. *Sexuality in childhood and adolescence*. Dallas: Houghton Mifflin, 1980.

Diepold, J. H. Adolescent sexual behavior: A review of taboo (1943–1976). Unpublished paper, Institute for Sex Research, Indiana University, 1976.

Diepold, J. H., & Young, R. D. Empirical studies of adolescent sexual behavior: a critical review. Unpublished paper, Institute for Sex Research, Indiana University, 1976.

Finkel, M., & Finkel, D. Sexual and contraceptive knowledge, attitudes and behaviors of male adolescents. *Family Planning Perspectives,* 1975, *7*, 256–260.

Gagnon, J. H. *Human sexualities.* Glenview, Ill.: Scott, Foresman, 1977.

Gordon, S., Scales, P., & Everly, K. *The sexual adolescent: Communicating with teenagers about sex.* North Scituate, Mass.: Duxbury Press, 1979.

Hogan, R. M. *Human Sexuality.* New York: Appleton-Century-Crofts, 1980.

Hudis, P. M., & Brazzell, J. F. Significant others, adult role expectations and the resolutions of teenage pregnancies. Unpublished paper, Department of Sociology, Indiana University, 1981.

Hunt, M. Sexual behavior in the 1970s—part II: Premarital sex. *Playboy,* 1973, *20*, 74–75.

Hunt, M. *Sexual behaviors in the 1970s.* Chicago: Playboy Press, 1974.

Hyde, J. S. *Understanding human sexuality.* New York: McGraw-Hill, 1979.

Janda, L. H., & Klenke-Hamel, K. E. *Human sexuality.* New York: Van Nostrand, 1980.

Jessor, S. L., & Jessor, R. Transition from virginity to non-virginity among youth: A socio-psychological study over time. *Developmental Psychology,* 1975, *11*, 473–484.

Jurich, A., & Jurich, J. The effect of cognitive moral development upon the selection of premarital standards. *Journal of Marriage and the Family,* 1974, *36*, 736–741.

Kantner, J. F., & Zelnik, M. Sexual experience of young unmarried women in the United States. *Family Planning Perspectives*, 1972, *4*, 9–18.

Katchadourian, H. A., & Lunde, D. T. *Fundamentals of human sexuality.* New York: Holt, Rinehart & Winston, 1975.

Kinsey, A. C., Pomeroy, W. B., & Martin, C. E. *Sexual behavior in the human male.* Philadelphia: Saunders, 1948.

Kinsey, A. C., Pomeroy, W. B., Martin, C. E., & Gebhard, P. H. *Sexual behavior in the human female.* Philadelphia: Saunders, 1953.

Kirby, D., Alter, J., & Scales, P. *An analysis of U.S. sex education and an evaluation* (5 vols., U.S. DHEW Report). Bethesda, Md.: MATHTECH, 1979.

Kolodny, R. C., Masters, W. H., Johnson, V. E., & Biggs, M. A. *Textbook of human sexuality for nurses.* Boston: Little, Brown, 1979.

Langdell, J. I. Adolescent sexual preoccupations. *Medical Aspects of Human Sexuality,* 1980, *14*, 90, 95–96, 99, 102.

Lieberman, J. E. Vanguard, rearguard or resistance? *Jounal of Current Social Issues,* 1978, *15*, 46–51.

Lieberman, J. E., Mahoney, C. S., & Poppen, P. Adolescent sex and birth control: The first time. Paper presented at the annual meeting, American Public Health Association, Washington, D.C., 1977.

McCary, J. L. *McCary's Human Sexuality* (3rd ed.). New York: Van Nostrand, 1978.

McCreary-Juhasz, A. Understanding adolescent sexual behavior in a changing society. *Journal of School Health,* 42, 149–154.

McCreary-Juhasz, A. A chain of sexual decision-making. Paper presented at the National Council on Family Relations Annual Meeting, 1973.

Meeks, J. E. *The fragile alliance; an orientation to the outpatient psychotherapy of the adolescent.* Baltimore: Williams & Wilkins, 1971.

Miller, P. Y., & Simon, W. Adolescent sexual behavior: Context and change. *Social Problems*, 1974, *22*(1), 58–76.

Mitchell, M. *The counselor and sexuality*. Boston: Houghton Mifflin, 1973.

Money, J., & Ehrhardt, A. *Man and woman, boy and girl*. Baltimore: Johns Hopkins University Press, 1972.

Offer, D. Attitudes toward sexuality in a group of 1500 middle class teenagers. *Journal of Youth and Adolescence*, 1972, *1*(1), 81–90.

Piaget, J. Intellectual evaluation from adolescence to adulthood. *Human Development*, 1972, *15*, 1–12.

Planned Parenthood Federation of America. *Eleven million teenagers: What can be done about the epidemic of adolescent pregnancies in the United States?* New York: Author, 1976.

Reiss, I. L. *Premarital sexual standards in America*. New York: Free Press, 1960.

Reiss, I. L. *Premarital sexual standards* (SIECUS Discussion Guide #5). New York: SIECUS, 1976.

Reiss, I. L. Changing sociosexual mores. In J. Money and H. Musaph (Eds.), *Handbook of sexology*. New York: Excerpta Medica, 1977.

Reiss, I. L., Banwart, A., & Foreman, H. Premarital contraceptive usage: A study and some theoretical applications. *Journal of Marriage and the Family*, 1975, *37*, 619–630.

Rosen, R. A. H., & Martindale, L. J. Contraception, abortion and self-concept. Paper presented at the Annual Meeting of the American Sociological Association, 1976.

Scales, P. Males and morals: Teenage contraceptive behavior amid the double standard. *The Family Coordinator*, 1977, *26*, 211–222.

The SIECUS/UPPSALA principles basic to education for sexuality. *SIECUS Report*, 1980, *8*, 8–9.

Simon, S. B., & Clark, J. *Beginning values clarification: A guidebook for the use of values clarification in the classroom*. San Diego: Pennant Press, 1975.

Simon, S. B., Howe, L. W., & Kirschenbaum, H. *Values clarification: a handbook of practical strategies for teachers and students*. New York: Hart, 1972.

Simon, W., Berger, A., & Gagnon, J. H. Beyond anxiety and fantasy: The coital experiences of college youth. *Journal of Youth and Adolescence*, 1972, *1*, 203–222.

Simon, W., & Gagnon, J. H. On psychosexual development. In D. L. Grummon & A. M. Barclay (Eds.), *Sexuality: A search for perspective*. New York: Van Nostrand Reinhold, 1971.

Sorensen, R. C. *Adolescent sexuality in contemporary America*. New York: World, 1973.

Van Ardale, K. Personal communication. December 8, 1980.

Vener, A. M., & Stewart, C. S. Adolescent sexual behavior in Middle America revisited: 1970–1973. *Journal of Marriage and the Family*, 1974, *36*, 728–735.

Waechter, E. H., & Blake, F. G. *Nursing care of children*. Philadelphia: Lippincott, 1976.

Walsh, R. H. Sexual attitudes, standards and behavior: A current assessment. In H. A. Otto (Ed.), *The new sex education*. Chicago: Follett, 1978.

Weiner, I. B. *Psychological disturbance in adolescence*. New York: Wiley-Interscience, 1970.

Whitman, F. L. Childhood predictors of adult homosexuality. *Journal of Sex Education and Sex Therapy,* 1980, *2,* 11–16.

Wolf, L. Homosexuality: Especially in adolescence. In M. N. Bernard, B. J. Clancy, & K. E. Krantz (Eds.), *Human sexuality for health professionals.* Philadelphia: Saunders, 1978.

Yankelovich, D. E. *The new morality: A profile of American youth in the 70's.* New York: McGraw-Hill, 1974.

Zabin, L. S., Kantner, J. F., & Zelnik, M. The risk of adolescent pregnancy in the first months of intercourse. *Family Planning Perspectives,* 1979, *11,* 215–222.

Zelnik, M., & Kantner, J. F. Sexual and contraceptive experience of young unmarried women in the United States, 1976 and 1971. *Family Planning Perspectives,* 1977, *9,* 55–71.

Zelnik, M., & Kantner, J. F. Contraceptive patterns and premarital pregnancy among women aged 15–19 in 1976. *Family Planning Perspectives,* 1978, *10,* 135–142.

Zelnik, M., & Kantner, J. F. Sexual activity, contraceptive use and pregnancy among metropolitan-area teenagers: 1971–1979. *Family Planning Perspectives,* 1980, *12,* 230–238.

Zelnik, M., Kim, Y. J., & Kantner, J. F. Probabilities of intercourse and conception among U.S. teenage women, 1971 and 1976. *Family Planning Perspectives,* 1979, *11,* 177–184.

5. Sexuality and Adulthood

Elizabeth M. Lion

VALUES CLARIFICATION EXERCISE

A person who reaches adulthood is allowed and encouraged by our society, under carefully prescribed conditions, to develop sexual roles and relationships. The following exercise is a way of examining what you have learned, what you believe, and what choices you have made about sex and sexuality in adulthood.

Here is a list of incomplete sentences. Write down your first reaction.

For young adults, sex is:
Sexually, older adults are:
Orgasm is:
Penile–vaginal intercourse is:
Premarital intercourse is:
Adults who masturbate:
If I were totally free sexually, I would:
Menopause seems:
Fellatio is:
I enjoy sex when:
Good sex doesn't mean:
Anal intercourse is:
Women who engage in extramarital sex:
Homosexual men are:
Homosexual women do:

Look at your responses. Did you complete all the sentences? Did you write your first reaction or did you write what you thought you should write? Did you write anything that made somebody right and somebody wrong? Did you write anything that surprised you? Pleased you? Disappointed you?

If you are willing, share your responses with someone close to you or with a group of people who are also willing to share. Discuss what you have learned about yourselves and each other. Was the group able to distinguish what is known about sex from what is believed? Were any opinions and beliefs shared by several people in the group? Discuss how differences were tolerated. Discuss how toleration of differences could affect nurse–client interaction.

BEHAVIORAL OBJECTIVES

After completing this chapter, you will be able to

- Describe the critical growth crises of young and middle adulthood.
- Explain the two basic functions of sexuality in adulthood.
- Describe the major physiologic changes occurring in the sexual response cycle of men and women.
- Identify five positions for sexual intercourse.
- Compare the incidence and practice of masturbation in men and women.
- Compare time of onset and physiosexual changes in the climacteric of men and women.
- Identify the frequency and use of fantasies by men and women.
- Compare the frequency of sexual outlet for men and women.
- Contrast the patterns of traditional and person-centered marriage.
- Identify the effect of education and religiousness on the frequency of marital intercourse.
- Describe the relationship between frequency of marital intercourse and marital satisfaction.
- Discuss this statement: The greatest sexual liberation has occurred among married people.
- Discuss the increased freedom to vary sexual positions and behaviors.
- Interpret the increase in the prevalence and frequency of premarital intercourse.
- Discuss the data on the incidence of extramarital relationships.
- Debate: An objective study of the advantages and disadvantages of extramarital relationships is needed.
- Describe five categories for homosexual relationships.
- Identify the sexual practices of men and women in homosexual relationship.
- Describe the role of the nurse as educator-counselor about sex and sexuality with adult clients.

ADULTHOOD AND THE LIFE CYCLE

We spend one-quarter of our lives as infants, children, and adolescents and three-quarters of our lives as adults. *Adults* are usually defined as people who have grown to full size and stature, are considered mature enough to accept responsibility for themselves, and have reached the age set by law that qualifies them for full legal rights. *Early adulthood* begins when a person is about 18 years old and ends when a person is about 35 years old. The years between 35 and 60 are considered *middle adulthood*, and 60 years and over is considered *late adulthood* (see Chapter 6).

Erikson (1963) conceptualized stages of psychosexual development. Each stage has a critical growth crisis that involves physical, psychologic, and social changes associated with new and unsettling thoughts, ideas, and feelings that are resolved as understanding and insight are gained and new attitudes and behaviors are considered, experimented with, and learned. The critical growth crisis for the young adult is to launch involved, mutual, and reciprocal social, sexual, and occupational roles and relationships. During this time, the young adult moves away from his or her family of origin and toward his or her family of procreation. The young adult explores his or her capacity to merge with and commit to self and others and to establish a full physiologic and fused psychologic intimacy with a sexual partner of his or her choice.

The critical growth crisis for middle adulthood involves the tasks of actively participating in caring for, teaching, and counseling the next generation; and involvement in producing, creating, contributing to, and leaving behind ideas, products, and works of art. Successful completion of the tasks results in the enrichment of life and ensures continuity of the culture and species. The women's movement has challenged society's proscriptions that tended to confine women to the roles of childbearer and childrearer. Presently, both men and women are developing parenting roles and searching for meaningful work roles.

Adulthood, like infancy, childhood, and adolescence, has pattern, pace, and growth crises of its own. An adult is not a finished product. An adult is a developing being–a person in process. "Who am I as a sexual person?" and "What does it mean to be male or female?" were the questions with which the adolescent grappled, and "What to be?" "How do I integrate the boy or girl I was with the man or woman I have become, and the adult or parent, or spouse I will become?" are the questions with which the adult will struggle (Anderson & Carter, 1978). During early and middle adulthood, the physiologic growth of adolescence is completed and the physiologic changes of aging begin. During this time, the adult person will be devoted to launching, living, renewing, and reinvesting in his or her social, sexual, and occupational roles and relationships.

SEXUALITY AND ADULTHOOD

Sexuality in adulthood fulfills two basic functions: (*1*) to procreate—to reproduce the species; and (*2*) to recreate—to give and receive physiologic and psychologic pleasure. Sexuality in adulthood is characterized by a wide variety of sexual behaviors that are influenced by a myriad of physiologic, psychologic, and social variables. Sexual behavior is affected by sex, age, race, marital status, educational level, occupational class, rural-urban background, religious affiliation, religiousness and parental occupational class. The nature of these variables make it difficult to measure or use them as predictors of sexual behavior. The meaning of and value and individual adult places on sexuality and sex are influenced by the unique interplay of physiologic, psychologic, and sociologic factors within his or her cultural and subcultural setting.

In the last 30 years, study of and research about sex and sexuality have been acceptable for scientific inquiry and have significantly changed what we know about sexual behavior of the developing adult. Yet adulthood remains burdened with folklore, myths, stereotypes, and misconceptions. Cameron (1972) found that young adults (age 18-25) are believed to be more physically capable: that they have, attempt, and desire sex more; and that they have more strength and vigor than the middle (age 40 to 55) and older (age 65 to 79) adult. Middle-aged adults are considered more knowledgeable about sex and more skillful in the sex act. Women of all ages are considered to have less sexual desire, knowledge, skill, and physical capacity than men. Older adults are perceived as almost sexless. Study and research have challenged many of these beliefs, but changes in personal and societal attitudes come slowly and often with considerable pain and much difficulty.

THE HUMAN SEXUAL RESPONSE IN ADULTHOOD

The Sexual Response Cycle

Our understanding of the changes that occur to both men and women as a result of effective sexual stimulation is based on the pioneering study of Masters and Johnson (1966). They divided the sexual response cycle into four phases: (*1*) the excitement phase, which begins with responses to sexual stimulation; (*2*) the plateau phase, in which sexual tension and physical responses heighten; (*3*) the orgasmic phase, which is the intense and pleasurable climax of sexual tension; and (*4*) the resolution phase, during which there is a release of muscular tension and a return to the unstimulated state (Figures 5.1 and 5.2).

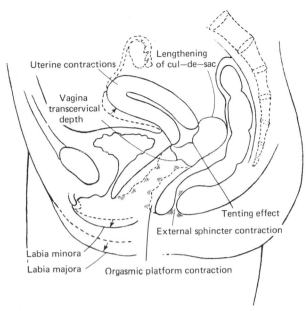

Figure 5.1. Female pelvis: orgasmic phase. From Masters, W. H., & Johnson, V. E. *Human sexual response.* Boston: Little, Brown 1966, p. 77. Reprinted with permission of Masters & Johnson Institute, St. Louis, Missouri.

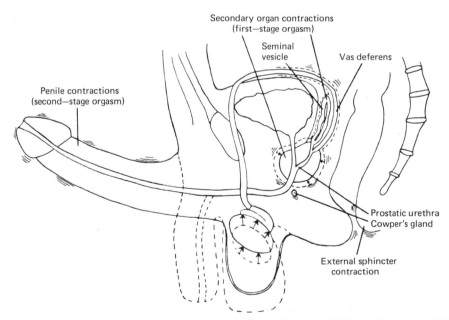

Figure 5.2. Male pelvis: orgasmic phase. From Masters, W.H., & Johnson, V.E. *Human sexual response.* Boston: Little, Brown and Company, 1966, p. 184. Reprinted with permission of Masters & Johnson Institute, St. Louis, Missouri.

The two fundamental responses to sexual stimulation are vasocongestion and myotonia, which build and resolve during the four phases. *Vasocongestion* is the engorgement of blood vessels and the increases of blood flow into the tissues. When sexual stimulation begins, the amount of blood entering the tissues is greater than the amount leaving and the result is enlargement and color changes in the involved tissue. Penile erection and the analogous vaginal lubrication are the result of vasocongestion.

Myotonia is increased muscle tension or tone that occurs throughout the body during sexual excitement. The facial grimaces, spasmodic contractions of the hands and feet, and muscular spasms that occur during orgasm are dramatic examples. During orgasm there is an involuntary climax of sexual tension increment, and the muscles relax and the blood vessels empty.

Human sexual response is elicited by a variety of stimuli, including visual, olfactory, gustatory, and fantasy. This response is a highly individual and variable process and not every sexually responsive person experiences each or all of the responses. The sexual response cycle is not a rigid pattern for sexual response.

Bragonier and Bragonier (1979) state that "the only true authority regarding a person's sexual satisfaction in any given episode is that individual, for himself or herself" (p. 10). What has been observed and studied about human sexual response is applicable to heterosexual, homosexual, and masturbatory behavior. Perhaps the only difference is that masturbation often leads to physiologic responses that are more intense (Sarrel, 1975).

Major Physiologic Changes During Each Phase of the Human Sexual Response Cycle

Masters and Johnson (1966) described for each phase of the human sexual response cycle physiologic responses common to as well as particular to men and women.

Excitement phase (varies from a few minutes to hours): During the excitement phase, both men and women experience increased muscle tension in their arms and legs and some tensing of the abdomen late in the phase. In about 75% of women and 25% of men, the *sex flush* (measlelike rash) appears over the epigastrium and spreads over the breasts. A moderate increase in blood pressure and heart rate occurs.

In men, there is an increase in the length and width of the penis, and penile erection occurs, which may be lost and regained several times during a prolonged phase. The scrotum elevates and its skin thickens and tenses. There is a partial elevation and increase in the size of the testes. In about 60% of men, nipple erection occurs.

In women, the breasts enlarge, the veins of the breasts become defined, the nipples become erect, and swelling of the aerola occurs. Vaginal lubrication (beads of moisture) begins. The vaginal barrel extends and distends, and the color changes from purple-red to deep purple. The clitoris increases in length and width. The labia majora flatten and separate away from the opening. The labia minora thicken and extend the vaginal barrel about 1 cm.

Plateau phase (30 seconds to 3 minutes): In the second phase (plateau), there is further increase of muscle tension for both men and women. Facial grimaces and involuntary muscular contractions of arms and feet occur. The sex flush is well developed and more widespread late in the phase. Blood pressure continues to rise and recorded heart rates average 100 to 175 beats per minute.

In men, there is an increase of penile engorgement at the coronal ridge. The erection is stable and a deepening of the red-purple color may occur. The testes continue to increase in size (50% over the unstimulated state) and full elevation to a position against the perineum occurs. Two to three drops of mucoid fluid from Cowper's glands appear at the tip of the penis.

In women, there is further increase in size of the breasts and marked aerolar engorgement. The clitoris withdraws under its hood and shortens. The red color of the labia minora intensifies and there is full elevation of the uterus. The engorgement of the outer third of the vagina builds the orgasmic platform, and the inner two-thirds increases only slightly in width and depth. One or two drops of mucoid fluid from the Bartholin glands are secreted.

Orgasmic phase (3 to 10 seconds): The orgasmic phase is considered the pleasurable peak of the sexual experience. For both men and women, hearing, vision, taste—all the senses—are diminished or lost. There is a reduction of voluntary muscle control. There are involuntary spasms of muscle groups throughout the body, and involuntary contraction of the rectal sphincter at 0.8-second intervals. The sex flush persists and its degree may parallel the intensity of the orgasmic experience. Blood pressure reaches its highest level and heart rates of 110 to more than 180 beats per minute have been recorded. Respiration may be as high as 40 per minute.

In men, emission of semen, resulting from contractions of the vas deferens and accessory organs, occurs, and ejaculation, involving contractions of the entire length of the penile urethra spaced at 0.8-second intervals, continues for several seconds. The first three to four contractions are the most intense and are followed by contractions of reduced frequency, intensity, and expulsive force. There are no observable changes in the scrotum or testes.

In women, the uterus and orgasmic platform contract 3 to 15 times at 0.8-second intervals. The first three to six contractions are intense and are followed by contractions of reduced frequency and intensity. There are no observable changes in the breasts, clitoris, labia majora, or labia minora.

Resolution phase (10 to 15 minutes with orgasm, may be 12 to 24 hours without orgasm): The resolution phase is primarily characterized by a reversal of the processes that resulted in vasocongestion. For both men and women, all signs of muscle tension (myotonia) are gone within five minutes. There is a rapid disappearance of the sex flush in reverse order of appearance. The blood pressure and heart rate rapidly return to normal.

In men, nipple erection subsides slowly and may last as long as one hour. Penile erection is lost in two stages: (1) with the reduction of vasocongestion, 50% of the size of the erect penis is lost within a minute or less after orgasm; (2) complete reduction of vasocongestion and return of the penis to unstimulated size may require several minutes or longer. The return of the scrotal sac to its wrinkled appearance and full descent of the testes occurs rapidly in most men.

In women, the clitoris returns to normal position within 5 to 10 seconds of orgasm. The labia majora return rapidly to normal thickness and midline position. The reduction of vasocongestion in the labia minora is rapid and the color returns to light pink in 10 to 15 seconds. The uterus returns to normal position in the pelvic cavity. There is a reduction of the orgasmic platform and a relaxation of the vaginal walls accompanied by a return to their normal color in 10 to 15 minutes. A lack of orgasm may result in the sexual organs remaining congested and genital and pelvic discomfort may be experienced.

Differences in Men and Women

The response cycles of men and women are more similar than different; however, there are differences. Women demonstrate a wider variability than men in their sexual response patterns (Figures 5.3 and 5.4). Pattern A (Figure 5.4) shows the entire response moving without interruption into first orgasm and then into second and possibly more without dropping to plateau level. Pattern B shows a gradual increase to arousal during the excitement phase, a fluctuating plateau with small uplifts toward orgasm, and a slow return to prearousal levels. Pattern C depicts a rapid rise in excitement followed by one intense orgasm. Though Masters and Johnson (1966) identified only one pattern for men it must be remembered that men experience orgasm in many ways.

The *refractory period* (temporary resistance to sexual stimulation) in the man's cycle is a significant difference in sexual response of men and women. The duration of the period is directly related to age—from a few moments to several hours or days. It has been speculated that the refractory period allows time for the prostate and seminal vesicles to recover and secrete more fluid.

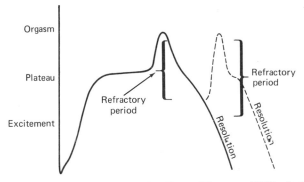

Figure 5.3.   Male sexual response cycle. From Masters, W.H., & Johnson, V.E. *Human sexual response.* Boston: Little, Brown and Company, 1966, p. 5. Reprinted with permission of Masters & Johnson Institute, St. Louis, Missouri.

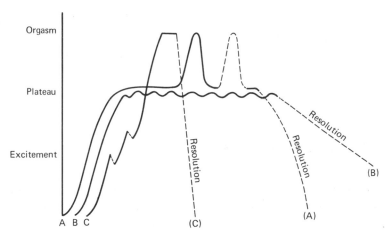

Figure 5.4.   Female sexual response cycle. From Masters, W.H., & Johnson, V.E. *Human sexual response.* Boston: Little, Brown and Company, 1966, p. 5. Reprinted by permission of Masters & Johnson Institute, St. Louis, Missouri.

Multiple orgasms are experienced by women with greater frequency than by men. Women are not limited by a refractory period and can be rapidly stimulated repeatedly to orgasm, although many women are satisfied with one orgasm. The potential for multiorgasmic response remains throughout a woman's life.

Women do not ejaculate. However, research by Sevely and Bennett (1978) suggests that women may ejaculate from the female prostatic glands surrounding the urethra.

Myths and Misconceptions

Women do not experience two kinds of orgasm. Masters and Johnson have clearly shown that the same events follow clitoral, vaginal, and, in some women, breast stimulation.

There is no physiologic reason to abstain from intercourse during menstruation. Some women report that orgasm is effective in relieving dysmenorrhea. The choice to abstain involves personal preference and aesthetic or religious reasons.

There is no correlation between the skeletal build of a man and the size of his penis, either in the flaccid or erect state (Masters & Johnson, 1966). Since there is much less variation in size of the erect penis, it follows that a large flaccid penis will undergo less increase in size and girth than a small one. Functional capacity, potency, fertility, and enjoyment are not related to the size of the penis (Boyarsky, 1980). The size of the penis does not make a man a better sexual partner nor necessarily give a partner more stimulation.

Simultaneous orgasm need not be a measure of a satisfactory sexual experience (Bragonier & Bragonier, 1979). Orgasms are basically involuntary responses, and efforts to synchronize the attainment may diminish or deprive the partners from fully experiencing their own orgasms.

POSITIONS FOR INTERCOURSE

As a general term, *sexual intercourse* can refer to any communication between people that involves a sexual response (Haeberle, 1978). As a specific term, *sexual intercourse* refers to direct physical contact involving the sex organs of at least one of the participants that involves a sexual response (Haeberle, 1978). *Manual intercourse* refers to the contact of the sexual organs of one partner with the hand(s) of the other; *oral–genital intercourse* refers to the contact of the sexual organs of one partner with the mouth of the other; *femoral intercourse* is the insertion of the penis between the thighs of a partner; *mammary intercourse* is the placing of the penis between the breasts; *genital intercourse* refers to contact between the sex organs of two persons; and *anal intercourse* refers to placing of the penis in the anus.

Oral–Genital Intercourse

Because of the body position suggested by the inverted numerals, the street-language term for simultaneous oral–genital contact is "69." In this position, the partners are lying abdomen-to-abdomen with their heads in opposite directions. Other positions include lying side-by-side, using a thigh to support the head; or one partner lying on his or her back while the other partner kneels astride with head toward the partner's feet (Comfort, 1972). These positions can be comfortable and satisfying to men and women, and can be used by partners of the same and different sexes. Some partners use oral–genital stimulation as part of foreplay and others continue it to orgasm.

Some people believe that oral–genital intercourse is immoral because it serves no reproductive function; in some states oral–genital contact is illegal. Some people consider oral–genital contact unsanitary, and many people who use oral–genital contact wash the genitalia with soap and water first.

Vaginal–Penile Intercourse

Vaginal–penile intercourse can be performed in a wide variety of positions (see Chapter 9 for positions during pregnancy). The basic positions are face-to-face, man above; face-to-face, woman above; face-to-face, lying side by side; and rear entry. Vaginal–penile intercourse can be performed with both partners standing, sitting in a chair, or with one partner partially on a bed or table while the other partner stands on the floor (Comfort, 1972).

No one vaginal–penile position is normal. Each society has a position that is commonly used for vaginal–penile intercourse, and members of that society consider that position the normal one for all people. Among young people, Hunt (1974) found that every penile–vaginal position is used without exception. Any position is normal, acceptable, healthy, and suitable if it is mutually satisfying to both partners. With mutual trust and experimentation, sexual partners can discover almost countless variations. What is mutually satisfying and preferred can change with age, weight, pregnancy, and state of health.

Anal Intercourse

The anus is an *erogenous zone* (an area of the body that is particularly responsive to sexual stimulation), and many men and women engage in and enjoy anal penetration. Anal intercourse is also considered immoral and some states have laws against *sodomy* (anal intercourse between two men).

Anal intercourse can be performed in different positions, and is commonly practiced by homosexual men. In a rear-entry position, the partner lies on his or her stomach while being approached from behind. In a face-to-face position, one partner lies on his or her back with knees raised to sides of chest while being approached.

The anus is surrounded by a strong sphincter muscle that must be relaxed before entry. A lubricant and gentle pressure are suggested. To avoid vaginal infection from bacteria normally found in the anus, a thorough washing of the penis after anal contact, or the use of a condom, is suggested.

MASTURBATION IN ADULTHOOD

Masturbation (any deliberate bodily self-stimulation that produces a sexual response) is a sexual behavior engaged in by adult men and women. Kinsey, Pomeroy, and Martin (1948) and Kinsey, Pomeroy, Martin, and Gebhard (1953) reported that masturbation is the second most important source of sexual gratification for the average American man (first is heterosexual intercourse) and the most reliable form of sexual activity for reaching orgasm for the average American woman. It is used regularly by nearly all single men and a majority of single women, and married adults today use it more frequently than those of previous generations (Hunt, 1974).

The incidence of masturbation in the total population of men is 95%. Kinsey (1948) reported 45% and Hunt (1974) reported 63% of men have masturbated by the age of 13. Kinsey also reported that 96% of the men who had attended college, 95% who had attended high school, and 89% who had attended only grade school had masturbated. Athanasiou (1976) estimated that the average man under 35 masturbates 75 to 100 times per year, and those over 35, 33 to 50 times a year. Kinsey reported that 95% of the men surveyed used manual stimulation of the genitals for sexual arousal.

About 50% to 90% of all women masturbate at some time in their lives. Kinsey (1953) reported 15% and Hunt (1974) reported 33% of all women had masturbated by the age of 13. Kinsey (1953) reported that 63% of college, 59% of high-school, and 34% of grade-school females had masturbated. Hite (1976) found that 82% of the women in her sample masturbated regularly. Kinsey et al. (1953) and Athanasiou (1974) reported that women masturbate about once every two to four weeks. In Kinsey's (1953) study, 84% of the women used manual stimulation of the genitals for sexual arousal, while a few others used thigh pressure, muscular tension, or fantasy without physical sensation.

In men, the frequency of masturbation decreases in the teenage years, while in women it increases and tends to remain constant during middle age (Kinsey et al., 1953). Hunt (1974) found almost no differences in the occurrence of masturbation among men who were regular churchgoers (92%), irregular churchgoers (92%), and nonchurchgoers (93%). Among women, churchgoing seemed to have a restraining effect. The occurrence of masturbation for regular churchgoers was 51%, irregular churchgoers 69%, and nonchurchgoers 75%.

CLIMACTERIC AND MENOPAUSE IN ADULTHOOD

Women

Menopause refers to the cessation of the menstrual periods. It is the final phase in the woman's reproductive ability and is considered complete after one year of no menstrual bleeding. *Climacteric* refers to all of the physiologic changes that occur as the woman changes from the fertile to the nonfertile phase, and it is the period initiated by decline of ovarian function and terminated by complete menopause. The term *change of life* refers to the entire climacteric period rather than just to the event of menopause. Fifty percent of women experience menopause between the ages of 45 and 50, 25% before 45, and 25% after 50 (Sloane, 1980).

The most significant change in the normal physiologic process of menopause is the permanent and irreversible atrophy of the ovaries accompanied by a decline in estrogen and progesterone production. Examination of vaginal smears have shown an estrogenic effect to persist for a decade or more beyond menopause in nearly 80% of all postmenopausal women (McLennan & McLennan, 1971).

Many women pass through the climacteric with little discomfort and only 10% have severe symptoms. The most common symptoms of menopause are vasomotor instability ("hot flashes"), thinning of the vaginal lining, difficulty sleeping, dizziness, irritability, nervousness, headache, and depression. Of all the symptoms, only two have been established as "uniquely characteristic of menopause"—vasomotor instability and thinning of the vaginal lining (Cooke & Dworkin, 1979; Sloane, 1980).

Vasomotor instability is experienced as hot flashes, which begin as a sensation of warmth over the upper part of the chest and spreads, wavelike, over the neck, face, and extremities. Hot flashes occur suddenly and unpredictably and are often followed by profuse perspiration and chills. They are over in 15 to 60 seconds, vary in intensity, come singly or in series, are harmless, and will eventually disappear. Hot flashes are not symptoms of a disease but rather symptoms of the normal and healthy process of menopause (Cooke & Dworkin, 1979; Reitz, 1977). Reitz (1977) urges women to discuss hot flashes with their family and friends. When the woman shares these experiences she no longer feels ashamed and can accept the hot flashes as part of herself. Physical exercise, good nutrition, and food supplements can sometimes alleviate menopause symptoms (Seaman & Seaman, 1978). Moderate doses of ginseng extract and vitamin E may be helpful for some women. Sedatives or mild tranquilizers taken for a short time may be helpful. Reitz (1977) feels that "there is a clear relationship between a healthy body and an easier menopause" (p. 31).

As a result of diminished estrogen, which decreases vascularity and causes atrophy of the mucous membrane, the vaginal epithelium becomes thin, pale, and dry during climacteric. Only 25% to 35% of women have so much thinning in the vaginal lining that they experience discomfort during intercourse. When the thinning is not severe, the symptoms may be relieved by the use of a sterile water-soluble jelly, such as KY. Continued frequent sexual activity helps maintain vaginal lubrication. When thinning is severe, local treatment with estrogen-containing vaginal suppositories is effective (Sloane, 1980).

Estrogen replacement therapy (ERT) can alleviate the symptoms of vasomotor instability and thinning vaginal lining; however, the wisdom of administering ERT except for severe and incapacitating symptoms is being challenged. Studies have shown there is a strong association between ERT and edometrial cancer and that ERT may increase the risk of breast cancer (Hoover, Gray, & MacMahon, 1976; Ziel & Finkle, 1975). Breast tenderness, weight gain, and edema are possible side effects of ERT.

All women considering ERT should be given information and encouraged to evaluate the potential risks and benefits and come to their own decision. If ERT is chosen, the treatment is usually short-term and the low-dose estrogen is best taken orally on a cyclical basis with progesterone.

A persistent stereotype of menopausal women has them uninterested in, unable to participate in, and ineligible for sexual activity and relationships. The stereotype is harmful and wasteful. Physiologically, there is no reason why the menopausal woman cannot participate in sexual activities, for she is fully capable of orgasmic response, particularly if she has had regular and frequent stimulation. Increased sexual desire and activity can occur during a woman's forties and fifties, and the woman may seek to enhance and enrich her sexual experiences. The older woman may be a sought-after sexual partner because of her life's experiences and her fewer anxieties about sex and sexuality. The menopausal woman who has good feelings about herself and is in a satisfying sexual relationship may experience little or no change in the pattern of her sexual activities (Masters & Johnson, 1966).

Men

When male menopause is discussed, such terms as "male climacteric," "metaphase," "mid-life crisis," and "mid-life transition period" are preferred. For men there is no dramatic change in circulating male hormones. The male climacteric entails the end of producing sperm but not semen, and the slow gradual rate of change may extend from the forties to the seventies. Symptoms commonly reported are predominately psychologic: moodiness, impatience, worry, headaches, fatigue, hypochondria, and depression. Men do not appear to have discomforting physical symptoms, but their psychologic and sociologic changes can be as unsettling as those of the menopausal woman. The changes involve struggles with self, irrational fear of aging, decreased opportunities for job changes or advancement, threat of competition by younger men, anxiety about waning sexual performance, and economic pressures of retirement. As in women, the period is a time for reassessment, reinvestment, and diversification.

Physiosexually, the size and firmness of the testicles diminish, ejaculate fluid becomes thinner and less copious, and the prostate may develop benign or malignant tumors. Changes in sexual response include the need for longer periods of stimulation for erection and orgasm, diminished urgency of ejaculation, reduction in number of orgasmic contractions, and lengthening of refractory periods.

The role diminishing male hormones play in the man's syndrome of symptoms is not clear. When testosterone replacement is administered, some men show a decrease in the psychologic symptoms and improvement in sexual functioning and others report no particular benefit (Kaplan, 1974). The most effective sexual treatment is continued frequent sexual activity. The middle-aged man with healthy attitudes and accurate information about his sexual potentials can appreciate the opportunity for satisfying and imaginative foreplay provided by the longer periods required for stimulation. In fact, middle-aged men with the ability to control ejaculation and to prolong intercourse may have distinct advantages over younger men (McCary, 1973).

SEXUAL FANTASIES

Sexual fantasies (fanciful products of the imagination that take place without conscious direction) occur in adult men and women. Fantasy is a common, natural, and acceptable human experience. Sexual fantasies can occur during masturbation, during encounters with a sexual partner, or in the absence of sexual activities. Friday (1973, 1980) asserts that the fantasies of women are as varied, vivid, and vigorous as those of men. Although some adults prefer to keep their sexual fantasies private, Comfort (1972) suggests that sexual partners consider sharing their sexual fantasies to focus on sexual arousal and enhance sexual feelings and experience.

In the Kinsey (1948, 1953) samples, almost 100% of the men and 65% of the women reported having erotic dreams sometime in their lives. Hunt (1944) reported the frequency of use of six categories of sexual fantasies during masturbation by adult men and women: (*1*) intercourse with strangers was a relatively common fantasy and was used by 47% of all men and 21% of all women; (*2*) intercourse with more than one person of the opposite sex at the same time was used by 33% of the men and 18% of the women; (*3*) doing something you would never do in reality, a catch-all category, was acknowledged as being used by only 19% of the men and 28% of the women; (*4*) being forced to have sex was used by 10% of the men and 19% of the women—this fantasy was rarely used by older persons of either sex and was much more common among those under 25; (*5*) forcing someone to have sex was acknowledged as being used by 13% of men and 3% of women; and (*6*) having sex with someone of the same sex was used by 7% of the men and 11% of the women.

Sexual fantasies are normal and most adults are able to distinguish between what they imagine and what they choose to do. Sexual fantasies are considered maladaptive only when they interfere with work productivity and are used in place of interaction with others.

FREQUENCY OF SEXUAL OUTLET

In Kinsey's (1948, 1953) surveys, *sexual outlet* referred to the total number of orgasms achieved during an average week through masturbation, sexual fantasies, petting (conscious sexually oriented physical contact that does not involve intercourse), intercourse, homosexual activities, and animal contacts.

Kinsey (1948) calculated that, among men between adolescence and age 85, the mean frequency of total sexual outlet was about three orgasms per week. For men, the average number of orgasms experienced per week was related to the age group. The highest levels of sexual activity was achieved before 30. After 30 there was a steady decline in frequency of orgasm.

Kinsey (1953) found the frequencies of total sexual outlet for women were lower than for men in all comparable age groups. The prepubescent women, up to the age of 15, were sexually inactive and rarely orgasmic. Women between the ages of 15 and 38 showed a steady increase in frequency of total sexual outlet to a peak at age 30. The rate was maintained until age 40 with a slight decrease in the 40 to 50 age group and a steady, steep decline between the ages of 40 and 80. The data demonstrate that the period of decline in men's sexual activity, after age 30, occurs simultaneously with the period of peak sexual activity in women, ages 30 to 40 and after age 45. The data seem to confirm Sheehy's

(1976) assertion that men and women between the ages of 30 and 40 have diverging sexual life cycles that begin to converge at ages 40 to 45.

MARRIAGE AND SEXUALITY

Most people spend the major part of their adult lives married (see Chapter 7 for a discussion of single, celibate, divorced, and widowed adults). *Marriage* is the state in which a man and woman are formally united for the purpose of living together with certain legal rights and obligations toward each other. Traditionally, marriage is the legal, and often religious, prerequisite to sexual union. Within marriage sex receives social approval and religious blessing and becomes one of the four legal rights and responsibilities married people have toward each other. Bearing of children, domestic and economic services, and property are the other three legal rights and responsibilities (Murray & Zentner, 1979).

The pattern of marriage in contemporary America is changing. The women's movement, the need for women to work outside the home, increased lifespan, increased leisure time, and presentation of alternatives and options in popular books, magazines, movies, and television have compelled and enabled changes.

In the traditional marriage, roles and relationships are fundamental and rigid. The man is strong and competent—the decision maker, the social and economic provider, a supportive and devoted husband, an authoritarian father, and an informed and active sexual partner. To complement, the woman is warm and attractive, a receiver, a housekeeper, a manager of time and money, a supportive, loyal, and devoted wife, a nourishing and nurturing mother, and an uninformed, submissive, and passive sexual partner. In the family, commitments are honored, responsibilities fulfilled, sacrifices made, sexual privacy maintained, sexual exclusivity expected, and monogamy respected.

The nontraditional or person-centered marriage has flexible roles and relationships and recognizes that values, life-styles, jobs, and needs of persons and families vary widely. The people in this type of marriage are growth oriented and place emphasis in personal freedom, inner awareness, independence, equality of the sexes, and self-actualization. The roles are designed and the relationships shaped by the strengths, growth needs, hopes, expectations, and visions of the persons involved. The roles and relationships are open ended and can be negotiated and renegotiated. The partners are free to examine their minds, bodies, and feelings, sex is discussed openly, experimented with, playful and pleasurable, and sexual exclusivity is negotiable. The commitment is to the sharing of experiences, personal growth, mutual respect, and caring.

Each marriage has its own unique pattern. Some marriages are strongly traditional, others are open and flexible, and others combine elements of each pattern. There is no such thing as an average American marriage. In every time period, Americans have followed a variety of patterns that reflect political and economic as well as social and sexual conditions and changes (Broderick, 1977).

MARRIAGE AND SEXUAL BEHAVIOR

Marital Intercourse

In the Kinsey (1948) population of men, marital intercourse provided 85% of the total sexual outlet for married men. For college-educated men, marital intercourse provided 85% of the total outlet during early marriage and dropped to 62% in the middle fifties. Among men with a high-school education, marital intercourse provided 82% of sexual outlet in the early years and rose to 91% of the total by the late forties. For grade-school-educated men, about 80% of the total outlet came from marital intercourse; this rose to about 90% in the late forties and early fifties. The reason for the striking difference in the incidence of marital intercourse and total sexual outlet between college- and grade-school-educated men is not clear. The difference is probably best explained by the personal and marital sexual experiences and adjustments of the men in each group as well as the impact of the prohibitions and sanctions within the subcultures of the group.

Among Protestant men (the only group for which sufficient data was available) Kinsey (1948) reported that the frequency of marital intercourse was greater for the less devout than for the more devout. Perhaps the more devout could not set aside their early strict religious training even within the approved and sanctioned circumstances of marriage. Hunt (1974) reports that although religiousness inhibits marital intercourse, it is the devoutness of the wife and not the husband that reduces frequency.

For married women between the ages of 16 and 35, Kinsey (1953) found that marital intercourse provided 84 to 89% of total sexual outlet. After age 35, there was a gradual decline in frequency; and when married women were 46 to 50 years old, only 73% of the total outlet was provided by intercourse. This decline in marital intercourse was the only sexual outlet among women that showed a gradual decline with advancing age, and occurred at a time when women's sexual desire had reached a peak. However, men's sexual desire had peaked between the ages of 16 and 25 and it was probably the aging of men that caused the decline in frequency of women's marital intercourse.

Kinsey (1953) reported that the incidence of total sexual outlet for married women was a bit higher for the college educated than for the grade-school or high-school groups. The religious background of the women had a definite and consistent effect on their total sexual outlet after marriage. The more devout women experienced 4% to 12% more of their total outlet in marital intercourse than did the women who were less devout. For devout women, a pattern of frequent marital intercourse developed more slowly than for less devout women; however, unlike the findings for Protestant men, once the pattern was established no further correlation existed.

Tavris and Sadd (1977), in their survey of female sexuality, found that the frequency of marital intercourse declined with a woman's age and length of marriage, with the greatest decline occurring after the first year. Twenty per cent of newly married wives reported they had sexual intercourse more than four times a week; that proportion dropped to 12% of women married one to four years, 7% of women married five to seven years, and 5% married eight years or longer. The majority of women who responded reported that they were satisfied with the frequency of marital intercourse. Only 4% thought the frequency too high, and 38% felt the frequency was not high enough. With few exceptions, the relationship between frequency of marital intercourse and satisfaction with marital intercourse was evident. Although frequency decreased in later years of marriage, satisfaction with marital intercourse did not.

Hunt (1974) reported a positive relationship between subjective ratings of sexual pleasure and emotional closeness. Men and women who rated their marriages as very close nearly always rated their marital intercourse as very pleasurable in the past year. Among the men and women who rated their marriage not close or very distant, 60% of the women and 40% of the men found marital intercourse unrewarding or even unpleasant. Hunt (1974) reported that contemporary marriages involve higher frequencies of marital intercourse than did those of a generation ago; and wives report such increases in every age group for comparable groups in the Kinsey data. Hunt (1974) contends that "sexual liberation has had its greatest effect, at least in numerical terms, within the safe confines of the ancient and established institution of monogamous marriage" (p. 194).

Sexual Practices of Heterosexual Marriages

Not only are men and women having marital intercourse more frequently, they are finding greater mutual pleasure in their sexual interactions and engaging in a wider variety of sexual practices. There has been an increase in the average duration of *foreplay* (sexually pleasurable activities such as kissing, touching, caressing, and oral–genital contact that precede intercourse). Kinsey (1948) found that the foreplay of less-educated men was brief and the duration for college-educated men was 5 to 15 minutes. Hunt (1974) reported that the median duration of foreplay for single people under age 25 was 15 minutes, for those age 25 to 34 about 20 minutes, and for married people in both age groups about 15 minutes.

Kinsey (1948, 1953) reported that among married men and women with lower levels of education, mouth–breast contact and manual stimulation of the genitals were rarely used. Hunt (1974) reported that every form of foreplay was now occasionally used in a large percentage of marriages and that the largest percentage of increase was among the less-educated groups.

Cunnilingus (oral stimulation of the female genitalia) and *fellatio* (oral stimulation of the penis) were totally avoided by the majority of the less-educated men and women in Kinsey's studies (1948, 1953). Tavris and Sadd (1977) reported that an overwhelming majority of the women had experienced oral–genital contact as an occasional or frequent part of intercourse. Most of the women stated having enjoyed cunnilingus more than fellatio. Hunt (1974) has speculated "that within another generation there will be almost no American marriage at any age level, where these two practices will not be used" (p. 199).

Hunt (1974) found that most married men and women performed anal intercourse rarely, but that over 6% of the under-35 age group did so sometimes or often. Tavris and Sadd (1977) reported that almost half of the women had tried anal intercourse although much less frequently than oral–genital intercourse. Those who had tried anal intercourse experienced it as acceptable with someone with whom they shared trust, emotional closeness, and love.

Good Marriages and Bad Sex

In general, good marriages are associated with good sex. Mutually satisfying sexual activity can contribute to self-esteem and closeness and to stability in a marriage or a sexual relationship (Mann & Katsuranis, 1975). However, mutually satisfying sexual activity can occur in poor relationships and unsatisfactory sexual activity in good relationships. Self-esteem is most effectively supported and enhanced when the behaviors of both partners are congruent with their needs, expectations, and values. When mutually satisfying sexual activity occurs with a poor relationship, Lief (1980) states, there has been a "separation of lust and love, and sex is being used as a reassurance to ward off separation anxiety" (p. 111).

Frank, Anderson, and Rubinstein (1978) studied 100 predominately white, well-educated, and happily married couples. They examined the frequency of sexual problems experienced and the relation of the problems to sexual satisfaction. Although more than 80% of the couples reported that their marital and sexual relations were happy and satisfying, 40% of the men and 63% of the women reported sexual dysfunctions (impairment of sexual response cycle; see Chapter 8); and 50% of the women and 47% of the men reported such dysfunction as lack of interest and inability to relax. The conclusion reached was that the quality of the affective component of the relationship and not the quality of the sexual performance determined the partners' perception of the quality of their sexual activities.

Premarital Intercourse

Premarital intercourse is vaginal–penile intercourse that occurs before the partners are married. In this country, there are four standards of premarital sexual behavior (SIECUS, 1970). *Abstinence* is the standard that formally forbids intercourse to both men and women. *Double standard* allows men to have greater access to intercourse than women. *Permissiveness with affection* as a standard accepts intercourse for both men and women when a stable affectionate relationship is present. *Permissiveness without affection* accepts intercourse from both men and women when it is voluntary, regardless of affection.

Many societies tolerate, permit, or even encourage premarital intercourse within a variety of identifiable specifications about age, time, place, and circumstances. The organization of these societies is such that all children born outside marriage are fully provided for and are not socially disabled or stigmatized (Davenport, 1977). Traditionally, our society has imposed abstinence, demanded *continence* (self-restraint in sexual activity), and banned premarital intercourse. King, Balswick, and Robinson (1977) have documented the increasing rejection of the double standard and the growing feeling that premarital intercourse should not be forbidden. Most people are involved in premarital sex for only a brief period in their adult lives. Most men experience premarital intercourse for a five-to-six year period and most women for a one-to-two year period (Hunt, 1974).

Kinsey et al. (1948, 1953) found that the prevalence of premarital intercourse was markedly related to educational level in men but much less so in women, and that it had little relation to parental occupational class for either men or women. Among men, 98% of grade-school-educated, 84% of high-school-educated, and 67% of college-educated had had premarital intercourse; and 50% of the men who had intercourse while in college had had their first experience before starting college. Fifty percent of the women had had premarital intercourse, and 46% of them with only one partner—usually the man they married. The Kinsey et al. (1953) data showed that a major change occurred in the prevalence of premarital intercourse among women in the 1920s. Less than 20% of the women married before 1920 had had premarital intercourse, whereas about 50% of the women married after 1920 had experienced premarital intercourse.

Among both men and women premarital intercourse was more prevalent in the urban areas and much less prevalent among the more religiously devout.

Hunt's (1974) survey showed a definite increase in the prevalence and frequency of premarital intercourse among men and a striking increase in women. He reported that twice as many unmarried men and two to three times as many women were having premarital intercourse in their late teens and early twenties as compared to those in the Kinsey survey; also, the frequency of premarital intercourse had increased by about one-third for men and at least three times for women.

Tavris and Sadd (1977) found that eight out of ten married women said they had had premarital intercourse, with 68% of the women over 40 having done so compared to 96% of the women under age 20. Pietropinto and Simenauer (1977) reported that 32% of men today still want to marry women with no previous sexual partners, 20.5% would marry a woman who had had one or a few sexual partners she really loved, and 2.2% would want to marry a woman who has been sexually active with many men. Kinsey et al. (1953) found that 53% of women who had experienced premarital intercourse had only one partner. In Hunt's (1974) survey, the married men had a median of six partners before marriage, and among the married women, 54% had had only one partner. In the older half of Hunt's sample of women, a little more than one-third had had premarital intercourse, over half of these with only one partner. In the younger half of the sample, over two-thirds had experienced premarital intercourse, more than half had had only one partner. Thus, despite the increase in the prevalence and frequency of premarital intercourse, the youth had not fully abandoned deeply rooted sexual value systems. The young women were still likely to experience premarital intercourse with the man they expected to marry, and although men were more ready to engage in intercourse without affection, both men and women continued to value relational requirements for premarital intercourse.

Extramarital Relationships

Extramarital relationships refer to those situations in which a married person has sexual intercourse with someone other than his or her spouse. Extramarital sex can occur as part of an unexpected and casual encounter or be part of a deep and full emotional commitment. Most extramarital relationships are *nonconsensual*—the sexual intercourse has occurred without the knowledge of the spouse (see Chapter 7 for a discussion of consensual extramarital relationships). In our society extramarital relationships are often condemned and are considered immoral and illegal. A recent survey of adults found that 87% felt that extramarital intercourse was always or almost always wrong (Glenn & Weaver, 1979).

Regardless of the prohibitions against it, extramarital intercourse has been a common behavior.

Kinsey et al. (1948, 1953) reported that about half of the men and one-quarter of the women they surveyed admitted that they had had at least one extramarital relationship by age 40. Among less-educated men, the highest incidence of extramarital intercourse occurred in the youngest age group, with the number of persons involved steadily declining to 27% by age 40 and 19% by age 50. Among college-educated men, the lowest incidence of extramarital intercourse occurred in the youngest age groups (15% to 20%), with the percentages steadily increasing to about 27% by age 50. Among college-educated women the incidence of extramarital intercourse was higher after the age of 25.

The Kinsey et al. (1953) data suggested a correlation between religiousness and extramarital intercourse, with the more devout less likely to be involved than the less devout. The researchers also found a positive correlation between premarital and extramarital intercourse among both men and women. About 41% of the women who engaged in extramarital intercourse reported one partner, and about the same percentage reported two to five partners.

Hunt's (1974) study found the overall incidence of extramarital intercourse unchanged. Among married men under 25 there was a moderate change. Among women under 25, however, there was a dramatic increase from 8% to 24%. This increase brings the incidence of extramarital intercourse for women to just below the incidence for men under 25 and suggests an erosion of the marital double standard.

Tavris and Sadd (1977) found that 29% of all married women had had extramarital intercourse. Length of marriage increased the chances of a woman having extramarital intercourse among employed and nonemployed women, with the likelihood greatly increasing for women employed full-time outside the home. Among women in their late thirties, 53% of the employed women reported extramarital intercourse, compared to 24% of unemployed women who stayed at home. Although religious affiliation was not significant, religiousness was the strongest inhibiting factor against extramarital intercourse, with 15% of the more devout having reported extramarital intercourse compared to 36% of the less devout.

Pietropinto and Simenauer (1977) found that 43% of the married men had been involved in extramarital intercourse, 4% with the consent and knowledge of their wives. When married, divorced, and widowed men are combined, 45% have had extramarital intercourse. The investigators concluded that "it seems safe to say that cheating is not so much a phase some men go through as a general way of life for those who engage in it" (p. 281).

Men are likely to become involved in extramarital relationships in the first few years of marriage (Kinsey et al., 1948; Hunt, 1974), and women are doing so at an earlier age and earlier in their marriages (Hunt, 1974;

Tavris & Sadd, 1977). Knowledge of a spouse's extramarital intercourse can be personally painful and maritally discordant. It is believed, and reinforced by medical and nonmedical literature, that extramarital relationships represent a weakness in the marriage and reflect sick, inadequate, or neurotic behavior on the part of the participant. Myers and Leggitt (1975) found that extramarital intercourse occurred in both "good" and "bad" marriages, that motives for it were best understood by the participants, and that the final outcome was not predictable. English (1971) and Myers (1976) assert that extramarital relationships can be creative and rewarding; they urge an objective study of the advantages and disadvantages. In many cases, the partners survive the pain and the marriage disruption, for the confrontation of themselves and the dynamics of the marriage can be growth producing. Myers (1976) urges that health professionals be more objective, for each person is responsible for his or her own decisions based on the best information available and consistent with his or her own sexual value system.

Cohabitation

Cohabitation occurs when two people of different genders live together, have a sexual relationship, and are not married. The United States Census Bureau (1979) has estimated that 2.2 million unmarried men and women live together (though not all have sexual relationships). Clayton and Voss (1979) found that between the ages of 20 and 30 about 18% of unmarried men had cohabitated with a woman for at least 6 months, although only 50% of these were currently doing so. Macklin (1978) estimated that about 25% of all college students will cohabitate for a period of weeks or months. Cohabitation is more likely to occur in urban areas than in rural areas. Religiousness strongly inhibits cohabitation (Henze & Hudson, 1944).

Macklin (1978) found that marriage was not the initial goal at the beginning of a cohabitation relationship. Most cohabitants feel an emotional attachment for one another, usually exclude other romantic involvements, and may pledge sexual exclusivity. Sexual gratification is not a major component of the cohabitation relationship, for the cohabitants work to develop a total relationship but do not feel ready for marriage. Many cohabitants state they would like to marry someday and do so, but most do not marry each other (Newcomb, 1979).

The advantages of cohabitation are an opportunity to develop emotionally close and sexually gratifying relationships. Some economic benefits can also be derived from the pooling of resources. One of the disadvantages may be the strain of parental disapproval. Parents tend to be more conservative about cohabitation than are college students, and many cohabitants do not tell their parents about their living arrangements (Macklin, 1978). Some cohabitants may have difficulty renting or buying property, and the lack of legal procedures may make the resolving of property rights difficult should the relationship end. Termination of the cohabitation relationship is often accompanied by psychologic trauma. Cohabitation is increasing, and for many it has become the last step in the courtship process (Broderick, 1979).

HOMOSEXUAL RELATIONSHIPS

Homosexual relationships (two men or two women living together in a committed social and sexual affiliation) are without the supporting legal and economic structures or approved social models associated with heterosexual relationships and marriages. If homosexual partners choose to be married, there are some clergy who will solemnize the commitment, but ready access to a marriage license is denied. Stable, responsible, and even lifetime homosexual relationships are not protected by tax and inheritance laws. The social pattern of families to support homosexual partners or a partner in crisis is not fully developed.

Bell and Weinberg (1978) have proposed five categories for adult homosexual relationships:

Close Couples. These partners were closely bound to each other for sexual and interpersonal satisfaction and did little *cruising* (planned searching for a sexual partner). They were happy with their sexual lives and enjoyed spending their leisure time at home. Both the homosexual men (HM) and homosexual women (HW) were the most self-accepting and the happiest of the homosexuals interviewed.

Open Couples. The HM and HW in this relationship were less committed and less happy with their partners and sought social and sexual satisfaction with other people. The HM did more cruising than average, the HW cruised more than any other HW, and the personal and social consequences (arrest and public exposure) of cruising were worrisome to them. Generally, their social and psychologic adjustment was average, but they were less self-accepting and more lonely than close-couple homosexuals.

Functionals. These homosexual men and women resembled "swinging singles." They were the least likely to regret being homosexual, cruised frequently, were highly involved in the *gay* (homosexual) community, engaged in a wide variety of sexual practices, were interested in multiple partners rather than a committed relationship, and considered themselves sexually attractive. When compared to close-couple homosexuals they spent less time at home, saw their friends more often, and were more tense, unhappy, and lonely.

Dysfunctionals.   People in this group came close to fitting the stereotype of the tormented homosexual. They regretted their homosexuality, found little gratification in life, cruised frequently, reported a high number of sexual problems, worried about their sexual inadequacies and inability to maintain an affectionate relationship, and considered themselves sexually unappealing.

Asexuals.   These homosexuals were characterized by their lack of involvement with others. Their general psychologic adjustment was about the same as the general homosexual population, but they were older, described themselves as lonely, and led a solitary life. They reported few partners, low sexual activity, low sexual interest, narrow sexual repertoires, and a fair number of sexual problems.

Bell and Weinberg (1978) concluded that homosexual men and women in continuing relationships have behaviors that are similar to heterosexuals who are married.

SEXUAL PRACTICES OF HOMOSEXUAL RELATIONSHIPS

Homosexual Men

HM may use lips, tongue, and hands to kiss and play, caress nipples, manipulate each other's penises, perform sequential or concurrent fellatio, and have anal intercourse. The number of different sexual practices in which HM are willing to engage is often related to their age, how long they have been homosexually involved, the willingness of their partners to experiment, and the degree to which they accept their homosexuality (Bell, 1979).

Bell and Weinberg (1978) reported that 27% of white homosexual men (WHM) preferred receiving fallatio and 26% preferred anal intercourse. Almost 50% of black homosexual men (BHM) preferred anal intercourse and approximately 20% preferred receiving fallatio. Fifty percent of WHM and 66% of BHM reported having sex with other men at least twice a week, with two to three times a week the most common frequency.

Weinberg and Williams (1974) stated that religious HM were more likely to believe they were born homosexuals and less likely to have experienced the sexual practices common to homosexuals. Bell and Weinberg (1978) reported that BHM described themselves as conventionally religious more often than WHM. Both BHM and WHM said that being homosexual had not affected their religious feelings, although more whites than blacks said it had tended to weaken these feelings.

Homosexual Women

HW use lips, tongue, and hands to kiss and play, stimulate breasts and genitals, and engage in sequential and simultaneous cunnilingus and *tribadism* (body friction that simulates intercourse). Most HW partners do not use a strap-on penis or *dildo* (artificial penis). Bell and Weinberg (1978) found that 50% of HW reported cunnilingus as the preferred sexual practice. Among white homosexual women (WHW), the next preferred sexual practice was being masturbated by their partners, or mutual masturbation, and black homosexual women (BHW) reported that they enjoyed body rubbing. The most common frequency of having intercourse reported for BHW was twice or more a week, and for WHW once a week.

Weinberg and Bell (1978) found that more BHW than WHW described themselves as religious in the conventional sense. Most HW said that their homosexuality had not affected their religiousness in any way, although some said their religious feelings had been weakened because of their homosexuality.

The common belief that HM and HW assume masculine (active) and feminine (passive) behaviors during sexual activity was not supported by Bell and Weinberg's (1978) data. The reports of preferred techniques centered on the individual's rather than the partner's orgasm, which suggests that attributing activity or passivity to the participant's behavior is unwarranted.

THE NURSE AS EDUCATOR-COUNSELOR

Information and knowledge about trends and changes in sexual behavior is helpful for nurses. The three basic changes that have occurred in our society are "the legitimation of individual choice of sexual standards," "increased tolerance of sexual customs," and recognition that there is "no physiologic barrier to sexual equality" (Reiss, 1979, p. 92). Assimilation of this knowledge can help the nurse understand the pressures of social change operating on the client and on the nurse. Knowledge about the wide range of human sexual behavior can help the nurse alter or discard culturally induced stereotypes and proscriptions for behavior. Understanding the psychologic and physiosexual complexities of human sexual behavior prevents the nurse from using his or her own sexual value system as reference and enables the nurse to interact with clients in a nonjudgmental, accepting, and encouraging manner. The nurse will not label clients as "bad," "good," "abnormal," "nice," or "not so nice." The nurse will see and hear them as adults dealing with psychosocial and physiosexual changes that affect their sexuality. The nurse will recognize that the most effective resolution of discrepancies between personal and societal values comes from within clients and will assist them as they seek solutions that are most meaningful for themselves and those with whom they relate.

The role of the nurse in dispelling myths and misconceptions associated with adulthood is almost limitless. As an educator, anticipatory guidance—providing reliable information and letting the client know what may be expected—can help clients avoid or seek a variety of solutions to a potential problem. As a counselor, the nurse is an attentive and careful listener and promotes communication that is growth producing.

As sexual relationships are reconsidered or revitalized, sexual partners can be encouraged to make and take time for physical, emotional, sensual, and sexual pleasure. Information about sensual activities, such as showering together and body massage, can be offered. Reliable information about the sexual response cycle, alternative positions for intercourse, a variety of sexual practices, and masturbation and mutual masturbation as normal and healthy is helpful.

Anticipatory guidance about the normal and healthy process of menopause and climacteric, when obtained early in adulthood, is beneficial. During menopause and climacteric, counseling for both men and women "will be an intricate combination and interplay between the very real stresses that are typical . . . and the very real potential for finding new freedom and fulfillment beyond" (Smallwood & Van Dyck, 1979, p. 76).

It is essential for the nurse to acknowledge, accept, and be comfortable with sex and sexuality as a continuing and valued part of adulthood. The nurse as educator-counselor can help adult clients look at the opportunities and resources available to them as they take responsibility for informed decision making about their sexual functioning, roles, and relationships.

NURSING PROCESS

Client: Inez Owens. Chief complaint: "these hot flashes bother me."
Nurse: Sylvia Wagoner, nurse at a women's health center.

Assessment

Subjective Data

"This is my first time here. My friend Ruby told me to come."
"During the last 6 or 7 months, I've noticed my periods are different. The flow is less and the time between is longer."

"The last 2 or 3 months I've been having hot flashes like I've always
   heard about."
"Ruby tells me not to worry—but it's scary."
"The hot flashes usually just last a few moments. My chest gets warm and
   then the heat spreads up over me—like a wave—and my face gets so
   red and I feel embarrassed and sort of like there's nothing I can do."
"Sometimes they come in twos and threes. I can tell when it's going to be
   bad—my feet tingle first."
"When that happens at work, I feel sort of ashamed."
"Yes, I work—took the job when my last child struck out on his own. I
   really like my job—and really like getting paid for baking."
"You know—sometimes a hot flash happens when Jim and I are—what
   we call—making 'vigorous' love—and then I don't pay much attention at all and Jim says I'm his 'blushing bride' again."
"No—haven't noticed anything different about making love. Except with
   no kids around it feels sort of more free."
"Yes, I know. Ruby has told me to be careful. I wear my diaphagm like
   always."
"But these hot flashes—anything to worry about? Anything I can do?"

Objective Data

Age 52
Employed—baker at McMahon's Catering Service for 5 years.
Married 34 years, 2 children (none living at home), 2 grandchildren.
Husband—self-employed plumber.
Pelvic examination—pink, thinning vaginal walls characteristic of
   menopause.
Pap smear taken.
Change in rate and regularity of menstrual bleeding characteristic of
   menopause.
Contraception practiced—diaphragm.
Sexual functioning and relationship satisfactory.
Seeks reassurance and possible interventions for vasomotor instability
   (hot flashes).

Nursing Diagnosis

Lack of information about vasomotor instability related to menopause.

Planning

Listen attentively.
Encourage expression of feelings.
Offer feedback of expressed feelings.

Explain that emotional response is appropriate and commonly experienced.

Explain normal physiologic and psychosocial changes associated with menopause.

Explain that self-report of menstrual bleeding and findings of pelvic examination are normal and characteristic of menopause.

Explain that physiosexual changes of menopause do not interfere with sexual functioning.

Explain the intervention available for potential problem of thinning vaginal walls.

Explain that results of Pap smear will be discussed when returned.

Explain that vasomotor instability (hot flashes) is a normal, healthy change of menopause and is not harmful.

Support realistic assessment of vasomotor instability.

Encourage keeping a journal of occurrence of hot flashes.

Advise avoidance of stressful situations that aggravate vasomotor instability.

Encourage discussion of hot flashes with family, friends, and work associates.

Encourage attention to nutrition and regular exercise.

Explain that health habits contribute to maintenance of positive self-attitude and physical well being.

Encourage reading of books by Reitz (1977) and Cooke and Dworkin (1979).

Encourage acceptance of vasomotor instability as normal, healthy part of self during menopause.

Explain the treatment available for severe or prolonged episodes of vasomotor instability.

Indicate availability for further counseling.

Implementation

Borrow Cooke and Dworkin (1979) from Ruby's friend.
Borrow Reitz (1977) from library.
Discuss information about menopause with Jim.
Cut down on junk food such as snacks after and between meals.
Keep a journal about hot flashes.
Talk about journal and hot flashes with women at work.
Talk to friends about exercise programs.
Choose an exercise program.

Evaluation

Work pressure increases likelihood of hot flashes.
Talking about hot flashes helpful. Feelings of embarrassment diminished.

Lost three pounds.
Enjoying doing exercises demonstrated on popular TV program.

BIBLIOGRAPHY

Allen, L. D. Penile length. *Medical Aspects of Human Sexuality,* 1980, *14*, 107.

Anderson, R. E., & Carter, I. *Human behavior in the social environment: A social systems approach* (2nd ed.). Chicago: Aldine, 1978.

Athanasiou, R. Frequency of masturbation in adult men and women. *Medical Aspects of Human Sexuality,* 1976, *10*, 121–124.

Bell, A. P. The homosexual as patient. In R. Green (Ed.), *Human sexuality: A health practitioner's text* (2nd ed.). Baltimore: Williams & Wilkins, 1979.

Bell, A. P., & Weinberg, M. S. *Homosexualities: A study of diversity among men and women.* New York: Simon & Schuster, 1978.

Boyarsky, S. Penis size vs. body height. *Medical Aspects of Human Sexuality,* 1980, *14*, 7.

Bragonier, J. R., & Bragonier, B. J. The physiology of sexual function. In V. L. Bullough (Ed.), *The frontiers of sex research.* Buffalo, N.Y.: Prometheus Books, 1979.

Broderick, C. B. *Marriage and the family.* Englewood Cliffs, N.J.: Prentice-Hall, 1979.

Cameron, P. The generation gap: Beliefs about sexuality and self-reported sexuality. In W. R. Loft (Ed.), *Developmental psychology: A book of readings.* New York: Holt, Rinehart & Winston, 1972.

Campbell, C. *Nursing diagnosis and intervention in nursing practice.* New York: Wiley, 1978.

Comfort, A. *The joy of sex.* New York: Crown, 1972.

Cooke, C. W., & Dworkin, S. *The Ms. guide to a woman's health.* Garden City, N.Y.: Anchor Books, 1979.

Crooks, R., & Baur, K. *Our sexuality.* Menlo Park, Cal.: Benjamin/Cummings, 1980.

Davenport, W. H. Sex in crosscultural perspective. In F. A. Beach (Ed.), *Human sexuality in four perspectives.* Baltimore: Johns Hopkins University Press, 1977.

Diekelmann, N., & Dressen, S. Menopause. In N. Diekelmann (Ed.), *Primary health care of the well adult.* New York: McGraw-Hill, 1977.

English, O. S. Positive values of the affair. In H. A. Otto (Ed.), *The new sexuality.* Palo Alto, Cal.: Science and Behavior Books, 1971.

Erikson, E. *Childhood and society* (2nd ed.). New York: Norton, 1963.

Foster, A. L. Relationships between age and sexual activity in married men. *Journal of Sex Education and Therapy,* 1979, *1*, 21–26.

Francoeur, R. T., & Shapero, R. Recognition of alternatives to traditional monogamy in new religious and civil rituals. *Journal of Sex Education and Therapy,* 1979, *1*, 17–20.

Frank, E., Anderson, C., & Rubinstein, D. Frequency of sexual dysfunction in "normal" couples. *New England Journal of Medicine,* 1978, *299*, 111–115.

Friday, N. *Men in love.* New York: Delacorte Press, 1980.

Friday, N. *My secret garden.* New York: Trident Press, 1973.

Glenn, N. D., & Weaver, C. N. Attitudes toward premarital, extramarital, and homosexual relations in the United States in the 1970's. *Journal of Sex Research*, 1979, *15*, 108–118.

Greenblatt, R. B. Sexual peak in women. *Medical Aspects of Human Sexuality.* 1980, *14*, 5.

Haeberle, E. J. *The sex atlas: A new illustrated guide.* New York: Seabury Press, 1978.

Henze, L. F., & Hudson, J. W. Personal and family characteristics of cohabitating and noncohabitating college students. *Journal of Marriage and the Family*, 1974, *36*, 722–727.

Hite, S. *The Hite report.* New York: Macmillan, 1976.

Hoover, R. L. A., Gray, P. C., & MacMahon, B. Menopausal estrogens and breast cancer. *New England Journal of Medicine*, 1976, *295*, 401–405.

Hotchner, B. Menopause and sexuality: Gearing up or down. *Topics in Clinical Nursing*, 1980, *1*, 45–52.

Hunt, M. *Sexual behavior in the 1970's.* New York: Dell, 1974.

Kaplan, H. S. *The new sex therapy.* New York: Brunner/Mazel, 1974.

Katchadourian, H. A., & Lunde, D. T. *Biological aspects of human sexuality.* New York: Holt, Rinehart & Winston, 1975.

King, K., Balswick, J. O., & Robenson, I. E. The continuing premarital sexual revolution among college females. *Journal of Marriage and the Family*, 1977, *39*, 455–560.

Kinsey, A. C., Pomeroy, W. B., & Martin, C. E. *Sexual behavior in the human male.* Philadelphia: Saunders, 1948.

Kinsey, A. C., Pomeroy, W. B., Martin, C. E., & Gebhard, P. H. *Sexual behavior in the human female.* Philadelphia: Saunders, 1953.

Levinson, P. J. *The seasons of a man's life.* New York: Ballantine Books, 1978.

Levitt, E. Duration of intercourse. *Medical Aspects of Human Sexuality*, 1980, *14*, 7.

Lief, H. I. Good sex in bad marriages. *Medical Aspects of Human Sexuality*, 1980, *14*, 107–111.

McCary, J. L. Sexual advantages of middle-aged men. *Medical Aspects of Human Sexuality*, 1973, *8*, 139–142; 150–151; 153–155.

McCary, J. L. *McCary's human sexuality* (3rd ed.). New York: D. Van Nostrand, 1978.

McLennan, M. T., & McLennan, C. E. Estrogenic status of menstruating and menopausal women assessed by cervico-vaginal smears. *Obstetrics and Gynecology*, 1971, *37*, 325–331.

Macklin, E. Nonmarital heterosexual cohabitation. *Marriage and Family Review*, 1978, *1*, 1–12.

Mann, J., & Katsuranis, J. The dynamics and problems of sexual relationships. *Postgraduate Medicine*, 1975, *58*, 79–85.

Masters, W. H., & Johnson, V. E. *Human sexual response.* Boston: Little, Brown, 1966.

Murray, R. B., & Zentner, J. P. *Nursing assessment and health promotion through the life span* (2nd ed.). Englewood Cliffs, N.J.: Prentice-Hall, 1979.

Myers, L. Extramarital sex: Is the neglect of its positive aspects justified? In W. W. Oaks, G. A. Melchoide, & I. Ficher (Eds.), *Sex and the life cycle.* New York: Grune & Stratton, 1976.

Myers, L., & Leggitt, H. A new view of adultery. In L. Sross (Ed.), *Sexual issues in marriage.* Holliswood, N.Y.: Spectrum Publications, 1975.

Newcomb, P. R. Cohabitation in America: An assessment of consequences. *Journal of Marriage and the Family,* 1979, *41,* 597–602.

O'Neill, N., & O'Neill, G. Marriage: A contemporary model. In B. J. Sadock, H. I. Kaplan, & A. M. Freedman (Eds.), *The sexual experience.* Baltimore: Williams & Wilkins, 1976.

Petterson, M. Routine sex. *Medical Aspects of Human Sexuality,* 1980, *14,* 111.

Pietropinto, A., & Simenauer, J. *Beyond the male myth.* New York: Times Books, 1977.

Rainwater, L. Some aspects of lower class sexual behavior. *Medical Aspects of Human Sexuality,* 1968, *2,* 15–25.

Reed, D. M. Traditional marriage. In B. J. Saddock, H. I. Kaplan, & A. M. Freedman (Eds.), *The sexual experience.* Baltimore: Williams & Wilkins, 1976.

Reiss, I. L. Heterosexual relationships of patients: Premarital and extramarital. In R. Green (Ed.), *Human sexuality: A health practitioner's text* (2nd ed.). Baltimore: Williams & Wilkins, 1979.

Reitz, R. *Menopause: A positive approach.* Radnor, Pa.: Chilton Book Company, 1977.

Sarrel, P. M. Sexual physiology and sexual functioning. *Postgraduate Medicine,* 1975, *58,* 67–72.

Seaman, B., & Seaman, G. *Women and the crisis in sex hormones.* New York: Bantam, 1978.

Sevely, J. L., & Bennett, J. W. Concerning female ejaculation and the female prostate. *Journal of Sex Research,* 1978, *14,* 1–20.

Sex Information and Education Council. *Sexuality and man.* New York: Scribners, 1970.

Sheehy, G. *Passages: Predictable crises of adult life.* New York: Dutton, 1976.

Sloane, E. *Biology of women.* New York: Wiley, 1980.

Smallwood, K. B., & Van Dyck, W. G. Menopause counseling: Coping with realities and myths. *Journal of Sex Education and Therapy,* 1979, *1,* 72–76.

Steen, E. B., & Price, J. H. *Human sex and sexuality.* New York: Wiley, 1977.

Tavris, C., & Sadd, S. *The Redbook report on female sexuality.* New York: Delacorte Press, 1977.

U. S. Bureau of the Census. Marital status and living arrangements: March 1978. *Current Population Reports,* Population Characteristic Series P-20, No. 338 (May 1979):1–63.

Weinberg, M. S., & Williams, C. J. *Male homosexuals: Their problems and adaptations.* New York: Oxford University Press, 1974.

Williams, J. H. Sexuality in marriage. In B. B. Wolman & J. Money (Eds.), *Handbook of human sexuality.* Englewood Cliffs, N.J.: Prentice-Hall, 1980.

Witters, W. L., & Jones-Witters, P. *Human sexuality: A biological perspective.* New York: Van Nostrand, 1980.

Ziel, H. K., & Finkle, U. D. Increased risk of endometrial carcinoma among users of conjugated estrogens. *New England Journal of Medicine,* 1975, *293,* 1167–1170.

6.   Sexuality and Aging

Valerie Jackson Markley

VALUES CLARIFICATION EXERCISE

Most people in the United States have been socialized to believe that sex is an activity for the young, strong, and beautiful. It follows, then, that sex is not for the older, weaker, and not-so-beautiful aging person.

The following exercise will enable you to examine your thoughts, feelings, and attitudes about the sexuality and sexual activity of older people.

Write down the way you feel the nurse should respond in each of the situations. As you write the responses, note the feelings associated with the behaviors you prescribe for the nurses. Then discuss your responses and share your thoughts and feelings in a small group. Discuss the common elements and the differences in the behaviors prescribed by the members of the group. Was the group able to identify behaviors that were best or most appropriate for any of the situations? Did any members of the group change their views after the discussion? How could the attitudes and feelings expressed in the group affect the nursing care planned by the group?

> Mrs. Johnson, a thirty-two-year-old nurse, wife, and mother, is doing private duty in a 300-bed hospital with a man who is a 92-year-old professor emeritus in medieval history and who has been a widower for two years. The professor talks often about his wife and how much he misses her. He repeatedly pulls Mrs. Johnson toward him and begs her to kiss him and give him a hug. Mrs. Johnson should _____.

> Ms. Kinser is a community health nurse in a large metropolitan area. On her visit to the Kleindorfers' apartment in a senior-citizens' complex, she finds the front door open. After there is no response to her knocking at the door, she steps inside. She can hear soft noises coming from the bedroom and sees Mr. and Mrs. Kleindorfer engaged in love making; they do not notice her. Ms. Kinser should _____.

Mr. Moser is the evening charge nurse in the residential wing of a convalescent center. As he begins his 11 P.M. rounds, he notes Mrs. Putnum and Mr. Todd in bed and asleep with the side rails raised. Mr. Moser should _____.

Mrs. Justin is a mental health nurse who has a "life review" group every Wednesday morning at the senior-citizens' center. As she goes in for the group one Wednesday, she meets Mrs. Wilson, one of the regular group members, on her way out the door. Mrs. Wilson is 74 years old and has had a chronic problem with alcohol. She explains that she must get her hair set before her appointment that afternoon with her therapist, "an attractive man in his early thirties." Mrs. Justin should _____.

While Miss Hunter, a 20-year-old nursing student, is bathing Mr. Oliver, a 69-year-old man, he has an erection. Miss Hunter should _____.

Ms. Vilardi, a 26-year-old student nurse, is helping Amanda Evans, age 27, prepare for a Pap smear. During the sexual health history taking, the client says: "My mother, who is almost 70, a widow for five years, and a grandmother to my two kids and seven others besides, says she wants to move in with her boyfriend on his farm. My sister thinks it's funny, but I certainly don't. What do you think?" Ms. Vilardi should _____.

BEHAVIORAL OBJECTIVES

At the completion of this chapter, you will be able to

- Critique the myths and folklore about the aged.
- Describe the anatomical and physiological changes in the sexual response cycle of aging women and men.
- Explain the psychosocial adaptation to the anatomical and physiological changes in the sexual response cycle of aging men.
- Discuss the possible effects of hormone replacement therapy for aging women and men.
- Discuss sexual behavior in the aging woman and man.
- Describe how physiological changes and psychological perceptions of self affect the sexual behavior of aging women and men.
- Discuss how the restrictive environment of a nursing home affects the sexuality of the residents.
- Describe a plan of nursing care that attends to the sexuality of the aging woman and man.

In the United States today, almost 33 million people are 65 years of age or older. This is more than 11% of the total population. Every day at least 4,000 people reach this 65-year mark, and many of them have 15 or more years yet to live (Schrock, 1980). The number of people who will be living to old age continues to increase, and the nurse needs to be familiar with the process of aging and its implications for sexuality.

STEREOTYPES, MYTHS, AND MISCONCEPTIONS

Old age and retirement, like every developmental phase of life, has its benefits and its crises. Often the stereotypes, myths, and misconceptions regarding the sexuality of the aging person make it difficult to see anything positive about growing older.

The most prevalent and encompassing stereotype is that of the sexless old age. Our youth- and beauty-oriented American society endorses the stereotype that "sex is reserved for the young (and beautiful) while the old (and ugly) are relegated to rocking chairs and celibacy" (Foster, 1979, p. 26). There is also the myth that the elderly cannot make love even if they want to, and that, sex does not matter and is not important in the later years. Some people even view interest in sexual activity as abnormal for older people (Kuhn, 1976). Both women and men are included in the widespread myths about aging and sexuality. One myth is that aging inevitably leads to impotence; another is that menopause signals the end of a woman's active sex life. These myths are closely linked with the myth, and deep belief, that the primary function of human sexuality is procreation. This is possibly linked to the religious tradition that links sexuality only with reproduction.

Another common myth in our society is the notion that child molesting and sexual deviation is prevalent among older men. This is connected with the stereotypic thinking that has denied sexuality in the aging and chosen to view any expression of it as psychological deviance. What society considers virility at 25 becomes lechery at 65. The so-called dirty old man is probably the most maligned figure in our culture, yet Whiskin (1970) states that, paradoxically, "he tends to be the most benign . . . of individuals" (p. 170). In reality, the belief that men past age 60 are more likely than younger men to molest children has been proven incorrect by everyone who has made an effort to check the facts.

Masters and Johnson (1966) have made major strides toward demystifying these myths and stereotypes through their detailed laboratory studies of the sexual responses of older persons. They have documented not only the interest in sexual activity but also the actual performance of sexual intercourse in persons from 51 to 78 years of age. They were the first to observe the anatomy and physiology of the sexual response of older persons under laboratory conditions.

The myth of sexless old age is most damaging when it is reinforced by a society that denies or ignores the reality of sexual needs and interests of more than 11% of the population. As these myths and misconceptions are nourished, there is a danger that they will be accepted by more of the older age group and thus become a self-fulfilling prophecy. This must be guarded against for the sake of the present elderly and for those yet to join their ranks. These stereotypes tend to make elderly women and men feel uncomfortable and guilty about their sexuality rather than pleased that they are normal and able to enjoy this aspect of their being.

SEXUAL CHANGES WITH AGING

People begin as sexual beings in utero and remain sexual beings throughout their lives. It is true that physiological changes occur with time; there is a gradual slowing down, yet the changes are not dramatic. Because the changes are gradual, the body has the opportunity to adapt to them. There are vastly different individual responses to aging. People do not age according to a set pattern. In fact, they become more different or individualistic with the passing of time (Weg, 1975). The sexual performance of the aging man is primarily limited by physical factors, although the culture imposes some restrictions. By contrast, the aging woman, whose physical capabilities and responsiveness have not declined, is limited from sexual expression largely by cultural factors (Sviland, 1978a). There is often no partner available for her.

Nevertheless, in the absence of physical illness, much of the sexual dysfunction in older couples occurs as a result of a lack of information and understanding about the normal physiological alterations of aging. Our society neglects to prepare people for aging. Many persons are surprised and alarmed by the gradual changes in sexual functioning that occur as part of the normal aging process. They may take these rather minor changes as a sign that they are losing their sexual capability. Each partner may assume that the changes in the other (i.e., slower erection or reduced vaginal lubrication) occur in response to his or her own fading attractiveness or responsiveness. "Brief preventive counseling for men and women during their forties or fifties could be expected to alter significantly the number of persons who eventually experience sexual difficulty during their geriatric years because of lack of adequate information and unrealistic expectations" (Kolodny et al., 1979, p. 88). In fact, realistic preparation throughout the lifespan, beginning in the earliest years, would be a major step forward.

ANATOMICAL AND PHYSIOLOGICAL CHANGES IN THE SEXUAL RESPONSE CYCLE OF WOMEN

In the middle years, women begin to acquire a different body contour; breasts sag somewhat and the abdomen becomes more creased. A small hump may appear near the nape of the neck. With the aging process the woman experiences a more absolute change in reproductive capability than the man. She experiences the end of fertility and of the hormonal cycles that characterize the second through the fifth decades of life. Kolodny et al. (1979) state that there is most likely a gradual decline in the capability of the woman to reproduce, beginning at age thirty.

Menopause, the cessation of menses, is the physiological transition phase from the child-bearing years to the older years. From 35 to 55 years of age, menses may begin to be irregular or less predictable. For some women the initiation of the menopause is delayed until age 50. Menopause usually occurs somewhere between 48 and 51 years of age in a wide variety of populations, but the individual differences in timing and pattern of menopause are great, particularly in the earlier range of these ages. This leaves about 25 years or longer remaining in the post-menopausal phase of the woman's life cycle. As Masters and Johnson (1966) point out, researchers have been unable to delineate the exact mechanisms that control the onset of the menopause and characterize the events associated with alterations in hormonal secretion during this period.

It is speculated that the eggs within the ovaries become less sensitive to the pituitary gonadotropins, resulting in reduced production of estrogens, which decreases the frequency of ovulation during menstrual cycles in the years just before menopause (Kolodny et al., 1979; Weg, 1975). The hypothalamus responds to this reduced estrogen secretion by increasing the supply of gonadotropin-releasing factor, causing an increase in the production of LH (luteinizing hormone) and FSH (follicle stimulating hormone). Nevertheless, the ovaries are not able to produce greater amounts of estrogen even in response to this powerful stimulus, and as a result a state of equilibrium is reached in which high levels of gonadotropins are circulating but the ovaries are synthesizing less estrogen and progesterone than during the reproductive years (Kolodny et al., 1979).

Only about 40% of women going through menopause have any recognizable symptoms at all, and not more than 10 or 15% are disturbed enough to seek treatment (Runciman, 1975). Many women do experience symptoms related to menopause however, including vasomotor instability or hot flashes, atrophic changes in the skin, genitals, and breasts, and psychological symptoms ranging from irritability to depression. These symptoms are affected by the change in the hormonal equilibrium, the deficiency in estrogen supply, and the societal programming that women are expected to experience certain symptoms during menopause (Kolodny et al., 1979).

After menopause, the physical evidence of chronic estrogen deficiency may appear in several ways. There is a decrease in vaginal length and width. The vaginal walls lose their rough, corrugated look and take on a light pinkish color. The thinning and drying of the vaginal mucosa results in decreased lubrication. There is also a reduction in Bartholin gland secretion. The vagina loses its ability to secrete acid, so there is a greater tendency toward vaginal infections. These changes may lead to *dyspareunia* (pain during intercourse), which can be relieved by local application of estrogen creams or by systemic replacement of estrogen and progesterone. Women who never experienced discomfort during sexual intercourse may have vaginal burning, pelvic aching, or vague lower-body distress. They may also complain of burning and irritation on urination and have an increased number of urinary tract infections. With the shrinkage in the size of the vaginal barrel there is a loss of elasticity in the vaginal walls analogous to the decrease in tissue elasticity in many parts of the body that is part of the normal aging process. The woman who is sexually inactive after menopause is particularly subject to these changes in the vaginal barrel (Kolodny et al., 1979; Burnside, 1975b).

The changes that occur in the breasts with aging are caused by a combination of decreased tissue elasticity and estrogen deficiency. Mechanical factors are mainly responsible for breast drooping, and the actual decrease in breast tissue mass is due to lowered estrogen stimulation (Kolodny et al., 1979). In spite of these changes it is interesting to note that the aging breast may maintain the capacity for lactation. In some cultures postmenopausal women function as wet nurses (Slome, 1956).

When the woman's general health is good, aging does not alter sexual interest or the capacity to be orgasmic (Kinsey et al., 1953). Masters and Johnson (1966) studied 34 postmenopausal women from 51 to 78 years of age and reported these women to be highly functional sexually. However, in comparison to women in the reproductive years there were some differences in their patterns of sexual response (Table 6.1). It was found that the vasocongestive increase in breast size that typically occurs during sexual excitement in younger women was reduced or absent in the postmenopausal women. The sex flush occurred less frequently and was more limited in distribution in older women. Generalized tonic spasm of muscles (myotonia) was decreased, the vagina expanded less during sexual stimulation, and vaginal lubrication was reduced in amount and required a longer time for production. These changes were increased by lack of regularity in sexual activity after menopause. Masters and Johnson also found that aging women had a higher incidence of painful uterine contractions. However, these symptoms are more likely to occur when intercourse is infrequent—once a month or less. Regular and frequent sexual activity results in a higher capacity for sexual performance (Kolodny et al., 1979).

PSYCHOSOCIAL ADAPTATION TO CHANGES IN THE SEXUAL RESPONSE CYCLE OF WOMEN

As sexual partners, women experience few physical changes as they age, and their level of interest and capacity change only slightly. Most older women, if appropriately stimulated, are able to respond to the four phases of the sexual response cycle: the excitement phase, the plateau phase, the orgasmic phase, and the resolution phase. More time is required for lubrication of the vulva and vaginal areas, but the clitoral response does not take longer. Nipples and breasts are still responsive to stimulation (Table 6.1). There is no vaginal erogenous tissue, as noted by Kinsey et al. (1953) and Masters and Johnson (1966). "With clitoral stimulation the contractions start in the fundus of the uterus, move in both directions and move down to the vaginal area as well. But it is the clitoral stimulation that is the sensate focus for orgasm in the female, young or old, and a capacity that does not change" (Weg, 1975, p. 11).

During the first stage of excitement, the sex flush decreases in intensity and extent in aging women, probably because the muscle fibers in the blood vessels are not as responsive to autonomic stimulation. The plateau phase may last longer. "Orgasm is as satisfying and as real and involves the same muscles and the same tissues as ever before. Differences relate to the contractions of the orgasm of the older woman which may be more spasmodic rather than regular, fewer in number and may even cause some pain" (Weg, 1975, p. 11). Resolution occurs more quickly. "It takes longer to respond and the seconds of extreme satisfaction and pleasure involved in orgasm are over more quickly, but fulfilling and satisfying" (Weg, 1975, p. 11). Sviland (1978b) reports that approximately 15% of elderly women show an increase in sexual capacity with aging.

In the Kinsey et al. (1953) studies, most women were found to become less inhibited over the years and to develop a greater interest in sexual activity. Many felt a sense of liberation after menopause, when the possibility of pregnancy was no longer a factor. Kinsey also noted that a large part of the sexual interest in the postmenopausal period is directly related to the sexual habits established during the procreative years. After marriage ends, the woman's desire to continue intercourse and to seek out sexual activity is greatly dependent on her previous capacity to reach orgasm. Pfeiffer and Davis (1972) concur that enjoyment of sexual relations in the younger years, rather than frequency or level of sexual interest in younger years, seems to be of particular importance in determining the extent of sexual interest and frequency of intercourse in a woman's later years.

Christenson and Gagnon (1965) analyzed data from interviews with 241 married and postmarried women in the 50-to-70-year age group. They found that at age 60, 70% of the married women and 12% of the postmarried women engaged in intercourse. Because the incidence of intercourse could be attributed largely to the sexual performance of the husbands, data was collected about the incidence of women masturbating. Reported masturbation rates were higher for the postmarital women, with 25% of the single women aged 70 still masturbating. Christenson and Gagnon (1965) also found that women with husbands younger than themselves had a higher rate of intercourse than did the women with older husbands. However, the orgasmic capacity of women tended to be higher when the husbands were of the same age.

Table 6.1. Changes with Age in Sexual Response Patterns[a]

	Younger Women	Older Women		Younger Men	Older Men
Breasts	Nipple erection; Increase in size, areolar engorgement, flush prior to orgasm	Same; Intensity of reactions diminishes	Breasts	Nipple erection	Diminishes
Sex Flush	Vasocongestive skin response to tension	Diminishes	Myotonia	Increased muscular tension; involuntary muscular contractions	Responses may diminish
Myotonia	Muscular tension increases	Response diminishes	Rectum	Rectal sphincter contractions during orgasm	Decrease in frequency
Urinary System	Minimal distention of external urinary meatus during orgasm	Meatus gapes with orgasm of high intensity or with successive orgasms	Penis	Erection develops within 3–5 seconds of stimulation; full erection early in cycle	Erection takes 2–3 times longer over 50; full erection not attained until immediately prior to orgasm
Rectum	Rectal sphincter contractions with orgasm	Decrease		Ejaculatory control varies	Maintain erection longer without ejaculation
Clitoris	High degree of responsivity	Same		May attain and partially lose full erection, several times during cycle	When erection partially lost, difficulty in returning to full erection
Major Labia	Flatten, separate, and elevate with increased sexual tension	Response diminishes		Color change of glans penis	Diminished or absent
Minor Labia	Vasocongestive thickening; color change from cardinal-red to burgundy-wine before orgasm	Color change and thickening diminish		Forceful ejaculation; expulsive contractions during orgasm	Force diminishes; sensual experience may be reduced
Bartholin's Glands	Small amount of mucoid secretion during plateau	Response diminishes		Refractory phase variable	Prolonged refractory phase after orgasm before next erection; rapid penile detumescence

Organ		
Vagina	Walls well-corrugated, thickened, reddish-purple appearance; vaginal lubrication within 10–30 seconds of stimulation	Walls tissue-paper-thin, noncorrugated, pinkish; vagina shortens and expansive ability decreases; lubrication may take 1–3 minutes or more. Engorgement reduced but constriction response continues
	Orgasmic platform (swelling of outer vagina) develops during plateau, constricting vagina	
	Contractions (5–6) of platform during orgasm	Number of contractions decreases
	During resolution, slow collapse of expanded portion of vagina	Rapid collapse
Ejaculation	Two-stage, well-differentiated process	Single-stage expulsion of seminal fluid
	Prostatic contractions	Not clinically obvious
	Awareness of fluid emission and pressure	May experience seepage rather than expulsion; fewer and less viable sperm than younger men
		Response diminishes
Scrotum	Scrotal folding patterns obliterated with sexual tension	
Testes	Testicular elevation in late excitement or early plateau; increase in size	Diminished response
	Testicular descent during resolution	Rapid descent
Uterus	Uterine elevation during excitement and plateau	Reaction delayed and elevation not as marked
	Expulsive contractions (3–5) with orgasm	Decrease in number

Source: D. Stanford, All about sex after middle age, *American Journal of Nursing*, April, 1977. Reprinted with permission of American Journal of Nursing.

[a]Based on phases of sexual responses as described by V. E. Johnson and W. H. Masters, *Human Sexual Response*, Little, Brown and Co., © 1966: 1. Excitement—begins with responses to sexual stimulation, e.g., penile erection, nipple erection; 2. Plateau—sexual tension and physical responses heighten; 3. Orgasm—pleasurable, intense, involuntary climax of sexual tension; 4. Resolution—release of muscular tension, return of organs to unstimulated state; in males, accompanied by refractory period. Chart adapted from *Human Sexual Response* with permission of authors and publisher.

In 1973, Christenson and Johnson did a study of never-married women. This group of 71 single, white, professional women stated that their sexual activities (masturbation and intercourse) were diminished by the age of 55.

Sexual abstinence in the elderly woman is not biologically induced but is influenced by social and psychological factors. The availability of a socially sanctioned, sexually capable partner remains one of the most crucial factors in determining the woman's sexual activity (Newman & Nichols, 1970; Pfeiffer & Davis, 1972). On the average, women outlive men by seven years, and women tend to marry men who are about four years older than themselves. Therefore, women may expect to experience an average of 11 years of widowhood. Only a very small proportion of these widowed women remarry. According to the 1970 census, at age 65 there are 138.5 women for every 100 men in the United States, and at age 75 the figures jump to 156.2 women for every 100 men. Drawing from these statistics, Pfeiffer and Davis (1972) speculate that much of the decline in sexual interest among aging women is not physiologic but defensive and protective. Perhaps it is adaptive to inhibit sexual striving when little opportunity for sexual fulfillment exists.

ANATOMICAL AND PHYSIOLOGICAL CHANGES IN THE SEXUAL RESPONSE CYCLE OF MEN

In men there is no finite cessation of fertility associated with age. Spermatogenesis does diminish with advancing age, and beginning with the fifth decade there are fewer sperm and fewer viable sperm. Sperm production persists into the ninth decade and beyond; however, there is usually not as pronounced a decrease in sex steroid hormone levels in men as in women, although there is a gradual reduction in circulating levels of testosterone from about age 60 onward. "There is an even greater decrease in the amount of free testosterone in circulation because there is a concomitant progressive rise in the concentration of sex steroid binding globulin after age 50. Similarly, age-related changes in pituitary gonadotrophins show a gradually increasing pattern after age 40" (Kolodny et al., 1979, p. 82).

According to Kolodny et al. (1979) a small subgroup of men aged 60 years or older exhibits a syndrome that may be called the male climacteric. This condition is characterized by a varying combination of the following symptoms: listlessness, weight loss or poor appetite, depressed libido with a probable alteration in erection ability, impaired concentration, weakness and fatigue, and irritability. Usually men exhibiting the male climacteric syndrome have positive findings in at least four of these categories. Because these symptoms are primarily nonspecific and could be attributable to depression or a number of disease processes, the man should be carefully evaluated and his plasma testosterone level should be checked. A markedly subnormal level is necessary before testosterone replacement is advised. The treatment is considered successful if the associated symptoms are alleviated within two months. If the man does not show significant improvement, a complete medical history and physical should be done.

Masters and Johnson (1966) found through direct laboratory observation that the physiology of sexual response is altered in aging men as compared to younger men in several ways (Table 6.1). Generally, the older man requires more time and more direct genital stimulation to achieve an erection. Usually there is a modest decrease in the firmness of the erection in men over the age of 60. The intensity of the ejaculatory experience usually diminishes with age. This may be partially due to the decreased volume of the ejaculate, the increase in the size of the prostate gland, and the changes in the nerve supply to the genital area. Also, the testes become more flaccid, and the testicular tubules that store and carry the sperm are lined by more and more layers of cells so that the diameter of the openings is narrowed. Having attained an erection, an aging man can maintain the erection longer before orgasm and the need to ejaculate. Many men over 60 discover that sexual intercourse can be stimulating and satisfying without ejaculating with every intercourse. The refractory period, the time interval after ejaculation when the man is physiologically unable to ejaculate again, tends to increase with advancing age. The vasocongestion of the scrotum is decreased. There is a reduction of the sex flush. After the mid-fifties, the elevation of the testes is lessened in the excitement and plateau phases. When the spermatic cord relaxes, the contractile tone of the cremasteric musculature is lost more rapidly. Resolution, the coming down from the high of orgasm, occurs more quickly, as it does in older women. In the older man, expulsive contractions of the penis are decreased in intensity and duration (Gress, 1978). The penis itself does not change in general appearance. However, like women, men experience some generalized decrease in the firmness of all their muscles, even with exercise.

PSYCHOSOCIAL ADAPTATION TO CHANGES IN THE SEXUAL RESPONSE CYCLE OF MEN

Because sexual arousal occurs at a slower pace in the older man than in the younger one, the former is likely to engage in sexual foreplay in an unhurried manner. Once intromission has occurred, the older man has the ability to prolong intercourse for a considerably longer period of time without feeling the urge to ejaculate that plagues the younger man. Because prolonging the sexual act provides greater opportunity for each partner to attain sexual gratification, the older man holds an important key to being an effective lover. Furthermore, the older man has had a longer time to overcome his sexual inhibitions, probably has had more sexual experiences, and is likely to have gained finesse and imagination in his sexual approach (McCary & Hammett, 1978).

With age there is a decrease in the frequency of sexual relations. This is particularly apparent in men by age 50, and a greater decline noted in the sixth and seventh decades (Rossman, 1975). There are also fewer morning erections (Runciman, 1975). Male sexual function reaches its peak responsiveness around age eighteen and then shows a steady decline. Kinsey, Pomeroy, and Martin (1948) noted that there are no calculations in all the material on human sexuality that give straighter slopes than the data showing the decline with age in the total sexual outlet for men.

Sexual dysfunction is common at all ages, and at all ages the psychic causes predominate over organic ones. It is extremely important to realize that alterations in erectile ability are not a feature of aging and are never a result of chronologic age alone (Table 6.1). "Management of potency problems lies in sexual counseling and in avoidance of iatrogenic interference with function, which increases sharply with age" (Comfort, 1978, p. 186). Although the incidence of sexual dysfunction in men takes a sharp upturn after age 50, Masters and Johnson (1966) have had success in training men over 50 years of age to reestablish erectile ability. "Only approximately five percent of impotence seen in previously well-functioning males is of a nonreversible physical origin . . . . Much impotency diagnosed as organic attributable to aging is actually attributable to such psychological and environmental variables as performance anxiety, loss of interest, or partner unavailability" (Sviland, 1978b, p. 225).

Regularity of sexual activity throughout the lifespan can prevent many of the sexual performance problems that have been erroneously attributed to aging. Therefore, many authorities suggest that the aged man masturbate on a regular basis whenever a partner is unavailable (Sviland, 1978b). Pfeiffer and Davis (1972) found in their research a significant positive correlation between high levels of sexual activity in the younger years and greater sexual activity in the later years. The most important fact for the maintenance of effective sexuality for the aging man is consistency of actual sexual expression (Runciman, 1975).

Masters and Johnson (1966) listed six factors involved in the loss of sexual responsiveness in the aging man:

1. Monotony or boredom of a repetitive sexual relationship
2. Preoccupation with career or economic pursuits
3. Mental or physical fatigue
4. Overindulgence in food or drugs (alcohol is the greater problem)
5. Physical or mental infirmities of either the individual or his partner

(this is a less acute problem for the man than for the aging woman with a physically infirmed partner)
6. Fear of unsatisfactory performance associated with or resulting from any of the above

HORMONE REPLACEMENT THERAPY

Hormone replacement therapy has had very limited success in helping men to retain or regain their youthful vigor. The old notions of rejuvenation and resexualization with hormones are almost totally erroneous (Comfort, 1978). Studies establish that there is no relationship between declining sexual capacity and hormone levels. The administration of testosterone to older men is usually useless in restoring youthful sexual pep, because there is no reliable relationship between aging and diminished blood testosterone levels (Rossman, 1975).

Hormones have been used extensively in postmenopausal women, however. Estrogens have been used to lessen epidermal atrophy, to preserve skin elasticity, and to prevent osteoporosis. After menopause there is less estrogen; however, the adrenal glands continue to synthesize estrogens. The use of estrogen replacement therapy is controversial, because some research findings purport to show a relationship between estrogen therapy and the development of breast or endometrial cancer. Kolodny et al. (1979) note that the studies on this issue

> do not prove causality. Until adequate and carefully controlled prospective studies are conducted, it appears impossible to ascertain the actual facts. ... Therefore, in a manner consistent with sound patient management, the risks of endometrial carcinoma should be explained to each woman who might be considered for estrogen replacement therapy, and attention should be given to possible medical contraindications to the use of estrogens, including impaired liver function, porphyria, history of breast cancer or endometrial cancer, and history of thromboembolic disease or cerebrovascular disorders. When estrogen replacement therapy is employed, the lowest effective maintenance dosage should be found for each patient and regular periodic gynecologic examinations should be carried out. [p. 82]

SEXUAL BEHAVIOR AND AGING

In 1965 Rubin, in summarizing the scientific literature that pertained to sexuality in the aging, noted only 13 studies. Of the thousands of persons studied by Kinsey et al. (1948), only 126 were over 60. Although Kinsey reported that sexual activity continues with advancing age, he found that sexual interest and activity declined at a steady rate, starting in the mid-teens. Nevertheless, he found that four out of five men over the age of 60 were capable of intercourse. Pfeiffer and Davis (1972) conducted a factorial study and found that a high level of sexual enjoyment and activity in youth was positively correlated with a high level of sexual enjoyment and activity in the later years. Pfeiffer, Verwoerdt, and Wang (1969) reported that 15% of the men and women studied showed a steady rising rate of sexual interest and activity as they grew older. The three most significant studies of sexual behavior in the aging have been made by Kinsey et al. (1948), Pfeiffer, Verwoerdt, and Wang (1969) at Duke's Center for the Study of Aging, and Masters and Johnson (1966). All their findings clearly indicate that men and women in a state of general good health are physiologically able to have a satisfying sex life well into their seventies, eighties and beyond. Even when there is a decline in sexual activity, interest remains for most people.

De Beauvoir (1972) has poignantly stated that what is needed most for a man to continue to feel like a man when he is older is to be treated like a man. From a very early age, personal identity is closely linked with sexual identity. When sexual functioning is taken away from people, their body image—the way they feel about themselves—is attacked. It is very important to maintain a sense of being masculine or feminine. People grow up being touched, held, and caressed, and they learn to reach out, hug, and kiss as ways of expressing themselves. Then as they grow old, people are sometimes isolated—except when someone comes to do something to them. Yet no one is too old to respond to the warmth of another's touching, holding, and stroking, which is associated with sexuality (Broderick, 1975).

One's reaction to aging is largely determined by one's own perception of it and psychologic attitudes toward it. Sexual satisfaction is more closely related to how one deals with one's own sexuality than to how well the partner performs. Older people differ greatly in regard to their sexual values, interests, and abilities. There are, of course, some conditions in which sexual functioning in the aging may be impaired. Kolodny et al. (1979) group these situations into the following categories: "general sexual disinterest, sexual boredom, impaired physical sexuality, cultural inhibition, and attrition by disuse" (p. 86). Some people never experienced sexual activity as particularly rewarding or gratifying in their youth and look forward to old age as a reason or excuse to abstain. Others, however, claim disinterest as a cover-up for their anxieties concerning sexual inadequacies or to accommodate disinterest or dysfunction in the partner.

Sexual boredom may reflect a growing monotony due to lack of variation in sexual activity (including time, place, and positions for intercourse, mutual masturbation, etc.). Many people forget the value of romanticizing and foreplay, which are important at all ages. Boredom with the same sexual partner may be a factor. Runciman (1975) notes that with the introduction of a new sexual partner erection takes place more rapidly: "But as the male continues with the new partner, he will eventually turn back to the same level of functioning he had with his previous partner. For that reason I don't find the suggestion of extramarital activity a valid one for reconstituting lively sexual activity" (p. 63).

As Kolodny et al. (1979) repeatedly note, frequency and regularity of sexual activity is the most important factor in maintaining the ability to perform. They report that masturbation may help to maintain the function of vaginal lubrication, but it is not adequate in maintaining the size of the vaginal barrel in the woman or the ability for erection in the man.

Physical disabilities may disrupt sexual capability directly or indirectly. Most often the problems of chronic illness, such as fatigue or shortness of breath, are the problem. Sexual activity does increase heart rate, blood pressure, and respirations at the point of orgasm and ejaculation, but these functions rapidly subside thereafter. The average maximal heart rate, which was found to be around 120, lasted for 10 to 15 seconds. Burnside (1975b) states, "It can be argued that the psychological stresses of enforced celibacy may predispose to more anginal pain than the physical exertion of intercourse or masturbation" (p. 46). People who can walk two flights of stairs without excessive exhaustion should be able to engage in sexual activity. There is also evidence that sexual activity aids arthritics by increasing the output of cortisone by the adrenal glands (Weg, 1975). In addition, the psychologic value of sexual activity is significant and may help to bolster the self-image. However, many older people need encouragement and reassurance that sexual activity in the later years is normal and healthy and can be continued. As Hogan (1980) has stated, "Ignorance is one of the greatest deterrents to successful sexual function in all ages, but it is the most crippling in the aging" (p. 397).

The positive value of companionship to general physical health is demonstrated by the lower mortality rates of older married people compared to older single people (Sviland, 1978b). The goal of sexual relationships need not be intercourse, but may be the pleasure and gratification that can be shared by elderly people in a reaffirmation of their humanness. Orgasm is not necessarily the epitomy of sexual pleasure.

INTERVENTIONS FOR SEXUAL ENHANCEMENT

The nurse can intervene to help couples with problems with sexual functioning related to the aging process. As a starting point, the sexual history provides the nurse with data about the client's sexuality. In addition, it must be remembered that attitudes and values about sex and sexuality vary greatly among aging people. Although it is the responsibility of the nurse to introduce the topic of sex and encourage the client to discuss sex and sexuality, the client defines the problem and assumes the responsibility for implementing the therapy congruent with his or her sexual value system.

The time of day to be selected for sexual activity is an important consideration for nursing intervention with older people. Energy as well as hormones are stored up during sleep, so morning offers some advantages. If the morning is not selected, a nap before sexual activity is beneficial, as is a nap afterwards. The ideal time is a time when neither partner feels physically or mentally fatigued, is affected by heavy eating or drinking, or is aggravated by an argument, and when each partner is comfortable with the room temperature and environment.

The position used for intercourse is another important consideration. Intercourse is less strenuous for the partner lying on his or her back when the partner on top assumes a kneeling position. In this position the partner on his or her back does not have to bear the other person's full weight. Another position to consider is the man sitting on an armless chair with the woman on his lap facing him with her feet placed firmly on the floor. The side-by-side position is often least strenuous for both partners. As a protection to the bladder and urethra, the man can thrust his penis downward toward the back of the woman's vagina and in the direction of the rectum rather than toward the upper part of the vagina.

The use of a lubricant that dissolves in water (K-Y Jelly is one) can compensate for decreased vaginal secretions. Coconut oil or even a light cooking oil, are alternatives that can be considered. Vaseline should be avoided because it is not water soluble and can be a vehicle for vaginal infection. Comfort (1978) instructs against overlubrication in consideration for the man's need for stronger penile stimulation.

There are methods that help to reduce the problems of atrophic vaginitis and secondary cystitis. Careful hygiene, specifically a thorough washing of the vaginal area and the penis before intercourse, is very important. The bladder should be emptied before intercourse, as a full bladder is more easily irritated. Urinating after intercourse helps to flush the urethra mechanically. Routinely drinking large amounts of water and urinating frequently are helpful preventative measures. Wearing cotton underwear rather than synthetics help prevent infections by allowing air to circulate in the vaginal area. For the same reason, snug girdles, panty hose, and tight pants can also create an environment conducive to the growth of bacteria (Butler, 1976).

Aging people need to be educated about the importance of direct genital stimulation. Such stimulation gains increasing importance with age, because both women and men become less responsive to fantasy for genital arousal as they grow older (Comfort, 1978). Fantasy or visual images alone often provide a sufficient stimulus to excite a younger person to genital arousal. With older people, direct manual stimulation of the genitals is usually required for excitation. Some women have difficulty stimulating their partners, however, because they have been socialized to play a passive role in sexual activity. A change in the woman's role might also require accommodation on the man's part.

Certainly, as Masters and Johnson (1966, 1970) have demonstrated in their research, older people can benefit from sexual counseling and therapy. When a careful nursing assessment indicates a need for formal sexual therapy, the individual or couple should be informed of and offered the option of such help.

A wider range of sexual expression may need to be explored for the aging. When there is no available sexual partner, a client may need to be taught to masturbate effectively. However, many older people were raised to believe that masturbation is wrong and harmful, and an older person may choose not to listen to information that is emotionally charged.

The imbalance of the sexes is an overwhelming dilemma. There are more than 11 million women who are over 65 years old. Of this number, 6 million are widows and an additional 1.2 million are divorced or single (Butler, 1976). These women's sexual needs often cannot be satisfied through intimate relationships with men, because the men may not be available. Some of these women can be helped to find closer bonds with other women through warm, close relationships.

As another therapeutic measure, Burnside (1976) proposes "reminiscing therapy," which has proven to be particularly effective in helping groups of elderly people to look back over their lives, search for meaning, and relish memories of earlier times. Also, nurses can reach out to touch the elderly; they desperately need to be touched to reaffirm that they are alive and appreciated.

The need for love and affection is universal. Older people need affection, tenderness, and touch as long as they live. Burnside (1975a) asked, "Do we withhold affection, tenderness, and touch because we are afraid to get involved, are repulsed by the idea, or simply are insensitive?" (p. 49). She makes a plea that we closely examine our own ideas or mores and that we never make fun of ideas and behaviors that may be different from our own.

SEXUALITY OF NURSING-HOME RESIDENTS

Only 5% of the elderly live in institutional settings, yet it is essential to realize that these older people have the same needs, drives, and desires as their counterparts living in the community. All people share the same needs for affection, warmth, and sexual expression.

Men and women living in nursing homes, even long-time marital partners, have almost universally been sexually segregated. They have been denied privacy and given both overt and covert messages that old men and old women in institutions are not to be sexual. They have been discouraged from and even punished for any behavior that did not strictly follow this established norm.

In spite of their treatment, elderly people in nursing homes do have sexual thoughts, feelings, and behaviors, but nursing-home staff members are frequently distressed and do not know how to respond. "If sexual health care is to become an integral part of total care in the nursing home, the starting point must be the staff . . . their attitudes and values will determine the quality of care in this area" (Aletky, 1980, p. 59). Staff members are ready to develop administrative policies and treatment approaches to provide quality sexual health care when they have been able to: (1) examine their own sexual values, (2) begin communicating comfortably about sex, and (3) gain knowledge about sexuality and the aging (Aletky, 1980).

Sexual health is an important part of the residents' physical and mental well being. If the sexual area is to be discussed, Aletky (1980) suggests a beginning approach with residents similar to that for staff: that is, encouraging exchange of values and attitudes. Then education can be offered. Burnside (1975a) suggests nine ways nurses can improve the atmosphere of the aged person in regard to sexuality. She directs the nurse:

1. to become better educated about sexuality in all stages of human development
2. to increase self-awareness so that we can begin to change our own attitudes as necessary
3. to discuss sexuality openly with staff, peers, and students so that problems can surface and be handled with common sense and honesty but without embarrassment
4. to assess the milieu in which older people live and to manipulate that milieu to provide more opportunities for them to express their own sexuality
5. to strive to better understand the aged people's life-styles and the lives they have been accustomed to living. Many passed much of their lives during the era when sex was not discussed. We must listen when they do discuss sexuality
6. to study our own approaches and to consider our friendship, touch, companionship, and interest as therapeutic for the aged. Not all intimacy occurs in bed
7. to respect the aged, whatever their views on sexuality may be
8. to be more courageous about intervention on behalf of the aged in matters of sexuality
9. to consider the positive aspects of sexuality in the aged (pp. 52–53).

THE ROLE OF THE NURSE AS EDUCATOR-COUNSELOR

Nursing interactions in relation to sexual health with the aging person are based on the assumption that for the social, emotional, and physical well-being of older people, an active sex life should be maintained as long as possible (Pfeiffer, 1968). The sexual history provides the nurse with data about the client's perception of his or her sexuality, sex roles, and sexual relationships. Although it is the nurse's responsibility to initiate, permit, and encourage discussion about sex and sexuality, it is the client who defines his or her concerns and expectations, does the planning, and selects the interventions congruent with his or her sexual value system.

The nurse as educator actively chooses to confront the myths and misconceptions about old age and uses knowledge to help dispel them. The nurse provides information about the effect of the aging process on the body in general and the sexual organs in particular. The nurse discusses how aging affects the sexual response cycle and suggests adaptations that the partners can make. The nurse offers specific information about interventions that enhance sexual activity and expression.

The nurse as counselor is objective and accepting and listens with an attentive and empathetic ear. The nurse reassures the aging partner or partners that interest in sex is normal, good, and beneficial; the nurse helps to eliminate fear and shame. As counselor the nurse encourages holding, touching, and sharing expressions of concern, caring , affection, and love. The nurse uses touch as an important part of communication in interactions with aging people. Through touch the nurse affirms that the client is touchable and she responds to the client's need to be touched.

The nurse can interact as educator-counselor in sexual health with the significant others of the aged person. The nurse can provide information about the positive value of sex and sexuality for the aging person. The nurse can help the significant others work through their feelings about the sexual behavior of their aging relatives.

In the community, the nurse as educator-counselor can advocate that information about growth, development, and aging be presented at all levels of education. The nurse can also assume the advocacy role for social and political changes to benefit the sexual health of aging people.

NURSING PROCESS

Client: Mrs. Cunningham, age 63.
Nurse: Mrs. Justin, nurse in Dr. Doris Murdock's office.

Assessment

Subjective Data

"Charlie and I have always had a very happy relationship and a good sex life too."

"We've been married for 42 years and everything was fine until Charlie got sick a few months ago."

"I've always had good health, just as Dr. Murdock said on my last physical two months ago."

"Our sex life kind of dropped off for a while—about six months."

"Now Charlie is well again and wanting to pick up where we left off."

"It never hurt during intercourse before during all those years."

"The last few times I've had cramping feelings down there during intercourse, and when Charlie first begins, it feels like it is going to tear me up inside."

"Charlie is upset to think he is hurting me."

"I'm terribly afraid that I am getting too old and worn out and that our good sex life is finished."

Objective Data

63-year-old woman married 42 years.

Six-month period of no intercourse due to husband's recurrent respiratory infections.

Experienced feelings of cramping, hurting, and tearing during last three attempts at intercourse.

Places both hands on lower abdomen where cramping occurs "down there."

Tearing sensation is in vaginal tract.

Holds body tense.

Speech rapid and forced.

Pelvic examination shows thin pale vaginal walls—normal physiological changes of aging.

Record of last physical examination shows findings within normal limits.

Fears loss of intercourse as part of relationship.

Feelings of low self-esteem.

Feelings of inadequacy about her sexual functioning.

Nursing Diagnosis

Pain during intercourse related to normal physiological changes in aging sexual organs.

Anxiety related to alterations in patterns of sexual functioning.

Planning

Approach unhurriedly.
Listen attentively.
Touch judiciously.
Provide atmosphere of acceptance.
Affirm significance of intercourse in relationship with husband.
Encourage expression of feelings.
Explain that client's physical symptoms are commonly experienced in her developmental stage.
Explain that client's emotional response is appropriate and commonly experienced when alterations in patterns of sexual functioning occur.
Provide information about the anatomical and physiological changes in the male and female sex organs due to the aging process.
Provide information about changes in the male and female sexual response cycle due to the aging process.
Explain specific interventions to help alleviate pain and anxiety about intercourse.
Explain alternatives to intercourse, such as mutual masturbation and oral sex.
Encourage expression of feelings about sexual functioning with partner.
Encourage sharing of information with partner.
Encourage mutual decision making.
Indicate availability for further counseling, individual or joint.

Implementation

Share feelings about significance of sexual functioning with partner.
Discuss effects of aging process in male and female sex organs.
Discuss effects of aging process on male and female sexual response cycle.
Discuss possible interventions for enabling intercourse.
Make mutual decisions about interventions.
Initiate selected interventions.

Evaluation

Reports absence of pain with intercourse.
Reports satisfactory experimentation with selected interventions.
Reports enhancement of sexual relationship.
Reports acceptance of joint counseling.

BIBLIOGRAPHY

Aletky, P. J. Sexuality of the nursing home resident. *Topics in Clinical Nursing*, 1980, *1*, 53–60.

Berman, E. M., & Lief, H. I. Sex and the aging process. In W. W. Oaks, G. A. Melchoide, & I. Ficher (Eds.), *Sex and the life cycle*. New York: Grune & Stratton, 1976.

Broderick, C. Sexuality and aging: An overview. In I. M. Burnside (Ed.), *Sexuality and aging*. Los Angeles: Ethel Percy Andrus Gerontology Center, 1975.

Burnside, I. M. Sexuality and aging. In I. M. Burnside (Ed.), *Sexuality and aging*. Los Angeles: Ethel Percy Andrus Gerontology Center, 1975. (a)

Burnside, I. M. Sexuality and the older adult: Implications for nursing. In I. M. Burnside (Ed.), *Sexuality and aging*. Los Angeles: Ethel Percy Andrus Gerontology Center, 1975. (b)

Burnside, I. M. (Ed.). *Nursing and the aged*. New York: McGraw-Hill, 1976.

Butler, R. N., & Lewis, M. I. *Sex after sixty: A guide for men and women in their later years*. New York: Harper & Row, 1976.

Cabot, N. H. *You can't count on dying*. Boston: Houghton Mifflin, 1961.

Christenson, C. V., & Gagnon, J. H. Sexual behavior in a group of older women. *Journal of Gerontology*, 1965, *20*, 351–356.

Christenson, C. V., & Johnson, A. B. Sexual patterns in a group of never-married women. *Journal of Geriatric Psychiatry*, 1973, *1*, 80–98.

Comfort, A. *A good age*. New York: Crown Publishers, 1976.

Comfort, A. Drug therapy and sexual function in the older patient. In A. Comfort (Ed.), *Sexual consequences of disability*. Philadelphia: Steckley, 1978.

De Beauvoir, S. *The coming of age*. New York: Putnam, 1972.

Falk, G., & Falk, U. Sexuality and the aged. *Nursing Outlook*, 1980, *28*, 51–55.

Foster, A. L. Relationships between age and sexual activity in married men. *Journal of Sex Education and Therapy*, 1979, *1*, 21–26.

Gress, L. Human sexuality and aging. In M. U. Barnard, B. J. Clancy, & K. E. Krantz (Eds.), *Human sexuality for health professionals*. Philadelphia: Saunders, 1978.

Hogan, R. *Human sexuality: A nursing perspective*. New York: Appleton-Century-Crofts, 1980.

Kinsey, A. C., Pomeroy, W. B., & Martin, C. J. *Sexual behavior in the human male*. Philadelphia: Saunders, 1948.

Kinsey, A. C., Pomeroy, W. B., Martin, C. J., & Gebhard, P. H. *Sexual behavior in the human female*. Philadelphia: Saunders, 1953.

Kolodny, R. C., Masters, W. H., Johnson, V. E., & Biggs, M. A. Geriatric sexuality. In *Textbook of human sexuality for nurses*. Boston: Little, Brown, 1979.

Kuhn, M. E. Sexual myths surrounding aging. In W. W. Oaks, G. A. Melchoide, & I. Ficher (Eds.), *Sex and the life cycle*. New York: Grune & Stratton, 1976.

Laury, G. V. Sensual activities of the aging couple. *Medical Aspects of Human Sexuality*, 1980, *14*, 32–37. (a)

Laury, G. V. Sex in men over forty. *Medical Aspects of Human Sexuality*, 1980, *14*, 65–71. (b)

McCary, J. L., & Hammet, V. L. Quiz: Prevalent sexual myths. *Medical Aspects of Human Sexuality*, 1978, *12*, 109–116.

Marcus, I. M., & Francis, J. J. *Masturbation from infancy to senescence*. New York: International Universities Press, 1975.

Masters, W. H., & Johnson, V. *Human sexual inadequacy*. Boston: Little, Brown, 1970.

Masters, W. H., & Johnson, V. *Human sexual response*. Boston: Little, Brown, 1966.

Newman, G., & Nichols, C. R. Sexual activities and attitudes in older persons. In A. Shiloh (Ed.), *Studies in human sexual behavior: The American scene*. Springfield, Ill.: Thomas, 1970.

Pfeiffer, E., & Davis, G. C. Determinants of sexual behavior in middle and old age. *Journal of the American Geriatrics Society*, 1972, *20*, 151–158.

Pfeiffer, E., Verwoerdt, A., & Wang, H. S. Sexual behavior in aged men and women. 1. Observations on 254 community volunteers. *Archives of General Psychiatry*, 1968, *19*, 753–758.

Pfeiffer, E., Verwoerdt, A., & Wang, H. S. The natural history of sexual behavior in a biologically advantaged group of aged individuals. *Journal of Gerontology*, 1969, *24*, 193–198.

Rossman, I. Sexuality and the aging process: An internist's perspective. In I. M. Burnside (Ed.), *Sexuality and aging*. Los Angeles: Ethel Percy Andrus Gerontology Center, 1975.

Rubin, I. *Sexual life after sixty*. New York: Basic Books, 1965.

Rubin, I. Sex after forty—and after seventy. In R. Brecher & E. Brecher (Eds.), *An analysis of human sexual response*. Boston: Little, Brown, 1966.

Runciman, A. Problems older clients present in counseling about sexuality. In I. M. Burnside (Ed.), *Sexuality and aging*. Los Angeles: Ethel Percy Andrus Gerontology Center, 1975.

Shrock, M. M. *Holistic assessment of the healthy aged*. New York: John Wiley & Sons, 1980.

Slome, C. Nonpuerperal lactation in grandmothers. *Journal of Pediatrics*, 1956, *49*, 550–555.

Stanford, D. All about sex . . . after middle age. *American Journal of Nursing*, 1977, *77*, 608–611.

Sviland, M. A. Helping elderly couples become sexually liberated: Psychosocial issues. In J. Lo Piccolo & L. Lo Piccolo (Eds.), *Handbook of sex therapy*. New York: Plenum Press, 1978. (a)

Sviland, M. A. The new sex education and the aging. In H. H. Otto (Ed.), *The new sex education: The sex educator's resource book*. Chicago: Follett, 1978. (b)

Wasow, M., & Loeb, M. B. Sexuality in nursing homes. In I. M. Burnside (Ed.), *Sexuality and aging*. Los Angeles: Ethel Percy Andrus Gerontology Center, 1975.

Weg, R. B. Physiology and sexuality in aging. In I. M. Burnside (Ed.), *Sexuality and aging*. Los Angeles: Ethel Percy Andrus Gerontology Center, 1975.

Whiskin, J. E. The geriatric sex offender. *Geriatrics*, 1970, *25*, 169–172.

7. Variations in Sexuality

Collin C. Schwoyer

VALUES CLARIFICATION EXERCISE

In our society sexual behavior is often given labels. Usually these labels are associated with a judgment that makes the normalcy of the sexual behavior suspect. This exercise is designed to help you discover what information you have and what your feelings and attitudes are about people whose sexual behavior has been given a label.

Write your definition of normal sexual behavior. Once the definition is written, ask yourself if it answers such questions as: Who is an appropriate partner? Is a partner required? Is the behavior limited to one partner? What is the role of each partner? What is the gender of each partner? What is the appropriate age of each partner? What relationship do the partners have? What is the frequency of sexual interaction? What time of day is it? What objects are present?

The following is a list of sexual behaviors. Read the list and, using your own information, write a definition of each.

Singles   Incest
Celibacy   Transsexualism
Bisexuality   Sadomasochism
Transvestism   Bestiality
Homosexuality   Fetishism

How did you learn this information? Who were the people involved in the learning? Where did you learn this information? What were the circumstances?

From your own life experiences, have you known of or interacted with any person whose sexual behavior fits any of your definitions?

As you interacted with these people, how did you feel? Uncomfortable? Stimulated? Scared? Relieved? Interested? Angry? Embarrassed?

After you have examined your definitions and your reactions, share them with a group of peers. Discuss the similarities and the differences in the definitions and reactions. Discuss how differences were tolerated in the group. Consider how the differences and the similarities would affect the nursing care designed by each person in the group and by the group as a whole.

BEHAVIORAL OBJECTIVES

After completing this chapter, you will be able to

- Discuss the concept of sexuality as a continuum.
- Define celibacy.
- Define and describe the sexual life-styles of people without partners.
- Identify some psychologic sequelae of incestuous relationships.
- Characterize fetishistic behavior.
- Define homosexuality and describe the homosexual experience.
- Define bisexuality and identify three categories of bisexuality.
- Compare and contrast transvestism and transsexualism.
- Define and describe sadomasochism.
- Define and describe nymphomania and satyriasis.
- Define and describe bestiality.
- Explain professional nursing behavior when interacting with clients having variations in sexual behavior.

SEXUALITY AS A CONTINUUM

Children in all societies learn what is considered normal and abnormal, natural and unnatural, acceptable and unacceptable, moral and immoral about sexual behaviors. Usually this learning leads people to choose one behavior over any other behavior and to consider one behavior right and all other behaviors wrong. Rarely does one learn of a continuum of sexual behavior. The existence of such a continuum was expressed in the book *Sexual Behavior in the Human Male*:

> The world is not to be divided into sheep and goats. Not all things are black nor are all white. It is a fundamental of taxonomy that nature rarely deals with discrete categories. Only the human mind invents categories and tries to force facts into separated pigeonholes. The living world is a continuum in each and every one of its aspects. The sooner we learn this concerning human sexual behavior the sooner we shall reach a sound understanding of the realities of sex. [Kinsey et al., 1948, p. 639]

Sexuality as a continuum can be better understood if current knowledge about variations in sexual behavior is studied.

VARIATIONS IN LIFE-STYLES

Celibacy

Celibacy is defined in some dictionaries as the "state of being unmarried," but that definition means that a cohabiting couple would be considered celibate even if they engaged in sexual intercourse. *Celibacy* is a considered, conscious choice and the behavior that follows, not to engage in sexual activity. A person who vows not to partake of sex with others is celibate. People who want to have sexual interaction but aren't able to for a variety of reasons, such as impotence or lack of opportunities, are abstaining but are not celibate. Celibacy can take two forms: total abstinence from all sexual activity, or abstinence from sexual activity involving others but not excluding self masturbation. Involuntary sexual responses such as nocturnal emission are excluded from the definition of either total or partial celibacy.

Celibacy can be practiced for varying lengths of time. Some people vow to abstain from all sexual activity for a lifetime, whereas others pledge themselves to temporary celibacy for a self-determined period of time.

There are many reasons why people choose to be celibate. Some religious orders require celibacy of their members. A nun has said that celibacy "is a grace enabling me more easily to devote my entire being to God with an undivided heart, viewing life from a sacred perspective, as a means of growing in love and perceiving truth" (DeLora & Warren, 1977, pp. 300-301). Health may be a reason to practice celibacy. Victims of severe heart attacks may be advised to avoid becoming sexually aroused during recovery. Others, who practice holistic health beliefs such as yoga, may be celibate to achieve maximum psychic and physical energy levels.

Experimental celibacy is practiced by people who want to exercise another sexual option. It can be an investigation into another sexual lifestyle and provide experiences with which other sexual options can be compared. Social or political celibacy enables one to take time and energy for self-exploration and discovery or to devote oneself to a particular cause, such as feminism, without sexual pressures. Sexual relationships can create anxieties and distractions that keep people from getting in closer touch with themselves and each other.

People without Partners

Our society constantly reinforces the belief that heterosexual coupling is the only natural and necessary life-style. Advertisements in the media, as well as the media themselves, presume that people can be happy only when they are coupled. This emphasis is so strong that being single is often regarded as a negative state of existence. If someone passes age 25 or 30 without being married, that person is looked upon as being suspect; parents become anxious, and friends and acquaintances wonder why the person is single. Most current social activities revolve around married couples (Bischoff, 1976; Gagnon, 1977). Any form of heterosexual union is better accepted than living a single life-style. Any other form of adult life is considered pitiable—old maid, widow; maligned—homosexual; or possibly tolerable—playboy, bachelor, eccentric artist. Some people choose to be single, and others are forced into a single life-style because of the death of a spouse or divorce.

Although health professionals emphasize the importance of sexual intercourse with orgasm to the physical and mental well-being of married people, the health profession is generally silent on what contributions a salubrious sex life can make toward the health of the unmarried. When forced to take a stand, many professionals publicly condemn sex for the unmarried but privately condone it. Unmarried people have no alternative but to ignore conventional morality, which demands that sexual relations take place only in marriage (Gebhard, 1970).

Like other aspects of our society, being single has been changing in social acceptance during the past few decades. More and more people are choosing to remain single or to become single again. Attitudes of singles about their life-styles vary widely. Some are searching for a spouse, with increased desperation as the years go by. Others enjoy their life-style, finding it a viable, rewarding, enjoyable way of life, and plan never to marry. Some popular books contain the message that being single is a satisfying way of life. These books offer advice to the single person about dealing with loneliness, going out alone, maintaining a varied social life, coping with an unpredictable sex life, and realizing the full potential of their freedom (Edwards & Hoover, 1974).

Some singles choose to experiment with new life-styles, such as living with friends of the opposite or same sex or living communally in a family environment. To be single does not mean that one does not have family, friends, lovers, or sexual partners. The only thing different about single people is that they are not involved in a marriage. Thus, it appears that being single, both voluntarily and involuntarily, is becoming an acceptable life-style and that it is possible to be both single and whole.

The Widowed

Except for the rarity of the simultaneous death of husband and wife, becoming a widow or widower is an inevitable fact of married existence. Men die on the average of eight years earlier than women, and the ratio of widows to widowers has increased from less than two to one in the early 1900s to five to one in the 1970s (Hoult, Henze, & Hudson, 1978).

There is little current data on the sexual life of the widowed woman, and even less on the widowed man. Widows, who are usually older, have sex less often than divorced women. Widows are generally financially more secure than divorced women; thus they place less emphasis on engaging in sex as a prelude to marriage. According to a study by Gebhard (1970), more widowed than divorced women in all ages remain celibate. When widows do resume intercourse their frequency of intercourse is lower than that of divorced women of the same age range. Widows, however, are equally as likely as divorced women to reach orgasm in their postmarital sexual intercourse.

Although figures are not available, it is assumed that the percentage of widowed men who have postmarital intercourse, the frequency of intercourse, and the speed with which postmarital sexual activity is begun after the end of marriage are all higher than the comparable figures for widowed women. The reasons for this may be that there are more women than men in the later years, and that it is socially acceptable for men to be sexually aggressive and to date younger women (DeLora & Warren, 1977).

The Divorced

The proportion of marriages ending in divorce has almost doubled in the last quarter century. In the 1950s, the ratio of divorce to marriage was one to four; by 1977, however, that ratio had changed to one divorce to every two marriages (Glick, 1977). Divorced adults must learn how to be unmarried just as they had to learn how to be married. The unwritten rules of the sexual marketplace are often quite different from the ones they knew before they were married.

Recently divorced people have often gone through a period of relative sexual deprivation and many are left with a sense of having failed in interpersonal relations. The anger some divorced people feel for their former spouses may carry over into new relationships, leading a divorced person to avoid sexual contact for a time; or it may lead the divorced person to seek only degrading or emotionally noninvolved sexual contacts (Waller, 1967).

Between 82 and 90% of women under the age of 55 and between 81 and 100% of men under the age of 55 return to an active sex life after a divorce. The median rate of frequency of intercourse for divorced men is a little higher than that of married men of the same age, whereas the median frequency of intercourse for sexually active divorced women is approximately the same as the rate for married women in the same age range (Hunt, 1974).

Evidence suggests that some divorced people find their postmarital sexual intercourse more sensuous and varied than their marital sexual activity. Eighty percent of divorced women report reaching orgasm in most or all of their postmarital intercourse, a figure higher than that for married women. Divorced people are much more likely than married people to have tried such variations as rear-entry vaginal intercourse, anal intercourse, or oral–genital intercourse. According to Hunt (1974), approximately 90% of divorced people rate their postmarital sex as mostly pleasurable or very pleasurable.

Single Parents

With the rising divorce rates, there are many people who have to learn not only how to be single again but how to be a single parent. Because they are usually either divorced or widowed, it is assumed that the sex life of single parents is similar to that of other divorced or widowed people of the same age range. Single parents are not only divorced or widowed, they are parents as well, however, and more study is needed to understand how being a parent affects sexual behavior. The problems of being single and trying to socialize with new peers are more complex when children are present. The logistics of obtaining a sitter and scheduling an evening out pose problems that a childless single person does not have.

Patton and Wallace (1979), in their study of single parents, found that 92% of the men and 81% of the women they studied had engaged in intercourse after becoming single again. The single parents in this study disputed the popular belief that sexual freedom may be void of feelings—most who engaged in sex emphasized the importance of a close relationship.

The Never Marrieds

The explanations offered for being single are reasons for not being married rather than reasons for being single. There is absolutely no reason to presume or perpetuate the myth that never-married adults are unmarried because they lack some needed characteristic or are irresponsible, inadequate, or incompetent. Some people simply prefer to remain single and do so. For many, being single is a realistic option with many positive aspects not available to married people. Singles value being able to think and create without interruption, to have time to travel, to cultivate personal talents and skills, to relax, to entertain and be entertained, to make decisions, to use their time as they wish, and to have opportunities to move to new jobs and new places (Edwards & Hoover, 1974). Because social custom approves a man's initiative in seeking and asking the woman in marriage, rather than the reverse, more men than women may deliberately avoid marriage (Duvall, 1971).

Some adults remain single because of unavoidable family responsibilities, such as caring for a dependent single parent or helping to raise orphaned siblings or other dependent relatives. Because of the high value society places on physical vigor and beauty, some people remain single because they are physically unappealing (or perceive themselves that way), crippled, deformed, or chronically ill. Some adults feel sexually inadequate or have unusual sexual interests that make them unsatisfactory marriage partners. For others, the close sexual and intimate relationship of marriage is uncomfortable.

The opportunities for meeting other singles vary greatly, depending to a large degree on a person's work, sex, age, sexual orientation, home community, and personal attractiveness. The opportunity to find a casual or committed sexual relationship becomes more likely if the single person lives in a larger city where there are singles clubs, singles apartment complexes and bars, and dating services (Proulx, 1973). Probably the most disadvantaged person in this respect is the older woman with a low income who lives in a small town or rural area (DeLora & Warren, 1977). The never-married woman may have to contend with the image of being either frigid or promiscuous, whereas the never-married man may find the image of the perpetual bachelor sexually unrewarding and emotionally empty.

Incest

Incest is sexual relations between close relatives such as mother and son, father and daughter, or sister and brother. The definition can be extended to include such family members as in-laws, cousins, stepparents, uncles, and aunts; it can be further extended to include sexual relations between people for whom there are no legal sanctions against marriage. Some countries limit the legal definition of incest to members of the family in immediate ascending and descending order and to siblings (Maisch, 1972). Incest, particularly mother–son, is one of the few universally condemned sexual activities (Ford & Beach, 1951; Henderson, 1976). Ford (1967) contends that the prohibitions against incest serve at least two useful functions: First, they tend to cut down on competition within the family unit, on jealousies that might interfere with the functioning of this important social group; second, they ensure that mating will take place outside the family, thus widening the circle of people who will band together in cooperative effort.

The ability to respond sexually does not depend on the closeness or distance of the familial association. There is neither a natural impulse for incest nor a natural restraint against it. The prohibition is learned through demands made by society and culture and reinforced through social condemnation and legal constraints. The incest taboo is cultural, not biological (Bagley, 1968; Maisch, 1972).

A persistent argument against incest is that it will cause a degeneration in genetic quality. Experiments of inbreeding among animals and studies of children born of incestuous relationships negate this assertion. Inbreeding does increase the likelihood of inheritance of both good and bad traits, but the risk of defective offspring from recessive hereditary traits can be disregarded if the defective trait has not previously displayed itself in the family (Bagley, 1968; Ullerstam, 1966).

The most common reported type of incest is father–daughter. Bernstein (1979) believes, however, that sibling incest, while not often reported, is actually the most common. Mother–son incest is the most rare. Henderson (1976) and Masters (1963) estimated that there are about two incidents of convicted incest offenders per year per million population and that incest offenses make up 5% of all sex crimes. Hunt (1974) found that about 15% of his sample had incestuous childhood sex play, generally before puberty, and no incestuous activity afterwards. Because most cases go unreported, it is difficult to know the exact incidence of incest, but it is agreed that the actual figures are higher than the reported incidences (Ford & Beach, 1951; Henderson, 1976; Maisch, 1972).

Because research on incest is limited to those cases reported to the authorities, it is difficult to generalize the findings to the whole population. Some researchers have suggested that overcrowding, poverty, and social isolation may have a primary influence on the rate of incestuous activity. Kelly (1980) responds, however, that these findings tend to imply that incest is more common in lower socioeconomic groups; but the chances are good that it is simply detected and reported less often in higher socioeconomic groups because of the greater privacy and emphasis on respectability that they enjoy. Most families are reluctant to report cases of incest, wanting to deal with the situation themselves rather than expose family members to probings of outsiders and to the ridicule, stigmatization, and ostracism of the community.

The taboo against incest can be regarded as a continuum. Some people are so afraid of sexuality both in themselves and in children that they deny any facet of psychosexual or physical intimacy to any but married spouses. This aversion often includes the banning of all nudity, which teaches the child that the sexual organs are to be hidden and that intimacy between adult and child is to be strictly limited. At the other extreme are those people who not only grant children sexual independence but see traditional divisions of parent–child roles as restrictive and archaic. Some advocate that all prohibitions against incest be eliminated, contending that the incest taboo lacks a solid scientific foundation and hinders the development of intimacy between family members and that incest can in fact be a healthy part of family interaction.

Most families try to strike a balance between the two extremes: They recognize love, intimacy, bonding, and physical closeness but do not commit the error of imputing adult sexuality to the child (Gagnon,

1977). There is a clear-cut difference between parental love and parental abuse: The parent who loves has in mind the welfare and best interests of the child; the one who abuses is indulging himself or herself (Fontana, 1973).

The effects of incest are primarily psychologic; they are not only short-term but also long-term. The experience of incest may evoke strong negative emotions. Loneliness may occur because of the perceived ostracism associated with incest. Incest may create uncertainty and confusion about the relationship between family and sex roles. Victims of incest may experience guilt and blame themselves for the activity. Many victims feel angry because they were used. The emotional trauma inflicted upon a girl subjected to sexual activities by one of her family, especially her father, is often more severe than that resulting from rape by a stranger (Steen & Price, 1977).

Many professionals feel, and the limited research on the subject supports the idea, that parent–child incest is usually the symptom of deeper problems that involve not only the incest partners but the family as a whole. Traditionally, incest has been indicative of a breakdown in family roles. The child in an incestuous relationship often assumes the role previously assigned to the nonincestuous parent. The spouse of the incestuous parent may not only be aware of the situation but may actively encourage it as a means of maintaining minimal family peace and harmony. The child may at first accept this new role and the subsequent attention that accompanies it, but disclosure can follow if the child becomes tired of the relationship or angry at the parent (Weinberg, 1955).

Once incest is detected, the family unit is disordered. The father may be imprisoned, the mother possibly forced to rely on public assistance, and the child and other siblings perhaps placed in temporary shelter. Separation or divorce may result. Tremendous pressure is placed on the child, and by the time the process is completed the incestuous behavior has been made the most important thing that ever happened in the child's life. The man who is prosecuted for having an incestuous involvement with his child is often economically disadvantaged, a heavy drinker, unemployed, and considers himself religiously devout and politically conservative (Gebhard et al., 1965).

Many professionals are hard pressed to decide which is more traumatic to the victim: the incestuous experience itself or the aftermath of its revelation (Weber, 1977). To help resolve this problem, some jurisdictions refer incest offenders and their families to therapeutic alternatives rather than to criminal proceedings with their consequent family disruptions. The therapy is family oriented; it provides therapy and counseling for the child, mother, father, and other family members involved, as well as practical assistance and emotional support. Therapy for the child is aimed at relieving her own feelings of guilt over the abuse and family breakup and helping her deal with her anger and resentment toward both parents. For the incestuous parent the counseling emphasizes taking responsibility for behaviors and the effects that follow. Both parents are helped to recognize the marital and family situations that are often the primary causes of sexual abuse. Preliminary results of this approach have been extremely positive (Weber, 1977).

Consensual Extramarital Relations

Changing sexual, social, and political values exert strong pressures on the institution of marriage. Some couples choose to continue the traditional marriage relationship and practice both monogamy and fidelity. *Monogamy* means that two people have decided to become a pair and value one another more than all others; *fidelity* excludes the possibility of having sex with another person. These couples have a strong, lasting bond between each other that does not include sexual activity outside marriage. For others marriage has become an institution that not only enhances and encourages social and intellectual growth and development but also allows for mutually agreed upon sexual experimentation with others. Extramarital sexual relations have always occurred, sometimes in secrecy, other times in culturally approved outlets such as concubinage. *Consensual extramarital relations* exist when both partners are informed about and supportive of sexual involvements outside their marriage bonds.

Consensual extramarital relations can take several forms. *Group marriage* refers to a living and sharing arrangement in which three or more people are linked together not only by shared sex but by a commitment toward future growth with one another. Close intimate contact with people who share similar expectations provides a unique opportunity for personal growth and development. Some participants feel that multiple parenting and increased sibling interactions are beneficial to the children. The pooling of economic resources can be considered an additional benefit (Constantine & Constantine, 1973).

A second form of consensual extramarital relations is *open marriage*, in which a primary relationship exists but there is emotional or sexual freedom outside the relationship. Open marriage can be completely free, with no restrictions placed on what happens outside, or it can be controlled, with certain restrictions placed on what, when, where, or with whom other activities can occur. Some partners agree that no information will be exchanged, whereas others require exchange of information about sexual activities that lead to emotional involvement.

Swinging, unlike other forms of consensual extramarital relations such as open marriage, where mutual participation is not characteristic, refers to a shared form of extramarital sexual sharing in which a husband and wife participate simultaneously and in the same location (Crooks &

Bauer, 1980). The husband usually initiates swinging, with the wife often becoming an enthusiastic participant. Swinging rarely involves any sexual activity between men, but sexual contact between women is common. By stressing the sexual side of extramarital activity, swinging makes these occasions safe for marriage by "defusing emotional involvement and exclusivity" (Gagnon, 1977, p. 230). Swingers tend to be middle class and upper middle class, Caucasian, politically conservative, and generally typical of the population of middle America (Bartell, 1970; Smith & Smith, 1970). Research indicates that probably only 2% of couples have tried swinging (Hunt, 1974).

VARIATIONS IN FREQUENCY AND STIMULUS

Fetishism

Fetishism is that condition in which genital sexual excitement is aroused by an inanimate object or a body part that is not a primary or secondary sex characteristic (Stoller, 1977). Common articles used are shoes, gloves, stockings, fur or leather items, jockstraps, panties, and brassieres. Body parts involved include the buttocks, thighs, ankles, feet, and hair. For most people, these items or body parts *may* be present as stimuli, but to someone with a fetish a particular object or body part *must* be present for genital sexual arousal or orgasm.

Some developmental dynamics of fetishism may include early masturbatory experiences involving specific pieces of clothing, body parts, or objects or a strong identification with what the object or body part represents. The major characteristic of fetishistic behavior is the exclusivity of the stimulus. This limits the availability of partners willing to engage in such activity and may interfere with the development of relationships. In some people the fetishistic attraction is so strong that the object or body part substitutes for personal interaction with a living sexual partner (Weinberg, 1976). For that reason, prostitutes are often hired to engage in the fetish experience. Although it is not known how many people engage in fetishistic behavior, it is generally agreed that most of them are men (Steen & Price, 1977).

Mild fetishistic interests exist in most people. It is not unusual to become sexually aroused by the sight or feel of underwear or by touching a person's hair. Some people can integrate their fetishistic needs into their sexual encounters with others in an enjoyable manner that causes neither partner inconvenience or unpleasantness. Fetishism is of concern only when it interferes with relationships or leads a person to illegal or offensive acts (Kelly, 1980). Fetishistic behavior itself is not against the law. Other activities that often accompany a fetish, such as voyeurism, theft, rape, or force, are, however, illegal.

Homosexuality

Homosexuality may be defined as the "emotional attachments involving sexual attraction and/or overt sexual relations between individuals—male or female—of the same sex" (Bell, 1973, p. 2). The term *homosexual* is used to describe someone who has a clear preference for partners of the same sex (Haeberle, 1978). Bell and Weinberg (1978) state that the homosexual experience is so diverse, the variety of its psychological, social, and sexual correlates so enormous, and its originating factors so numerous that to use the words "homosexuality" or "homosexual" as if they meant more than simply the nature of a person's sexual object choice is misleading and imprecise. In terms of psychologic, sociologic, and other personality adjustment factors, the homosexual is basically indistinguishable from the heterosexual (Bell, 1979; Bell & Weinberg, 1978; Fisher, 1972).

Homosexuals have existed throughout history and in all cultures and ages. Some cultures look more favorably upon homosexuality than others, and many cultures distinguish between same-sex affection and same-sex sexual activity: Hand-holding and affectionate kissing between people of the same gender may be considered normal and expected.

Kinsey et al. (1948, 1953) found that homosexuality and heterosexuality were not separate entities but were part of a continuum. Some people, between 4 and 8% of men and between 1 and 6% of women, are exclusively homosexual in behavior; some people, between 10 and 13% of men and between 8 and 20% of women, are homosexual in their behavior part of the time; others, around 18% of men and between 1 and 11% of women, are both homosexual and heterosexual in their behavior; and some people, around 63% of men and around 75% of women, are exclusively heterosexual in their behavior. Kinsey et al. also found that 37% of men and between 11 and 20% of women experimented with homosexual activity at some point in their lives past puberty.

The possible causes of homosexuality (like the causes of heterosexuality) are not known; many have been suggested but none withstand careful examination. The search for biological factors has included physical examinations, chromosome and endocrine studies, metabolic and fasting blood sugar determinations, glucose tolerance tests, and measurements of the sella turcica (Coppen, 1959; Kallman, 1952; Parr & Swyer, 1960; Rosanoff & Murphy, 1944). This research sometimes reveals slight biological differences between the homosexual and the heterosexual samples; however, the findings, more often than not, are contradictory (Beach, 1949; Ellis, 1963; Lang, 1940; Pare, 1956; Rubin, 1961; Secor, 1950; Sevringhaus & Chornyak, 1945). Some research has found that male homosexuals have less androgen than male heterosexuals, other research has indicated the opposite, and still other research has revealed no differences. Because of the makeup of the samples usually used in such research, however, the findings should not be generalized from the sample to the populations from which they were drawn (Bell, 1979; Warren, 1977). The general consensus seems to be that biological causation of homosexuality remains unproven and lacking in scientific evidence (Bell, 1979; Committee on Homosexual Offenses and Prostitution, 1957; Hooker, 1972; Katchadourian & Lunde, 1975; Money & Ehrhardt, 1972; Weinberg & Williams, 1974).

Research into the psychosocial aspects of homosexuality has been equally ambivalent. The official policy of both the American Psychiatric Association and the American Psychological Association is that homosexuality in and of itself is not a mental illness. Many members of both organizations, however, still strongly believe that homosexuality is a symptom of mental illness or social maladjustment.

Freud theorized that all people pass through certain stages on the way to a heterosexual identity. Although he did not regard it as an illness, Freud suggested that the homosexual was "arrested" in one of the developmental stages of infancy usually the oral or the anal—and that psychoanalysis might be of some help in discovering those blocks (Freud, 1951). Psychoanalytic theory since then has held homosexuality to be a mental illness and has implicated early childhood experiences and relationships with parents as having some importance in the development of a homosexual identity (Socarides, 1968). Followers of psychoanalytic theory generally "assume that adult homosexuality is psycho-pathologic" and that the background of male homosexuals frequently includes a dominant and overprotective mother and a passive and detached father (Bieber, 1962).

A constant criticism of research based on psychoanalytic theory is that its sample is usually drawn from patient or institutionalized populations and then generalized to the whole homosexual population (Klaich, 1974). Silverstein's (1981) study, using a noninstitutionalized and nonpatient sample, found that whereas parental relationships may influence the ways in which a child adapts to his or her sexual orientation, they rarely if ever cause a child's sexual orientation.

Hooker (1957) did the first major research that compared heterosexuals and homosexuals who were not in therapy and found no significant differences in intrapsychic or interpersonal functioning. Other research suggests that homosexuals function at least as well as heterosexuals: "Homosexual adults who have come to terms with their homosexuality, who do not regret their sexual orientation and who can function effectively sexually and socially, are no more distressed psychologically than are heterosexual men and women" (Bell & Weinberg, 1978, p. 216). Other researchers have found that there are some areas, such as coping skills and centering abilities, in which homosexuals might be better off psychologically than heterosexuals (Francher & Henkin, 1973; Freedman, 1975).

Some theorists hold that energy now directed toward finding the possible causes of homosexuality should be directed instead to the recognition and acceptance of the human potential of homosexuality and the homosexual person (Bell, 1974; Hooker & Chance, 1975; Hopkins, 1969; Marmor, 1970). Despite the positive support from many groups and associations, the homosexual person still faces a myriad of problems. Most of these are psychosocial in nature and are similar to those problems experienced by other minority groups. In general, our society condemns homosexuality, and homosexuals experience a broad range of difficulties, such as job discrimination, arrests and imprisonment, alienation from friends, family, and peers, housing discrimination, insurance difficulties, lack of legal protection, physical assaults, and even blackmail. Certain elements in our society advocate even further societal and legal prohibitions against homosexuality, viewing it as a threat against traditional moral standards.

Whereas members of other cultural, racial, ethnic, and oppressed groups can usually identify with their group from an early age (thus forming positive role models and a sense of belonging and community), the homosexual person, from the time of first homosexual awareness, generally has no positive examples or sense of community to which he or she can relate. The only role models available to most gay people are either the mythical and stereotypical ones passed down in folklore or the negative ones presented by the media in news exposés. Lacking exemplary role models, many homosexuals either fall back on stereotypes for some form of self-identity or vastly overemphasize those characteristics that they feel tend to dissociate them from the homosexual stereotype. Many people, with any degree of homosexual orientation, are hesitant to disclose any aspect of their sexuality, even to medical professionals, for fear of being labeled or stereotyped.

Stereotypes of homosexuals are no more representative than stereotypes of Italians or Irish people. You don't have to be Italian to be an opera singer or Irish to be a police officer or homosexual to be a hairdresser. A common belief is that homosexuals cannot relate to the opposite sex. This belief does not acknowledge that a warm and close relationship can exist between a man and a woman without sexual stimulation. One of the most prevalent and damaging beliefs about homosexuals is that they are child molesters. Research has shown that there are fewer cases of child molestation involving homosexuals than those involving heterosexual friends of the family (Fisher, 1972).

Coming out is a term used to indicate the acceptance of one's own homosexuality in a positive, self-affirming, and enlightened manner. At this point one views oneself as *gay* or *lesbian*, which is a positive, self-applied statement, and not "homosexual," a label often viewed as being negative, demeaning, or derisive. The first step in the coming out process is to come out to oneself: to acknowledge and accept one's homosexual orientation as part of one's humanity and say, "This is who I am." The next step may involve seeking out other gay people and sharing with them an openness that seems impossible elsewhere (National Gay Task Force, 1979). For the person involved, coming out is a critical time of life, at which one risks rejection by family, friends, and peers and possibly future employment opportunities and religious affiliations. This is balanced by the person's need to be honest, not only with himself or herself but with family, friends, and significant others. Sexuality plays an important part in a person's life and coming out enables a gay person to realize full sexual identity and human potential.

Once a person is out and it is no longer traumatic or innovative to say to friends and to the world, "I am gay," then the joy, the victory, the sheer relief of being one's self is no longer such an overwhelming part of day-to-day reality (Young, 1975). Once out, a person can decide whether or not to become a part of gay liberation, a movement which stresses gay identity, gay pride, and gay activism. The movement challenges traditional cultural restrictions on the degree of love and caring permitted between members of the same gender, and may be viewed as part of a broader cultural trend that stresses individual self-realization rather than conformity to socially imposed patterns (National Gay Task Force, 1979).

One of the most difficult aspects of coming out is telling one's parents. Their reaction can involve rejection, acceptance, or initial shock and willingness to stay with and work on their feelings. Like their gay offspring, the parents often need understanding, empathy, and mutual support. In order to promote this network of support, a national organization, Parents of Gays, was formed. Parents of Gays works toward mutual growth and understanding not only between child and parent but between parents and parents. They have a commitment to help their gay daughters and sons by actively working for the same human rights, liberties, and opportunities enjoyed by others.

The range of relationships available to gay people runs the gamut from marriagelike unions that last for decades to the self-styled loner who views traditional relationships as repressive (Chapter 5). Most gays, however, tend to look for a primary partner, a primary relationship in which intimacy, personality, and friendship, as well as sexuality, can be shared over a long period of time. Such relationships provide a bulwark against loneliness and a sense of social definition in a society that still, by and large, recognizes the couple as its essential human unit. Some gays want same-sex relationships to be legalized and gay couples granted all the benefits of heterosexual marriages. Others feel that marriage of the conventional sort is failing even among heterosexuals. These gays, increasingly conscious of the positive differences between themselves and heterosexuals, are rejecting the model of marriage as the pattern for their relationships. Other gay people are experimenting with nontraditional relationships, with some deliberately choosing a single, partnerless life-style, much like a never-married person (Silverstein & White, 1977; Sisley & Harris, 1977).

Bisexuality

A *bisexual* or *ambisexual* person is usually attracted to and engages in sexual relations or relationships with partners of both sexes. A bisexual person feels comfortable in sexual interactions with both men and women without doubts or concerns about his or her own masculine or feminine identity. If "bisexual" is defined as a person who has had at least one sexual experience with a man and one with a woman, Kinsey, Pomeroy, and Martin (1948) found about 60% of men were heterosexual, around 40% were homosexual, and about 36% were bisexual. Kinsey et al. (1953) found that about 17% of single women were bisexual.

Klein (1978) identified three categories of bisexuality: transitional, historical, and sequential. *Transitional* is the term applied to the small percentage of people who use bisexuality as a bridge from homosexuality to heterosexuality or heterosexuality to homosexuality. The transition period can be very short or can last for many years and involves change in emotions, ideals, and behavior. For some of these people, bisexuality often becomes the norm, although a few do complete the move from one end of the continuum to the other. *Historical* bisexuality encompasses people who have lived predominantly heterosexual or homosexual lives, but whose histories include bisexual experiences or fantasies. Klein found *sequential* bisexuality "quite common." This category involves people whose sexual relations are with only one gender at any given time.

Self-identification is an important factor in bisexuality. Persons may feel they are bisexual (have erotic dreams about and romantic attachments to people of both sexes) even though they engage in sexual relations with partners of only one sex. Other persons who have had a significant amount of sexual experiences with partners of each sex may actively choose to label themselves homosexual or heterosexual (Blumstein & Schwartz, 1976).

Although there seems to be an increasing acceptance of bisexual identity and life-style, the bisexual person may be viewed with suspicion and hostility and be pressured by homosexuals and heterosexuals to "make up your mind" or "get off the fence." For the bisexual person, sexual orientation is not an either/or situation, for he or she feels open to the widest possible variety of human and sexual relations and relationships.

Transsexualism

Benjamin & Ihlenfeld (1970) state that the *transsexual* is a person who feels that his or her psychologic gender is the opposite of his or her anatomic gender. There may be a male body with a female psychology, or a female body with a male psychology. "The emotional makeup and personality orientation of these people is in keeping with, and totally appropriate to, the psychologic gender; thus the psychologic gender is in constant and intense conflict with the anatomic gender" (Benjamin & Ihlenfeld, 1970, p. 9). *Hermaphroditism* (in which the embryonic or fetal differentiation of the reproductive system fails to reach completion as either entirely female or male) is rarely present.

The term "transsexual" is relatively new, but references to the condition are found in many historical sources. The Greeks had a goddess, Venus Castina, for transsexuals, and there are many examples of crossgenderisms in all cultures and ages.

No one knows the exact number of transsexuals in the United States. Benjamin and Ihlenfeld (1970) estimate that there are around 10,000, though reported incidences of transsexualism have risen in the past decade. Seventy-five percent of all transsexuals are women who feel trapped in a man's body. Some famous man-to-woman transsexuals are Christine (George) Jorgenson, Jan (James) Morris, René (Richard Raskind) Richards, and Wendy (Walter) Carlos.

All transsexuals do not share common backgrounds or feelings, but clinical research has identified some general characteristics. Rarely are any hormonal imbalances or cytogenetic errors present. Early childhood history shows strong cross-gender identification that may include crossdressing, playing with toys associated with the opposite gender, and taking on the mannerisms and behaviors of the opposite gender. Transsexuals often report a lonely childhood with no playmates of either gender.

The United States has several clinics that help in the identification and treatment of gender disorders. Care is taken at these clinics to ensure that other sexual problems are not confused with transsexualism. Fewer than 7% of transsexuals who go to an established, reputable clinic obtain a complete sex-change operation. The screening process for determining who is eligible for the operation is quite stringent, requiring psychologic evaluation, counseling, hormone treatment, living in the desired gender for from 6 to 18 months, and informing significant others. Benjamin and Ihlenfeld (1970) explain that the role of the professional is to assess the client and the intensity of the problem, to explore with the client alternative modes of living and to try to persuade the client to do without the irrevocable surgery, with all its risks and uncertain results. As a rule, however, most of the clients have tried, to a greater or lesser degree, alternative courses of living before seeking surgical intervention, and they are usually sure that surgery alone can salvage their lives. The cost of the operations is high, $5,000 and up, and medical insurance usually does not cover these costs.

Those transsexuals not choosing to have a sex-change operation sometimes attempt to minimize the discrepancy between their anatomic and psychologic genders by cross-dressing, taking hormones, having breast augmentation or reduction surgery, living in areas and finding employment they feel appropriate to their desired gender role, and taking on a name to match their new identity.

Transvestism

Stoller (1977) defines *transvestism* as a condition in which a man becomes genitally sexually excited by wearing feminine garments. The term "transvestism" literally means "cross-dressing," but it refers only to sexually stimulating cross-dressing, not to other situations in which opposite-gender clothing is worn, such as transsexualism, drag (homosexual parody cross-dressing), or female impersonation. (See Table 7.1 for a comparison of transsexualism, transvestism, and drag.) At this time, research identifies transvestism as a phenomenon only in men.

The transvestite regards himself as male and has no desire to change his gender. He enjoys his penis as the symbol of his maleness. The erotic and love object of most transvestites is a woman. Transvestites are almost always overtly heterosexual and may marry and have children.

Transvestism exists in two forms—partial and total. Partial transvestites, from the time the condition first manifests itself, find only one type of garment exciting. Total transvestites start with a single garment but gradually the condition spreads so that they occasionally wish to dress completely as women (Stoller, 1977). If the attraction did not include actually wearing the garment in question, the behavior would be classified as fetishism (DeLora & Warren, 1977).

Most total transvestites assume two personalities—one male, the other female. When in female attire they assume traditional feminine qualities and wish to be regarded as female. When they are in the male role, their masculine qualities are evident. Sometimes this behavior is kept secret from the spouse, with the transvestite cross-dressing only when alone or away from home. There are, however, situations in which the wife not only knows of the transvestite behavior but even becomes actively involved in helping create the female image.

Transvestism is practiced for its own sake, not for the benefit of others, as are drag or female impersonation. The rare homosexual who wants to dress in drag wants only to amuse or to baffle other people and would not cross-dress without an audience. Female impersonators perform as much

Table 7.1. Differentiation of Three Types of Males Who Cross-Dress

	Transsexualism	Transvestism (Commonest Type)	Homosexual (in drag)[a]
Biological Sex	Male	Male	Male
Gender Identity	Female	Male with fetish	Male (no fetish)
Sexual Object Choice	Male	Female	Male
Cross-Dressing	Public & private	Private (usually)	Public
Object of Cross-Dressing	Daily living	Erotic stimulation	Entertainment/attention
Characteristics of Cross-Dressing	a. Complete b. Nonattention	a. Usually incomplete b. Emphasis on undergarments	a. Exaggerated/flashy b. May or may not be complete c. Emphasis on outer garments
Desire to Change Sexes	Strong Seeks sex change Surgery	Minimal	Minimal
Gratification from Cross-Dressing	Role consonance	Primarily sexual	Primarily social

SOURCE: Reprinted with permission of Bruce A. Baldwin, Ph.D., Clinical Associate Professor in the Department of Psychiatry, University of North Carolina School of Medicine.

[a]Note that only a minority of homosexuals cross-dress, probably no more than 10% of those who define themselves as homosexuals.

for their own enjoyment as for audience reactions. The transvestite has a greater investment in his own performance and may have no interest whatever in other people's reactions (Tripp, 1975). Most transvestism is practiced in private and at home or by secretly wearing an article of female clothing.

Sadomasochism

Sadism can be defined as the preference for or the necessity of inflicting physical or psychological pain upon a sexual partner in order to achieve sexual arousal or gratification; *masochism* is the sexual preference in which pain inflicted by a sexual partner is associated with or becomes the source of sexual arousal, sometimes becoming a necessary part of sexual gratification (Gagnon, 1977). It is important to realize that pain per se is not attractive to the masochist and, generally, not to the sadist, unless it occurs in an arranged situation. Accidental pain is not perceived as pleasurable or sexual. These definitions are specific to sexual behavior and exclude cruel and inhuman treatment of a nonsexual nature.

The word *sadism* comes from the name of the Marquis de Sade, a late eighteenth-century French nobleman and author, who wrote extensively of his cruel erotic fantasies and experiences. One of de Sade's favorite pastimes was to whip women hung from the ceiling while his servant manually stimulated his genitals. The term *masochism* is derived from the name of a nineteenth-century German novelist, Leopold von Sacher-Masoch, whose greatest pleasure came from being mistreated by the women in his life (Ullerstam, 1966). The two terms, sadism and masochism, were used independently to describe sexual behaviors until Richard von Kraft-Ebing, an early twentieth-century Austrian sexologist, created the term *sadomasochism* (SM), stating that the two behaviors are mirror images of each other.

Although sadism and masochism have been viewed as discrete and different sexual variations, they occur together in many people, with one preference dominating the other. The selection of sadism or masochism can be a flexible one. Townsend (1974) stated that the difference is not as sharp and clear as one would wish; in his opinion, every sadist has also practiced masochism.

SM is not an either/or situation—it is a continuum. Many couples engage in some body biting, scratching, or pinching during sexual arousal and intercourse—sometimes without being aware of such activities until after they occur. Some people cannot tolerate such experiences. Other people seek out pain or the giving or receiving of humiliation or punishment as a part of a sexual encounter. How much a person chooses to participate in the pain-pleasure continuum varies from time to time and from one person to another.

The dynamics of SM are not really known. Tripp (1975) stated that the enjoyment of sadomasochistic techniques is usually limited to people who have had exceptionally strong social training in either the be-kind-to-others direction or the sex-is-sinful viewpoint, or both. Ths establishment of a firm taboo is required to transform the act of violating it into an erotic excitement. Thus, a taboo that successfully restrains the activity of many people acts as a special incitement for many others. Hyde (1979) feels that conditioning is one of the likelier explanations. The child has learned to associate pain or spanking with sexual arousal, and possibly this sets up a lifelong career as a masochist.

Whatever the dynamics, Kinsey et al. (1948, 1953) found that 3% of women and 10% of men had a definite of frequent erotic response to sadomasochistic stories and that over 25% of both men and women had definite or frequent erotic response to being bitten during sexual foreplay. Hunt (1974) found that 5% of men and 2% of women obtained sexual pleasure from inflicting pain and that 3% of men and 5% of women obtained sexual pleasure from receiving pain. IIunt also found a difference in age among SM practitioners: those under 35 comprised two-thirds of the SM respondents.

Various degrees of intensity are characteristic of SM. For some people the main effects of SM are psychologic. They want to fantasize that they are really slaves or masters or that a particular erotic experience is happening to them. For others, the physiologic differentiation between pain and pleasure begins to diminish, so that what is pain to others becomes pleasure to them. Ford and Beach (1951) observed that for all animals, including human beings, sexual excitement is closely related to other forms of intense emotional arousal. Sensations of pain associated with sexual intercourse may inhibit sexual response and divert the person from sexual activities, or the emotional response to pain may intensify effects of other stimuli, producing an increased sexual fervor. Which effect will be produced depends upon the physiological constitution and previous experience of the person under consideration.

There are many variations of SM. *Bondage* is a version that consists of being tied up with ropes, handcuffed, or otherwise secured, to create the feeling of being restricted. *Discipline* consists of one partner voluntarily submitting to the control of another for brief periods of sexual play. In *leather sex*, a fetish that often accompanies SM, the bondage, discipline, or humiliation is accompanied by the participants wearing leather garments such as pants, garters, belts, shoes, restricting harnesses, or hoods. SM is usually carried on under elaborate rituals, with the partners engaging in active role playing, such as master–slave, teacher–student, parent–child, cop–prisoner. The average SM session is staged: The masochist must allegedly have done something meriting punishment, and there must be threats and suspense before the punishment is meted out. The phenomenon is a planned ritual in which the masochist is in charge and has specialized instructions for the sadist to follow—the sadist is merely servicing the masochist (Weinberg, 1976). People practicing SM need not engage in sadomasochistic activities for every sexual encounter. SM may be an occasional and carefully programmed experience that is engaged in only when time, conditions, and accommodating partners are available.

Nymphomania and Satyriasis

Nymphomania and *satyriasis* are psychiatric terms used to describe compulsive behavior in which there is an extraordinarily high level of sexual activity and sex drive, to the point that the person is perceived as sexually insatiable and sexual activity overwhelms all other concerns and interests. The sexual behavior of people with nymphomania (women) and satyriasis (men) is not a matter of choice; rather, the person is driven by an inner, pathological need to seek continual sexual release, even though this activity leaves the person with strong negative feelings (Kelly, 1980). The incidence of nymphomania and satyriasis is extremely low. Fewer than one-eighth of 1% of medical patients in a study conducted by Levitt (1973) were concerned with excessive desire for intercourse, and there is little likelihood that even these few could have been truly classified as nymphomaniacs or satyrs.

What is an extraordinarily high level of sexual activity cannot be easily measured. Frequency of intercourse is highly variable, influenced by such factors as age, education, personal preference, and availability of a partner. Chesser (1971) reported that the Aranda of Australia have intercourse three to five times each night and that the polygamous Chagga of Tanganyika do not regard it as unusual to have intercourse ten times a night. Kinsey et al. (1948, 1953) found that in the United States the rate of intercourse was four times a week for people in their twenties, dropping to three times a week at 30, twice a week at 40, and once a week at 60. These figures do not express the full range of frequency that actually exists.

Satyriasis has received little attention, because a high level of sexual activity in men is often regarded as admirable and even ideal. Nymphomania, on the other hand, has been subjected to a great deal of interpretation rooted in prejudice, double standards, and male chauvinism (Kelly, 1980). Although there is little agreement on the possible causes of nymphomania and satyriasis, they may usually be seen as symptoms of deep emotional conflict.

The labels are often applied by people who see the sexual desires and demands of their partners as being beyond what they consider normal. The terms "nymphomania" and "satyriasis" tend to be subjective and pejorative.

Bestiality

Bestiality occurs when a human has sex with a nonhuman animal (Ford & Beach, 1951). Throughout human history there have been mythological and religious themes dealing with this behavior—Leda and the swan, Europa and the bull, Persephone and the serpent. Most sexual contact with animals is usually the result of experimentation or the lack of an available human contact during periods of intense sexual arousal (Kelly, 1980).

Bestiality is rare. Kinsey et al. (1948, 1953) found that about 8% of the men in their survey had at least some sexual contact with animals and that about 3% of the women had an erotic experience with animals, with only one-half of 1% of women having orgasm. The men usually had experiences with farm animals, and the women usually had experiences with household pets. Most contacts occurred well before the age of 20, with extremely few contacts of an extended or frequent nature. There are no long-term consequences associated with sexual contacts with animals. Rarely does bestiality represent severe psychologic disturbances or a continuing pattern of sexual fixation.

THE NURSE AS EDUCATOR-COUNSELOR

The nurse who interacts with clients who do not have a socially sanctioned sexual partner needs to maintain a holistic view in helping the client resolve sexual issues and concerns. The nurse needs to be non-judgmental, to show acceptance of the person, to express care and concern, to affirm the client's wholeness and integrity, and to acknowledge that the issues and concerns expressed are real, valid, and appropriate (Turner, 1980).

When the nurse deals with a variation in sexual behavior, the interplay between what the nurse knows and what the nurse feels should be given particular attention. When the nurse recognizes that the sexual behavior, and not the client's statement of the problem, has become the center of or blocks data gathering, the nurse has the responsibility to stop to assess his or her own feelings and behaviors. The nurse who begins to make judgments about whether the sexual behavior is right or wrong or good or bad for society should renew his or her professional commitment to guiding clients in solving their problems using their own sexual value system.

When a young woman states that she is concerned about being pregnant with her brother's child, the nurse–client interactions should not be based on shock, disbelief or any other preconceived notion. The interaction should be based on what the nurse knows about the phenomenon of sexual relations between brother and sister, and data should be gathered on how the client perceives the situation; how she feels about herself, about the pregnancy, and about her brother; what information she is seeking; what help she wants; and what action or solution she is considering. When a young man in an emergency room reports a bleeding, torn rectum, the nurse's intervention should be directed toward treating the injury and providing suggestions for prevention of future injuries; judgments about the young man and advice or prohibitions about the behavior that may have caused the injury should be withheld. When a young woman reports distress in a relationship with a married man, the nurse gathers data about the client's feelings of distress and should not suggest, even subtly, that the client has broken a societal proscription.

Pogoncheff (1979) was concerned about homosexual clients being denied their right to total, high-quality nursing care. An adaptation of her guidelines for helping to ensure rights of homosexual clients and avoiding unnecessary conflict between client and staff are given in Figure 7.1.

The development of professional behavior with clients having variations in sexual behavior reflects a deep caring and concern for human beings and a readiness, willingness, and ability to learn, grow, and change as knowledge is acquired and understanding is experienced.

The following questions should be used as a basis for discussion in a client-care conference and as part of an educational program to help develop professional behavior in the care of clients with variations in sexual behavior:

1. What do I know about the client's sexual behavior?
2. How was the information gathered? From the client? From the physician? From a written report? From a significant other? From nursing staff?
3. Who knows about the client's variation in sexual behavior? Nursing staff? Medical staff? Other clients?
4. Does the client seem at ease with her or his variation in sexual behavior? Talk about it? Act obvious about it? Maintain reserve?
5. What are the attitudes of the nursing staff toward the client? Upset? Concerned? Uncomfortable? Anxious? Accepting? Rejecting? Unconcerned?
6. What are the attitudes of the family, friends, and significant others toward client? Unaware? Upset? Accepting? Concerned? Rejecting? Unconcerned? Uncomfortable?
7. What are the attitudes of other clients? Unaware? Upset? Concerned? Uncomfortable? Accepting? Rejecting? Indifferent?
8. Is the client's behavior being attributed to the variation in sexual behavior rather than to a general personality trait?
9. Are the attitudes of the nursing staff negatively influencing the therapeutic environment?
10. What does the nursing staff know and think about the variation in sexual behavior in general?
11. Is the staff treating the variation in sexual behavior rather than the health problem?

Figure 7.1. Assessment of feelings, behaviors, and nursing care related to variations in sexual behavior. Adapted with permission from Pogoncheff, E. The gay patient. *RN*, 1979, *42*, 46–52.

NURSING PROCESS

Client: Warren Strycker—chief complaint is difficulty sleeping and concentrating.

Nurse: Julie Bascom—nurse at Northhampton Holistic Health Center in a large urban area.

Assessment

Subjective Data

"I've been having a lot of headaches recently."
"I've not been sleeping well."
"I can't seem to concentrate on anything."
"I'm worried because my roommate, George, is up to his neck in political activism."
"I don't think he should be so involved."
"Gay activism can really cause you a lot of problems."
"People get to know George, talk about him, and then they'll talk about me, too."
"I'm not sure I'm ready for others to know about my being gay."
"George and I have been friends for a long time, and people know we're friends, but my friends don't know I'm gay."
"I'm scared my friends and employer will find out, and I don't know how they feel—and I'm not ready to deal with that."
"I've tried talking with George about it, but he just says that it's something he has to do."
"I love George, I want to be with him, but I'm more private—I don't want to go public."

Objective Data

Age 25, college graduate, manages camera store.
Verbalizes concern about roommate's political activities.
Verbalizes fear of gayness being discovered.
Speaks softly and sighs frequently.
Difficulty sleeping and concentrating.
Physical examination—within normal limits.
Vital signs—normal.

Nursing Diagnosis

Anxiety related to fear of public disclosure of gayness through partner's political activities.

Planning

Express empathy.
Express warmth and friendliness.
Provide an atmosphere of acceptance.
Inform that physical examinations are within normal limits.
Offer feedback of client's expressed feelings.
Encourage maintenance of positive self-attitude.
Encourage expression of thoughts and feelings to roommate.
Explain the importance of offering emotional support to each other.
Encourage clarification of personal expectations of relationship.
Encourage discussion of the effects of partner's political activities on personal need for privacy about gayness.
Encourage recognition and acceptance of partner's individuality.
Encourage mutual problem solving.

Implementation

Initiate discussion of feelings with roommate.
Show acceptance of roommate's values.
Discuss personal expectations of relationship.
Discuss thoughts and feelings about balancing need for political activities with the need for privacy about gayness.
Reaffirm love and respect for partner.
Express importance of maintaining mutual support.
Make appointment at Gay Community Center for partner counseling.

Evaluation

Reports normal sleeping patterns.
Reports level of concentration satisfactory.
Reports stabilization of relationship.
Reports mutual involvement in counseling.

BIBLIOGRAPHY

Bagley, C. Incest behavior and incest taboo. *Social Problems*, 1968, *16*, 505–508.
Bartell, G. Group sex among mid-Americans. *Journal of Sex Research*, 1970, *6*, 113–130.
Bates, D. Sadomasochists discuss their pleasure . . . and pain. *Sexology*, 1975, *42*, 11–14.

Beach, F. A. *Hormones and behavior.* New York: Hoeber, 1949.

Beach, F. A. (Ed.). *Human sexuality in four perspectives.* Baltimore: Johns Hopkins University Press, 1977.

Bell, A. P. *Homosexuality* (SIECUS Study Guide No. 2, rev. ed.). New York: SIECUS, 1973.

Bell, A. P. Research in homosexuality. Paper presented at the Stony Brook Conference, Stony Brook, New York, June 1974.

Bell, A. P. The homosexual as patient. In R. Green (Ed.), *Human Sexuality* (2nd ed.), Baltimore: Williams & Wilkins, 1979.

Bell, A. P., & Weinberg, M. S. *Homosexualities.* New York: Simon & Schuster, 1978.

Benjamin, J. Should surgery be performed on transsexuals? *American Journal of Psychotherapy,* 1971, *25,* 74–82.

Benjamin, H., & Ihlenfeld, C. L. The nature and treatment of transsexualism. *Medical Opinion and Review,* 1970, *6,* 9–11.

Benjamin, H., & Ihlenfeld, C. Transsexualism. *American Journal of Nursing,* 1973, *73,* 457–461.

Bernstein, G. A. Physical management of incest situations. *Medical Aspects of Human Sexuality,* 1979, *13,* 67; 71; 75; 79; 83; 87.

Bieber, I., Dain, H. J., Dince, P. R., Drellich, M. G., Grand, H. G., Gundlach, R. H., Kremer, M. W., Rifkin, A. H., Wilbur, C. B., & Bieber, T. B. *Homosexuality.* New York: Vintage Books, 1962.

Bischoff, L. *Adult psychology* (2nd ed.). New York: Harper & Row, 1976.

Black, M. One mother's journey. *Journey of Current Social Issues,* 1978, *15,* 55–58.

Blumstein, P. W., & Schwartz, P. Bisexuality in women. *Archives of Sexual Behavior,* 1976, *5,* 171–181.

Bode, J. *View from another closet.* New York: Hawthorn, 1976.

Boston Women's Health Book Collective. *Our bodies, ourselves* (2nd ed.). New York: Simon & Schuster, 1976.

Browning, D. H., & Boatman, B. Incest. *American Journal of Psychiatry,* 1977, *134,* 69–72.

Bullough, V. L. *Sexual variance in society and history.* New York: Wiley, 1976.

Butler, S. *Conspiracy of silence.* San Francisco: New Glide Publications, 1978.

Chesser, E. *Strange loves.* New York: William Morrow, 1971.

Committee on Homosexual Offenses and Prostitution. *Report of the Committee on Homosexual Offenses and Prostitution.* London: Her Majesty's Stationery Office, 1957.

Constantine, L., & Constantine, J. *Group marriage.* New York: Macmillan, 1973.

Coppen, A. J. Body build of male homosexuals. *British Medical Journal,* 1959, *5164,* 1443–1446.

Crooks, R., & Bauer, K. *Our sexuality.* Menlo Park, Cal.: Cummings, 1980.

DeLora, J. S., & Warren, C. A. *Understanding sexual interaction.* Boston: Houghton Mifflin, 1977.

Duvall, E. *Family development.* Philadelphia: Lippincott, 1971.

Edwards, M., & Hoover, E. *The challenge of being single.* Los Angeles: Tarcher, 1974.

Ellis, A. Constitutional factors in homosexuality. In H. G. Biegel (Ed.), *Advances in sex research.* New York: Harper & Row, 1963.

Ellis, A., & Abarbanel, A. (Eds.). *The encyclopedia of sexual behavior* (rev. 2nd ed.). New York: Hawthorn Books, 1967.

Erickson Educational Foundation. *An outline of medical management of the transexual.* Baton Rouge: Author, 1973.

Erickson Educational Foundation. *Religious aspects of transexualism.* Baton Rouge: Author, 1973.

Erickson Educational Foundation. *Counseling the transexual.* Baton Rouge: Author, 1976.

Erickson Educational Foundation. *Guidelines for transexuals.* Baton Rouge: Author, 1976.

Fisher, P. *The gay mystique.* New York: Stein & Day, 1972.

Fontana, V. J. *Somewhere a child is crying.* New York: MacMillan, 1973.

Ford, C. S. Culture and sex. In A. Ellis & A. Abarbanel (Eds.), *The encyclopedia of sexual behavior* (rev. 2nd ed.). New York: Hawthorn Books, 1967.

Ford, C. S., & Beach, F. A. *Patterns of sexual behavior.* New York: Harper & Row, 1951.

Francher, J. S., & Henkin, J. The menopausal queen. *American Journal of Orthopsychiatry*, 1973, *43*, 670–674.

Freedman, M. Homosexuals may be healthier than straights. *Psychology Today*, 1975, *8*, 30–32.

Freud, S. Letter to an American mother. *American Journal of Psychiatry*, 1951, *107*, 787.

Gagnon, J. H. *Human sexualities.* Glenview, Ill.: Scott, Foresman, 1977.

Gagnon, J. H., & Simon, W. (Eds.). *Sexual deviance.* New York: Harper & Row, 1967.

Gebhard, P. Postmarital coitus among widows and divorcees. In P. Bohannon (Ed.), *Divorce and after*. New York: Doubleday, 1970.

Gebhard, P., Gagnon, J., Pomeroy, W., & Christenson, C. *Sex offenders.* New York: Harper & Row, 1965.

Gebhard, P., & Johnson, A. B. *The Kinsey data.* Philadelphia: Saunders, 1979.

Glick, P. E. Updating the life cycle of the family. *Journal of Marriage and Family*, 1977, *39*, 5–13.

Green, G., & Greene, C. *S–M.* New York: Grove Press, 1974.

Green, R. (Ed.). *Human sexuality: A health practitioner's text.* Baltimore: Williams & Wilkins, 1979.

Green, R., & Money, J. *Transsexualism and sex reassignment.* Baltimore: Johns Hopkins University Press, 1969.

Greenblatt, R. B. The sexually insatiable Catherine the Great. *Medical Aspects of Human Sexuality*, 1980, *14*, 87.

Gross, L. (Ed.). *Sexual behavior.* Flushing, N.Y.: Spectrum, 1974.

Haeberle, E. J. *Sex atlas.* New York: The Seabury Press, 1978.

Henderson, D. J. Incest. In B. J. Sadock, H. I. Kaplan, & A. M. Freedman (Eds.), *The sexual experience.* Baltimore: Williams & Wilkins, 1976.

Holmes, D. J. *Psychotherapy.* Boston: Little, Brown, 1972.

Hooker, E. The adjustment of the male overt homosexual. *Journal of Projective Techniques*, 1957, *21*, 18–31.

Hooker, E. Homosexuality. In J. M. Livingood (Ed.), *National Institute of Mental Health task force on homosexuality: Final report and background papers.* Rockville, Md.: National Institute of Mental Health, 1972.

Hooker, E., & Chance, P. Facts that liberated the gay community. *Psychology Today,* 1975, *9*, 52–55.

Hopkins, J. Lesbian personality. *British Journal of Psychiatry,* 1969, *115,* 1433–1436.

Hoult, F., Henze, L., & Hudson, J. *Courtship and marriage in America.* Boston: Little, Brown, 1978.

Hunt, M. *Sexual behavior in the 1970s.* Chicago: Playboy Press, 1974.

Hyde, J. S. *Understanding human sexuality.* New York: McGraw-Hill, 1979.

Jay, K., & Young, A. *After you're out.* New York: Links, 1975.

Jones, C. R. *Understanding gay relatives and friends.* New York: Seabury Press, 1978.

Kallmann, F. J. Comparative twin study on the genetic aspects of male homosexuality. *Journal of Nervous and Mental Disease,* 1952, *115,* 283–298.

Katchadourian, H. A., & Lunde, D. T. *Fundamentals of human sexuality* (2nd ed.). New York: Holt, Rinehart & Winston, 1975.

Kelly, G. F. *Sexuality.* Woodbury, N.Y.: Barron's, 1980.

Kinsey, A. C., Pomeroy, W. B., & Martin, C. E. *Sexual behavior in the human male.* Philadelphia: Saunders, 1948.

Kinsey, A. C., Pomeroy, W. B., Martin, C. J., & Gebhard, P. H. *Sexual behavior in the human female.* Philadelphia: Saunders, 1953.

Klaich, D. *Woman plus woman.* New York: Simon & Schuster, 1974.

Klein, F. *The bisexual option.* New York: Arbor House, Priam, 1978.

Kolodny, R. C., Masters, W., Hendryx, J., & Toro, G. Plasma testosterone and semen analysis in male homosexuals. *New England Journal of Medicine,* 1971, *285,* 1170–1174.

Kraft-Ebing, R. von. *Psychopathia sexualis.* New York: Pioneer, 1943.

Lang, T. Studies on the genetic determination of homosexuality. *Journal of Nervous and Mental Disease,* 1940, *92,* 55–64.

Lawrence, J. C. Homosexuals, hospitalization and the nurse. *Nursing Forum,* 1975, *14,* 304–317.

Levitt, E. E. Nymphomania. *Sexual Behavior,* 1973, *3,* 13–17.

MacDonald, A. P. Homophobia. *Homosexual Counseling Journal,* 1976, *3,* 23–33.

Maisch, H. *Incest.* New York: Stein & Day, 1972.

Mandetta, A., & Gustaveson, P. *Abortion to zoophilia.* Chapel Hill: Carolina Population Center, 1977.

Marmor, J. Homosexuality and objectivity. *SIECUS Newsletter,* 1970, *6,* 1–5.

Marshall, D. D., & Suggs, R. C., Eds. *Human sexual behavior.* Englewood Cliffs, N.J.: Prentice-Hall, 1971.

Masters, R. E. L. *Patterns of incest.* New York: Julian Press, 1963.

Masters, W. H., & Johnson, V. E. *Homosexuality in perspective.* Boston: Little, Brown, 1979.

McCary, J. L. My most unusual sexual case: Nymphomania. *Medical Aspects of Human Sexuality,* 1979, *13,* 74–75.

Menninger, K. A. Contemporary attitudes toward animals. In G. B. Wilbur & W. Muensterberger (Eds.), *Psychoanalysis.* New York: Wiley, 1951.

Mims, F. H., & Swenson, M. *Sexuality.* New York: McGraw-Hill, 1979.

Money, J., & Ehrhardt, A. A. *Man and woman/boy and girl.* Baltimore: Johns Hopkins University Press, 1972.

Money, J., & Tucker, P. *Sexual signatures*. Boston: Little, Brown, 1975.

Moore, S. L. My most unusual sexual case: Satyriasis. *Medical Aspects of Human Sexuality*, 1980, *14*, 111.

Morris, Jan. *Conundrum*. New York: Harcourt Brace Jovanovich, 1974.

National Gay Task Force. *Twenty questions about homosexuality*. New York: Author, 1979.

One couple's S/M follies. *Sexology*, 1977, *43*, 44–49; 61; 81.

Panor, R. *The unmarried father*. New York: Springer, 1971.

Pare, C. M. Homosexuality and chromosomal sex. *Journal of Psychosomatic Research*, 1956, *1*, 247–251.

Parents and Friends of Gays. *About our children*. Los Angeles: Author, 1978.

Parr, D., & Swyer, G. I. Seminal analysis in 22 homosexuals. *British Medical Journal*, 1960, *5209*, 1359–1361.

Patton, R. D., & Wallace, B. C. Sexual attitudes and behaviors of single parents. *Journal of Sex Education and Therapy*, 1979, *1*, 39–41.

Pogoncheff, E. The gay patient. *RN,* 1979, *42,* 46–72.

Proulx, C. Sex as athletics in the singles complex. *Saturday Review/Society*, May 1973, 23–29.

Rinzema, J. *The sexual revolution*. Grand Rapids, Mich.: Eerdmans, 1974.

Robinson, P. *The modernization of sex*. New York: Harper/Colophon, 1977.

Rosanoff, W. R., & Murphy, F. E. The basal metabolic rate, fasting blood sugar, glucose tolerance, and size of the sella turcica in homosexuals. *American Journal of Psychiatry*, 1944, *101*, 97–99.

Rubin, I. Homosexuality: Conflicting theories. In I. Rubin (Ed.), *The third sex*. New York: New Book, 1961.

Sadock, B. J., Kaplan, H. I., & Freedman, A. M. (Eds.). *The sexual experience*. Baltimore: Williams & Wilkins, 1976.

Scanzoni, L., & Mollenkott, V. R. *Is the homosexual my neighbor?* San Francisco: Harper & Row, 1978.

Secor, H. W. Can hormones cure homosexuals? *Sexology*, 1950, *16*, 721–727.

Sevringhaus, E. L., & Chornyak, J. A study of homosexual adult males. *Psychosomatic Medicine*, 1945, *7*, 302–305.

Shope, D. F. *Interpersonal sexuality*. Philadelphia: Saunders, 1975.

Silverstein, C. *Man to man*. New York: William Morrow, 1981.

Silverstein, C., & White, E. *The joy of gay sex*. New York: Crown, 1977.

Sisley, E. L., & Harris, B. *The joy of lesbian sex*. New York: Crown, 1977.

Smith, J., & Smith, L. Co-marital sex and the sexual freedom movement. *Journal of Sex Research*, 1970, *6*, 131–142.

Socarides, C. W. *The overt homosexual*. New York: Curtis Books, 1968.

Spensley, J., & Bartes, J. T. Adolescent boys who wear girls' clothes. *Medical Aspects of Human Sexuality*, 1973, *7*, 136; 142–143; 146; 148; 151–152; 156.

Steen, E. B., & Price, J. H. *Human sex and sexuality*. New York: Wiley, 1977.

Stoller, R. J. Sexual deviations. In F. A. Beach (Ed.), *Human sexuality in four perspectives*. Baltimore: Johns Hopkins University Press, 1977.

A symposium—should homosexual be a diagnosis. *American Journal of Psychiatry*, 1973, *130*, 1207–1216.

Thompson, C. J. *The mysteries of sex*. New York: Causeway, 1974.

Townsend, L. *Leatherman's handbook*. New York: Freeway Press, 1974.

Tripp, C. A. *The homosexual matrix.* New York: McGraw-Hill, 1975.

Turner, N. Sexual issues in separation and divorce. *Topics in Clinical Nursing,* 1980, *1*, 39–44.

Ullerstam, L. *The erotic minority.* New York: Grove Press, 1966.

Waller, W. *The old love and the new.* Carbondale: Southern Illinois University Press, 1967.

Warren, C. A. Fieldwork in the gay world. *Journal of Social Issues,* 1977, *33*, 93–107.

Weber, E. Sexual abuse begins at home. *Ms.,* April 1977, *5*, 64–67; 105.

Weinberg, G. *Society and the healthy homosexual.* New York: St. Martin's Press, 1972.

Weinberg, M. S. (Ed.). *Sex research.* New York: Oxford University Press, 1976.

Weinberg, M. S., & Bell, A. P. *Homosexuality.* New York: Harper & Row, 1972.

Weinberg, M. S., & Williams, C. J. *Male homosexuals.* New York: Oxford University Press, 1974.

Weinberg, S. *Incest behavior.* New York: Citadel Press, 1955.

Withersty, D. J. Sexual attitudes of hospital personnel. *American Journal of Psychiatry,* 1976, *133*, 573–575.

Young, A. On human identity and gay identity. In K. Jay, & A. Young (Eds.), *After you're out.* New York: Links, 1975.

8. Sexual Dysfunction and Therapeutic Approaches

Penelope L. Wadleigh

VALUES CLARIFICATION EXERCISE

The following series of questions is designed to help you discover what you know about sexual dysfunction and what you believe about sex therapy.

Respond to the following questions. Write down your answers and share your feelings with another person and with a group of your peers or colleagues.

1. What does sex therapy mean to you? Are the people in sex therapy sick? Does sex therapy take a long time?

2. Do you believe sex therapists are health professionals? Are all health professionals educationally prepared to be sex therapists? Does a sex therapist require clinical preparation? Would the sex of the therapist matter to you? Does the sex of the therapist affect the therapy?

3. For what reason do you think people enter sex therapy? How are people who enter sex therapy different from other people?

4. For whom do you believe sex therapy should be available? Single people? Married people? Heterosexuals? Homosexuals? Transsexuals? Bisexuals?

5. How would you describe a sexual dysfunction? Do sexual dysfunctions have signs and symptoms? What signs and symptoms are specific to sexual dysfunction?

6. Could sex therapy affect a person's life? How? Are the outcomes of sex therapy the responsibility of the therapist? The therapist and the clients? The clients?

BEHAVIORAL OBJECTIVES

After reading this chapter you will be able to

- Identify the main objective of sex therapy.
- Describe the time-limited approach of sex therapy.
- Contrast the dual-sex-therapist approach to sex therapy and the solo-therapist approach.
- Describe conjoint therapy.
- Describe sensate focus.
- Describe erectile dysfunction.
- Discuss a treatment format for erectile dysfunction.
- Describe premature ejaculation.
- Discuss a treatment format for premature ejaculation.
- Describe retarded ejaculation.
- Discuss a treatment format for retarded ejaculation.
- Describe vaginismus.
- Discuss a treatment format for vaginismus.
- Describe general sexual dysfunction.
- Discuss a treatment format for general sexual dysfunction.
- Describe orgasmic dysfunction.
- Discuss a treatment format for orgasmic dysfunction.
- Identify physiologic and psychologic causes of dyspareunia.
- Describe inhibited sexual desire.
- Discuss a treatment format for inhibited sexual desire.
- Describe sexual aversion.
- Discuss the role of the nurse with clients with possible sexual dysfunction.

ORIGINS OF SEX THERAPY

The treatment of human sexual dysfunction has undergone a significant evolution since the advent of directive sex therapy introduced by Masters and Johnson's 1970 publication, *Human Sexual Inadequacy*. Before that time, sexual therapy followed the psychoanalytic model, which views adult sexual dysfunction as either the symptom of an underlying personality conflict or the manifestation of a destructive interpersonal transaction (LoPiccolo & LoPiccolo, 1978; Kaplan, 1974). The theoretical model proposed by Masters and Johnson (1970) depicts a *sexual dysfunction* as an adverse modification of a person's innate physiological reflexes. Within this framework, a sexual dysfunction is not regarded necessarily as a symptom of an underlying personality conflict. Rather, a *dysfunction* is described as a modified response to effective sexual stimulation by the theory of interdigital systems. The theory describes a relationship between two totally separate systems—biophysical and psychologic—that are believed to constitute the human sexual response. From this perspective, a sexual dysfunction can result when one or both systems fail to contribute positively to psychosexual input.

Masters and Johnson (1970) report that the majority of people treated in their sexual therapy program did not manifest psychiatric problems. Because a sexual dysfunction can exist independently of an intrapsychic conflict, they propose that the sexual dysfunction may not be the symptom but the disease itself.

CONCEPTS OF SEX THERAPY

Focus and Approach of Therapeutic Intervention

The notion that sexual dysfunction is itself the disease prompted the development of innovative sexual therapy methods that depart widely from those of traditional psychotherapy. The focus of therapeutic intervention shifted from the identification and resolution of intrapsychic conflicts to direct intervention with the sexual dysfunction. Direct sex therapy does investigate psychological factors that influence a sexual dysfunction, but only to the extent necessary to relieve the dysfunction and to ensure its eradication (Kaplan, 1974). The main objective of sex therapy is to mitigate the client's sexual dysfunction.

This limited objective of sex therapy has given rise to another departure from psychoanalytic method—the time-limited approach. Typically, psychoanalysis requires years, and it is concluded when the client's unconscious personality conflict is resolved and the person's sexual functioning is stable and reasonably permanent. In contrast, sex therapy is often time limited. For example, Masters and Johnson's (1970) program rigidly adheres to a two-week time limit involving daily therapy sessions, and the expectation is that when the time period is concluded, the sexual dysfunction will be alleviated.

Dual Sex-Therapy Team

Sex therapy programs often use a therapist team composed of two members, one woman and one man. Masters and Johnson (1970) originally advocated the use of a dual sex-therapy team and believe it is an essential component of treatment for sexual dysfunctions. First, they believe women and men cannot really understand each other's sexuality or dysfunctions. This notion applies to therapists as well as to clients. The dual sex-therapy team can function as individual men or women interpreters of sexual experiences for clients of the opposite sex. Second, sex therapy is based on a program of education, an important aspect in changing behavior. The presence of a dual sex-therapy team can enhance the instructional process. Many therapy sessions are directed toward the client's learning about the physiologic and psychologic aspects of sexual responses. In its interpreter role, the dual sex-therapy team translates and clarifies for clients portions of the educational sessions that may otherwise be misunderstood. Third, the dual-sex-therapist approach can also provide clients with support. The presence of a therapist of the same gender can enhance a client's personal comfort and facilitate open communication. For example, a man client may be constrained by fear that a woman therapist will not understand or be sympathetic to his sexual point of view. The presence of a man therapist can provide tacit and explicit support to the man client. The therapist team can also provide a model of good feelings and communication between members of the opposite sex.

The dual-sex-therapist team can be an effective technique in a sex therapy program. Kaplan (1974) contends, however, that although there are advantages to using dual-sex-therapy teams, this approach is not always essential to the successful treatment of sexual dysfunctions. She and her co-workers at Cornell University believe that one therapist of either sex who is sensitive, well trained, experienced, and specifically sensitive to the sexual response and reactions of the opposite gender can adequately conduct sex therapy.

There are many differences of opinion among professionals about the advisability of using a dual-sex-therapy team. Empirical research has not yet shown which therapist approach, solo or dual, yields the most effective results in the sex-therapy program.

Conjoint Therapy

Conjoint sex therapy is the simultaneous treatment of both sexual partners throughout the course of their sex-therapy program. Conjoint programs were pioneered in 1959 by Masters and Johnson. The conjoint therapy innovation was based on the notion that there is no such thing as an uninvolved partner in a relationship crippled by a sexual dysfunction.

Additional support for this innovative belief is provided by the fundamental premise of sex therapy: Complete sexual functioning reflects suitable physical and behavioral interaction between two people. LoPiccolo and LoPiccolo (1978) emphasize that a sexual dysfunction is a shared disorder for which each partner has a mutual responsibility for effecting change and resolution. In contrast, psychoanalysis treats one person in isolation from the sex partner. Such an approach fails to consider the crucial component of complete sexual functioning—the partner's direct influence on the attainment of suitable sexual interactions (Masters & Johnson, 1970).

Sensate Focus

Many clients engaged in sex therapy are often not aware of their physical perceptions or psychologic feelings when giving or receiving erotic stimulation. Nor have many clients previously communicated to their sex partner what type of sexual stimulation they prefer. Often clients also need an opportunity to experiment with new erotic stimulation techniques that can enable them to learn new means of achieving erotic arousal and enhance their sexual communication abilities.

Sensate focus exercises that are specifically designed and directly prescribed by the sex therapist provide a couple with an opportunity to learn experientially new techniques that are sexually stimulating and that enhance interpersonal communication. The exercises may include giving body massages, taking bubble baths, gentle fondling, or stroking the body. The therapist may or may not initially prohibit touching the genitalia, depending upon the client's sexual dysfunction. Sensate focus exercises are intended to be low keyed and nongoal directed. They are meant to enable people to participate in the sexual activity, to learn about themselves and their partner during sexual contact, and to communicate with each other.

SEXUAL DYSFUNCTIONS OF MEN

Erectile Dysfunction

Erectile dysfunction can be defined as a man's inability to obtain or maintain an erection of sufficient firmness to initiate or complete sexual intercourse (Masters & Johnson, 1970). Erectile dysfunction is of two types, primary and secondary. A man with *primary erectile dysfunction* has never been able to achieve enough penile rigidity to initiate coitus. A man with *secondary erectile dysfunction* has had the ability to achieve at least one successful coital initiation and completion but has lost this ability. Erectile dysfunction does not mean that a man's erectile capacity is entirely absent, for many of these men do have transient erections, particularly during their sleep (Kolodny et al., 1979). Thus, the basic meaning of erectile dysfunction is that the quality of a man's erection does not allow him to initiate or complete sexual intercourse.

Causes of Erectile Dysfunction

Both primary and secondary erectile dysfunction may have physiological causes. Masters and Johnson (1970) indicate that physiologic factors rarely cause primary erectile dysfunction. Kolodny et al. (1979) state that only approximately 10 to 15% of men with erectile dysfunctions appear to have a physiologic basis for their impotence.

Even though physical factors seldom cause erectile dysfunction, a thorough physical examination is necessary to rule out the presence of contributing physiologic factors (Kaplan, 1974; Kolodny et al., 1979). Acquiring a thorough sexual history is also helpful to the therapists, supplementing the information gathered during the physical examination. The combination of the medical and sexual data can provide the therapists with information to help establish a temporal relationship between the occurrence of a medical or psychologic event and the onset of the client's impotence (Kaplan, 1974).

Establishing this temporal relationship can help the therapist determine the possible causes of the client's impotence. Kolodny et al. (1979) contend that erectile dysfunction that begins insidiously and progressively becomes more manifest typically has a physical origin. Erectile dysfunction that occurs suddenly is more apt to have a psychologic origin. Kaplan (1974), however, points out that the establishment of a temporal relationship between the onset of erectile dysfunction and the presence of a physiologic or psychologic factor may be impossible. Even if a temporal relationship between an event and the onset of erectile dysfunction cannot be established, most sex therapists agree that the data acquired from medical and sexual histories provide valuable and necessary information to formulate a treatment plan. It is necessary to ascertain as precisely as possible the causes of the client's erectile dysfunction in order to treat him effectively. Treatment must be based upon correction of the cause of the sexual dysfunction.

An estimated high percentage of all cases of erectile dysfunction are precipitated by psychologic factors. Kolodny et al. (1979) report that in 85 to 90% of their clients treated for erectile dysfunction, psychologic factors contributed to the development of their erectile difficulties.

Treatment of Erectile Dysfunction

Sensate focus (pleasuring) is the initial phase of treatment for erectile dysfunction. This is based on the idea that the man needs to experience sufficient erotic pleasuring without a compelling need to achieve an erection (Masters & Johnson, 1970). The sensate focus exercises provide the man with an opportunity to relax and enjoy erotic pleasures that do not require an erection. These exercises give his partner a chance to learn which of the stimulating techniques are enjoyable to him. For example, the therapist instructs the couple to engage in sex play that mimics sexual foreplay, but forbids the touching of the genitals. In this manner the couple's attention is diverted away from the penis and its responses. The couple engages in sexual behaviors that provide pleasure, such as touching, stroking, or massaging each other's body. The man is specifically instructed to direct his attention away from achieving an erection. He is instructed to relax, enjoy, and become aware of the erotic physical sensations provided by his partner. These therapeutic directions are given in an attempt to stop the man from *spectatoring*, a phenomenon that is characterized by a man involuntarily approaching his sexual encounters as an anxious observer who watches and evaluates his penis's performance (Masters & Johnson, 1970). While spectatoring, an impotent man awaits an erection, watches it occur, and continually evaluates its quality. The psychologically demanding role of spectator inhibits his erection. Often, during sensate focus, an erection occurs spontaneously. The event provides wonderful evidence to the man that his sexual ability is not gone forever. From such an experience, a man can regain confidence that his problem can be solved (Kaplan, 1974). If an erection does not occur, however, the man can be assured by the therapist during therapy sessions that he was specifically instructed not to attempt an erection and that lack of one signifies having successfully completed the prescribed task. Accordingly, the therapist can instill a sense of success that can aid in the process of eliminating the man's performance anxieties.

Sensate focus exercises are intended to provide the partners with the necessary environment and tools to achieve success. One erection is not considered a cure for erectile dysfunction. The new behaviors of erectile confidence developed from the sensate focus experiences need to be permanently incorporated into the couple's sexual repertoire. The ultimate goal of sex therapy is to achieve this confidence and permanence (Masters & Johnson, 1970; Kaplan, 1974).

After the initial establishment of an erection, the partners are directed to engage in sexual tasks that provide them with opportunities to experiment with the erectile response. Masters and Johnson (1970) indicate that experimentation with the erectile response demonstrates to the man that an erection (a) can be achieved, (b) will last, and (c) can be regained with confidence if lost. Acquiring erectile confidence can alleviate the man's fear of failure. Masters and Johnson suggest the use of the "teasing" technique to diminish performance fears and reinforce erectile confidence. The partners are directed to participate in sex play until an erection occurs. Once an erection is accomplished, erotic stimulation is to cease and the man is to be distracted until the erection is lost. The cycle of reinstituting sex play that fosters an erection, removing erotic stimulation, and allowing the erection to dissipate is to be repeated in a nondemanding fashion. Repeated success during this task improves the man's confidence and helps ameliorate his performance fears.

As therapy progresses—with performance fears diminished and spontaneous erectile competence restored by sensate focus and "teasing" techniques—methods of vaginal intromission are practiced. Initially, the woman mounts and attempts vaginal intromission of the penis. Masters and Johnson (1970) point out that initial intromission attempts should be conducted by the woman. They are to be accomplished in a nondemanding fashion to minimize the man's anxiety, while the man remains passive to prevent distraction from his sensate input. Masters and Johnson state that if attempts at vaginal intromission are initially unsuccessful, no sense of failure is to be instilled into the man. Repeated attempts are to be made with no emphasis on the man's performance. A series of successful attempts of intromission and vaginal containment are to be accomplished before pelvic movements are instituted.

In the woman-on-top position, pelvic movements are to be initiated by the woman in a nondemanding fashion, so not to threaten the man's erectile confidence (Masters & Johnson, 1970; Kaplan, 1974). Initially, orgasms are not to be attempted. As vaginal containment and the woman's pelvic movement is repeatedly accomplished successfully, the man is encouraged to move. Slow penile thrusts can now be attempted. Gradually, as vaginal containment no longer threatens the man, the movements can progress to active thrusting to the point of an orgasm.

Treatment of erectile dysfunction basically attempts to ameliorate the sexual dysfunction by alleviating fears of performance in the man and establishing erectile confidence during therapeutic sexual tasks and psychotherapeutic sessions. Masters and Johnson's (1970) treatment statistics indicate a failure rate of 66.6% for primary impotence and 26.2% for secondary impotence from the clinical application of their therapy format. Kaplan (1974) believes that an excellent prognosis can be offered to reasonably healthy men.

Relapse after sex therapy has been reported in the literature. Masters and Johnson (1970) believe that it is a man's own susceptibility to the causative factors of erectile dysfunction that determines his level of sexual functioning. As a point of encouragement, Kaplan (1974) states that clients who experience a recurrence of the sexual dysfunction can reenter sex therapy and anticipate successful results.

Premature Ejaculation

To date, a universally acceptable definition for the male sexual dysfunction of premature ejaculation has evaded physicians, psychologists, and sex therapists. The problem most often encountered when attempting to construct a definition of this sexual dysfunction is one of quantifying the period of time a sexually aroused man should be able to endure vaginal containment before experiencing an ejaculation.

Kinsey, Pomeroy, and Martin (1948) found that 75% of the men they studied ejaculated within two minutes after vaginal containment. Stewart et al. (1979) indicate that an ejaculation can occur within 30 to 60 seconds after achieving an erection; however, that phenomenon is rare. Kaplan (1974) refers to a definition of premature ejaculation that quantifies the time span as 30 seconds and states that various sex-therapy clinics subscribe to different time limits, which can range from one and a half to two minutes. The number of penile thrusts that occur before a man's orgasm is also commonly used as a quantifiable criterion for premature ejaculation. Ability to withstand ten thrusts before orgasm is reportedly used as the criterion by one therapy clinic (Kaplan, 1974).

Masters and Johnson (1970) describe a *premature ejaculator* as a man who has not achieved sufficient ejaculatory control to enable him to withstand vaginal containment long enough for his sexual partner to achieve an orgasm during at least 50% of their sexual contacts. Kaplan (1974) stated that "the crucial aspect of prematurity is the absence of voluntary control over the ejaculatory reflex, regardless of whether it occurs after two thrusts or five, whether it occurs before the female reaches orgasm or not" (p. 290). Most men who report difficulties with prematurity say they have no such problem during oral sex or masturbation. Probably the best definition is self-definition. If a man is concerned about his ejaculatory control or feels it is interfering with his sexual relationships, or if his partners believe that it is a problem, then the ejaculation is premature and dysfunctional. Thus premature ejaculation can be defined as an ejaculation that occurs before the man desires to have it (Julty, 1979).

Causes of Premature Ejaculation

A variety of theories about the causes of premature ejaculation have been formulated. Kolodny et al. (1979) point out that to date no reliable research has been generated that can specify with certainty the causes of premature ejaculation. Many sex therapists have stated that there could be a learned component in premature ejaculation that results in the man becoming conditioned to ejaculate rapidly (Kolodny, Masters, & Johnson, 1979; Masters & Johnson, 1970). Other traditional theories have suggested that this sexual dysfunction is the result of a man's excessive sensitivity to erotic sensation. Kaplan (1974) contends that a man's inability to perceive premonitory orgasmic sensations is the factor that precludes the establishment of a desired level of ejaculatory control.

Treatment of Premature Ejaculation

The most successful techniques for treating premature ejaculation are modifications of the so-called stop–start technique proposed by James Seman, a urologist, in 1956. Masters and Johnson (1970) employ a squeeze technique and Kaplan (1974) advocates a modified start–stop technique. All of these techniques foster the man's awareness of his premonitory ejaculatory sensations and thereby teach him methods of voluntarily controlling his ejaculatory reflex.

Kaplan's (1974) method for the treatment of premature ejaculation includes a psychiatric evaluation of both partners. A detailed sexual history is obtained, and the relationship is evaluated. The partners are acquainted with the sex therapy procedures and advised that the prognosis for therapeutic resolution of premature ejaculation is excellent if they adhere to the prescribed tasks. Kaplan clearly indicates a need to establish early with the partners their need to accept responsibility for successful therapy. The partners are seen conjointly from once or twice a week for a total of six to twelve sessions.

The partners, in the privacy of their home, are directed to engage in limited foreplay that will elicit an erection. While the woman orally or manually manipulates the penis, the man is told to focus his attention on the pleasurable erotic sensations he receives. The man is to communicate to his partner his perception of premonitory ejaculatory sensations. At that time, erotic penile manipulation is to cease. When premonitory ejaculatory sensations cease, the woman reinstitutes erotic stimulation of the penis; she then removes them again once the man again perceives warning sensations. The procedure is to be repeated three times before the man is permitted to ejaculate (during the fourth experience). Kaplan (1974) points out that no attempt to control the ejaculation voluntarily should occur during the initial three experiences because such attempts could possibly deter a man from perceiving erotic sensations before an ejaculation.

By requiring the man to focus his attention only upon the erotic sensations before orgasm, the technique attempts to allow him to perceive and experience the premonitory erotic sensations needed for regulatory power. Once the man is capable of recognizing his premonitory ejaculatory sensations during dry manual manipulation, use of a lubricant such as KY jelly, is introduced. Use of a lubricant can more realistically simulate the penile sensations produced during vaginal containment.

Kaplan (1974) indicates that after three to six therapeutic experiences, each consisting of three stop–start maneuvers and one including ejaculation, men typically report a noticeable improvement in their ejaculatory control, Once ejaculatory control has been established, the couple progresses to vaginal intromission and ejaculation during vaginal containment. The woman-on-top position is initially used, because ejaculatory control is achieved more slowly in the man-on-top position. The start–stop maneuvers are again employed during vaginal containment maneuvers in the woman-on-top and lateral coital positions. Kaplan (1974) reports that ejaculatory control is generally attained in these coital positions within three to four weeks and that control is achieved in the man-on-top position after formal sex therapy is concluded.

Kaplan (1974), while recognizing the simplicity of her treatment regimen, points out that resistance to therapy from either partner is typically encountered. She believes that resistance stems from underlying anxiety in either partner and can be treated successfully during the concurrent therapeutic sessions.

The therapy cure rate reported by Masters and Johnson (1970) of 186 clients is 98%, and Seman (1956) reports a 100% cure rate for eight clients. Kaplan (1974) indicates that success is anticipated when a treatment format emphasizes teaching the man objective recognition of premonitory sensations, and that permanent amelioration can be anticipated by most clients.

Retarded Ejaculation

"Ejaculative impotence" (Cooper, 1968), "ejaculatory incompetence," (Masters & Johnson, 1970), and "retarded ejaculation" (Kaplan, 1974), are all labels found in the literature denoting the male sexual dysfunction *ejaculatio retardata*. *Retarded ejaculation* may be defined as a specific impairment of the ejaculatory reflex mechanism in which the man (a) perceives and reacts to erotic stimulation and (b) achieves an erection but (c) is unable to ejaculate. The severity of the dysfunction ranges from an occasional inability to ejaculate in specific situations to complete absence of an ejaculatory experience.

Masters and Johnson (1970) reported after treating 510 clients during 11 years of clinical therapy that only 17 men had complained of retarded ejaculation. Today the sexual dysfunction is not considered such a rarity. Although no reliable statistics are available to describe the overall incidence of the dysfunction, sex-therapy programs report an increase in the number of clients whose primary difficulty is retarded ejaculation.

There are two clinical categories of retarded ejaculation: primary and secondary. A man with *primary retarded ejaculation* has experienced the dysfunction since the onset of his sexual contacts. A man who had a sexual history free of ejaculatory inhibition before the onset of his sexual disability is regarded as suffering from *secondary retarded ejaculation*.

The etiology of retarded ejaculation can be categorized either as physical or psychologic. Kaplan (1974) points out that the cause of this dysfunction can be attributed to few diseases. Even those disease processes that interfere with androgen levels do not selectively modify the ejaculatory reflex to render it operational only in specific situations or under certain circumstances. Some neurologic disorders can modify the ejaculatory reflex, but they are rarely said to cause only retarded ejaculation. Although the dysfunction rarely has a physical cause, sex therapists must be aware of the possibility and conduct the necessary procedures to rule out their presence.

Treatment of Retarded Ejaculation

Sex therapy for the amelioration of retarded ejaculation is aimed at extinguishing the inhibitory process precluding uninhibited ejaculation. Kaplan (1974) indicates that this can be achieved through a program of behavioral deconditioning methods without necessarily resolving the underlying processes that give rise to the man's sexual dysfunction, unless the conflicts per se interfere with the deconditioning.

Sex therapy currently uses a combination of psychotherapeutic sessions and a series of individualized prescribed sexual tasks designed to desensitize the man systematically by employing erotic fantasy or stimulation. The client is instructed to ejaculate under whatever conditions he prefers. Gradually, ejaculatory behavior is modified and directed toward intravaginal ejaculation. Therapy does not proceed upon a fixed routine, and it is modified to suit each person's needs (Kaplan, 1974).

Ejaculation produced by the partner is considered by Masters and Johnson (1970) and Kaplan (1974) to be a critical landmark in therapy. Gradually, vaginal intromission and containment just before ejaculation are accomplished. Eventually, ejaculation can occur from vaginal friction during vaginal containment.

Masters and Johnson (1970) have reported that of 17 men seen in their program, ten were treated successfully. Other sex-therapy programs have not reported any descriptive statistics. Kaplan (1974) points out that the consensus among clinical sexologists is that the prognosis for therapeutic resolution of retarded ejaculation is directly related to its severity (primary or secondary) and the associated marital or psychologic pathology.

SEXUAL DYSFUNCTIONS OF WOMEN

Vaginismus

Vaginismus is a psychophysiologic sexual dysfunction of women characterized by the presence of conditioned involuntary muscular spasms or constriction of the vaginal outlet and the outer third of the vagina. The muscular response may involve all of the musculature of the vaginal outlet, the vaginal barrel, or the entire musculature of the female perineum.

The woman's coital function may be impeded either partially or totally by vaginismus depending upon the muscles involved and the severity of the spasms. In the presence of muscular spasms, penile penetration is possible but difficult and causes much discomfort for the woman. When the spasms are severe, the resulting vaginal constrictions may render penile insertion or penetration impossible. Regardless of the degree of muscular spasm, women affected by vaginismus face either recurrent episodes of painful intercourse (dyspareunia), or the inability to have sexual intercourse. Masters and Johnson (1970) point out that many marriages have never been consummated as a result of vaginismus.

Vaginismus may affect women of any age or any socioeconomic group. The prevalence of the disorder is unknown. Even though a woman's ability to participate pleasurably in sexual intercourse is directly affected by vaginismus, her sexual desire and capacity remain normal, appropriate vaginal lubrication can occur, and her ability to achieve an orgasm is not compromised.

Causes of Vaginismus

The exact cause of vaginismus is unknown. Kolodny et al. (1979) indicate that both physical and psychologic factors can contribute to the development of the disorder. Psychologic factors appear to be most operative in the dysfunction's etiology, however. Masters and Johnson's (1970) clinical observations have indicated that the development of vaginismus may be related to a variety of psychosexual inhibiting influences, such as an orthodox religious background, an episode of sexual trauma, or a woman's homosexual identification before attempting heterosexual contact. Kolodny et al. point out that vaginismus may subsequently develop from a variety of organic causes, such as sexual contact in the presence of an unhealed episiotomy, or pelvic pathology, such as hymenal abnormalities, genital infections that give rise to sore lesions, obstetric trauma, or atrophic vaginitis. Kaplan (1974) believes that vaginismus may be caused by a variety of stimuli, such as pain during coitus or fear of men. Accordingly, any stimulus that a woman associates with painful intercourse or that elicits a fear of vaginal penetration may cause vaginismus.

Masters and Johnson (1970) specify that an accurate diagnosis of vaginismus cannot be made by established interrogative techniques. Any suspicion of vaginismus must be validated by a direct pelvic examination. The diagnosis of vaginismus is only appropriate after the pelvic examination has revealed the presence of involuntary muscular spasms or constriction upon manual examination, or when the response is elicited merely by a woman's anticipation of vaginal intromission.

Treatment of Vaginismus

The characteristic involuntary vaginal muscle spasms of vaginismus are regarded by most sex therapists as a conditioned response to penetration attempts into the vagina. The majority of sex-therapy regimens for vaginismus primarily direct therapeutic interventions toward modifying the conditioned response of the vaginal musculature. Kaplan (1974) indicates that the psychologic causes are dealt with only to the extent that they impede the therapeutic process of desensitization. Vaginal dilatation exercise is the typical method used to desensitize the spasticity-prone vaginal musculature. The method used by Masters and Johnson (1970) is reported to be a successful approach. The format is designed to allow the therapist to intervene therapeutically with the physiologic and psychologic aspects of the dysfunction.

Masters and Johnson's (1970) approach includes (a) conjoint therapy; (b) a thorough explanation of the dysfunction—what it is, how it developed, and how it can be ameliorated; (c) reassurance that the dysfunction can be treated successfully; (d) a clinical demonstration of the physical existence of the muscular spasms to both of the clients; (e) gradual desensitization of the spastic vaginal musculature by the use of Hegar dilators; and (f) the direct dissemination of information to combat sexual misconceptions.

Masters and Johnson (1970) suggest that the therapeutic intervention for vaginismus should be preceded by a clinical demonstration to the partners of the vaginal muscle spasm phenomenon. During a chaperoned pelvic examination, the male client is gloved and encouraged to experience the vaginal muscle spasms around his finger. The experience can also clarify the degree of the muscular involvement to the woman.

Upon completion of the clinical demonstration, the partners are familiarized with the set of Hegar dilators to be used in the vaginal desensitization process. The dilators are used to assimilate penile penetration. Repeated gentle insertion of a dilator results in a diminishing of the vaginal spasms. Gradually, as the vaginal reaction decreases, larger dilators can be introduced, until vaginal containment is accomplished comfortably while using a large dilator.

To date, any conjoint therapy mode that uses a progressive vaginal dilation technique to extinguish the woman's conditioned muscular response can successfully eradicate vaginismus (Kaplan, 1974). Masters and Johnson (1970) have reported a 100% success rate, and Kaplan (1974) and co-workers also report perfect results from their program at Cornell.

General Sexual Dysfunction

The term *general sexual dysfunction* has been suggested by Kaplan (1974) to describe women who receive little, if any, erotic pleasure from sexual contact. Generally dysfunctional women are capable of and do have orgasms but are essentially void of the erotic and physiological premonitory sensations of orgasm. General sexual dysfunction can be divided into two categories—primary and secondary. Women suffering from *primary gen-*

eral sexual dysfunction have never experienced erotic sensations during sexual contact. Women affected by *secondary general sexual dysfunction* have experienced erotic arousal during sexual contact at some time in the past, but have for some reason lost that ability.

No disease process or physical impairment has been directly implicated in causing general sexual dysfunction. Disease processes rarely affect a woman's sexual ability, except to the extent that a disease is debilitating. The majority of cases of general sexual dysfunction are caused by psychologic factors.

Kaplan (1974) offers a psychosomatic model to explain the dynamics of the development and maintenance of general sexual dysfunction. Physiologically, a woman's sexual arousal is a visceral response that is controlled by the autonomic nervous system. Any emotion—anxiety, fear, hate—can interfere with or modify the functions of the autonomic nervous system. Accordingly, a woman's ability to be sexually aroused is vulnerable to any impairment of the autonomic nervous system. If a woman's anxiety is high, there is a strong likelihood that her reflexive genital vasocongestion, which forms the basis of the female sexual response, will be impaired. The typical result is the inability to respond sexually. The source of the impeding anxiety or emotions is irrelevant. The effect is the impairment of a woman's ability to abandon herself and respond sexually to erotic stimulation.

Treatment of General Sexual Dysfunction

Sex therapy for general sexual dysfunction attempts to facilitate the dysinhibition of arousal by modifying the woman's inhibited sexual system (Kaplan, 1974). By participating in specific sexual tasks designed to evoke erotic enjoyment, such as sensate focus and genital stimulation, sexually nonresponsive women can learn how to experience erotic sensations and to respond sexually.

Typically, the partners engage in sensate focus exercises that are void of genital contact. When the woman acknowledges having felt erotic sensations during the body caressing and stroking exercises of sensate focus, the partners are directed to incorporate genital play. During genital play, the man is cautioned not to proceed in a demanding manner.

When the woman also desires sexual stimulation from genital play, sexual intercourse can be initiated. Again, the partners are instructed to participate in intercourse in a nondemanding manner. The woman is directed to focus her attention upon the erotic vaginal and clitoral sensations perceived during intercourse. The positions used for intercourse vary. Masters and Johnson (1970) suggest the woman-on-top position, which enables the woman to direct intercourse toward her preferences.

However, Kaplan (1974) states that any position can be used that enables the woman to respond to physical stimulation and become erotically aroused.

Although they are specifically designed to invite a woman's arousal, the prescribed sexual tasks also offer the partners an opportunity to become aware of each other's sexual needs and reactions and thus to improve communication between them.

Once open communication occurs, the client's resistances during therapy can be identified and dealt with effectively in the concurrent psychotherapeutic sessions. Most resistances are learned defense mechanisms that block the woman's perception of erotic feelings. Deep-rooted psychologic conflicts are not dealt with by sex therapy except to the extent that they interfere with a woman's sexual responsiveness.

Kaplan (1974) indicates that many women have attained sexual responsiveness after participating in sex therapy specifically designed to ameliorate general sexual dysfunction. The clinical failures of sex therapy characteristically involve clients with deep-rooted hostility or conflicts that inhibit the sexual response. Many generally dysfunctional women also suffer from orgasmic dysfunction. Often the successful elimination of a woman's sexual inhibition can alleviate orgasmic dysfunction.

Orgasmic Dysfunction

Orgasmic dysfunction is probably the most prevalent female sexual dysfunction. *Orgasmic dysfunction* refers to the inability of a woman to achieve orgasm.

A woman with *primary orgasmic dysfunction* has never been able to achieve an orgasm. A woman suffering from *secondary orgasmic dysfunction* has achieved orgasm, but has lost this ability. Further differentiation is also made by categorizing orgasmic dysfunction either as situational or absolute. If a woman has been unable to achieve an orgasm under any circumstances, by clitoral manipulation or during intercourse, the dysfunction is considered absolute. However, if the woman is able to achieve an orgasm in specific situations or under certain circumstances, such as automanipulation, or with a specific sexual partner, the dysfunction is considered situational.

Unlike the woman with general sexual dysfunction, the woman with orgasmic dysfunction is sexually responsive and may seek out sexual contact and respond with erotic feelings. In terms of the sexual response cycle, she may experience vaginal lubrication and genital vasoconstriction, and she may often enjoy penetration and intercourse. However, she does not move beyond the plateau stage, for the orgasmic component is inhibited.

Causes of Orgasmic Dysfunction

Only 8% of all women are totally nonorgasmic. It is more common for women to be situationally nonorgasmic. Some of these women have unconscious fears of letting go in the presence of a man or a specific man. Fear of rejection if the woman is sexually aggressive or an obsessive concern with giving pleasure may inhibit orgasm. The woman may have unconscious conflicts about penetration and intercourse. Some women can achieve orgasm with masturbation alone but not with a partner, and still others can achieve orgasm with a partner only with direct clitoral stimulation.

In rare instances, physical factors can cause orgasmic dysfunction. Clitoral adhesions or weak or incompetent pubococcygeal muscles can contribute to the development and maintenance of a woman's orgasmic dysfunction. Involuntary inhibition of the orgasmic reflex is the major causative factor of a woman's orgasmic dysfunction. Because the woman's orgasmic reflex can be conditioned easily, women readily develop orgasmic dysfunction after participation in several experiences of intercourse in which the orgasm was consciously withheld (Kaplan, 1974). After a woman consciously denies herself an orgasm several times, the inhibition process seems to become automatic, and the ability to achieve an orgasm spontaneously is lost, even if the woman is relaxed and sexually responsive.

According to Kaplan (1974), three prerequisites must be met before a woman can respond sexually. First, she needs adequate erotic stimulation. Second, the woman must be relaxed enough during a sexual experience to respond to sexual stimulation and to be able to abandon herself to erotic pleasure. Third, a learned orgasmic inhibition process must not be negatively interfering with the woman's orgasmic reflex.

The type of erotic stimulation required to stimulate women varies from woman to woman. Each individual woman's erotic needs can vary with each of her sexual experiences. The woman needs to communicate to her sexual partner which type of stimulation is necessary to enable her to become erotically aroused. Kaplan (1974) believes that if a woman wants to be sexually responsive, she must assume the responsibility of communicating to her partners which type and quality of erotic stimulation she actually needs. In addition to taking such responsibility, the woman must not believe that sexual assertiveness is reserved solely to men. A woman must develop a degree of sexual autonomy if she is to become a responsive recipient of erotic stimulation and actualize her erotic potential.

A woman's inability to develop the necessary sexual autonomy is believed to be largely dependent upon cultural and religious influences (Masters & Johnson, 1970; Kaplan, 1974). The fear of rejection by her partner if she behaves aggressively or the anxiety or guilt about her sexual activities that an orthodox religious background may instill can often prevent a woman from sexually abandoning herself to an orgasm. Mead (1949) found that in the woman the potential for orgasm is a cultural factor. If a society considers orgasmic release for the woman important, then the essential love making techniques that ensure the woman's orgasm will be learned and practiced. If a woman's orgasm is considered unimportant, the members of the culture will not practice techniques essential to orgasmic release in the woman, and the woman is likely to be nonorgasmic.

Treatment of Orgasmic Dysfunction

The whole spectrum of orgasmic dysfunctions—absolute to situational —can be successfully treated by sex therapy. The therapeutic interventions—sexual tasks and psychotherapeutic sessions—vary according to the dysfunction's specific etiology. The interventions used can also be modified to meet the specific needs of an individual client or the needs of the partner's sexual systems. Sex therapy for the treatment of primary, absolute, secondary, or situational orgasmic dysfunction consists of an integration of specifically designed prescribed sexual tasks and psychotherapeutic sessions.

Treatment of a woman's orgasmic dysfunction focuses on diminishing her involuntary control over her orgasmic reflex. Through a variety of techniques, the client is taught to focus her attention on the premonitory sensations and to allow them to progress freely. Concurrent psychotherapeutic sessions serve to foster the client's awareness and resolution of psychological and transactional problems that impede her orgasmic response. Specifically designed sexual tasks are prescribed to enable the woman to learn or relearn how not to inhibit her orgasmic reflex. Kaplan (1974) points out that the prescribed sexual tasks are not just exercises to learn erotic techniques. They are sexual experiences designed specifically to foster constructive communication and to make the partners aware of each other's special sexual needs.

Treatment of Absolute Primary Orgasmic Dysfunction

The philosophy of the sex-therapy program at Cornell University regarding absolute primary orgasmic dysfunction is that the orgasmic reflex has been inhibited, not destroyed. Treatment is based on enabling the affected client to become distracted from the forces that inhibit her from achieving an orgasm. It is believed that if a woman can be sufficiently stimulated to attain intense erotic arousal, she can be distracted from the inhibitory forces by her erotic arousal and achieve an orgasm. Treatment procedures are designed to maximize a woman's state of erotic arousal and minimize the factors that inhibit her orgasmic response (Kaplan, 1974).

The psychotherapeutic session conducted concurrently with the prescribed sexual tasks are used as a means to identify remote psychologic conflicts and to ameliorate them to the extent that the conflicts impede restoration of a client's sexual functioning. In addition, other resistances, such as guilt, shame, fear, and sexual role problems can also be identified and dispelled during the sessions. The sex therapist also attempts to treat the couple's transactional problems, which interfere with the woman's orgasmic response. Communication—verbal and physical—is also a focus during the sessions. Therapists strive to enhance a couple's ability to communicate with each other.

Initially, treatment consists in helping the woman achieve her first orgasm. Achieving an orgasm demonstrates to the woman that she is indeed capable of attaining an orgasm. Attaining the first orgasm is believed to be a crucial step toward extinguishing the inhibition of the orgasm.

If, during conjoint efforts, a woman is unable to achieve an orgasm, she is asked to use automanipulation techniques. Achieving an orgasm through masturbation is used therapeutically to remove the woman from the inhibitory force of an audience—her partner—which is known to be a major inhibiting factor. If the client is unable to achieve orgasm by a manual technique, a vibrator is used. Kaplan (1974) believes that a vibrator should be used only when other techniques have failed. Clients are also cautioned against continual use of a vibrator, since it is difficult during sexual intercourse to attain the amount of clitoral stimulation that can be achieved by using a vibrator.

The time initially required for a woman to reach orgasm by automanipulation is usually quite lengthy—sometimes hours. Once the process has been reduced to a reasonable time, the client is instructed to achieve an orgasm with her partner. The couple is instructed to engage in sexual intercourse in their usual fashion to enable the man to achieve orgasm. When the man is relieved sexually, the woman is relieved of the pressure to perform quickly. After the man has ejaculated, he is instructed to manually manipulate the woman to orgasm. The woman is instructed to be consciously not attentive of the inhibitory forces which might be operating to inhibit her orgasm during her partner's manipulation.

Kaplan (1974) reports that virtually all the clients suffering from absolute primary orgasmic dysfunction who are treated by the sex-therapy format of Cornell University do achieve an orgasm, and many go on to enjoy a sexually satisfying relationship with their sexual partners.

SEXUAL DYSFUNCTIONS OF MEN AND WOMEN

Dyspareunia

Dyspareunia is the experience of pain by either men or women on intromission and during and following intercourse (Masters & Johnson, 1970; Mims & Swenson, 1980). In women the pain may be felt around the vaginal entrance and clitoris, in the vagina, and deep in the pelvis and lower abdomen (Wabrek & Wabrek, 1975). In men the pain is felt on the surface of the penis or in the internal anatomy such as the penile urethra, prostate, or bladder (Munjack & Oziel, 1980).

There are many physical causes of dyspareunia in both men and women; however, in women the majority of cases are related to complex psychologic factors. In men, psychologic factors are more likely to be associated with erectile and ejaculatory dysfunctions than with dyspareunia. Abarbanel (1978) identified fears—fear of erotic stimuli, fear of rejection, fear of failure, fear of fantasized conflicts based on beliefs and myths—as the common denominator associated with psychogenic dyspareunia. For some women the fears are based on actual pain experienced in previous intercourse, and the fear of the reoccurrence of that pain becomes translated into the pain itself.

In women physical causes of dyspareunia may involve an intact hymen or irritated remnants of it, painful scars from an episiotomy, or infection of the Bartholin glands. Clitoral pain may result from inflammation (trichomonas) and adhesions. Vaginal or vulval infections (trichomonas, monilia, venereal warts) and irritation from chemical contraceptives, douche preparations and feminine hygiene aerosol deodorants can lead to painful intercourse. Lack of lubrication is a common cause of dyspareunia. Pelvic infection (gonorrhea), endometriosis, and ovarian cysts can cause painful intercourse.

Cystic abnormalities of the cervix, benign neoplasms (polyps and papillomas) and malignancies of the cervix give rise to pain on intercourse. Uterine pathology such as myoma or sarcoma of the uterus, fixed retroversion, and tearing of the broad ligaments supporting the uterus are associated with dyspareunia.

In uncircumcised men, inadequate washing may allow material to collect under the foreskin of the penis and cause painful intercourse. *Phimosis*, a condition in which the foreskin cannot be retracted over the glans, may be so painful as to make intercourse impossible. An allergy related to vaginal douches, creams, jellies, and foam can cause dyspareunia. *Priapism* is a condition characterized by persistent and painful erection of the penis. *Peyronie's disease*, produced by induration and fibrosis of the corpora cavernosa of the penis, can result in an upward bowing of the penis as well as a gradually increasing angulation to the left or right of the midline. Both of these conditions lead to painful intercourse and both require medical and sometimes surgical treatment.

Occasionally some men have a true hypersensitivity of the penile glans and complain of irritation from their clothes or bodily contact. Masters and Johnson (1970) report there are some men who cannot tolerate the normal pH levels of the vagina and experience blistering and peeling of the surface of the penile glans. For these men the only treatment that can be offered is protective covering.

Lesions or tumors of the testicle, such as hydrocele or carcinoma, can cause pain. Gonorrhea can produce stricture formation along the length of the penile urethra that can result in pain during urination or ejaculation that sometimes radiates to the bladder and prostate.

Data about the physical causes of dyspareunia should be collected and assessed before any attempt is made to identify psychologic factors involved. A careful and detailed sexual history identifying when, where, and how the pain began should be taken. A thorough physical and pelvic examination should be performed, noting in particular any manipulation that causes discomfort, aching, or pain. The medical diagnosis is made and treatment prescribed by the physician, and the nurse consults and collaborates with the physician in the design of effective nursing care.

After the selected medical or surgical treatment and plan of care have been implemented, there should be a reevaluation of any remaining dyspareunia. When pain has been associated with intercourse over a long period of time, a conditioned expectation and physical avoidance response can be produced that may require a therapeutic relearning intervention (Fordney-Settlage, 1979).

Inhibited Sexual Desire

Inhibited sexual desire is probably the most prevalent sexual dysfunction (Kaplan, 1979). *Inhibited sexual desire* is recognized as a separate clinical entity and defined as a psychosexual dysfunction with persistent and pervasive low sexual desire. Inhibited sexual desire is a state marked by simultaneously low levels of sexual receptivity and initiatory sexual behavior (Kolodny, Masters, & Johnson, 1979). The actual frequency in the population is not known. Lief (1977) states that 32 of 115 clients (27%) seen at the Marriage Counseling Center in Philadelphia were given the primary diagnosis of inhibited sexual desire; the rate among female clients (37%) was approximately twice that observed in male clients (18.79%). Inhibited sexual desire is an important diagnostic distinction, for it makes clear that the sexual response cycle is triphasic—that the desire phase precedes the excitement and orgasm stages. Each component is believed to be distinct and capable of being inhibited separately.

Inhibited sexual desire is not to be confused with the phenomenon that can occur when partners have disparate levels of sexual interest. From a practical point of view, clients suffering from inhibited sexual desire have no sexual desire (Kolodny, Masters, & Johnson, 1979). The dysfunction may be situational—desire for sexual activity with a specific sex partner may be affected while the desire for sexual activity with another partner or under other circumstances is unaffected. People with inhibited sexual desire may be quite functional sexually or may have concomitant difficulty in mechanisms of sexual arousal or orgasm. Partners often cope with inhibited sexual desire by establishing a sexual repertoire founded upon the notion of acceptable accommodation—the affected partner is capable of performing and accommodating the unaffected partner sexually. In these instances there is an acceptable accommodation, and no sexual problem results.

In some instances, another sexual dysfunction coexists with inhibited sexual desire. In such situations, inhibited sexual desire may have developed and may serve as a mechanism to cope with the other sexual dysfunction (Kolodny, Masters, & Johnson, 1979). Clinically, when inhibited sexual desire coexists with another dysfunction, it is very difficult, if not impossible, to determine which dysfunction is the primary disorder.

The causes of inhibited sexual desire may be either organic processes or psychosocial factors. Almost any chronic disease process, such as diabetes or arteriosclerotic heart disease, may affect sexual desire (see Chapter 14). Inhibited sexual desire may arise as a result of depression, a traumatic experience, fears or inhibitions, or interpersonal difficulties. Incest or rape often precede the development of inhibited sexual desire. A person's fears of failure or rejection also may elicit an inhibition of sexual desire. Partners in conflict are likely to experience diminished sexual attraction for each other, and one or both partners may develop an impaired or inhibited sexual desire. Inhibited sexual desire has also been referred to as sexual anorexia, because, while in conflict, people typically experience a loss in their sexual appetites. Kolodny, Masters, & Johnson (1979) point out that a person's sexual expectations may preordain the pattern of sexual behavior. For example, a man who adheres to the culturally ordained notion that the man should always initiate sexual contact may experience a discomfort when his sexual partner initiates sexual contact. In such a case, the man may situationally react by developing an inhibited sexual desire with that specific sexually assertive partner.

Treatment of Inhibited Sexual Desire

A detailed sexual history must be obtained from each client who is seeking therapeutic intervention for inhibited sexual desire. An intensive psychotherapeutic approach is required to treat a client suffering from inhibited sexual desire successfully. A client's desire to change needs to be assessed before treatment is instituted. If the inhibited partner does not sincerely desire change, the therapeutic tasks may be sabotaged and the treatment may fail.

Therapy usually begins with the partners being given information about the possible etiology of the sexual dysfunction. It is believed that knowing the etiology may foster the development of insights that are often necessary in bringing about change. Kolodny, Masters, & Johnson (1979) caution therapists not to overextend their "interpretive license" when formulating an etiology, because a precise etiology is often very difficult to determine. Therapy proceeds conjointly with particular emphasis being placed on the relationship—no individual partner should ever be singled out as "okay" or "not okay."

Therapy formats are always individualized, but they combine specifically designed and structured prescribed sexual tasks with concurrent psychotherapeutic sessions. During the psychotherapeutic sessions, any negative effects derived from culturally imbued expectations, such as sex-role stereotypes, can be treated effectively.

Therapy places a particular emphasis on enhancing a couple's ability to communicate physically and verbally. The partners are repeatedly encouraged to identify and verbalize their feelings. Such efforts help to build the couple's communication skills. Initially, the goals of sexual arousal and orgasm are purposely removed from sensate-focus exercises. Participation in sexual activity during sensate focus is eventually permitted, but it is stopped if either partner experiences boredom or fatigue, or if any form of discomfort is elicited from sexual contact. Affected clients can achieve a sense of sexual freedom during therapy when it becomes apparent that they are not responsible for their partner's ability to become aroused.

A sex therapy format for inhibited sexual desire is not generalizable, because each client's etiology will necessitate a unique format. However, through the combined use of specifically designed and structured sexual tasks that afford an affected client opportunities to change his or her sexual behavior experientially, and through the support and direction obtained from the psychotherapeutic sessions, satisfactory therapeutic outcomes can be expected.

Sexual Aversion

Sexual aversion is a consistent negative reaction of phobic proportions to sexual activity or the thought of sexual activity (Kolodny, Masters, & Johnson, 1979). Although sexual aversion is infrequently encountered, it does occur in both men and women, and is far more common in women. The person with sexual aversion is not sexually dysfunctional—the man is fully potent and able to ejaculate, and the woman is able to experience orgasm. Sexual aversion does not involve a strong distaste for sex or an intense dislike for a specific sexual activity. The person with sexual aversion experiences irrational and overwhelming anxiety at the thought of sexual contact. While the response may be internalized and not overt, it can sometimes be observed through profuse sweating, nausea, vomiting, diarrhea, and palpitations. Although sexual aversion can be situational, occurring only with a particular partner or a heterosexual contact, the diagnosis is made only when there is a consistent phobic reaction to all aspects of sexual contact with another person.

ROLE OF THE NURSE AS EDUCATOR-COUNSELOR

Today, people are more openly concerned about their sexual health. Accordingly, nurses need to have an understanding of the physiology of sexual health, the associated symptomology of sexual dysfunctions, and the psychosocial ramifications of a sexual dysfunction. The nurse is not a sex therapist. When confronted with a client's expressed anxieties, fears, and concerns, the nurse can use data-gathering skills to contribute to the determination of the presence of a sexual dysfunction; as educator-counselor, the nurse actively participates in the process of referral.

The nurse can discuss with the client the kinds of results that have been obtained from sex therapy and the time frame involved. It might be helpful for the nurse to assure the client that he or she has the right to expect information and explanation about an acceptable treatment plan and that the client has the right to expect the therapist to be nonjudgmental and nonsexist and to have a respectful attitude toward the client's sexual value system.

The sex therapist can be viewed as a helping professional whose knowledge and skills are focused on helping men and women, as individuals or couples, deal more effectively with their sexual problems. The sex therapist has knowledge and skills in general counseling and psychotherapy, psychiatric social work, or psychiatric nursing. The sex therapist has knowledge of the physiology and psychology of sexual function and dysfunction coupled with education and clinical training in counseling and therapy. The sex therapist must also have education and clinical training in marital, family, or group therapy. The nurse, with additional training and education, can be prepared to function as a sex therapist. The American Association of Sex Educators, Counselors and Therapists (AASECT) is the largest national group that certifies sex educators, sex counselors (who work within agencies), and sex therapists. The AASECT will provide lists of qualified sex therapists. Local mental health groups or medical associations or university centers are prepared to provide information about qualified sex therapists available within the community.

NURSING PROCESS

Client: Ben Leigh—being discharged after herniorrhaphy.
Nurse: Ralph Barter—staff nurse on surgical nursing unit.

Assessment

Subjective Data

"I'm not looking forward to leaving the hospital and sleeping at home."
"She—my wife—wonders if my operation will make things worse."
"She used to like to have sex often, and so did I—but now—"
"She says that I go too fast—that I get it over too soon."
"She says when we first got married, and even before, we took more time
        and it was better for her."
"Lately, it's been worse—nothing I do seems to help."
"We talk, and she talks, and I try, and I can't last any longer. She says
        even less."
"She gets upset—and I—well I sure as hell don't feel good about it."
"Even going to where we spent our honeymoon didn't help."
"Once we gave up sex for a little while—and it was worse."
"She wants me to slow down, and I tell her to hurry up."
"She says she wants us to go see a sex therapist. What do you think?"

Objective Data

25 years old.
Married two years.
Employed—electrician.
Uneventful recovery from herniorrhaphy.
Discharge order written.
Verbalizes inability to control ejaculation.
Worried over partner's reaction.
    Anxiety.
    Lowered self-esteem.

Nursing Diagnosis

Seeks information about partner's suggestion of sex therapy related to
        possible sexual dysfunction (premature ejaculation).

Planning

Approach unhurriedly.

Provide an atmosphere of acceptance.

Express empathy.

Reassure verbally.

Encourage expression of feelings.

Listen attentively.

Explain that the client's emotional response is appropriate and commonly experienced.

Offer feedback of client's expressed feelings.

Recognize the use of appropriate defense mechanisms.

Support a realistic assessment of the situation.

Advise against causing defensive responses in others.

Advise that significant persons express acceptance of one another.

Advise that significant persons express love for one another.

Explain the importance of recognizing tension within oneself.

Explain the need for realistic expectation of others.

Encourage identification of value of sex, sexual functioning, and the sexual relationship.

Explain the difference between freedom from anxiety and freedom from problems.

Explain the importance of maintaining a positive self-attitude.

Encourage mutual problem solving.

Explain that relaxation is essential for successful sexual response.

Explain that sexual response normally varies.

Explain possible psychological causes of inability to control ejaculation.

Provide information about sex therapy.

Provide information about effectiveness and limitations of sex therapy.

Provide information about community resources for sex therapy.

Encourage discussion of sex therapy with family physician and friends.

Implementation

Initiate discussion with partner.

Share feelings about acceptance and love with partner.

Discuss value of sex, sexual functioning, and the sexual relationship.

Discuss information about sexual response and inability to control ejaculation.

Discuss information about sex therapy.

Discuss selection of sex therapist with family physician.

Discuss selection of sex therapist with family friends, friends who have had experience with sex therapy.

Select sex therapist.

Make appointment with sex therapist.

Evaluation (six months later)

Reports satisfaction with selection of sex therapist.
Reports satisfaction with sex therapy.
Reports satisfaction with treatment for premature ejaculation.
Reports enhancement of sexual relationship.

BIBLIOGRAPHY

Abarbanel, A. R. Diagnosis and treatment of coital discomfort. In J. LoPiccolo & L. LoPiccolo (Eds.), *Handbook of sex therapy*. New York: Plenum Press, 1978.

Bergler, E. Frigidity in the female: Misconceptions and facts. *Marriage Hygiene*, 1974, *1*, 16–21.

Caird, U., & Wincze, J. P. *Sex therapy: A behavioral approach*. New York: Harper & Row, 1977.

Campbell, C. *Nursing diagnosis and intervention in nursing practice*. New York: Wiley, 1978.

Chambless, D. L., & Goldstein, A. J. Behavioral psychology. In R. J. Corsini (Ed.), *Current psychotherapies* (2nd ed.). Itasca, Ill.: Peacock, 1979.

Cooper, A. J. A factual study of male potency disorders. *British Journal of Psychiatry*, 1968, *114*, 719–731.

Cooper, A. J. The causes and management of impotence. *Postgraduate Medical Journal*, 1972, *98*, 548–552. (a)

Cooper. A. J. Diagnosis and management of "endocrine impotence." *British Medical Journal*, 1972, *2*, 34. (b)

DeLora, J. A., & Warren, C. A. B. *Understanding sexual interaction*. Boston: Houghton Mifflin, 1977.

Fordney-Settlage, D. S. Clitoral abnormalities. *Medical Aspects of Human Sexuality*, 1975, *9*, 183–184.

Fordney-Settlage, D. S. Pelvic examination of women: Genitorectal examination of men. In R. Green (Ed.), *Human sexuality: A health practitioner's text*. Baltimore: Williams & Wilkins, 1979.

Frank, E., Anderson, C., & Rubinstein, D. Frequency of sexual dysfunction in "normal" couples. *New England Journal of Medicine*, 1978, *229*, 111–115.

Friedman, D. E. The treatment of impotency by brietal relaxation therapy. *Behavior Research and Therapy*, 1968, *6*, 257–261.

Friedman, M. Success phobia and retarded ejaculation. *American Journal of Psychotherapy*, 1973, *27*, 78–84.

Hogan, D. R. The effectiveness of sex therapy: A review of the literature. In J. LoPiccolo & L. LoPiccolo (Eds.), *Handbook of sex therapy*. New York: Plenum Press, 1978.

Huffman, J. W. Sex and endometriosis. *Medical Aspects of Human Sexuality*, 1971, *5*, 186–204.

Husted, J. B. Desensitization procedures in dealing with female sexual dysfunction. In J. LoPiccolo & L. LoPiccolo (Eds.), *Handbook of sex therapy*. New York: Plenum Press, 1978.

Julty, S. *Men's bodies: Men's selves*. New York: Delta, 1979.

Kaplan, H. S. *The new sex therapy.* New York: Brunner/Mazel, 1974.

Kaplan, H. S. Hypoactive sexual desire. *Journal of Sex & Marital Therapy*, 1977, *3*, 3–9.

Kaplan, H. S. An interview: Inhibited sexual desire. *Medical Aspects of Human Sexuality*, 1979, *13*, 26–47.

Kaplan, H., & Kohl, R. Adverse reactions to the rapid treatment of sexual problems. *Psychosomatics*, 1972, *13*, 185–190.

Kaplan, H. S., Kohl, R. N., Pomeroy, W. B., Offit, A. K., & Hogan, B. Group treatment of premature ejaculation. In J. LoPiccolo & L. LoPiccolo (Eds.), *Handbook of sex therapy.* New York: Plenum Press, 1978.

Katz, S. Ejaculation without pleasurable sensation. *Medical Aspects of Human Sexuality,* 1975, *9,* 76.

Kinsey, A. C., Pomeroy, W. B., & Martin, C. E. *Sexual behavior in the human male.* Philadelphia: Saunders, 1948.

Kinsey, A. C., Pomeroy, W. B., Martin, C. E., & Gebhard, P. H. *Sexual behavior in the human female.* Philadelphia: Saunders, 1953.

Kockott, G., Dittmar, F., & Nusselt, L. Systematic desensitization of erectile impotence: A controlled study. In J. LoPiccolo & L. LoPiccolo (Eds.), *Handbook of sex therapy.* New York: Plenum Press, 1978.

Kolodny, R. C., Masters, W. H., & Johnson, V. E. *Textbook of sexual medicine.* Boston: Little, Brown, 1979.

Kolodny, R. C., Masters, W. H., Johnson, V. E., & Biggs, M. A. *Textbook of human sexuality for nurses.* Boston: Little, Brown, 1979.

Lazarus, A. A. Overcoming sexual inadequacy. In J. LoPiccolo & L. LoPiccolo (Eds.), *Handbook of sex therapy.* New York: Plenum Press, 1978.

Leiter, E. Ejaculatory pain. *Medical Aspects of Human Sexuality*, 1976, *10*, 157.

Levine, S. B. Some thoughts about the pathogenesis of premature ejaculation. *Journal of Sex and Marital Therapy*, 1975, *1*, 326–334.

Linton, E. Honeymoon cystitis. *Medical Aspects of Human Sexuality*, 1971, *5*, 111–116.

Lief, H. I. Inhibited sexual desire. *Journal of Sex and Marital Therapy*, 1977, *11*, 94–95.

LoPiccolo, J. Treatment of sexual concerns by the primary care male clinician. In R. Green (Ed.), *Human sexuality: A health practitioner's text* (2nd ed.). Baltimore: Williams & Wilkins, 1979.

LoPiccolo, J., & LoPiccolo, L. (Eds.). *Handbook of sex therapy.* New York: Plenum Press, 1978.

Lowe, J. C., & Mikulas, W. L. Use of written material in learning self-control of premature ejaculation. In J. LoPiccolo & L. LoPiccolo (Eds.), *Handbook of sex therapy.* New York: Plenum Press, 1978.

Marmor, J. Impotence and ejaculatory disturbances. In B. J. Soccock, H. I. Kaplan, & A. M. Freedman (Eds.), *The sexual experience.* Baltimore: Williams & Wilkins, 1976.

Masters, W. H., & Johnson, V. E. *Human sexual response.* Boston: Little, Brown, 1966.

Masters, W. H., & Johnson, V. E. *Human sexual inadequacy.* Boston: Little, Brown, 1970.

Mead, M. *Male and female: A study of the sexes in a changing world.* New York: Dell, 1949.

Mims, F. H., & Swenson, M. *Sexuality: A nursing perspective.* New York: McGraw-Hill, 1980.

Munjack, D., & Kanno, P. An overview in frigidity: Treatment, effect, and effectiveness. *Comprehensive Psychiatry*, 1976, *17*, 401–413.

Munjack, D. J., & Oziel, L.J. *Sexual medicine and counseling in office practice: A comprehensive treatment guide.* Boston: Little, Brown, 1980.

Newell, A. G. A case of ejaculatory incompetence treated with a mechanical aid. In J. LoPiccolo & L. LoPiccolo (Eds.), *Handbook of sex therapy.* New York: Plenum Press, 1978.

Razani, J. Ejaculatory incompetence treated by deconditioning anxiety. In J. LoPiccolo & L. LoPiccolo (Eds.), *Handbook of sex therapy.* New York: Plenum Press, 1978.

Reckless, J., & Geiger, N. Impotence as a practical problem. In J. LoPiccolo & L. LoPiccolo (Eds.), *Handbook of sex therapy.* New York: Plenum Press, 1978.

Rosenbaum, M. B. Treatment of sexual concerns by the primary care female clinician. In R. Green (Eds.), *Human sexuality: A health practitioner's text* (2nd ed.). Baltimore: Williams & Wilkins, 1979.

Saltzman, L. Interesting sexual cases: Premature ejaculation. *Medical Aspects of Human Sexuality*, 1972, *6*, 119–127.

Satterfield, S. B., & Stayton, W. R. Understanding sexual function and dysfunction. *Topics in Clinical Nursing*, 1980, *1*, 21–32.

Seman, J. H. Premature ejaculation: A new approach. *Southern Medical Journal*, 1956, *49*, 353–357.

Semmens, J. P., & Semmens, J. F. Dyspareunia. *Medical Aspects of Human Sexuality*, 1974, *8*, 85–86.

Steen, E. B., & Price, J. H. *Human sex and sexuality.* New York: Wiley & Sons, 1977.

Stewart, F. H., Stewart, G. K., Guest, F. J., & Hatcher, R. A. *My body, my health: The concerned woman's guide to gynecology.* New York: Wiley, 1979.

Wabrek, A. J., & Wabrek, C. J. Dyspareunia. *Journal of Sex and Marital Therapy*, 1975, *1*, 234–241.

Wabrek, A. J., & Wabrek, C. J. Vaginismus. *Journal of Sex Education*, 1976, *2*, 21–24.

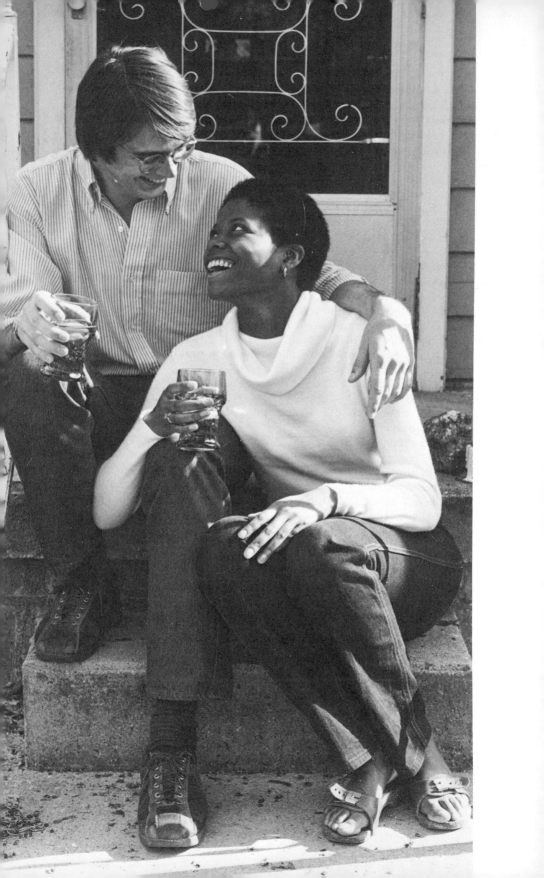

9. Sexuality and Reproductive Decision Making

Marguerite Supko Casey

VALUES CLARIFICATION EXERCISE

In our society, the puritan tradition remains influential. Although the tradition is not antisex, it is antipleasure. The purpose of these exercises is to have you examine your feelings and convictions about sex as procreation and sex as recreation.

Write your answers to the following questions. Examine your answers and note which you have strong feelings about. Identify your pattern of beliefs and consider how you arrived at it. Give some thought to how your beliefs influence your behavior.

1. Do you believe that people have a right to make decisions about reproduction?
2. Do you feel that preventing conception is primarily a woman's obligation?
3. Which of the following factors do you think is most important when a person chooses a contraceptive: lack of side effects, effectiveness in preventing pregnancy, or acceptability to both partners? Which factor is most important to you?
4. What do you think is the most appropriate contraceptive for adolescent girls? boys?
5. Do you think contraceptive counseling should be available to single men? women?
6. What do you think is the significance of intercourse in a relationship in which the partners are infertile?
7. How do you react to this statement: Contraception is practiced in order to free sexual relations from the consequences of unwanted pregnancy?

8. In what way do you think infertility can affect a person's concept of himself or herself as a sexual being?
9. For whom do you think infertility poses a greater emotional problem—men or women?

Discuss your feelings and beliefs with a group of peers or colleagues. How are the feelings and beliefs expressed in the group similar? How are they dissimilar? How could the feelings and beliefs expressed affect a nurse–client interaction in which information about fertility control is being sought by a 16-year-old girl? A 45-year-old woman? A 65-year-old man? An unmarried couple? How could the feelings and beliefs expressed affect a nurse–client interaction in which information about promotion of fertility is being sought by a married couple childless for six years? An unmarried couple childless for two years? A married couple of which the husband has children by a previous wife? A married couple of which the wife has children by a previous husband? An unmarried couple of which the husband is physically disabled? A married couple of which the wife is physically disabled?

BEHAVIORAL OBJECTIVES

After completing this chapter, you will be able to

- Discuss the effects of modern technology on reproductive decision making.
- Discuss the effects of sexuality on contraception.
- Identify the factors that influence contraceptive choice.
- Identify the three factors that influence contraceptive effectiveness.
- Define contraception effectiveness rates.
- Discuss the risks associated with contraception.
- Briefly describe hormonal, barrier, mechanical, behavioral, and surgical methods of contraception.
- Discuss the contraceptive choices of adolescents.
- Give the rationale for establishing contraceptive services for men.
- Discuss the relationship between sexuality and infertility.
- Discuss the possible effects of infertility and infertility assessment on sexual behavior.
- Illustrate the roles of the nurse as educator-counselor in conception control and infertility management.

REPRODUCTIVE DECISION MAKING

The complexities of fertility and infertility have puzzled human beings for centuries. Historically, the management of reproduction has burdened the inventiveness of many cultures and societies. Cultural, religious, and legal standards of morality influence prevention, curtailment, or promotion of childbearing.

It is only within the past decade that the decision to reproduce has been seen as a right belonging to women. A woman's right to plan whether or not to conceive has become the crux of the decision-making process in fertility control. Information on fertility control has become available to a majority of the population. It is possible not only to choose to reproduce but also to choose when and how often to reproduce or not to reproduce at all.

For approximately 10 to 15% of couples who want children, the concern is not fertility control but infertility management. For these couples, although reproductive decision making remains inherent in their sexual relationship, the problems and solutions are different.

Modern technology affects the choices available to the fertile and infertile woman. For the fertile woman there is increased opportunity to limit conception; for the infertile woman there is increased opportunity to promote conception. For both, there is increased opportunity and sanction to control bodily function in a way that is congruent with their self-image, self-concept, and sexual value system.

Whether the concern is fertility control or infertility management, it is the responsibility of the nurse to recognize the uniqueness of the client's concerns. Nursing care must reflect the selective and stated needs, desires, and expectations of each client.

SEXUALITY AND CONTRACEPTION

The development of reliable methods of contraception has had a profound effect on human sexual behavior. Contraception has enabled some people to assume the responsibility for separating procreative from recreative sexual behavior. Intercourse can now be viewed as a form of intimate communication with conception being a selective condition. For those people who perceive themselves as responsible for planning or preventing pregnancy, the ability to make this decision often enhances their self-esteem and self-image.

Some people use contraception out of necessity rather than personal choice. Economic deprivation or ill health, for example, may prevent a couple from having the children they want. There are also people whose sexual value system will not allow the separation of sex from reproduction. For these people, too, contraception is not a choice.

EFFECTIVENESS RATES OF CONTRACEPTIVE METHODS

The effectiveness of a birth-control method is frequently a major concern for people considering or using a contraceptive. Effectiveness is best understood through the information provided by theoretical and actual effectiveness rate. *Theoretical effectiveness rates* represent the maximum effectiveness of a birth-control method when used with absolute consistency and exactly as the instructions direct—they assume that the users of the method are consistent and diligent in its use. *Actual-use effectiveness rates* represent the use of the method with and without error. They mean that the method has been used consistently as well as inconsistently and that instructions have been followed sometimes and sometimes not followed. These rates take into account that some users may be inconsistent and careless in the use of the method.

Effectiveness rates for each method of contraception are calculated by gathering data on a group of sexual partners who use a particular method for a specified length of time and counting the pregnancies that occur. Effectiveness rates are determined in terms of pregnancies per 100 women per year of use. An effectiveness rate of 97% means a failure rate of 3%, or that three pregnancies have occurred in 100 women for the year studied (Table 9.1). The difference between theoretical effectiveness rate and actual-use effectiveness rates indicates the margins of error for that particular method. Both theoretical and actual-use rates should be given to people inquiring about methods of contraception. The use of theoretical rates for one method and actual-use rates for another gives inaccurate, unreliable, and biased information.

RISKS ASSOCIATED WITH CONTRACEPTION

The risks involved in the use of various methods of contraception may be a major concern for the potential or active user. How will this method affect my health? Are there any serious consequences from using this method? Some risks are caused directly by the contraceptive method—birth-control pills do cause blood-clotting disorders that can result in hospitalization. There are other indirect risks, such as when the method fails and the client becomes vulnerable to the medical risks of pregnancy or abortion. For every 100,000 full-term pregnancies, some 14.9 women

Table 9.1. Method Effectiveness: Theoretical and Actual-Use Rates (Pregnancies per 100 Woman Years)

	Theoretical failure rate	Actual-use failure rate	Death rate per 100,000 women	Event cost 1981[a]
No protection	80	80	14	0
Legal abortion[a]	0	0	3.2	$125–250
Tubal ligation[a]	0.04	0.04	1–2	$350–400
Vasectomy[a]	0.15	0.15	0	$ 75–150
Oral contraceptives	1.0	2–3	0.3–3.0	$5–7
Condom	3	15–20	2–5+	$3
Diaphragm	3	20–25	3	$9+clinic visit ($18)
Spermicidal Foam	3	30	3–4	$5–6
Withdrawal	15	20–25	?	0
Rhythm	15	35	?	0
Spermicidal jelly[b]				$6

[a]Based on cost estimates at Wishard Memorial Hospital, Indianapolis, Indiana. Ranges are given because the procedures are affected by individual needs and alterations.

[b]Spermicidal jelly must be used with a diaphragm.

SOURCE: Adapted from Hatcher, R. A., Stewart, G. K., Stewart, F., Guest, F., Stratton, P., and Wright, A. H. *Contraceptive Technology 1978–1979* (9th ed.). New York: Irvington Publishers, 1978. With permission from Irvington Publishers, Inc., 1980

die each year as a direct result of pregnancy (Cates & Tietze, 1978). Risks are best understood in relation to illness (morbidity) or death (mortality) during the reproductive years.

Information about risks should be presented in terms of both what is known and what has yet to be learned. The information should be made applicable to the client's state of health and personal concerns. The information is reliable and specific and contributes to growth and responsible decision making.

Factors that influence a person's choice of a method of contraception include his or her health status, life style, and habits (Stewart et al., 1979). The choice of a contraceptive is influenced by such issues as effectiveness, risk, accessability, ease in use, and cost. The choice is often determined by the method or combination of methods that best meets the person's perceived and stated needs.

Although the choice of a contraceptive method is a significant one, the actual effectiveness of the method depends on three factors of equal importance: (1) theoretical effectiveness of the method, (2) consistency of use, and (3) correct use by the sexual partners. The choice of an effective method of conception control must be accompanied by a commitment to vigilant and accurate contraceptive behavior.

The following list of questions can be helpful to people considering the use of a given contraception. A "yes" answer to any or several of the questions could affect how, when, or whether the chosen method is used (Hatcher et al., 1978, p. 24).

- Am I afraid of using this method of birth control?
- Would I really rather not use this method?
- Will I have trouble remembering to use this method?
- Have I ever become pregnant while using this method?
- Are there reasons why I will be unable to use this method as prescribed?
- Do I still have unanswered questions about this method?
- Has my mother, father, sister, brother, or a close friend strongly discouraged me from using this method?
- Will this method make my periods longer or more painful?
- Will prolonged use of this method cost me more than I can afford?
- Is this method known to have serious complications?
- Am I opposed to this method because of my religious beliefs?
- Have I already experienced complications from this method?
- Has a nurse or doctor already told me not to use this method?
- Is my partner opposed to my using this method?
- Am I using this method without my partner's knowledge?
- Will the use of this method embarrass me?
- Will the use of this method embarrass my partner?

• Will my partner or I enjoy intercourse less because of this method?
• Will this method interrupt the act of intercourse?

METHODS OF CONTRACEPTION

Contraception is not birth control but conception control. The person considering conception control needs information on available contraceptive methods, effectiveness rates, associated risks, accessibility, contraindications, and the possible effects on sexual behavior.

Hormonal Contraception

Contraceptive pills are hormonal contraceptives taken orally. Synthetic estrogen and progesterone are combined in pill form. When taken in adequate dosage, the estrogen suppresses the development of the ovum within the ovaries, and the progesterone suppresses the release of the mature ovum into the fallopian tubes.

The pill has additional contraceptive effects. The low continuous levels of progestin apparently change the cervical mucus so that sperm cannot enter the uterus. Even if ovulation and fertilization did occur, both components of the pill change the endometrium in such a manner than implantation would be unlikely.

Oral contraceptives are prescribed in either combined or sequential form. In the combined form (20- or 21-tablet packs), estrogen and progestin are contained in a tablet that is taken daily from the fifth to the twenty-fourth day of the cycle. The sequential form consists of 15 or 16 tablets containing only estrogen that are taken daily, after which five tablets containing estrogen and progestin are taken over the next five days. After two or three days of suspended use, withdrawal bleeding occurs. Resumption of the drug takes place on the fifth day of the new cycle. There is also a 28-tablet pack that contains 21 tablets of combined drug and seven placebo tablets. This allows for a tablet to be taken every day without interruption. Withdrawal bleeding occurs during the seven days in which the placebo is being taken. This method eliminates the necessity of calculating calendar days.

The pill can be started any time during the first seven days of a natural cycle. Starting the pill on the first Sunday after a normal menstrual period begins is the easiest schedule to understand. This regimen will result in the use of a new pack of pills every fourth Sunday and the avoidance of menstrual periods on weekends.

The pill is to be taken at a regular time each day. If a woman misses taking a pill, she should take one at the time she remembers it and should take the next pill at the scheduled time. If she misses two days, she should take two pills as soon as she thinks of the omission and then take two on the scheduled time the following day; a backup contraceptive should also be used until the next menses begins. When a client misses three or more pills, she should not take a pill until after the next menses occurs and she should use the backup contraceptive through the first 14 days of the new pill cycle.

The only significant reason for failure is the missing of one or more tablets during the cycle of medication (Pritchard, 1971). Women who choose to use the pill should be provided with a backup method such as foam, condom, or diaphragm. Information about a backup method should be presented and demonstrated as carefully and thoughtfully as with the method of choice.

The pill may cause unpleasant side effects such as nausea, weight increase, spotting or irregular bleeding, and tenderness of the breasts. Contraindications for use occur when a woman is over 40 years old, smokes, or has a history of circulatory problems, high blood pressure, migraine headaches, epilepsy, diabetes, or asthma.

Some people believe their sexual desires may be affected by the pill. Masters and Johnson (1966) reported that a reduction in a woman's sexual drive occurs after taking the pill for 18 to 30 months. Brazonier (1976) reported that it is unclear whether there is an increase or decrease in the sexual desire of women using oral contraceptives. Some women report that freedom from the fear of pregnancy increased their desire for intercourse; others do not experience this. For those women who feel safe about using the pill, it is easy to use, accessible, highly effective, and inexpensive.

The so-called morning-after pill is used for selective conditions. This preparation consists of a high dosage of estrogen used after intercourse to prevent implantation of the fertilized ovum. Although it is not suitable for use as routine or long-term contraception, the morning-after pill can be used in cases of ruptured condom, perforated diaphragm, and unprotected intercourse in a variety of circumstances (Green, 1977).

Barrier Contraception

Condom

Barrier contraceptives are used by many people who choose not to risk alterations in their body chemistry, who feel the need for only occasional protection, or who need a backup method for oral contraceptives.

Perhaps the oldest and still the most commonly used mechanical barrier is the condom. The condom is a pliable casing that fits over the erect penis and prevents the ejaculate from entering the vagina. Terms used to identify this contraceptive include "rubber," "sheath," and "prophylactic." The condom is probably the regular method used by 10 to 20% of couples currently practicing contraception in this country. Condoms are sold in pharmacies as well as in men's lavatories. To add sensuousness to this contraceptive, manufacturers produce condoms in various colors and textures.

The incorrect use of the condom probably accounts for the unplanned pregnancy that may occur when this method is used (Figure 9.1). Stewart et al. (1979, pp. 82–83) present nine rules for correct use of a condom:

1. Use a condom every time intercourse occurs.
2. Place a condom on before the penis makes any contact near or within the vagina.
3. Leave space at the tip of the condom to collect semen.
4. Hold the rim of the condom securely as the penis is withdrawn from the vagina.
5. Withdraw the penis before erection subsides.
6. Check the condom for leakage before it is discarded.
7. Store condoms away from heat.
8. Do not lubricate condoms with petroleum jellies such as Vaseline.
9. Use a condom only once and discard it.

How the sexual partners perceive the use of the condom can affect its use. Some sexual partners object to the medicinal smell and to the feel of the condom. Other partners state that the condom impairs the sensation of insertion and thrusting of the penis. Still others feel that the application of the condom interrupts the flow of sexual activity. Some men claim difficulty in maintaining an erection when using a condom.

Some of these objections can be overcome by having the sexual partner look at and handle the condom as well as share in the selection of the brand, color, and cost of condom. The partners can experiment with the woman placing the condom on the penis as part of foreplay.

Vaginal Spermicide

About 4 million American women use vaginal spermicides (Stewart et al., 1979). Spermicides are chemical preparations with two actions: to obstruct access to the cervix physically and to kill the sperm by breaking down their surfaces on contact. The sperm-killing action is the more important contraceptive effect.

Spermicides in the form of foams, jellies, creams, or suppositories can be purchased in pharmacies without prescription. They are inserted deep

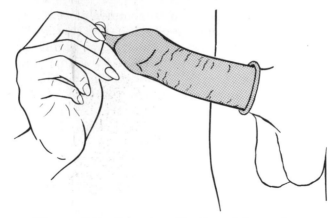

Figure 9.1. Correct application of the condom.

into the vagina. Foam comes with an applicator for insertion. Jellies and creams are usually used in conjunction with other types of contraceptives, such as the diaphragm.

Contraceptive foam must be inserted 15 to 30 minutes before intercourse and must be reapplied if intercourse is repeated. Douching should not be practiced for at least eight hours after ejaculation has occurred. Because leakage may occur, the woman may want to insert a tampon if intercourse has taken place during the active part of her day. The man may make insertion of the foam a part of the foreplay. This is also suggested when the woman feels uncomfortable about touching her own genitalia. Foam can be objectionable to those who desire oral–genital sex. This objection can be overcome by delaying the application of foam until after oral–genital intercourse occurs.

Diaphragm

A diaphragm consists of a latex cup-shaped dome that is mounted on a flexible circular ring. It is approximately the size of the palm of a hand. Before being inserted into the vagina, a spermicidal jelly or cream is placed all over the rim as well as in the cup (Figure 9.2). The latex dome covers the cervix and holds the spermicidal jelly or cream directly against the cervix. The diaphragm must be fitted by a skilled practitioner and may be obtained by prescription.

Instructions for using the diaphragm include demonstration of insertion and removal. The diaphragm must be inspected before and after each use and should be refitted after a pregnancy (six to eight weeks postpartum) or a significant weight loss or gain.

The diaphragm can be inserted up to six hours before intercourse and

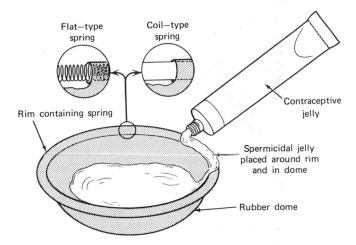

Flat—type spring   Coil—type spring

Rim containing spring

Contraceptive jelly

Spermicidal jelly placed around rim and in dome

Rubber dome

Figure 9.2. The diaphragm

must remain in place for six to eight hours or more after intercourse (Figure 9.3). Douching should not be done until the diaphragm is removed. The diaphragm can contain menstrual flow for several hours and thus can make intercourse possible for those who object to it during menstruation. The insertion of the diaphragm can be integrated into foreplay.

There are no life-threatening risks directly related to using the diaphragm. No contraindications exist; however, women or men who are allergic to latex or spermicides may not be able to use this method.

Some women report that the use of the diaphragm helps them in sexual decision making. Comfort in discussing the use of the diaphragm with a potential sexual partner may be an indication of readiness and willingness to be sexually intimate (Crooks & Baur, 1980). Sharing information and expressing feelings about contraceptives and their use during intercourse can enhance sexual intimacy.

Mechanical Contraception: Intrauterine Device

An intrauterine device (IUD) is a small, lightweight, inert plastic object that is inserted into the uterine cavity. All IUD's have nylon strings that trail out of the uterus through the cervix and into the vagina. The strings must be checked once a week for the first three months and then at least once a month, after each menstrual period, to ensure that the IUD has not been lost. The woman or her sexual partner can check to be sure the device is in place before intercourse. When the IUD string cannot be

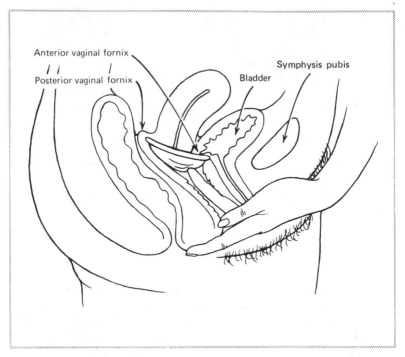

Figure 9.3. Correct insertion of the diaphragm

found, the woman must immediately use a backup method until the presence or absence of the device can be ascertained.

In general, contraindications for using an IUD include previous pelvic inflammatory disease (PID), the presence of uterine fibroids, congenital uterine anomalies, or severe cervicitis (Green, 1977). It is not clearly understood how this device works but it is believed to prevent implantation.

Some men object to the feel of the string during intercourse and some women report having mild, moderate, or severe lower abdominal cramps after the IUD is inserted. These objections or discomforts may require the removal of the IUD and selection of another contraceptive method. Using and IUD does not interrupt sexual activity and requires no extra equipment or supplies except on the days when a backup method is advised.

Behavioral Contraception: Abstinence, Withdrawal, and Rhythm

Abstinence and withdrawal are probably the oldest and most frequently used forms of contraception. Abstinence, withdrawal, and rhythm are valid approaches to contraception; almost everyone relies upon one of these three methods at some time in their lives, and abstinence is probably everybody's first method of contraception. *Abstinence* (the use of self-restraint and self-discipline from sexual activities considered inappropriate or unsuitable) guarantees the absence of conception. Abstinence does not mean denial of sexual activity or sexual expression, but it does mean purposeful avoidance of penile–vaginal intercourse. Sexual partners remain free to participate in oral sex, mutual masturbation, and other forms of sexual activity that are mutually satisfying and pleasurable.

Abstinence is the control of conception through the control of behavior. It is a viable choice for sexual partners who choose to control the sexual behavior that leads to conception and it allows experimentation with and selections of behaviors that enhance sexual intimacy but are free of conception risk.

Withdrawal, or coitus interruptus, is a form of conception control in which the man withdraws the penis before ejaculation. McCary (1966) stated that the bulk of the spermatozoa are contained in the first few drops of the ejaculation. Withdrawal can fail as a contraceptive method when even a few drops of semen enter the vagina. Some sexual partners feel that the crucial timing necessary for effectiveness of this method increases anxiety and lessens enjoyment. Withdrawal, like other forms of behavioral contraception, requires commitment to the method and cooperation by the sexual partners.

Rhythm involves estimating the time period in the menstrual cycle when the woman is ovulating and therefore fertile. As a general rule, ovulation usually occurs at approximately the same date in any given menstrual cycle. In theory, if the date of ovulation can be ascertained, abstinence from vaginal–penile intercourse on that day and for two days before and after would prevent conception.

Menstrual cycles vary and the probable date of ovulation can be estimated by keeping a record of dates of menstruation. It is suggested that a menstrual record be kept for 12 months to determine the fertile (unsafe) and infertile (safe) periods.

When partners commit themselves to the rhythm method, effectiveness is enhanced when the man participates actively in sharing the data collecting as well as by being aware of the cycle timetable. Sharing information can bring the sexual partners closer together. Medvin (1978) states that men who become involved in the process find it exciting rather than mechanical.

The basal body temperature method requires the woman to record her temperature each day at the same time for at least three months. The temperature is best taken upon awakening and before any activity— getting out of bed, using the bathroom, or even answering the telephone. A drop in temperature usually precedes ovulation by about 12 to 24 hours and is followed by a rise for at least three days. These days are considered to be the fertile, or unsafe, period. Because the time immediately before ovulation can also be an unsafe time, relying solely upon a rise in temperature risks conception. Abstinence or the use of another method of birth control is suggested throughout the first half of the menstrual cycle, or at least as soon as the temperature drops, and until it has been elevated for at least three days in a row (Stewart et al., 1979). Data about basal body temperature can be used to increase the accuracy of the estimated day of ovulation for sexual partners using the rhythm method.

The cervical mucus or Billings method depends upon the recognition of changes in the cervical mucus that occur during the menstrual cycle. The cervical mucus undergoes five characteristic changes. The first change follows menstruation, when there is very little cervical mucus and the vagina and the cervix are dry. Change two occurs before ovulation, when the mucus becomes cloudy, white, and sticky. The third change occurs around ovulation, when the mucus becomes less viscous and clear. The fourth change occurs after ovulation, when the amount of mucus decreases and it is cloudy and sticky again. The fifth change occurs just before menstruation, when the cervical mucus is thin, watery, and clear. The fertile or unsafe period is roughly from the beginning of change two through the first four days of change four (Billings, 1973). One month of daily observation and noting of the characteristics of cervical mucus by one or the other of the sexual partners is recommended before relying solely on this method of conception control.

Behavioral methods of conception control require the sexual partners to collect data and become thoroughly familiar with the woman's fertility cycle and to make mutual decisions regarding the timing of vaginal–penile intercourse. The acceptance of responsibility and the development of a caring and sharing attitude deepens the relationship and nourishes sexual intimacy (Medvin, 1978).

Surgical Contraception: Sterilization

Sterilization is a surgical procedure that permanently prevents conception. For men, the primary technique is vasectomy, which involves severing the vas deferens. For women the surgical procedure involves ligating the fallopian tubes. Five different procedures that can be used: (1) laparoscopy, (2) postpartum tubal ligation, (3) vaginal tubal ligation, (4) abdominal tubal ligation, and (5) minilaparotomy.

Sterilization is thought to be 100% effective (Hatcher et al., 1978). Although surgical reconstruction may be attempted, there is no guarantee that it will be successful in restoring fertility, and results are often disappointing. Permanent infertility is the expected outcome of a sterilization procedure. Vasectomy and tubal ligation do not affect hormonal functioning and therefore do not directly affect sexual interest or capacity. For the woman the menstrual periods should be unchanged and for the man there is no noticeable difference in the ejaculate. The woman may find herself more responsive and less inhibited during intercourse because she has no reason to fear an unwanted pregnancy. She may, however, experience a feeling of loss and depression if her sexual self-image and self-concept are strongly influenced by her ability to bear children.

Men who undergo vasectomy frequently fear the effects of other methods of contraception on their sexual partners (Ager et al., 1974). If the man's sexual partner has pressured him into having a vasectomy, the procedure has a greater chance of creating an emotional problem for him (Erikson, 1954). If the man's sense of masculinity was dependent on his capacity to impregnate a woman, he may experience feelings of loss, depression, and anger.

The vasectomy may have an effect upon the relationship. When a relationship is not burdened with problems and the vasectomy has been freely selected, it is unlikely to cause difficulties. However, if the relationship has problems, the vasectomy may be just one more problem with which to contend (Swenson, 1975).

Because sterilization is permanent, it is a highly personal decision. Informed consent and counseling are necessary prerequisites to the sterilization procedure. The decision to become sterile must be free of pressure from either family, friends, significant others, or health professionals. Each person should be helped in reaching his or her own conclusions about how feelings about sterilization may be affected by a change in economic circumstances, a change in marital situation, the possible loss of present children, or involvement with a new sexual partner.

ADOLESCENTS AND CONTRACEPTION

Because of the increase in the number of adolescents who are sexually active by the age of 15 or 16 (many by the age of 12), premarital pregnancies have become a major public-health concern (Alan Guttmacher Institute, 1976). Some people fear that information about and accessibility to contraceptives for adolescents will encourage sexual activity among teenagers. A review of the research indicates, however, that teenagers participate in sexual activities for a number of physical, social, and psychological reasons that have little to do with knowledge of or accessibility to contraceptive services (Chilman, 1980). Review of the literature also shows that teenagers are often sexually active for a year or more before they seek contraceptive services (Chilman, 1980).

Zelnik and Kantner (1980) report that in 1979, by the age of 18, 6 out of 10 women and 7 out of 10 men living in a metropolitan area had had premarital intercourse. Even though more teenagers (age 15–19) are practicing contraception and doing so consistently and early, the number of premarital pregnancies continues to rise. This rise is partially due to the fact that those teenagers who use contraceptives are choosing less effective methods, such as withdrawal, rather than more effective methods, such as the pill.

Contraceptive information needs to be tailored to the behavioral patterns of the individual adolescent. Older adolescents have acquired more knowledge of and experience with their bodily functions than younger adolescents. Among younger adolescents, the sexual partners' attitudes and degree of control within the relationship influence when information about contraception is sought and the type of contraceptive used.

Zelnik and Kantner (1975) have shown that the role of the teenage man is especially important in sexual decision making within adolescent relationships. Education and counseling about contraception needs to be directed to include the adolescent man (Scale, Etelis, & Levits, 1977).

Counseling the young person through the turbulent adolescent period is based on the recognition that one of the primary developmental tasks of this period is to develop the competence to establish intimate interpersonal relationships. The adolescent needs not only information about the technology of contraception but also help in acquiring communication and behavior skills regarding the use of contraceptives in a sexual relationship (Chilman, 1980).

Education and counseling about contraceptives should help adolescents determine how sexually active they really want to be or if they want to be sexually active at all. The adolescent often needs support in learning that initiating or stopping sexual activity involves choice and control over impulses and action that may be uncomfortable or unsuitable for that time and with that person. Responsible decision making about contraception means learning to ask such questions as "How do you feel about contraception?" "What kind of contraception do you use?" or "Do you—do we—need time to apply it?"

MEN AND CONTRACEPTION

Contraceptive information has been directed toward women; men have been assigned a nonparticipatory role. Mutual involvement and satisfaction with the choice of contraceptive is a prerequisite to effective and consistent use. It brings greater equality into the relationship and enhances the sexual partners' understanding of one another (Medvin, 1978).

The women's movement has made it possible for men to reexamine their traditional roles. Men are participating in childbirth and parenting and have begun to insist that they participate in contraception planning as well (Swanson, 1980). For true shared responsibility, men need to know as much as possible about contraception. Effective contraceptive services must include them and be made available to men. Sharing sexual responsibility and accountability for contraception means that men are informed and active participants in contraception planning (Julty, 1979).

SEXUALITY AND INFERTILITY

There are no signs or symptoms of infertility. A person is unaware of the state of his or her fertility until he or she is unable to conceive a child. Then and only then does the need to confront infertility arise. Infertility involves not only the sexual partners but also their families, friends, and significant others who have made an emotional investment in the partners' childbearing capacity. Society has expectations that sexual partners will bear children, and the infertile partner may feel the pressure of these unfulfilled expectations.

The notion that conception may occur after any unprotected act of intercourse is prevalent. Actually, in more than half of partners known to be fertile, conception does not occur until after the third menstrual cycle of unprotected intercourse (Hemsleigh, 1978). By nine months 80% of partners establish a pregnancy. Most specialists consider the 15% of the partners remaining infertile after a year of unprotected intercourse to be in need of evaluation (Pfeffer, 1980).

Green (1977) defines *infertility* as the failure to conceive after a year or more of sexual intercourse. *Absolute infertility*, or *sterility*, indicates an inability to conceive. *Relative infertility* indicates a diminished ability to conceive and includes a possibility that conception can occur.

Effects of Infertility on Sexual Behavior

Infertility may have a profound effect upon the individuals' perception of their gender identity. Being able to conceive a child may be considered synonymous with being a woman or a man. The inability to conceive may be perceived as a loss of self-worth.

When a diagnosis of infertility is confirmed, each of the partners may have to deal with the effect the problem has on himself or herself as well as on the relationship. Mazor (1980) states that the recognition of being infertile may evoke feelings of shock and disbelief, embarrassment, anger, depression, and grief. Resolving the problems related to this personal loss depends upon facilitation of the grieving process.

Linked to the gender identity conflict may be a conflict over one's perception of one's own sexuality. Some people equate fertility with sexuality. Sexuality is not fertility but a concept that is emotionally integrated with fertility. Separating sexuality from fertility is part of the complexity surrounding the resolution of problems of infertility. Successful separation of these concepts may contribute to a more positive attitude of oneself.

Self-worth can be enhanced through open dialogue between the partners. Feelings of being defective or prematurely old and useless can be linked to disappointment in the inability to produce a member of the future generation. Adoption may satisfy the desire to have a child, but the problems of infertility remain. Overcompensation may result from an attempt to be the perfect parent or to have a perfect child. There is no evidence to support the notion that adoption affects the conception rate (Mazor, 1980).

Coping successfully with infertility depends heavily upon the partners' ability to accept disappointment and loss as well as to manage frustration and anger. The fertile partner may suppress anger and disappointment. Suppressed feelings, shame, guilt, and embarrassment may lead to disinterest in the sexual act. Evaluative procedures may also cause a decrease in sexual interest as well as impotence. Transient ejaculatory disturbances resulting from infertility workups are believed to occur in more than half of all cases (Mazor, 1980).

Sexual intercourse may become more like the sharing of a work responsibility than the sharing of intimacy. If a diagnosis of infertility is made there may be a time when the partners' feelings about sex are sad, negative, and threatening (Menning, 1977).

Menning (1977) makes several suggestions that may help the partners appreciate sex for its own sake. Each needs to be receptive to and sensitive of the needs of the other partner. A change in time, positions, and location may serve to break up old associations with unfulfilled expectations and may revitalize the sexual exchange. Sexual counseling may facilitate change in communications and behavior. Finally, once again, the partners need to look to each other in a caring way and again believe in sex for its personal pleasure and partnership fulfillment.

Infertility Assessment

The assessment of sexual partners who are concerned about their infertility is done in a carefully planned progression beginning with a complete health history and a careful physical examination.

The sexual history deserves special attention and care. Sexual dysfunction, such as premature ejaculation or impotence, is responsible for a large number of infertility cases. Some practices are detrimental to conception: for example, lubricants and douches used after intercourse may kill sperm. Intercourse more often than once a day may deplete the sperm count. Intercourse occurring less often than every second day during the middle of the cycle is likely to miss ovulation.

Sterility is not due to a single cause but generally is the result of multiple factors. Laboratory studies should be performed on both sexual partners. Studies are done on the woman to ascertain whether there are malfunctioning of the ovaries and uterus, obstructed fallopian tubes, and conditions within the female genital tract that interfere with sperm transport. Studies are done on the man to ascertain the presence of impaired production of spermatozoa, disorders in secretory function of the accessory sex glands, and obstruction of sperm ducts.

Assessment of infertility continues over several months or years and involves financial and emotional commitment. The affected partners need to know that the diagnosis and treatment of infertility may involve a long and complex process that can add strain to their personal, economic, and sexual lives.

ROLE OF THE NURSE AS EDUCATOR-COUNSELOR

The nurse has an active role as educator-counselor in reproductive management. In this role the nurse recognizes and respects the right of each person either to control conception or promote his or her fertility and to make choices about reproductive management that are consistent with his or her own sexual value system. The nurse must also realize that both men and women make responsible decisions about reproductive management and that these decisions may be subject to reevaluation as changes occur in the sexual relationship, in sexual partners, or in life circumstances.

The nurse as educator provides information to dispel myths and misconceptions about the body and the body processes involved in conception control and infertility management. As counselor, the nurse listens for the concerns, anxieties, and conflicts that the client expresses as he or she deals with sex for procreation and sex for recreation.

As educator-counselor in conception control, the nurse provides accurate information about each of the contraceptive methods available, indicates the options, reviews the risks, and presents the advantages and disadvantages. The nurse guides each person toward the selection of a contraceptive method that is best suited to his or her perceived needs or intended goals.

The nurse must be particularly sensitive in working with adolescents. As adolescents come to grip with feelings that are new, pleasant, different, scary, and unusual to them, they need support that allows them to express their concerns. The nurse can help adolescents cope with sexual decisions by accepting their feelings, being nonjudgmental about their behavior, and guiding them in responsible decision making. The nurse can help adolescents make decisions based on their own innermost feelings and their own developing sexual value system. Adolescents need help in distinguishing sex as an emotional experience from sex as a response to individual or group pressure. Adolescents often seek assurance that it is normal, healthy, and acceptable not to have sex.

Sexual partners who have committed time and energy to infertility management need clear information about the many and different diagnostic procedures and the prescriptions about timing of intercourse. These couples need sensitive counsel and support so that their personal self-esteem and the dignity of their sexual relationship is not impaired or injured by the demands made for the diagnosis and treatment of infertility. Self-help groups, such as the national group RESOLVE, and group support and counseling can contribute to the feelings of wholeness and continuity for infertile partners (Menning, 1976).

Nurses must recognize that conception control and infertility management are a major part of the delivery of sexual health care and should be ready to develop the knowledge base and interpersonal skills necessary to make a significant contribution to the delivery of that care.

NURSING PROCESS: CONCEPTION CONTROL

Client: Fern Dowling, 22 years old, divorced six months, one child—15 months old.

Nurse: Joe Nolting, staff nurse-practitioner at a family-planning clinic in the midwest.

Assessment

Subjective Data

"I'm here for birth control."

"When I was married, I used foam or he used a condom." "He didn't like condoms, so most of the time it was me and the foam. But I was always nervous so I used a douche afterward just to be safe."

"I need something better now because I'm going with a guy and neither of us wants me to get pregnant."

"We plan on getting married someday, but neither of us is ready for that yet."

"I want a birth-control that won't hassle me or him even though he says he'll use a condom if he really has to."

"I don't want the pill because my friend used it and had problems and my boyfriend said he heard you shouldn't use them if you smoke."

"Yes, I do have lots of problems with my periods, mostly cramping and heavy flow the first two days."

Objective Data

Induced abortion at 16.
Lives with 15-month-old daughter in two-bedroom apartment in suburbs.
Works evenings as waitress in large hotel downtown.
Receives child-support payments irregularly.
Indicates tips supplement salary satisfactorily.
Nearest relative 150 miles away.
Neighbor cares for child in her own apartment during hours client works.
Believes first pregnancy resulted from inadequate contraception.
Will not consider use of pill.
History of late menarche, dysmenorrhea, menorrhagia.
Partner prefers not to use condom.

Nursing Diagnosis

Seeking reliable contraceptive method because of sexual relationship.

Planning

Obtain menstrual history.
Obtain medical history.
Perform pelvic and breast examination.
Discuss methods of contraception using samples and visual aids.
Discuss effectiveness rate, risks, advantages and disadvantages, and contraindications.
Encourage mutual decision making.
Discuss mutual responsibility in fertility control.
Discuss relationship of choice of method, accurate use, and vigilant practice.
Advise that negative comments from others be regarded with minimal significance.
Explore feelings about methods presented and facilitate a choice.

Measure for diaphragm and demonstrate application of spermicidal jelly on plastic model.

Explain procedure for insertion and removal of diaphragm. Observe client insert and remove diaphragm.

Explain use of diaphragm as part of foreplay.

Schedule reappointment for evaluation of method in two weeks.

Implementation

Initiate discussion of choice of contraceptives with sexual partner.
Explain choice of diaphragm as contraceptive method to sexual partner.
Initiate discussion of mutual responsibility in fertility control.
Discuss correct use of diaphragm and vigilant practice.
Discuss insertion of diaphragm as part of foreplay.
Encourage sharing feelings.
Encourage participation in mutual decision making.
Schedule follow-up appointment at family planning clinic.

Evaluation

Reports partner's positive attitude toward method chosen.
States partner prefers not using condom.
Partner receptive to insertion of diaphragm as part of foreplay.
Reports vigilant practice.
Reports satisfaction with chosen method.

NURSING PROCESS: INFERTILITY

Client: Monique Shawnasee, 28 years old, married six years, no children.

Nurse: Meg Thornbird, nurse working with gynecologist specializing in infertility management.

Assessment

Subjective Data

"We've been trying to get pregnant for three years."
"We both come from large families and having children is important to us as well as to our relatives."

"We didn't try to have children right away because I had my shop but now that my shop is established I don't need to spend as much time there."

"My family as well as his seems to put more and more pressure on us."

"His family really gets to me—says my shop is more important than he is."

"I can't seem to tell them that we've been trying everything we know for so long that it isn't like they think it is."

"I can't and won't tell them about us wanting and trying."

"He doesn't discuss it with them because he knows how I feel about it and he feels the same way."

"He says it's no one's business."

Objective Data

Client is owner of successful boutique.

Husband is football coach of small private university.

IUD insertion before marriage six years ago, used for six months.

Removal of IUD because of severe cramping and intermittent bleeding.

Tried foam and condom. Method found to be sexually inhibiting.

Used pill for two years without interruption; stopped three years ago.

Has used no contraceptive for three years.

Menses regularly occurring every 30–32 days.

Menstrual flow heavy first day, moderate for three days, scant brownish discharge follows for approximately three days.

Intercourse experienced two times per week; female-on-top position preferred.

Douches occasionally immediately after intercourse.

Believes pleasure with sexual act is diminishing.

Difficulty in expressing feelings—drops eyes, remains quiet for long periods, and repeats statements several times.

Nursing Diagnosis

Seeking information about fertility due to couple's inability to conceive.

Planning

Obtain medical history.

Perform physical examination.

Discuss myths surrounding infertility.

Explore sexual self-concept.

Discuss feelings regarding sexual partner (husband).

Discuss feelings about sexual relationship.

Discuss methods for determining fertile period.

Discuss record keeping.

Discuss significance of planned intercourse.

Discuss mutual responsibility and commitment to prescribed sexual regimen.

Encourage mutual discussion about maintaining sexual relations as a pleasure bond.

Provide information about counseling services.

Schedule appointment in one month.

Indicate availability for further information and counseling.

Implementation

Initiate discussion and ventilation of feelings.

Discuss data obtained from history and physical examination.

Discuss methods of determining fertile period.

Explain record keeping.

Discuss use of counseling service.

Share feelings about prescribed sexual regimen.

Schedule appointment with counseling service.

Partners arrange time for appointment in one month.

Evaluation

Reports compliance with sexual regimen.

Reports satisfactory record keeping.

Indicates satisfaction with counseling service.

Reports enhancement of sexual relationship.

BIBLIOGRAPHY

Ager, J., Werley, H., Allen, D., Shea, F., & Lewis, H. Vasectomy: Who gets one and why? *American Journal of Public Health*, 1974, *64*, 680–686.

Alan Guttmacher Institute. *Eleven million teenagers: What can be done about the epidemic of adolescent pregnancies in the United States.* New York: Author, 1976.

Behrman, S. J., & Kistner, F. *Progress in infertility* (2nd ed.). Boston: Little, Brown, 1975.

Belleny, E. L., Billings, J. J., & Catarinick, M. *Atlas of the ovulation method.* Collegeville, Md.: Liturgical Press, 1974.

Belsky, R. Vaginal contraceptives: A time for reappraisal? *Population Reports* (Ser H., No. E). Washington, D.C.: George Washington University Medical Center, 1975.

Billings, J. J. *Natural family planning: The ovulation method.* Collegeville, Md.: Liturgical Press, 1973.

Bloom, L., & Houston, K. The psychological effects of vasectomy for American men. *The Journal of Genetic Psychology*, 1976, *128*, 173–182.

Boston Women's Health Book Collective. *Our bodies, ourselves* (2nd ed.). New York: Simon & Schuster, 1976.

Brazonier, J. R. Influence of oral contraception on sexual response. *Medical Aspects of Human Sexuality*, 1976, *10*, 130–143.

Cates, W., & Tietze, C. Standardized mortality rates associated with legal abortions: *Family Planning Perspectives*, 1978, *10*, 109–112.

Cooke, C. W., & Dworkin, S. *The Ms. guide to a woman's health.* Garden City, N.Y.: Anchor Books, 1979.

Chilman, C. S. *Adolescent sexuality in a changing American society.* Washington, D.C.: Department of Health, Education, and Welfare, 1980.

Crooks, R., & Baur, K. *Our sexuality.* Menlo Park, Cal.: Benjamin/Cummings, 1980.

Diamond, M. Sex and reproduction: Conception and contraception. In R. Green (Ed.), *Human sexuality: a health practitioner's text* (2nd ed.). Baltimore: Williams & Wilkins, 1979.

Dor, J., Homburg, R., & Rabaw, E. An evaluation of etiologic factors and therapy in 665 infertile couples. *Fertility and Sterility*, 1977, *28*, 92–94.

Dumm, J. J., Piotrow, P. T., & Dalsimer, I. A. The modern condom—A quality product for effective contraception (Population Report H-21). Washington, D.C.: George Washington University Medical Center, 1974.

Elder, R. G. Orientation of senior nursing students toward access to contraceptives. *Nursing Research* 1976, *25*, 338–345.

Erikson, M. H. The psychological significance of vasectomy. In H. Rosen (Ed.), *Therapeutic abortion.* New York: Julian Press, 1954.

Goldsmith, S., Gabrielson, M. O., Gabrielsen, I., Matthews, V., & Potts, L. Teenagers, sex, and contraception. *Family Planning Perspectives*, 1972, *4*, 32–38.

Gordon, S. *The sexual adolescent.* North Scituate, Mass.: Duxbury Press, 1973.

Green, T. H., Jr. *Gynecology, essentials of clinical practice* (3rd ed.). Boston: Little, Brown, 1977.

Harrison, M. *Infertility, a couple's guide to causes and treatments.* Boston: Houghton Mifflin, 1977.

Hatcher, R. A., & Adams, J. B. Solving the teenage pregnancy problem. *Medical Aspects of Human Sexuality*, 1980, *14*, 15–18; 23.

Hatcher, R. A., Stewart, G. K., Stewart, F., Guest, F., Stratton, P., & Wright, A. H. *Contraceptive technology 1978–1979* (9th ed.). N.Y.: Irvington Publishers, Inc., 1978.

Hemsleigh, P. Infertility. In M. V. Barnard, F. J. Clancy, & K. E. Krantz (Eds.), *Human sexuality for health professionals.* Philadelphia: Saunders, 1978.

Himes, N. E. *Medical History of Contraception.* New York: Schocken Books, 1970.

Hogan, R. *Human sexuality: a nursing perspective.* New York: Appleton-Century-Crofts, 1980.

Huber, S. C. IUD's reassessed—A decade of experience. *Population Reports* (Ser B., No. 2). Washington, D.C.: George Washington University Medical Center, 1975.

Huggins, G. Contraceptive use and subsequent fertility. *Modern Trends,* 1977, *28,* 603–611.

Hunt, W. B. *Adolescent fertility—Risks and consequences* (Population Report, J-154). Washington, D.C.: George Washington University Medical Center, Department of Medical and Public Affairs, 1976.

Jaffe, F. S., & Dryfoos, J. G. Fertility control services for adolescents: Access and utilization. *Family Planning Perspectives,* 1976, *8,* 167.

Julty, S. *Men's bodies/men's selves.* New York: Delta, 1979.

Kahn, H., & Tyler, C. IUD-related hospitalization: United States and Puerto Rico. *Journal of the American Medical Association,* 1976, *234,* 53–56.

Kistner, R. W. The infertile woman. *American Journal of Nursing,* 1973, *73,* 1937–1943.

Klaus, H., Goebel, J., Woods, R. E., Castles, M., & Zimny, G. Use-effectiveness and analysis of satisfaction levels with Billings's ovulation method: Two-year pilot study. *Fertility and Sterility,* 1977, *28,* 1038–1043.

Kremer, J. Infertility: Male and female. In J. Money & H. Musaph (Eds.), *Handbook of sexology: Procreation and parenthood.* New York: Elsevier, 1978.

Lee, R. V. The case for chastity. *Medical Aspects of Human Sexuality,* 1980, *14,* 57–58.

Lidz, R. W. Conflicts between fertility and infertility. In M. F. Nortman & C. C. Nadelson (Eds.), *The woman patient: Medical and psychological interfaces.* New York: Plenum Press, 1978.

Masters, W. H., & Johnson, V. E. *Human sexual response.* Boston: Little, Brown, 1966.

Mazor, M. D. Psychosexual problems of the infertile couple. *Medical Aspects of Human Sexuality,* 1980, *14,* 32; 39; 43; 47–49.

Medvin, M. R. Natural birth control: A man's view. In E. Bauman, A. Brint, L. Piper, & P. Wright (Eds.), *The holistic health handbook.* Berkeley, Cal.: And/Or Press, 1978.

Menning, B. E. *Infertility, a guide for the childless couple.* Englewood Cliffs, N.J.: Prentice-Hall, 1977.

Menning, B. E. RESOLVE: A support group for infertile couples. *American Journal of Nursing,* 1976, *76,* 2.

Mims, F. H., & Swenson, M. *Sexuality: A nursing perspective.* New York: McGraw-Hill, 1980.

Nofziger, M. *A cooperative method of natural birth control* (3rd ed.). Summertown, Tenn.: The Book Publishing Company, 1979.

Peck, E., & Senderowitz, J. *Pronatalism: The myth of mom and applie pie.* New York: Crowell, 1974.

Pfeffer, W. H. An approach to the diagnosis and treatment of the infertile female. *Medical Aspects of Human Sexuality,* 1980, *14,* 121–122.

Phillips, J., Hulka, J., Keith, D., Hulka, B., & Keith, L. Laparoscopic procedures: A national survey for 1975. *Journal of Reproductive Medicine,* 1977, *18,* 219–225.

Pritchard, J. A., & Hellman, L. M. *Williams obstetrics* (14th ed.). New York: Appleton-Century-Crofts, 1971.

Robbie, M. O. Health care for adolescents. Contraceptive counseling for the younger adolescent woman: A suggested solution to the problem. Part III, *JOGN Nursing,* 1978, 7, 29–33.

Ross, M. A., & Piotrow, P. T. Birth control without contraceptives. *Population Reports* (Ser I., No. 1). Washington, D.C.: George Washington University Medical Center, 1974.

Ryder, N. B. Contraceptive failure in the United States. *Family Planning Perspectives*, 1973, 5, 133–142.

Scales, D., Etelis, R., & Levitz, N. Birth control counselors' involvement of young males in contraceptive decision making. *Journal of Community Health,* 1977, 3, 54–60.

Stewart, F. H., Stewart, G. K., Guest, F. J., & Hatcher, R. A. *My body, my health: The concerned woman's guide to gynecology.* New York: Wiley, 1979.

Stycos, J. M. Desexing birth control. *Family Planning Perspectives*, 1977, 9, 286–292.

Swanson, J. M. Knowledge, knowledge, who's got the knowledge? The male contraceptive career. *Journal of Sex Education and Therapy,* 1980, 2, 51–56.

Swenson, I. Psychological consideration in vasectomy: A review of literature. *JOGN Nursing,* 1975, 4, 29–32.

Taylor, D. Contraceptive counseling and care. In R. T. Mercer (Ed.), *Perspectives on adolescent health care.* Philadelphia: Lippincott, 1979.

Tietze, C., & Lewit, S. Use-effectiveness of oral and intrauterine contraception. *Fertility and Sterility*, 1971, 22, 508–513.

Tyrer, L. B. Checking for IUD strings. *Medical Aspects of Human Sexuality*, 1980, 14, 21, 87–88.

Vaughan, B., Trussell, J., Menken, J., & Jones, E. F. Contraceptive failure among married women in the United States, 1970–1973. *Family Planning Perspectives,* 1977, 9, 251–258.

Whelan, E. M. *A baby? . . . maybe.* New York: Bobbs-Merrill, 1975.

Woods, N. F., & Luke, C. Sexuality, fertility, and infertility. In N. F. Woods (Ed.), *Human sexuality in health and illness* (2nd ed.). St. Louis: Mosby, 1979.

Wortman, J., & Piotrow, P. The vaginal approach. *Population Reports* (Ser C., No. 3). Washington, D.C.: George Washington University Medical Center, 1973.

Zelnik, M., & Kantner, J. Attitudes of American teenagers to abortion. *Family Planning Perspectives*, 1975, 7, 89–91.

Zelnik, M., & Kantner, J. Sexual and contraceptive experience of young unmarried women in the United States, 1976 and 1971. *Family Planning Perspectives,* 1977, 9, 55–71.

Zelnik, M., & Kantner, J. Sexual activity, contraceptive use and pregnancy among metropolitan-area teenagers: 1971–1979. *Family Planning Perspectives*, 1980, 12, 230–237.

10. Sexuality During Pregnancy, the Postpartum Period, and Lactation

Elizabeth M. Lion

VALUES CLARIFICATION EXERCISES

In general, our society is comfortable with the reproductive aspects of sexuality. Poets, artists, and songwriters depict loving mothers, contented babies, and happy families. This exercise is meant to have you look at and work with the feelings, attitudes, information, and beliefs that you have about the meaning of pregnancy and the sexual roles of the pregnant woman and her partner.

React to these statements and questions. Pay attention to the feelings you have and make note of them. As you respond, ask yourself these questions: How did I come to these beliefs? How did I acquire this information? Are my beliefs shared by other members of my family? Do my beliefs protect me from anything? Do my beliefs make somebody right and somebody wrong?

1. Which of these phrases best describes your concept of a pregnant woman: A person who will give birth to another person? A woman heavy with child? A wife bearing her husband's child? A mother-to-be? Is your concept different from any of these? How would you phrase your concept?

2. How does being pregnant affect a woman's sexual interest, desire, and functioning? What should be a pregnant woman's concern about her partner's sexual interest, desire, and functioning during pregnancy? After pregnancy?

3. Does sexual activity during pregnancy affect the baby? Should sexual activity be restricted by health professionals at any time during pregnancy? After pregnancy? For what reasons?

4. How do you feel when a woman says she prefers to nurse her child?

How do you feel when a man says he would prefer his sexual partner not to nurse?

5. How do you feel when you see a woman nursing a child in your home? at church? at a restaurant? on the job? Happy? Pleased? Embarrassed? Curious? Detached? Interested? Disgusted? Degraded? Angry? Scared? Uncertain? Militant? Helpless? Giggly? Shocked?

Now share your responses and reactions with a group of peers and colleagues. Were there any beliefs that most of the group shared? Was there a range of beliefs shared by the group? How had the information been acquired? How could beliefs or information affect nurse–client interactions?

BEHAVIORAL OBJECTIVES

After completing this chapter, you will be able to

- Identify the objective and subjective effects of pregnancy on the female sexual response cycle.
- Summarize the findings of studies on sex and sexuality during pregnancy.
- Explain the relationship of body image and pregnancy.
- Discuss the need for physical closeness during pregnancy.
- Summarize the findings of studies about the possible association between intercourse and the various complications of late pregnancy, delivery, and the puerperium.
- Summarize the findings of studies about the possible relationship between orgasm and premature labor.
- Explain the relationship of birth behavior to coital orgasm.
- Identify the objective and subjective effects of the postpartum period on the female sexual response cycle.
- Summarize the findings of studies on sex and sexuality during the postpartum period.
- Discuss the sensual and sexual effects of breast-feeding on the mother, the family, and society.
- Discuss the reactions of sexual partners to pregnancy and the postpartum period.
- Illustrate sexual health history taking with the pregnant woman and her sexual partner.
- Discuss the role of the nurse as educator-counselor for sexual health during and after pregnancy.

SEXUALITY AND PREGNANCY

Until recently, there has been a lack of objective information about sex and sexuality during pregnancy. For the pregnant woman, child bearing became the primary focus and her sexuality was ignored. If intercourse was mentioned at all, health professionals indicated that it was uncomfortable for the woman and potentially harmful to the unborn child. Also ignored was the sexuality of her partner and the couple's desire or need for continued sexual sharing, caring, and intimacy.

SEXUAL RESPONSE DURING PREGNANCY

Masters and Johnson (1966) did the first study of sexual activity during pregnancy. As part of their study, they evaluated the anatomical and physical changes in the woman's sexual response cycle during pregnancy and the postpartum period. The subjects were six women—two nulliparas (women who have not produced viable offspring) and four multiparas (women who have had two or more pregnancies which resulted in viable offspring). (See Chapter 5 for discussion of sexual response cycle in nonpregnant women.) The findings of the study are summarized in the following sections.

Breasts

Masters and Johnson (1966) reported that the breasts of these women rapidly increased in size during the first trimester as a result of significant increases in the vascular and glandular components of the breasts. During the first trimester, when the nulliparous women responded to sexual stimuli the venous congestion of their breasts became more obvious than when the women were not pregnant. In the first trimester all the women had breast tenderness, and for the nulliparous women this was severe. During the second and third trimesters the breast tenderness decreased for all the women.

Genital Organs

Pregnancy increased the vascularity of the pelvic viscera. All six women reported an awareness of increased sexual tension toward the end of the first trimester or during the early stages of the second trimester. Four women reported abdominal cramping and aching during and after orgasm in the first trimester, and two women complained of low backache. All the women reported a subjective awareness of increased uterine irritability. During the second trimester, all six women reported an awareness of a strong sexual drive marked by an increased interest in intercourse and manipulative activity and intense orgasmic experience.

Excitement Phase

During the excitement phase, the reaction of the major labia of the nullipara followed the usual pattern (Chapter 5). For the multipara, there was a tendency toward excessive engorgement and edema in the major labia, and the minor labia distended to two to three times their unstimulated state. During the third trimester, the minor labia were chronically engorged with blood and fluid, and excitement-phase distention was difficult to demonstrate. All six subjects reported increased vaginal lubrication and the appearance of light mucoid discharge toward the end of the first trimester that continued throughout pregnancy.

By the end of the first trimester the uterus of a pregnant woman is so enlarged that it has become an abdominal organ. After the uterus is elevated into the abdomen, vaginal expansion and distention during sexual excitement continue as in the nonpregnant state. The tenting phenomenon in the transcervical vaginal depth cannot be observed, however.

Plateau Phase

During the plateau phase, the change from pink to red in the skin color of the minor labia, if orgasm was to occur, was the same for the pregnant as for nonpregnant women. In both the nulliparas and the multiparas the severe vasocongestion in the entire vaginal barrel resulted in the development of a more pronounced orgasmic platform. The more advanced the pregnancy, the more severe the venous engorgement and the more pronounced the development of the platform.

Orgasm

Orgasmic platform contractions can be identified during both the first and second trimesters. During the third trimester the orgasmic platform in the outer third of the vagina may be so congested and the entire vaginal barrel so edematous that objective evidence of contractile efficiency is reduced. During the third trimester, the uterus, instead of contracting regularly during orgasmic experience, may go into tonic spasm for as long as one minute. Fetal heart tones were slowed during this period, but there was no further evidence of fetal distress.

Resolution Phase

Resolution-phase reaction during pregnancy differs from that in the non-pregnant state in that the vasocongested pelvis frequently is not relieved completely with orgasm. Masters and Johnson (1966) concluded that the residual pelvic vasocongestion, together with the pelvic pressures of the second- and third-trimester uterus, may account for the high levels of sexual tensions frequently maintained during these stages of pregnancy.

SEXUALITY DURING PREGNANCY

There have been several major studies about women's feelings and sexual behavior during pregnancy and the postpartum period. In addition to the six women studied for sexual response, Masters and Johnson (1966) studied 111 women during pregnancy and the postpartum period. In this group were 43 nulliparous women, 7 of whom were unmarried, and 68 parous women, 2 of whom were unmarried.

In the first trimester, 33 of the nulliparous women reported reduction in sexual tension and effectiveness accompanied by nausea, sleepiness, and chronic fatigue. Twenty-six reported fear of injury to the unborn child as affecting their physical response to intercourse, four reported significant increase in sexual interest and demand for increased rate of performance, and six reported no change. The seven unmarried women reported little or no eroticism during the first trimester. As a group, the 68 parous women reported little change in sexual tension or effectiveness.

During the second trimester there was an increase in eroticism and effectiveness of performance regardless of parity or age. The increased eroticism was reported by women not only as interest in sexual encounters but also as planning for sexual encounters, fantasies of encounters, and sexual dream content. Four unmarried women reported heightened sexual awareness and increased frequency of masturbation as compared with first-trimester activity and their pattern before pregnancy.

During the third trimester the nulliparous women experienced a significant decrease in coital frequency compared with the second trimester. For 31 of the nulliparous women, continence varying from four weeks to three months in length had been prescribed by the physician. Although they were strongly influenced by medical restrictions, 33 of the women reported gradual loss of interest in sexual activity throughout the third trimester.

Continence had been prescribed by physicians for 46 of the parous women for periods ranging from three months to four weeks. Forty-one of the women described a significant reduction in eroticism and frequency of sexual performance. Frequently, parous women admitted that contending with their physical stress and size and with existing children kept them in such a state of chronic exhaustion that they seldom sought the opportunity for sexual intercourse. When directly approached, however, they found that their effectiveness in and capacity for sexual performance surprised them.

Sixty-eight of the 77 women for whom intercourse had been medically restricted were concerned about their husbands' sexual needs. Seventeen of the nulliparous women and 32 of the parous women reported making deliberate attempts to relieve their husbands during the period of medical restrictions. Twenty of the women reported that their husbands withdrew from sex late in the second or early in the third trimester. They attributed the withdrawal to the appearance of their large abdomens, the husbands' concern for their personal comfort, and fear of injury to the unborn child.

Solberg, Butler, and Wagner (1973) interviewed 260 women in the immediate postpartum period to gather data about their sexuality during pregnancy. Unlike the Masters and Johnson study (1966), the most significant finding was a steady and consistent linear decrease in sexual intercourse during pregnancy for the majority of the women. Also, Masters and Johnson reported a distinct association between parity and sexual interest levels in the first trimester, whereas the Solberg study reported no significant difference in sexual-interest level between nulliparous and parous women throughout pregnancy.

Solberg, Butler, and Wagner (1973) found that the frequency of intercourse was significantly age related, with younger women tending to be more active. Length of marriage was significant; frequency of intercourse tended to decrease with length of marriage. Frequency of intercourse during pregnancy was not related to race, religious preference, or whether or not the pregnancy was planned. The variable most consistently associated with frequency of intercourse was the woman's level of sexual interest during pregnancy as compared with the level of her interest before the pregnancy. Only in the last month of pregnancy was there no significant relationship between sexual interest and activity.

The Solberg study found that the rate of orgasm with intercourse decreased as the pregnancy progressed. There was also a general decrease in the strength or intensity of orgasm compared with prepregnancy experience. A consistent percentage of women reported an increase in orgasmic intensity at all stages of pregnancy, however. As with frequency of intercourse, the rate of orgasm throughout the pregnancy was not significantly related to sexual interest.

Other sexual behaviors engaged in to reach orgasm were studied. There was a decrease in the number of women who masturbated during pregnancy and in the number who used manual stimulation by the partner, but the rates of orgasm did not change. The number of women who used oral–genital stimulation did not change during pregnancy, but the rate of orgasm declined in the advanced stages of pregnancy.

The positions used for intercourse during pregnancy changed as the pregnancy progressed. There was a notable decrease in the use of the male-on-top position and an increase in use of the side-by-side position and rear entry. Variability in positions used tended to decrease throughout the pregnancy.

Women reporting a change in degree or intensity of their sexual experience were questioned about the reasons for the change. Their reasons were: physical discomfort, 46%; fear of injury to baby, 27%; loss of interest, 23%; awkwardness having coitus, 17%; recommendation of physician, 8%; reasons extraneous to pregnancy, 6%; loss of attractiveness in woman's own mind, 4%; recommendation other than physician, 1%; and other reasons, 15%.

Falicov (1973) studied the nature, frequency, and timing of the changes in sexual adjustment, the underlying factors, and the attitude toward these changes in a group of 19 primigravidas (women pregnant for the first time). The women were interviewed five times during their pregnancies and twice during the postpartum period. By the end of the first trimester, 14 had experienced a moderate or marked decrease in coital frequency, sexual desire and involvement shortly after conception. Tiredness, sleepiness, and heartburn were the reasons mentioned for the decline in sexual involvement, and increased severity of the symptoms was associated with decreased sexual activity. Some somatic complaints related to sexual functioning were mentioned by six women. These included changes in the sexual organs, such as the vagina feeling smaller, which made penetration uncomfortable, and a feeling of vaginal numbness, which interfered with experiencing orgasm. For 10 women, fear of harming the fetus inhibited sexual enjoyment.

In the second trimester, coital frequency and sexual satisfaction were slightly increased but continued at below the prepregnancy levels. Sexual desire remained at the diminished first-trimester levels. Nausea and heartburn decreased, but tiredness, breast tenderness, and genital discomfort were reported to interfere with sexual readiness. The need to change positions or modify movements because of the enlarging abdomen interfered with sexual satisfaction. The fear of harming the fetus remained for nine women.

During the seventh and eighth months, seven women reported fluctuations in sexual desire. Half of the women who had reported decreased eroticism found intercourse more relaxed and enjoyable in spite of heaviness and clumsiness. The fear of harming the fetus had abated. Despite a relative increase in sexual interest, by the eighth month 15 of the 18 women had stopped having intercourse. Five of the couples had been advised to do so by their physicians. The other ten had read or had heard that sexual abstinence was recommended. Two couples subsequently stopped at three weeks before their due date, and one couple did not stop.

The attitudes of the wives and husbands to the changes in sexual adjustment ranged from intense frustration and resentment to almost indifferent acceptance. In the first trimester, half of the couples accepted the decline in sexual activity as a natural part of pregnancy, but over one-third of the couples found it difficult to adjust to unanticipated changes. By the second trimester, sexual interaction had come to be regarded by 10 women as an avenue for affective communication rather than for erotic stimulation. Their husbands seemed to accept this attitude and the temporary necessity for it. For four husbands the quickening seemed to introduce a third human being, which slightly disturbed sexual intimacy and possibly inhibited their sexual initiative. During the first part of the third trimester, seven women expressed frustration and resentment at having to abstain from sexual relations, nine women said they had adjusted but felt guilty about their husbands' forced abstinence, particularly because eight husbands stated their impatience and frustration. A few husbands appeared to be attracted to the maternal qualities of their wives' abdomens, but others expressed a longing for their wives' non-pregnant looks.

Tolor and DiGrazia (1976) studied 216 women seen by obstetricians and gynecologists in office practice. The subjects were divided into four groups: 54 first-trimester women, 51 second-trimester women, 56 third-trimester women, and 54 women who were six weeks postpartum. Each woman was given a questionnaire seeking information about present and previous sexual behavior and administered an attitude-toward-sex scale, measuring sexual conservativism versus liberalism. The physicians placed no restrictions on sexual activity during the pregnancy except when such complications as bleeding occurred.

The three groups of pregnant women reported a decline in their desire for intercourse and a decrease in frequency, with the lowest level occurring in the third trimester, when almost one out of three women abstained. First- and second-trimester women seemed satisfied with the prevailing sexual activity rate, whereas third-trimester women were less satisfied and preferred to have either more sexual activity or less. There was a significantly greater incidence of multiple orgasms in the second-trimester women and a significantly greater incidence of no multiple orgasms in third trimester women. There was a significant decline in interest levels in sex as pregnancy progressed. The degree of conservatism or liberalism in sexual attitudes was not found to be significantly related to sexual behavior or attitudes toward sex during pregnancy.

Bing and Coleman (1977) asked several hundred couples who had access to childbirth education or human sexuality education to report their experiences during pregnancy, labor, and the postpartum period. Detailed replies were received, and the respondents' statements were used to exemplify the goal of honest and sensitive communication between the pregnant woman and her sexual partner about sex and sexuality during and after pregnancy. The four typical patterns of interest in sex reported were: steady increase; down in the first trimester, up in the second, and down in the third; more or less steady decline with some fluctuations; and no change. Steady increase was the most frequently reported pattern (Figure 10.1).

In the first trimester, the couples reported a new freedom to enjoy intercourse related to the joy of being pregnant and the absence of contraception. There were also reports of the couples dealing with sleepiness, nausea, fatigue, and the fear of harming the fetus (Figure 10.2). The couples reported that generally the second trimester was the most comfortable period of pregnancy. The initial adjustment to being pregnant had been made, feelings of nausea and fatigue had passed, fear of harming the fetus had gone, and the abdomen was not large enough to present an obstacle to intercourse. The couples reported experimenting with and discovering new positions and dealing with the anxiety of premature labor. Some women reported feelings of inwardness and self-absorption with the pregnancy and feelings of being awkward, ungainly, and ugly. Some men reported negative responses to the enlarged abdomen and swollen breasts of their wives. Some couples reported finding beauty and joy in the pregnant figure.

In general, the data from these studies and reports indicate a decline in sexual interest and activity, with some increased interest in physical closeness as the pregnancy progresses. The data do contain reports of women with heightened sexuality throughout the pregnancy, and heightened sexuality during the second trimester, however. Pregnancy appears to be a unique event in terms of each woman's sexuality and must be treated as such. Knowledge of the most likely effects of pregnancy can help dispel anxiety and assist the pregnant woman and her sexual partner in dealing with their own experience and in seeking their own solutions to the common problems of pregnancy.

BODY IMAGE AND PREGNANCY

Throughout pregnancy, a woman is confronted with progressive bodily changes and profound changes in personal, interpersonal, and social roles. These changes alter her self-image and therefore her sexual self-concept and sexual behavior. Some investigators have sought to prove that nausea and vomiting during pregnancy are organic, others that they are psychologic, and each investigator has claimed an effective treat-

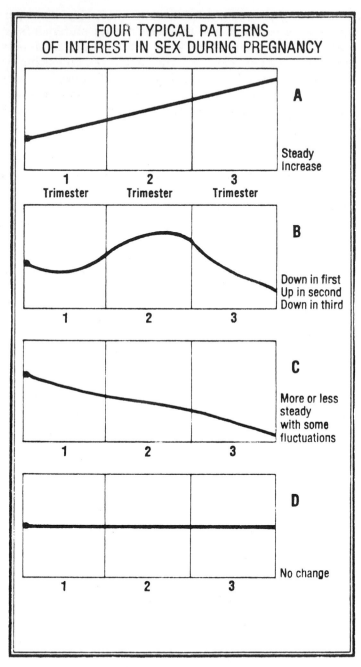

Figure 10.1. From *Making Love During Pregnancy* by Elizabeth Bing and Libby Coleman. Copyright © 1977 by Elizabeth Bing and Libby Coleman. Reprinted with permission of Bantam Books, Inc. All rights reserved.

266

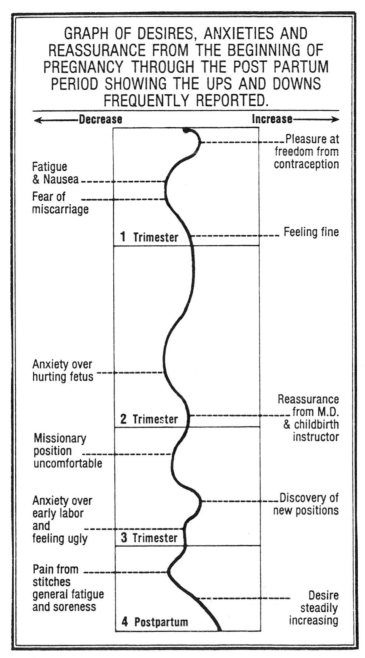

Figure 10.2. From *Making Love During Pregnancy* by Elizabeth Bing and Libby Coleman. Copyright © 1977 by Elizabeth Bing and Libby Coleman. Reprinted with permission of Bantam Books, Inc. All rights reserved.

ment. Semmens (1971) investigated the relationship of a woman's view of her sexual self-concept and behavior and the incidence of nausea and vomiting. A psychosocialsexual profile was administered to 200 pregnant women who requested treatment for nausea and vomiting, 80 women with excessive weight gain, and a control group of women who had no nausea with their past or present pregnancies.

The quantitative profiles of the women with nausea and vomiting indicated that 92% enjoyed intercourse and 75% had orgasms. Eighty-five percent of the women with nausea and vomiting saw themselves as attractive and evaluated their sexuality in a favorable fashion similar to that of the control group. Ninety-three percent of the weight gainers enjoyed intercourse and 60% had orgasms. Only 50% saw themselves as attractive, 40% thought their husbands felt they were unattractive, about 60% felt that their husbands were more interested in the children they produced than in them, and 16% questioned their husbands' fidelity.

In the qualitative profiles of the group with nausea and vomiting, the short-term duration of personal concerns and conflicts suggested that nausea and vomiting represented a reaction to forces that interfered with the projection of self-image. Their anxieties were caused by life situations, family, friends, and society, which threatened the self-image they had selected. In contrast, the weight gainers listed similar concerns and conflicts but reflected increased depth of involvement, and the chronic nature of their problems and frustrations was best exemplified by their poor concept of their own sexuality. Semmens (1971) concluded that successful treatment depended on understanding the woman's total sexuality and assisting her in the adoption of acceptable and realistic self-images.

Anticipatory guidance is helpful (Iffrig, 1974). The pregnant woman needs information beforehand about what to expect. By imagining in advance what pregnancy will be like, she is able to lower her anxiety and develop a readiness for a healthy reaction. Physical and psychologic changes can be described in detail, and the pregnant woman can be given an opportunity to ask questions about her feeling and anxieties and to rehearse, in an accepting atmosphere, what might be coming.

PREGNANCY AND THE NEED FOR CLOSENESS

Bing and Coleman (1977) noted, through the words of pregnant women and their sexual partners, that physical closeness, holding, cuddling, and caressing help partners share their joys and sorrows and stay in touch with each other's changing needs. Being held or cuddled may relieve a woman's feeling of anxiety or depression, gratify dependency needs, afford a sense of closeness, and reassure her that she is loved.

Security, protection, comfort, contentment, and love are words women have used repeatedly in describing the feelings derived from being held (Hollender, 1971; Hollender, Luborsky, & Harvey, 1970). Hollender and McGehee (1974) conducted a study to determine if the wish to be held increases during pregnancy, is influenced by race, or differs during first and second pregnancies. Fifty women, 25 black and 25 white, filled out a body-contact questionnaire at their first prenatal clinic visit. More than half of the women noted a change in their wish to be held (31), and of those who did, approximately three out of four reported an increased desire (23). The white group tended to score higher on the wish to be held or cuddled than the black group, but the finding could be due to differences in marital status rather than racial factors (14 of the 17 single women were black). Approximately as many women in their second pregnancy reported an increase in the wish to be held as did those in their first.

Tolor and DiGrazia (1976) found a high incidence of a woman's need for close physical contact in 216 women divided into first-, second-, and third-trimester and six-weeks-postpartum groups. The question "When I make love I like to be held" elicited a response of "always" from more than 70% of the women. When women were asked to complete the statement, "On those occasions when I am not in the mood for sexual intercourse, I now prefer . . . " "just to be held" was by far the most frequently selected alternative.

The data from these studies and reports suggested that during pregnancy, the need for physical closeness is high. The need for closeness may be a significant topic to include in discussions with partners preparing for or experiencing pregnancy.

INTERCOURSE DURING PREGNANCY

Masters and Johnson (1966) state that for the majority of women there is no reason to refrain from intercourse during the first trimester. However, women with poor obstetrical histories may be cautioned to refrain from intercourse and orgasm during these months. During the second trimester, there is no reason to refrain from intercourse for the overwhelming majority of women. Late in the third trimester, when the presenting part is engaged and the cervix descends into the main axis of the vagina, intercourse may produce vaginal and abdominal discomfort. Vigorous thrusting may cause the penis to strike the cervix. This direct contact between the erect penis and the vasoconstricted predelivery cervix may result in spotting or bleeding after intercourse. Although the woman can control the depth of penetration by placing her hand on the shaft of the penis, Masters and Johnson (1966) recommend restriction of intercourse if spotting and bleeding occur. Any substantial bleeding, at any time during the pregnancy, is a contraindication to intercourse until the source of the bleeding is diagnosed and the bleeding is satisfactorily managed.

In the third trimester, the enlarged abdomen can be an obstacle to intercourse. The pregnant woman and her sexual partner can be encouraged to experiment and discover new positions and techniques. They may find individual variations of the woman-on-top position (Figure 10.3), the side-lying position (Figure 10.4), the rear-entry position (Figure 10.5), and the rear-entry position with woman masturbating (Figure 10.6) comfortable and enjoyable. The pregnant woman and her sexual partner need not be limited to intercourse as their primary method of sexual activity. A range of expressions—caressing, touching, kissing, oral sex, and manual stimulation of erotic areas—are available.

One of the major reasons for discontinuing sexual intercourse is the fear of harm to the fetus, either by infection or by bringing on labor prematurely. The earliest study to examine the effects of intercourse in late pregnancy was done by Pugh and Fernandez (1953). They studied 500 women admitted to a general hospital and found no significant relationship between the time of last intercourse before delivery and puerperal infection or premature rupture of fetal membranes. Among the

Figure 10.3.   Woman on top position.

Figure 10.4. Side lying position.

women who had experienced premature labor, there was a statistically significant difference between those who had had intercourse shortly before delivery and those who had not, when compared with all other women. However, the investigators questioned whether a cause-and-effect relationship existed, since the median time of last intercourse before delivery was 21 days. The conclusion was that intercourse was not responsible for the various complications of late pregnancy, delivery, and the puerperium frequently attributed to it.

In the study by Solberg, Butler, and Wagner (1973), none of the 260 women noticed the immediate onset of labor after intercourse or orgasm. Birth weight, gestational age at delivery, and Apgar scores at one minute were all independent of intercourse and orgasm in the last trimester. Lukesch (1976) interviewed 239 women in the immediate postpartum period regarding sexual behavior during pregnancy. No relationship was found between sexual intercourse in late pregnancy and complications of childbirth.

Naeye (1979) analyzed the data from 26,886 births from 1959 to 1966 to determine whether intercourse was involved in amniotic fluid infections. The frequency of infection was 156 per 1,000 births when mothers reported intercourse once or more per week during the month before delivery and 117 per 1,000 when no intercourse was reported. The percentage of infected infants who died was 11.0 when there was intercourse and 2.4 when there was no intercourse. The findings indicated that intercourse during pregnancy may increase the frequency and severity of the amniotic fluid infections and thus increase the fetal and neonatal mortality rate. The reasons have not been determined, but it is possible that a greater number or variety of bacteria reach the amniotic fluid after inter-

Figure 10.5. Rear entry position.

Figure 10.6.   Rear entry position with woman masturbating.

course. When the reasons for association of intercourse with amniotic fluid infection are known, it may be possible to recommend preventive measures. It may be that "fastidious" perineal cleansing by the sexual partners or use of condoms can reduce the frequency and improve the outcome of the infections. Specific advice will have to await the results of further studies.

One other way in which intercourse might possibly be related to premature labor is through the effects of prostaglandins, a group of fatty acid derivatives present in human semen. Prostaglandins have been used intravaginally to stimulate uterine contractions (Speroff & Ramwell, 1970). Semen, it has been postulated, may have the property of inducing labor (Goodlin, Keller, & Raffin, 1971). At the present time, however, there is no real evidence linking prostaglandins in human semen with premature labor, nor is there specific evidence that rules out an association.

The data from these studies suggest that although there appears to be no relationship between intercourse in late pregnancy and early labor, there may be a relationship between intercourse and amniotic fluid infections. Specific directions for prevention of infection await development.

ORGASM IN PREGNANCY

Studies have been done on the possible relationship between orgasm and premature labor. Goodlin, Keller, and Raffin (1971) studied 200 women who experienced orgasm during the second and third trimesters. The relative risk of premature labor or ruptured membranes was 15% in those women who experienced orgasm after the thirty-second week of pregnancy. In those women who had had previous premature deliveries, there was a 21% risk of premature delivery. However, 85% of these women were not orgasmic after the thirty-second week of pregnancy, so their poor reproductive history also appears to be a variable.

In the Seattle study by Solberg, Butler, and Wagner (1973) of 260 women, the prematurity rate of the 138 women who had orgasms after the seventh month was less than 6%, which is not significantly different from that in women who did not have orgasms after the seventh month.

The possible relationship of orgasm to premature labor might be through the mechanism of induced uterine contractions. Masters and Johnson (1966) demonstrated the existence of uterine contractions during orgasm and reported that there is more severe uterine contractile response during an orgasm induced by manual stimulation than by intercourse. They have also commented on the similarity of uterine contractions in orgasm to the contractions in labor.

Fox and Knaggs (1969) found oxytocin in blood samples of women taken one minute after orgasm. The release of oxytocin may be instrumental in the uterine contractions that are associated with female orgasm. Fox, Wolf, and Baker (1970) measured the intrauterine pressure changes during orgasm in comparison to pre- and postorgasmic pressures. Contractions at the peak of orgasm produced an increase in uterine pressure four times that of the pressure in peak resting uterine contractions. Intrauterine pressure fell sharply after orgasm and gradually returned to regular uterine contractions that were present initially. In some women postorgasmic uterine contractions were sufficiently painful to discourage intercourse (Goodlin, Keller, & Raffin, 1971).

Perkins (1979) indicated that there was no association between coitus, orgasm, or other sexual experiences and the onset of labor in 25 women delivering premature infants. This same study also showed that among 155 pregnant women, being orgasmic was associated with lower rates of early deliveries, and masturbation was consistently associated with a lower risk of prematurity through all stages of pregnancy.

At the present time, the relationship of orgasm to premature labor is unclear. Although there may be some findings suggesting a relationship, the studies that looked at reasonably large samples of pregnant women found no relationship between orgasm and premature labor.

It is clear, however, that orgasm produces uterine contractions. This may present problems to habitual aborters, women who threaten to abort, or women who may enter premature labor. Since there may not be any sure way to determine who may enter premature labor, it seems sensible to recommend that orgasm, whether by masturbation or intercourse, be prohibited for women who have previously delivered prematurely or who are found on vaginal examination to have a dilated cervix or any finding suggesting either premature labor or an unusually small fetus (Butler, Reisner, & Wagner, 1979).

INTRAPARTUM SEXUALITY

Intrapartum sexuality involves the pregnant woman and her partner in two contemporary battles. On one side, obstetricians tend to represent birth as medically and surgically risky. On the other side, feminists push for the woman's right to have knowledge, control, and mastery of the birth process and the man's right to have a significant participatory role in and access to the birth of his child. The outcome has yet to be decided.

Newton (1973) maintains that women are trebly sensuous. Men can form reproductive relationships only with women and only through one act—intercourse. Women can engage in three reproductive acts— intercourse, childbirth, and nursing—that involve two people. These acts are interrelated, physiologically and psychologically, through three basic characteristics. They share a neurohormonal level in which oxytocic substances are involved. Each reproductive act is sensitive to environmental factors, for unsheltered and disquieting emotions may be inhibiting. All three acts trigger caretaking behavior—affectionate partnership formation between woman and man and woman and child—so essential to human reproduction.

Women who have had a birth experience without anesthesia or analgesia have reported ecstasy and orgasm during the second stage of labor. Masters and Johnson (1966) reported that some women who have had babies describe the sensation of imminent orgasm as a "feeling of receptive opening." Twelve women in their study who had given birth without anesthesia or analgesia "reported that the second stage of labor felt like the sensations just before orgasm but greatly exaggerated." Newton (1973) shows the relationship between birth behavior and behavior during intercourse (Table 10.1).

Undisturbed, undrugged childbirth or some form of prepared childbirth may not be chosen by or available to the pregnant woman or partners. It is important, however, for the nurse to know the sensual and sexual aspects of uninhibited acts of partuition.

POSTPARTUM SEXUAL RESPONSE

The six subjects in the Masters and Johnson (1966) study of sexual response during and after pregnancy had uncomplicated deliveries, and all their babies were reported to be in good health. The women were examined three times after delivery. Three of the six women nursed through the fourth postpartum month.

At the first examination, between the fourth and fifth weeks, the

Table 10.1. Relation of Birth Behavior to Coital Orgasm

	Undisturbed, Undrugged Childbirth	Sexual Excitement
Breathing	In the first stage of labor breathing becomes deeper during contractions.	During the early stages of sexual excitement, breathing becomes faster and deeper.
Vocalization	There is a tendency to make noises and grunts in the second stage of labor.	There is also tendency to make gasping, sucking noises as orgasm approaches.
Facial expression	During the second stage of labor, the face takes on an intense, stressed look, which often makes observers assume the woman is suffering great pain. As birth climax approaches, the face looks like that of an athlete undergoing great strain.	As orgasm approaches, the face gets what Kinsey et al. call a "tortured expression"—mouth open, glassy eyes, tense muscles. The face looks like that of an athlete under great physical strain.
Uterine reactions	The upper segment of the uterus contracts rhythmically during labor.	The upper segment of the uterus contracts rhythmically during sexual excitement.
Cervical reactions	Loosening of mucus plug from os of cervix is one of the standard signs of early labor.	In sexual excitement, cervical secretion may loosen mucus plug which ordinarily lies at os of cervix thus opening it for spermatozoa.
Abdominal muscle reactions	These contract periodically in second stage labor; a strong urge to bear down develops as delivery approaches.	During sexual excitement, abdominal muscles contract periodically.
Position	The usual position for delivery in our society is with the woman flat on her back with legs wide apart and bent.	The birth position is commonly used for coitus—a woman on her back with legs bent and wide apart.
Central nervous system reactions	Women tend to become uninhibited during parturition, particularly as the baby descends the birth canal. Veneers of conventional behavior disappear in the later stages of labor.	During coitus, inhibitions and psychic blockages are relieved and often eliminated.
Strength and flexibility	Delivery of the baby through the narrow passage calls for unusual strength and body expansion.	In sexual excitement unusual muscular strength develops. Many persons become capable of bending and distorting their bodies in ways they could not otherwise.

Sensory perception	In labor the vulva become anesthetized with full dilation so that the woman often must be told of the birth of the baby's head. During undrugged labor, uninhibited by fear, there is a tendency to become insensitive to surroundings as delivery approaches. Amnesia develops. Suddenly, a delivery complete, the woman becomes wide awake.	In coitus the whole body of the sexually aroused person becomes increasingly insensitive even to sharp blows and severe injury. As orgasm approaches, loss of sensory perception is nearly complete—sometimes leading to moments of unconsciousness. After orgasm there is a sudden return of sensory acuity.
Emotional response	After the birth of the baby there is a flood of joyful emotion. Read describes it as "complete and careless ecstasy."	After orgasm there is often a strong feeling of well being.

Reprinted with permission from Newton, N., Interrelationships between sexual responsiveness, birth, and breast-feeding. In J. Zubin & J. Money (Eds.), *Contemporary Sexual Behavior: Critical Issues in the 1970s.* Baltimore: The Johns Hopkins University Press, 1973, pp. 79–80. Copyright © 1973 The Johns Hopkins University Press.

episiotomies were healed, the cervixes had closed, and the uteri were still abdominal organs. As expected, the uteri of the nursing mothers were smaller and better involuted. Although four of the six women reported significant levels of eroticism, the physiological reaction of their pelvic organs was reduced in rapidity and intensity of response. Lubrication developed more slowly and was less profuse, and vaginal distention occurred more slowly and was less marked. Vaginal walls were thin and normal rugae flattened, and the color of the minor labia was much less vivid. The pattern of steroid starvation was particularly true for the nursing mothers. Vasocongestion of the orgasmic platform was significantly reduced, and although the women reported satisfaction from the orgasmic experience, the orgasmic contractions were markedly reduced.

At the six- to eight-week examination, there was little variation from the physiologic finding at the first examination. Sexual tensions were reported at nonpregnant levels, particularly among the nursing mothers. Steroid starvation may have had more of an effect on the physiologic patterns than on psychologic levels of tension. In nursing mothers, milk was observed to run from both nipples during and immediately following an orgasmic experience.

At the end of the third postpartum month an entirely different picture was presented. All six women evidenced return of ovarian hormone function, although the nonnursing group was ahead of the three nursing mothers. Vaginal rugae had returned, the uterus had descended into the pelvis, the major and minor labia began to respond more readily, vaginal lubrication had returned to nonpregnant levels, and expansion of the vaginal barrel had returned to prepregnancy dimensions. Subjectively the women could not discern significant differences between the orgasmic experiences at the three-month examination as compared with those at the four- to five-week examination. Physiologically, however, the third-month experiences were increased in intensity and duration as compared with those evaluated four to five weeks after delivery.

POSTPARTUM SEXUALITY

Masters and Johnson (1966) interviewed 101 women in the third month after delivery. The feelings of eroticism reported bore no direct relationship to the parity or age of the woman but could be related directly to the act of nursing. The highest level of postpartum sexual interest in the first three months after delivery was reported by the group of nursing mothers. For the 47 women who described low levels of sexuality, the greatest expressed concern was personal fear of permanent physical harm if intercourse was resumed.

With the exception of the women for whom intercourse was medically prohibited and the members of the unmarried group, all women returned to intercourse within six weeks to two months after delivery. Despite medical prohibition, there was resumption of intercourse within three weeks after delivery by high-tension women or by wives responding to their husbands' demands. Eleven women described significantly increased sexual pleasure derived from the tenderness of the episiotomy area or the tightness of the postpartum vaginal barrel.

Forty-eight women reported concern for their husband's sexual tension during the postpartum period of continence, particularly when added to a predelivery period of continence. Those women who had provided relief for their husbands during third trimester continence continued to do so. Four women who had not approached their husbands before delivery did so after delivery.

Falicov (1973) studied 18 couples at two and seven months postpartum. Twelve of the 18 couples resumed intercourse within two months. Six couples rapidly regained prepregnancy levels of sexual activity. Six couples did not return to their previous levels because of tension, fatigue, and physical discomforts such as breast soreness and soreness of the episiotomy site. The six couples who did not resume intercourse at the six- to 8-week postpartum period included four of the five women who were bottle feeding. Reasons stated for nonresumption were fatigue, lack of interest, tenderness of episiotomy site, and lack of time.

Five of the 18 women reported increased eroticism primarily as a result of increased sensitivity of the breasts. The experience of nursing seemed to heighten breast eroticism for 6 of the 13 women, but two women who were not nursing noticed heightened sensitivity as well. Most of the women who had resumed intercourse reported that achieving orgasm was more difficult than before pregnancy. The contributing factors were tension, fatigue, and anxiety about perceived changes in their sexual organs. Displays of affection and eagerness by the husbands were important in resuming intercourse.

By seven months postpartum, the frequency of intercourse for the whole group was still lower than before pregnancy. This appeared to be the result of fatigue and psychologic tension, since sexual desire and eroticism had returned to normal or heightened levels. Nine women reported that their capacity for arousal and orgasm increased, and four of the six nursing women felt heightened sexual desire and frustration at the lower frequency of sexual relations.

In general, the timing and resumption of postpartum sexual activity seemed related to the women's present physical conditions and their husbands' attitudes toward abstinence. For some women, a high degree of past sexual interest combined with present breast-feeding was positively related to increased sexual desire.

Kenny (1973) studied 33 women during the breast-feeding and weaning periods. Thirty percent of the women reported that the childbirth experience made them more interested in sex, 52% reported that there was no difference, and 18% felt less interested than before pregnancy. Seventy-five percent reported sexual functioning to be similar to pre-pregnancy levels. Fifty-two percent believed that intercourse could be safely resumed when vaginal discharge stopped, even if this was before the six-week checkup. Desire returned for most women by four weeks, and 42% were then interested, although only 12% felt it was safe. Women who had been married longer, with more children and more breast-feeding time, reported an earlier return of sexual interest and felt it safe to resume intercourse earlier. Most women reported that their sexual interest after weaning was essentially unchanged, and no one reported a decrease. All of the women reported breast-feeding as enjoyable.

Tolor and DiGrazia (1976) analyzed data on 55 postpartum women, comparing the data with those obtained from three groups of similar size composed of women in the first, second, and third trimesters. The decline in desire for intercourse that was seen in pregnant women was reversed in the postpartum phase. There was a relatively high incidence of inter-course after childbirth, with one out of every three women reporting that she had intercourse four or more times each week. Postpartum women were more satisfied with the prevailing level of sexual activity than were third-trimester women, but 31% of the postpartum women desired still higher levels of activity. The postpartum group reported more frequent multiple orgasms than the pregnant group. There was an increased pref-erence for oral sexual activity and decreased preference for clitoral stimu-lation among the postpartum women. Interest in intercourse declined in the pregnancy group until the postpartum period, at which point it peaked.

Effects of Obstetrical Operative Procedures

There can be emotional sequelae associated with obstetrical operative procedures (Daly, 1976). The need for episiotomies is being questioned. In Europe, deliveries by midwives had no higher incidence of pelvic relaxa-tion, tears, or harm to the baby. Episiotomies contribute to postpartum discomfort and the immediate benefit is not obvious. Many women view an episiotomy as an assault on their bodies and react with anger. Some women react negatively to forceps. A woman may fantasize that these instruments are destructive to herself and her baby or feel that the in-strument represents a failure on her part. These feelings can contribute to a depression during the postpartum period. Women on whom ce-sarean sections are performed may feel threatened and anxious be-cause they did not have their babies normally.

Although the cervix and the vagina of a woman who has a delivery by cesarean section have not been through the anatomic process of birth, the hormone changes are the same. Women who have deliveries by cesarean section report vaginal tenderness and dryness (Bing & Coleman, 1977). To the postpartum course is added the tiredness and fatigue associated with recovery from major surgery and the discomfort of the abdominal incision when intercourse is resumed.

PREGNANCY EFFECT

As part of her exploration of female sexuality, Sherfey (1973) discussed the so-called pregnancy effect. The heightened sexuality of women after pregnancy, and the fact that many women experience their first orgasm during intercourse at this time, have been given psychologic explanations. The reasons postulated include a lessening of anxiety about femininity and the maturing experience of successful pregnancy, labor, and care of the newborn infant.

Sherfey (1973) examined the physiologic outcomes of pregnancy and theorized that orgasmic competence after a first pregnancy has more to do with the greatly increased vascularity of the entire pelvis induced by the pregnancy hormones with the resultant growth of new blood vessels and varicosities than with psychologic factors. In addition, the effect of the androgen and the androgenic action of progesterone, both of which are secreted during pregnancy, is to increase responsiveness of the clitoral system and strengthen the muscles of orgasmic response. Pregnancies increase the volume capacity of the pelvic venous bed, increase the volume of the sexual edema, enhance the capacity for sexual tension, and improve orgasmic intensity, frequency, and pleasure. Sherfey concludes that the pregnancy effect enhances sexual pleasure and serves as insurance that the woman will remain sexually, and hence reproductively, active.

In general, after childbirth there is a return to normal sexual desire and sexual activity. Factors that influence the return are: anxiety about obstetrical healing, fatigue and tension resulting from a new role, the attitude of the sexual partner, and the experience of nursing. The woman's heightened postpartum sexuality represents a genuine recovery and expression of her own sexual desire and capacity.

SEXUALITY AND LACTATION

Pryor (1973) states that erotic feeling may be felt at the beginning and end of nursing and that sustained sexual pleasure can be a part of the nursing experience. Francis (1976) maintains that a woman who has not successfully breast-fed leaves an important part of her sexuality unfulfilled. Successful breast-feeding is described as a joyous, sensuous relationship in which the mother offers her breast not only for nourishment but also to provide comfort and love, receive caresses, and enjoy skin-to-skin contact. Newton (1973) described several similarities between intercourse and breast-feeding. Uterine contractions occur during both breast-feeding and sexual excitement. Breast stroking and nipple stimulation with nipple erection are part of both sexual stimulation and breast-feeding. The older infant shows total body response through rhythmic movements of hands, feet, fingers, and toes. Erection of the penis is common in male babies. Both sexual and breast-feeding contact involve vascular and thermal changes in the skin and can trigger the milk-letdown reflex. Similar emotions are experienced during sexual arousal and uninhibited breast-feeding. Orgasm has been experienced during breast-feeding. There may be a relationship between an accepting attitude toward sexuality and an accepting attitude toward breast-feeding. Added to this may be the similarities between the nursing songs of the mother and the soft, contented sounds of the baby and the spontaneous noise sometimes made during intercourse.

Kenny (1973) asked 33 women to complete a questionnaire about their recollections of their sexual behavior during pregnancy and breast-feeding. The more experienced breast-feeders in the group tended to report that frequency of intercourse and orgasm were about the same during both periods. The less experienced mothers reported a decrease in frequency of intercourse and a decrease in frequency of orgasms in the last trimester of breast-feeding. Kenny (1973) hypothesized that women who breast-fed more were or became more physical and sensual than other mothers.

All the women reported that they enjoyed breast-feeding. The major psychological reasons for this feeling were "closeness to baby" and "emotional fulfillment," and the major practical reasons were that breast-feeding was "convenient" and "easy." Eighty-seven percent of the younger married women and 59% of the older married women found breast-feeding an "exceptionally meaningful experience." Further, it was the younger married and one-child mothers who felt more at ease breast-feeding in a group of friends of mixed sex. Most women reported that their sexual interest after weaning was about the same. No one reported a decrease in sexual interest after weaning.

In the Masters and Johnson (1966) study of 101 women, the 24 women who nursed reported sexual stimulation induced by breast-feeding. Six of the women expressed guilt about the arousal and were anxious to relieve fear of perverted sexual interest by resuming intercourse with their husbands. Eight previously nulliparous women and 17 parous women rejected nursing during the postpartum period. A major factor was the rejection of nursing by 17 husbands. Thirteen of these women expressed fear of loss of their figures. Personal rejection of the process as degrading was expressed, and six women who had previously attempted nursing expressed fear of the high levels of eroticism stimulated by breast-feeding.

The rigid pattern of breast-feeding as currently practiced in the United States places restrictions on time, place, and mother–child interactions (Newton, 1971). Western industrial societies limit sensory contact between mother and child—mother and child are separated at birth, baby sleeps alone, and women wear restrictive clothing. These practices discourage the discovery of the sensuous nature of breast-feeding.

A range of physical, psychological, and sociological factors plays a part in the decision to nurse or not to nurse. Using a systems model in which the individual family and society interact dynamically, Bentovim (1976) offered a possible explanatory model of the input, output, and feedback of emotions aroused about the breast and breast-feeding. The model separates the multiple factors of the individual, family, and society that affect the decision-making process. The model depicts the variables that act as precipitating factors in the decision to attempt breast- or bottle-feeding during pregnancy, delivery, and the postpartum period. The consequences of the decision between breast-feeding and bottle-feeding and the consequences for mother, infant, family, and society are listed. Sexually related variables in the women include lack of embarrassment about nudity, tolerance of rather than shame about masturbation and sex play, and masculine rather than feminine strivings. Sexually related family variables include marital status, length of marriage, belief in natural functions, support of the women's movement rather than traditional views of dominance and submissiveness, and openness rather than modesty about sexuality. Societal variables include women's occupational roles and the opportunity to breast-feed, role of the breast as sexual rather than feeding object, and the prerequisites of sexual modesty in the community. Sexually precipitating factors in the decision to breast-feed include response to breast change with pleasure versus shame, neurohormonal changes, and response to milk letdown and milk flow. Sexually related consequences for the infant involve a total body pleasure response. Consequences for the family and society range from marital satisfaction and confirmation of parental role to incongruity and from acceptance to rejection of the breast as a sexual or feeding object.

Familiarity with the model prevents the nurse from arriving at simplistic answers about breast-feeding and enables the nurse to incorporate sexual aspects into the decision-making process about whether or not to breast-feed. The model compels nurses to use physical, psychological, and sociological facts about breast-feeding as they plan nursing care for the individual, family, and society.

The first consumer organization structured to help women with birth-related problems in a technological society was the LaLeche League, started in 1956 by a group of nursing mothers. They were alarmed at the failure of health professionals to recognize and understand the needs and expectations of women who choose to nurse their children. Many of the original members attributed part of their success in nursing their later children to removing themselves from the care of health professionals and giving birth at home (Seiden, 1978). Through the principle of group support, women who are nursing or who have nursed successfully share, teach, help, educate, and support the woman contemplating nursing or the woman new at the experience. The LaLeche League is an international organization and a community resource that advocates breast-feeding, provides basic information, and gives support to women who desire to breast-feed their babies.

REACTION OF THE SEXUAL PARTNER DURING AND AFTER PREGNANCY

The feelings and needs of the woman's sexual partner must be given attention during and after pregnancy. Pregnancy is centered within the woman, but it happens through, with, and to the man as well. Pregnancy can precipitate emotional changes and compel the man to come to grips with a new family and socioeconomic role—that of father. He may feel and want to expose the tender, gentle, and nurturing qualities he finds within himself, but these qualities may be alien to him and to his social role (McNall, 1976). The man may feel conflict between the need to respond in a personally appropriate and socially acceptable way to fatherhood and the need to demonstrate his masculinity. It has been demonstrated that childbirth preparation classes and being present at delivery can have a positive effect on the father's perception of his role as father and his relationship to his wife (Cronenwett & Newmark, 1974).

Seventy-nine husbands cooperated with Masters and Johnson (1966) and were interviewed at the end of the third postpartum month after interviews with their wives had been completed. Thirty-one of the men stated they had withdrawn slowly and almost involuntarily from sexual intercourse at the end of the second or early in the third trimester of pregnancy. The husbands gave no consistent reason other than fear of causing physical injury to the fetus or the wife.

Seventy-one of the men were married to women whose physicians had prohibited intercourse from four weeks to three months before delivery. Twenty-one of these men stated that they understood, agreed with, and honored the prohibition. Twenty-three men did not understand the reason, were not sure the physician had said it, or wished he had explained it to them as well as to their wives. The major concern expressed after delivery by the entire group was how soon active intercourse could be reinstated without physical harm or emotional distress to their wives.

Eighteen of the 71 husbands for whom intercourse with their wives had been prohibited from four weeks to three months before delivery reported that they sought sexual intercourse outside the marriage. Twelve of the men who reported extramarital activities during the predelivery period continued to do so after delivery. Six of the men engaged in extramarital activity during the postpartum continence period, and three of these men said it was the first time they had done so.

Rainwater (1969) found that working-class fathers saw pregnancy as a confirmation of their masculinity and that it was during pregnancy that husbands were the most considerate of, close to, and interested in their wives. Shereskefsky and Yarrow (1973) studied the reactions of 60 young, middle-class, urban families to pregnancy. After fetal movement was felt, half of the husbands were reluctant to engage in intercourse for fear of harming the baby. Some men were envious of the pregnancy and the woman's body, and others were uncomfortable about being seen with the woman because the pregnant figure was a public statement of a private sexual activity.

Since ways of expressing love and affection often differ for men and women, Wegsteen and Wagner (1977) saw the pregnant woman's decreased sexual interest and her increased need for affection as a possible source of conflict between the woman and her sexual partner. Traditionally women are socialized to express affection in nonsexual but physical ways such as hugging. For men, strong cultural traditions socialize them to equate sexual activity with affection. Even in a close and caring relationship, when the woman refuses or does not respond to sexual advances by her partner, he may experience feelings of frustration, rejection, and depression.

Bing and Coleman (1977) provided insight into the sexual conflicts, fears, and anxieties experienced by the sexual partners of pregnant women. The partner may wish for the woman's body to remain the same. The enlarged abdomen and swollen breasts may be strange and even overwhelming and may make him feel temporarily pressured and inadequate. He may consider running away from the social, emotional, and economic responsibilities of being a father. Even if he does not leave, he may withdraw emotionally and perhaps feel replaced by the fetus. It may be that the man does not want his well-established patterns of intercourse to be disturbed. He may feel embarrassed about relaxing and enjoying sensual pleasure for its own sake. Mutual masturbation may feel childlike and unclean and not appropriate for a man about to become a father. He may feel guilty about receiving sexual gratification when his partner does not. New positions may embarrass him or elicit a deep-seated fear that if he tries them he may fail. He may feel that he will be unable to satisfy his partner in any but the usual positions.

Sensitivity to the conflicts, fears, and anxieties of the sexual partner of a pregnant woman is essential for competent sexual health care. The nurse as educator-counselor needs to provide information to help dispel the myths and misconceptions and encourage the partners to attend to each other as they share the experiences of new, different, and even frightening feelings and behaviors. The partners who are able to deal with the unavoidable conflicts and fears have the opportunity to grow with each other and learn new ways and levels of relating to each other.

ASSESSMENT OF SEXUAL HEALTH DURING PREGNANCY

The ideal time to promote an exchange of information and the sharing of thoughts and feelings between the pregnant woman and the sexual partner is during sexual health history taking. This is an ideal time for the nurse to allow the partners to discuss sexual concerns and anxieties and to let the partners know that education and counseling about sexuality are components of their health care. The nurse must not make assumptions about the relationship and the pregnancy. The pregnancy may be planned, eagerly anticipated, and part of a strong and caring relationship, or it may be unplanned, unwanted, and part of a shaky and disturbed relationship.

Additional questions and pregnancy-related categories can be added to the adult sexual health history (Chapter 2). Additional data about sexual knowledge and attitudes are appropriate. The additional categories are physical status of the man, relationship status, breast-feeding, labor and delivery, and family planning.

Sexual Knowledge and Attitudes

Inquiry into how information and attitudes about sex and pregnancy were acquired is helpful:

What have you heard from family and friends about sex during pregnancy? about sex after pregnancy?
How do you feel about sex during pregnancy? after pregnancy?
How did you find out about the normal changes that take place in a woman's body during and after pregnancy?

How do you feel about trying other positions as the pregnancy progresses?

How do you feel about masturbation and oral sex during pregnancy?

How do your thoughts and feelings about sex differ from those of your partner?

Sexual Role, Sexual Being, Sexual Function

Additional data about the physical and emotional changes of pregnancy can be gathered:

How does being pregnant make you feel about yourself?

To the woman: How do you feel about the normal changes that are happening to your body?

To the man: How do you feel about the changes you see happening to her body?

Physical Status of the Man

Physical assessment of the pregnant woman is of paramount importance and includes a meticulous menstrual and obstetric history. However, because physical health affects sexual health, questions about the physical health of the sexual partner are important (Zalar, 1976):

How do you feel about your physical health?

How do you feel about your health in general?

Have you noticed any differences in your health lately?

Do you feel there is anything about your health it would be helpful for me to know?

Relationship Status

Pregnancy affects not only the partners but also the sexual role, being, and function of the relationship:

How has being pregnant changed your lives?

How do you think having a child will change your lives?

What plans has being pregnant changed?

What plans will having a child change?

How are you going to handle the change now? later?

Breast-feeding

It is helpful to open discussion about breast-feeding early in the pregnancy:

Have any of your family, friends, or neighbors breast-fed their children?
How do you feel about breast-feeding?
What are your thoughts and feelings about breast-feeding at home? on the job? in public?
Do you feel breast-feeding might be appropriate for you?

Labor and Delivery

It is helpful, also, for the woman and her sexual partner to consider, early in the pregnancy, the options available to them for labor and delivery:

Where were you born? hospital? home? birth center?
What are your thoughts and feelings about how the baby should be born?
Have any of your family, friends, or neighbors attended childbirth education classes?
To the woman: What are your feelings about having your partner support you through labor and delivery?
To the man: What are your feelings about being a support to your partner during labor and delivery?
At this time, what plans would you like to make about labor and delivery?

Family Planning

It is often helpful and appropriate to introduce the topic of family planning for discussion and consideration:

At this time, how do you feel about more children?
Have you thought about changing your methods of contraception after the delivery?
Are there any questions about family planning you want to ask me?

The sexual health history is the means by which the nurse gathers data for planning sexual health care during and after pregnancy. Taking the history gives the nurse an opportunity to introduce and activate the role of educator-counselor and to encourage the partners to learn more about each other and their relationship.

THE NURSE AS EDUCATOR-COUNSELOR

The nurse, as educator-counselor in sexual health care, has an active role during all the stages of pregnancy, the postpartum period, and lactation. As an educator, the nurse can provide information and anticipatory guidance to the pregnant woman and her sexual partner about the biopsychosocial changes that occur. The following are important considerations:

1. Changes in body contours that may alter the woman's concept of herself as well as her partner's perception of her as a sexual being.
2. Changes in the woman's sexual response cycle during and after pregnancy.
3. Fluctuations in the woman's interest in sex and frequency of intercourse during and after pregnancy.
4. Alternative positions or sexual activities that enable comfortable and satisfying sexual communication as changes in body contour occur.
5. Lactation as possible enhancement of sexuality, with sexual arousal during nursing and involuntary leakage of milk from breasts during sexual activity.

The pregnant woman and her sexual partner need anticipatory guidance about intercourse during and after pregnancy, and the nurse can provide factual and reasonable guidelines. Information about and reasons for continuing, maintaining, changing, or prohibiting intercourse or other sexual activity is presented to both partners. The nurse encourages mutual discussion and expression of feelings and allows time for mutual exploration of alternatives and decision making. The following guidelines may be offered to clients:

1. Sexual activity that is psychologically satisfying, physiologically safe and comfortable, and mutually pleasurable may be continued during and after pregnancy.
2. At the present time, there is no evidence that sexual intercourse should be prohibited in the last part of a normal, uncomplicated pregnancy.
3. Spotting or frank bleeding is a contraindication for intercourse until the source of the bleeding is diagnosed and managed.
4. Masturbation as well as intercourse should be prohibited if there is concern that orgasmic response might induce premature labor.
5. Intercourse in the postpartum period can be resumed when uterine bleeding and discharge have ceased, when the woman feels perineal comfort, and when both partners are psychologically capable and ready.

Kegel exercises for the pubococcygeus (PC) muscle are now taught in childbirth education classes and are recommended to tighten the PC muscle, maintain muscle tone, and prevent weakening of the pelvic floor. The PC muscle is one of the muscles that contract during orgasm, and in some women the muscle may be lacking in tone after childbirth. Kegel exercises were developed for women with the common problem of urinary incontinence and were designed to tighten the PC muscle to prevent expelling urine when sneezing or coughing (Kegel, 1952). Women have found that these exercises increase sensitivity in the vaginal area and heighten sexuality (Barbach, 1975).

Instructions for Kegel Exercises

1. Locate the PC muscle by sitting on a toilet with knees as far apart as possible.
2. Start the flow of urine and practice stopping and starting the flow until you are familiar with how the PC muscle functions.
3. Contract the PC muscle and hold for three seconds. Relax the muscle for three seconds and contract again.
4. Perform 10 three-second contractions at three different times of the day.
5. If there is any discomfort or tightness, reduce the number of contractions but do not stop the exercise. Like any muscle being exercised for the first time, the PC muscle may get a little stiff at first.

The nurse knows that how the pregnant woman and her sexual partner respond to the pregnancy depends on their individual, social, and cultural learning and experiences. As a counselor, the nurse is sensitive to and appreciates the changes that can take place in sexual roles and relationships during and after pregnancy. The nurse listens to the pregnant woman and her sexual partner and assists them in mixing and matching their individual needs, desires, expectations, and goals. In each nurse–client interaction, the nurse individualizes education and counseling to meet the sexual health care needs defined by the pregnant woman and her sexual partner as they deal with the common changes and problems occurring during and after pregnancy.

NURSING PROCESS

Client: Marilyn Picconi—three days after a cesarean section
Nurse: John Rawles—nursing student assigned to mother-child care on maternity unit

Assessment

Subjective Data

"This is my third child but my first cesarean section."
"Don't feel as well as the other times—not as fit and ready to go."
"I'm tired and get more tired easily."
"My abdomen—the incision is uncomfortable; in fact, I ache all over."
"My husband and I have talked about it."
"I certainly didn't expect anything like this."
"I'm nursing this baby too. I like to nurse—good body experience for both
    of us, but that's all I have energy for."
"The last two times we started making love again when the bleeding
    stopped—about 3 weeks."
"But should we wait longer or something because of the cesarean sec-
    tion?"

Objective Data

29 years old, married, housewife.
Two children, 3 and 5 years old, both vaginal deliveries.
Postoperative cesarean section—three days—progress satisfactory.
Baby in good condition.
Nursing experience satisfactory.
Feeling of fatigue and discomfort unexpected and unlike previous im-
    mediate postpartum experiences.
Intercourse resumed three weeks after vaginal deliveries.
Information about resumption of intercourse after cesarean section
    sought.

Nursing Diagnosis

Concern about unexpected feelings of fatigue related to postoperative
    course of cesarean section delivery.
Inadequate information about resumption of intercourse in the postpar-
    tum period after cesarean section delivery.

Planning

Communicate acceptance of feelings of fatigue and discomfort.
Provide information about postoperative course following major abdomi-
    nal surgery.

Inform that fatigue and discomfort are normal.

Reassure that fatigue and discomfort will subside.

Use positive suggestion for fatigue and discomfort relief.

Explain that guidelines and recommendations for resuming intercourse after cesarean section are the same as for vaginal delivery.

Inform that hormonal change will occur as in vaginal delivery.

Suggest alternative positions for intercourse if weight on abdomen at incision is uncomfortable.

Suggest use of water-soluble lubricant for vaginal tenderness or dryness.

Encourage expression of feelings.

Encourage mutual decision making.

Indicate availability for further information or counseling.

Implementation

Understand postoperative course of major abdominal surgery; share information with husband.

Review guidelines and recommendations about resuming intercourse in postpartum period with husband.

Use third trimester "off-the-belly" positions for incisional discomfort.

Obtain lubricant.

Make mutual decisions about resuming intercourse.

Evaluation

Reports feelings of well being.

Reports satisfactory resumption of intercourse.

BIBLIOGRAPHY

Barbach, L. G. *For yourself: The fulfillment of female sexuality.* New York: New American Library, 1975.

Bentovim, A. Shame and other anxieties associated with breast-feeding: A systems theory and psychodynamic approach. In *Ciba Foundation symposium: Breast-feeding and the mother* (Vol. 45). New York: Ciba Foundation, 1976.

Bing, E., & Coleman, L. *Making love during pregnancy*. New York: Bantam Books, 1977.

Boston's Women's Health Book Collective. *Our bodies, ourselves* (2nd ed.). New York: Simon & Schuster, 1976.

Butler, J. C., Reisner, D. P., & Wagner, N. N. Sexuality during pregnancy and postpartum. In R. Green (Ed.), *Human sexuality: A health practitioner's text* (2nd ed.). Baltimore: Williams & Wilkins, 1979.

Campbell, C. *Nursing diagnosis and intervention in nursing practice*. New York: Wiley, 1978.

Clark, A. L., & Hale, R. W. Sex during and after pregnancy. *American Journal of Nursing*, 1974, *74*, 1430–1431.

Cronenwett, L. R., & Newmark, L. L. Father's responses to childbirth. *Nursing Research*, 1974, *23*, 210–217.

Daly, J. D. Psychological impact of surgical procedures on women. In B. J. Saddock, H. I. Kaplan, & A. M. Freedman (Eds.), *The sexual experience*. Baltimore: Williams & Wilkins, 1976.

Falicov, C. J. Sexual adjustment during first pregnancy and postpartum. *American Journal of Obstetrics and Gynecology*, 1973, *117*, 991–1000.

Fox, C. A., & Knaggs, G. S. Milk-ejection activity (ocytocin) in peripheral venous blood in women during lactation and in association with coitus. *Journal of Endocrinology*, 1969, *45*, 145–146.

Fox, C. A., Wolf, H. S., & Baker, J. A. Measurement of intravaginal and intrauterine pressures during human coitus by radiotelemetry. *Journal of Reproduction and Fertility*, 1970, *22*, 243–251.

Francis, B. Successful lactation and women's sexuality. *The Journal of Tropical Pediatrics and Environmental Child Health*, 1976, *22*, 151–152.

Goodlin, R. C., Keller, D. W., & Raffin, M. Orgasm during late pregnancy: Possible deleterious effects. *Obstetrics and Gynecology*, 1971, *38*, 916–920.

Hogan, R. *Human sexuality: A nursing perspective*. New York: Appleton-Century-Crofts, 1980.

Hollender, M. H. Women's wish to be held: Sexual and nonsexual aspects. *Medical Aspects of Human Sexuality*, 1971, *5*, 12–26.

Hollender, M. H., Luborsky, L., & Harvey, R. B. Correlates of the desire to be held in women. *Journal of Psychosomatic Research*, 1970, *14*, 387–390. Hollender, M. H., & McGehee, J. B. The wish to be held during pregnancy. *Journal of Psychosomatic Research*, 1974, *18*, 193–197.

Iffrig, M. C. Sr. Body image in pregnancy: Its relation to nursing functions. *Nursing Clinics of North America*, 1974, *7*, 631–639.

Kegel, A. H. Sexual functions of the pubococcygeous muscle. *Western Journal of Surgery*, 1952, *60*, 521–524.

Kenny, J. A. Sexuality of pregnant and breast-feeding women. *Archives of Sexual Behavior*, 1973, *2*, 215–219.

Kyndely, K. The sexuality of women in pregnancy and postpartum. *JOGN*, 1978, *7*, 28–32.

LaLeche League International. *The womanly art of breast-feeding*. Franklin Park, Ill: Author, 1963.

Lukesch, H. Sexual behavior during pregnancy. *Geburtshilfe Frauenheilkda*, 1976, *36*, 1081–1090.

McNall, I. K. Concerns of expectant fathers. In L. K. McNall & J. T. Galeener (Eds.), *Current practice in obstetric and gynecologic nursing.* St. Louis: C. V. Mosby, 1976.

Masters, W. H., & Johnson, V. E. *Human sexual response.* Boston: Little, Brown, 1966.

Morris, N. M. The frequency of sexual intercourse during pregnancy. *Archives of Sexual Behavior*, 1975, *4*, 501–506.

Naeye, R. L. Coitus and associated amniotic-fluid infections. *The New England Journal of Medicine*, 1979, *301*, 1198–1200.

Newton, N. Psychological differences between breast- and bottle-feeding. *The American Journal of Clinical Nutrition*, 1971, *24*, 993–1004.

Newton, N. Interrelationships between sexual responsiveness, birth, and breast-feeding. In J. Zubin & J. Money (Eds.), *Contemporary sexual behavior: Critical issues in the 1970's.* Baltimore: Johns Hopkins University Press, 1973.

Newton, N. Trebly sensuous woman. *Psychology Today*, 1975, *5*, 68–71; 98–99.

Perkins, R. P. Sexual behavior and response in relation to complications of pregnancy. *American Journal of Obstetrics and Gynecology*, 1979, *134*, 498–505.

Pryor, K. *Nursing your baby.* New York: Pocket Books, 1973.

Pugh, W. E., & Fernandez, F. L. Coitus in late pregnancy: A follow-up study of the effects of coitus on late pregnancy, delivery, and the puerperium. *Obstetrics and Gynecology*, 1953, *2*, 636; 642.

Quirk, B., & Hassanein, R. The nurse's role in advising patients on coitus during pregnancy. *Nursing Clinics of North America*, 1973, *8*, 501–507.

Rainwater, L. Sex in the culture of poverty. In C. B. Broverick & J. Bernard (Eds.), *The individual, sex, and society.* Baltimore: Johns Hopkins University Press, 1969.

Seiden, A. M. Overview: Research on the psychology of women: Gender differences and sexual and reproductive life. *American Journal of Psychiatry*, 1976, *133*, 995–1007.

Seiden, A. M. The sense of mastery in the childbirth experience. In M. T. Notman & C. C. Nadelson (Eds.), *The woman patient: Medical and psychological interfaces* (Vol. 1). New York: Plenum Press, 1978.

Semmens, J. P. Female sexuality and life situations: An etiologic psychosociosexual profile of weight gain and nausea and vomiting in pregnancy. *Obstetrics and Gynecology*, 1971, *38*, 559–562.

Shereshefsky, P. M., & Yarrow, L. J. *Psychological aspects of a first pregnancy and early postpartum adaptation.* New York: Raven Press, 1973.

Sherfey, M. J. *The nature and evolution of female sexuality.* New York: Vintage Books, 1973.

Solberg, D. A., Butler, J., & Wagner, N. N. Sexual behavior in pregnancy. *New England Journal of Medicine*, 1973, *288*, 1098–1103.

Speroff, L., & Ramwell, P. W. Prostaglandins in reproductive physiology. *American Journal of Obstetrics and Gynecology*, 1970, *191*, 1111–1130.

Tolor, A., & DiGrazia, P. V. Sexual attitudes and behavior patterns during and following pregnancy. *Archives of Sexual Behavior*, 1976, *5*, 539–551.

Wagner, N. N., & Solberg, D. Q. Pregnancy and sexuality. *Medical Aspects of Human Sexuality*, 1974, *8,* 53–54.

Wegsteen, L. A., & Wagner, N. N. Psychological aspects of sexuality during pregnancy. *Fertility and Contraception*, 1977, *1,* 51–54.

Woods, N. F. *Human sexuality in health and illness* (2nd ed.). St. Louis: Mosby, 1979.

Zalar, M. Sexual counseling for pregnant couples. *The American Journal of Maternal Child Nursing*, 1976, *3,* 176–181.

11. Problem Pregnancy and Induced Abortion

Elizabeth M. Lion

VALUES CLARIFICATION EXERCISE

Whether or not to terminate a problem pregnancy is a complex question involving medical, religious, moral, and legal issues. Becoming aware of your own feelings and attitudes is crucial, for these influence your interactions with clients experiencing a problem pregnancy and considering or requesting an induced abortion.

Read the following statements and consider the extent to which you agree, disagree, or are uncertain about them. There are no right or wrong answers, only your answers. The statements are intended as a process of self-discovery—an assessment of your feelings and attitudes.

For each statement circle whether you:

SA—Strongly agree   D —Disagree somewhat
A —Agree somewhat   SD—Strongly disagree
U —Are uncertain

1. Induced abortion should be available to any woman who requests it.
   SA A U D SD
2. A nurse with strong religious objections should not care for a client considering termination of a problem pregnancy.
   SA A U D SD
3. Life begins at conception.
   SA A U D SD
4. Welfare money should not be used for induced abortions.
   SA A U D SD
5. Induced abortion should be allowed only in case of rape or incest.
   SA A U D SD

6. The rights of women to control their bodies supersede the rights of the embryo or fetus.

SA   A   U   D   SD

7. The consent of the sexual partner should be required for an induced abortion.

SA   A   U   D   SD

8. Induced abortion is a lesser evil than bringing an unwanted child into the world.

SA   A   U   D   SD

9. Induced abortion is murder.

SA   A   U   D   SD

10. Induced abortion should be permitted if there is a strong possibility that the fetus is retarded or deformed.

SA   A   U   D   SD

11. Once quickening is felt by the mother, there is human life.

SA   A   U   D   SD

12. The availability of induced abortion increases sexual promiscuity.

SA   A   U   D   SD

13. Life begins at birth.

SA   A   U   D   SD

14. After the first trimester, induced abortion should be prohibited except when the mother's health is endangered.

SA   A   U   D   SD

15. Induced abortion should be available to women when recommended by a physician.

SA   A   U   D   SD

16. A nurse with strong convictions about a woman's right of choice should not care for a client considering termination of a problem pregnancy.

SA   A   U   D   SD

17. A nurse involved in the care of a client considering an induced abortion would probably choose to terminate a problem pregnancy if it were her own or his partner's.

SA   A   U   D   SD

18. Parents of teenage daughters should be involved in the decision-making process when termination of a problem pregnancy is considered.

SA   A   U   D   SD

19. Induced abortion is a surgical procedure associated with considerable personal risk.

SA   A   U   D   SD

20. Readily available contraceptive services would decrease the number of abortions performed.

SA   A   U   D   SD

21. Availability of induced abortion promotes irresponsible sexual behavior.

SA A U D SD

Examine your answers and respond to these questions. What issues do I have strong feelings about? What issues am I sensitive about or make me feel uncomfortable? What attitudes do I have? How did I come by these attitudes? Parental teaching? Religious beliefs? Peer-group information? Other? Are these attitudes useful to me? How could these attitudes influence my interactions with clients? What would happen to me if I changed one or more attitudes? What would happen to the nursing care I give?

After you have assessed your feelings and attitudes, share your assessment with a peer or group of peers and note the extent of the similarities and dissimilarities. Discuss how differences are tolerated by the group. Consider how the differences and similarities might affect the nursing care designed by individuals in the group and by the group.

BEHAVIORAL OBJECTIVES

After completing this chapter, you will be able to

- Define problem pregnancy.
- Define induced abortion.
- Describe five procedures for induced abortion.
- Discuss the legal and political issues surrounding induced abortion since its legalization in 1973.
- Identify the socioeconomic characteristics of women who seek induced-abortion services.
- Relate the availability of induced-abortion services to the use of them in the United States.
- Outline five steps in successful decision making about a problem pregnancy.
- Identify the sociodemographic characteristics of women who delay decision making and the psychosocial factors involved.
- Name three factors present in the decision to refuse induced abortion.
- Discuss the effect of induced abortion on contraceptive practice.
- Relate contraceptive failures and risk taking to repeat abortion.
- Discuss the psychologic consequences of induced abortion.
- Discuss the use of induced abortion services by adolescents in the United States.
- Outline the role of the nurse as a counselor for a client considering induced abortion.

DEFINITION OF PROBLEM PREGNANCY AND INDUCED ABORTION

"Unplanned" and "unwanted" are words often used to define a problem pregnancy. When used singly or even in combination, the words define one aspect of pregnancy, but they do not convey how the pregnancy affects the woman. Thus the term *problem pregnancy* is preferred. It is a pregnancy a woman experiences as disruptive to her physical, mental, emotional, or social well-being.

Abortion is the termination of a pregnancy by the premature expulsion from the uterus of the products of conception—a fertilized ovum, embryo, or nonviable fetus. In a *spontaneous*, or *involuntary*, abortion, the expulsion comes about by means of natural or unknown causes. In an *induced*, *voluntary,* or *elected* abortion the expulsion comes about by means of deliberate action intended to terminate the pregnancy.

PROCEDURES FOR INDUCED ABORTION

The procedures used for induced abortion are safe when they are performed by a competent physician, and the earlier in the pregnancy an abortion is performed the safer it is. The risk of complications increases each week that the induced-abortion procedure is delayed. Modern abortion techniques involve less health risk to a woman than full-term delivery of a baby. Neither sexual nor reproductive function is affected. The probability that complications of induced abortion will require major surgery is less than 1 in 500. The procedure can be performed in a physician's office, a specialized clinic, or a hospital. Descriptions of commonly used procedures follow.

Menstrual Extraction/Menstrual Induction (from 0 to 6 Weeks of Pregnancy)

The terms *menstrual extraction* and *menstrual induction* refer to endometrial aspiration via the vagina. Menstrual extraction does not require cervical dilation or more than local anesthesia; it can be done in a physician's office. A flexible plastic tube is inserted into the uterine cavity and gentle pressure is applied by means of a mechanical pump or manually, using a large syringe. The procedure takes from one to ten minutes, depending on the length of gestation. The woman may feel ready to resume activities after only a brief rest. She is usually advised to abstain from sexual intercourse for one week to ten days and then to return for a checkup. There is the possibility of retained tissue or even retained pregnancy, which would make another procedure necessary. Since pregnancy may now be ascertained as early as one week after conception, the use of endometrial aspiration as an abortion procedure may increase.

Dilation and Evacuation (D and E) (from 6 to 14 Weeks of Pregnancy)

Vacuum aspiration abortions account for 80% of all induced-abortion procedures done in the United States. Vacuum aspiration is the accepted technique for terminating pregnancy during the first trimester. The procedure can be performed under local anesthesia, although general anesthesia may be used. The procedure is usually performed in a specialized clinic or hospital. The cervix is dilated and a plastic tube is inserted into the uterine cavity. The tube is attached to an electric suction-pump machine (that makes a distinct loud noise), and the products of conception are withdrawn. The procedure usually takes from five to fifteen minutes. The total amount of tissue and blood withdrawn at five to six weeks of pregnancy is about 20 grams; at 11 to 12 weeks the amount is about 100 to 150 grams (Stewart, Stewart, Guest, & Hatcher, 1979). After suctioning, the physician may use a standard curette to make certain all the tissue has been removed. Risks of this procedure include perforation of the uterine wall, hemorrhage, and infection.

Most women say cramping occurs during or after the procedure, but it usually does not require analgesia. When local anesthesia is used, most women are able to move about soon after the procedure, and in many clinics it is routine for the client to walk to the recovery area. Most women feel ready to leave after an hour of observation. When general anesthesia is used, the woman is awakened from general anesthesia and is transferred to a recovery room, where observation for signs of bleeding are made and vital signs are closely monitored. The woman is usually ready to be released three to four hours after the procedure.

Dilation and Curettage (D and C) (from 12 to 14 Weeks of Pregnancy)

Dilation and curettage is an alternative method for performing a first-trimester abortion. The D-and-C abortion procedure is similar to the dilation of the cervix and curettage (scraping) of the endometrial lining of the uterus used to diagnose diseases of the uterus or to correct excessive or prolonged bleeding. A local or general anesthesia is used, and the procedure usually takes about 15 to 20 minutes. The cervix is dilated and the products of conception are removed using a standard curette. When general anesthesia is used, the woman is observed and monitored in the recovery room. The woman may be released from the hospital from several hours to one day after the procedure. A longer recovery period is usually associated with a D and C than with the suction abortion. The woman is informed that a vaginal discharge is part of the healing process and is told to avoid the use of tampons and to abstain from sexual intercourse for two to three weeks. A follow-up visit is scheduled.

Amniocentesis Abortion: Saline, Prostaglandins, or Urea (from 15 to 24 Weeks of Pregnancy)

Amniocentesis refers to the procedure in which a hollow needle is inserted into the fluid-filled amniotic sac surrounding the fetus in order to remove amniotic fluid or introduce medication. The procedure is performed under aseptic conditions, and the risks involved are infection, hemorrhage, retained placenta or tissue, and water intoxication. Because the woman is asked to report unusual sensations, general anesthesia is not used. About 6% of all induced abortions in the United States are done using this procedure.

A slender hollow needle or plastic tube is inserted through an anesthetized area in the lower abdomen into the amniotic sac. Saline, urea, or prostaglandins are inserted through the tube into the amniotic sac surrounding the fetus, and the tube is withdrawn after the solution is injected. Most women have a period of several hours after amniocentesis before the abortive process (labor) begins. Once the symptoms of abortion appear (abdominal pain, vaginal bleeding, rupture of the amniotic sac), oxytocics may be administered intravenously to strengthen uterine contractions and minimize blood loss. The products of conception, a relatively small but recognizable fetus, are most often expelled as in a spontaneous, complete abortion. The expulsion may occur as early as six to eight hours after the introduction of the selected solution or as late as 36 to 48 hours. The expulsion is usually not associated with pain, tearing does not occur, and an episiotomy is not required. After a three-to-four-hour period of observation, most women are able to go home. Women who undergo this induced abortion procedure are asked to prepare for a 48-hour stay in the hospital.

Hysterotomy (after 15 Weeks of Pregnancy)

Hysterotomy is major surgery and is rarely used as an abortion technique. It involves an incision through the abdominal wall and uterus to remove the fetus. Sometimes a tubal sterilization can be carried out at the same time. A general or spinal anesthetic is used and the woman can expect several postoperative days in the hospital. The postoperative complications that can occur are similar to those occurring after any abdominal surgery. As is true of other induced abortion procedures, reproductive and sexual function are not affected; however, future deliveries may be done by cesarian section.

LEGAL AND POLITICAL ENVIRONMENT

In the early 1800s, there was no abortion legislation in the United States and advertisements for abortion services appeared in urban and rural newspapers and magazines. In the 1830s, abortion became a statutory crime for the first time. By 1900 almost all jurisdictions had restricted and even criminalized abortion (Mohr, 1978). In 1967, elective abortion became available again when Colorado broadened the conditions for permissible abortion. By 1973, 15 states and the District of Columbia had adopted similar statutes (Tietze & Lewitt, 1969).

On January 22, 1973, the United States Supreme Court announced two decisions—*Roe* v. *Wade* and *Doe* v. *Bolton*—that made induced abortion legal throughout the country. The court ruled that, during the first trimester, state and federal law may not impose any restriction, qualification, or prerequisite on how, when, or where an induced abortion is performed. The question of terminating a pregnancy is to be resolved solely by the pregnant woman and her physician.

The court stated that during the second trimester the state has an interest in promoting the health of the mother and may regulate the conditions under which induced abortions are performed but may not limit the reasons for which women may have induced abortions.

As for the state's interest in protecting the fetus, the court held that the word *person* as used in the Constitution applied only after birth and that therefore the Fourteenth Amendment's provision that no person shall be deprived of life, liberty, or property without due process does not apply. The Supreme Court stipulated that neither courts nor legislatures could, by adopting a single theory of when life begins, override a woman's constitutional right to choose abortion.

The Supreme Court ruled that in the last trimester the state has an interest in the potentiality of human life and may regulate and even forbid abortion except where it is necessary for the preservation of the life or health of the mother.

This landmark decision did not address the issue of the state requiring consent from someone other than the pregnant woman. In June, 1976, the Supreme Court held unconstitutional statutes requiring a husband's consent for a wife's induced abortion or parental consent for a minor's induced abortion (Pilpel, Zuckerman, & Ogg, 1977). Although the law seems clear that there can be no successful suit against a physician or health facility for providing induced abortion service to an adult or minor on her own consent, some physicians and health facilities do request that a consent be signed by the husband or parent. If such a request is unacceptable to the pregnant woman, she may have to search for a physician or health facility requiring only her consent for care.

On June 20, 1977, the Supreme Court ruled that neither the Constitution nor the federal Social Security Act requires the states to use public funds to subsidize induced abortions for indigent women. The court also stated that public hospitals are not obligated to provide abortion services (Alan Guttmacher Institute, 1977). These decisions placed equal accessibility to services, regardless of economic circumstances, into state and federal political arenas.

In December, 1977, the United States Congress attached the Hyde Amendment to the Department of Health, Education, and Welfare labor-appropriation bill. This amendment restricted federal funding of induced abortions for economically disadvantaged women except (1) when necessary to preserve a woman's life, (2) when necessary to prevent severe and long-lasting physical health damage when so determined by two physicians, or (3) for victims of rape or incest reporting promptly to a law-enforcement agency or public-health facility. In January, 1978, the Department of Health, Education, and Welfare announced that federal health-care funds may be used to pay for induced abortions performed on victims of rape or incest if the incidents are reported within sixty days. Reports could be made by the victim or by any third party, including private health facilities to which the victim may have gone for medical treatment (Alan Guttmacher Institute, 1978).

On February 19, 1980, the Supreme Court granted a review of *Harris* v. *McRae*. The question presented was whether or not the federal law (Hyde Amendment) that prohibits federal financing of induced abortions violates the religious-freedom guarantee of the First Amendment and equal-protection component of the Fifth Amendment's due-process clause (*Harris* v. *McRae*, 1980a).

On June 30, 1980, the Supreme Court decided that states participating in federal health-care funding (Medicaid) are not required to fund medically necessary abortions for which federal reimbursement is made unavailable by the Hyde Amendment. The Court has also decided that the Hyde Amendment does not violate the religious-freedom guarantees of the First Amendment and does not impinge on a woman's due-process liberty interests (*Harris* v. *McRae*, 1980b).

The January, 1973, Supreme Court decision made induced abortion legal, and abortion thus became part of the delivery of health care. This decision escalated moral uncertainties, exacerbated the ethical dilemmas of health professionals, and amplified the discord in society's acceptance of abortion as a human right. The woman searching for her own solution to a problem pregnancy does so in a changing sociocultural climate and a stormy political and legal scene.

DECISION MAKING AND PROBLEM PREGNANCY

Sociodemographic Aspects

Attitudes concerning the acceptability of abortion still vary widely. Education, religion, religiousness, total number of children intended, and attitudes toward women's roles are important predictors of abortion attitudes. It is true that public support for unrestricted abortion is not unanimous; however, public opinion has continuously moved in the direction of the least restrictive circumstances (Jones & Westcoff, 1978).

Between 1973 and 1977, four million women—1 of every 11 women of reproductive age—obtained more than five million abortions (Forrest, Tietze, & Sullivan, 1978). In 1977, the 50 states and the District of Columbia reported 1,079,430 abortions to the Center for Disease Control, a 9% increase over 1976. The national abortion ratio rose 4%, from 312 per 1000 live births in 1976 to 325 per 1000 live births in 1977, or almost one abortion for every three live births. The trend toward redistribution of abortions into states that had restrictive abortion laws before 1973 appeared to have leveled off; the same proportion of women obtain the procedure out of state (10%) as in 1976 (Table 11.1) (Center for Disease Control, 1979).

As in previous years, women who obtained abortions in 1977 were most often young, white, unmarried, and of low parity. Sixty-five percent were less than 25 years of age; 65% were white. Seventy-six percent of all women obtaining abortions were unmarried at the time of the procedure, and 53% had no living children. Curettage continued to be the most widely used procedure for reported legal abortions, accounting for 94% of abortions performed in 1977. Women continued to seek abortions at earlier gestational ages; over half (51%) of all abortions were performed at less than eight menstrual weeks of pregnancy, and 92% of abortions were induced within the first 12 weeks. Compared with 1976, the percentage of dilation and evacuation (D and E) and hypertonic saline instillation procedures after 12 weeks gestation decreased, whereas the percentage of prostaglandin and other instillation procedures increased (Center for Disease Control, 1979).

In 1977, 33 women died from abortions, compared with 27 in 1976, 47 in 1975, 53 in 1974, 56 in 1973, and 90 in 1972. Compared with 1976 there was a rise in the annual number of legal abortion deaths; 15 women died after legally induced abortion in 1977, compared with 11 in 1976, 29 in 1975, 25 in 1974, 25 in 1973, and 24 in 1972. In 1977 there were four deaths after illegally induced abortions and 14 deaths after spontaneous abortions. The death-to-case rate for legal abortions rose from 1.1 per 100,000 abortions in 1976 to 1.4 in 1977 (Center for Disease Control, 1979).

In August, 1977, when federal funds for financing abortions for Medicaid-eligible women were restricted, an estimated 295,000 abortions

Table 11.1. Summary of Characteristics of Women Receiving Abortions in the United States, 1972–1977

Characteristics	% Distribution[a]					
	1972	1973	1974	1975	1976	1977
Residence						
Abortion in-state	56.2	74.8	86.6	89.2	90.0	90.0
Abortion out-of-state	43.8	25.2	13.4	10.8	10.0	10.0
Age						
≤ 19	32.6	32.7	32.7	33.1	32.1	30.8
20–24	32.5	32.0	31.8	31.9	33.3	34.5
≥ 25	34.9	35.3	35.6	35.0	34.6	34.7
Race						
White	77.0	72.5	69.7	67.8	66.6	66.4
Black and others	23.0	27.5	30.3	32.2	33.4	33.6
Marital Status						
Married	29.7	27.4	27.4	26.1	24.6	24.3
Unmarried	70.3	72.6	72.6	73.9	75.4	75.7
Number of Living Children						
0	49.4	48.6	47.8	47.1	47.7	53.4
1	18.2	18.8	19.6	20.2	20.7	19.1
2	13.3	14.2	14.8	15.5	15.4	14.4
3	8.7	8.7	8.7	8.7	8.3	7.0
4	5.0	4.8	4.5	4.4	4.1	3.3
≥ 5	5.4	4.9	4.5	4.2	3.8	2.9
Type of Procedure						
Curettage	88.6	88.4	89.7	90.9	92.8	93.8
Intrauterine instillation	10.4	10.4	7.8	6.2	6.0	5.4
Hysterotomy/Hysterectomy	0.6	0.7	0.6	0.4	0.2	0.2
Other	0.5	0.6	1.9	2.4	0.9	0.7
Weeks of Gestation						
≤ 8	34.0	36.1	42.6	44.6	47.0	51.2
9–10	30.7	29.4	28.7	28.4	28.0	27.2
11–12	17.5	17.9	15.4	14.9	14.4	13.1
13–15	8.4	6.9	5.5	5.0	4.5	3.4
16–20	8.2	8.0	6.5	6.1	5.1	4.3
≥ 21	1.3	1.7	1.2	1.0	0.9	0.9

SOURCE: Reprinted with permission. Center for Disease Control, *Abortion surveillance, annual summary, 1977* (Atlanta: Center for Disease Control, 1979).
[a]Excludes unknowns.

had been financed by federal funds through the Medicaid program in fiscal year 1977 (Center for Disease Control, 1979). The Abortion Monitoring in Sentinel Hospitals (AMSH) project, initiated by CDC, was designed to monitor any substantial increase in the number of Medicaid-eligible women seeking self-induced or non-physician-induced abortions. Preliminary results indicated that the states where most Medicaid abortions had been performed before the federal funding cutoff were then using state funds for performing abortions; therefore, the projected excess morbidity and mortality of Medicaid-eligible women did not occur. The restriction of public funds was found to be significantly associated, however, with gestational age at the time of abortion. In nonfunded states, Medicaid-eligible women with complications after legally induced abortions had a 1.9-week-later mean gestational age than their counterparts in funded states. Moreover, Medicaid-eligible women in nonfunded states had a 2.4-week-later mean gestational age than non-Medicaid-eligible women in the same states. The CDC (1979) concluded that the restriction of public funds for abortion did not cause large numbers of Medicaid-eligible women to choose non-physician-induced or self-induced abortions; however, they may have delayed their abortions to raise enough private funds for the procedure.

In three of five comparable studies, no link was found between previous induced abortions and later unfavorable outcomes such as stillbirths, ectopic pregnancies, complications of delivery, low birth weight, ill health or congenital malformations in the newborn, or increased neonatal deaths. Teenagers and women who have never given birth do not appear to be at greater risk than other women for unfavorable subsequent pregnancy outcomes as the result of induced abortions. Preliminary results of one study show an increased incidence of miscarriage and other problems associated with prior D and C but not with D and E. In another study, however, no evidence of an association between miscarriage and prior induced abortion was found (Five Studies, 1978).

In 1977, about 560,000 women who wanted and needed abortion services were unable to obtain them, primarily because the services were unavailable in their own or nearby communities. An estimated 458,000 women who did obtain abortions had to travel outside their home counties for service—340,000 to counties within their state and 118,000 to other states (Forrest, Tietze, & Sullivan, 1978).

In 1976, abortion providers were identified in 698 counties, or one-fifth of all U.S. counties. Eight of ten public hospitals and six of ten Catholic private hospitals do not provide abortion services. In 1976, 16% of abortions were performed in nonhospital clinics, the major provider of abortion services, and 35% by hospital providers. An estimated 9% of ob-gyn specialists perform abortions in their offices (Forrest, Tietze, & Sullivan, 1978).

The availability of abortion services remains highly concentrated on the east and west coasts and in relatively few other metropolitan areas. In several states, legal abortion is almost as unavailable as illegal abortion was. In 1974, New York and California, where just one-fifth of all U.S. women of reproductive age reside, accounted for nearly two-fifths of all abortions reported, whereas in such states as Louisiana, Mississippi, North Dakota, and West Virginia, virtually no abortions were reported (Weinstock, Tietze, Jaffe, Dryfoos, 1975). The requirements of skill at health-care seeking and extensive travel restrict and penalize poor, rural, young, and black women, who are a major portion of the women who are in need and underserved.

The Decision-Making Process

Women decide to terminate pregnancies for many reasons. Rape and incest are commonly used to justify induced abortion, but they account for less than 1% of abortions; medical reasons account for less than 2%. The vast majority of women give social and personal reasons: "I am not married," "I cannot afford a child now," "A child would interfere with my education," "I feel unable to cope with a child now," "I already have enough children," "I think I'm too young to have a child." Most women give more than one reason. The majority (63%) who choose induced abortion make their decision soon after they acknowledge they are pregnant. Only about 25% decide just before the induced abortion, and about 8% had decided on that course of action before they got pregnant (Diamond et al., 1973). Whatever the reasons given, the solutions considered, or the choices made, there is no psychologically painless way to cope with a problem pregnancy.

In a recent study, most of the 329 women who experienced first-trimester induced abortions reported conflicting emotions. Elevation of both anxiety and depression were strongly related to the problem pregnancy. Few women had perceived themselves as proabortion. The most trying time was the period after the pregnancy had been confirmed but before termination. Women who underwent abortions typically were involved in monogamous sexual relationships, whatever their marital status, and their male partners were considered the main source of emotional support. For these women, abortion was a difficult solution to a pregnancy perceived as an insurmountable problem. Freeman (1978) concluded that induced abortion is not an unusual choice of a few atypical women but rather an experience undergone by average women who describe themselves in terms of traditional feminine concepts and who are emotionally stable.

Swigar, Quinlan, and Wexler (1977) compared the characteristics of 100 women who sought abortion but chose not to follow through with 100 women who proceeded with the abortion. The women who chose not to have the abortion were more indecisive, expressed greater concern about the procedure and its consequences, were less educated (as were their partners), and received more negative comments from their partners.

In a comparison between women who selected abortion and women who carried a problem pregnancy to term, it was found that the women who selected induced abortion were more oriented to future planning, had higher personal aspirations, and were more idealistic about marriage and eventual motherhood. The researchers concluded that the only identifying characteristic of the woman who selects induced abortion may be a problem pregnancy that she has decided not to continue (Steinhoff, Smith, & Diamond 1972).

In a study about advice in the abortion decision, a group of abortion, obstetric, and nonhospital control subjects reported on the process of decision making that led to having an induced abortion, carrying a pregnancy to term, and engaging in significant behavior not related to a pregnancy. When compared with the women in the obstetric and control groups, the women in the abortion group sought two fewer persons for advice and sought advice from professionals and persons outside their immediate families. Control subjects reported significantly greater difficulty making their decisions than abortion subjects, but control subjects and obstetric subjects felt greater satisfaction with their decisions. The reported differences may be caused by the nature of the decision. For the women in the nonhospital control group, the decision, outcome, and consequences largely involved themselves. Although the decision of the women in the obstetric group affected more people, family and friends usually responded positively to the mother and the expected child. The decision to abort usually confronts issues of personal self-esteem, family reputation, and traditional values. Fear or uncertainty about the reaction of family and friends may result in dissatisfaction in the decision about induced abortion. The process in the decision about induced abortion usually involved conflict between the expectations society has about women and about pregnant women, and the expectations the woman has of herself as a woman with a problem pregnancy. To discern the extent of this conflict is to understand better the advice sought and the formation of the decision (Luscutoff & Elms, 1975).

Bracken and Kasl (1975a) outline five steps a woman follows in making a successful decision about problem pregnancy. The first step is to acknowledge the pregnancy. This may not be easy and is generally preceded by denying, ignoring, or explaining away the usual symptoms. The second step is to formulate alternative outcomes. The woman recognizes for herself the three possible choices—continue the pregnancy and assume single or married parenthood, continue the pregnancy and relinquish the child for adoption, and terminate the pregnancy. The third step is to choose to continue or terminate the pregnancy. At this point multiple factors and personal conflicts are considered, and the more factors and conflicts dealt with, the more successful the decision. The fourth step is to make a commitment to the choice made. If the decision is to continue the pregnancy, the woman begins prenatal care or contacts an adoption agency and moves toward long- and short-term economic plans. If the decision is to terminate the pregnancy, the woman selects a suitable abortion service and gathers information about the process ahead. Whatever the choice, she contacts and interacts with the people who support her decision. The fifth step is to adhere to the decision. The woman who makes a firm decision, is comfortable with it, believes it is right for her, and has the support of significant others has the best outcome.

DELAYED DECISION MAKING AND PROBLEM PREGNANCY

The advantages of first-trimester induced abortion make it important to learn why some women with problem pregnancy delay their decision making. Women who demonstrate delayed decision making about problem pregnancy are usually young, single primigravidas experiencing their first abortions. Black women, women in lower socioeconomic groups, those with lower levels of completed education, and the unemployed tend to delay induced abortion (Bracken & Kasl, 1975b, 1976; Bracken & Swigar, 1972). Late induced abortions occur most frequently among economically, educationally, and socially disadvantaged women and especially among very young teenagers. Tietze and Murstein (1975) view this fact as a reflection of the inexperience of the very young in recognizing the symptoms of pregnancy, their unwillingness to accept the reality of their situation, their ignorance about where to seek advice and help, and their reluctance to confide in adults.

Kerenyi, Glascock, and Horowitz (1973) suggest that internal and external conflicts are additional reasons for delayed decision making. External conflicts include lack of information on availability or location of services, bureaucratic delays, and inaccurate physician or clinic diagnosis. Internal conflicts include ambivalence, fear of telling parents or partner, and late recognition or denial of pregnancy until signs and symptoms become obvious.

The differential characteristics of 697 women requesting induced abortion were studied according to when in pregnancy they presented (Fielding et al., 1978) (Table 11.2). The greatest delay occurred among the unmarried and minimally educated. Fear, which was a characteristic of the young, poorly informed contraceptors, had the greatest impact on the delayed decision. Denial was more likely to be found among older and better-informed women. Physician delay and laboratory error were concentrated in the women presenting in the early part of the second trimester. Lack of information was uniformly distributed and not concentrated among those of limited education. Denial, ambivalence, fear, and menstrual irregularities were uniformly distributed and constituted the greatest proportion of reasons for delaying the decision longest.

In an analysis of women who had repeat abortions, Bracken and Kasl (1975b) found that the experience of a previous abortion did not change the psychologic reaction or make the decision to have an induced abortion easier. The decreased delay in obtaining induced abortion among these women was due to the shorter time they took to anticipate, suspect, and acknowledge pregnancy and locate the abortion clinic once the decision to abort was made.

The sociodemographic characteristics of women who delay the decision to abort can be identified, but how the psychosocial, cultural, and environmental factors influence decision making is not clear. Further study

Table 11.2. Women's Stated Reasons for Delay Seeking Repeat Abortion

Reason	Frequency	
	% of total	% of known
Denial	21.4	22.6
Menstrual irregularity	17.6	18.6
Physician delay	15.2	16.0
Ambivalence	14.8	15.6
Lack of information	7.6	8.0
Fear	7.1	7.5
Laboratory error	6.7	7.1
Financial	2.9	3.1
Unavailable resource	1.0	1.1
Continued pregnancy	0.5	0.5
Religion	0.0	0.0
Unknown	5.2	

SOURCE: Reprinted by permission of the C. V. Mosby Company. Fielding, W. L., Sachtele-ben, M. R., Friedman, L. M., & Friedman, E. A. Comparison of women seeking early and late abortion. *American Journal of Obstetrics and Gynecology*, 1978, *131*(3), 304–310.

is needed of how the woman's resources for dealing with decisional conflict, lack of information about induced abortion, and lack of health-seeking skills influence decision making.

INDUCED ABORTION REFUSED

There are two kinds of induced abortion refusals. A request for an induced abortion may be denied, or a woman with a problem pregnancy may change her mind and carry the pregnancy to term after the request has been granted. In the United States there has never been a study of women with problem pregnancies who were denied abortion or the children they had to bear.

Swigar et al. (1976) and Swigar, Quinlan, and Wexler (1977) have done the only follow-up studies of women who changed their minds. There were no statistically significant demographic or gynecologic differences between women who decided to carry a problem pregnancy to term and a control group of women who implemented their plans for induced abortion during the same period. The most influential factor in the woman's or partners' decision to refuse induced abortion was the public controversy about the morality of obtaining induced abortion. The second most important factor was the sexual partner's desire for a baby, and the third was fear of the procedure and possible complications.

INDUCED ABORTION AND CONTRACEPTION

Discussions about induced abortion often reflect the concern that relatively easy access to abortion will lead to neglect of contraception. Information available from New York City about women over age 20, most of whom were married, suggests that after induced abortion there is general or more effective practice of contraception (Tietze, 1975). Using the 1965–1975 data on the proportion of white women fifteen to forty-four years of age using contraception, Tietze (1977) noted an increase rather than a decrease in contraceptive practice following the 1973 Supreme Court decision. In a nationwide sample, the percentage of sexually experienced and active teenage women reporting the use of contraceptives at last intercourse increased from 45.4 to 63.5% between 1971 and 1976 (Zelnik and Kantner, 1977, 1978). Research literature suggests that women who have had induced abortions are more likely to use contraceptives and women who use contraceptives are more likely to resort to induced abortion in case of contraceptive failure (Moore, 1974).

REPEAT INDUCED ABORTION

The use of services for repeat induced abortion is viewed with dismay and considered a problem. State and federal officials have said it is disturbing to have recipients of federal payments come back for additional induced abortions.

Lee (1969) studied 69 women who had had an illegal induced abortion performed by a physician before the 1973 Supreme Court decision. The women were described as "well-educated, intelligent, and sophisticated," and each had obtained medical advice about contraception. Of these 69 women, 28 (42%) later had a second abortion, and nine of the 28 (32%) had a third.

In 1974, in New York City, repeat abortions accounted for more than one-fifth of all resident abortions—although the repeat abortion rate remained constant over the years, at 66 repeat abortions to every one thousand first-time abortions (Pakter, Nelson, & Swigar, 1975). The Center for Disease Control (1979) reported that of the women who had had abortions in 1977, 17% had had one previous abortion, 3% had had two abortions, and 1%, three or more abortions. The proportion of women reporting one or more induced abortions ranged from 9% in Nebraska to 32% in the District of Columbia.

Women who had repeat induced abortions were compared with women having first-time induced abortions, pregnant women carrying to term, and nonpregnant women at risk of conception (Schneider & Thompson, 1976). Each of the women who had a repeat induced abortion was matched with a woman in each of the other three populations for parity, marital status, and age. The study showed that women who have had one induced abortion tend to increase subsequent use of contraception and are more likely to continue it than women about to have their first induced abortion; however, they are less consistent and accurate in their contraceptive practices than are sexually active nonpregnant women. Women seeking repeat induced abortions are more frequently dissatisfied with themselves, more often perceive themselves as victims of "bad luck," feel unable to control their lives, especially in areas of sexuality and reproduction, and more frequently express negative feelings toward the current induced abortion (Leach, 1977).

For most couples, contraception and its practice involve risk-taking or chance behavior. The behavior is not a thoughtless act. It involves balancing risks and probabilities. Luker (1975, 1977) states that risk taking is an active reconsideration of the costs and benefits of contraception compared with the costs and benefits of pregnancy, and it is often accompanied by misconceptions about the degree of risk. It is postulated that a certain irreducible proportion of problem pregnancies "inevitably arise from the interplay between contraceptive technology and human behavior" (Cobliner, Schulman, & Smith, 1975).

One study demonstrated that if 100 women rely on a method that provides 98 to 99% effectiveness after a first induced abortion, about 21 to 51 will probably have at least one more problem pregnancy within 10 years. Some 69 to 97 out of 100 women who rely upon foam or condoms, which have 90 to 95% effectiveness, will face a problem pregnancy at least once more within 10 years. Even within the first year, a significant number of repeat problem pregnancies can be expected (Tietze, 1974). These statistics make it inappropriate to view repeat induced abortion as indicative of a psychologic problem or careless contraceptive behavior. Repeat induced abortion rates may reflect nothing more than statistical odds (Stewart et al., 1976).

PSYCHOLOGIC CONSEQUENCES OF INDUCED ABORTION

The myth of frequent and severe consequences of induced abortion persists. Each year there are about 4,000 documented incidents of postpartum psychoses requiring hospitalization in the United States—between 10 and 20 per 10,000 deliveries. There should be a sizable number of hospitalized postabortion psychoses if induced abortion is as traumatic for some women as term delivery (Fleck, 1970). So-called postpartum blues are well known, typical depressive stress reactions to the end of a pregnancy. "Postabortion blues" have been observed to be generally brief and mild unless a serious mental disturbance was present before abortion (Osofsky, Osofsky, & Rajan, 1973). In a matched control study of women seeking either term deliveries or first- or second-trimester induced abortions, the researchers noted that "induced abortion appears to be a benign procedure compared to term birth, psychologically and physically" (Athanasiou et al., 1973).

In 1958, the Kinsey Institute reported the interviews of 44 women who admitted to having had induced abortion, and less than 10% reported psychological upset. Sixty percent of the women had premarital induced abortions and achieved orgasm in the first year of marriage, as compared with 52% of women without premarital induced abortion (Gebhard et al., 1958). Kummer (1963) surveyed 32 Los Angeles psychiatrists who frequently saw women after induced abortion. Seventy-five percent of the psychiatrists did not recall seeing a single woman with moderate or severe psychiatric sequelae. The other 25% had seen significant sequelae only rarely.

Niswander and Patterson (1967) studied 116 women who had induced abortions in 1963, 1964, or 1965. Ninety-five percent of the women were certain induced abortion had been the best solution under the circumstances. Minor doubts had been common, but few regrets remained after eight months. The women who were generally satisfied but suffered the greatest doubt were those who were married and who had induced abortion for medical reasons (maternal organic disease or rubella in the first trimester). The women most likely to be satisfied were unmarried and without dependable partner support. It appears that when a problem pregnancy occurs in a socially acceptable environment, the woman is more regretful of the induced abortion even though the pregnancy was potentially at the risk of her life or of a deformed child. On the other hand, if the problem pregnancy occurs in a socially unacceptable and nonaccepting environment, the induced abortion will rarely be regretted. The findings show that once the decision is made, the induced abortion is therapeutic—the client feels better and therefore functions more effectively.

A study was conducted to assess the effect of induced abortion on the emotional state of 57 unmarried women from 12 to 36 years old. The women were predominantly black, Protestant, multiparous, and of the low socioeconomic class. Mean preabortion scores on psychometric tests placed their emotional stress midway between normal and neurotic. Test scores obtained four weeks after induced abortion showed statistically significant reduction in distress, and 60% of the women stated they felt relieved and better. The conclusion was that these women did not experience psychologic ill effects from induced abortion performed in a permissive atmosphere (Jacobs et al., 1974).

The importance of the level of support of significant others for the decision to terminate a problem pregnancy was examined as a predictor of the reaction to the induced abortion in 489 women at a New York clinic. Reaction to the abortion was measured within an hour of the procedure. The overall short-term reaction to the induced abortion was quite positive for the whole group. Partner support was significantly more important in predicting a favorable reaction among older women, whereas parental support was a more powerful predictor among younger women (Bracken, Hachamovitch, & Grossman, 1974).

Freeman (1977) found that some women making a decision about induced abortion did not perceive themselves to be active and controlling their own lives and thus chose induced abortion out of perceived necessity. After abortion, however, these women felt that the experience resulted in a "different awareness about themselves," especially since for many it was their first experience with a major individual decision in which the consequences were important and affected others as well as themselves.

The literature and four case studies were used to analyze the decision-making process and the outcomes of induced abortion (Friedman, Greenspan, & Mittleman, 1974). The researchers concluded there is a greater likelihood of postabortion psychiatric illness when any of the following elements are present: strong ambivalence, coercion by family or health professional, medical indication (hereditary disease), concomitant severe psychiatric illness, and the woman's feeling that the decision was not her own.

Induced abortion cannot be seen as a minor procedure that lacks significance to the woman. It occurs as the result of a problem pregnancy—a crisis situation filled with anxiety, vulnerability, and dependence. According to Friedman et al. (1974), induced "abortion presents a double challenge because it is both the termination of a pregnancy and a surgical procedure, and any surgery causes a complex of feelings related to invasion of the body." The emotional responses of loss, sadness, guilt, regret, and anxiety are part of the normal reactions of any person to a stressful situation. In those rare instances in which postabortion psychiatric disturbances appear, they are more likely to relate to the degree of adjustment existing before the pregnancy than to the abortion procedure. Very few women with histories of severe psychiatric problems have difficulty with induced abortion—most remain the same, and some even improve (Friedman et al., 1974).

It seems possible that, for a vast majority of women, when dependable support is available, sensitive counseling is provided, the woman's decision is respected, and there is no interference with her right to make the decision she believes best for herself, induced abortion can represent a maturing experience of successful coping and crisis resolution.

INDUCED ABORTION IN THE TEENAGE YEARS

Each year more than one million 15- to 19-year-olds become pregnant. Two-thirds of these pregnancies are conceived out of wedlock. In addition, some 30,000 girls younger than 15 get pregnant annually (Alan Guttmacher Institute, 1976).

In 1974, 28% of these one million pregnancies resulted in marital births conceived following marriage, 10% resulted in marital births conceived before marriage, 21% resulted in out-of-wedlock births, 27% were terminated by induced abortion, and 14% resulted in miscarriage. Of the additional 30,000 pregnancies experienced by girls younger than 15, 45% were terminated by abortion, 36% resulted in out-of-wedlock births, 6% ended in marital births, and almost all of these resulted from pregnancies conceived out of wedlock (Alan Guttmacher Institute, 1976).

About one-third of all abortions in the United States each year are obtained by teenagers—50% by 18- and 19-year-olds, 45% by 15- to 17-year-olds, and 5% by girls 14 and younger. Between 1972 and 1975, the rate of induced abortion rose from 19 to 31 per 1000 for women under twenty. The abortion rate among all teenagers increased by more than three-fifths, and the abortion rate of girls under 15 nearly doubled over the four-year period. The rate among 18- and 19-year-olds is higher than the rate for women 20 to 24. The ratio of abortions per 1000 live births increased in a like manner (Alan Guttmacher Institute, 1976) (Fig. 11.1).

In a study of preadult fertility and family formation, Zelnik and Kantner (1972) found that blacks, when compared with whites, become sexually active earlier, are less likely to use contraception, prefer a younger age for marriage, and do not want any more children than whites. However, in 1976 black teenagers had slightly more births than white teenagers but many fewer abortions (Zelnik & Kantner, 1978).

A New York City study found that the demographic characteristics of teenagers having repeat induced abortions were similar to those of teenagers having first-time induced abortions. Although induced abortion was not the preferred form of fertility regulation, teenagers seeking repeat induced abortion more frequently stopped using one method of contraception without adopting another. Age, education, and parity were associated with the choice of specific methods (Cahn, 1976).

Perez-Reyes and Falk (1973) interviewed 41 adolescent girls under age 16 before and after a hospital abortion and found that about 33% said they were happy that they had the abortion and about 15% had unfavorable feelings of depression and guilt. They concluded, after interviews and testing, that the physical and mental health of the adolescents was considerably better after the abortion than it had been immediately preceding it.

Evans, Selstad, and Welcher (1976) interviewed 333 single adolescent girls before and six months after abortion. They found that about 20% regretted the decision, and these girls were most likely to be Catholic, Chicano, very young, conservative in their attitudes toward abortion, poor students, of low-income homes; and felt that abortion was forced on them.

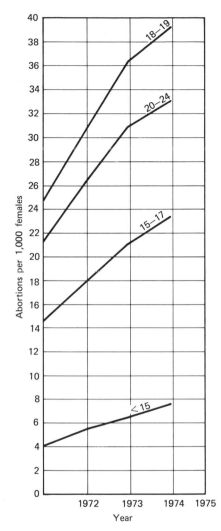

Figure 11.1. Number of legal abortions per 1,000 females aged 14–24, by age group, United States, 1972-1975. Reprinted with permission from *11 Million Teenagers: What Can Be Done About the Epidemic of Adolescent Pregnancies in the United States*, published by The Alan Guttmacher Institute, New York, 1976.

Legal abortion is not equally available in all parts of the country. The consequences for adolescents are indicated by the very different teenage abortion rates in the different states, ranging from three induced abortions per 1,000 live births in Mississippi to 1,300 induced abortions per 1,000 live births in New York (Alan Guttmacher Institute, 1976). Teenagers are underserved in family planning clinics, and 27% have had a pregnancy before receiving services (Day et al., 1976).

The national problem of teenage abortion requires the nurse to examine her feelings and abilities in the role of client advocate for families and communities requiring public health education and services. There is a need for better understanding of what teenagers need and want for effective contraception. There is a need for support of research for new, safer, and different techniques of contraception better suited to the frequently episodic nature of teenagers' sexual activity. There is a need for realistic sex education with emphasis on responsible separation of sexuality and reproduction. There is a need for a network of available and accessible family planning programs, adequate pregnancy counseling services, and induced abortion services (Alan Guttmacher Institute, 1976).

PROFESSIONAL PREPARATION FOR INDUCED ABORTION SERVICES

Because induced abortion is a surgical procedure, health professionals are involved in every phase from referral to follow-up care. Health professionals are crucial to equitable and effective provision of induced abortion services. Their attitudes and behavior directly affect the quality of care women considering induced abortion receive.

Nurses and all health professionals who have personal, moral, or religious objections to abortion should be free to decline to participate in induced abortion services without penalty or coercion. They have, however, the professional obligation to make appropriate referrals.

Clients considering induced abortion are best served by a health professional who has a sincere belief in the right of the client to make her own decision after she has explored all the options. The efforts of the effective health professional are not directed to influencing the decision made but to the process and quality of the decision itself.

Schools of nursing have been hesitant to plan laboratory experience for students in induced abortion services. Induced abortion is an important, legal, and reputable part of the delivery of health care. In a hospital in which the staff viewed induced abortion with disfavor, clients who had induced abortions perceived the nursing care as less than satisfactory (Harper, Marcom, & Wall, 1972). Nurses have the responsibility to recognize their own attitudes and beliefs and to plan and implement nursing care based on the physical and emotional needs of the client undergoing induced abortion. The care taught and learned can be positive and growth producing for the clients and the student and should be part of undergraduate and graduate nursing curricula (Goldman, 1971; Malo-Juevera, 1971; Mims & Swenson, 1980).

THE ROLE OF THE NURSE AS EDUCATOR-COUNSELOR

The client considering induced abortion is in conflict. The nurse-client interaction is based on crisis intervention in a safe and accepting environment. The emphasis is on promoting decision making, evaluating options, involving significant others, giving emotional support, and providing information (Sanders, Wagener, & Thompson, 1973). The nurse can be a reliable, accepting, and informed base of support as the client defines her needs and problems and seeks solutions involving the quality of her life.

The decision-making process is never easy. The nurse actively encourages exploration of each of the three options in terms of the client's present situation. It is helpful for the client to list the long- and short-term practical and emotional effects of each option on herself and her significant others. The client is urged to express her thoughts and feelings, to ventilate her anxieties, explore her ambivalence, confront discomfort, and avoid impulsive decision making.

The teenage client requires sensitive listening, teaching, and counseling. The nurse talks with the client—gives information, answers questions factually, and encourages the expression of thoughts about pregnancy, the physiologic toll of motherhood, and the realities of parenting, sexuality, reproduction, and contraception.

The nurse not only encourages the expression of feelings but also helps in acknowledging and dealing with feelings that may be frightening and embarrassing. The nurse can be a nonjudgmental and a reliable reference for the pregnant teenager who may have little experience or few resources to use in making a major decision in a short period of time (Dorin, 1978; Gedan, 1974). The client is urged to participate actively in the decision making and to assume responsibility for the implementation without coercion or passive submission. In making her own decision, the client gains a sense of her own ability to solve problems and makes a commitment to the decision.

Whenever possible, the nurse makes every effort to involve the people significant to the client—parents, relatives, husband, sexual partner, peers, and friends, encouraging them to express their feelings, conflicts, and anxieties. Factual answers to their questions and concerns and acceptance of their feelings is comforting and reassuring. The nurse can assist the client and her significant others is planning and structuring their caring and support.

More attention is being focused on how to counsel clients' partners. It is recognized that the partner is emotionally involved in the induced abortion experience. Anxiety, helplessness, guilt, a vacillating sense of responsibility, and regret are the concerns and feelings usually expressed (Gordon & Kilpatrick, 1977). A group of men initially indicated a desire to play a supportive and responsible but limited role. However, as information about contraception and the induced abortion procedures was gained, their responsiveness increased. Permitting men increased participation in their partner's experience is educationally and psychologically sound (Rothstein, 1977).

Confirming pregnancy by laboratory testing and pelvic examination is the first step in counseling for induced abortion. Interpreting the pregnancy test and diagnosing pregnancy remain the responsibility of the physician.

All counseling about induced abortion includes contraceptive counseling. The nurse must be thoroughly knowledgeable about all methods of contraception and community contraceptive services. The client needs to deal with the full reality of sexuality and reproduction and the implications for her own sexuality. The nurse helps the client make a responsible and informed choice about future contraception (Chapter 9).

Providing information about induced abortion procedures is an integral part of counseling. The nurse gives information about the relative risks of early as opposed to late termination and the time limits involved, how each of the procedures is performed, where they are available, and the estimated costs. The objective is to allay fears and enable the client to gain greater control over conflicts and anxieties elicited by the procedure. The nurse uses teaching skills to describe the procedures step by step—sights, sounds, smells, and touch. Anatomical charts and graphs can be effective teaching aids. Orienting the client to the physical environment, showing the actual instruments to be used in the procedure, and introducing the client to the personnel to be involved are suggested. This can be done individually or in small groups. The group process allows for the sharing of common fears and anxieties.

The information about amniocentesis abortion requires sensitive attention. The client needs preparation for the labor involved. Information about fetal growth and development is helpful preparation for the expulsion of a recognizable fetus. Some clients ask about the sex, and some clients ask to look at the fetus. The client needs to know she will not be alone. A nurse will be there to answer her questions and respond to her feelings.

For all clients, information about the procedure is incomplete without a description and discussion of the feelings likely to occur before, during, and after the procedure. Acceptance is provided for such feelings as fear, helplessness, sadness, grief, loneliness, loss, and relief. The client and significant others need reassurance that these feelings are normal, acceptable, and appropriate and can be expressed and worked through.

If the client chooses to continue the pregnancy, the nurse provides information on the necessary procedures for adoption and the location of adoption agencies and data on public and private agencies in the community concerned with the welfare of mother and child.

If the client chooses to terminate the pregnancy, the procedure is scheduled within a few days. Written consent is obtained, and the time of arrival and length of stay in the health facility stipulated. At all times the nurse is ready to repeat and clarify information, for anxiety decreases the receiving and retention of information.

Postabortion counseling begins before the procedure and always includes encouraging the client to use a 24-hour emergency telephone number. Rh immunization is routine. The client receives verbal and written information about the physical occurrences that are expected and normal, the signs and symptoms of possible complications, what she may do, and what she may not do. She should take her temperature twice a day and report an elevation, take a shower or bath, wash her hair, wear sanitary pads only, wear a snug bra day and night for two or three days if breast milk appears, and keep both the medical follow-up appointment and counseling session scheduled in two weeks. She should not, for two weeks, have sexual intercourse, douche, or use tampons.

The range of emotions likely to be experienced after induced abortion should be reviewed. The client may be angry at her partner—she may avoid sex or risk unprotected intercourse. She may feel loss and need help to grieve for the lost child. She may experience a sense of relief. She may be angry with herself and uncertain she did the right thing. She needs to be encouraged to use the counseling service as she works through these feelings. She needs to know that for most women the induced abortion experience heightens and strengthens their ability to promote their own mental and physical well-being.

NURSING PROCESS

Client: Nancy Pruitt, age 42, single (divorced twenty years ago after a six-month marriage), secretary. Pregnancy resulted from a sexual relationship with her employer.

Nurse: Josephine Fong, nurse and counselor at a Planned Parenthood facility in an eastern state.

Assessment

Subjective Data

"Five weeks late with my period and I'm never late."
"Dr. Ryan says I'm pregnant."
"Phil says he wants to marry me, but there's his wife and growing children. He keeps saying he has to wait until the children are older. Wonder what age is older?"
"Besides the office we see each other once or twice a week, but never on weekends. That's classic, too, isn't it? I really have to do something with that relationship."
"I'm very careful about the diaphragm. I always use it like I should—exactly."
"He wants me to have an abortion—he'll even pay for it. He says then

everything will be the same. He wants his world to be the same, but how about my world?"

"About the abortion—he's probably right, but I don't want things to be just the same. He'll have to listen to me some day."

"My mother just sat there and cried—as usual. This time I got mad at her. She's never any help—lovable but definitely not helpful."

"My two best friends, Ann and Liz, came through, though. Ann told me about this place."

"Some of me says—what my mother taught me—I should have the baby—but no. Maybe ten years ago I could have—but I don't think I can go it alone now."

"Adoption? No, I couldn't handle that. I'd feel even worse."

"Tell me about induced abortion. I'm pretty sure that's what I want."

Objective Data

Laboratory test positive for pregnancy (physician's report).
Pelvic examination confirms pregnancy (physician's report).
Sexual partner (Phil) is married and has children.
Wants change in relationship with Phil.
Expresses anger at mother.
Rules out adoption.
Not comfortable with single parenthood.
Seeks information about induced abortion.

Nursing Diagnosis

Lack of information about available options related to problem pregnancy.
Anger related to lack of emotional support from a significant other (mother).
Dissatisfaction in relationship with sexual partner (Phil) because of unproductive communication.

Planning

Encourage exploration of the three options available.
Provide verbal and written information about abortion procedures, specifying gestation-period time limits and relative risks.
Provide verbal and written information about community resources for prenatal care, adoption, maternal and child health, and induced abortion.

Review contraceptive methods and risk factors involved.
Encourage decision making.
Encourage expression of feelings with significant others.
Encourage acceptance of limitation in significant others.
Encourage reaching out for emotional support from significant others.
Encourage mobilization of support from significant others.
Encourage assessment of relationship with sexual partner.
Encourage request for change in relationship with sexual partner.
Encourage mutual problem solving.
Indicate availability of further counseling.
Encourage return visit.

Implementation

Make a list of the advantages and disadvantages of the three options.
Discuss the list and decision with significant others.
Make a decision.
Express feelings about lack of support with mother.
Request support from significant others.
Mobilize support from significant others.
Acknowledge different risk factors involved in contraceptive methods.
Make a list of what is acceptable and unacceptable in present relationship with sexual partner.
Request changes in present relationship with sexual partner.
Request mutual problem solving.
Contact free-standing induced abortion clinic.
Contact nurse (Planned Parenthood) about return visit after induced-abortion procedure.

Evaluation

On return visit three weeks after the abortion, client reports:

No regrets about decision—"believe it was right for me."
Induced abortion experience satisfactory—felt "well and cared for."
"No signs and symptoms of complications."
"Recovering as I expected."
"Feeling a little sad, but friends help."
Mother able to "give support requested."
Friends are "especially supportive."
Phil unwilling to consider any changes in relationship.
Mutual termination of relationship pending.
Will continue use of diaphragm and will request partner use condom in future sexual relationships.

BIBLIOGRAPHY

Alan Guttmacher Institute. *Eleven million teenagers: What can be done about the epidemic of adolescent pregnancies in the United States.* New York: Author, 1976.

Alan Guttmacher Institute. *Planned births, the future of the family, and the quality of American life.* New York: Author, 1977.

Alan Guttmacher Institute. *Washington Memo, January 13,* January 27, 1978.

Athanasiou, R., Oppel, W., Michelson, L., Unger, J., & Yager, M. Psychiatric sequelae to term birth and induced early and late abortion: A longitudinal study. *Family Planning Perspectives,* 1973, *5,* 227–231.

Bracken, M. B., Hachamovitch, M., & Grossman, G. The decision to abort and the psychological sequelae. *The Journal of Nervous and Mental Disease,* 1974, *158,* 154–162.

Bracken, M. B., & Kasl, S. V. Delay in seeking induced abortion: A review and theoretical analysis. *American Journal of Obstetrics and Gynecology,* 1975, *121,* 1008–1018. (a)

Bracken, M. B., & Kasl, S. V. First and repeat abortions: A study of decision making and delay. *Journal of Biosocial Science,* 1975, *7,* 473–491. (b)

Bracken, M. B., & Kasl, S. V. Psychosocial correlation of delayed decision to abort. *Health Education Monographs,* 1976, *4,* 6–44.

Bracken, M. B., & Sigar, M. E. Factors associated with delay in seeking induced abortion. *American Journal of Obstetrics and Gynecology,* 1972, *113,* 301–309.

Cahn, J. Correlation of repeat abortions. Presented at the Annual Meeting of the Planned Parenthood Federation of America, October 1976.

Cates, W., & Tietze, C. Standardized mortality rates associated with legal abortion: United States, 1972–1975. *Family Planning Perspectives,* 1978, *10,* 109–112.

Center for Disease Control. *Abortion surveillance,* 1974. Atlanta: Author, 1976.

Center for Disease Control. *Abortion surveillance, annual summary, 1977.* Atlanta: Author, 1979.

Clancy, B. The nurse and the abortion patient. *Nursing Clinics of North America,* 1973, *8,* 469–478.

Cobliner, G. W., Schulman, H., & Smith, V. Dynamics of contraceptive failures. *Journal of Biosocial Science,* 1975, *7,* 307–318.

Cronenwett, L. R., & Choyce, J. M. Saline abortion. *American Journal of Nursing,* 1971, *71,* 1754–1757.

Daubar, B., Zalar, M., & Goldstein, P. J. Abortion counseling and behavioral change. *Family Planning Perspectives,* 1972, *4,* 23–27.

Davis, A. J. Dilemmas in practice: Competing ethical claims in abortion. *American Journal of Nursing,* 1980, *80,* 1359.

Day, N., Brady, L., Faerstein, M., Stone, D., Radford, J., & Potts, L. *Improving family planning services for teenagers.* San Francisco: Urban and Rural Assistance Associates, 1976.

Diamond, J., Steinhoff, P. G., Palmore, J. A., & Smith, R. G. Sexuality, birth control, and abortion: A decision-making sequence. *Journal of Biosocial Science,* 1973, *1,* 221–225.

Doe v. *Bolton*, 93 Supreme Court 705 (1973), 41 USL Week 4233–4240 (No. 70-18), January 22, 1973.

Dorin, A. Adolescent sexuality: Adolescent depression: The nurse practitioner as counselor. *Pediatric Nursing*, 1978, *4*, 49–52.

Dunlop, J. L. Counseling of patients requesting an abortion. *The Practitioner*, 1978, *220*, 847–852.

Evans, J., Selstad, G., & Welcher, W. Teenagers: Fertility control behavior and attitudes before and after abortion, childbearing or negative pregnancy test. *Family Planning Perspectives*, 1976, *8*, 192–200.

Fielding, W. L., Sachtleben, M. R., Friedman, L. M., & Friedman, E. A. Comparison of women seeking early and late abortion. *American Journal of Obstetrics and Gynecology*, 1978, *131*, 304–310.

Five studies: No apparent harmful effect from legal abortion on subsequent pregnancies; D and C is possible exception. *Family Planning Perspectives*, 1978, *10*, 34–35; 38.

Fleck, S. Some psychiatric aspects of abortion. *Journal of Nervous and Mental Diseases*, 1970, *151*, 42–50.

Fonesca, J. D. Induced abortion: Nursing attitudes and action. *American Journal of Nursing*, 1968, *68*, 1022–1027.

Forrest, J. D., Tietze, C., & Sullivan, E. Abortion in the United States, 1976–1977. *Family Planning Perspectives*, 1978, *10*, 271–279.

Freeman, E. W. Influence of personality attributes on abortion experiences. *American Journal of Orthopsychiatry*, 1977, *47*, 503–513.

Freeman, E. W. Abortion: Subjective attitudes and feelings. *Family Planning Perspectives*, 1978, *10*, 150–155.

Friedman, C. M., Greenspan, R., & Mittleman, F. The decision-making process and the outcome of therapeutic abortion. *American Journal of Psychiatry*, 1974, *131*, 1332–1336.

Gebhard, P. H., Pomeroy, W. B., Martin, E. E., & Christensen, C. V. *Pregnancy, birth, and abortion.* New York: Hoeber, 1958.

Gedan, S. Abortion counseling with adolescents. *American Journal of Nursing*, 1974, *74*, 1856–1858.

Goldman, A. Learning abortion care. *Nursing Outlook*, 1971, *19*, 350–352.

Gordon, R. H., & Kilpatrick, C. A. A program of group counseling for men who accompany women seeking legal abortion. *Community Health Journal*, 1977, *13*, 291–295.

Harper, M. W., Marcom, B. R., & Wall, V. D. Abortion: Do attitudes of nursing personnel affect the patient's perception of care? *Nursing Research*, 1972, *21*, 327–331.

Harris v. *McRae*. 48 USL Week 3514 (No. 79-1268), February 19, 1980. (a)

Harris v. *McRae*. 48 USL Week 4941 (No. 79-1268), June 24, 1980. (b)

Jacobs, D., Garcia, C., Rickels, K., & Preucel, R. W. A prospective study on the psychological effects of therapeutic abortion. *Comprehensive Psychiatry*, 1974, *15*, 423–434.

Jekel, J. F., Tyler, N. C., & Klerman, L. V. Induced abortion and sterilization among women who became mothers as adolescents. *American Journal of Public Health*, 1977, *67*, 621–625.

Jones, E. F., & Westcoff, C. F. How attitudes toward abortion are changing. *Journal of Population*, 1978, *1*, 6–21.

Kay, B. J., & Thompson, C. W. N. An outcome evaluation of counseling services provided by abortion clinics. *Medical Care*, 1977, *15*, 858–868.

Keller, C., & Copeland, P. Counseling the abortion patient is more than talk. *American Journal of Nursing*, 1972, *72*, 102–106.

Kerenyi, T. D., Glascock, E. L., & Horowitz, M. L. Reasons for delayed abortion: Results of 400 interviews. *American Journal of Obstetrics and Gynecology*, 1973, *117*, 299–311.

Kummer, J. Post-abortion psychiatric illness: A myth? *American Journal of Psychiatry*, 1963, *119*, 980–983.

Leach, J. The repeat abortion patient. *Perspectives in Family Planning*, 1977, *9*, 37–39.

Lee, N. H. *The search for an abortionist*. Chicago: University of Chicago Press, 1969.

Liu, D. T., & Hudson, I. Karman Cannula and first trimester termination of pregnancy. *American Journal of Obstetrics and Gynecology*, 1974, *118,* 906–909.

Luker, K. *Taking chances: Abortion and the decision not to contracept*. Berkeley: University of California Press, 1975.

Luker, K. Contraceptive risk taking and abortion: Results and implications of a San Francisco Bay area study. *Studies in Family Planning*, 1977, *8*, 190–196.

Luscutoff, S. H., & Elms, A. C. Advice in the abortion decision. *Journal of Counseling Psychology*, 1975, *22*, 140–146.

Malo-Juevera, D. Preparing students for abortion care. *Nursing Outlook*, 1971, *19*, 347–349.

Mims, F. G., & Swenson, M. *Sexuality: A nursing perspective*. New York: McGraw-Hill, 1980.

Mohr, J. C. *Abortion in America*. New York: Oxford University Press, 1978.

Moore, E. C. *International inventory of information on induced abortion*. New York: International Institute for the Study of Human Reproduction, Columbia University, 1974.

Niswander, K. R., & Patterson, R. J. Psychologic reaction to therapeutic abortion. *Obstetrics and Gynecology*, 1967, *29*, 702–706.

Osofsky, J. D., Osofsky, H. J., & Rajan, R. Psychological effects of abortion: With emphasis upon immediate reactions and follow-up. In H. J. Osofsky & J. D. Osofsky (Eds.), *The abortion experience: Psychological and medical impact*. Hagerstown, Md.: Harper & Row Medical Division, 1973.

Pakter, J., Nelson, F., & Swigar, M. Legal abortion: A half-decade of experience. *Family Planning Perspectives*, 1975, *7*, 248–255.

Perez-Reyes, M., & Falk, R. Follow-up after therapeutic abortion in early adolescence. *Archives of General Psychiatry,* 1973, *28*, 120–126.

Personal experience at a legal abortion center. *American Journal of Nursing*, 1972, *72*, 110–112.

Pilpel, H. F., Zuckerman, R. J., & Ogg, E. *Abortion: Public issue, private decision*. Public Affairs Pamphlet No. 527. New York: Public Affairs Pamphlets, December, 1977.

Roe v. Wade. 93 Supreme Court 705 (1973), 41 USL Week 4213 (No. 70-18), January 22, 1973.

Rothstein, A. A. Men's reaction to their partner's elective abortion. *American Journal of Obstetrics and Gynecology*, 1977, *128*, 831–837.

Sanders. R. S., Wagener, J. M., & Thompson, G. E. Counseling for elective abortion. *Journal of the American College Health Association*, 1973, *5*, 446–450.

Schneider, S. M., & Thompson, D. S. Repeat abortion. *American Journal of Obstetrics and Gynecology*, 1976, *126*, 316–320.

Steinhoff, P. G., Smith, R. G., & Diamond, M. The Hawaii pregnancy, birth control, and abortion study: Social-psychological aspects. *Proceedings of Conference on Psychological Measurement in the Study of Population Problems*. Berkeley: University of California Institute of Personality Assessment and Research, 1972.

Stewart, G., & Hance, F. Legal abortion: Influences upon mortality, morbidity, and population growth. *Advances in Planned Parenthood*, 1976, *9*, 1–7.

Stewart, F. H., Stewart, G. K., Guest, F. J., & Hatcher, R. A. *My body, my health: The concerned woman's guide to gynecology*. New York: Wiley, 1979.

Swigar, M. E., Breslin, R., Pouzzner, M. G., & Quinlan, D. Interview follow-up on abortion applicant dropouts. *Social Psychiatry*, 1976, *11*, 135–143.

Swigar, M., Quinlan, D., & Wexler, S. Abortion applicants: Characteristics distinguishing dropouts—remaining pregnant and those having abortion. *American Journal of Public Health,* 1977, *67*, 142–146.

Tietze, C. The "problem" of repeat abortion. *Family Planning Perspectives*, 1974, *6*, 148–150.

Tietze, C. Contraceptive practice in the context of a non-restrictive abortion law: Age specific pregnancy rates in New York City, 1971–1973. *Family Planning Perspectives*, 1975, 7, 197–202.

Tietze, C. Abortion and contraception. *Family Planning Perspectives*, 1977, *9*, 12–15.

Tietze, C., & Lewitt, S. Abortion. *Scientific American*, 1969, *220*, 3–9.

Tietze, C,, & Lewitt, S. *Early medical complications of legal abortion: Highlights of the joint program for the study of abortion*. New York: Population Council, 1972.

Tietze, C., & Murstein, M. C. Induced abortion: 1975 factbook. *Reports on Population/Family Planning*, December 1975, No. 14 (2nd edition).

Villaneuva, C., & Clancy, B. Counseling and abortion. In M. U. Underwood, B. J. Clancy, & K. E. Krantz (Eds.), *Human sexuality for health professionals*. Philadelphia: Saunders, 1978.

Weinstock, E., & Tietze, C., Jaffe, F. S., & Dryfoos, J. G. Legal abortions in the United States since the 1973 Supreme Court decisions. *Family Planning Perspectives*, 1975, 7, 23–31.

Wulff, G. J. L., & Freeman, S. M. Elective abortion: Complications seen in a free-standing clinic. *Obstetrics and Gynecology*, 1977, *49*, 351–355.

Zelnik, M., & Kantner, J. F. Some preliminary observations on preadult fertility and family formation. *Studies in Family Planning*, 1972, *3*, 59–65.

Zelnik, M., & Kantner, J. F. Sexual and contraceptive experience of young, unmarried women in the United States, 1976 and 1971. *Family Planning Perspectives*, 1977, *9*, 55–71.

Zelnik, M., & Kantner, J. F. First pregnancies to women aged 15–19: 1976 and 1971. *Family Planning Perspectives*, 1978, *10*, 11–20.

12. Human Sexuality and Drugs

Roselle Vlcek Partridge

VALUES CLARIFICATION EXERCISE

The following client situation is designed to help you focus on some issues involved in dealing with the effects of drugs on sexual functioning. Nurses have personal beliefs about the use of therapeutic and recreational drugs and about the interaction of drugs and sex. As health-care providers, nurses must be sensitive to the client's convictions about taking therapeutic or recreational drugs and the client's perception of the sexual impact of drugs. Read this situation and answer the questions that follow it.

> Ken Gary is a 56-year-old married man who has returned for a routine three-month visit to check his progress after initial antihypertensive therapy of Aldomet for essential hypertension. He stated on questioning that he has adapted well in his new life-style, to a low-sodium diet, and to an increased daily exercise routine, and he is taking his medication at appropriate intervals. He has occasionally felt "run down," but this feeling has not stopped his participation in activities. He has had difficulty in attaining and maintaining an erection during sexual intercourse. This has been frustrating, both to him and to his wife, and has become worse this past month during the opening of a new store for which he is responsible. He believes the medication has caused the problem; he is upset and wants help now or he will quit taking the medication altogether. His blood pressure is within normal range at the present time.

What are your immediate reactions to this situation?

What personal and relationship attitudes and beliefs do you hold that you feel are involved in this client situation?

From where did your attitudes and beliefs come? How did you learn them? Do any of your attitudes or beliefs prevent you from responding, or hinder your ability to respond to the sexual needs of the client? Do your attitudes and beliefs enable you to respond to him easily? In what way?

Here is a list of possible reactions. Read them and compare them with your own responses.

Having sex is still important to him.
He should be pleased to have his blood pressure under control.
Having sex with him is still important to his wife.
His wife should be more understanding.
Maybe she's not sexually stimulating to him after all these years.
He's hit middle-age crisis.
He cares about his health because he came for his scheduled visit—he must really want to stay on his medication.
He's concerned about his wife's frustration.
I wonder if he'd be able to have an erection if he chose to have sex with someone besides his wife.
He's working too hard and worrying about work.
He's telling me this to get my sympathy.
He's looking for something to blame.
He'll have to just get used to doing without.

Are any of your reactions similar to these? How are they different? Do your reactions show acceptance of the client's concerns? What are your concerns for the future outcome of his drug therapy, his sexual functioning, and his sexual life?

What you think and feel about these issues will influence your communication with the client. In a group of your peers, try role playing your response to Ken Gary to gain insight into your reactions. Are your reactions similar to those of your peers? How are they similar? How are they different?

BEHAVIORAL OBJECTIVES

After completing this chapter you will be able to

- List the common effects of eight categories of recreational drugs on the sexual functioning of men and women.
- List the common effects of nine categories of therapeutic drugs on the sexual functioning of men and women.
- Give examples of information the nurse as educator-counselor can provide about therapeutic drugs and sex.
- Describe the role of the nurse as counselor about therapeutic drugs and sex.
- Describe the role of the nurse as educator-counselor about recreational drugs and sex.

SEXUAL FUNCTION AND DRUGS

Drugs are chemical substances that alter the functioning of cells of the body. The use of any pharmacologic agent or drug has an effect on many body functions and often on sexual function. Some drugs affect sexual function directly; others affect it indirectly by altering physiologic and psychologic responses. Actual effects vary from person to person, depending on individual biologic makeup, training, experiences, beliefs, expectations, and compliance. Therefore, the nurse should use information about drug effects on sexual functioning as a guide rather than as a prediction of response. Much data has been collected on how drugs effect the male sexual response. Few research studies have involved drug use and the female sexual response; therefore, data on this topic are limited. Research into the effect of illicit drugs on sexual function is also scant because of difficulties in controlling variables and in gaining legal sanction for such studies. Nurses need to be continually alert to new information dealing with the effects of drugs on sexual function and must carefully consider using this information in the education and counseling of clients.

Nurses administer medications and are responsible for evaluating client response to drugs. They need information about the expected action and side effects of drugs and how these affect sexual functioning. Nurses' attitudes about significance of functioning to personal well being determine how they respond to clients whose sexual function may be affected by drugs.

SEXUAL FUNCTION AND RECREATIONAL DRUGS

Recreational drugs are self prescribed drugs. They are used to refresh, to entertain, to enhance pleasurable activity, and to produce euphoria. Some of these drugs have social approval and legal sanction, where others have varying degrees of social approval and may be illegal to possess and use.

Legally and Socially Approved Drugs

Caffeine

Caffeine is a central-nervous-system stimulant that is found in such common household foods as coffee, cola, and chocolate. Caffeine in these substances can help people overcome fatigue in order to participate in sexual relations. Overuse of caffeine can trigger a nervous response, but this response only indirectly affects sexual functioning. The effects of caffeine on the body as a whole and on sexual activities are transient.

Nicotine

Cigarette smoke containing nicotine constricts blood vessels and reduces blood oxygen levels. This constricts blood flow to sex organs and limits the response of erectile tissues to stimulation. Reduced oxygen levels and reduced lung capacity impair general health and sexual response.

In heavy smokers (one or more packs per day), researchers have found a decrease in spermatogenesis and sperm mobility in men and an increase in miscarriage, stillbirths, and small-for-gestational-age neonates in women. General health and sexual function almost always improve after smoking is stopped (Stein & Price, 1977).

Alcohol

Alcohol is a central-nervous-system depressant that, in small amounts, is credited with release of inhibitions and enhancement of sexual function. Sexual performance is not enhanced after ingestion of moderate amounts of alcohol, and tactile reactions may be inhibited. Larger quantities of alcohol contribute to impotence, premature ejaculation (two to three minutes after arousal), vaginismus, and orgasmic dysfunction (see Chapter 8 for descriptions of these conditions). Alcohol affects the neurogenic reflex that produces erection (Lemere & Smith, 1973) and is probably the most common cause of secondary impotence (Newman, 1976).

A common myth in our society is that a drink will ensure mental release and physical relaxation, which will increase the pleasure of sexual relations. The continual use of alcohol or other recreational drugs during sexual contacts makes people believe that they are sexually inadequate without alcohol (Gallant, 1978).

The greatest problem with alcoholism is its destructive effect on the psychologic and socioeconomic functioning. Partners often object to the behaviors of the person who abuses the use of alcohol and rejects him or her sexually. This rejection may lead to impaired sexual functioning in one or both partners (*AMA Manual on Alcoholism*, 1973). The reported incidence of alcoholism is increasing among homosexuals, homemakers, and teenagers, and this increase is demanding more attention from society.

The effects of small amounts of alcohol on sexual functioning are transient. In men, prolonged and heavy use of alcohol can be associated with multiple neurotoxic manifestations, and destruction of the neurogenic reflex that mediates erection may occur. The prolonged effects of alcohol on the sexual function of women is unknown.

Antabuse

Antabuse disulfiran is an antioxidant used as a deterrent to treat alcoholism. Used together with alcohol, it produces unpleasant effects such as headache, nausea, vomiting, and palpitation. Antabuse may cause temporary impotence, leading to reluctance on the part of the alcoholic to use it as part of the treatment plan.

Illicit Drugs

Opiates

Opiates, such as heroin, methadone, morphine, opium, and codeine, are central-nervous-system depressants. The overall effect of opiates is to decrease basal metabolic rate, blood pressure, respiration, secretion of digestive fluids, and gastrointestinal tract motility. Opiates cause appetite and weight loss. These effects are associated with decreased sexual desire, decreased sexual activity, and decreased sexual enjoyment. While using one of these drugs, people may indulge in sexual behaviors that are atypical for them, such as extramarital relations, increased frequency of intercourse, increased number of sexual partners, and group sex. Prostitution may be practiced in order to support the drug habit. Any or all of these behaviors may become a source of self-condemnation or diminished self-esteem and may contribute to sexual dysfunction.

With chronic use, opiates decrease serum testosterone, causing impotence in men. Women may experience amenorrhea, dysmenorrhea, infertility, decreased sensation, and increased likelihood of spontaneous abortion (Money & Musaph, 1977). The psychologic side effects of opiate drug abuse usually require concentrated rehabilitation.

Amyl Nitrite

Amyl nitrite is a fast-acting vasodilator commonly used in the treatment of angina pectoris. The street term for this drug is "popper" or "snapper," referring to its form, which is an inhalable ampule. *Isobutyl nitrite* is its analog sold over-the-counter. For recreational use, the drug is taken at the start of sexual intercourse or just before orgasm to enhance mental reactions and intensify physical sensations. It is a popular drug with homosexual men because it relaxes the rectal sphincter for anal intercourse. Side effects include dizziness and typical nitrite headache. It is contraindicated for sexual purposes for anyone with cardiovascular disease because of potential adverse systemic effects (Kolodny et al., 1979). Women report that this drug has little effect on their sexual desire or sensations (Mims & Swenson, 1980). There are no long-lasting sexual side effects from amyl nitrite.

Amphetamines

Amphetamines are psychomotor stimulants and anorexiants. "Uppers" is a street language term for amphetamines. "Bernice," "Corine," "coke," and "flake" are street-language terms for the amphetamine cocaine. "Speed" is slang for methamphetamine. Because of their stimulant effect, amphetamines increase motor activity and mental alertness, overcome fatigue, elevate moods, and produce slight euphoria. Sexually they produce a heightened suggestability, for men a rapid and long-lasting erection, and for women an intensification of orgasm. Intravenous injection of speed produces an almost instantaneous onset ("rush," or "flash") of the drug's effect. For men, chronic use can lead to loss of sexual interest and impotence, which can be reversed after a period of abstinence from the drug. Women generally report a reduction in vaginal secretions resulting in discomfort or pain during intercourse. More research is needed about the chronic use of amphetamines in women (Stein & Price, 1977).

Hallucinogens

Lysergic acid diethylamide, (LSD or "acid") and mescaline phencyclidine (PCP or "angel dust") are two examples of hallucinogenic drugs. These drugs alter all perception of experience, including sexual perception. Users claim that sexual pleasure is enhanced by increased sensory awareness, lavish imagery, prolonged orgasms, intensified intimacy, and loss of inhibition. Although hallucinogens do alter perceptions, there is no evidence that they directly stimulate sexual desire. Hollister (1968) and Piemme (1976) suggest that hallucinogens do not allow for the focus of thoughts and energy necessary to initiate or complete sexual activity. Systematic research on the sexual effects of these drugs has not been done. Some users report a "bad trip" (an acute panic reaction) that is severely disturbing and has negative sexual effects. "Flashbacks" (transient reoccurrence of part of a prior drug experience) have been reported as a major problem among chronic users. Systematic research on sexual effects of these drugs has not been carried out.

Marijuana

Marijuana is classified as a sedative hypnotic. Common names for this drug are *pot* and *grass*. Marijuana users have reported increased sexual desire and delayed orgasm in men and intensification of orgasm in women; however, this was not borne out by research (Kolodny et al., 1979). Increased sense of touch, greater degree of relaxation, and being more in touch with one's partner are feelings that were actually enhanced by this drug.

Contradictory findings have been reported on the effect of marijuana on fertility, and more research is needed. Interviews with marijuana users reveal that they often use more than one drug simultaneously, thus confounding reactions attributed to marijuana (Stohs, 1978).

Marijuana can produce moderate psychologic dependence but it produces neither tolerance nor physical dependence. The psychic effect is dependant on the strength of the preparation used and the route of consumption. The effects on sexual behavior are transient.

SEXUAL FUNCTION AND THERAPEUTIC DRUGS

Therapeutic drugs are drugs prescribed by clinicians for the diagnosis and treatment of physical or mental conditions. The effect of any drug varies greatly from client to client. Each drug has its own dosage range, route of administration, rate of absorption, duration, and excretion; each client has his or her own age, weight, rate of metabolism, social milieu, personal suggestability, and compliance record. Because of legal sanction, research on the effects of therapeutic drugs on sexual function has been more widely performed than research on illicit drugs.

Before drug therapy is initiated, a sexual history of each client should be obtained to compare changes and possible causes for altered sexual function during therapy (see Chapter 2). If sexual dysfunction occurs, the drug therapy is potentially the source of the problem; however, further questioning will be needed at the time of dysfunction to determine if other possible causes, including altered social relationships, may be the source of change. Simultaneous use of illicit drugs or alcohol might also be a source of dysfunction. Inquiry about sexual concerns at each health-care visit facilitates discussion, enables mutual problem solving, and prevents chronic discouragement. For example, if the client has an erection upon awakening in the morning, impotence is unlikely to be drug induced. If sexual dysfunction is determined to be drug induced, the client needs reassurance of the source of this difficulty and an estimation of the chances for its reversibility (Kolodny et al., 1979). Drugs and dosage should be tailored to each client's needs, including sexual needs.

PHYSIOLOGIC CHANGES OF THE SEXUAL RESPONSE CYCLE WITH DRUG THERAPY

Therapeutic drugs can affect the entire central nervous system and specific parts of the autonomic nervous system. Neurologically, sexual organs, associated glands, and blood vessels are controlled by the two actions of the autonomic system—sympathetic (adrenergic) and parasympathetic (cholinergic). The two effects work together to affect the sexual response cycle. Adrenergic action produces ejaculation in the man through contraction of the prostate, seminal vesicles, and bulbocavernosus and ischiocavernosus muscles. Cholinergic action controls penile erection by causing congestion of the vascular sinuses in the corpora. Blockage of either of these systems by drugs interferes with sexual function. Ganglionic blocking agents interfere with both the sympathetic and parasympathetic systems, resulting in possible complete impotence (Woods, 1979).

Sex hormones, used in drug therapy, affect fertility and secondary sex characteristics, as well as sexual desire when hormonal blood levels are altered.

Sedatives and Hypnotics

Sedatives and hypnotics, including barbiturates, diazepam, chlordiazepoxide, and methaqualone, are the most widely prescribed medications in the United States. They are central-nervous-system depressants that, in low doses, produce mild depression resulting in sedation. Higher doses produce deeper depression and have a hypnotic or sleep-inducing effect. These drugs reduce inhibitions and decrease anxiety when taken in moderate doses. Their effects when taken in large dosages are varied: they may affect sexual performance, increase or decrease desire for sex, or modify discrimination in selecting sexual partners. In women, long-term use of barbiturates commonly causes menstrual disorders or loss of pleasure in sexual activity, resulting in difficulty in attaining orgasm.

Antipsychotics (e.g., chlorpromazine and thioridazine)

In men, impotence or inhibited ejaculation may occur. Women have a greater degree of sexual dysfunction than men (Gossip, Stern, & Connell, 1974). In contrast, Kolodny, Masters, and Johnson (1979) stated that many people who use barbiturates on a long-term therapeutic basis experience no alteration in sexual function.

Antipsychotic drugs act on the subcortical centers of the brain to produce a calming effect on aggressive, overactive, disturbed patients; to relieve the despondency of the severely depressed; to activate the immobile and the withdrawn, and to make such clients more accessible to psychotherapy (Lobel, Spratto, & Heckheimer, 1980).

Antipsychotics can decrease sexual function by blocking the peripheral cholinergic effect to sex glands, which may lead to dry ejaculation and erectile difficulties. Galactorrhea (spontaneous flow of milk from breasts) and gynecomastia (abnormally large mammary glands in the man) have also been seen. Decreased vaginal lubrication, amenorrhea (absence or abnormal stoppage of menses), and decreased sexual response may occur in women. The sexual side effects of thorazine have been noted in persons of all ages. In general, side effects disappear when the drugs are discontinued.

Antidepressants

These include MAO inhibitors—pargyline and tranylcypromine; tricyclic antidepressants—imipramine, desipramine, and lithium. MAO inhibitors' primary mode of action is to interfere with the enzyme monoamine oxidase in the brain, which breaks down norepinephrine and other chemicals involved in nerve impulse transmission. These drugs are used to elevate the mood of depressed clients.

Tricyclic antidepressants act on the central nervous system to increase the levels of neurotransmitters (e.g., norepinephrine) at the synapse and to relieve depression (Lobel, Spratto, & Heckheimer, 1980). The exact action of lithium is unknown, and it is used exclusively in the management of manic-depressive clients. The symptoms of decreased sexual desire and impaired sexual function are frequently associated with depression. As the depression is successfully treated the client functions better emotionally and sexually.

MAO inhibitors have been associated with impotence or inhibited ejaculation in men and difficulty achieving orgasm in women (Seagraves, 1977). Tricyclic antidepressants have produced impotence and ejaculatory difficulties plus delay in orgasm in both sexes. Lowered testosterone levels have been reported (Sanchez et al., 1976).

Lithium has not been systematically studied for its effect on sexual function. Hollister (1975) reported that lithium carbonate has been associated with disturbed sexual function in clients treated with this drug. In general, sexual symptoms subside when the dosage is reduced or the medication discontinued.

Antihypertensives

Antihypertensives (e.g., guanethidine, reserpine, and methyldopa) reduce blood pressure and decrease cardiac output by stimulating pressor receptors in the carotid sinus and heart. These actions result in decreased arterial resistance and increased peripheral vasodilation. Antihypertensives modify sympathetic-nervous-system response and can cause impotence, retrograde ejaculation, and some decrease in sexual desire. Many of these responses are dose dependent. The sedative effect of the drugs contributes to depressed sexual desire (Kolodny et al., 1979). These symptoms are relieved and adequate control of the blood pressure maintained after the drug is discontinued, dosage reduced, another medication substituted, or a combination of drugs used (Kolodny, Masters, and Johnson, 1979). Adjustment to the revised medication regimen usually requires one to two weeks. Some clients stop taking the drugs abruptly, particularly to regain sexual function. They should be cautioned that there is the likelihood that blood pressure may rapidly increase.

Diuretics (thiazides and spironolactone)

The basic action of diuretics is to increase renal excretion of sodium and chloride, which increases the secretion of urine. Impotence and gynecomastia may be caused by diuretics in about 5% of male clients taking these drugs (Greenblatt & Koch-Weser, 1973). Amenorrhea and breast soreness may appear in women. Return to normal function occurs within two months after discontinuing the drug (Levitt, 1970).

Antihistamines

Antihistamines (e.g., diphenhydramine hydrochloride, promethazine hydrochloride, chlorpheniramine maleate) antagonize the action of histamine. They usually prevent the increased capillary permeability that leads to edema, itching, and smooth muscle contraction. They may also have a depressant effect on the central nervous system that may result in drowsiness. Sexual desire can decrease through the sedative effect of antihistamines. Vaginal lubrication is also decreased by anticholinergic action (Kolodny, Masters, and Johnson, 1979). Sexual effects of antihistamine are relieved when the drugs are discontinued.

Antispasmodics

The primary effect of antispasmodic drugs (e.g., methantheline, glycopyrolate) is relaxation of the smooth muscle of the gastrointestinal and biliary tracts, ureter, and uterus. Antispasmodics act to inhibit parasympathetic-nervous-system function, causing vasoconstriction of blood vessels in sex organs and leading to impotence and decreased vaginal lubrication (Mims & Swenson, 1980).

Cytoxic Drugs

Cytoxic drugs (e.g., cyclophosphamide) are chemicals that destroy cells or prevent their multiplication, thus slowing down the disease process. Cytoxic drugs interfere with normal cells as well as neoplastic cells; however, neoplastic cells are more active and multiply more rapidly than normal cells, so they are more likely to be affected by the action of cytoxic agents (Loebl, Spratto, & Heckheimer, 1980).

Because of the drugs' lack of selectivity in action, amenorrhea and decreased spermatogenesis may occur. Spermatogenesis gradually returns after discontinuation of drug treatment (Sharins & DeVita, 1973).

Cytoxic drugs are used in cancer chemotherapy, which is reported to decrease sexual desire and potency. Information from well-controlled studies is not available, however (Stohs, 1978).

Corticosteroids

Corticosteroids (e.g., prednisone, hydrocortisone acetate, prednisolone) are a group of natural hormones produced by the adrenal cortex that influence many metabolic pathways and all organ systems. When taken in high doses and used over long periods of time, corticosteroids can decrease spermatogenesis and precipitate latent diabetes mellitis, increasing susceptibility to vaginal and other infections. More definitive research on these effects is needed (Kolodny, Masters, & Johnson, 1979).

THE ROLE OF THE NURSE AS EDUCATOR-COUNSELOR

The nurse has an important role in successful drug therapy. The nurse as educator-counselor can provide reliable information and guidance about drugs and their benefits or detrimental effects as the client participates in decisions about treatment and assumes responsibility for his or her own health.

The nurse is responsible for knowing the actions, uses, expected outcomes, contraindications, precautions, and adverse side effects of the drugs he or she administers. The nurse as health-care provider needs ready information about the possible direct or indirect side effects drugs may have on sexual interest, response, and performance. This information is shared with the client and his or her sexual partner, because both persons' responses may be significant to the client's acceptance and reaction to the therapy. Information about a possible alteration in sexual function associated with drugs should be presented positively and followed by a statement that reassures, encourages further questions, and offers individual attention: "Eighty percent of the people taking this medication experience no sexual side effects. If such a problem occurs with you, just let me know and we can easily make an adjustment in your medication to restore things to normal" (Kolodny, Masters, & Johnson, 1979). When discussing drug effects upon sexual function with the client, the nurse must be alert to changes in social situations or to new emotional stresses that may be the real source of alteration in sexual behavior patterns. Reassuring the client of the reversibility of drug side effects may lead to greater client cooperation and acceptance of the plan of treatment.

The nurse who has information about sexual effects of drugs and is comfortable with his or her sexuality can help a client cope with conflicting feelings about discontinuing a drug that is causing altered sexual response at the risk of symptom control. The nurse must accept and understand the client who refuses medication adjustment because symptom control is valued more than sexual well-being. When the physician's and client's beliefs and attitudes about the interaction of sex and drugs differ, the nurse can encourage discussion and facilitate mutual decision making about the regimen (Hogan, 1980).

The nurse as educator-counselor can provide information and guidance about recreational drugs to individuals, families, and communities. The information must be factual, reliable, and based on what has been observed and studied and is yet to be researched. The nurse can provide information that sex and sexuality are natural expressions of the total personality and total interpersonal relations and that healthy and pleasurable sex is attainable without the use of drugs to stimulate or enhance the sexual potential.

People who experiment with recreational drugs need reliable information about the physiologic, psychologic, and legal consequences of drug use. The experimenter has potential for problems, and parents who are worried and anxious about their children's use of drugs should be referred to community outreach programs. The person who claims social use of recreational drugs and who shows evidence of any significant psychological problem can be referred to an appropriate community counseling center or self-help group. The person with problems of recreational drug abuse or addiction may need intensive and extended rehabilitation assistance with individual counseling, encounter groups, and residential care, with self-help as part of the program. State and local health departments, mental-health associations and clinics, police departments, physicians, nurses' associations, religious centers, and other city information services can provide information about programs available in a particular area.

NURSING PROCESS

Refer to the client situation at the beginning of this chapter. The following process is based on that information. The client is Ken Gary. The nurse is Karen Windsor, who works with a physician in family practice.

Assessment

Subjective Data

"I'm on a low sodium diet."
"I do my exercises every day."
"But sometimes I feel rundown."
"I'm doing all the things I used to do."
"But I can't keep it up when my wife and I go to it."
"My wife and I are bothered because I can't keep a hard-on."
"It's gotten worse this last month."
"I've been responsible for opening a new store in the chain."
"Has this medication got anything to do with what's happening to me?"

Objective Data

Male, 56 years old, married 30 years.
Began antihypertensive therapy three months ago.
Blood pressure is within normal range at this time.

Nursing Diagnosis

Alteration in patterns of sexual functioning due to inability to maintain erection.

Planning

Encourage to express feelings about sexual functioning.
Encourage to express concerns about sexuality.
Accept feelings expressed about change in sexual function.
Show acceptance of sexual partner's reaction as appropriate and normally
    experienced.
Assess potential causes of changes
    Drug induced—does he have erection in morning without sexual
        contact? Does he have erection with masturbation?
    Attitudinal changes about self since diagnosis of hypertension?
    Changes in relationship with significant other in past three months?
    Sexual contacts with people other than wife?
    Taking any other drugs or ingesting alcohol?
Provide information about varying dosage or change of drugs.
Adjust medication dosage.

Encourage experimentation with sensuality (touching, holding, body massage, self-stimulation).
Encourage use of alternative positions.
Indicate availability for further counseling.
Indicate availability for joint counseling.

Implementation

Arrange time and initiate discussion with wife.
Express feelings with wife.
Share expectations about sex and sexual function with wife.
Make appointment for joint counseling.
Take adjusted dosage of prescribed medication.

Evaluation

Reports taking new dosage of medication.
Reports improved sexual function.
Reports sensate focus, position experimentation as satisfactory.
Plans to continue joint counseling with wife.

BIBLIOGRAPHY

AMA Manual on alcoholism. Chicago: American Medical Association, 1973.

Beaumont, G. Untoward effects of drugs on sexuality. In S. Crown (Ed.), *Psychosexual problems: Psychotherapy, counseling, and behavioral medication.* London: Academic Press, 1976.

Gallant, D. Sexual survey #14: Current thinking on recreational drugs and sex. *Medical Aspects of Human Sexuality,* 1978, *12*, 80–81.

Gay, G., & Sheppard, C. Sex crazed dope fiends: Myth or reality. In E. Harms (Ed.), *Drugs, youth: The challenge today.* New York: Pergamon Press, 1975.

Gossip, M. R., Stern, R., & Connell, P. H. Drug dependence and sexual function: A comparison of intravenous users of narcotics and oral users of amphetamines. *British Journal of Psychiatry,* 1974, *124*, 431–433.

Greenblatt, D., & Koch-Weser, J. Gynecomastia and impotence: Complications of spironolactone therapy. *Journal of the American Medical Association,* 1973, *223*, 82.

Hogan, R. M. *Human sexuality: A nursing perspective.* New York: Appleton-Century-Crofts, 1980.

Hollister, L. E. *Chemical psychosis, LSD, and related drugs.* Springfield, Ill.: Thomas Y. Crowell, 1968.

Hollister, L. E. Drugs and sexual behavior in men. *Life Science,* 1975, *17*, 661–668.

Kaplan, H. S. *The new sex therapy*. New York: Bruner/Mazel, 1974.

Kolodny, R., Masters, W. A., & Johnson, V. E. *Textbook of Sexual Medicine*. Boston: Little, Brown, 1979.

Kolodny, R., Masters, W., Johnson, V., & Biggs, M. *Textbook of human sexuality for nurses*. Boston: Little, Brown, 1979.

Lemere, F., & Smith, J. Alcohol induced sexual impotence. *American Journal of Psychiatry*, 1973, *130*, 212–213.

Levitt, J. Spironolactone therapy and amenorrhea. *Journal of the American Medical Association*, 1970, *211*, 2014–2015.

Loebl, S., Spratto, G., & Heckheimer, E. *The nurse's drug handbook* (2nd ed.). New York: Wiley, 1980.

MacLennan, A. (Ed.). *Women: Their use of alcohol and other legal drugs*. Toronto: Addiction Research Foundation of Ontario, 1976.

Mims, F., & Swenson, M. *Sexuality: A nursing perspective*. New York: McGraw-Hill, 1980.

Money, J., & Musaph, H. *Handbook of sexology*. Amsterdam: Excerpta Medica, 1977.

Newman, J. (Ed.). *Sexual counseling for persons with alcohol problems: Proceedings of a workshop*. Pittsburgh: University of Pittsburgh, 1976.

Piemme, T. E. Sex and illicit drugs. *Medical Aspects of Human Sexuality*, 1976, *10*, 85–86.

Sanchez, R. S., Murthy, G. G., Mehta, J., Shreeve, W. W., & Singh, F. R. Pituitary-testicular axis in patients on lithium therapy. *Fertility and Sterility*, 1976, *27*, 667–669.

Schneider, J., & Kaffarnik, H. Impotence in patients treated with clofibrate. *Atherosclerosis*, 1975, *21*, 455–457.

Seagraves, R. Pharmacological agents causing sexual dysfunction. *Journal of Sex and Marital Therapy*, 1977, *3*, 157–176.

Sharins, R., & DeVita, V. Effect of drug treatment for lymphoma on male reproductive capacity: Studies of men in remission after therapy. *Annals of Internal Medicine*, 1973, *70*, 216–220.

Stein, E., & Price, J. *Human sex and sexuality*. New York: Wiley, 1977.

Stohs, S. Drugs and sexual function. *U.S. Pharmacist*, 1978, 11–12, 52–66.

Witters, W. L., & Witter, P. J. *Drugs and sex*. New York: Macmillan, 1975.

Woods, N. F. *Human sexuality in health and illness* (2nd ed.). St. Louis: Mosby, 1979.

13. Sexually Transmitted Diseases

Roselle Vlcek Partridge

VALUES CLARIFICATION EXERCISE

The following situation is designed to help you focus on some issues involved in dealing with clients with sexually transmitted diseases. You and the client hold values that influence your responses, and becoming aware of your own values is helpful. Read the following situation and respond to the questions asked. As you write your responses, note the feelings you experience.

> Robert Swenson is a 23-year-old business major at a university. He comes to the student health center for these symptoms: burning on urination for the past three days, white discharge from penis, and some pelvic pain. He says he's been living with his "future wife" for six months. About a week ago he had a "one-night stand" with a woman he had known back home.

Write your immediate reactions.

List attitudes and beliefs you hold about relationships that you feel are involved in this client situation.

From where do you think these attitudes and beliefs came? How did you learn them? Do any of your attitudes and beliefs prevent or hinder your ability to plan and implement care for this client? Do your attitudes and beliefs enable you to plan and implement care for this client easily? In what way?

Here is a list of possible reactions. Read them and compare with your own responses.

He's got a real problem!

He came in for treatment quickly—he is a responsible lover.

Wonder if his future wife has got it now or is she the source?

He knows how to take care of his sexual needs. He just needs info on VD.

Why didn't he use a condom?
Wonder if this has ever happened to him before?
Doesn't he get enough from the future wife?
Is the problem sexual or communication?
They've got a problem now even before marriage.
How will this affect their relationship? Maybe they've agreed that sex outside their relationship is OK.
How will he explain this to his future wife?
Will his future wife stay with him and work it out or will she leave him?
Wonder if his future wife plays around too?
What does the old girl friend mean to him?
Wonder if old girl friend got gonorrhea from another one-night stand or this time?
He's awful for doing that to his future wife—or did she do that to him?

Are any of your reactions similar to these? How are they different? Are your judgments for or against the client? Do your reactions show acceptance of the client? Acceptance of his behavior? What are your concerns about the future wife? How do you feel about the girl from back home? What feelings do you have for the future relationship of the client and his future wife? For the client and the girl back home? For the client himself? Your values can affect your plan of care and communication with this client, both verbal and nonverbal.

In a group of your peers, share your responses and reactions. Note the similarities and the differences in the responses and reactions within the group. Role play the situation. The person playing the nurse should gather data. When you are the nurse, how does your value system affect your response to the client and the data you gather? In the group, discuss how the value systems of the other members affect the data gathered.

BEHAVIORAL OBJECTIVES

After completing this chapter you will be able to

- Give examples of psychologic and sociologic factors that affect treatment of people with sexually transmitted diseases (STDs).
- State six selected personally administered measures that prevent or lessen transmission of STDs.
- Summarize the significant symptoms and disease process of 14 selected STDs.
- Explain the impact of STDs on the present and future sexual behavior of a person.

- Explain the impact of the appropriate health care for persons infected with an STD, their sexual partners, and significant others.
- List possible sources of infection of STDs.
- Describe the nurse's role as educator-counselor of clients who have STD.

SEXUALLY TRANSMITTED DISEASES

Sexually transmitted diseases (STDs) are communicable diseases that are transmitted primarily by sexual contact. They were referred to in the past as *venereal diseases* (VD); however, "sexually transmitted diseases" is currently the term of choice.

Because of the method by which the microorganisms that cause these diseases are primarily transmitted, clients with STDs are subject to judgments on their sexual behavior by potential and current sexual partners as well as by those responsible for their medical care. Thus, STDs can be considered medical afflictions with social complications. This is especially true for those STDs that are asymptomatic in one or both sexes, and are therefore reliant upon human communication for awareness of infection and treatment.

The purpose of the list below is to acquaint the reader with the selected STDs that have been identified by the Center for Disease Control as most likely to be encountered by health professionals. The prevalence of each infection varies with geographical region and the type of population seen in particular health settings. Each will be discussed in this chapter.

1. Gonorrhea
2. Syphilis
3. Lymphogranuloma venereum
4. Granuloma inguinale
5. Chancroid
6. Nonspecific urethritis (NSU)
7. Trichomoniasis
8. Vulvovaginal candidiasis
9. Genital herpes infection
10. Condyloma acuminata (genital warts)
11. Pediculosis pubis
12. Scabies
13. Hepatitis B infection
14. Nonspecific vaginitis

PSYCHOSOCIAL FACTORS AFFECTING TREATMENT

For centuries, STDs had been viewed as the result of shameful, forbidden, dirty conduct. These diseases were believed to be punishment for promiscuous sexual conduct. Such moralistic, judgmental attitudes still affect many people's decisions to seek a cure for STDs. Although the treatment process is relatively simple and effective, the fear of judgment by those involved in the health-care system and condemnation by the community is widespread. By law, the names of people having specific STDs (gonorrhea, syphilis, chancroid, lymphogranuloma venereum, and granuloma inguinale) must be reported to the state communicable disease office for the purpose of finding and treating sexual contacts and recording the evidence of these diseases. This fact may trigger fear of disclosure or fear of breach of confidentiality and may provide an excuse for not seeking treatment.

Society often continues to provide inaccurate, vague, moralistic education about both sexuality and STDs on the assumption that ignorance about sex will prevent participation in sexual behaviors. This attitude seems to be changing, as consumers demand increasingly greater knowledge about STDs and their prevention. The public needs such education to decrease confusion about sexual behaviors and STD. The idea of responsible health care for both oneself and one's sexual partner is evolving.

Common emotional responses in the client to the diagnosis of STD include confusion, embarrassment, guilt, and anger. The client often is ashamed to admit that sexual behavior has led to this infection. The client is usually most anxious on the first visit for treatment of an STD. This anxiety rapidly diminishes in one week of so, after treatment produces relief of symptoms. Social relationships may be altered by the reaction of the sexual partner, spouse, or family upon learning of the diagnosis of STD. Depending upon the nature of the relationship, a crisis of confidence may be triggered with concomitant anxiety and depression. Relationships can be destroyed, or there may be little reaction (Money, 1977).

The manner of approach to treatment in the health-care setting often determines the patient's level of cooperation and compliance with the health-care provider. Clients who perceive their care as moralistic, judgmental, and insulting will probably be uncooperative. Impersonal treatment will also be perceived in long waiting times, hurried examinations, and overquestioning, all of which further hinder cooperation.

The client may view inquiries about contacts as invasive, which may elicit uncooperative responses despite the fact that the health-care provider is simply fulfilling a responsibility required by law. Ironically, it is estimated that private physicians treat 80% of all STD but report only

10% of these cases seen in their practices, hoping to protect their patients from shame and embarrassment (Montreal Press Inc., 1973). This of course hinders health officials' efforts at stopping transmission of STD.

SOCIOSEXUAL FACTORS CONTRIBUTING TO STD TRANSMISSION

In addition to the previously discussed psychosocial factors, other elements contribute to the prevalence of STD. Gonorrhea is the most common communicable disease in the United States (2,000,000 estimated cases per year), and syphilis is the third most prevalent communicable disease (STD Fact Sheet, 1977). These statistics reflect the increase in adolescent sexual relations. The highest incidence of STD is found in the 20-to-24-year-old population, and the greatest increase in STD is seen in the college population (Money, 1977).

The larger the number of sexual partners a person has the greater the chance of acquiring STD. Indiscriminate choice of sex partners is found in all age groups and in homosexual men, who have shown increased rates of STD since 1970 (Henderson, 1977). The incidence of oral–genital sex has also increased; more cases of oral sites of infection are reported as a result.

Current methods of birth control also may contribute to the rising incidence of STD. The increased use of oral contraceptives possibly heightens susceptibility to infection in women because of the alteration of the normal vaginal pH, which enhances growth of infectious microorganisms (Mims, 1980). Intrauterine devices for birth control have been transmission agents for infection into the uterus and pelvis (Ory, 1978). Concurrently, the use of condoms, which have been shown to block or deter the transmission of STD organisms, has decreased. This is also somewhat true of the use of the diaphragm with jellies, creams, and foams, which have a chemical antibacterial effect in the vagina as well as a mechanical blocking function.

New strains of gonorrhea probably imported from Vietnam by members of the armed services, are more resistant to penicillin therapy. Also, asymptomatic carriers of gonorrhea, especially women (80%) and homosexual men (anal infection 50% to 95%), unwittingly increase the spread of disease (Ginsburg, 1980).

Until recently, public-health STD control programs have neither received sufficient funding nor been directed at high-risk populations, including adolescents and young adults, novice prostitutes, alcohol and drug users, and people living in large urban areas. Black people are at high risk because of their reluctance to use the health-care system as it exists (Darrow, 1976). Finally, increased mobility of the population spreads STD rapidly and widely. This is true of members of the armed forces, truckers, immigrants, and tourists. The health-care consumer movement and grass-roots education have been more effective in reaching high-risk populations and inducing people to seek treatment than have been mass screening techniques, and new funds are therefore being directed to these areas.

PREVENTION OF TRANSMISSION OF SEXUALLY TRANSMITTED DISEASES

Education about prevention of STD transmission is within the domain of the nurse. Sexually responsible people have to know how STDs are transmitted and how to prevent their transmission. Only abstinence from sexual contact is 100% effective, but chances of acquiring infection can be reduced by the following:

1. Using a condom may help prevent the spread of gonorrhea during vaginal and anal intercourse, if the lesion is only on the penile shaft and the condom is applied before the partners' genitals touch. Sexually active women should carry condoms for their own protection and use birth control foams, creams, or jellies, which also slow the transmission of STDs by blocking the passage of organisms into the pelvis. A variety of sensual, colored condoms are available, which are more appealing than uncolored ones (Montreal Health Press, 1973). Contrary to popular belief, female douching after intercourse is an ineffective preventive measure and douching is contraindicated if a vaginal foam, cream, or gel was used for birth control. Frequent douching is harmful, because it changes the vaginal chemical balance, thus allowing organisms to multiply.

2. Washing the genitals with soap and water before and after sexual intercourse may decrease the number of organisms present. An oil-based soap should not be used. Washing is of questionable value for women (Hubbard, 1973).

3. An inspection of the genitalia of both partners before sexual contact, including milking the penis, may show visual signs of infection. Sores or discharge, if present, are an indication of the presence of STDs, and genital contact should be avoided in such cases (Mayhew, 1976). There are STDs that would not be evident on inspection, however.

4. Urinating soon after sex may help protect the man (Hart, 1977).

5. If transmission of the disease has occurred, penicillin or tetracycline tablets should be taken as soon as possible to prevent infection, but a prescription is required and users can become sensitized to the drug.

6. Testing for STDs should be performed as soon as exposure is suspected, and abstinence should be practiced until negative tests are reported or treatment is completed.

SEXUALLY TRANSMITTED DISEASES IN BRIEF

This section describes in greater detail the 14 STDs listed earlier. Note that it is possible to contract more than one STD at once and that no immunity develops to any of these infections.

Gonorrhea (GC, a Dose, Clap, Runs, Morning Whites, Drip, Stain, Hot Piss)

Gonorrhea is caused by the bacteria *Neisseria gonorrhoeae*, a gram negative diplococcus, and is communicable before symptoms appear. It is detected by identifying the bacteria on a smear slide or by culturing it in an anaerobic environment for from 24 to 48 hours. These bacteria die four to five seconds after leaving the body if exposed to drying, cooler temperatures, or antiseptics. Seventy-five percent of people exposed to gonorrhea for the first time become infected. The incubation time is two to ten days after exposure.

Symptoms in the man: burning on urination, cloudy or white urethral discharge with faint odor of mushrooms and accompanying swelling of glans, discomfort in pelvic area or rectum revealing proctitis or prostatitis which can lead to sterility. Twenty percent of infected men are asymptomatic.

Symptoms in the woman: vaginal discharge and cystitis. Sixty percent of women are asymptomatic until the infection advances into salpingitis, which produces abdominal pain, low backache, fever, pelvic inflammatory disease (PID), or abscesses of the Bartholin or Skenes glands. A gentle examination is required because of pain.

Gonorrhea can become systemic in two months, causing acute arthritis, tenasynovitis, or pericarditis. If not treated and cured early, it may lead to sterility and ectopic pregnancy as a result of blockage of the fallopian tubes through chronic infection.

Pharyngitis can be caused by the gonorrhea bacteria if transmitted during oral sex, and rectal infection can occur after transmission during anal sex. Any potential site of infection must, therefore, be cultured.

A pregnant woman with gonorrhea may pass on the disease to the newborn during birth. The child may acquire an eye infection that may lead to blindness. Ophthalmia neonatorium is prevented by prophylactic use of silver nitrate eye drops or an appropriate antibiotic.

The most frequent treatment for any other site of gonorrhea infection is high doses of quick-acting intramuscular penicillin in conjunction with probenicid. Massage of the site of injection increases absorption and decreases soreness. Disease symptoms take two to three days to disappear. Sexual contact is prohibited until culture results are negative—usually a period of one to two weeks.

Men may have residual burning on urination even after a negative culture and will need reassurance that they are no longer infected. Infected people should refrain from genital, oral, or anal intercourse and from masturbation to prevent transmission of the disease and irritation of the infection site. Consumption of alcohol, coffee, and tea should be avoided until the infection is cleared, because these liquids are irritating to the urethra. All sexual partners should be notified of their exposure and checked for possible infection.

Syphilis (Syph, Lues, the Great Pox, Bad Blood, Old Joe, the Sore)

Syphilis is caused by a spirochete, *Treponema pallidum*, which attacks arterioles throughout the body, causing systemic infection and destruction of tissue. It is curable in the primary and secondary stages; however, because it mimics many diseases, it is easily misdiagnosed and inappropriately treated. It is acquired through sexual contact or through placental transfer of the bacteria to the fetus (transfer does not occur before the eighteenth week of gestation).

The incubation period is 7 to 90 days after exposure, during which time the client is not infectious. This period is followed by the primary stage of syphilis, during which one or more chancres are found at the site where the organism invaded the body, usually at the genitalia. These lesions have the appearance of eroded, watery ulcers and are usually painless. Occasionally chancres appear at sites of abrasion. These sores are painful and unusually shaped. Chancres can also be found on breasts, tongue, lips, fingers, cervix, anus, rectum, and abdominal skin. The chancres, which are the major mode of transmission of bacteria, heal spontaneously, and it is possible that the infected person will not notice them, especially if they are located on the cervix or hidden by the scrotum. Transmission may also occur through semen, vaginal discharge, saliva, or blood during sexual contact.

The secondary stage of syphilis develops three to six weeks after the initial chancre heals. At this time, a generalized body reaction occurs, with a cherry-red skin rash (in black people the rash is greyish-blue in color) particularly prevalent on the palms of the hands and soles of feet. Chancres reoccur. The client undergoes enlarged lymph glands, hair loss, as well as flulike symptoms of irritability, fever, loss of appetite, and nausea, which last for a few days.

During this stage, the blood test for syphilis (VDRL) becomes weakly positive and remains so for some time even after treatment. Other diseases may cause a false positive VDRL, including hepatitis, mononucleosis, chronic collagen disease, narcotic addiction, and alcoholism; therefore, additional blood tests are necessary to confirm the presence of syphilis.

A slide smear test, taken from a chancre, is also performed, because this location is the greatest source of bacteria. Possible false-negative results from the bacterial smear may occur if alcohol, Merthiolate, penicillin, or ointments have been used on the site before examination. Chancres can reappear and are communicable at various times during the secondary stage for up to two years. After this stage the person is no longer infectious and has entered a latent period.

Two to forty years later, the tertiary stage of syphilis may begin, during which the spirochete invades the vital organs of the body, destroying tissue in the heart, brain, bones, and liver. Twenty-five percent of untreated persons develop tertiary syphilis. At this stage the disease can only be arrested, not cured.

The treatment for syphilis is the use of long-acting penicillin over several days to weeks, depending on the stage of the disease. There is a body reaction within twelve hours of treatment in which any existing chancre swells for a few hours and a fever of 101°F to 102°F (38.3°C to 38.8°C) occurs. Response to treatment should be evaluated at one month, three months, and one year. With successful treatment, the VDRL test becomes negative 6 to 12 months after the primary stage or 12 to 18 months after the secondary stage. More extensive follow-up is required in the latent phase.

As with all STDs, the sexual partners of the infected person must be informed immediately of their exposure to syphilis to begin observation of and treatment for the disease. Infected persons should avoid sexual contact until one month after treatment is concluded.

Lymphogranuloma Venereum

Lymphogranuloma venereum represents 5 to 6% of all cases of sexually transmitted disease. It usually occurs in tropical areas, and is caused by *Bedsonia* or *Clamydia* organisms. The incubation period is between one week and three months after sexual contact. In both men and women a primary ulcer appears. The ulcer is small, smooth, superficial, and wet and may be surrounded by tiny warts. It is usually found on the penile glans or shaft, vulva, or rectum, and it lasts for 4 to 10 days. Then the organism infects the lymph glands in the groin and in front of the rectum. The glands become large, sore, red, and tender; they may ulcerate, are slow in healing, and cause unsightly scarring. In the woman, the labia may swell and can block the vagina.

The treatment for lymphogranuloma venereum is with sulfonamides or tetracycline. Response is slow and the infection can last for years.

Granuloma Inguinale

Granuloma inguinale is the least common STD, is found in tropical areas of the United States, and is caused by the *Klebsiella* group of bacteria. After its incubation time, which is 8 to 100 days after sexual contact, a painless papule forms, ulcerates, and becomes a granulomatous mass. Tissue is friable and beefy red, and inguinal subcutaneous tissue swells. Eventually, scarring occurs, with distortions, elephantiasis, and ulceration of underlying tissue. Treatment is with broad spectrum antibiotics. This is a reportable disease in particular states.

Chancroid

A *chancroid* is a soft, sore ulcer on the genitalia caused by *Hemophilus ducreyi* bacteria. It is transmitted by oral–genital, genital, or anal sex and may involve lymph glands. The disease can also be transmitted by bacteria-contaminated fingers, towels, clothing, or instruments, and can be prevented by washing after sexual conduct. Outbreaks are frequent in tropical environments. The incubation time is three to eight days after exposure. The disease is communicable as long as there is any pus present in the lesions. A chancroid is treated with tetracycline or sulfa drugs. This infection is reported in most states.

Nonspecific Urethritis

Nonspecific urethritis (NSU), or nongonorrhea urethritis (NGU), can be caused by several organisms, including *Chlamydia* and *Mycoplasmas*. This condition has become the most rapidly increasing STD in recent years. The major finding is a mucopurulent discharge from the urethra that is usually slightly less copious than that associated with gonorrhea. Symptoms of urinary tract infection may occur, including burning on urination, increased frequency and urgency of urination, and irritation of the urethral area. Some persons are asymptomatic. A microscopic examination of the discharge is necessary to distinguish between NSU and gonorrhea and to determine which treatment is appropriate. The incubation time is three to five days after sexual contact. A weakened physical status contributes to a person's susceptibility. NSU may follow a gonococcal infection and may produce mild to moderate pain. Treatment is with tetracycline. Penicillin is of no value in this infection. No treatment should be started until a specimen of the urethral discharge is taken to be certain appropriate treatment is used. Despite adequate bacterial response to treatment, symptoms may persist and concern the patient. As with gonorrhea, intercourse, masturbation, alcohol, coffee, and tea should be avoided.

Trichomoniasis

Trichomoniasis, an amoebic infection, has a 4- to 28-day incubation period. The amoeba can live for several hours on moist surfaces at room temperature, so they can be transmitted by toilet seats and wash cloths that have been in contact with infected persons, as well as by sexual contact. The symptoms, which occur only in the woman, include a foamy white, yellow, or green discharge with a foul odor, and reddened vaginal mucosa that is itchy, and edema of the vulva. Since it is commonly carried under the foreskin of the uncircumcised penis and in semen, there is often a ping-pong transmission between steady sexual partners causing continued reinfection and resulting in the necessity of treating both partners.

To diagnose, a wet prep, obtained using a normal saline-soaked cotton swab in the vaginal area, is examined microscopically for the Trichomonas. Treatment is with oral metronidazole (Flagyl), which stains the urine a dark shade. Possible gastrointestinal side effects are aggravated by smoking or drinking alcohol.

No sexual intercourse should occur until both partners are treated for one week, unless a condom is used. Metronidazole should be avoided if the patient is in the first half of pregnancy or is breast feeding, because it passes across the placenta barrier or through breast milk and produces teratogenic effects.

Candidiasis Albicans, or Monilia

This is a yeastlike fungal infection. It produces a white cottage-cheese like discharge or clear watery discharge and reddened, dry, irritated itching vaginitis, balanitis, or cutaneous lesions on the penis. Intercourse is often painful. The natural habitat of these microorganisms is in the mouth, intestines, and vagina. A woman is more susceptible to the growth of this fungus if she is diabetic, pregnant, is taking birth control pills or antibiotics, or douches excessively (more than once per week), since these situations disturb the normal acid environment of the vaginal flora and enhance the conditions necessary for candida growth. This fungus can be transmitted by contact with genitals, fingers, mouth, or dildo. Sexual activity may not pass the candida from partner to partner, but can transmit the agent from one area to another of the same person's body. Candida is diagnosed by microscopic exam of the discharge on a wet-mount slide. Treatment is with nystatin, miconaxole, or clotrimazole intravaginal cream.

Suggestions for prevention of infection include wearing cotton underwear, careful hand washing before and after handling genitals of self and sex partner, and not using perfumed douches. A vinegar douche (two tablespoons of vinegar to one quart water) or similar product can also help prevent infection in the susceptible woman, although it does not cure an established infection.

This fungus does infect the neonate during passage through the vaginal canal, causing thrush of the mouth.

Herpes Progenitalis Type II

This infection is caused by a small intracellular virus that is incurable, although it may fluctuate between active and dormant phases. The infection is more common in women. The incubation period varies from 24 hours to three months and the lesion is active for 10 to 20 days. Antibodies form one to four weeks after the initial infection but will not prevent recurrence of the disease. The virus penetrates intact mucous membranes, causing small, painful red lumps and patches that enlarge, become blisters, and break open. These lumps and patches are found on the shaft of the penis, the scrotum, perineum, vulva, and cervix and can cause extreme local pain with sexual intercourse. Side effects include groin lymph node enlargement, fever, headache, loss of appetite, and nausea.

If contracted during pregnancy, this virus can cause miscarriage or stillbirth. Fifty percent of newborns infected at the time of vaginal delivery become sick, develop encephalitis, and will die or be severely affected (Hart, 1977). Cesarean delivery is performed to prevent the transmission of infection from the mother's lesion to the newborn.

Although no curative treatment is available, care for the Herpes II client is symptomatic. Chemicals may be used to dry the blisters, and sitz baths, local anesthesia, analgesia, and bed rest may all promote comfort. Herpes lesions heal in three to four weeks. Condoms should be used to prevent transmission of the active virus during intercourse. An increased incidence of cancer of the cervix in women who have been infected by the herpes virus has been noted, and such women should have a Pap smear at least yearly.

Venereal Warts (Condyloma Acuminata)

Venereal warts are a virus-caused inflammation producing a soft, painless, warty growth singly or in clusters around the genitals and anus. The warts have a pink cauliflower appearance in moist areas or are small, hard, and yellow-gray in dry areas, such as the penile shaft. They are most commonly found in the uncircumcised man.

The warts proliferate during pregnancy but may spontaneously disappear after pregnancy. The incubation time from the moment of exposure is two to three months. Treatment is with podophyllum applied carefully to the wart area and washed off with soap and water six hours after application. This medication should not be used during pregnancy, since it crosses the placental barrier and its safety has not been established. Cautery or cryosurgery may also be used to treat venereal warts.

Pubic Lice (Crabs, Itch)

Pubic lice are seen as yellow-gray- to rust-colored specks or black dots of excretia on the skin in the pubic area. Because lice rarely survive over 24 hours off the host, they are passed by both sexual and nonsexual close contact between people. Kwell soap (*gamma benzene hexachloride*) is used to destroy the lice by working up a lather for four to five minutes and then rinsing. Other chemicals used are A-200 pyrinate and benzyl benzoate lotion. Repeating the treatment in 7 to 10 days is necessary to destroy developing nits. Any sex partner needs to be examined for lice, and all bedding and underwear must be washed.

Scabies

Scabies, often called the seven-year itch, is caused by a mite and is often associated with unclean living conditions. It is transmitted by skin contact or by clothing and bedding. The itching increases when the host is warm, for example, after a bath or in bed.

Treatment is with benzyl benzoate lotion after bathing and must be repeated in one week. All contacts must be treated.

Hepatitis Type B

This infection is caused by a virus found in the digestive system. Sexual behaviors involving anal and oral intercourse cause transmission of this virus. The incubation time is 60 to 180 days after sexual contact. The signs of the disease appear gradually with gastrointestinal symptoms and progress to jaundice. Diagnosis is by blood test. There is no treatment, other than symptomatic, for this disease, which is communicable during the incubation period and for several days after symptoms appear.

Nonspecific Vaginitis (NSV)

This condition is frequently caused by *Corynebacterium* or *Hemophilus* bacteria. A gray, chalky, white, or yellow, thin, foul-odored discharge is produced. Periodic vaginal bleeding and irritation of the vulva can occur. Diagnosis is made by microscopic examination of the discharge for characteristic cells. Both partners are treated with oral ampicillin or metronidazole.

HEALTH TEACHING AND SEXUALLY TRANSMITTED DISEASES

Frequently, the nurse is the health-care provider who receives inquiries about sexual concerns. This requires the nurse to be aware of attitudes about human sexuality—both her own and the client's. Nurses are in an excellent position to offer education about sexual health and to provide counseling when needed, because they tend to have opportunities to work more closely with patients than do physicians.

An honest, open approach will gain the client's confidence and help create an atmosphere conducive to interpersonal confidence and cooperation. Clients, especially teenagers, will be wary of authoritarian, ambiguous, or judgmental statements and nonverbal cues. For example, avoid assumptions about the number of sexual partners and their gender, using such neutral terms as *partner* or *contact*, unless the client uses *he* or *she*. Even then, never assume exclusively heterosexual or homosexual activity.

A client being examined for a possible STD may be suffering from guilt and anger at real or perceived judgmental cues from the self, partners, family, and peer group, and the nurse's sensitivity to the client's reactions may help the client and partners cope with these feelings. A nurse may offer to role play partner encounters with a client or volunteer to counsel the client and sexual partner together.

Nurses may use a discussion about sexuality as an opportunity to provide counseling or referral for relationship problems, sexual dysfunction, pregnancy, and contraception, as well as the need for self-breast exams, Pap smears, and testes checks. The client's right to privacy about personal affairs must be respected, however.

Finally, the nurse must stress the need for retesting for STDs until negative results are obtained and the need for the names of all sexual partners in order to arrest transmission.

More information about STDs is available for patients from:

VD Hot Line: 1-300-272-2577
National Communication Service Corps (day hours): 1-800-523-1885
Planned Parenthood agencies

Local or state public health agencies, department of communicable disease

Local STD clinics

American Social Health Association

NURSING PROCESS

    Client: Robert Swenson.

    Nurse: Patricia Newhart, nurse at student health center.

Assessment

Subjective Data

"It burns when I urinate."

"There's a white discharge coming from my penis."

"I've been living with my future wife for six months."

"Don't know how Gail (future wife) will react to my having had sex with someone else. I had this one-night stand with an old girl friend from home about a week ago. She has been the only other person I've had sex with since Gail and I began living together. I've had sex with Gail three times this past week. God, I hope she's not infected. I had regular vaginal intercourse with both of them."

"Neither one knows I have these symptoms or that I've come here for help."

"I'm not allergic to penicillin."

Objective Data

Positive diagnosis of *Neisseria gonorrhoeae* from urethral smear.

Vague pelvic pain.

Able to state symptoms of gonorrhea but does not know treatment.

No previous history of gonorrhea or other sexually transmitted disease.

Nursing Diagnosis

Lack of information about treatment and prevention of gonorrhea related to diagnosis of *Neisseria gonorrhoeae*.

Possible conflict in relationship with partner (Gail) due to sexual contact outside the relationship.

Possible conflict in relationship with partner (Gail) because either may have transmitted gonorrhea.

Planning

Express acceptance of problem and feelings.
Emphasize value of seeking early treatment.
Explain course of treatment—medication regimen and follow-through.
Explain need to vary sexual activity until negative smear is obtained.
Initiate drug therapy as prescribed by medical protocol.
Discuss need to inform both sexual partners of possible infection.
Explore the options available to inform sexual partners.
Encourage decision making.
Encourage expression of feelings with sexual partner (Gail).
Encourage mutual decision making between sexual partners about relationship.
Present information about counseling services available.

Implementation

Arrange personal time for treatment regimen.
Make commitment to course of treatment.
Inform both partners of exposure to gonorrhea.
Express feelings about having gonorrhea to sexual partner, Gail.
Initiate discussion with sexual partner, Gail, about relationship.
Modify sexual activity.

Evaluation

Reports that relationship with sexual partner, Gail, continues but is undergoing change.
Reports that both partners have been informed and are under medical treatment.
Reports no further symptoms.
Discusses preventive measures.

BIBLIOGRAPHY

Breecher, E. M. Prevention of the sexually transmitted diseases. *Journal of Sex Research*, 1975, *11*, 318–328.

Bureau of State Services Technical Information Services. *STD summary.* Public Health Service Center for Disease Control, Atlanta, Georgia, 1979.

Darrow, W. *Venereal disease, the victimless crime.* Abstract of a speech presented at Center for Disease Control, Atlanta, Georgia, January 7, 1979.

Dunlop, E. Some moral problems posed by sexually transmitted diseases. *British Journal of Venereal Diseases*, 1973, *49*, 203–204.

The Gay Health Collective of Boston. *VD facts for gay women and men.* Gay Health Collective of Boston and Massachusetts Department of Public Health, 1979.

Ginsberg, M. Gonorrhea among homosexuals. *Medical Aspects of Human Sexuality,* 1980, *14,* 45–46.

Hart, G. *Sexual maladjustment and disease.* Chicago: Nelson-Hall, 1977.

Henderson, R. Improving sexually transmitted disease health services for gays: A national perspective. *Sexually Transmitted Diseases*, 1977, *4*, 58–62.

Hubbard, C. *Family planning education: Parenthood and social disease control.* St. Louis: Mosby, 1973.

Mayhew, A. (Ed.). *Our bodies, ourselves* (2nd ed.). New York: Simon & Schuster, 1976.

Mims, F., & Swenson, M. *Sexuality: A nursing perspective.* New York: McGraw-Hill, 1980.

Money, J., & Musaph, H. *Handbook of sexology.* Amsterdam: Excerpta Medica, 1977.

Morton, B. *VD: A guide for nurses and counselors.* Boston: Little, Brown, 1976.

Montreal Health Press, Inc. (Eds.). *VD handbook.* Montreal, Quebec: Editor, 1973.

Nicholas, L. Venereal disease in pediatrics. *Medical Aspects of Human Sexuality,* 1978, *12,* 30–45.

Ory, H. A review of the association between intrauterine contraceptive devices and acute pelvic inflammatory disease. *Journal of Reproductive Medicine,* 1978, *12,* 30–204.

Pearsall, F., & Rosenwerg, N. (Eds.). *Sex education for the health professional.* New York: Grune & Stratton, 1978.

Pariser, H. Frequently overlooked signs of the early stages of venereal diseases in man. *Medical Aspects of Human Sexuality,* 1978, *12,* 121–122.

Rodin, P., & Goldmeir, D. Sexual problems seen by venerologists. In S. Crown (Ed.), *Psychosexual problems; psychotherapy, counseling, and behavior modification.* London: Academic Press, 1976.

Rowan, R., & Gilette, P. *The gay health guide.* Boston: Little, Brown, 1978.

Venereal Diseases Control Division. *STD fact sheet* (34th ed.). Public Health Service Center for Disease Control (HEW pub. no. [CDC] 79-8195), 1977.

14. Sexuality and Chronic Illness

Caroline M. Myer

VALUES CLARIFICATION EXERCISE

Our American culture values youth, wholeness, normality, and attractiveness of the body. Each of those valued attributes, to a greater or lesser degree, is a significant part of the mental image a person has of his or her body. It is not surprising then that a chronic illness that affects body appearance or function affects a person's perception of himself or herself. This exercise is meant to help you understand how a chronic illness might affect how you perceive your body and how that perception can influence your sexual roles and relationships.

Imagine that you have been married for six months. Just before your wedding you became aware of an increased appetite followed by an increased thirst and increased output of urine. The weakness and fatigue that you experienced during your honeymoon has persisted and increased. Two weeks ago you stubbed your right large toe; it is still so swollen and red that wearing your favorite shoes is painful. You are aware, too, that your genital area is red and itchy. Your family physician makes the diagnosis of diabetes mellitus.

As you read your symptoms and diagnosis did you feel shock? Denial? Anger? Sadness? Fear? Anxiety? Confusion? Emptiness? Helplessness? Loneliness?

With what symptoms did you find it most difficult to deal? The symptoms involving your appetite? Your thirst? Your urine output? Your right large toe? Your genital area?

How do you see yourself in relation to your sexual partner? Do you feel worthy of the relationship? Do you see yourself continuing the relationship? Do you feel the relationship should be terminated? How does what you expect to get from the relationship change? How does what you expect to give to the relationship change?

How do you see your sexual partner responding? Does what you want from your sexual partner change? Have your feelings about your sexual partner changed?

Now share your responses and reactions with a small group of your peers or colleagues. Are there any responses or reactions that seem to occur more frequently than others? Are the responses or reactions of the group members affected by their age? Their sex? Their life experiences?

Compare how the potential change in body image affected the self-worth of the individual members of the group. Compare how the potential change in body image affected sexual relationships for members of the group.

Discuss what each of you have learned about the relationship, your body image, your sexual self-esteem, and your sexual concepts. Discuss planning and implementing nursing care for a client with an alteration in body image related to a chronic illness from what you have learned about yourself and each other.

BEHAVIORAL OBJECTIVES

At the completion of this chapter you will be able to

- Discuss the relationship of body image and health disruptions.
- Discuss the effects of grief associated with the loss of an established body image on sexuality.
- Discuss the impact of myocardial infarction on the sexual behavior of the client during the acute phase, and early and late convalescence.
- Explain the cardiac cost of intercourse and masturbation.
- Discuss the direct and indirect evidence that relates the fear of recurrent heart attack and sexual activity.
- Discuss the practice of advising against specific positions for intercourse for the client after a myocardial infarction.
- Explain the aim and therapeutic goal of cardiac rehabilitation.
- Outline a sexual activity program for a client with umcomplicated myocardial infarction.
- Discuss the information given to a client about resumption of sexual activity after a myocardial infarction.
- Discuss the psychologic consequences of a myocardial infarction on the client's significant others.
- Explain the purpose of Heart Clubs.
- Describe the role of the nurse as educator-counselor in providing sexual health care to the client with a myocardial infarction.
- Discuss the varied psychologic reactions to the alteration in body image associated with diabetes.

- Discuss the occurrence and pathogenesis of erectile dysfunction in diabetic men.
- Explain the process of identifying the psychologic or organic basis of impotence in diabetic men.
- Describe the medical and surgical treatment of impotence in diabetic men.
- Discuss the occurrence and pathogenesis of orgasmic dysfunction in diabetic women.
- Describe the treatment of sexual dysfunction in diabetic women.
- Describe the effect of diabetes on the fertility and sterility of diabetic men and women.
- Discuss genetic counseling for diabetic men and women.
- Describe the role of the nurse as educator-counselor in the sexual health care of people with diabetes.

BODY IMAGE AND HEALTH DISRUPTIONS

Body image is the way a person sees himself or herself in the world. It is that internalized mental picture one has of oneself, derived dynamically and involving personal perceptions of one's body. A person's body image develops over a span of years and has a psychologic and physiologic foundation. Body image influences a person's self-concept and self-esteem and has an impact on his or her sexual self and, in turn, on sexual functioning, sexual roles, and sexual relationships.

A chronic illness is an impairment of health that requires an extended period of care and attention and hinders one from pursuing normal, usual, and selected activities. A chronic illness can have acute episodes but these usually are of limited duration, and the major task of the person and his or her significant others is coping with the continuing aspects of the chronic illness. A chronic illness can alter the internal or external appearance and functioning of the body. The alteration may be perceived as a movement away from wholeness and normality and thus may disturb security and threaten self-esteem.

Awareness of, information about, and diagnosis of chronic illness affects the person's body image. The person will use mental and emotional energy to protect the established image of body and its functioning. Any alteration that is not consistent with the established body image may be accompanied by loss of self-esteem, feelings of abandonment and powerlessness, loss of control, loss of competence in the sexual role, and disturbance of interpersonal relationships.

The emotional investment a person makes in the functioning of the involved body part will affect how he or she responds to the alteration (Bower, 1977). For many, the heart is the symbol of life and is central to body functioning. Responses to heart attack may range from denial, with the person refusing to modify activity, to "immobilizing fear", with the person too frightened to return to work, leisure activities, sex, and society (Bower, 1977, p. 81). In diabetes mellitus, the innermost level of bodily experience is affected and may profoundly influence the way a person sees and feels about himself or herself. The person may experience feelings of increased vulnerability and sense a loss of control of the body and its functions.

Alterations in body appearance and function may progress slowly or rapidly. If the alteration progresses slowly, the person may have time to adapt to the alteration and grieve the loss of the established body image. A person's characteristic coping patterns influence how he or she will adapt to the alteration. A person who has always used denial may continue to do so and will hinder rather than facilitate adaptation. Whatever the rate of alteration, the person is forced to change his or her mental and emotional picture of the self. The person must acknowledge the illness and assimilate the resulting changes into his or her body image and self-concept.

Adaptation to alterations in the body's appearance and function depends upon the nature of the alteration, the meaning of the alteration to the client, the client's coping ability, the response of his or her significant others, and the assistance available to him or her and significant others as the alterations occur (Bower, 1977). Knowledge about the concept of body image can help the nurse predict and anticipate reactions and to prepare clients with chronic illness for possible and expected alterations in body image.

MYOCARDIAL INFARCTION AND SEXUAL BEHAVIOR

A heart attack is a *myocardial infarction* (MI)—a sudden blockage of one of the coronary arteries. The heart as the beat of life is probably uppermost in the mind of the person undergoing a heart attack. The person must cope with the sudden loss of his or her intactness, and while, physically, the damage is not visible, the heart is no longer as reliable as it once was. Little is known about sexual behavior during the immediate acute phase of the heart attack. However, when the threat of death is no longer present, the person will begin to deal with what changes the heart attack will make in his or her life. Concerns about job and work habits, sexuality, and sexual functioning are typical (Kolodny et al., 1979). Cassem and Hackett (1971) report that men studied on a coronary care unit were greatly concerned about impotence; their conversations contained themes of sexual prowess and function, and a few of the men acted out sexually toward women nurses. During the fourth and fifth days, when their conditions had stabilized, it was not unusual to find clients depressed and grieving their loss of intactness and independence.

Wishnie, Hackett, and Cassem (1971) comment that weakness, insomnia, and boredom are frequently experienced by the myocardial infarction client during early convalescence. The client may rigidly conform to the initial restrictions on activity and an exaggerated dependency may develop. Bruh, Wolf, and Phillips (1971) stated that depression, like fear and anxiety, is not an uncommon reaction and may lead to decreased interest in sexual activity.

Several studies have reported substantial decrease in sexual activity after a myocardial infarction. Klein et al. (1965) interviewed 20 men between 3 and 48 months post-MI and found that only five men had returned to pre-MI sexual activity; seven men reported complete abstinence and eight men said that their sexual activity had decreased. Tutle, Cook, and Fitch (1964) interviewed men one to nine years after MI and reported that 10% of the men were impotent, about 60% had a marked and lasting reduction of levels of intercourse, and only about 30% returned to their pre-MI levels. The investigators concluded that the change in behavior was based on misinformation and fear.

Block, Malder, and Haessly (1975) interviewed 88 men and 12 women about their sexual practices before and after MI. The investigation reported that the monthly mean frequency of sexual intercourse before the MI was 5.2, as compared to 2.7 after the MI in spite of the fact that almost all of the men and women had resumed otherwise normally active lives. The reasons given by the subjects for the decrease in sexual activity were anxiety, depression, lack of desire, fear of another attack or sudden death, and decision of the sexual partner. Abramov (1976) reported a high incidence of depression among women who had heart attacks. Hellerstein and Friedman (1970) found a significant decrease in sexual activity in a group of men who had experienced heart attacks when compared to a matched group of MI-prone men.

Wishnie, Hackett, and Cassem (1971) stated that the problems that develop after MI hinge largely on the misunderstanding of the MI and on misinterpretation of the physician's orders. Eliot and Miles (1975) contend some clients assume that if their physician does not mention the possibility of sexual activity it must be because sex is beyond their present physical capabilities. Koller et al. (1972) found that the client with an MI received advice about reducing or stopping smoking and doing mild physical exercise but very little information about sexual functioning. These clients relied upon inadequate information, fear, opinions or superstitions, and reduced sexual activity even to the point of abstinence. Koller et al. stated that reduced sexual activity can lead to or cause conflicts in relationships, frustration, and irritability that may hinder rehabilitation and even increase the chances of further cardiac involvement.

It would appear that the reasons underlying the development of sexual difficulties after MI are not organic in nature but largely a result of anxiety, avoidance, depression, poor self-esteem, misconceptions, and unreliable and inadequate information.

Cardiac Cost of Intercourse

There are two common and prevalent fears associated with a heart attack—the fear that another MI will occur during intercourse and the fear of sudden death during intercourse. There is also the belief that a person who has had a heart attack must greatly reduce his or her physical activity. Even though evidence points to the fact that there is no increase in mortality due to early and gradual return to full activity, including sexual activity, there remains a cultural bias that makes changes in treatment regimens difficult (Levy & McGill, 1975).

Masters and Johnson (1966) performed laboratory studies on the physiologic effects of intercourse on healthy subjects and found that sexual activity is accompanied by marked cardiovascular fluctuations. During excitement, there is a gradual increase in respiratory and heart rates and a mild elevation of the blood pressure. During plateau, recorded heart rates averaged from 100 to 175 beats per minute. Blood pressure increases from 20 to 80 mm Hg (systolic) and 10 to 50 mm Hg (diastolic). The respiratory rate accelerates as high as 40 breaths per minute. The physiologic parameters return to baseline rates within one to two minutes during the resolution phase.

Hellerstein and Friedman (1970) provided the first significant experimental findings on the physiologic impact of sexual intercourse on men with diseased hearts. The subjects for the study were 48 postmyocardial men, average age 53; and 48 normal but MI-prone men, average age 48. Data were obtained during 24- to 48-hour monitoring periods with a portable electromagnetic tape recorder that continuously recorded electrocardiogram (EKG) information on tape. Of the 91 subjects, 14 engaged in sexual activity while being monitored.

Hellerstein and Friedman (1970) found that the mean maximal heart rate during orgasm was 117.4 beats per minute (BPM) with a range from 90 BPM to 144 BPM. This dropped to 96.9 BPM one minute after orgasm and to 85.0 BPM two minutes after orgasm. The mean maximal heart rate during the performance of usual occupational or professional activity was 120.1 BPM, just slightly more than that during sexual activity. EKG changes and symptoms during intercourse and usual occupational activities were comparable in frequency and severity. The investigators concluded that conjugal sex in a middle-aged man with a partner of 20 years or more in the privacy of their own bedroom demanded only modest physical requirements and was similar to walking up one flight of stairs, walking briskly, or performing tasks in many occupations.

Douglas and Wilkes (1971) offer further support for sexual activity after MI. The energy expenditure of a person at rest requires an oxygen consumption of approximately 3.5 ml/kg body weight/min. This activity level is equal to one metabolic equivalent or 1 MET. Exercise above this level can then be described in multiples of METs. Douglas and Wilkes gave the mean energy cost in METs of some common activities: sleeping, .8; walking uphill on a 5% grade at three miles per hour, 4.0; sexual foreplay, 3.5; orgasm, 4.7 to 5.5. Mackey (1978) stated that during pre- and postorgasmic periods, the energy cost is 3.7 METs. The heart rate correlates with the number of METs and is a convenient way of determining oxygen consumption and thus physical work (Green, 1975; Mackey, 1978). Average middle-aged men who have recovered from an uncomplicated MI have a maximum capacity of 8 to 9 METs and are equal to the energy demands of sexual intercourse (Eliot & Miles, 1973).

Cardiac Cost of Masturbation

Wagner and Sivarajan (1979) reported the preliminary data from a study about the cardiac cost of masturbation. The study subjects were 10 healthy young men. At the time of orgasm by masturbation the heart rate does not go above 130 BPM and it rises to the 110 to 130 BPM level only for brief moments. This is in contrast to the cardiac cost of up to 180 BPM for intercourse of people in this same age and health group. It is intended that data about the cardiac cost of masturbation for young healthy women and cardiac clients be collected and reported also.

For many men, the return of sexual arousal symbolizes the intactness of their masculinity and is a positive sign in terms of a continuing sex life (Wagner & Sivarajan, 1979). Masturbatory activities ranging from partial erection to full tumescence and ejaculatory release are controlled by the client. When a heart rate of 110 to 130 beats per minute will do the client no harm, masturbation can be suggested as an acceptable activity before resumption of intercourse for clients whose personal convictions and values permit it.

Fear of Recurrent Heart Attack

The only factual information available on the possibility of sudden death during intercourse is from a study by Ueno (1973), who did autopsies on 5,559 cases of sudden death over a 4½ year period. He reported that 34 (0.6%) of the deaths were specifically precipitated by sexual activity. The 18 men were with partners who were on the average 20 years younger than they, and the two women were with partners three years older. Three of the 34 deaths occurred after masturbation. Twenty-five percent (9) of the deaths occurred in hotel rooms, and 77% (27) of the sexual relations were extramarital. One-third (6) of the victims were noted to have been in a drunken state.

The evidence suggests that nonmarital sexual relations may lead to greater cardiac expenditure. There is indirect evidence that sudden death during intercourse may be more a function of stress than of sexual activity alone (Massie, Rose, Rypp, & Whelton, 1969). Such death usually occurs when the sexual partner is not the spouse, the surroundings are unfamiliar, and sexual intercourse occurs after a large meal and alcohol intake. Wagner and Sivarajan (1979) point out that sexual activity with a new or newer partner is particularly stress producing. A man resuming sexual activity with his wife after a 10-year abstinence would be at risk. The facts seem to indicate that chances of a sudden death during intercourse, particularly within a comfortable relationship and atmosphere, are relatively small. Open discussion about the fact of recurrent MI and sudden death during sexual intercourse requires tact. Perhaps such phrases as "usual partner," "comfortable about having sex," "familiar surroundings" might be helpful.

Positions for Intercourse

Because of the detrimental effect of isometric exercises, MI clients are sometimes cautioned against such activities as lifting any objects, carrying suitcases, and shoveling snow, all of which involve this type of muscular work (Douglas & Wilkes, 1975). For this reason, many post-MI men have been advised against the man-on-top position so as to avoid using their arms to support their body for a sustained period of time. Nemec, Mansfield, and Kennedy (1976) studied eight normal men aged 24 to 40 to determine if intercourse carried out in the man-on-top position would be more stressful than the man-on-bottom position.

The mean maximal heart rate responses during orgasm in the man-on-top position was 114 beats per minute; in the man-on-bottom position it was 117 beats per minute. Blood pressure response during sexual activity in the man-on-top position was 112/66 mm Hg at rest, increased to 163/81 mm Hg at orgasm, and returned to 121/71 mm Hg two minutes after orgasm. In the man-on-bottom position it was 113/70 mm Hg at rest, 161/77 mm Hg at orgasm, and 121/77 mm Hg two minutes after orgasm. The pressure–rate product (systolic blood pressure & heart rate), which is an indirect measure of myocardial oxygen consumption, was also calculated. In the man-on-top position, pressure–rate product was 67 at rest, 189 at orgasm, and 82 two minutes after orgasm, and the corresponding values for the man-on-bottom position were 65, 183, and 77, respectively.

Nemec, Mansfield, and Kennedy (1976) found no significant differences in heart rate or blood pressure as a function of position during intercourse and concluded there was no basis for advising cardiac clients to use the man-on-bottom position for intercourse.

Sexual Rehabilitation Programs

A systematic exercise program has become an accepted form of treatment for post-MI clients. A physically fit person can perform a given level of work at a lower heart rate and systolic blood pressure than an unfit person. Information that the aim of an exercise program is to improve cardiovascular performance by reducing heart rate and blood pressure responses for any given amount of workload and that exercise rehabilitation helps sexual rehabilitation as well is helpful information for the client and his or her sexual position. Hellerstein and Friedman (1970) found that participation in a systematic exercise program produced significant improvement in physical fitness, blood pressure, mood, frequency, and quality of sexual activity.

Stein (1977) studied 16 men, 12 to 15 weeks post-MI, before and after a 16-week bicycle ergometry training program and compared the results with those of six post-MI men who did not receive training. The mean peak heart rate during sexual activity for both groups of men was 127 beats per minute, with a range of 120 to 130. After the 16 men completed the training, a decrease in mean peak heart rate during intercourse to 120 beats per minute was observed. No such change occurred in the six men who did not undergo the training program. Stein (1977) concluded that peak heart rate during intercourse, and possibly also myocardial oxygen requirements, declines as the man's level of fitness is enhanced.

Siewicki and Mansfield (1977) closely evaluated the customary recommendations that if post-MI clients can climb two flights of stairs without symptoms, they can resume sexual activity with their usual partner. Thirty normal men aged 20 to 39 performed the two-flight test, which consisted of climbing 20 steps in 10 seconds, or two steps per second. The mean maximal heart rate during the two-flight test was 127 beats per minute and the mean maximal blood pressure was 145/72. The mean maximal pressure–rate product was 190 and similar to that reported by Nemec, Mansfield, and Kennedy (1976). The investigators concluded that the physical exertion of the men in the study was similar in energy to that of sexual activity, and that the two-flight test is probably a useful method to ascertain if post-MI clients are ready to resume sexual activity.

Hellerstein and Friedman (1970) reported that 40% of their study sample reported awareness of a very rapid heart beat during intercourse. Awareness of very rapid heart beat occurs in people who have not had heart attacks, and is rarely thought of as a sign of impending danger. The post-MI client who is more physically fit as a result of a systematic exercise program is less likely to experience rapid heart pounding and breathlessness during sex and thus is less likely to misinterpret rapid heart beat as an unusual response to sexual activity (Friedman, 1978).

Douglas and Wilkes (1975) state that within 48 hours after a heart attack, clients who are free of pain show no signs of complications and those whose resting pulses are between 50 and 90 are ready to start on a systematic exercise program. The program is prescribed by the physician, and the activities begin with passive range-of-motion exercises and move to ambulation and moderate exercises with resumption of work and usual and sexual activities as a goal.

Watts (1976) advocates for the client with uncomplicated MI the sexual activity program shown in Figure 14.1. The program incorporates general activity level, cardiac education, and sexual counseling and activities, and specifies a role for a nurse clinician. The sexual activity begins with masturbation, moves to mutual pleasuring and nondemanding sexual activity, and progresses to intercourse. Opinions and practices vary as to when a post-MI client may resume intercourse. There are some physicians who give permission for intercourse eight weeks after infarction; Green (1975) questions whether a limit of eight weeks is necessary. The program, however, can provide a possible format for consideration as each client is individually assessed and evaluated.

Information Concerning Resumption of Sexual Activity

Before a client is given information concerning the resumption of sexual activity, his or her physician is consulted. In order to provide information suitable and appropriate to the individual client, the sexual history is reviewed (Chapter 2) and data is gathered about the following: usual or preferred type and time of sexual activity; usual and preferred amount and variety of sexual activity; previous consumption of alcohol and food associated with sexual activity; previous episodes of decreased sexual urge or desire, impotence (man), and ejaculatory dysfunction (man); previous occurrences of any chest pain, fatigue, or sleeplessness after sexual activity (Mims & Swenson, 1980). These data supply information about what is comfortable and normal; what is preferred and valued by the client and his or her sexual partner is the best starting point.

The following information related to the resumption of sexual intercourse should be shared with the client and his or her sexual partner:

External environment: The room should be at a comfortable temperature. Extremes of temperature and extremely high humidity make maintaining steady temperature difficult.

Personal environment: The client should feel comfortable with himself or herself and be at ease with his or her sexual partner. Tension, anxiety, and uncertainty contribute to stress.

Food and alcohol: The client should wait at least two to three hours after eating a heavy meal or drinking alcohol before engaging in sexual activity. Digestion of large amounts of food or ingestion of alcohol (a depressant) requires additional output of energy.

CONVALESCENT PHASE: IN HOSPITAL—WEEK 3

Activity level

General: Walk hall two to three times per day at normal walking pace; receive family
visitors; shave

Sexual: Masturbation to partial erection

Education

Cardiac: Heart rate should not exceed baseline of 20 bpm

Contraindications to above activities: faintness, dyspnea, diaphoresis,
tachycardia

Teach patient to take pulse and pace himself

Sexual counseling: Interview patient, spouse, and couple prior to discharge

CONVALESCENT PHASE: POST-HOSPITAL—WEEKS 4 TO 6

Activity level

General: Maintenance of hospital activity program

Begin slowly, daily walks on level surface

Sexual: Self-stimulation to partial erection

Couple begins sensate pleasure for one another with quiet nondemanding
stroking of back, face, arms, legs; focus on self-pleasure, exclude genital
areas (do not attempt sexual intercourse or stimulation to ejaculation
despite occurrence of erection)

Both partners must be well-rested prior to exercises

Education: Contraindications to above activities include dyspnea, faintness, rapid
pulse, fatigue, emotional upset

Take pulse prior to, during, and after stroking episodes

Sessions three times per week for 20 minutes

Telephone contact with nurse clinician regarding problems or progress;
office visit with physician

CONVALESCENT PHASE: 7 TO 9 WEEKS

Activity level

General: Continue all previous activities; physician may order treadmill test

Sexual: Masturbation to full erection

Husband and wife on alternate occasions stroke the other's pelvic area,
under the direction of the other; focus attention on each other

Education: Note previous complications; sessions three times per week for 20 minutes each; contact with nurse clinician for support and guidance

CONVALESCENT PHASE: 10 to 12 WEEKS

Activity level

General: Continue daily walks and moderate exercises; climb two flights of stairs;
work to tolerance

Sexual: Masturbation to ejaculation

Couple engage in manipulative play

Oral–genital sex if accepted as marital norm

Sexual intercourse in position comfortable for couple (avoid isometrics)

Education: Adequate pacing of activities; check pulse

Avoid sudden exercise or competitive efforts

Note unusual symptomatology

Avoid clustering of other physical activities with coital activity (e.g., eating,
drinking, fatigue, emotional upsets)

Suggest couples read *Sound Sex and the Aging Heart*

Telephone contact with physician or nurse clinician

Figure 14.1.   Sexual activity program for patient with uncomplicated myocardial infarction. Reprinted with permission from Watts, R. J. Sexuality and the
middle-aged cardiac patient. *Nursing Clinics of North America,* 1976, *11,* 349-
359.

Fatigue: Fatigue can impair sexual functioning. The best time for sexual activity is when a person is well-rested. Intercourse in the morning, when the client is fresh and rested, can be considered; a nap before intercourse can be planned. A rest period after intercourse can enhance sensuality and prepare for increased physical exertion after intercourse.

Position: The position used should be comfortable and nonstrenuous. Recommendation for a change in position can be anxiety provoking, and the needs, preferences, expectations, and usual practices of the client and his or her sexual partner are important considerations. The on-top position may be modified by supporting more of the weight with the knees and legs. Sidelying position may be used. The man can sit in a low, armless chair, head resting on a pillow, with his partner sitting on his lap and both partners' feet touching the floor. The partners may be encouraged to try touching, holding, body massage, and self-stimulation to lessen performance demand and increase mutual pleasuring.

Warning signs: A client must report and consult with a physician if any of these symptoms occur in association with sexual activity:

- Rapid heart and respiratory rate persisting 20 to 30 minutes after sexual activity.
- Heart palpitation continuing 15 minutes after intercourse.
- Chest pain during or after intercourse.
- Sleeplessness after sexual activity.
- Extreme fatigue on the day after intercourse.

Angina pectoris: Clients who occasionally have mild chest pain or discomfort associated with angina (ischemic heart disease) during intercourse may benefit from taking nitroglycerin before intercourse (Kolodny et al., 1979).

Medications: Clients on antihypertensives, tranquilizers, antidepressants, and hypnotics should know that these medications can affect sex and sexuality (Chapter 12).

The client's usual sexual partner should be a participant in the giving and sharing of information. The discussion should be private and the nurse's comfort with the subject and his or her open and direct manner can have a positive effect on the interaction. During the discussion, the nurse needs to remember that the information is intended to facilitate and enable sexual activity, not inhibit or prohibit.

The Effect of Myocardial Infarction on the Sexual Partner

One of the most important factors in determining how well a post-MI client will function sexually is how well his or her sexual partner is functioning, for fear and anxiety from either partner may have negative effects on sexual activity. In a study of the psychologic consequences of a heart attack on 65 wives of male clients, Dominian and Shelton (1973) found that feelings of loss, depression, and guilt were present. The period of convalescence was very stressful to the wives, and they attributed the stress to a fear of recurrent infarction and to marital tension caused by their husband's increased irritability and dependency.

Papadapaules et al. (1980) found that 100 wives of post-MI men had fears and concerns about inadequate sexual instructions, risk of sexual activity, sexual difficulties of the husband, change in sexual patterns, partner's symptoms during intercourse, and emotional relationships of the married partners. The fear experienced by these wives was not necessarily allayed by information given. Fear did not seem to prevent a return to sexual activity; however, fear may have affected both the frequency and quality of the sexual activity the partners shared.

If the wife assumes some of her husband's former responsibilities within the family, sexual roles are clouded and sexual relating and sexual relationships may be disturbed. Wishnie, Hackett, and Cassem (1971) reported that conflicts are noted even if the home life has previously been stable; if a marital problem was already present, it tended to worsen.

It appears that anticipatory guidance, including direct and specific information and counseling, can be helpful and valuable to the MI client's sexual partner, and individual, private discussion times should be arranged.

Heart Clubs

In some areas, Heart Clubs have been started for clients with myocardial infarction. Through guest speakers and group discussion, an attempt is made to help and support members as they attempt to reconstruct and resume their social, occupational, and sexual roles and relationships. As with most groups, some members participate and are positive role models, others are participant observers, and others withdraw. The discussion of mutual concerns and the sharing of, listening to, and acknowledging of similar concerns, frustrations, anxieties, and expectations can be helpful to a diminished sexual self-concept and self-esteem.

THE ROLE OF THE NURSE AS EDUCATOR-COUNSELOR

Providing reliable and current information through anticipatory guidance and teaching is of particular importance in the sexual health care of the client with an MI. Sensitive counseling is needed as the client copes with anxiety, anger, and depression in the process of modifying body image, reconstructing sexual self-image, and reorganizing a continuing sexual life. Through openness to feelings, direct information, and acceptance of the client's perception of sex, the nurse assures and reassures the client and his or her significant others that their thoughts, feelings, and fears are normal, helps them understand the impact of the MI on their sexual lives, and assists them as they make responsible decisions about sex and sexuality based on reliable information.

The role of educator-counselor begins in the coronary care unit, where the nurse assumes the responsibility of opening discussions of sex and sexuality and, through anticipatory guidance, assures the client that most people are able to resume their usual, even though modified, activities after convalescence, including sexual activity. As the client progresses and cardiac rehabilitation is considered, it is helpful to have clients associate sexual activity with other physical activities by telling them that they can resume full sexual activity when they meet a specific level of exercise tolerance and to arrange for their significant others to be participant-observers of the exercise program. It is helpful for post-MI clients and their significant others to know about the cardiac cost of masturbation and that the cardiac rate, blood pressure, and respiratory rate increase rapidly during sexual activity but that the increase is not significantly different from that experienced during other types of exercise and daily activities. Information about the male and female sexual response cycle and the amount of energy required for sexual intercourse can be helpful; and, when appropriate, so can information about the effect of aging on the response cycle (Chapter 6).

A client's expression of fear and anxiety about sex should never be answered with "don't worry," and a vague comment such as "take it easy" is inappropriate. The nurse chooses instead to recognize the fear and anxiety as real, legitimate, and important and responds with understanding and open discussion of the feelings and with direct reliable information. As educator-counselor, the nurse is sensitive to the client who reports either no problems or increased frequency of intercourse and high levels of pleasure, for such reports may identify the client who may be denying the heart attack, who may be pushing himself or herself beyond current capacity for physical effort, or who may not be following the guidelines offered. The client may be coping with grief, anxiety, altered sexual self-image, and lowered self-esteem. The nursing intervention is not based on "no's" and "stops," but on the acknowledgment of feelings and anticipatory guidance and counseling about the altered sexual self-image. The nurse listens, accepts, and guides as the client searches for an acceptable set of sexual behaviors that reflect his or her altered body image. The nurse who understands the impact of altered body image on sexuality and is comfortable with open and direct discussion can make a major contribution to the sexual health care of the post-MI client.

NURSING PROCESS

Client: Wyatt Chan—39-year-old man, six weeks post-MI.
Nurse: Amy Baxter—nurse in cardiac rehabilitation program at local hospital.

Assessment

Subject Data

"My wife thinks I'm not well enough to have intercourse."
"I have erections and she knows it, but she thinks intercourse is too dangerous."
"She thinks I'll have another heart attack in bed."
"I don't think my days for having sex are over. I want to—and I think I can."
"We used to have sex four and sometimes five times a week."
"We both enjoyed it—at least I think she did—I know I did."
"I try to hold her and love her like before, but she moves away or has something else to do."
"It's supposed to be OK for us to have intercourse, but she says she's afraid to."
"It doesn't help when she won't even touch me. I feel really bad and unsure about my heart, too."
"Now I just don't know what to do."
"Even the little work I do on the farm tires me."
"My appetite?—not very hungry these days."
"Sleep? Not like I used to."

Objective Data

39 years old, married 18 years, wife 37 years old.
Farms own land—200 acres.
Has four daughters, ages 16, 14, 11, 3.
Post-MI 6 weeks.
Participant in cardiac rehabilitation program.
Passed exercise tolerance criterion.
Fatigue, loss of appetite, sleeplessness.
Lowered eyelids, lowered voice pitch.
Lowered self-esteem.
Powerlessness.

Nursing Diagnosis

Depressive symptoms due to delay in resuming intercourse associated
  with sexual partner's reported fear of recurrent heart attack during
  sexual activity.

Planning

Express empathy.
Encourage expression of feelings.
Accept feelings as legitimate and important.
Offer feedback about feelings.
Touch judiciously.
Explain that emotional response is appropriate and commonly experi-
  enced by others.
Review progress in cardiac rehabilitation program and physical and
  heart readiness to resume intercourse.
Review information about risks of another MI attack during sexual activ-
  ity.
Review energy expenditure of masturbation and intercourse.
Review guidelines for resumption of intercourse.
Encourage movement toward resumption of intercourse.
Encourage sharing of information with partner.
Encourage expression of feelings of significance of intercourse and delay
  in resumption.
Encourage listening to partner's fears and sexual concerns.
Advise that significant persons express acceptance of one another.
Suggest partner be participant-observer at scheduled exercise session.
Suggest attending Heart Club meeting to interact with people who have
  had similar experiences.
Indicate availability for further counseling.
Indicate availability for individual or joint counseling with partner.

Implementation

Initiate discussion with partner.
Discuss information about cardiac rehabilitation and general physical
  and heart readiness to resume intercourse.
Discuss information about risks of another heart attack during sexual
  activity.
Discuss guidelines for resuming intercourse.
Share feelings about delay in resuming intercourse.
Share feelings about significance of intercourse as recognition of whole-
  ness and health, and as an expression of acceptance and love.

Accept feelings expressed by partner as real and important.
Make appointment for partner's attendance at exercise session.
Suggest attendance at Heart Club meeting.
Suggest individual or joint counseling with nurse.

Evaluation

Reports discussing information.
Reports sharing of feelings.
Reports attendance of partner at exercise session.
Reports attendance at two meetings of Heart Club.
Reports satisfaction with joint counseling session.
Reports resumption of sexual intercourse.

DIABETES, BODY IMAGE, AND SEXUALITY

Diabetes mellitus is a chronic, complex disease characterized by alterations of carbohydrate, protein, and fat metabolism, the development of microvascular complications (thickening of the capillary basement membranes), neuropathy (peripheral sensorimotor defects, segmental demyelination), and macrovascular complications (large vessel disease) (Chaney, 1977). During the last 10 years, there has been a 50% increase in the incidence of diabetes, with diabetes probably occurring in 1 out of 50 people (Jones, Dunbar, & Jerovic, 1978).

In diabetes mellitus the initial alteration in body image is usually not visible; however, the person is faced with the loss of a complex, coordinated, and controlled functional activity and may feel the loss of wholeness, a sense of failure, and the threat of being found inadequate (Roberts, 1976). For some, the diagnosis may be experienced as less threatening than a heart attack and less calamitous than cancer. This feeling of relief or escape may be followed by a reactive depression, however. For some people, the change in bodily function, the medical treatment, the hospitalization, the multiple and varied interventions involved in nursing care, and the reactions of family may precipitate such feelings as social ineptitude and uneasiness and personal embarrassment and humiliation.

The control and management of diabetes can significantly alter the normal activities of daily living. Although the health teaching of a person with diabetes emphasizes leading a normal life, it also specifies an activity plan, regulates dietary intake, requires urine testing, stresses skin and foot care, warns about the signs of hypoglycemia and hyperglycemia, and may mandate oral or subcutaneous medication. Some people with diabetes may become upset, anxious, and depressed at the seeming end-

lessness of their difficulties. Some follow the health prescriptions ritualis-
tically and with meticulous care. Others may react with denial; they may
not test their urine or follow their diet and may be careless about their
medication. Adolescents may resist the requirements of the diabetic
regimen that can make them appear different from their peers. Older
people may have difficulty in changing established habits and routines.
Whatever the behavior, the person struggles to grasp and understand the
personal, interpersonal, social, and sexual significance of the alterations
in body function and image.

For the person with diabetes, return to preillness state is not possible
and adjustment to the chronicity of the illness is a major task. The person
with diabetes must mourn the loss of his or her established body image;
deal with loss of or changes in customary control over self, physical environment, and time; and find new ways of approaching sexual roles and
relationships. The delivery of sexual health care to the person with diabetes and his or her significant others requires that the nurse understand
and balance the interrelationships between physiologic and psychologic
factors.

DIABETES AND SEXUAL DYSFUNCTION IN MEN

Erectile Dysfunction

Erectile dysfunction (secondary impotence, Chapter 8) is the inability to
achieve or maintain an erection long enough to engage in satisfactory
intercourse. This dysfunction was associated with diabetic men as early
as 1798. In a group of 198 diabetic men from 16 to 92 years of age, Rubin
and Babbott (1958) reported that 50% of the men who had diabetes for
less than one year had erectile dysfunction. Among those who had diabetes from one to five years, 43% were impotent, and among those with
diabetes for more than five years, 45% were impotent. Of those who
became impotent, 30% did so within one year of the diagnosis of diabetes,
and 60% were impotent within five years. No relationship was seen between the age at onset of diabetes or the severity of the disease and the
incidence of impotence. Other complications of diabetes were no more
frequent among men who became impotent than among those who did
not.

Kolodny et al. (1974) studied 175 men between the ages of 18 and 83
with previously diagnosed diabetes. Eighty-five of the 175 men (48.6%)
were impotent. In the group of men with impotence the mean age was
53.2 years, and in the group with no impotence the mean age was 44.4
years. There was no apparent correlation between duration of diabetes
and presence or absence of impotence. In 14 men, impotence had been an

initial manifestation of diabetes and preceded the diagnosis of diabetes; eight of these men regained normal potency after medical treatment.

The men who required the use of insulin and who were impotent used an average daily dose of 40.4 units, whereas the men who were not impotent used an average dose of 42.3 units. The incidence of vascular disease was evidenced by both retinopathy and nephropathy, and hypertension was similar in the group of impotent men and the group of nonimpotent men. The incidence of neuropathy was significantly greater in the group of impotent men (37.6%) than in the group of nonimpotent men (21.1%). Typically, the onset of impotence was gradual, progressing over a period of six months to a year with a period of time during which there was decreased firmness of the erection but not total absence of erectile response.

The studies by Rubin and Babbott (1958) and Kolodny et al. (1974) report a markedly higher prevalence of erectile dysfunction in men with diabetes than the prevalence figures reported in the general population (Kinsey, Pomeroy, & Martin, 1948). The findings of these two studies confirm a lack of correlation between the occurrence of impotence and the control, duration, and severity of the diabetes. Age, however, seems to be a significant factor in the prevalence of erectile dysfunction, with older men more likely to be reported as impotent. The development of impotence in diabetic men is usually progressive, and sexual interest is usually maintained; transient episodes may disappear when the diabetes is controlled; and impotence may be the initial manifestation of diabetes (Rubin & Babbott, 1958; Ellenberg & Weber, 1966).

Retrograde Ejaculation

Retrograde ejaculation is a condition in which the seminal fluid is discharged into the bladder rather than to the outside through the urethra. It may be a cause of infertility. This disorder is found in 1% to 2% of diabetic men (Kolodny et al., 1979). Retrograde ejaculation occurs as a result of autonomic neuropathy involving the neck of the urinary bladder (Ellenberg & Weber, 1966). The internal sphincter of the bladder does not close effectively, and the seminal fluid mixes with the urine in the bladder and is expelled from the body with urination. The diagnosis is made when no ejaculation or spermatozoa are found in a condom used during intercourse and numerous spermatozoa are found in a urine specimen collected after the same intercourse (Kolodny et al., 1979).

In the diabetic man with erectile impotence, the physiologic mechanism subserving orgasm and ejaculation is usually intact, so that the man may achieve both with a flaccid or semitumescent penis (Schiavi, 1979). Retrograde ejaculation may occur during intercourse or masturbation and the man may report diminished or absent ejaculate or diminished or absent sensations associated with the passage of seminal fluid through the distal urethra.

Klebanow and MacLeod (1960) analyzed the quality of the seminal fluid of 19 men, all of whom had diabetes for more than 12 years. These investigators found that nine of the men produced no seminal fluid in spite of normal orgasmic sensation, and, in the urine of six men, they found spermatozoa but not in the quantity usually associated with retrograde ejaculation. They theorized that ejaculatory dysfunction resulting from an abnormality in the ejaculatory phase of the sexual response cycle was often a progressive phenomenon among diabetic men.

Faerman et al. (1974) found histologic evidence of autonomic neuropathy in the neural fibers of the corpora cavernosa in impotent diabetic men examined at the time of autopsy. Campbell (1975) and Lawrence and Abraira (1976) reported a frequent association between erectile impotency in diabetic men and peripheral autonomic neuropathy. Ellenberg (1971, 1978) attempted to study the possible association between erectile impotence and peripheral autonomic neuropathy. His work was based on the recognition that the autonomic pathways involved in micturition and erection are identical. Because there is no direct method of objectively measuring impotence, neurogenic bladder studies were performed, on the assumption that involvement of these nerves would be reflected simultaneously by abnormalities in both areas. Ellenberg reported a much higher rate of neuropathic bladder dysfunction in impotent diabetic men (37 of 45) than in nonimpotent diabetic men (3 of 30). This evidence suggests that erectile dysfunction in the diabetic man is due to impaired transfer of the nervous impulse that leads to penile artery dilation, thus hindering engorgement of the corpora cavernosa and spongeosum (Jones et al., 1978).

Psychogenic and Organic Impotence

Accurate identification of the psychogenic or organic basis of diabetic impotence is crucial because the identification determines the treatment and prognosis. Diabetic men who experience erectile problems must be carefully evaluated. The man with diabetes is just as vulnerable to psychogenic causes such as anxiety and depression as any other man. Data gathered during history taking can provide information for differential diagnosis.

Erectile problems of an organic basis are characterized by a progressive development and a continued sexual interest and drive. The erectile problem is present during both masturbation and intercourse and there is a decrease in the frequency and degree of early-morning and spontaneous erections. In psychogenic erectile problems, the onset tends to be sudden, the problem may occur periodically, be associated with specific circumstances, and may be a response to a stress. If the basis for the erectile problem is psychogenic, erection is possible during masturbation and there is no decrease in the frequency or degree of early morning erections.

The monitoring of nocturnal penile tumescence (NPT) is a method for systematic, objective differential diagnosis of psychogenic or organic impotence. In normal (organically intact) men, a close temporal relationship exists between rapid eye movement sleep (REM) (or dreaming sleep) and penile tumescence. There is an age-related gradual decline in total erection time with nocturnal tumescence, which constitutes 32% of sleep in the 13-to-15 age group and 20% in the 60-to-69 age range (Karacan et al., 1975; Karacan et al., 1976). At puberty, about 90 minutes of sleep time is associated with full tumescence, between the ages of 30 and 39 the minutes are reduced to about 45, and they are further reduced to less than 15 minutes between the ages of 60 and 69. Although NPT and dreams often occur at the same time, there is no evidence that NPT is consistently related to sexual dreams. Both REM sleep and NPT are more prominent in the later than in the earlier portion of a normal night of sleep. Men have erections on awakening in the morning because they have awakened from REM-related NPT, not because bladder pressure stimulates erection.

The use of NPT for differential diagnosis assumes that the man who complains of impotence but who has a normal NPT for his age has psychogenic impotence, whereas the man who complains of impotence and who has abnormal NPT for his age has organic impotence (Karacan et al., 1977). In psychogenic impotence, the man's REM erections appear as normal in amount and degree and are markedly different when compared to the man's performance during intercourse while awake. In organic impotence the maximum nocturnal erections attained correspond to the man's performance while awake (Fisher et al., 1975). Clinicians are urged to use assessment of NPT for every man who complains of or seeks treatment for impotence.

Treatment of Impotence in the Diabetic Man

When transient episodes of impotence are associated with poor metabolic control, appropriate carbohydrate management can restore good physical condition and normal sexual function. Myers (1977) noted that in some diabetic men impotence is associated with early morning hypoglycemic reactions and reported that two or three Life Savers taken before sexual activity make a difference. Of 10 clients (ages 25 to 50), eight were able to resume sexual activity after this Life Saver therapy.

Impotence that occurs when the diabetes is well controlled is likely to be permanent, and the prognosis for recovery of sexual function is poor once erectile dysfunction becomes severe. At present, there is no known cure for impotence due to diabetic neuropathy. Sexual counseling for the diabetic man, regardless of the degree of organic involvement, is of vital significance, and his sexual partner should be included.

The diabetic man and his sexual partner need to know that usually the impotence associated with diabetes is not a sudden and unchanging condition but that, just as other symptoms in other chronic illnesses vary, the severity of the erectile dysfunction will also vary. For both partners, the counseling is directed toward examining and working through low self-esteem, anger, and guilt. The counseling is designed to encourage exploration and experimentation of sexual alternatives to vaginal–penile intercourse (Chapter 5). More than 95% of impotent diabetic men are able to ejaculate (Kolodny et al., 1979) and even when ejaculation does not occur, holding, caressing, stroking, and cuddling can provide emotional intimacy and physical gratification. Renshaw (1978) emphasizes that at least some part of diabetic impotence is functional and not organic, and advocates the use of sex therapy (Chapter 8) in all cases of diabetic erectile dysfunction. For those cases in which sex therapy does not assist the diabetic man, the therapy itself will have provided a reassessment of the relationship and his desire to perform not only for himself but also for his partner.

Progress has been made in the past two decades with surgical implantation of penile prosthetic devices for organic impotence. Two types of penile prostheses are used. The Small-Carrion prosthesis consists of two semirigid plastic rods implanted from the perineum into the corpora cavernosa (Small, 1976). The simple implantation results in a permanent erection. Through the use of broad-banded athletic supporters, jockey shorts, or a light, tight-fitting corset, the erection will remain undetected when the man is fully clothed. However, the permanent erection may be socially unacceptable to the client or his partner. Scott, Bradley, and Temm (1973) developed a hydraulic device that simulates erectile tumescence by pumping fluid into two cylindric chambers implanted into the corpora cavernosa. The pump is activated when the man compresses the bulb in the scrotum and causes the cylinders to expand and produce penile tumescence. The erection is released when the man presses a valve in the lower portion of the scrotal bulb, which allows the fluid to flow from the penile cylinders back to the reservoir. Although the surgical procedure takes longer and the device costs more than the Small-Carrion prosthesis, the natural appearance of the penis is a major advantage.

For the man with diabetes there may be a higher operative and postoperative risk, greater difficulty in wound healing, and greater susceptibility to infection. Before such prostheses are surgically implanted, a careful assessment is required. An organic base for the impotence and no concomitant prostate or genitourinary problems need to be confirmed. The man should have a prediabetic history of adequate sexual functioning with maintained sexual urge and desire and some orgasmic capacity. The ability to satisfy the partner may be as strong as the desire for wholeness and self-satisfaction. The diabetic man needs to understand that the prosthesis does not provide or reinstate arousal, ejaculation, or orgasm. Assessment of self-concept and body image can contribute to understanding the client and contributing to his care before and after the implantation. To the man who is able to enjoy and obtain satisfaction from his partner's sexual arousal, it can be "exhilarating once more to share closely his partner's orgasm" (Renshaw, 1978 p. 439).

A willing sexual partner is important, and the partner's inclusion in education and counseling before and after surgery is crucial. Maddock (1980a) advocates the assessment of the potential impact of the surgery and the restored potency upon the sexual partner as well as the assessment of the potential impact of the prosthetic device upon the couple's pattern of sexual behavior. Maddock reported that whether or not the surgery was deemed successful by the man was a function of how his sexual partner responded to the implantation.

DIABETES AND SEXUAL DYSFUNCTION IN WOMEN

Orgasmic Dysfunction

Kolodny (1971) published the first study of the effect of diabetes on the sexual functioning of diabetic women. He compared 125 sexually active diabetic women and 100 sexually active nondiabetic women ranging in age from 18 to 42 to determine the prevalence of sexual dysfunction. The two groups were carefully matched in age, religion, education, marital status, parity, frequency of intercourse, and self-estimation of sexual interest. A significant difference in the prevalence of sexual dysfunction was noted. Forty-four (35.2%) of the diabetic women and six (6%) of the nondiabetic women were nonorgasmic. None of the nonorgasmic women in the control group had ever experienced orgasm. Forty of the 44 nonorgasmic diabetic women had previously been orgasmic and had become nonorgasmic gradually over a period of six months to a year. Typically, the time of onset was four to eight years after the diagnosis of diabetes had been made. Usually, sexual interest was maintained, but most of the women complained it took a longer period of direct stimulation for them to reach high levels of arousal. In contrast to the studies of diabetic men, there was a direct correlation in the diabetic women between the duration of the diabetes and the prevalence of sexual dysfunction. There was no significant relationship between the sexual dysfunction and other complications of diabetes (neuropathy, retinopathy, vaginitis).

Six of the 44 nonorgasmic diabetic women and all of the nonorgasmic women in the control group reported difficulty with vaginal lubrication. Two of the diabetic women became orgasmic when the use of a water-soluble lubricant was advised and instruction given to both sexual partners. Chronic candidal vaginitis caused pain and interfered with orgasm in two diabetic women. One of the women returned to orgasmic function after treatment of the candidal infection. Kolodny (1971) suggested that several factors such as neuropathy, susceptibility to infection, microvascular changes, and the psychosocial adaptation to chronic disease may be involved in the cause of sexual dysfunction in diabetic women.

Ellenberg (1977) reported a study that tested the hypothesis that diabetic neuropathy was responsible for impairment of sexual functioning. He compared the sexual functioning of 54 diabetic women characterized as having a neuropathic disorder to that of 46 diabetic women without such evidence based on neurologic evaluation and bladder-function tests. The ages of both groups were comparable (24 to 73 years), as was the duration of diabetes (1 to 53 years). Forty-four (81%) of the 54 women with neuropathy and 38 (79%) of the 46 women without neuropathy reported the presence of sexual desire and orgasmic reaction. These findings were comparable to those for the nondiabetic female population as reported by Kinsey (1953) and Hite (1976). Ellenberg concluded there was no difference in sexual desire and orgasmic reaction between the diabetic women with neuropathy and the diabetic women without neuropathy.

The reasons for the differences between the studies done by Kolodny and Ellenberg are not clear. More study of the changes in the sexual response cycle of diabetic women is needed.

Treatment of Sexual Dysfunction in the Diabetic Woman

No effective therapy exists for reversing sexual dysfunction associated with diabetic neuropathy or vascular disease. Sexual dysfunction should not be viewed as an inevitable complication of diabetes, however. Careful screening for possible remedial causes, such as drugs, infection, and other physical diseases, should be done. A complete sexual history should be obtained to distinguish psychologic problems from organic disorders.

Good diabetic control may succeed in restoring sexual interest and function associated with poor physical condition. Candidal vaginitis can be treated with mycostatin vaginal suppositories and good diabetic control. Decreased vaginal lubrication may be corrected by increasing sexual stimulation before penetration and by the use of water-soluble lubricants. The diabetic woman and her sexual partner should know that sexual dysfunction usually develops slowly after several years of the disease and varies in intensity at onset. Counseling of the diabetic woman and her sexual partner should emphasize that wholeness and attractiveness are unaffected by sexual dysfunction and that emotional warmth and intimacy and physical gratification are possible within a sexual relationship without orgasm and despite irreversible organic changes.

FERTILITY, STERILITY, AND GENETIC COUNSELING

Disturbances of fertility and sterility in diabetic men and women may affect their sexual self-concepts and sexual roles and relationships. Anticipatory guidance can provide information that can help in coping with anxieties about pregnancy and uncertainties about the outcomes of pregnancy.

Diabetic women have irregular menses and a greater frequency of abortions, stillbirths, malformed infants, and high-birth-weight babies, but 80% of women with diabetes successfully complete their pregnancies (Rubin & Murphy, 1958; Brooks, 1977). The perinatal mortality rate among fetuses of diabetic women has been reported as being five to seven times that of a control population (Brooks, 1977). In diabetic men, reduced sperm counts or, occasionally, *aspermia* (absence of semen or spermatozoa) and abnormal spermatogenesis (development of mature spermatozoa) have been reported (Shoffling et al., 1963; Ellenberg, 1971).

Genetic counseling for the diabetic person and his or her sexual partner may help them understand the consequences of genetic transmission of the disease. If a nondiabetic person with no family history of diabetes and a diabetic person had children, the children would probably all be carriers. If both partners are diabetic the incidence of diabetes in the children is usually 70%. If one parent has diabetes and the other is a carrier the incidence is 50%, and if one partner has diabetes the incidence is 25%.

ROLE OF THE NURSE AS EDUCATOR-COUNSELOR

The role of the nurse in the sexual health care of the diabetic person begins as educator. The nurse provides information—teaches, explains, distinguishes, clarifies—so that the client has reliable information to use and is able to build a sound knowledge base about diabetes. The nurse provides information about the day-to-day tasks involved in good diabetic control and prevention of infection and helps the client formulate long-term goals for health management. The nurse provides information about possible complications of the disease and the likelihood of sexual difficulties. For the adolescent, diabetic teen clubs and diabetic camps may be helpful in providing information about daily living and support for developing a positive self-image. As educator, the nurse is attentive, empathetic, and accepting as the client struggles and adapts to the chronic physical disabilities of diabetes. The nurse understands and helps the client learn that the complications of diabetes are not necessarily preventable and that the occurrence of a complication does not mean the client has failed to comply with the prescribed medical regimen.

As a counselor, the nurse is sensitive to such emotional responses as anxiety, anger, depression, withdrawal, and dependence associated with alteration in body image. The emotional adaptation the client makes will depend on the significance of the alteration to his or her sexual self-esteem and self-concept. The emotional adaptation will affect sexual interest and performance and influence sexual roles and relationships. As counselor, the nurse is receptive, supportive, and empathetic and encourages expression of feelings and open discussion about sex and sexuality as the client and his or her sexual partner confront the sexual difficulties of diabetes. Knowledgeable and sensitive counseling may enable the diabetic person and his or her sexual partner, committed to giving and receiving pleasure, to explore their options, discuss the consequences, and make decisions congruent with their sexual value system.

NURSING PROCESS

Client: Brenda Johnson, client medical diagnosis of diabetes mellitus, having biweekly check-up of diabetic control.

Nurse: Robert Bradley, nurse working with Dr. Emily Owens in family practice clinic.

Assessment

Subjective Data

"My genital area has started to be red and itchy again."

"When it's like this, I don't really want to have sex."

"And when I do, it doesn't feel good—it hurts."

"The redness and itching stopped when I first started on insulin every day and watched what I ate."

"But it has started again—only it seems worse—there's white stuff now."

"Eric says it's my fault because I don't follow the diet."

"That's easy for him to say—there's nothing the matter with him."

"Having diabetes is bad enough without having problems with him and sex."

"We weren't going to have children for two years, but now—with me . . . well . . . things are different now."

"My urine has been positive only a couple of times these last two weeks."

"What's my blood sugar today?"

"Cooking is not as much fun as it used to be."

"And I guess I do snitch some of the desserts I make for Eric—my mother taught me how to make very special desserts."
"At least at work I can still keep up—almost."
"I'm really feeling . . . low . . . these days."

Objective Data

22 years old, married one year.
Diabetes mellitus diagnosed six months ago.
Diaphragm and condom contraceptive choice.
NPH insulin (U100), 35 U q.d.
1800 calorie ADA diet.
Urine—2+ sugar, negative acetone.
Blood sugar—180 mgm.
Vaginal examination—thick white patches on vaginal mucosa and thick white cheeselike discharge present. Vulva and perineum red and swollen.
Vaginal culture obtained.
Sitting slumped in chair.
Personal appearance—not as well-groomed as in previous visits.
Sensitive to comments made by partner.
Lowered eyelids, low-pitched voice.
Sense of helplessness.
Depression.
Lowered self-esteem.

Nursing Diagnosis

Alterations in patterns of sexual desire and response related to vaginal infection.
Alteration in nutrition due to changes in body requirements associated with diabetes mellitus.
Lowered self-esteem due to alteration in body image associated with diabetes mellitus.

Planning

Provide atmosphere of acceptance.
Express empathy.
Reassure verbally.

Explain that the client's emotional response is appropriate and commonly experienced.

Emphasize the person's value as an individual.

Emphasize person's normal characteristics.

Explain and offer hope that alterations in activities of daily living will be learned.

Encourage acceptance of alterations in activities of daily living.

Support realistic assessment of situation.

Encourage use of normal coping mechanisms.

Refrain from criticizing negatively.

Advise that significant people express love for each other.

Advise that significant people express acceptance of each other.

Explain the importance of offering emotional support to each other.

Encourage touching, holding, caressing for emotional intimacy and physical warmth and comfort.

Encourage mutual problem solving.

Review importance of diabetic control for prevention of infection and for optimal health.

Identify significance of alterations in food preparation and intake.

Review carbohydrate management.

Provide information (recipes) for low-carbohydrate desserts.

Explain cause of vaginal infection.

Review hygienic measures to decrease potential for vaginal infection.

Explain use of prescribed medications—mycostatin (vaginal suppository) and nystatin ointment (perineum).

Explain the reason for intended effect of therapy.

Encourage expression of feelings about effect of vaginal infection on sexual desire and response.

Encourage identification of significance of conception, child bearing, and parenting.

Review the effect of diabetes on fertility and identify genetic component.

Indicate availability for further individual counseling.

Advise that partner be included in counseling session.

Implementation

Cleanse vaginal area as directed.

Begin prescribed use of mycostatin vaginal suppository and nystatin ointment to perineum.

Initiate discussion with partner.

Share feelings of love and acceptance.

Participate in touching, holding, and caressing.

Discuss use of prescribed drugs.

Share feelings about effect of vaginal infection on sexual desire and response.

Discuss meaning of alteration in food preparation and intake.

Discuss plans to prepare special low-carbohydrate desserts.

Ask partner to share these desserts.

Urge mutual counseling session.

Arrange personal time.

Make appointment for counseling with husband.

Evaluation (six weeks later)

Reports absence of redness and itching.

Vaginal examination—vaginal and perineal tissue normal.

Reports return of sexual desire and normal pattern of sexual response.

Reports satisfaction in the preparation and sharing of low-carbohydrate
desserts with partner.

Reports ongoing discussion about significance of conception, child bearing, and parenting with partner.

Requests further joint counseling.

BIBLIOGRAPHY

Abramov, L. A. Sexual life and sexual frigidity among women developing acute
myocardial infarction. *Psychosomatic Medicine*, 1976, *38*, 418–425.

Block, A., Malder, J. P., & Haessly, J. E. Sexual problems after myocardial infarction. *American Heart Journal*, 1975, *90*, 536–537.

Bower, F. L. *Distortions in body image in illness and disability*. New York: Wiley,
1977.

Brooks, M. H. Brief guide to office counseling: Effect of diabetes on female sexual
response. *Medical Aspects of Human Sexuality*, 1977, *11*, 63–64.

Bruh, H., Wolf, S., & Phillips, B. Depression and death in myocardial infarction:
A psychosocial study of screening male coronary patients over nine years.
Psychosomatic Research, 1971, *15*, 305.

Campbell, C. *Nursing diagnosis and intervention in nursing practice*. New York:
Wiley, 1978.

Campbell, I. W., & Clarke, B. Sexual dysfunction in diabetic men. *Medical Aspects of Human Sexuality*, 1975, *9*, 157.

Cassem, N. H., & Hackett, T. P. Psychiatric consultation in a coronary care unit.
Annals of Internal Medicine, 1971, *95*, 9–14.

Chaney, P. *Managing diabetes properly*. Horsham, Pa.: Internal Communications
1977.

Davis, II. K. Sexual dysfunction in diabetes: Psychogenic and physiologic factors.
Medical Aspects of Human Sexuality, 1978, *12*, 48–65.

Dominian, J., & Shelton, M. Psychological stress in wives of patients with myocardial infarction. *British Medical Journal*, 1973, *2*, 98–103.

Douglas, J. E., & Wilkes, T. D. Reconditioning cardiac patients. *American Family Physician*, 1975, *11*, 123–129.

Eliot, R. S., & Miles, R. R. Brief guide to office counseling: Advising the cardiac patient about sexual intercourse. *Medical Aspects of Human Sexuality*, 1973, *9*, 49–50.

Ellenberg, M. Impotence in diabetes: The neurologic factor. *Annals of Internal Medicine*, 1971, *75*, 213–219.

Ellenberg, M. Sexual aspects of the female diabetic. *Mount Sinai Journal of Medicine*, 1977, *44*, 495–500.

Ellenberg, M., & Weber, H. Retrograde ejaculation in diabetic neuropathy. *Annals of Internal Medicine*, 1966, *65*, 1237–1246.

Faerman, I., Glover, L., Fox, D., Jadzensky, M. N., & Rappaport, M. Impotence and diabetes: Histological studies of the autonomic nervous fibers of the corpora cavernosa in impotent diabetic males. *Diabetes*, 1974, *23*, 971–976.

Fisher, C., Scheavi, R., Lear, H., Edwards, A., Davis, D. M., & Watkin, A. P. The assessment of nocturnal REM erection in the differential diagnosis of sexual impotence. *Journal of Sex and Marital Therapy*, 1975, *1*, 277–289.

Friedman, J. M. Sexual adjustment of the post-coronary male. In J. LoPiccolo & L. LoPiccolo (Eds.), *Handbook of sex therapy*. New York: Plenum Press, 1978.

Green, A. W. Sexual activity and the postmyocardial infarction patient. *American Heart Journal*, 1975, *89*, 246–252.

Griffith, G. G. Sexuality and the cardiac patient. *Heart and Lung*, 1973, *2*, 70–73.

Harding, A. L., & Morefield, M. Group interaction for wives of myocardial infarct patients. *Nursing Clinics of North America*, 1976, *11*, 339–347.

Haswell, G. L. Chronic illness and sexuality. In M. U. Barnard, B. J. Clancy, & K. E. Krantz (Eds.), *Human sexuality for health professionals*. Philadelphia: Saunders, 1978.

Hellerstein, H. K., & Friedman, E. H. Sexual activity and the postcoronary patient. *Archives of Internal Medicine*, 1970, *125*, 987–999.

Hite, S. *The Hite report*. New York: The Macmillan Co., 1976.

Hogan, R. M. *Human sexuality: A nursing perspective*. New York: Appleton-Century-Crofts, 1980.

Hoth, J. R. Sex and the heart patient: A nursing view. *Topics in Clinical Nursing*, 1980, *1*, 75–84.

Johnston, B. L., Cantwell, J. D., Watt, E. W., & Fletcher, G. F. Sexual activity in exercising patients after myocardial infarction and myocardial revascularization. *Heart and Lung*, 1978, *7*, 1026–1031.

Jones, D. A., Dunbar, C. F., & Jerovic, M. M. *Medical–surgical nursing: A conceptual approach*. New York: McGraw-Hill, 1978.

Karacan, I. Advances in the psychophysiological evaluation of male erectile impotence. In J. LoPiccolo & L. LoPiccolo (Eds.), *Handbook of sex therapy*. New York: Plenum Press, 1978.

Karacan, I., Salis, P. J., Thornby, J. I., & Williams, R. L. The ontogeny of nocturnal penile tumescence. *Waking and Sleeping*, 1976, *1*, 27–44.

Karacan, I., Scott, L. B., Salis, P. J., Attia, S. K., Ware, J. C., Altinel, A., & Williams, R. L. Nocturnal erections, differential diagnosis of impotence, and diabetes. *Biological Psychiatry*, 1977, *12*, 373–380.

Karacan, I., Williams, F. L., Thornby, J. I., & Salis, P. J. Sleep-related tumescence as a function of age. *American Journal of Psychiatry*, 1975, *132*, 932–937.

Kinsey, A. C., Pomeroy, W. B., Martin, C. E. *Sexual behavior in the human female*. Philadelphia: Saunders, 1948.

Kinsey, A. C., Pomeroy, W. B., Martin, C. E., & Gebhard, P. H. *Sexual behavior in the human female*. Philadelphia: Saunders, 1953.

Klebanow, D., & MacLeod, J. Semen quality and certain disturbances of reproduction in diabetic men. *Fertility and Sterility*, 1960, *11*, 255–261.

Klein, R. F., Dean, A., Wilson, M., & Bogdonoff, M. The physician and post-myocardial involusion. *Journal of the American Medical Association*, 1965, *194*, 123.

Koller, R., Kennedy, J. W., Butler, J. C., & Wagner, N. N. Counseling the coronary patient on sexual activity. *Postgraduate Medicine*, 1972, *51*, 133–136.

Kolodny, R. C. Sexual dysfunction in diabetic females. *Diabetes*, 1971, *18*, 858–866.

Kolodny, R. C., Kahn, C. B., Goldstein, H. H., & Barnett, D. M. Sexual dysfunction in diabetic men. *Diabetes*, 1974, *23*, 306–309.

Kolodny, R. C., Masters, W. H., Johnson, V. E., & Biggs, M. A. *Textbook of human sexuality for nurses*. Boston: Little, Brown, 1979.

Lawrence, A. M., & Abraira, C. Diabetic neuropathy. A review of clinical manifestations. *Annals of Clinical Laboratory Science*, 1976, *6*, 78–83.

Lawson, B. Easing the sexual fears of the cardiac patient. *RN*, 1971, *4*, 1601–1605.

Leonard, B. J. Body image changes in chronic illness. *Nursing Clinics of North America*, 1972, *7*, 687–695.

Levy, R., & McGill, A. Target behaviors for task groups on cardiac rehabilitation. Proceedings of the MHLI Working Conference on Health Behavior, May 1975. BHEW Publication (NIH) 76-868. Washington, D.C.: United States Department of Health, Education, and Welfare, 1975.

Mackey, F. G. Sexuality and heart disease. In A. Comfort (Ed.), *Sexual consequences of disability*. Philadelphia: Strickley, 1978.

Maddock, J. W. Assessment and evaluation protocol for surgical treatment of impotence. *Sexuality and Disability*, 1980, *1*, 39–49. (a)

Maddock, J. W. *The evaluation and follow-up of surgical treatment of impotence*. Paper presented at First National Conference on Sexuality and Physical Disabilities, Ann Arbor, Michigan, November 1980. (b)

Marble, A., White, P., Bradley, R. F., & Hall, L. P. *Joslin's diabetes mellitus* (11th ed.). Philadelphia: Lea & Febiger, 1971.

Massie, R., Rose, E. F., Rupp, J. C., & Whelton R. W. Viewpoints: Sudden death during coitus—fact or fiction. *Medical Aspects of Human Sexuality*, 1969, *3*, 22–26.

Masters, W. H., & Johnson, V. E. *Human sexual response*. Boston: Little, Brown, 1966.

Melman, A. The diagnosis and therapy of impotence associated with diabetes. *Sexuality and Disability*, 1978, *1*, 52–56.

Mims, F. H., & Swenson, M. *Sexuality: A nursing perspective*. New York: McGraw-Hill, 1980.

Moore, K., Folk-Lighty, M., & Nolen, M. J. The joy of sex after a heart attack. *Nursing 77*, 1977, *7*, 53–55.

Murray, R. L. E. Principles of nursing intervention for the adult with body image changes. *Nursing Clinics of North America*, 1972, *7*, 697–707.

Myers, S. A. Diabetes management by the patient and a nurse practitioner. *Nursing Clinics of North America*, 1977, *12*, 415–426.

Naughton, J. Effect of chronic illness on sexual performance. *Medical Aspects of Human Sexuality*, 1975, *9*, 110–114.

Nemec, E. D., Mansfield, L., & Kennedy, J. W. Heart rate and blood pressure responses during sexual activity in normal males. *American Heart Journal*, 1976, *92*, 274–277.

Norris, C. M. Body image: Its relevance to professional nursing. In C. E. Carlson & B. Blackwell (Eds.), *Behavioral concepts and nursing intervention* (2nd ed.). Philadelphia: Lippincott, 1970.

Papadapaules, C., Larrimore, P., Cordin, S., Shelly, S. T. Sexual concerns and needs of the post coronary patient's wife. *Archives of Internal Medicine*, 1980, *140*, 38–41.

Puksta, N. S. All about sex . . . after coronary. *American Journal of Nursing*, 1977, *77*, 602–605.

Renshaw, D. C. Impotence in diabetes. In J. LoPiccolo & L. LoPiccolo (Eds.), *Handbook of sex therapy*. New York: Plenum Press, 1978.

Roberts, S. L. *Behavioral concepts and the critically ill patient*. Englewood Cliffs, New Jersey: Prentice-Hall, Inc., 1976.

Rubin, A., & Babbott, D. Impotence and diabetes mellitus. *Journal of the American Medical Association*, 1958, *168*, 490–500.

Rubin, A., & Murphy, W. P. Frequency of congenital malformations in the offspring of nondiabetic and diabetic individuals. *Journal of Pediatrics*, 1958, *53*, 579–585.

Satterfield, S. B. Sexual rehabilitation for the postcoronary patient. *Topics in Clinical Nursing*, 1980, *1*, 85–89.

Scalzi, C. C. Nursing management of behavioral response following an acute myocardial infarction. *Heart and Lung*, 1973, *2*, 62–69.

Scalzi, C., & Dracup, D. Sexual counseling of coronary patients. *Heart and Lung*, 1977, *7*, 840–845.

Scheingold, L., & Wagner, N. *Sound sex and the aging heart*. New York: Human Science, 1974.

Schiavi, R. C. Sexuality and medical illness: Specific reference to diabetes mellitus. In R. Green (Ed.), *Human sexuality: A health practitioner's text*. Baltimore: Williams & Wilkins, 1979.

Schoffling, K., Federlin, K., Ditschuneit, H., & Pfeiffer, E. F. Disorders of sexual function in male diabetics. *Diabetes*, 1963, *12*, 519–527.

Scott, F. B., Bradley, W. E., & Temm, G. W. Management of erectile impotence: Use of implantable inflatable prosthesis. *Urology*, 1973, *2*, 80–82.

Siewicki, B. J., & Mansfield, L. W. Determining readiness to resume sexual activity. *American Journal of Nursing*, 1977, *77*, 604.

Small, M. P. Small-Carrion penile prosthesis. *Mayo Clinic Proceedings*, 1976, *51*, 336–338.

Smith, C. A. Body image changes after myocardial infarction. *Nursing Clinics of North America*, 1972, *7*, 663–668.

Stein, R. A. The effect of exercise training on heart rate during coitus in the postmyocardial infarction patient. *Circulation*, 1977, *55*, 738–740.

Tobis, J. S. Cardiovascular patients and sexual dysfunction. *Archives of Physical Medicine and Rehabilitation*, 1975, *56*, 10–15.

Tutle, A. B., Cook, W. L., & Filch, E. Sexual behavior in postmyocardial infarction patients. *American Journal of Cardiology*, 1964, *13*, 140–153.

Ueno, M. The so-called coition death. *Japanese Journal of Legal Medicine*, 1963, *17*, 330–340.

Wagner, N. N., & Sivarajan, E. S. Sexual activity and the cardiac patient. In R. Green (Ed.), *Human sexuality: A health practitioner's text* (2nd ed.). Baltimore: Williams & Wilkins, 1979.

Watts, R. J. Sexuality and the middle aged cardiac patient. *Nursing Clinics of North America*, 1976, *11*, 349–359.

Wishnie, H. A., Hackett, T. P., & Cassem, N. H. Psychological hazards of convalescence following myocardial infarction. *Journal of the American Medical Association*, 1971, *215*, 1292–1296.

Wood, R. Y., & Rose, K. Penile implants for impotence. *American Journal of Nursing*, 1978, *78*, 234–238.

Woods, N. F. *Human sexuality in health and illness*. St. Louis: Mosby, 1979.

Woods, N. F., & Herbert, J. M. Sexuality and chronic illness. In N. F. Woods, *Human sexuality in health and illness* (2nd ed.). St. Louis: Mosby, 1979.

Young, L. E. Nursing interventions with obese cardiac patients. *Nursing Clinics of North America*, 1978, *13*, 449–456.

15. Sexuality and Surgery

Josephine Novo Osborne

VALUES CLARIFICATION EXERCISE

Every Monday through Friday in hospitals throughout the United States, the surgery schedule is posted and clients are prepared for operative procedures that make use of the best technology available. In the preparation of these clients for surgery, the physical problem may be considered paramount and although the client's psychosocial concerns may receive attention, the sexual concerns are often considered as private matters. Nurses' beliefs affect their perceptions of their clients' sexuality and affect how information and counseling is provided for people undergoing surgery.

The following exercises have been designed to help you explore your own feelings and attitudes about surgery and its influences on sexuality. Read and react to the following situations. Note your feelings and write down your reactions.

Your friend tells you that she felt a lump in her breast while showering last evening. She tells you that she is going to leave it alone for awhile, because it may go away. How do you respond? How do you feel about her response to the discovery of the lump in her breast? How do you feel you would respond if you discovered a lump in your own breast? What happens to your feelings about yourself when you imagine a lump in your breast?

You arrive home from work at 4:30 P.M. and the phone rings. It is your mother. She tearfully tells you that her Pap test has come back positive. What is your response? Are you embarrassed? Ashamed? Annoyed? Disgusted? Worried? What do you say to your mother? How would you feel if it were your wife? Your unmarried sister? How do you imagine you would feel if it were your Pap test that came back positive?

You are a nurse working with a surgeon and have been asked to talk to Mr. Jones about the outcome of his prostatectomy. Mr. Jones, a 68-year-old man, is three days postoperative. The surgeon believes that Mr. Jones will not be able to have an erection for at least six months. While you are talking to Mr. Jones, he interrupts you and says, "Please, I am an old-fashioned man. I don't want to talk about this." What is your response to him? Do you feel embarrassed? Angry? Sad? Do you feel helpless? Hopeless? Do you feel empathy? Frustration? What do you want to do now?

Your boyfriend has just told you that he has cancer of the testes and he is scheduled to have them removed by a surgeon next week. What do you say to him? How do you feel? Do you feel scared? Worried? Angry? Do you feel like you would like to end the relationship? How do you imagine you would feel if it was your husband? Your brother? Your father?

With a group of your peers or colleagues, share the reactions and feelings noted for each situation. Role play the situations. The same participants should play each role—the sender of the message and the receiver. Discuss the different or similar feelings elicited and thoughts generated during the role playing.

Describe the actions and other participants used to express your feelings and help you understand your attitudes and responses. Describe the possible use of these helpful actions in nurse–client interactions about sexuality and surgery.

BEHAVIORAL OBJECTIVES

After reading this chapter, you will be able to

- Explain how alterations in body image may affect sexual roles and relationships.
- Give examples of the emotional investment a person can make in various parts of the body.
- Describe the impact a hysterectomy, a oophorectomy, or a mastectomy may have on a woman's self-concept and sexual functioning.
- Explain the functions of community resources in the process of recovery from a mastectomy.
- Explain the postoperative exercise that can be taught to a woman who has had a mastectomy.
- Identify the possible effects on sexual roles and sexual functioning of men and women who have a relocation of body orifice.
- Discuss the information about preparation for sexual activity that can be given to an ostomate.
- Explain the functions of the ostomy team.

- Give examples and explain the functions of community resources for the ostomate.
- Explain the possible effects that types of prostatectomies may have on the sexual functioning of men.
- Identify the increased stress associated with surgery for cancer.
- Explain the role of the nurse as educator-counselor in the case of clients undergoing surgery to their sexual organs.

BODY IMAGE AND SURGERY

Body image, as defined in Chapter 14, involves emotional investments of varying degrees in parts of the body. The pianist and the fashion model, the football player and the swimmer, the telephone operator and the waiter, vary in how they view their bodies and what importance they place on each body part. Surgery, like chronic illness, has a strong impact on that emotional investment because the body image changes.

Time is needed to process the full impact of loss—loss of function or relocation of external or internal body parts. Before surgery, the person may be dealing with the anxiety of the surgery and may be neither willing nor ready to cope with the sexual consequences of the surgery. Changes in body structure or functioning that occur abruptly are far more traumatic emotionally than those that occur gradually. The person requiring a leg amputation after an automobile accident will likely experience more stress than one who loses a leg because of secondary side effects from diabetes. When a person suddenly finds himself or herself without the presence or function of a body part, he or she will react emotionally to the trauma or surgery.

Coping responses to the surgery and the resulting body changes are unique to each person. For example, a person may demonstrate denial, experience loss of self-esteem, express feelings of emasculation, feel less feminine, or verbalize feelings of being punished. An example of denial is, "I think this lump in my breast is just due to my excess drinking of coffee—if I cut back on coffee, the lump will go away." "I will never be the same again, my wife will not want me anymore," is an example of a decrease in self-esteem and emasculation after an orchiectomy (removal of the testes). An example of being punished can be heard from a woman, after hearing that her Pap smear came back positive, saying, "I heard that early intercourse can cause the uterus to be cancerous . . . I should not have become sexually active so early. It's my fault." These responses express the person's feelings about body image, and they affect sexual functioning. The nurse as educator-counselor can help the client cope with alterations in body image.

SURGERY AND THE SEXUAL ORGANS OF WOMEN

Hysterectomy

It is estimated that 700,000 women have a *hysterectomy* (removal of the uterus) each year (Butts, 1979). By the nature of this procedure, each of these women experiences a loss of an internal body part and will undergo a change in body image.

Krueger et al. (1979) noted factors that influence adjustment to hysterectomy, including age, culture, background, educational level, sexual partner's attitude, family situation, preoperative preparation, and whether cancer was involved. They found that problems after a hysterectomy were greatly influenced by the reasons for the surgery, how the woman had coped with previous losses, what she told herself about how the operation would affect her relationship with others, and how those significant others responded to her pre- and postoperatively. The following tentative cultural generalizations about some women's responses to a hysterectomy can guide the nurse's practice when working with patients of different ethnic groups.

In a study by Cosper, Fuller, and Robinson (1978), it was found that black women did not change their beliefs about being a woman nor did they feel their partner's attitudes change toward them after their hysterectomy. Roeske (1978) found that Mexican-American women may not want a hysterectomy because they feel their husbands will reject them or they will be told that they are "no good anymore." The fear of losing her husband to another woman can lead a woman to postpone the surgery.

Wren (1978) cites that after a hysterectomy women frequently develop psychosexual problems, such as loss of self-esteem, and physiologic problems, such as hot flashes, dry vagina, and dyspareunia (painful intercourse), as well as a variety of urinary infections. He further stated that there was a greater incidence of postoperative depression, restlessness, and sleeplessness in women who had had hysterectomies as compared with women of the same age group who had other abdominal operations.

For some women, the loss of the uterus is associated with the loss of what menstruation meant to them. It may represent the loss of the mythic monthly cleansing effect or the loss of the rhythm of life. And for other posthysterectomy women it is the loss of the symbol that initiated them into womanhood (Woods, 1979).

Among other fears expressed by hysterectomy clients are worries about becoming overweight, masculinized, and unresponsive sexually (Polivy, 1974). These are worries that clients may find difficult to express. Clients wonder about their incision. They ask questions like, "Will I have an ugly scar?"

On the other hand, there are many women who feel relief after a hysterectomy. They are no longer worried about becoming pregnant and find that their sexual activity as well as orgasmic responses improve. A woman who was plagued by heavy menstrual bleeding or by fears of a spreading cancer may be relieved (Eskew, 1980).

Sexual Response Cycle after Hysterectomy

Morgan (1978) notes that during arousal there will be fewer vaso-congestive changes in the pelvis because of the absence of the uterus. During sexual excitement, there will be the absence of the elevation of the uterus, and the ballooning of the vagina will be limited by the inelasticity of the surgical scar. The extra response of sexual tension that occurs during the plateau phase may not be felt postoperatively.

Women who were formerly aware of uterine contractions during orgasm will note the absence of this sensation. Morgan also points out that in a vaginal hysterectomy the placement of the surgical scar may make intercourse uncomfortable if the scarred area is struck by the penis during intercourse.

A common belief is that as long as the ovaries remain after a hysterectomy, the woman will not experience a decrease in her estrogen production. Some evidence indicates, however, that a hysterectomy can cause a disturbance in the blood supply to the ovaries and creates a decrease in estrogen production (Krueger et al., 1970). A woman who has a decrease in estrogen level may complain of hot flashes and dry vagina. This decrease in estrogen production should not influence her sexual capacity or enjoyment, because the androgens produced by the adrenal glands are the primary influences of the sexual drive (Coope, 1975).

Significant Others and Hysterectomy

The responses of significant others will affect the woman's psychosexual adaptation. Melody (1962) found that a depressive reaction in 11 women after a hysterectomy was precipitated by social experiences that were perceived as acts of disapproval or rejection by significant others. Roeske (1978) spoke about the negative attitude that a sexual partner may have toward a woman without a uterus. The thought that emerges is, "If a woman does not have a uterus is she really a woman, and if she is not really a woman what am I if I have intercourse with her?" The critical issue according to Roeske is the partner's sexual self-concept and the emotional investment made in the presence of a uterus.

Oophorectomy

When a woman has a hysterectomy she may have an oophorectomy (removal of an ovary) at the same time. In addition to the loss of her uterus, she will now experience a loss of estrogen. Occasionally, oophorectomies are performed without a hysterectomy. At that time, an alteration in body image will occur and a body adjustment to decreased estrogen production.

With the removal of the ovaries, the estrogen supply in the body will be markedly decreased, although there will continue to be some circulating estrogen supplied by the adrenal glands. The decrease in the estrogen supply should not influence the patient's sexual functioning postoperatively. Massler and Devansen (1978) found that postsurgical sexuality was more dependent on the quality of the presurgical sexuality than on the presence of functioning ovaries. Lack of estrogen supply can result in thinning vaginal walls leading to bleeding with intercourse, susceptibility to vaginal infections, and diminished vaginal lubrication.

Resumption of Intercourse after Pelvic Surgery

A woman may need to postpone intercourse after pelvic surgery, depending on the healing process. For some people this may be 4 to 6 weeks. Positions for intercourse that allow deep vaginal thrusting need to be avoided until healing is complete and the thrusting can take place without discomfort or pain. The suggested limitation on genital intercourse need not limit hugging, holding, caressing, masturbation, or oral–genital contact. The woman often needs the reassurance and affirmation that these touches and gestures give to her.

The woman will need to share her feelings and reactions to the surgery with some helpful supportive person or significant other. The nurse needs to be alert to a sign of depression and seek out the preferred person to assist in this problem when it occurs.

Mastectomy

When the wives of President Ford and Vice-President Rockefeller underwent mastectomies within a short period of time of each other, the awesome realization that carcinoma of the breast strikes 1 in 13 women in the United States was forced into public knowledge. The breast as a sexual body part affects body image, with all its accompanying ramifications, and loss of a breast affects a woman's sexual self-concept, sexual functioning, and sexual relationships. The following quote is an example of the loss experienced following a mastectomy:

> I'd been home for three weeks. He wanted to make love . . . I knew it . . . but I couldn't stand the thought. He came toward me smiling and put his hand

on my breast . . . I ran into the other room and slammed the door. All I could think about was the breast that wasn't there anymore.

This statement suggests that a client about to undergo a mastectomy may need counseling. Witkin (1978) stated that when she had her mastectomy 20 years ago the advice given her husband was to behave "as though nothing unusual, terrifying, or traumatic had occurred" (p. 20). She and her husband proceeded as though life could go on and nothing different needed to happen in their relationship. But the fact was that a new adjustment was required by both partners and that "communication of real feelings was thwarted and the marriage almost broke up" (p. 21).

The breast, to many women, is a symbol of femininity. It is a significant part of their gender identity and is important to their sex role. It influences their interpersonal communications and represents their capacity to be sexual. After a mastectomy, women may perceive themselves as handicapped and consequently will respond as a handicapped person in areas dealing with their sexuality. These responses spill over into other aspects of living, such as parenting and work roles, and the woman's total self-image can be diminished (Abt, McGurrin, & Heintz, 1978). Wabrek, Wabrek, and Burchell (1979) feel that the woman who has had a mastectomy must cope with multiple problems: the possibility of recurring cancer, the way the operation will affect her relationship with significant others, adjusting and relating to a strange body with only one breast, and her own changed sexuality.

Familial factors contribute to the development of breast cancer. Women whose mothers or sisters have had breast cancer are twice as likely to develop it as women with no familial history of the disease (HEW, 1979). Women who started their menstrual periods at an early age are more likely to develop it. A woman faces the ordeal of adjusting to her changed body image after a mastectomy, and the meaning she attached to this lost part will play a significant role in her adjustment.

Sex Role and Significant Others

The loss of a breast, with its accompanying grief, affects a woman's sex role and her sexual relationship. Without the adequate support of nurses and significant others, her adaptation becomes more problematic. In a study conducted by Abt, McGurrin, and Heintz (1978), it was found that most women desired more pre- and postoperative sexual counseling than was usually provided, and 50% of the women in their sample of 47 postmastectomy clients felt they received poor information from the professional staff. The women sampled experienced changes in sexual self-image, attitudes, and behaviors, and the changes were made more easily when they received "candid supportive counseling on sexual implications of mastectomy" (p. 43). The researchers went on to say that the mass media and communications by the "American Cancer Society (Reach for Recovery) also seem to avoid the issue of the sexual behavior of the mastectomee and hold up an idealized image of normalcy as a reasonable goal for recovery" (p. 43). It seems that health professionals and significant others who try to facilitate healthy adaptation and a return to normal may minimize the problems and needed changes of the mastectomy client. The reality of the situation is that a marked physical and psychologic change has occurred.

When a woman has a mastectomy, it is a crisis situation in her life. She will need to cope with an entirely new situation, one for which she has no specific coping skills but that will tax all of her previous coping strategies. If she has had success in the past coping with new situations and if she has the ability to mobilize support from her environment, she is more likely to adapt well to the crisis. Important variables in her adaptation are whether guidance and counseling are given to her and her family, particularly her sexual partner, and the time she is given to grieve her lost part.

There are three areas of concern to the woman: physical, cosmetic, and emotional (Askin, 1975). In the physical concern, there is the need to obtain and maintain shoulder motion, to prevent postural deformities, and to reduce the possibility of lymphedema (swelling of the arm on the involved side). The cosmetic concern involves the fitting of a prosthesis as soon postoperatively as possible—sometime within two to three days after surgery—and, for some women, the possibility of breast reconstruction. Currently, there are an increasing number of reconstructive techniques (mammoplasty) being used by plastic surgeons (U.S. Dept. of HEW, 1979, pp. 41–45). The emotional aspects of the surgery can involve both partners. The woman may feel guilty and see the breast cancer as punishment for sexual transgressions. The man may feel guilty because he views his handling of the breast as the cause of the cancer. These reactions can be dealt with by counseling the woman alone, the sexual partner alone, the woman and her partner together, several women together, or several partners together (Wabrek, Wabrek, & Burchell, 1979). Wabrek, Wabrek, and Burchell encouraged the woman and her sexual partner to be counseled together whenever possible.

Witkin (1978), interviewed 41 women who were coming to a clinic for chemotherapy or checkup after their mastectomies, found that sexual counseling could greatly help a woman's recovery. Once a woman realizes that she is not going to die, her psychosexual concerns dominate her thinking, and her ability to adjust to her crisis depends upon her perception of her partner's acceptance of her. Witkin demonstrated that the sexual partner should be involved in the whole process of counseling, if possible, from finding the tumor through the recovery. If there is a presurgical marital problem or family discord, an appropriate referral to a counselor can be made. During hospitalization the nurse can have the client view her incision early and participate in dressing changes. The sexual partner or significant others can be invited to participate in the procedure. It is best to do this while the client is still in the hospital, so that necessary guidance can be carried out while the client is under the direct observation of nurses (Comfort, 1978; Wabrek, Wabrek, and Burchell, 1979; Witkin, 1978). Sexual partners need to be assured that touching, holding, and caressing are helpful and even vital. Witkin asserted that without exception the "sexual role and functioning of the woman was experienced by her not merely as being important but as central issues in her psychological recovery" (p. 22).

Although the responses of the woman's sexual partner and her significant others are extremely important, even more important is the client's perception of those responses. Some partners are afraid to hug the woman because of fear of hurting the incision. The woman, with her vulnerable self-esteem, may interpret this as rejection (Green & Mantell, 1978).

Abt, McGurrin, and Heintz (1978) stated that adaptation to the consequences of a disease is more problematic when the problem is associated with death, sex, or mutilation. The client who has a mastectomy must deal with all three of these issues. Most people associate cancer with pain and death, and this association makes the loss of a breast more complex.

Single women have potential self-image problems, too. Some single women who have had a mastectomy are blocked from entering into sexual relationships (Kent, 1975), and some may choose to interact with many sexual partners (Comfort, 1978). One woman known to this writer stated that "I have to have frequent sexual partners to remind me that I can still attract a man." The single woman who has a mastectomy is faced with the issue of when she should reveal this information, how much she should reveal, and to whom. After a mastectomy, a single woman may say, "I don't know what to tell my boyfriend. He may think I am inviting him for sex . . . I only want him to know."

The mother of an adolescent girl faces another concern. The mother may be worried about the genetic factors in the development of breast cancer and may feel guilty because her daughter may be vulnerable to breast cancer. A woman who had a mastectomy asked about her daughter's chances of developing breast cancer. She had been "worried sick" for months.

Community Resources for Mastectomy Clients

Because of the lack of educational programs available to the woman who has just discovered a lump in her breast, a group of nurses at the Georgetown University Medical Center in Washington, D.C., has started a volunteer program called Nursupport. "The program is designed to assist women from the time a possible symptom of breast cancer is discovered through the progression of the disease. The nurses offer emotional support to the woman by listening to her fears, answering her questions, referring her to a physician, and even walking with her into the physician's examining room if she wishes. Women also are provided with information on breast cancer and guidance regarding the treatment, rehabilitation, and reconstruction options available to them during all stages of the disease" (U.S. Dept. of HEW, 1979, pp. 102–103). This is a unique type of support found at one health facility, but this help is needed and the nurse can facilitate and advocate the establishment of such programs.

The Reach to Recovery organization has volunteers who visit a woman who has had a mastectomy during her hospital stay. A volunteer for this organization is generally three years postoperative and is physically healed and psychologically adjusted to her mastectomy. Opportunities to discuss sexual role and behavior as well as the practical aspects of living are provided to the woman who has recently had a mastectomy. Reach for Recovery is a program of the American Cancer Society and is a valuable community resource.

Continuity of Sexual Activity for Mastectomy Clients

Joint visits for hospitalized clients and their sexual partners are encouraged if it is assessed that it would be beneficial to the woman who has had a mastectomy. If early intercourse is viewed by the woman as evidence that her husband does love, accept, and want to be close to her, it is beneficial to her emotional recovery to provide an opportunity for this to happen. Early intercourse is encouraged if the client views it as positive.

When a woman has had an unsatisfactory relationship or has been without one, the nurse can discuss with her the possibility of masturbation. Witkin (1978) found that some of her clients felt that it was remarkably liberating to become aware of the permissibility and acceptability of masturbating.

When the woman returns to her home, she is encouraged to view herself nude in the mirror and to talk about her feelings with a nurse-counselor (Green & Mantell, 1978). This behavior can be helpful in her struggle to cope with her changing body image.

It is best to avoid pressure to the woman's chest during intercourse. A good guideline is to question the partners about their preferred position before surgery and to suggest that they modify this position enough to avoid unnecessary pressure to the chest (Wabrek, 1979). Some women are so eager to please that they will not inform the sexual partner of pain when it happens. An example of this occurred to one woman who stated that she felt she wanted everything to be the same as before so she didn't tell her partner of the pain. Consequently, she almost developed a revulsion for intercourse. The client needs to be reminded that her sleeping positions may need to be changed because of the removed breast. This change in sleeping position may influence the sexual feelings of the partners either negatively or positively. The nurse should be prepared to deal with negative feelings if the partners see a change in sleeping positions as a problem (Wabrek, Wabrek, & Burchell, 1979). Some couples find that changing places in bed is different in a pleasurable way.

Postoperative Recommendations after a Mastectomy

The postoperative client can benefit from some specific exercises. Green and Mantell (1978) list activities done in private and some in a group with other postmastectomy clients. They include the following:

1. Water play—water play can be used to increase sensory discrimination, stimulate sexual arousal, and release sexual tension. Lying in a warm bubble bath or standing in a shower, gently soaping the entire body surface, is a nonthreatening means of tactile exploration of one's own body and can be less intimidating to those women unaccustomed to self-pleasuring. Altering water pressure with a shower massage to sore or tense areas may be both pleasurable and soothing. Practicing repeated contraction and relaxation of different muscles (thigh, pelvis, abdomen, or buttocks) can be sexually arousing for some women.

2. Mirror-image—(a) by posing before a mirror in various gradients of light, ranging from dim to bright sunlight and regulating the amount of light to the optimal level of comfort, a woman can progressively desensitize her reactions and explore feelings about her altered body image. (b) Standing before a full-length mirror, preferably a three-paneled one, the woman articulates her feelings about the aesthetics and function of each body part. By this means, she can increase her self-awareness of positive as well as negative feelings. With each subsequent exposure, disparity between her expectations and reality is reduced.

3. Role playing—by repeatedly role playing her concept of the ideal feminine image, a woman may gradually incorporate some of the admired traits as part of her new self-concept.

4. Personification (Gestalt technique)—by holding a two-way conversation with her missing breast, reviewing the significant role her breasts played in her life (e.g., wearing her first bra, initial experiences in sex play, and breast feeding), the mourning process can be facilitated.

Group exercises include the following:

1. Body meditation—lying in a comfortable position, fully clothed and with eyes closed, women are instructed to touch, massage, and caress those parts of their bodies that conjure up negative feelings. After com-

pletion of the exercise, the support provided by group feedback will contribute to the dissipation of such feelings.

2. Human-figure drawing—women are given a lapboard, colored markers, and paper. Each is instructed to draw her own image. The drawings are then passed to other group members, each of whom writes her interpretation of the feelings expressed by the figure in the picture. The drawing is returned to its creator, who then talks about what she intended to express and her reactions to the group's comments. This exercise is particularly effective for those women who are unwilling or unable to articulate their feelings.

3. Mirror image—the body-image exercise done in private before a three-way mirror is equally effective when executed individually in front of a group. This exercise provides many women with their first social nude experience and is a prime opportunity for viewing other mastectomees. Looking at others with their explicit permission in a safe, structured setting is beneficial for gaining a perspective of one's body contours in relation to others. Because the affected site is always hidden from others' view, women imagine that their own mutilation is unique and much worse than that of others who have had the same surgery. (From: Comfort, A. *Sexual Consequences of Disability*. Philadelphia: George F. Stickley Company, 1978, pp. 213–214.)

BODY IMAGE AND THE RELOCATION OF A BODY ORIFICE

When people experience changes in their excretory function, such as those changes that occur with ostomies (relocation of body orifice), former childhood conflicts about the excretory organs may be relived. Body parts associated with excretory functions are often labeled "dirty" and "bad." Further, in our society excretory functions are considered a private matter. The toilet is a place where privacy is often demanded and the bathroom is one room in the house where a lock is frequently used.

Persons who have had an ostomy may question their sexuality. They may ask questions such as "Am I still attractive?" "Do I smell?" "Will I be able to have sex?" When a relocation of an orifice is associated with the possibility of cancer, there is also the fear of death.

The type of ostomies most common today are colostomy, ileostomy, and urinary ostomy, or ileal conduit. All involve a relocation of a body orifice and a change in body image.

Ileostomy surgery for ulcerative colitis or Crohn's disease (regional ileitus) generally does not require extensive incising around the perineal area, so nerve damage may not result. The $S_2S_3S_4$ nerves supply the penis to produce an erection. When these nerves are damaged, the man will be impotent (see Chapter 16).

An ostomy affects a person's body image in the same way other surgeries do. The person's growing-up experiences with excretory functions will be significant complicating factors, however. Parental and societal attitudes toward excretory organs are frequently interrelated with one's sexuality (Dlin & Fisher, 1976). The way people handle their physiologic excretory functions is controlled by family rules, societal norms, and group sanctionings. The culture determines how excretions will be handled, where they are to be placed, and the places where it is permissible for those functions to occur. The trauma of suddenly having to change this ritualistic pattern of dealing with excretory functioning can be devastating. The person will feel a lowered self-esteem, his or her sexual self-concept will be vulnerable, and the sexual role and relationships can be seriously disrupted. The person is faced with the task of incorporating into the body image a new orifice and a new appliance, such as an ostomy bag.

In such highly stressful situations, perceptions can sometimes become impaired. The person may cope with the altered body image by denying that the alteration has occurred. In people with ostomies, personification (a "not me" phenomena) as a way of dealing with an ostomy may occur. When this defense is used, the painful loss and the feelings associated with that loss are repressed; that new part of the body not belonging to the person is given a name—such as calling the ostomy "Charlie" (Pasqueli, 1975). This naming of the new body part does not allow a change in body image to occur in the person's perception of the self. Through this name the client separates the stoma from the self, denies being different from before, and continues to hold the same sexual expectations of the self and others. This personification delays the needed acceptance of a new orifice and way of functioning.

A urinary diversion is frequently done for cancer of the bladder, and dysfunction of the sexual organs can occur because of nerve damage. Impotence, orgasmic dysfunction, and sterility are frequently encountered (Gambrell, 1973). These problems may be irreversible, depending on the extent of the nerve damage. If the urinary diversion occurred in childhood, perhaps for a congenital anomaly, the man will have an erection, but he may be sterile and may not ejaculate.

Sexual Roles and Functioning for the Ostomate

The influences that an ostomy may have on sexual role and functioning are multidimensional, encompassing social, psychologic, and physical factors. In the man, physical and psychologic factors are particularly important in initiating and sustaining an erection (Chapter 16). Whenever trauma or actual nerve damage occurs, impotence and the possible resulting sterility can be a concern, particularly if the client believes that having an erection is equal to being a man. In conditions in which the sacral nerves 2, 3, and 4 are damaged, as in a urinary diversion or a colostomy, the man will frequently be unable to have an erection (Klompus, 1980). For the man who had an ileostomy, the picture is different. Having an ostomy because of colitis can be different in that sexual dysfunction can vary from no problem at all to some dysfunction—some difficulty with erection or ejaculation. This complication is an uncommon one (Babb & Kieraldo, 1977). If the rectum was removed, the client may be impotent temporarily (Gambrell, 1973). The age and mental state of the client seem to be more significant factors in sexual dysfunction than any other variable (Babb & Kieraldo, 1977).

Fasth et al. (1978) found unchanged or improved sexual relationships after an ileostomy in the majority of the people they studied. Seventy percent of the men and 87% of the women said their sexual lives improved. Out of 122 people, only 19 men (29%) and 7 women (12%) has some impaired sexual functioning. For the men, the sexual problem was described as impotence and the loss of ejaculation. For the women, impairment consisted of dyspareunia or inability to achieve orgasm or both.

Fasth et al. (1978) stated that the reasons for the development of sexual dysfunction for the man with an ostomy, particularly an ileostomy, are still debatable. They believe that "it appears unlikely that in males impotence is caused by trauma to the pelvic nerves" (p. 10). The fear of failure or marital or sexual relationship problems may be a more likely reason for sexual difficulties.

The male ostomate has varying sexual responses ranging from full potency to complete loss of orgasm. Those who are orgasmic will generally have a retrograde ejaculation in which the seminal fluid is propelled backwards into the bladder. This retrograde ejaculation causes the urine to have a milky color. Other problems frequently encountered are impotence, sterility, and ejaculatory incompetence (Ward, 1976).

The nurse must pay particular attention to the client's response to his surgery as well as to the responses of his significant others to his surgery. Temporary or permanent impotence may be brought about through fear of failure, fear of offending the sexual partner, or depression from the losses experienced (Eardley, 1976; Fasth et al., 1978). Before serious sexual dysfunction is considered to be permanent, a complete assessment of client–partner communication should be undertaken. The physical injury, the reason for the surgery, the sexual partner's attitude toward the surgery, and prior sexual history should be assessed. The client's general state of health should be considered, because blood loss and the results of surgery can leave a person debilitated and thus affect sexual functioning.

The person who has had an ostomy should wait at least 12 to 18 months after surgery before determining whether or not sexual impotence is permanent. When the impotence is assessed to be permanent and the conditions for a prosthesis are met, a prosthesis can be made available (see Chapter 14).

The woman who has had an ostomy fares much better than the man in relation to sexual functioning. She is generally able to have intercourse, be orgasmic, and remain fertile. Frequently, her sexual responses may be enhanced, because the ostomy took care of a diseased organ or physical problem (Fasth, 1978). If the ostomy was performed because of a malignancy and more extensive surgery was necessary, such as a bilateral oophorectomy or a hysterectomy, then sterility does follow. Although it is generally accepted that women should not have a physical reason for sexual dysfunction postoperatively, they still may have emotional responses to altered body image. Women may fear that they are unlovable, untouchable, and that their sexual relationships will be lost. An important thing to emphasize to the woman who has recently had an ostomy and to her sexual partner is that sexual activity need not be stopped. The sexual activity may occur as soon as the incision is healed and when the woman feels strong enough. When the rectum has been removed, there might be some rectal pain around the perineal area for several months, varying with each person, but this pain usually does not interfere with intercourse (Norris & Gambrell, 1972). Some women complain of dyspareunia (painful intercourse).

Pregnancy is possible for the woman who has a stoma and generally can occur within two years after surgery; however, a limit of two babies is usually imposed. The physical condition of the woman and the philosophy of the attending physician are determining factors. A common problem in pregnant women is an enlargement of the stoma as the abdomen enlarges to accommodate pregnancy and the resulting difficulty of a proper fitting appliance to cover the stoma (Norris & Gambrell, 1972).

Sexual Activity and the Ostomate

An important point that is often stated and restated to ostomates and the health professionals involved in their care is, "There are many ways of making love and achieving orgasm and there are many ways of making love without orgasm and achieving satisfaction" (Norris & Gambrell, 1972, p. 8).

The effect of the relocation of a body orifice cannot be underestimated: It changes the person's life style and has an impact on the family. Previous expectations of self and others must make way for a new way of living.

The following advice is offered to the ostomate in preparation for sexual activity. Cleanliness and attractiveness of the body are important. Bathing and using perfumes are frequently helpful in preparing for lovemaking. Pleasing clothing, soft lights, and music can heighten sensuality and sexuality. If the appliance is worn during sexual activity, special attention should be given to its security. The person may need to develop a good sense of humor, for it is not unusual to have an ostomy make noises during intercourse. It would be best for the person to avoid gaseous foods or any foods that contribute to unexpected noises (Gambrell, 1973; Norris & Gambrell, 1972).

Clients can be referred to the United Ostomy Association. There are local chapters throughout the United States, or the national office can be reached by writing to the United Ostomy Association, Inc., 1111 Wilshire Boulevard, Los Angeles, California 90017. The association has many pamphlets that can be helpful to the client. Some sample pamphlets include "Sex, Courtship and the Single Ostomate"; "Sex, Pregnancy and the Female Ostomate"; and "Sex and the Male Ostomate." The organization has, in addition to this literature, volunteers who come and speak to the new ostomate and give first-hand information to the ostomate. As Ward (1976) stated, "An ostomy is not a disease, not a handicap, not a disability. It is an abnormality, an alternative way of accomplishing a natural and normal function. The ostomy must be accepted and dealt with in the same manner as eye glasses, dentures, hearing aids or pacemakers. While there have been many ostomate mothers and fathers, there is yet no report of an infant having been born wearing an ostomy appliance" (p. 5).

The Ostomy Team

The ostomy team (whose members have received specific and specialized training in the care of clients with an ostomy) has an opportunity to be available to clients before and after the surgery. They provide anticipatory guidance about the surgery and the care that the client will receive before and after surgery. They can begin the crucial discussion of how the surgery will change body functioning and image. They can begin to provide information about the specific equipment and materials that will be used to care for the new body orifice. The client can be encouraged to discuss the feelings associated with the alteration of body part and how these feelings will affect his or her self-worth and acceptability. Through the development of trust with the client and his or her sexual partner and significant others, the ostomy team members are able to discuss emotionally laden topics. Sitting down with the client indicates that time has been planned for the interaction. Before surgery, it is appropriate to discuss with the client what he or she knows and needs to know about the surgery. The client gives clues about what he or she is ready to discuss about sexuality. A client may say, "I won't need to use that anymore" (pointing to his penis) or, "I'm not worth much anymore to anyone."

The sexual partner, the family, and significant others are important resources. The ostomy team encourages those intimately involved with the client to remain with the client during dressing changes or other procedures. These significant people can be helpful in assisting the client in adjusting to the altered body image. It should be emphasized that all questions are significant to the person who does the asking. Answering questions directly and sensitively at the time they are asked saves time, conserves energy, and avoids negative emotional output. Time for exchanging reliable information about the ostomy and for expressing feelings and concern must be planned with the client, family, and significant others.

SURGERY AND THE SEXUAL ORGANS OF MEN

Men must contend with alterations in body image when surgery involves their sexual organs. The importance of the testes and penis to the identity of a man has been discussed frequently in the psychologic literature. "Surgical procedures can threaten potency, fertility and excretory control. A procedure may affect the sexual self image of the patient and the reflected image imposed by the environment on the man. Doubts, guilt, recrimination, and even hate may appear" (Freedman, Kaplan, & Saddock, 1977). Depression may result from a testectomy or orchiectomy, a vasectomy (removal of the vas deferens), or a prostatectomy (removal of all or part of the prostate gland).

Procedures occurring for cancer of the genital area, such as a penectomy (removal of the penis), are difficult to accept. Men who have lost their penises are anxious and acutely ashamed of their altered body image and feel a loss of social face and a loss of masculinity. As a result, there is a high incidence of suicide in this population (Freedman et al., 1977).

Prostatectomy

It has been estimated that one out of every ten men who live long enough will have a prostatectomy (Boyarsky & Boyarsky, 1978). This is a common surgical procedure that is done in increasing numbers because the elderly population is increasing. Enlargement of the prostate is a common occurrence in aging men.

Hargreave and Stephenson (1977) interviewed 252 men after they had a prostatectomy. Ninety-eight of these men reported full potency before their prostate operation; 44 men reported partial potency. The incidence of total impotence after a prostatectomy was 4% if the man was fully potent before surgery. This percentage increased if there was failing potency before the prostatectomy.

Several patients reported that they were afraid to try intercourse and attributed total or partial impotence to this fear. Zohar et al. (1976) found that "all potent patients who were given a preoperative explanation about sexual function remained potent postoperatively but not so when no explanation was given" (p. 333).

Types of Prostatectomies and Effects on Potency

Currently, three types of prostatectomy surgery are performed—perineal, suprapubic or retropubic, and transurethral. The transurethral, commonly called the TUR, is the most often performed. The TUR causes problems with potency in only approximately 9 or 10% of men; however, there is an interference with ejaculation (Shrom, 1979). Retrograde ejaculation can occur. When the surgery is more extensive, as in cases of malignancy, the incidence of impotence is considerably higher, depending on the involvement of nerve pathways to the penis and surrounding tissue (Shrom, 1979; Boyarsky & Boyarsky, 1978; Mims & Swenson, 1980; Hogan, 1980). From the data it is generally believed that routine prostatectomies should not interfere with potency in the majority of men.

Postoperative problems related to the surgery fall into three areas—physical, psychologic, and social. Along with the problems of potency the client is likely to worry about his "milky" urine. He needs to be reassured that this is damage only to the bladder sphincter, and that the semen has backed up into the bladder during ejaculation (Boyarsky & Boyarsky, 1978). When a more extensive type of prostatectomy is performed, such as the open method (perineal), the client experiences urinary incontinence. This method is rarely used. For a more complete discussion, see Chapter 16. Erections and orgasms should not be a problem unless the client has nerve or blood-supply interference.

Windle and Robert (1974) demonstrated the importance of considering the patient's sex life before a prostatectomy. Clients who had sexual difficulties after a prostatectomy were likely to have had similar problems before surgery. Boyarsky and Boyarsky (1978) emphasized that the client's previous sex habits and increase in sex should be assessed thoroughly before surgery and that postoperative sexual problems tended to fall into the area of psychologic rather than physical difficulty. Gold (1969) stated that a sexual history should be undertaken with emphasis on the relationship with the significant other. This gives a clearer picture of difficulties that may arise after surgery.

In the realm of psychologic functioning, the client is likely to experience some fears either in the area of his sexuality or his life in general, particularly if he had had a friend who had difficulty with prostatectomy surgery or is aware of the problems that accompanied these procedures in the past. At the turn of the century, clients suffered excessive blood loss, serious infections, and problems with impotence. The mortality rate was as high as 40% (Boyarsky & Boyarsky, 1978). Because the operative procedure is often performed in people who are over 50 years old, other problems cause anxieties for the client, such as decreasing interest in sexual activity or fear of death, if the surgery was the result of cancer. Gold and Hotchkiss (1969) believe that age is more of an influence on later sexual activity than is the operation itself.

Other psychologic difficulties can occur as a result of lack of information to the client postoperatively. He is left to wonder what is happening to him. The disease process itself can cause worries, and when the fears resulting from the problem are not all vented, they tend to become magnified. It is not uncommon to hear complaints of depression after this procedure.

Sexual Functioning after Prostatectomy

The nurse is responsible for knowing the following information when discussing with the client the possible effects of a prostatectomy on his sexual functioning:

1. Sexual abilities should remain the same if perineal or radical prostatectomy is not used.
2. There will be an absence of ejaculation and the presence of a milky urine, but erections, orgasms, and sexual satisfaction should be unimpaired, particularly after four to six weeks postoperatively.
3. Communication between the patient and his sexual partner helps to alleviate any irrational fears and beliefs the sexual partner may hold. Keep in mind that sexual functioning before the onset of the illness greatly determines the postoperative outcome.
4. The pathophysiologic changes that have occurred are variables that influence potency. Secondary effects, such as infection or increased blood loss, have an effect postoperatively if the client is fatigued.
5. Emotional responses to the illness are commonly experienced.

THE NURSE AS EDUCATOR-COUNSELOR

Body image develops over time, and adaptation to alterations in body image also require time. Each client has his or her own unique pattern of adaptation that involves individual coping skills, responses and interactions with significant others, and cultural values to which the client is accustomed.

The nurse must be aware that some behaviors exhibited during recovery from the surgery are associated with the process of mourning for the lost, changed, or relocated body part. Some clients feel that other people will reject them; consequently, they may respond with hostility to those around them. A pervasive sense of helplessness can trigger hostility in clients. The nurse needs to keep the following in mind:

1. Internal changes are generally less distressing than external ones that can be seen by others.
2. Certain body parts are endowed with more emotional significance than others.
3. Previous conflict about certain body parts can be reawakened after surgery.
4. There can be a loss of self-esteem accompanying the loss or relocation of body parts that can affect the client's belief in his or her capacity to resume previous sex roles and sexual attitudes.

The nurse discusses with the client the impending changes, gathers data about previous responses to stress, and evaluates the coping response in terms of active or passive coping patterns. Active coping may involve a willingness to talk to another person with a colostomy before the operation in order to get some understanding of the way to deal with the new ostomy. With passive coping the client may say, "Forget about any talking until after it's all over."

The nurse should seek out and work with the client's family or significant others to present reliable information and sensitive counseling that will provide reassurance in coping with the changing body image. The nurse needs to provide anticipatory guidance about the process of grief.

During interactions with the client, the nurse should ask about and listen to the personal meaning and significance of the body part, how the client perceives the loss or relocation, and how it will affect his or her sexual role and relationship.

The nurse explores beliefs and feelings about other losses, recalling that coping with previous losses will influence the present response. The nurse should assess how realistically the client evaluates the present situation. Nursing intervention paves the way for the client's "work of worrying," a necessary process that helps the client through the change in body image.

During nurse-client interactions, the nurse helps the client realistically to see and develop his or her own strengths and potential and reinforce the idea of self-care. The nurse further coordinates with other health professionals to promote and support the change in body image, so that arrangements for continuity of care may be made for when the client returns to the home and community.

NURSING PROCESS

Client: Leslie Munroe, early afternoon admission to 3 West, scheduled for gynecologic surgery the next morning.

Nurse: Denise Walsh, staff nurse, assigned to admit client and take nursing history.

Assessment

Subjective Data

"Just a couple of days ago I was busy getting to know my new students and getting the classes started right and taking care of my family, and now you're talking to me about an operation in the morning."

"I've got lots of responsibilities. I've got lots of things that must be done."

"I've got three children—two away at college, and only one home, but she needs attention."

"I haven't thought about wanting any children for years, but now I realize that part of my life is really over."

"And my period—that's probably over too. Funny, my shopping list will change. What a silly thing to think about."

"My husband tells me not to worry. He says I'm the mother of his children and that he cares for me and that I'm his wife forever—but I wonder if he's just saying that."

"My husband and I—in bed—you know—will it be different?"

"My children—I wonder how they will see me?"

"I wonder, and worry too, that if everything has to go—uterus and ovaries—maybe I'll look different, you know—older—sooner."

"I'm not sure—I just don't know."

Objective Data

T 98.4, P 80, R 18, B/P 130/80.

45 years old, married, college professor.

Three children, ages 20, 18, 15 (two oldest in college—150 miles away)

Medical history and physical: menarche age 12, 29-day cycle with four-to-five-days moderate flow, last menstrual period seven days ago; dysmenorrhea past 18 months; profuse midcycle bleeding past four months; fatigue; general malaise; nonmovable abdominal mass in lower right quadrant.

Scheduled for surgery 8:30 A.M.—exploratory laparotomy with possible hysterectomy and possible bilateral oophorectomy.
Lowered eyelids—lowered voice pitch.
Infrequent eye contact.
Verbalizes impending loss.

Nursing Diagnosis

Anticipatory grief about altered body image related to possible loss of sexual organs (uterus, ovaries).

Planning

Express empathy.
Listen attentively.
Touch judiciously.
Explain that emotional response is appropriate and commonly experienced.
Encourage expression of feelings about possible loss of uterus.
Encourage expression of feelings about possible loss of ovaries and associated hormonal function.
Communicate comfortable feelings about discussion of possible losses.
Offer feedback about expressed feelings.
Identify symbolic meaning of sexual organs and associated functions.
Describe the normal stages of grief.
Emphasize value as person and woman.
Offer affirmations of wholeness as person and woman.
Advise that significant persons express love for one another.
Advise that significant persons express acceptance of one another.
Encourage expression of feelings about possible losses with sexual partner.
Encourage expression of feelings about possible losses with significant others at home and away from home.
Explain the importance of offering emotional support to one another.
Encourage reduction of demands on self.
Encourage use of normal coping mechanisms.
Support realistic assessment of situation.
Encourage planning one day at a time.
Discuss scheduled operative procedures.
Present changes gradually.
Explain gradual resumption of activities of daily living and sexual activi-

ties to presurgery levels during recovery and convalescence as real expectation.

Offer the following information only if receptive:

1. function of uterus in relation to sexual response cycle, and other physiologic processes
2. role of estrogen replacement therapy
3. alternate positions for intercourse after surgery

Allow time for thought comprehension.

Indicate availability for further teaching and counseling.

Indicate availability for teaching and counseling with sexual partner and significant others.

Obtain feedback about messages communicated.

Implementation

Telephone significant others at home, share feelings, and request presence before and after surgery tomorrow.

Telephone significant others away from home, share feelings, establish a schedule for telephone calls after surgery, and arrange for visit home during recovery.

Initiate discussion with sexual partner during visiting hours.

Share feelings about love and acceptance.

Share feelings about possible losses.

Share information about gradual resumption of activities of daily living and sexual activities during recovery and convalescence.

Evaluation (three weeks after surgery)

Reports presence of "family" before and after surgery "felt good."

Reports telephone calls from "children away from home just what I needed."

Reports "all my children will be home for Thanksgiving."

Reports discussion about "sex after surgery" with sexual partner (husband) was "easier than I thought it would be . . . should have known he would listen and help both of us get started again."

Reports "grappling" with the picture of herself as "almost the same on the outside but different on the inside."

Reports plans for gradual return to activities of daily living "proceeding as planned and on schedule."

BIBLIOGRAPHY

Abt, N., McGurrin, M., & Heintz, L. The impact of mastectomy on sexual self-image, attitudes and behavior. *Journal of Sex Education and Therapy*, 1978, *4*, 43–46.

Asken, M. Psychoemotional aspects of mastectomy: A review of recent literature. *American Journal of Psychiatry*, 1975, *132*, 56–59.

Babb, R., & Kieraldo, J. Sexual dysfunction after abdominoperineal resection. *Digestive Diseases*, 1977, *12*, 1127–1129.

Binder, D. P. Sex, courtship and the single ostomate. California: United Ostomy Association, Inc., 1973.

Boyarsky, L., & Boyarsky, R. Prostatectomy, sexual disabilities and their management. In A. Comfort (Ed.), *Sexual consequences of disability*. Philadelphia: Stickley, 1978.

Butts, P. Meeting the special needs of your hysterectomy. *Nursing*, 1979, *79*, 40–47.

Campbell, C. *Nursing diagnosis and intervention in nursing practice*. New York: Wiley, 1978.

Comfort, A. (Ed.). *Sexual consequences of disability*. Philadelphia: Stickley, 1978.

Coope, J. The post-hysterectomy syndrome. *Nursing Times*, August 1975, *71*, 1285–1286.

Corbeil, M. Nursing process for a patient with a body image disturbance. *Nursing Clinics of North America*, March 1971, *6*, 156–157.

Corman, M., Veidenheimer, M., & Coller, J. Impotence after prostatectomy for inflammatory disease of the bowel. *American Society of Colon and Rectal Surgeons*, 1978, *21*, 418–419.

Cosper, B., Fuller, S., & Robinson, G. Characteristics of post-hospitalization recovery following hysterectomy. *Journal of Obstetrics, Gynecology, and Neonatal Nursing*, 1978, *7*, 7–11.

Derick, V. The psychological hurdles of new ostomates: Helping them up and over. *Nursing*, 1974, *74*, 52–55.

Dlin, B., & Fisher, K. Psychiatric aspects of colostomy and ileostomy. In J. Howells (Ed.), *Modern perspectives in the psychiatric aspects of surgery*. New York: Brunner/Mazel, 1976.

Downie, P. A. Rehabilitation of the patient after mastectomy. *Nursing Mirror*, 1975, *140*, 58–59.

Drüner, H., Palmtag, H., & Wersching, M. Assessment of genitourinary dysfunction after rectal surgery. *British Association of Surgical Oncology*, 1978, *4*, 145–151.

Eardley, A. Post surgical problems. *Nursing Mirror*, February 1976, *142*, 58–59.

Eskew, P. Personal communication, 1980.

Fasth, S., Felipsson, R., Hellberg, R., Hulten, L., Linhagen, J., Nordgrens, S. Sexual dysfunction following proctocolectomy. *Annales Cherurgial et Gynaecologiae*, 1978, *67*, 8–12.

Finkle, A. The relationship of sexual habits to benign prostate hypertrophy. *Medical Aspects of Human Sexuality*, 1967, *1*, 24–25.

Finkle, A., & Prian, D. Sexual potency in elderly men before and after prostatectomy. *Journal of American Medical Association*, 1966, *196*, 125–129.

Fisher, S. Body experience before and after surgery. *Perceptual and Motor Skills*, 1978, *46*, 699–702.

Ford, A., & Alexander, O. Sexual behavior and the chronically ill patient. *Medical Aspects of Human Sexuality*, 1967, *1*, 54–70.

Freedman, A., Kaplan, H., & Sudock, B. *Comprehensive Textbook of Psychiatry*. New York: The Williams & Wilkins Co., 1975.

Gambrell, E. *Sex and the male ostomate*. Los Angeles, Cal.: United Ostomy Association, 1973.

Gennser, G., Owman, G., Owman, T., & Wehlin, S. Significance of adrenergic innervation of the bladder outlet during ejaculation. *Lancet*, 1969, *1*, 154.

Gold, F., & Hotchkiss, R. Sexual potency following simple prostatectomy. *New York State Journal of Medicine*, 1969, *69*, 2987–2989.

Gonick, P. Urologic problems and sexual function. In W. Oaks, G. Melchiodi, & I. Fischer (Eds.), *Sex and the life cycle*. New York: Grune & Stratton, 1976.

Green, C., & Mantell, J. The need for management of the psychosexual aspects of mastectomy. In A. Comfort (Ed.), *Sexual consequences of disability*. Philadelphia: Stickley, 1978.

Gruendemann, B. The impact of surgery on body image. *Nursing Clinics of North America*, 1975, *10*, 635–642.

Hampton, P., & Tornasky, W. Hysterectomy and tubal ligation: A comparison of the psychological aftermath. *American Journal of Gynecology*, 1974, *119*, 949–952.

Hargreave, T., & Stephenson, T. Potency and prostatectomy. *British Journal of Urology*, 1977, *49*, 683–688.

Herr, H. Preservation of sexual potency in prostatic cancer patients after pelvic lymphadenectomy and iodine 125 implant. Paper presented at the *American Urological Association Convention*, Washington, D.C., May 1978.

Hogan, R. *Human sexuality: A nursing perspective*. New York: Appleton-Century-Crofts, 1980.

Kattreider, N., Wallace, A., & Horowitz, M. A field study of the stress response syndrome: Young women after hysterectomy. *Journal of the American Medical Association*, 1979, *242*, 1499–1503.

Kent, S. Coping with sexual identity crisis after mastectomy. *Geriatrics,* October 1975, *30*, 145–146.

Klompus, W. Sexual function after surgery for lower bowel disease. *Medical Aspects of Human Sexuality*, 1980, *14*, 89–95.

Krueger, J., Hassell, J., Goggins, D., Ishimatsu, T., Pablico, M., and Tuttle, E. Relationship between nurse counseling and sexual adjustment after hysterectomy. *Nursing Research*, 1979, *28*, 145–150.

Kübler-Ross, E. On death and dying. New York: Macmillan, 1969.

Labby, D. Sexual concomitants of disease and illness. *Postgraduate Medicine*, 1975, *58*, 110.

Lazaras, R., & Galeman, D. Positive denial: The case for not facing reality. *Psychology Today*, 1980, *13*, 44–60.

Lindensmith, S. Body image and the crisis of enterostomy. *The Canadian Nurse,* November 1977, *73*, 24–27.

Littlefield, V. The surgical patient's sexuality. *AORN*, 1977, *26*, 649–658.

Madorsky, M., Hshamalla, M., Schussler, I., Lyons, H., & Miller, G. Post-prostatectomy impotence. *Journal of Urology*, 1976, *115*, 401–403.

Massler, D., & Devansen, M. Sexual consequences of gynecological operations. In A. Comfort (Ed.), *Sexual consequences of disability*. Philadelphia: Stickley, 1978.

May, R. Sexual dysfunction following rectal excision for ulcerative colitis. *British Journal of Surgery*, 1966, *53*, 29.

Meikle, S., Brody, H., & Pysh, F. An investigation into the psychological effects of hysterectomy. *Journal of Nervous and Mental Disease*, 1977, *164*, 36–41.

Melody, G. Depression reactions following hysterectomy. *American Journal Obstetrics and Gynecology*, 1962, *83*, 410–413.

Mims, F., & Swenson, M. *Sexuality: A nursing perspective*. New York: McGraw-Hill, 1980.

Morgan, S. Sexuality after hysterectomy and castration. *Women and Health*, 1978, *3*, 5–10.

Murry, R. Body image development in adulthood. *Nursing Clinics of North America*, December 1972, 7, 617–630.

Norris, C., & Gambrell, E. Sex, pregnancy and the female ostomate. Los Angeles, Cal.: United Ostomy Association, 1972.

Pasqueli, E. Personification: Patient and nurse problem. *Perspectives in Psychiatric Care*, 1975, *13*, 58–61.

Polivy, J. Effects of mastectomy on a woman's feminine self-concept. *Journal of Nervous and Mental Disease*, 1977, *164,* 77–87.

Polivy, J. Psychological reactions to hysterectomy: A critical review. *American Journal of Obstetrics and Gynecology,* 1974, *118,* 417–429.

Richards, D. A post-hysterectomy syndrome. *Lancet*, 1974, *2*, 983.

Rollin, B. *First, you cry*. Philadelphia: Lippincott, 1977.

Roeske, N. Hysterectomy and other gynecological surgeries: Psychological view. In M. Natman & C. Nadelson (Eds.), *The Woman Patient*. New York: Plemun Press, 1978.

Shrom, S., Lief, H., & Wein, A. Clinical profile of experience with 130 consecutive cases of impotent men. *Urology*, 1979, *13,* 511–515.

United States Department of Health, Education, & Welfare. *The breast cancer digest*. Washington: U.S. Government Printing Office, 1979.

Wabrek, A. J., Wabrek, C. J., & Burchell, R. C. Marital and sexual counseling after mastectomy. In R. Green (Ed.), *Human sexuality: A health practitioner's text* (2nd ed.). Baltimore: Williams & Wilkins, 1979.

Ward, E. *Sex and the ostomate*. Paper presented at Institute for Sex Research, Bloomington, Indiana, July 28, 1976.

Windle, R., & Robert, J. Ejaculatory functioning after prostatectomy. *Proceedings Royal Social Medicine*, 1974, *67*, 1160.

Witkin, M. Psychosexual counseling of the mastectomy patient. *Journal of Sex and Marital Therapy*, 1978, *4*, 20–28.

Witkin, M. Psychosexual myths and reality of mastectomy. *Medical Aspects of Human Sexuality*, 1979, *13,* 65–79.

Wolf, S. Emotional reactions to hysterectomy. *Post Graduate Medicine*, 1970, *47*, 156.

Wood, N. Influences on sexual adaptation to mastectomy. *Journal of Obstetrics, Gynecology, and Neonatal Nursing*, 1975, *4,* 33–37.

Woods, N. F. *Human sexuality in health and illness* (2nd ed.). St. Louis: Mosby, 1979.

Wren, B. Counseling the hysterectomy patient. *Medical Journal of Australia*, 1978, *1,* 87–89.

Zohar, J., Meiraz, D., Maoz, B., & Durst, N. Factors influencing sexual activity after prostatectomy: A prospective study. *Journal of Urology*, 1976, *116*, 332–334.

16. Sexuality and Spinal Cord Injury

Jane M. Egan
Josephine Novo Osborne

VALUES CLARIFICATION EXERCISE

Each year, especially during the spring and summer season, people take advantage of fresh air and sunshine. Motorcycle trips, automobile races, and swimming events become principal means of recreation and escape from daily life stresses. Although pleasurable and useful, these activities are dangerous. An accident during one of the recreational activities can result in serious injuries to the head and spinal cord.

The following exercises are planned to assist you in examining your thoughts and feelings about the sexuality of people with spinal cord injuries. Write your initial responses to these questions.

Imagine yourself waking up in the middle of the night unable to move your legs because they feel as if they have fallen asleep. How do you feel? Do you tell yourself it's only temporary? How do you reassure yourself that the loss of function and feeling is only temporary? Do you hear yourself saying, "I'll be okay in a few minutes?"

Imagine receiving a phone call from a friend telling you that a mutual friend has been in an automobile accident and has sustained a neck injury. What is your first reaction? Are you relieved that you were not in the car? Do you feel sad? Sorry? Curious? Anxious? Concerned? Distant? Terrified? Guilty? Fearful?

You are asked to care for a 30-year-old married man who is paralyzed from the waist down because of a motorcycle accident. How do you feel about taking care of him? Do you feel pity? Sad? Sorry? Curious? Anxious? Concerned? Distant? Terrified? Guilty? Shame?

You are asked to care for a middle-aged woman who states that she is a homosexual. She is paralyzed from the shoulders down. What is your first response? Do you feel pity? Sorry? Sad? Curious? Anxious? Concerned? Distant? Terrified? Guilty? Ashamed?

Look at the responses that you have chosen. Are the responses under each situation the same? Does the situation of the person involved in the situation affect your response? Is one of the situations more threatening to you than the others?

Share your responses with a group of peers or colleagues. How are your responses similar to those of the members of the group? How do they differ? Are there any responses that occur more frequently than others? Is the group more threatened by any one of the situations? Discuss how your responses and the group's responses could influence behavior and thus nursing care.

BEHAVIORAL OBJECTIVES

After completing the chapter, you will be able to

- Describe the impact of spinal cord injury on sexual self-concept and sexual functioning.
- Describe the coping behaviors exhibited by people with spinal cord injury (SCI).
- Discuss the effect myths and misconceptions about the sexuality of the SCI person can have on nurse's perception of client's sexual functioning.
- Explain how different levels of spinal cord injury affect reproductive capabilities in men and women.
- Explain the psychologic and physiologic preparation for sexual activity for the SCI person.
- Explain the techniques of sexual intercourse that are available to the SCI person.
- Explain the role of the nurse as educator-counselor for the SCI person.

BODY IMAGE AND SPINAL CORD INJURY

"The first time I realized I couldn't get a hard on, I didn't feel macho anymore." With these words, a 26-year-old paraplegic man realized that he was different, and he imagined his masculinity was lost. Injury from a motorcycle accident changed how he felt about himself as a person and sexual being. In a sexually aware society, such an alteration in body image may result in a person feeling depressed, devastated, and dehumanized. Not being able to perform like others will lower a person's self-esteem and change his or her self-concept.

Self-concept and self-esteem mirror the person's adaptation to the environment. The responses and appraisal of significant others strongly affect the self-concept of the spinal-cord-injured person. The interrelationship of self-concept and self-esteem influences the way in which spinal-cord-injured people view themselves. Their altered body image has to include the use of a wheelchair for mobility, and they must adapt to changes in their bowel, bladder, and sexual functioning.

Coping Behaviors

People with spinal cord injuries must deal with a crisis situation. They experience various responses to the injury as adaptation occurs. Shock is the immediate response, followed by the feelings of being overwhelmed by the loss of function. An inability to carry out the simple tasks of daily care leaves them confused and helpless. Loss of personal control increases the need for reassurance and trust. Extreme degrees of helplessness and dependency are not uncommon. This is demonstrated by emotional outbursts or by excessive demands on the staff and family. The nurse often experiences some confusion about these behaviors, forgetting that such behaviors are the person's attempts to hold things together.

Weller and Miller (1977) have discussed stages of adaptation that can be observed. The first stage is characterized by disbelief that the injury has occurred and it has "really happened to me." This can lead to the use of denial, which is a defense mechanism that is beneficial and initially comforting. Lazarus (1979) states that "illusion and self-deception can have positive value in a person's psychological economy" (p. 50). He goes on to say that with a spinal cord injury the hope of moving can have many useful effects, since a person's rehabilitation depends on his or her struggle to move forward. It is important to give people the time they need to assimilate the loss.

Defense mechanisms provide psychologic comfort for people by bringing about an initial period of reorganization during which the full impact of the situation cannot serve a useful purpose. It is important to realize, however, that persistent use of defense mechanisms is maladaptive and can prevent the client from preparing for a threatening event.

As spinal-cord-injured clients begin their recovery process, they begin to acknowledge their losses. The realization that the injury has occurred and is permanent triggers further feelings of helplessness and hopelessness. These feelings can be overwhelming, causing the injured to lash out angrily at those around them or to hold back the anger in an effort to maintain their integrity. Development of anger is to be expected after the loss of function. People may value keeping their cool and may show anger in subtle ways, such as making demands on others in a biting voice or, indirectly, refusing to eat meals when served, or sleeping through the time for physical therapy.

Later on in their recovery, a deep sense of grief can be seen in spinal-cord-injured people. The enigma of total disability engenders despair that is expressed in symptoms of depression. These symptoms may include loss of appetite, sleeplessness, mood changes, crying spells, and loss of interest in the environment. Clients may stay in this stage for a long period of time; they become vulnerable to drug and alcohol abuse. Loss of sexual interest occurs during this period, accompanied by personal neglect. Sexual relationships are impaired, and the partner is often left to determine the cause of the problem, especially when the injured person rejects the partner. The process of working through the discord in sexual relationships and other losses occurs during hospitalization for rehabilitation but may set the stage for problems after discharge from the hospital.

The last stage of adjustment may occur early in the process of rehabilitation, may take approximately one to two years post injury, or may never happen. This stage is characterized by the client's recognition of his or her own personal worth as a viable human being who has power over what happens to the self, despite acknowledgment of handicaps. Behaviors observed during this stage are the ability to perform activities of daily living and the establishment and maintenance of meaningful relationships, which includes sexual activities.

Myths and Misconceptions about Sexuality and Spinal Cord Injury

Conine et al. (1979) discussed sexual myths and misconceptions related to sexuality and spinal-cord-injured people (Table 16.1). It is important to be aware of these myths and misconceptions so that a clear understanding of the sexual functioning of the SCI person can be developed.

NEUROLOGICAL ASPECTS OF SEXUAL FUNCTIONING

In order to understand the actual physiologic process that occurs after a spinal cord injury, the nurse needs to have a clear understanding of the neurologic aspects of sexual response. Sexual functioning involves the complex action of the spinal reflex arc, which includes the afferent and efferent pathways as well as the corticomotor and ascending pathways. In the man, erection occurs as a result of parasympathetic stimulation arising from the S_2–S_4 cord level, and the impulse travels through the

Table 16.1. Myths and Misconceptions about Sexuality and SCI (Held by 10% or More of the Subjects)

- Actual physical loss of sexual function in persons with SCI is very prevalent.
- Sexual functioning is not important to persons with SCI.
- Sexual activity is not as important as walking to some paraplegics.
- A child born to a woman with SCI is likely to have deformities.
- The ability for erection and ejaculation will not return if it is lacking three months after injury.
- The menstrual period of a woman with SCI may cease after the trauma and will never resume.
- Female sexual neurophysiology does not include sequential events of erection, emission, and ejaculation.
- Persons with SCI are not frustrated or unhappy if they fail to experience orgasm or climax.
- Erections occur more often in persons with SCI who have a complete lower-motor-neuron lesion than those with a complete upper-motor-neuron lesion.
- For men with SCI, vibrators are useless for causing erection firm enough to achieve intromission.
- Men with SCI who have suprapubic catheters cannot engage in penile–vaginal vaginal intercourse.
- Women with SCI must remove indwelling catheters before engaging in penile–vaginal intercourse.
- Men with SCI who have subrapubic catheters cannot engage in penile–vaginal intercourse because the catheter can be pulled out.
- Most women with quadriplegia who have complete lesions would not need lubricants for penile–vaginal intercourse because reflexes provide adequate vaginal moisture.
- It is necessary for the able-bodied partner to assume the dominant position during penile–vaginal intercourse.
- The technique of a woman placing a man's flaccid penis into her vagina and manipulating an erection is known as the "semen-squeeze."
- When a man with SCI ejaculates, he will experience orgasm.
- If the man with SCI can ejaculate, he is likely to be fertile.
- Caesarean sections are necessary in women with SCI because their uterine muscles will no longer contract.

SOURCE: Reprinted from *Physical Therapy* 1979, *59:*397, with the permission of the American Physical Therapy Association.

splanchnic pelvini nerves to the penis. Erection can be psychologically or reflexly induced.

Cortical afferent stimuli, especially from the thalamic and limbic systems, facilitate the psychic stimulation in the sexual response cycle. Light touch and pressure, important in the excitement stage of the sexual response in both men and women, are conducted via the pudendal nerve and sacral plexus.

Spinal cord injuries are divided into two categories, quadriplegia and paraplegia. *Quadriplegia* is an injury to the cord above the level of T_4 and causes paralysis of all four extremities. *Paraplegia* is an injury to the cord below the T_4-level and results in paralysis of the lower extremities. Injuries are further divided into upper and lower motor neuron lesions. These are subdivided into complete and incomplete lesions. The number of nerve fibers that are severed in the cord determines whether the injury is complete or incomplete. The location of the injury determines whether it is an upper motor neuron or lower motor neuron injury. An *upper motor neuron* (UMN) injury is characterized by a loss of voluntary function and an increase in muscle spasm and hyperreflexia as a result of injury to the cord itself. The reflex arcs are intact but are no longer connected to the control centers, the brain and spinal cord. Such injuries are found above the L_1 vertebral level. *Lower motor neuron* (LMN) lesions occur below the T_{12} level. Lower motor neuron injuries involve the S_2, S_3, S_4 nerve roots, not the spinal cord, and affect bowel, bladder, and sexual functioning. LMN injuries are characterized by muscle flaccidity and hyporeflexia.

SPINAL CORD INJURY IN MEN

Generally, the higher the cord lesion, the more likely the chances are that the client will experience both reflexogenic and psychogenic erections (Figure 16.1). For *reflexogenic* erection, the man must have direct local stimulation of the glans penis. The majority of men with UMN lesions can experience this erection at any time, day or night, but the erection will be of such short duration that intercourse is impossible (Comarr & Gunderson, 1975). When the man is able to have a *psychogenic erection,* it occurs because impulses from the brain sometimes bypass the injured part of the spinal cord and are conducted via the autonomic nervous system (Woods, 1979). In *psychogenic erection,* there is arousal as a result of such mental processes as fantasy and imagery. Men can have psychogenic erections and yet not have reflexogenic erections. In the spinal-cord-injured person, erections of the penis can occur as a response to cerebral stimuli transmitted via the autonomic nervous system. Genitopelvic and cerebro-cognitional eroticism can function independently of one another.

In order to evaluate the sensory components of the pudendal nerves and the possibility that the man has intact sacral segments, several tests are performed. These tests include touch, pressure, and pinprick on the scrotum, penis, and penile skin as well as anal tone and the bulbocavernosus reflex. If all are normal, it is presumed that there are intact S_2, S_3, S_4 segments, which implies reflexogenic erection (Klompus, 1980).

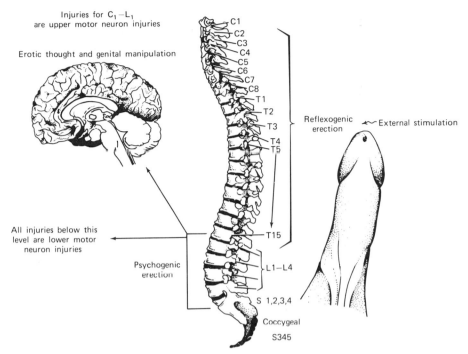

Injuries for C₁–L₁ are upper motor neuron injuries

Erotic thought and genital manipulation

All injuries below this level are lower motor neuron injuries

Psychogenic erection

Reflexogenic erection

External stimulation

C1 C2 C3 C4 C5 C6 C7 C8 T1 T2 T3 T4 T5 T15 L1–L4 S 1,2,3,4 Coccygeal S345

Figure 16.1. Reflexogenic and psychogenic erections. Drawn by Jane M. Egan, M.S.N., and James Lingeman, M.D. For more details concerning complete or incomplete lesions, see Table 16.2.

Stabilization of the cord injury cannot be fully determined until at least six months after the injury.

For seminal emission and ejaculation to occur, it is essential that the sympathetic nervous system at T_{11} to T_{12} cord level be intact and that the sensory pathways at the S_2 through S_3 nerve roots also be intact. The process of *seminal emission* includes peristalsis of the smooth muscles of the vas deferens, seminal vesicles, and prostate, which leads to deposition of sperm and seminal fluid into the posterior urethra. *Ejaculation* is the expulsion of the ejaculate (sperm and seminal fluid) brought about by contractions of skeletal muscles, especially the lower pelvic muscles, the urethra, and the penis. Additionally, mucus production, which begins in the excitement stage, is necessary for sperm life and mobility as well as for enhancing comfort during intercourse. Parasympathetic pathways at S_2 and S_4 nerve roots must be intact for successful mucus secretion in both men and women (Table 16.2). Neurologic injury can interfere with the process of emission, ejaculation, and mucus production depending on the site of the neurological involvement.

Due to autonomic denervation, reflex emission of ejaculate may be dribbling in nature and true ejaculation may not occur, because of lack of muscle power for ejaculation. Also, there may be retrograde ejaculation.

If the man is fertile but unable to ejaculate effectively, prostatic massage or electrical simulation can be used to obtain semen for artificial insemination of his sexual partner.

Sterility in the man occurs as a result of loss of testicular temperature regulation secondary to autonomic denervation or as a result of hormonal disturbances.

If impotence is present secondary to parasympathetic denervation, there are other means of helping the spinal-cord-injured man to perform sexually. A new method of treatment is the penile prosthetic implant. Two implantable devices are available (see Chapter 14).

SPINAL CORD INJURY IN WOMEN

Spinal-cord-injured women, regardless of the level of injury, experience no menstrual period for about six months, but it then spontaneously resumes. In about 50% of young women, the menstrual period is not interrupted. If there was menstrual irregularity before the injury, sometimes the menstrual period becomes regular after the injury. If the woman is approaching menopause or is in menopause, she will probably not continue to menstruate after the injury.

If the woman is still fertile, the use of contraceptives is necessary. The pill is contraindicated because of the risk of blood clotting or other neurologic sequelae. Intrauterine devices are not recommended because of the spinal-cord-injured woman's inability to feel pain. In many instances, contraception is left to the woman's partner.

Women with spinal cord injuries can experience orgasm if there is residual innervation in the pelvis. They may experience some frustration because of the lack of physical sensations but most women seem to prefer allover body touching, especially about the breasts, neck, and ears, which are especially sensitive to sexual arousal. Muscle spasms may cause problems during arousal but can be managed by medications, positioning, or elimination of visual distractions.

Women with denervation of pelvic structures can experience orgasm through the use of sexual fantasy. Indeed, many spinal-cord-injured women use sexual fantasy to enhance sexual arousal.

SCI women have no apparent interference with fertility and are capable of becoming pregnant whether they are paraplegic or quadriplegic. Most are able to have vaginal delivery and do not need a caesarean section unless there are anatomic abnormalities or other physiologic problems. Women whose lesions are above T_{10} have a painless labor, but contractions are normal. Women with lesions below T_{10} experience normal sensations of pain during labor and may have increased muscle spasms and ankle clonus during labor.

In women with an injury about the level of T_4, autonomic dysreflexia problems are likely to occur during the final stage of labor. These problems can be overcome by means of the administration of beta adrenergic receptor blocking drugs. However, such a complication must be carefully monitored to prevent cardiac arrythmias, intercranial bleeding, and extreme hypertension.

All spinal-cord-injured women are able to breast-feed successfully and may exhibit the usual letdown reflex while nursing their babies. The characteristic joys, pleasures, and anxieties about breast-feeding are experienced by SCI women.

SEXUAL ACTIVITY FOR THE SPINAL-CORD-INJURED CLIENT

Preparation

For people who are disabled, sexual activity requires planning. Certain preparations must be made in relation to bowel and bladder control. If the disabled person has a suprapubic catheter, the catheter should be securely taped to the abdomen. If an ileal diversion is the means for urinary control, it is necessary that the ileostomy appliance be checked to see that it is securely adhered to the skin. The drainage tubing from the appliance should be taped to the abdomen to prevent dislodging the apparatus. For those SCI clients who use intermittent catheterization or who crede' the bladder (emptying the bladder by applying pressure to the lower abdomen directly over the bladder area), it is important to empty the bladder before any sexual activity.

If a Foley catheter is worn, it can either be left in place or removed before intercourse. In the man, the catheter may be bent and folded along the shaft of the penis, where it will cause no harm to his partner, as the vagina easily accommodates the penis with the catheter folded in this way. Any lubricant that is water soluble can be used when the catheter is in place. It is important that caution be used during the act of intercourse so that the catheter does not pull out of the bladder.

The routine used for bowel care is usually sufficient to prevent any problem. Accidents can occur, however, if the bowels are full or partially full, and a discussion of the possibility of such an accident is appropriate before intercourse. The discussion should include the expression of feelings and decisions made about how the partners will deal with the accident, so that sexual activity is not totally disrupted.

If spasticity is a problem, medications to prevent its occurrence may be taken in advance so that the drug effect is at its height when needed. For

Table 16.2. Paraplegia and Quadriplegia

Lesions	Possible effects on sexual functioning	Presumed pathogenic mechanism	Accompanying common problems
Lesions are divided into	Erection (reflexogenic). Occurs as a result of external stimulation applied below the level of spinal cord lesion (generally to some area in pelvis or pelvic organs). Reflexogenic erection occurs more often in those people with complete upper-motor-neuron lesion at any level, with maximal evidence at the cervical level.	In absence of sacral cord function, reflexogenic erection is believed to originate from thoracic lumbar segments of cord. Psychogenic erection only experienced when lesion is below 12th thoracic vertebra (T12). When lesion is below T5 to T6 (and complete), erection is absent and probably due to vascular insufficiency of cord	Low levels of muscular strength spasticity
Upper motor neuron complete			Muscular contracture
Upper motor neuron incomplete			Incontinence
			Chronically infected testes
Lower motor neuron complete			Retrograde ejaculation
			Social isolation
Lower motor neuron incomplete	Erection (psychogenic). Erection achieved through the use of either erotic thought or direct bodily and/or genital manipulation. Psychogenic erection may occur with incomplete lesion.		Depression (lower androgen supply)
			Loss of self-esteem
			Altered body image
			Performance anxieties
	Ejaculatory difficulties (reported ejaculation occurs in 7–27%. Higher incidence of ejaculation in lower lesion)	Absence of sacral cord function, pudendal nerve, and sacral plexus needed for ejaculation	Injury above T4 may cause hyperreflexia headaches from rise in blood pressure during sexual activity

Infertility (males)   Reflex emission may be dribbling in nature and lack projected power for impregnation

Inability of body to control temperature in scrotum to produce sperm (electroejaculation sometimes used to obtain semen for artificial insemination if sperm are normal)

Fertility (females unchanged)

Orgasmic response is usually changed   Orgasm achieved if there is some residual pelvic innervation or if patient has reassigned sensation from a neurologically intact portion of the body to the genitalia and experience orgasm in a fantasy. Many report this type of orgasm is satisfying and leads to resolution of sexual tension

SOURCE: T. H. Anderson & T. Cole, Sexual counseling of the physically disabled, *Postgraduate Medicine*, 1975, Copyright © 1975 by McGraw-Hill, Inc. Used with permission.

some men, spasticity may be a welcome adjunct to obtaining penile erections, however. In such cases it would be unadvisable to take any medications to decrease spasticity.

The spasticity experienced by the SCI man and woman affects the selection of the position for intercourse. The sexual partners may need to experiment to find the best position—the one that will either decrease spasticity or prevent it from being a problem. Some SCI clients find that moderate exertion or exercise before sexual activity may help decrease spasticity. For some SCI clients, the use of a water bed is indicated, because body movements are amplified and spasticity seems to be lessened with this kind of bed (Rabin, 1979; Mooney, Cole, & Chilgren, 1975).

General Techniques

Sexual activity is most enjoyable when the sexual partners are mentally and physically relaxed. It is important that the time for sexual activity be chosen when there is less chance of distraction and both partners are relaxed. Because it is difficult for the partner of the SCI person to assume the role both of caregiver for bowel and bladder and of sexual partner and lover, it may be helpful to arrange for an outside person to attend to the nursing needs. Such people as visiting nurses, aides, or family members may assist with that care.

Listening to music, using soft lights, reading sexy books together are all means of setting the atmosphere for sexual activity. For some people, taking a shower together not only helps to relax the SCI person but it also heightens receptivity because of cleanliness.

If the SCI partner is unable to undress or to remove an appliance, it may be necessary to ask the able-bodied partner to assist in such preparation. Talking together and touching in a sensuous way while undressing may bring more comfort and fun to such activities.

The able-bodied partner can position him or herself in such a way that the SCI partner can experience pleasurable touching and feeling. Stroking the partner's breasts, vagina, or penis, either one at a time or simultaneously, can provide a stimulating massage. Such massage can be done with the hands or with a battery powered stimulator. (Many types of stimulators are available on the market.) Many sexual partners find that it is fun and exciting to experiment with various body oils. If the partners choose to use oral–genital stimulation, sensations are enhanced by licking or sucking each other on various parts of their bodies. Some SCI individuals find that they develop new erogenous zones or heightened sensations in areas just above the level of the spinal cord injury. These areas include the nipples (men and women), the neck, the ears, the shoulders, or the rectal area. Finding out where each partner can be turned on can be fun as well as rewarding for both sexual partners.

Specific Techniques for Men

Although it is not necessary for the man to have an erection for successful sexual functioning, some SCI men feel the need to have an erection. The partner can manipulate the penis with a hand or by any other means that is comfortable for the couple to help achieve an erection. Some men find that use of a vibrator stimulates an erection. For others, stimulation around the rectal area, either by kissing or by using a vibrator, will stimulate an erection. It is necessary that the patterns of rhythm and pressure of stimulation be continued during sexual activity to prevent loss of erection. For some men, the occurrence of spasticity or a change in position will cause the loss of an erection, so that must be attended to during the sexual activity. For some men who cannot maintain an erection long enough to promote intromission, the condom can be stretched around the base of the penis and held with stretchable tape. This maintains engorgement and prevents detumescence. It may be that masturbation by the SCI man by himself or with his partner may be a means of finding new and different ways of being sexually expressive without necessarily maintaining an erection.

For men who desire penile–vaginal intercourse, the technique of "stuffing" can be used. This technique involves having the man tuck his flaccid penis into the partner's vagina. As the woman voluntarily contracts her pubococcygeus muscles, she can hold the penis in her vagina and often cause a reflex erection by the combination of her hip motion and vaginal muscle action.

The man can have a fantasized orgasm by mentally transposing feelings from specific sensory areas to the sexual parts. Guided imagery and fantasy of preinjury sexual functioning can be used to achieve orgasm in this manner.

The paraplegic man can use the on-top position by doing pushups with the arms and can achieve a downward thrusting motion by rocking or shifting his weight back and forth. If his partner assumes the on-top position, however, she will have more freedom for hip and pelvic movement. The able-bodied partner will also be more comfortable not having to support the weight of the injured partner.

Oral–genital sex can be effectively performed either in bed or in the wheelchair. The partners may find that this technique is the only means that the SCI man has to bring his partner to orgasm.

Specific Techniques for Women

The SCI woman may find it satisfying to have her genital area stimulated digitally or with a vibrator. She may find that mutual masturbation with her partner may be the most satisfying activity for her. For women who do not have vaginal sensation but have heightened sensation in the breasts, the neck, the ears, fantasy and imagery may help to produce lubrication and orgasm.

Many women are concerned about their attractiveness and their ability to perform sexually. They are capable of being the aggressor in sexual activity and may assume either the on-top or on-bottom position. They may need a greater amount of time than they did before the injury to arrive at satisfaction, but they can achieve as much satisfaction as able-bodied women.

Many women enjoy being held, petted, and touched, and they must be allowed time for sensory input. SCI women need to communicate to their partners what is stimulating and what causes pain. They may find that masturbation and self-exploration can give them knowledge about themselves.

While some women may experience pelvic sensation, others may attain more arousal by stimulation of the breasts, neck, or upper body at the time of penile intromission. For some women, a change in position may provide the pressure needed for adequate clitoral stimulation. This, plus breast stimulation, may lead to orgasm.

Penile penetration, even with a Foley catheter in place, should not be prohibited. If the woman cleans her catheter and handles it properly, her partner should not be exposed to any infection.

Some women experience increased sexual drive just before or during the menstrual period. It is useful for the partners to discuss their feelings about sexual activity during menstruation and to proceed accordingly.

Some women may prefer oral–genital sex exclusively, as it gives them more satisfaction and allows greater opportunity for orgasm. Some homosexual women prefer oral–genital sex rather than mutual masturbation because of the involvement of both partners.

Finally, the SCI woman can achieve multiple orgasms and thus great degrees of sexual satisfaction. Whatever means are used for sexual enhancement and sexual enjoyment, the woman can be a positive, contributing partner.

THE ROLE OF THE NURSE AS EDUCATOR-COUNSELOR

The nurse caring for SCI clients is often involved in bathing them, assisting with activities of daily living, or establishing bowel and bladder routines. This care includes touching, looking at, and being with the SCI person. During this interaction, SCI clients may show anxiety or concern about sexuality and sexual functioning. The SCI man may flirt with the female nurse, make sexual comments, tell sexy jokes, or ask personal questions about the nurse's sexual life. He may make such remarks as "I'll never be the same man again," "Guess my pretty face won't matter to anyone anymore," "I bet you're a foxy lady," "Does your boyfriend lay you?" "Are you AC or DC?" The nurse can use these remarks to initiate open discussion about sex and sexuality.

In helping the SCI client to cope with the alterations in body image that have occurred, the nurse must remember that sexual intercourse is part of being sexual and not the goal to attain in a person's sexuality. The significance of being loved, being man or woman, worker or provider, giver or receiver, has greater significance for the SCI client. The role of the nurse is that of educator-counselor, and the nurse can be an effective force in helping SCI clients realize their full potential as human beings with satisfactory sexual functions, productive sexual roles, and fulfilling sexual relationships.

The nurse as educator-counselor gathers information about the SCI client's attitudes and beliefs about sexual practices and relationships. This data includes:

1. Presence or absence of sexual relationship
2. Acceptability of alternative sexual expressions
3. Acceptability of masturbation
4. Responsibility for orgasm
5. Acceptability of artificial insemination
6. Acceptability of abortion
7. Attitudes about homosexual behavior
8. Acceptability of mechanical devices to enhance sexual expression.

The nurse must always consider the sexual concerns and specific sexual goals of the SCI client and his or her sexual partner when discussing sexuality or planning care. The nurse helps the SCI client and his or her partner to develop positive self-concepts in order to establish a meaningful, satisfying sexual relationship. The use of audiovisual aids (films, film strips) must always be accompanied by discussion. Visual aids without discussion are not effective and may even contribute to misunderstanding.

While caring for the SCI man, the nurse may observe that he is having a reflexogenic erection. In this situation, the nurse needs to recognize the wholeness and normalcy of such a physiologic reaction. Humor can be used appropriately. This may be an opportunity to encourage the SCI client to feel comfortable about asking questions. The nurse should give permission for the discussion. The nurse should always project a positive attitude about the client's sexual capabilities, or he may feel rejected, withdraw, and stop asking questions.

The role of the nurse as educator begins with information about how the level of cord injury and the extent of involvement of sacral nerve roots affects physiologic sexual functioning. The nurse also provides information about the degree of muscle spasticity, the involved sensory levels, and the amount of bladder and bowel control present. The client is informed that it will take approximately six months to determine the degree of sexual functioning he or she will have, although some indication of sexual functioning can be ascertained at the end of the period of spinal shock.

The SCI client may be grieving the loss of body functions, and the energy needed for this grief may consume the energy available for interest in other body functions, such as sex. Some SCI clients continue to use denial and feel that the loss of sexual functioning is not permanent. These people will not be interested in any discussion of sexual functioning and alternate life-styles. SCI clients may use indirect methods of indicating their concerns, such as nonverbal behavior or indirect questions.

The role of educator includes a discussion of the male and the female sexual response cycle. The nurse can encourage the use of thoughts, feelings, and fantasies to enhance sexual arousal. The nurse-educator must never assume that the SCI client is well informed about sexual anatomy and physiology and how the spinal cord injury has affected it. The nurse encourages the use of thoughts, feelings, or fantasies to enhance sexual arousal and gives specific information about techniques that can be used in sexual arousal.

As the SCI client copes with the impact of the alteration in body image, the nurse as counselor offers reassurance that sexual expression can be a meaningful part of life. Being in a wheelchair does not limit one's sexual attractiveness or ability to be a sexual partner. The nurse emphasizes that the alteration in body image does not change the capacity for emotional commitment or the responsibility for the giving and receiving of pleasure.

NURSING PROCESS

Client: Joseph Li, paraplegic, due to motorcycle accident one month ago.

Nurse: Jane Clayburgh, nurse on neurosurgical unit in a large teaching hospital.

Assessment

Subjective Data

"I was just coming back from a great party."
"My wife told me not to ride the motorcycle."
"She got mad at me and left the party early."
"We just bought a new house and I just changed jobs."
"We've been married one year and my wife wants a baby."
"We both want a baby—I can picture myself with my son."

"My wife and I really used to go at it—in bed was great—the greatest."
"I used to work out in the gym regularly. My physique is a turn-on."
"Can I—can we ever have that again?"
"What grabs you about your boyfriend?"

Objective Data

24 years old.
Married one year.
One-month post-SCI.
College graduate, computer programmer.
Wife college graduate, personnel manager at a local industry.
T_{10} injury, client in Minerva body jacket.
Comments on physical strength and sexual prowess.
Directs sexual remarks at nurse.
Seeks information about sexual functioning.

Nursing Diagnosis

Lack of information about sexual functioning related to alteration in body image due to spinal cord injury (T_{10}).

Planning

Listen attentively.
Provide atmosphere of acceptance.
Encourage expression of feelings.
Offer feedback of the client's expressed feelings.
Refrain from negative response to sexual remarks.
Confirm emotional response as appropriate and commonly experienced.
Explore client's perception of altered body image on sexual functioning, sex role, and sexual relationship.
Explore client's perception of altered body image on occupational role.
Explore client's perception of altered body image on reproductive capabilities and role of parent.
Explain the anatomy and physiology of the male and female sexual response cycle.
Explain how T_{10} injury affects the sexual response cycle.
Encourage expression of feelings with wife.
Advise that significant person express love and acceptance of one another.
Indicate availability for further information about preparation for and techniques of sexual activity.
Encourage involvement of wife in further discussion of sex and sexuality.

Implementation

Initiate discussion about sexual functioning with wife.

Express feelings of love and acceptance.

Share information about male and female sexual response cycle.

Share information about how T_{10} injury affects sexual functioning in relationship.

Encourage mutual expression of feelings.

Encourage mutual decision making.

Request that wife be included in future discussion of sexual function, role, and relationship.

Explore with wife significance of pregnancy and role of parent.

Explore with wife significance of occupational role of husband.

Make appointment with nurse-counselor.

Evaluation

Reports satisfaction with information obtained.

Reports counseling session supportive of coping with change of sexual and occupational role.

Describes male and female sexual response cycle.

Identifies changes in sexual response cycle due to T_{10} injury.

Requests information about preparation for and techniques of sexual activity.

ACKNOWLEDGMENT

The completion of this chapter was facilitated by the special assistance of Judith Alfred, Chief Librarian at VA Medical Center, Indianapolis, Indiana.

BIBLIOGRAPHY

Anderson, T. H., & Cole, T. Sexual counseling of the physically disabled. *Post Graduate Medicine,* 1975, *58,* 117–127.

Berkman, A., Weissman, R., & Frielich, M. Sexual adjustment of spinal cord injured veterans living in the community. *Archives of Physical Medicine and Rehabilitation,* 1978, *59,* 29–33.

Blanchard, M. G. Sex education for spinal cord injury patients. *Supervisor Nurse,* 1976, *7*(2), 20–26.

Bregman, S. Sexuality and the spinal cord injured woman. University of Maryland, Rehabilitation Counseling Department, 1975.

Bregman, S., & Hadley, G. Sexual adjustment and feminine attractiveness among spinal cord injured women. *Archives of Physical Medicine and Rehabilitation,* 1976, *57,* 448–450.

Burke, D. C., & Murray, D. D. *Handbook of spinal cord medicine.* New York: Raven Press, 1975.

Campbell, C. *Nursing diagnosis and intervention in nursing practice.* New York: Wiley, 1978.

Cole, T. M. Sexuality and physical disabilities. *Archives of Sexual Behavior,* 1975, *4,* 389–403.

Comarr, A. E., & Gunderson, B. B. Sexual function in traumatic paraplegia and quadriplegia. *American Journal of Nursing,* 1975, *75,* 250–255.

Comarr, A. E., & Vigue, M. Sexual counseling among male and female patients with spinal cord and/or canda equina injury, Part I. *American Journal of Physical Medicine,* 1978, *57,* 107–122.

Comarr, A. E., & Vigue, M. Sexual counseling among male and female patients with spinal cord and/or canda equina injury, Part II. *American Journal of Physical Medicine,* 1978, *57,* 215–227.

Comfort, A. (Ed.). *Sexual consequences of disability.* Philadelphia: Stickley, 1970.

Conine, T. A., Disher, C. A., Gilmore, S. L., & Fischer, B. A. Physical therapists' knowledge of sexuality of adults with spinal cord injury. *Physical Therapy,* 1979, *59,* 395–398.

Crewe, N., Athelstan, G., & Krumberger, J. Spinal cord injury: A comparison of pre-injury and post-injury marriages. *Archives of Physical Medicine and Rehabilitation,* 1979, *60,* 252–256.

Fitting, A. F., Salisbury, S., Davies, N. H., & Maychin, D. K. Self-concept and sexuality of spinal cord injured women. *Archives of Sexual Behavior,* 1978, *7,* 143–156.

Higgins, G. E., Jr. Sexual response in spinal cord injured adults: A review of the literature. *Archives of Sexual Behavior,* 1979, *8,* 173–196.

Hogan, R. M. *Human sexuality: A nursing perspective.* New York: Appleton-Century-Crofts, 1980.

Klompus, W. H. Sexual function after surgery for lower bowel disease. *Medical Aspects of Human Sexuality,* 1980, *14,* 89–95.

Lazarus, R. S. Positive denial: the case for not facing reality. *Psychology Today,* 1980, *13*(6), 44–60.

LoPiccolo, J., & LoPiccolo, L. (Eds.). *Handbook of sex therapy.* New York: Plenum Press, 1978.

Mooney, T. O., Cole, T. M., & Chilgren, R. A. *Sexual options for paraplegics and quadriplegics.* Boston: Little, Brown, 1975.

Rabin, B. J. *The psychology of disability.* Santa Ana, Cal.: Joyce Publications, 1979.

Rabin, B. J. *The sensuous wheeler.* San Francisco: Multi Media Resource Center, 1980.

Weller, D. J. & Miller, P. M. Emotional reactions of patient, family, and staff in acute-care period of spinal cord injury: Part 1. *Social Work in Health Care,* 1977, *2,* 369–377.

17. Sexuality and Violence: Rape

Elizabeth M. Lion

VALUES CLARIFICATION EXERCISE

In our society, there are a number of different feelings and attitudes about rape. Rape is at times condemned as a monstrous criminal act, and at other times, it is sloughed off with a knowing wink as a minor skirmish in the battle of the sexes. The following questionnaire and suggested activities can help you assess what you know and what you believe about rape and to recognize the depth and intensity of your feelings about the rape victim and the rape offender.

For each of the following statements, circle whether you: SA—strongly agree; A—agree somewhat; U—are uncertain; D—disagree; or SD—strongly disagree. As you circle your answers, it might be helpful to remember there are no right or wrong answers—only an opportunity for you to assess what you know, believe, and feel about rape.

1. Rape is legally defined as carnal knowledge of a person by force against her will.

   SA   A   U   D   SD

2. Rape is an unplanned crime of passion.

   SA   A   U   D   SD

3. Rape is a premeditated crime of violence.

   SA   A   U   D   SD

4. Group rape represents sexual exploitation of women and is the result of deviant sexual behavior.

   SA   A   U   D   SD

5. Group rape is aggressive behavior in which the participants condone the use of force.

   SA   A   U   D   SD

6. Fifty-six percent of reported rapes occur outside the home.

   SA   A   U   D   SD

7. Most rapes involve black men and white women.

   SA   A   U   D   SD

8. A rape cannot be committed against a prostitute or a lesbian.

   SA   A   U   D   SD

9. A woman can avoid rape by staying at home.

   SA   A   U   D   SD

10. If a woman refuses to report a rape, it probably means she is dealing with feelings of guilt or shame.

    SA   A   U   D   SD

11. Single women between the ages of 17 and 24 are the most frequently reported rape victims.

    SA   A   U   D   SD

12. Women are raped because they ask for it by seductive dress or provocative behavior.

    SA   A   U   D   SD

13. Women with marginal reputations are raped more frequently than women with good reputations.

    SA   A   U   D   SD

14. Women are taught that rape is the most terrible thing that can happen to them.

    SA   A   U   D   SD

15. Women cannot be raped unless they want to be.

    SA   A   U   D   SD

16. Women fantasize rape and really want to be raped.

    SA   A   U   D   SD

17. Women actually enjoy rape.

    SA   A   U   D   SD

18. A woman's testimony that a rape has occurred is sufficient evidence that a rape did occur.

    SA   A   U   D   SD

19. Many women falsely accuse men of rape.

    SA   A   U   D   SD

20. Innocent men have gone to jail because hysterical women are motivated to invent stories about rape.

    SA   A   U   D   SD

21. Corroborative (confirming) evidence is needed to protect men against women who are likely to make false charges of rape.

    SA   A   U   D   SD

22. Rapists are members of lower-class subcultures.

    SA   A   U   D   SD

23. Rapists are violent, aggressive members of the community.

    SA   A   U   D   SD

24. Rapists are usually under the age of 30.

    SA   A   U   D   SD

25. Rapists are sexually unfulfilled men carried away by a sudden uncontrollable urge.

   SA A U D SD
26. Rapists are emotionally disturbed and therefore are not really responsible for their behavior.

   SA A U D SD
27. Rapists are always strangers to their victims.

   SA A U D SD

Examine your answers and ask yourself: What do I know about rape? What do I believe about the rape victim? The rape offender? How did I acquire my information? How did I come by my beliefs? Where are my strong feelings? How could my beliefs or knowledge influence the nursing care of a woman who states she has been raped?

You may now be interested in sharing with a peer or a group of peers what you have learned about your knowledge, beliefs, and feelings. You may decide to discuss these questions. What does the group know about rape? The rape victim? The rape offender? What does the group believe about rape? The rape victim? The rape offender? How is what is known and believed different? Similar? Is the group interested in more information about rape, the rape victim, or the rape offender? How would what the group knows and believes about rape influence the nursing care planned by the group of an alleged rape victim?

BEHAVIORAL OBJECTIVES

After completing this chapter, you will be able to

- Identify the historical origins of rape as a social and political issue.
- Compare the legal definition of rape with several personal and social definitions of rape.
- Summarize the incidence and reporting of forcible rape in 1978 in terms of classification, number of reported offenses, rates of increase, places of occurrence, and arrests.
- Discuss the legal aspects of corroboration and resistance standards for the crime of rape.
- Discuss the data given on rape as a sociocultural phenomenon.
- Describe the typology of rape.
- Discuss attitudes and beliefs commonly held by members of our society about rape and rape victims.
- Discuss the impact of rape on the family and significant others of the rape victim.
- Discuss the psychosexual aspects of the rape behavior of rape offenders.

- Discuss the psychologic patterns of response of rape victims.
- Summarize the biologic consequences of rape.
- Identify specific cognitive, verbal, and physical coping mechanisms of rape victims.
- Identify the five categories of rape crisis requests.
- Describe the characteristics of the phases of the rape trauma syndrome.
- Discuss age-specific stresses of the rape crisis victim.
- Identify the five categories of rape counseling requests.
- Discuss the origin, purpose, and goal of rape crisis centers.
- Explain the medico-legal care process of the rape victim.
- Describe the role of the nurse as a rape counselor.

HISTORICAL PERSPECTIVE ON RAPE

In the past decade, the women's movement has compelled our society to confront rape as a social and political issue. Women themselves have defined rape as a traumatic event with long- and short-term effects on the victim's physical, mental, and emotional well-being. Rape is now recognized as a national and local problem and as a personal crisis with profound psychosocial consequences. The treatment of rape victims includes medical and nursing intervention, counseling intervention, and legal intervention by the police and the courts. In some communities, hospital, law enforcement, and legal personnel have recognized their interdependent responsibilities and have coordinated their services to ensure effective and humanistic interaction with the rape victim.

LEGAL AND SOCIAL DEFINITIONS OF RAPE

Any discussion about rape must begin with an exploration of the definitions of rape, because the care, treatment, and counseling of the rape victim are dependent on the social meaning and personal understanding of the crime. Rape is defined legally as carnal knowledge of a person by force and against that person's will (Evrard, 1971). The specific terminology of the legal definition may vary, but in most jurisdictions three elements are necessary to constitute a rape: (1) sexual intercourse, (2) force, and (3) nonconsent. The slightest penetration by the male organ constitutes sexual intercourse; neither complete penetration nor emission is required. If the offender uses another part of the body (finger, tongue) or some other object (bottle, broomstick) for vaginal penetration, the crime is classified not as rape but as attempted rape, sodomy, or carnal abuse (MacNamara & Sagarin, 1977).

The concept of force includes the use of actual physical force to overcome the victim's resistance or the use of threats that result in compliance because of fear of death or grave bodily harm. The concept of nonconsent is subject to interpretation by assuming that certain social relationships—husband-wife, lovers, employer-employee—imply a willingness for a sexual relationship (Notman & Nadelson, 1976). Putting together the elements of cases that have been successfully prosecuted in the U.S. court system, Brownmiller (1975) defined rape as "the perpetration of an act of sexual intercourse with a female, not one's wife, against her will and consent, whether her will is overcome by force or fear resulting from the threat of force, or by drugs or intoxication; or when, because of mental deficiency, she is incapable of exercising rational judgment, or when she is below an arbitrary age of consent" (p. 368).

Griffin (1971) defined rape as experienced by women within a sociocultural context. She saw rape as "an act of aggression in which the victim is denied her self-determination", an act of violence that carries with it the threat of death, and a "form of mass terrorism" in which the victims are declared the cause of the rape because they are not respectable women or they are in the wrong place at the wrong time (p. 20). Women are taught that rape is the worst thing that can happen to them, and the awareness that some men rape provides sufficient threat to keep all women in a continual state of intimidation (Brownmiller, 1975). Bard and Ellison (1974) state that rape is the "ultimate violation of self," short of murder (p. 68). Hilberman (1976a) states that rape is an "act of violence and humiliation in which the victim experiences an overwhelming fear for her very existence as well as a profound sense of powerlessness and helplessness that few other events in life can parallel" (p. 436). Metzger (1976), herself a rape victim, defines rape as a "ritual of power" that degrades and dehumanizes (p. 408). She views rape as the ultimate expression of the negative attitudes toward and contempt for women of all ages. Abarbanel (1979) describes rape as a "violation of body integrity, a hostile invasion into the life sphere reserved for positive relationships," a threat to life, and a form of victimization that may leave the survivor stigmatized (p. 226)."

Rape is best understood as a crime against the person and a display of power and anger in the sexual mode. For the virgin, the prostitute, the aged woman, the child, the housewife, the divorcee, the lesbian, the personal experience is the same—a life-threatening crisis and a violent dramatization of power and dominance.

In these definitions, women are the rape victims and men are the rapists because that is the most common occurrence. In prisons, men frequently express violent aggression and exert power by raping other men, and women rapists of other women apparently exist. Rape is violence and a ritual of power directed at a person, and the victim, whether man or woman, experiences loss of control, helplessness, and fear.

INCIDENCE AND REPORTING OF RAPE

According to the Uniform Crime Report (F.B.I., 1978) an estimated total of 67,131 forcible rapes was recorded in 1978. Forcible rape continued, as in prior years, to comprise less than 1% of the total crimes reported and accounted for 6% of the total volume of violent crimes. The southern states recorded 34% of the total volume of forcible rapes; the western states reported 27%; the north central states 22%; and the northeastern states 17%. More rapes occurred in the summer, with August the peak month.

The number of forcible rape offenses in 1978 was up nearly 7% over 1977 and up 21% over 1974. During 1978, 40% of the forcible rapes occurred in cities with 250,000 or more inhabitants, a 6% increase in volume over the previous year. In the suburban areas, forcible rape offenses rose 5%, and the rural areas registered a 2% increase over 1977. In 1978, an estimated 60 out of every 100,000 females in this country were reported rape victims, a 5% increase over 1977 (F.B.I., 1978).

Total 1978 arrests for forcible rape increased 2% from 1977 figures and 8% from those for 1974. During 1978, 54% of the forcible rape arrests were of males under the age of 25, and 28% of the arrests were in the 18-to22-year age group. Forty-eight percent of the people arrested for forcible rape in 1978 were white, 48% were black, and all other races comprised the remainder (F.B.I., 1978).

Forcible rape has been recognized by law enforcement officials as one of the most underreported of all crimes. It is estimated that between 50% and 90% of rape cases go unreported (Amir, 1971; Schultz, 1975). Although rape is the fastest-growing crime against persons, it has the lowest proportion of cases closed by arrest (Center for Women Policy Studies, 1975). In 1970–1971, 950 rape cases were reported to the police in Denver, and only 41 cases were brought to trial (Giacinti & Tjaden, 1973). Although the Uniform Crime Report attributes the underreporting to the victims' fear of their rapists and their embarrassment about the rapes, it is also probably the painful, humiliating, and stigmatizing process involved in the effort to identify and convict rapists that discourages victims from reporting. Reporting a rape involves police interrogation and filing a report. Victims of rape report being leered at and harassed by the police they have called for help. Victims report that the sexually explicit questions asked seem irrelevant to finding the rapist (Weiss & Borges, 1973).

Rape is the only violent crime for which corroboration remains mandatory in many jurisdictions. *Corroboration* is defined as evidence independent of the mere assertion of the fact, not merely supporting evidence that might be used to strengthen the prosecutor's case but primary evidence required to prove that the offense occurred (Hibey, 1975). The assumption is that women make false charges of rape against men and that an additional protection for the accused is necessary. The consequence is that the testimony and the character of the victim become the central object of inquiry and not the rape itself. According to Slovenko (1973) and Brownmiller (1975), the moral character of the victim may be used as a defense in rape cases under the assumption that a woman of questionable sexual history is likely to have consented. Kalven and Zeisel (1971) found that a jury often weighs evidence concerning the woman's prior sexual behavior in reaching a verdict in charges of rape.

Once the rape is reported, the victim becomes involved in a complex legal process over which she has little control, for it is the state, not the victim, that brings the charges. Consent is usually the primary factor in determining the guilt of the accused. Most laws demand a high degree of resistance from the rape victim. In a charge of robbery, it is understood that the property was taken from the person without his or her consent, and there is no need to prove that fear of death or grave bodily harm was involved. Although some people successfully resist robbery, others are killed in the attempt, so no one is urged to fight a robber. Even a person who wants to resist and is trained to fight may be unable to do so when confronted with a situation that he or she perceives as dangerous (Center for Women Policy Studies, 1975).

Increasing public awareness has resulted in some states amending laws concerning mandatory corroboration. Resistance standards have been revised to be dependent on reasonable fear, and laws prohibiting the use of information about the victim's prior sexual behavior, except under specific circumstances, have been enacted. Such changes eliminate the distinctions between victims of rape and victims of other crimes and may increase the number of sexual assaults reported (Gates, 1975; Wood, 1975).

SOCIOCULTURAL CONTEXT OF RAPE

Amir (1971) studied 646 rape victims and 1,292 rape offenders through police records in Philadelphia. The victims varied in age from infants to old women, but most of them were in the 15-to-24 age group. The median age of the rapists was 23, but the 15-to-19 age group was the most likely to commit rape. The majority of the rapes reported were intraracial, with the victims and the rapist of the same race.

The Philadelphia study reported that 56% of all rapes occurred in the home, 18% occurred in open spaces, 11% occurred in other indoor locations, and 15% occurred in automobiles. Three-quarters of the rapes involved one or two assailants—single rape 57%, pair rape 16%—with group rape (three or more assailants) comprising 27% of the cases. Of the total number of rapes, 71% were planned in advance and only 16% could be considered unplanned. Group rapes were planned in 90% of the cases and single rapes in 58% of the cases. In only half of the cases was the rapist a stranger to the victim; the remainder included casual acquaintances, neighbors, boyfriends, family friends, and relatives.

Amir (1971) found that physical force was present in 86% of cases, the remainder involving various kinds of nonphysical force, such as coercion and intimidation, with or without weapons. He found that rape offenders tended to be young members of a subculture in which masculinity is expressed by displays of aggression. Rape was carried out not for sexual satisfaction but as an antisocial act to demonstrate group membership.

TYPOLOGY OF RAPE

Groth, Burgess, and Holmstrom (1977) analyzed descriptions of rape from accounts of 133 convicted rapists and 92 adult rape victims in order to develop a typology of rape. The investigators reported that in all cases of forcible rape three components are present: power, anger, and sexuality. They found that either power or anger dominates and that rape is not an expression of sexual desire but the use of sexuality to express power and anger.

The researchers identified two major categories of rape: power rape and anger rape. In power rape, the offender seeks power and control over his victim through intimidation by means of a weapon, physical force, or threats of bodily harm. Rapists who fall into the power-rape category can be subdivided on the basis of whether the major goal is assertion or reassurance. The power-assertive rapist regards rape as an expression of his virility, mastery, and dominance. He commits the offense to resolve doubts about his sexual adequacy and masculinity. By placing a woman in a helpless, controlled position in which she cannot refuse or reject him, he attempts to salvage his foundering sense of adequacy.

In anger rape, the rapist expresses anger, contempt, and hatred for his victim by beating her, sexually assaulting her, and forcing her to perform or submit to additional degrading acts. Rapists who fall into the anger-rape category can be subdivided into two groups on the basis of whether or not the degradation of the victim represents conscious rage or pleasure on the part of the rapist. The anger-retaliation rapist commits rape as an expression of his hostility and rage toward women. His motive is revenge and his aim is degradation and humiliation. The anger-excitation rapist derives pleasure, thrills, and excitement from the suffering of his victim. He is sadistic, and his aim is to punish, hurt, and torture his victim. In the total of the cases studied, 65% were power rapes and 35% were anger rapes. The investigators concluded that "rape is a sexual behavior in service of nonsexual needs and, in that sense, is clearly a sexual deviation" (p. 1239).

SOCIETY AND RAPE VICTIMS

Jones and Aronson (1973) tested the hypothesis that a socially respectable person is seen as being at fault in a crime in which he or she was the victim. This so-called just-world hypothesis is based on two assumptions: that individuals believe people deserve what they get and get what they deserve, and that the more respectable the victim, the greater the need to attribute fault to his or her actions since it is more difficult to attribute fault to his or her character. The study subjects were 234 undergraduate men and women at the University of Texas. The students were presented with a written account of a rape. They were asked to recommend a prison term for the rapist and to rate, on a 21-point scale, the extent to which the victim might have been at fault. The description of the victim in the cases varied as to whether the victim was a virgin, a married woman, or a divorcee, and the crime was sometimes described as rape and sometimes as an attempted rape.

The results supported the investigators' predictions that when the victim of the rape was a married woman or virgin (most respectable), more fault was attributed to her than when the victim was a divorcee. When sentencing the rapist, the group assigned a significantly longer prison term to the person who had raped the married woman than the divorcee. The investigators explained the result in view of the belief that injuring a highly respectable person is a more serious crime than injuring a less respectable person. The investigators also offered the explanation that as the consequence of a crime becomes more severe, the greater the need is to attribute fault to the victim. Because the rape of a married woman may be seen as affecting her husband and the family, there may be need to attribute more fault to her. There was no significant difference between the fault attributed to a victim when the rape was actual or when the rape was attempted. Apparently only the character of the victim determined the perception of how much fault the victim had in the crime. Although the perception of how much the victim suffered might have determined the prison sentence for the rapist, it did not determine the fault attributed to the victim. There were no sex differences in these data. Women were just as severe as men in attributing fault to the victim.

In his study of victims of violent crime and society's attitudes toward victims, Symonds (1975) found a marked reluctance and resistance to accept the innocent or accidental nature of victim behavior. Such questions as "Didn't you know this neighborhood is dangerous to walk in after dark?" "Did you have your door locked?" or "Why didn't you scream?" imply that the victim could have prevented or avoided her injuries.

Symonds sees this early response to victims as a basic need for all people to find a rational explanation for violent crimes. Exposure to violent and irrational behavior makes one feel helpless, and the belief that the victim has done or neglected to do something that contributed to the crime makes one feel less helpless. Questions about the cause of the crime are directed toward the victim, since the criminal is not available for questioning.

Symonds also studied the roots of the word "victim." It originally meant a beast selected for sacrifice, and the word is closely tied to the concept of the scapegoat. The word *victim* has unpleasant associations, and people generally are reluctant to associate or be identified with victims. As a result, people develop an illogical, ritualistic defense against being a victim: "If you act good, nothing bad will happen to you. Therefore, if something bad does happen to you, you were not acting good. If you act right, nothing wrong will happen; if something wrong happens, therefore, you were not acting right." In general, this belief explains why victims who fight back seem to obtain greater social acceptance than victims who follow society's rules and comply with the criminal's demands. This double-bind attitude is particularly evident toward victims of rape.

When rape victims discuss the way the community responded to their plight, seeming indifference is their most common complaint, and it is frequently directed toward the police. Symonds (1975) contends that the victim's expression of distress is heard by the listener as a demand that something be done as well as a criticism that the listener failed to protect the victim from the crime. The seeming indifference on the part of the police denies the victim the comfort she may have expected and also denies the victim's criticism that the police have failed to do their job of protecting her from the crime.

Symonds concludes that when a person suffers an injury from a criminal, that person is a victim of a crime; and when society responds by ignoring, excluding, and even accusing the victim of contributing to the crime, that person then becomes a victim of society. This contradictory attitude of society results in the victim feeling isolated and helpless and part of a hostile world. The growing awareness that anyone can be a victim of a violent crime has caused society to become more sympathetic to the victim. Any effort made to help the victim and reduce the feelings of isolation and helplessness also reduces his or her secondary psychologic trauma.

IMPACT OF RAPE ON FAMILY AND SIGNIFICANT OTHERS

Medea and Thompson (1974) and Brownmiller (1975) recognize that the attitude about rape and the reaction of the family and significant others to the rape are of great significance to the victim. One of the first concerns of the victim is whether or how to tell her husband, parents, boyfriend, or lover about the rape. Because of preconceived notions about rape and the role of the victim in rape, the significant people in the victim's life may isolate and reject her (Hilberman, 1976b). Many families decide to keep a rape a secret in order to protect both the victim and the family, but the unresolved feelings and issues may become a problem for the family and the victim at a later date (Peters, 1977).

Husbands often divorce their wives after rape (Brownmiller, 1975; McCartney, 1980). Husbands are often inconsiderate and rejecting, misplacing their anger at the rapist on to their wives. Some husbands see their wives as soiled and sexually undesirable and feel disgust. Some husbands suspect that the wife was deliberately unfaithful. Others blame the victim for not resisting enough, and still others feel that she has overreacted to a simple sexual act. In some cases, a husband, in an attempt to understand his wife's experience, will explore his own feelings, and the sharing of feelings may add stress to the marriage (McCartney, 1980).

To what extent the lack of support from significant others affects the rape victim is not clear, but it is clear that at a time of personal crisis the victim's usual support system may be disrupted.

RAPE OFFENDERS AND RAPE BEHAVIOR

Myths and misconceptions about rapists range from their being sexually unfulfilled men carried away by a sudden uncontrollable urge to their being competent men in search of sexual gratification. Some people even believe that rapists are usually innocent men "led on" by provocative women.

In a study of a sample consisting of 170 convicted rapists, Groth and Burgess (1977b) reported a relatively high rate of sexual dysfunction at some point during the sexual assault. Impotence, the most common type of sexual dysfunction, was experienced by 27 (16%) of the rapists. Some experienced "conditional impotence," being able to have an erection only after the victim stimulated him manually or orally or put up a struggle. Twenty-six (15%) reported retarded ejaculation (difficulty or failure to ejaculate during intercourse). Five (3%) reported premature ejaculation. In a general population of men seeking treatment for sexual dysfunction, Masters and Johnson (1970) reported impotence as the primary complaint and described retarded ejaculation as an infrequent complaint.

Practically none of the rape offenders reported similar physiologic dysfunction in their nonassaultive, consenting sexual relations. The dysfunction appears specific to the context or situation of rape. The medicolegal implications of the study suggest that although the presence of sperm can confirm the occurrence of sexual intercourse, its absence does not prove that intercourse did not occur, for the absence of sperm may be caused by sexual dysfunction on the part of the rapist. The evidence implies that, for the rapist, rape may be an unsuccessful or pathological act that reflects his emotional disturbance (Nadelson, 1977).

Abel et al. (1977) studied the components of rapists' sexual arousal in 20 male subjects. The erections of rapists and nonrapists were measured during audio descriptions of rape and nonrape sexual scenes. On the basis of these measurements, rapists could be separated from nonrapists because the rapists developed erections from listening to rape descriptions, whereas the nonrapists did not. The method also documented those rapists with the highest frequency of rape and those who injured their victims.

Using the subjects' histories, the investigators were able to describe a continuum along which were placed men who have displayed increasingly aggressive sexual behavior (Figure 17.1). Along the same continuum were also placed erection responses specific to these clinical histories, indicating a decreasing arousal from descriptions of mutually enjoyable intercourse and increasing arousal from purely aggressive cues. On the far right of the continuum was the nonrapist. Toward the left of the continuum was the rapist with a history of forcing himself on his victim when compliance was not forthcoming. Further to the left, the clinical histories progressed to the sadist category. This continuum, from right to left, changed as aggression served to suppress erections (nonrapists), only mildly suppressed erections (rapists), and was necessary to the development of erections (sadists). Descriptions of mutually enjoyable intercourse produced good erections in nonrapists and rapists but failed to generate arousal in sadists. Although the measurement of erection to various cues did not provide information about the etiologic factors in the development of rape behavior, it did provide an accurate measure of the behavior being examined—the disposition to rape.

Symonds (1976) suggested there was a need to study the rapists' goals and behavior in order to understand the psychologic responses of the rape victim. He classified criminals who rape into two major categories: compulsive rapists and predatory rapists. Compulsive rapists seek symbolic gratification of deep-seated unresolved sexual problems. Through an atmosphere of terror and implied violence, they made the victim "voluntarily" give herself to them. Some compulsive rapists demand utter submission, and any act of protest produces rage in the criminal with tragic consequences for the victim.

The second category is predatory rapists. They are impulsive people who have little or no emotional reserve. Frustration of their impulses brings on anger, rage, and acting out behavior. Because predatory criminals are primarily interested in ripping off the victim, when they rape they demand submission to their wishes. Unlike the compulsive rapist, the predatory rapist does not want the victim to talk to him. His intention is to strip the victim of her property and pride, to invade her body, and to remain anonymous. Predatory rapists rape after robberies and they often act in groups.

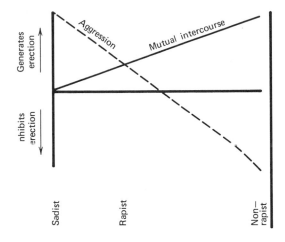

Figure 17.1. Hypothesized components of rapists' sexual arousal. Reprinted with permission from Able, G. G., Barlow, D. H., Blanchard, E. B., & Guild, D. The components of rapists' sexual arousal. *Archives of General Psychiatry,* 1977, *34,* 895–903. Copyright 1977, American Medical Association.

Symonds (1976) concluded that there is often a good deal of overlap in the categories—some compulsive rapists are also predators. The whole spectrum of mental and emotional illness is found in rapists. What all rapists have in common is their use of terror, intimidation, and violence to achieve the subjugation of the victim.

The main goal of most rapists is the acquisition of power, and it is generally agreed that most rapists are potential murderers. When asked about their motivations to rape, rapists mentioned several factors: (*1*) their difficulties in relating to women, (*2*) their general discomfort with meaningful interpersonal relationships, (*3*) their sense of inadequacy, and (*4*) their feelings of low self-esteem (Ryan, 1971). Most men who rape use alcohol or other drugs, act in the evening and on weekends, attack with physical force to daze or shock the victim, and are described by victims as hostile.

Groth and Burgess (1977a) obtained data on 133 convicted rape offenders of adult victims. In no case did the man have to rape for the purpose of sexual gratification. At least one-third of the offenders were currently married and engaging in regular sexual intercourse with their wives. Of those offenders who were not married, the majority were actively involved in sexual relations with one or more women and had access to prostitutes or other sexual outlets. The offenders did not appear to make any initial efforts to negotiate a consenting sexual relationship with their victims. Thirteen (10%) of the convicted offenders effected the assault through verbal threat alone, 24 (18%) through intimidation with a weapon, 52 (39%) through physical strength, and 37 (28%) through physical violence. Fifty-three percent of the offenders had at least one previous conviction for rape, 63% of the recidivists showed an increase in force and aggression during their assaults over time, and none showed a decrease. Fifty-three (40%) of the offenders appeared to manifest to various types of personality disorders. For 31 (23%) of the offenders, their sexual offenses constituted an exception to an otherwise noncriminal life history.. But for the majority of the offenders (102, or 77%), the rapes were but another aspect of multiple conflicts with the law, both sexual and nonsexual.

Groth and Burgess (1977a) conceptualize rape behavior as stemming more from the internal dynamics operating in the rapist rather than from external events occurring outside him. The rape offender is viewed as a psychologically disordered to dangerous person. Such a view may help to encourage more referrals to mental-health agencies as an intrinsic part of the rapist's rehabilitation.

PSYCHOLOGIC PATTERNS OF RESPONSE OF RAPE VICTIMS

The first significant clinical study of the responses of rape victims was reported by Sutherland and Scherl (1970). Their sample consisted of 13 social workers, ranging in age from 18 to 24 years, who were victims of rape while in their working environment. The women were seen within 48 hours of the rape in a community mental-health facility, and the psychologic healing process of each of the victims was followed by a therapist.

The investigators found in all the women a similar pattern that they described as a three-phase process. Phase 1, or the acute reaction, was characterized by signs of acute distress, including shock, disbelief, emotional breakdown, and disruption of normal behavior patterns. The victims were unable to talk about what had happened and were uncertain about telling those close to them, much less reporting the crime to the hospital or police. Guilt was experienced, and five victims delayed telling anyone about the rape or seeking legal or medical assistance. Those women who felt there was no seduction or willing compliance involved immediately phoned the police or went to a nearby facility. Some feared that poor judgment had precipitated the rape. The idea of notifying family, friends, and significant others and hearing their possible responses created great anxiety in the women. During this period of disruption, the victims were confronted with having to decide whether to press charges, the possibility of having to identify the assailant, anxiety about publicity, and the possibilities of becoming pregnant and contracting a sexually transmitted disease.

Phase 2, that of outward adjustment, began within several days to weeks after the rape. In an attempt to overcome her anxiety and to regain control, the victim returned to her normal life patterns. The victim behaved as though the crisis was resolved, thus reassuring herself and others that she needed no help. The investigators labeled this period "pseudo-adjustment" and believed that in it the victim manifests denial or suppression. The personal impact of what has happened is ignored in the interest of protecting the self and others, and the victims have very little interest in gaining insight through professional help during this phase.

Phase 3, that of integration and resolution, may come unrecognized. Depression was prominent along with the need to integrate the event with the victim's view of herself and to resolve her feelings about the rape and the rapist. Her earlier readiness to understand the man's problems is replaced by anger toward him for having "used" her and anger toward herself for in some way having permitted or tolerated this "use." During this period the woman may have obsessive thoughts about the assault, concerns about the influence of the rape on the rest of her life, and a real need to consult with a professional to resolve her conflicting feelings.

Symonds (1976) described the psychologic patterns of response of rape victims. The pattern of traumatic psychologic infantilism begins with shock and disbelief and is the first and immediate response of all people to sudden violence. When realization sets in, the vast majority of victims experience fright that borders on panic. With the panic there is a heightened distortion of perception and judgment. Most learned behaviors disappear, and the victim responds with the adaptive patterns of early childhood.

The behavior of the vast majority of women during their contact with rapists demonstrates the frozen-flight response of psychologic infantilism. The response looks like cooperative behavior: the victim may smile, even initiate acts, and may appear relaxed and calm. The frozen-fright response may confuse the rapist, the victim's family, her friends, the police, and even the victim herself. But the frozen-fright response has its roots in profound terror: The victim submits in order not to be killed. Because of frozen fright, rape victims make submitting signs to the rapist in order to inhibit his aggressive action. Because the rapist is alienated from the victim's needs, however, submitting gestures are generally ignored.

Many victims experience anger as well as fright. Fright and anger occurring at the same time may be dangerous to the victim if the rapist threatens imminent violence for noncompliance, however. As long as there is hope of survival, fright always overrides anger and submitting behavior occurs. When anger is incompletely submerged, Symonds (1976) states that passive-resistance patterns of a frightened, angry person develop. The victims cry, are slow to obey, and do not hear or seem to understand what is being demanded. Some verbal examples are: "Why do you want me to do this?"; "I'm pregnant"; "My mother just died"; or "You're a nice person. You wouldn't want to do anything you would be ashamed of."

Passive patterns of resistance are an attempt to stop the rapist's behavior by trying to induce guilt or appeal to the rapist's conscience. Although there have been reports that these responses have worked, generally they fail to stop the rape, and instead of making the rapist feel guity, they often make him angry.

Active patterns of resistance are directed to produce fear in the rapist, that is, fear of being hurt, caught, or exposed. This may stop the attack if done early in the contact. In active patterns of resistance there is no appeal to the rapist's inner feelings of conscience. It is a fight for survival. Sometimes the victim's belief that the use of force is imminent leads to active physical resistance. Active, physical, aggressive behavior is culturally and socially disapproved of, and this disapproval is so imprinted on women's behavior that even when they are specifically trained, some women cannot initiate aggressive physical defense, much less attack. Responding with anger usually requires the victim to ignore major aspects of being socialized as a woman (Queens Bench Foundation, 1976).

Symonds (1976) contends that what determines a rape victim's pattern of resistance, if any, is early life experiences. Those people with little or no exposure to violence in early life generally display passive resisting patterns, particularly verbal ones. If they do resist actively, they generally use the verbal response. Those from the lower socioeconomic class or those who have had early exposure to violence are more likely to employ physical patterns of resistance.

BIOLOGIC CONSEQUENCES OF RAPE

Physical Trauma

Burgess and Holmstrom (1973) reported on the physical trauma of 80 rape victims who came to Boston City Hospital. In the general physical examination of the rape victims, 147 marks of bruises or lacerations were visible on the head, face, throat, chest, abdomen, back, arms, and legs, with facial trauma and lacerations the most prevalent. During gynecologic examination, 57 more marks were found on the perineum, hymen, vulva, vagina, cervix, and anus with cervical, vulval, and perineal bruises the most frequent. Close to half the women were threatened with a weapon. Bruises to the body were made by the weapon or the rapist's hands or fists. Struggles on the ground often resulted in abrasions of the legs, arms, and back. Twelve of the 80 victims required medical, surgical, or orthopedic consultation in addition to x-ray services to confirm a secondary diagnosis. Eight of the 80 victims did not receive speculum/pelvic examinations. Copious vaginal bleeding required immediate vaginal packing and hospitalization of one victim. The hymen ring was intact and thus just a swab of the vaginal wall was taken from four clients. Two victims were not examined because of their pain and anxiety, and one client refused a speculum/pelvic examination. Ten of the 80 victims were raped during their menstrual periods and were further traumatized by the tampon being pushed deep into the vagina.

Hayman and Lanza (1971) studied the severe injuries connected with 2,190 females brought to medical examination in a general hospital in the District of Columbia. The age of the study population ranged from six months to 91 years, with the peak at ages 14 to 15 years. Eighty-five percent were black, although blacks comprised 67% of the estimated female population. Of the 82 clients classified as having severe physical injuries, 24 were admitted to the hospital. Six children and one adult were hospitalized for vaginal or perineal lacerations and one child and 16 adults for injuries such as abrasions, lacerations, fractures, and stab wounds. Fifty-eight women and girls required major treatment in the emergency room. Many hundreds required treatment for minor injuries. There were four proved instances of murder from physical assault, including rape, and three more in which rape was suspected.

Soules et al. (1978) studied 110 rape victims over a period of four months in Denver, Colorado. They found general physical trauma (bruises, lacerations, scratches) present in 45% (59) of the victims. General trauma was three times as common as genital trauma. Signs of genital trauma (hymenal tears, vaginal lacerations, perineal ecchymosis) were present in 13% (14) of the victims, and many victims were reported to have both types.

Woodling, Evans, and Brodbury (1977) examined the data from five studies of rape victims in Washington, D.C.; Dade County, Florida; and San Francisco and Ventura, California. Injuries in the form of large bruises, lacerations, minor fractures, or joint pain occurred in 10% to 46% of the reported cases. Major physical injuries, including fractures, subdural hematomas, cerebral concussions, skull fractures, and intra-abdominal injuries, that required hospitalization occurred in 4% to 15% of the rapes reported. Many of the more seriously injured victims have sustained their injuries after rather than during the rape. These studies prove that there is a significantly high incidence of extragenital and genital injury among rape victims.

SEXUALLY TRANSMITTED DISEASES

Sexually transmitted diseases, which may be acquired from the rapist, are a serious concern of the rape victim. The victim's risk of contracting gonorrhea is approximately 3 to 5%, of contracting syphilis about 0.25% (Abarbanel, 1979). In the sample studied by Hayman and Lanza (1971), there were 76 cases of gonorrhea, five cases of syphilis, one of whom was a 4-year-old child, and one case of lymphogranuloma venereum. Voight (1972), in his Copenhagen study, found acquisition of sexually transmitted disease in 0.8% of the total population of 650 women and children. Of the 418 girls under 15 years of age, there were three cases of gonorrhea (0.07%) and no cases of syphilis. Whatever the risk of sexually transmitted disease, the potential acquisition requires attention during the medical treatment of a rape victim.

Rape-Induced Pregnancy

Pregnancy is a potential consequence of rape. In their study population, Hayman and Lanza (1971) found 39 pregnancies preceding the rapes, and 13 subjects were found to be pregnant as a result of the rape. Induced abortion was performed on 10, and three carried to term. Weiss (1975) reported that there is about a 10% chance of conception for the victim on the day she ovulates and a 4% chance of conception if the rape occurs any other time during the menstrual cycle. Tietze (1960) reported that the risk from a single episode of unprotected intercourse is approximately 3 to 5% higher at midcycle that at other times.

If menstrual and contraceptive history and the occurrence of the assault indicate the client is at risk for pregnancy, the emergency preventive measures and the options available should be presented to her.

Vaginismus and Dyspareunia

Masters and Johnson (1970) discussed the onset of vaginismus (involuntary spasm or constriction of the musculature surrounding the vaginal outlet and the outer third of the vagina) subsequent to rape in three women. One woman became vaginismic after a gang rape that made extensive surgical repair of the vaginal canal necessary. Two women who were physically forced by male members of their families to provide sexual release for men they did not know became vaginismic as adults. Masters and Johnson noted that trauma initiating involuntary vaginal spasm can be either physiologic or psychological or both, and that forced sexual activity can have serious and long-lasting consequences.

Masters and Johnson reported on three women who experienced dyspareunia (occurrence of pain during intercourse) after gang-rape experiences. In all three cases, superficial and deep lacerations had been sustained throughout the vaginal barrel and other soft tissues of the pelvis. Included in the soft-tissue lacerations were tears of the broad ligaments sufficient to produce severe symptoms of dyspareunia. For years, each of the three women was told by medical authorities that the pain with intercourse was associated with the psychologic trauma of the gang rape. Before obtaining surgical repair of the broad ligaments, these three women underwent a combined total of 21 years of crippling dyspareunia.

COPING BEHAVIORS OF RAPE VICTIMS

The reported coping behaviors of 92 women diagnosed as having rape trauma were analyzed. Burgess and Holmstrom (1976) found that the victims of rape resorted to specific cognitive, verbal, and physical coping behaviors that occurred in four time phases: a period of early awareness of danger, the period just before the rape, the period during the rape, and the period just after the rape.

Some victims described an early awareness of danger as the threat of attack was perceived. The coping task was to react quickly to the warning. Their strategies included mentally assessing the situation and determining possible alternatives such as escape or keeping the man calm. Some employed verbal tactics and tried to talk themselves out of the situation. Physical actions included fighting and fleeing. Some victims were physically paralyzed and overpowered. Some were stunned and surprised because the rapist was known as a friend. Some were psychologically paralyzed—they blacked out or could think only of death.

At the moment of the actual rape, the victim realized that the sexual attack was inescapable and the coping task was to survive. Cognitively, victims often coped by directing their attention to some specific thought to keep their minds off the reality of the rape. Remaining calm was one strategy used so as not to provoke additional violence. Memorizing details about the rapist and recalling advice people had given on the subject of rape was helpful. Memories of previous violent situations provided alternatives for some. Praying for help decreased stress and tension. Compliance was a chosen strategy.

Victims combined verbal and affective responses by screaming and yelling. This tactic served both to relieve tension involuntarily and to deter the assailant. Several victims believed that talking with the rapist during the attack helped them avoid additional violence. Sarcasm was used, especially if that was the victim's usual style. Some victims tried to gain control of the situation by frightening the rapist, and the strategy was sometimes partially successful.

The victims reported that they physically struggled and fought with their assailants. Some victims quickly discovered that struggling and fighting were just what the rapist wanted.

Psychologic defense mechanisms were another way of coping. These included denial, disassociation, suppression, rationalization, and resignation.

Physiologic responses during the rape included choking, gagging, nausea, vomiting, pain, urinating, hyperventilating, and losing consciousness.

Immediately after the attack, the coping task was to escape from the rapist, and some victims concentrated on how to get help. Bargaining for freedom sometimes took place. The rapist sometimes apologized to gain sympathy or tried to persuade the victim not to tell. The victim coped by remaining silent or agreeing to the instruction or by promising not to tell. If the victim freed herself, she often felt mastery, because she had survived.

The identification of coping behaviors is pivotal in the case of the rape victim. As the victim recounts the rape, the nurse hears and acknowledges the victim's coping behaviors. With understanding, the nurse supports the victim's coping style so that the victim can see herself as a person who was able to do something in a highly stressful situation. Such recognition and confirmation is vital, for it provides the victim with positive expectations of her ability and capacity to restore herself to a pre-crisis level of functioning.

RAPE CRISIS REQUESTS

Rape is perceived by the victim as a life-threatening crisis. The work of Lazare et al. (1972) suggests that the nurse should approach the rape victim as a customer of emergency services with an immediate and legitimate crisis request. Requests are defined as the client's hopes and desires for help. With this approach, the nurse's initial responsibilities are to pay attention to the victim, regard the victim as a person of dignity and worth, and listen carefully for the victim's particular rape crisis request.

Analysis of the crisis request of 146 victims admitted to the emergency service of Boston City Hospital yielded five categories (Burgess & Holmstrom, 1974a):

1. Medical intervention: "I need a physician." The victims who made this request viewed the emergency services and hospital staff in a traditional medical role.
2. Police intervention: "I need a policeman." These victims saw the police as authorities in the traditional role of defending, supporting, and protecting the community against crime.
3. Psychologic intervention: "I need to talk to someone." These victims viewed the emergency service as providing both emotional support

and medical care and wanted to talk to someone about what had happened and requested a supportive person.

4. Uncertainty: "I'm not sure I want anything." These victims tended to be unsure about what to do, sought other opinions, and were swayed by the thoughts, feelings, and actions of other people. They seem to be gathering information and usually consented to someone accompanying them to the police station or hospital.

5. Control: "I need control." These victims arrived at the emergency service in an incoherent and distraught state. This group included people high on alcohol or drugs, the psychotic, and the mentally retarded. The victims were unable to verbalize their needs or wants and required management interventions until they were in better control of themselves.

When the nurse identifies and understands the rape victim's crisis request, an accepting and receptive communication pattern is established. When the nurse responds to the crisis request, the victim regains a sense of physical safety and assumes control over what has happened to her and what will happen to her.

RAPE TRAUMA SYNDROME

On the basis of their work with 146 rape victims, Burgess and Holmstrom (1974b) identified a rape trauma syndrome. The rape trauma involves two phases: (1) an immediate and acute phase in which the victim's lifestyle is completely disrupted, and (2) a long-term phase in which there is a reorganization process back to the precrisis level of functioning. The syndrome includes the physical, emotional, and behavioral reactions that occur as a result of the rape trauma.

The immediate and acute phase is characterized by confusion, disruption, and disorganization. The victims deal with invasions of privacy of person and personal space. The acute phase includes many physical symptoms: gastrointestinal irritability, changes in sleeping patterns, genitourinary discomfort, soreness, muscular tension, and exhaustion. Financial disruption occurs because of medical bills and loss of earnings. If there was a robbery, the victim grieves over her lost possessions. Family and friends who were supportive may withdraw to deal with their own feelings.

Emotional reactions include anxiety, fearfulness and minor mood swings. The emotional responses fall into two categories: an expressed style and a controlled style. In the expressed style, words are used to ventilate anger and fear, and crying is a form of nonverbal expression. The controlled victim appears calm and collected with little external evidence of distress, the apparent calmness reflecting disbelief and exhaustion. Some women have multiple responses. The primary reaction is fear of physical injury and loss of life; the primary defense is to block thoughts from her mind. Attempts to undo the event are reflected in fantasies of how the victim might have handled the situation differently and avoided the assault.

The acute phase lasts from a few days to a few weeks with gradual merging into the long-term reorganization process, which lasts from a few months to several years. It is characterized by reprocessing, reorganizing, and restructuring. Sleep disruption continues. Flashbacks, nightmares, and transitory phobias are common. Flashbacks occur at unexpected moments and the rape is seen mentally and experienced emotionally. Two kinds of nightmares occur. Whatever the content, in one nightmare the victim is helpless and powerless, and in the other the victim is in control and has mastered the situation (Burgess & Huntington, 1978).

Changes in life-style are prominent, with impaired level of functioning at work, home, and school. Many women feel the need to get away and move to another residence or city, whereas others are afraid to leave their homes and give up independence by returning to their families. Sexual fears are common, associated with a decline in interest in sex and withdrawal from the victim's sexual partner.

Victims need to recapitulate the rape and their reactions to it with significant others, and they find that some of these people are unable to listen, refuse to listen more than once, or show avoidance, fear, and hostility. If the victim decides on legal proceedings, it is during the preparation for the trial that she feels most isolated and lonely (Burgess & Huntington, 1978). Victims work at restructuring their relationships, reorganizing their lives, performing routine tasks, and resuming their occupational roles and responsibilities, although this is often an uneven course of action.

Two subdiagnostic categories of rape trauma syndrome are compounded reaction and silent reaction (Holmstrom & Burgess, 1975). In compounded reaction to rape, the victim experiences not only the symptoms described for rape trauma but also reactivated symptoms of previous behavior, such as a physical or psychiatric illness or a reliance on alcohol or drugs. In the second category, the silent reaction, various symptoms occur but without the victim's ever mentioning to anyone that she has been raped. The following symptoms should alert a nurse to the possibility of an earlier and unresolved rape: increased anxiety during history taking, reports of abrupt changes in relationships with men, distinct changes in sexual behavior and feelings about the self as a sexual being, and sudden onset of phobic reactions or nightmares.

The identification of a rape trauma syndrome provides a logical framework for the collection of biopsychosocial data about the rape victim for nursing diagnosis and the planning of nursing care during the acute and long-term phases of rape trauma.

AGE-SPECIFIC STRESSES OF RAPE CRISIS VICTIMS

The stresses the rape crisis victim faces include age-specific stresses that vary with her developmental stage. These life-stage considerations have been described by Notman and Nadelson (1976) and Burgess and Holmstrom (1974c). The young single woman may be sexually inexperienced and her encounters with men limited to the trusting, caring figures of her childhood or to high school dates. If the rape is this woman's first sexual experience, she is likely to be quite confused about the relationship between sexuality, violence, and humiliation. If she is going through the process of separating from her family and establishing an independent identity, the rape may disrupt her sense of adequacy and ability to care for herself. Relatives and friends may offer to care for her and, although they are supportive and reassuring, they may hinder autonomous growth. The integrity of her body is also at issue and is seen in her concerns about the pelvic examination, which may be a new experience and can be perceived as being another rape. The woman who has an ongoing sexual relationship may choose not to tell her partner because of fear that the rape might disrupt their relationship. Her silence may protect the relationship but leave her feeling anxious, guilty, and without support.

The divorced or separated woman is in a difficult position because her life-style, morality, and character are often frequently questioned by others. The rape experience may serve to confirm the victim's feelings of inadequacy about functioning in an independent manner. The woman with children must decide what, how, and when to tell them, because the event may be known in the school and in the community. The middle-aged woman will have concerns about her independence. She may already be in a crisis phase about her life role, with changes in her relationship to husband and children. Her husband may be in his own midlife crisis and may be less responsive and supportive of her emotional needs than he was formerly. The misconception that an older woman has less to lose by a rape than does a younger woman may seriously hinder the older woman's ability to resolve the crisis.

It is difficult to predict all the long-term needs of the rape victim. The feelings aroused may lead to behavior that seems out of character and puzzling. Some of the issues that reemerge in women at some later time are mistrust and avoidance of men, sexual disturbances, phobic reactions, and anxiety and depression, often precipitated by seemingly small events that symbolize the original trauma.

Woodling et al. (1977) concluded that no matter how brutal or demeaning the attack, the single most important determinant of eventual emotional health is whether a suspect is identified and successfully prosecuted. Those victims in cases in which a suspect was not identified or prosecuted have more phobic reactions, are more fearful of male strangers, and have more interpersonal problems after the rape.

RAPE COUNSELING REQUESTS

Burgess and Holmstrom (1974a) studied the counseling requests of 146 rape victims served by the emergency service of Boston City Hospital. During follow-up telephone contact, the crisis requests changed to counseling requests, and five categories were identified:

1. Confirmational concern: "It's nice to know you are available." These victims volunteered minimum information. They were satisfied that the counselor was concerned and available if needed. They tended to be guarded and controlled in their emotions and verbal responses. They did not ask advice or volunteer information about the degree of personal or social disruption the rape had caused.
2. Ventilation: "It helps to talk about this." These victims viewed the counselor as someone with whom to share the burden, and they felt relieved after talking. They usually talked spontaneously about the rape experience with strong focus on feelings. The counselor allowed the victim to talk freely and, when asked, could give the victim some assistance in gaining control of her life.
3. Clarification: "I want to think this through." The victims with this request specifically want to think through the crisis and settle it for themselves. They talk easily, answer questions in detail, ask questions, seek out referrals given, and are definitive in their actions.
4. Nothing wanted: "I don't need the counseling services." These victims were not followed, and none of the victims in this category indicated any wish for follow-up. Each told the counselor at the hospital that she would be fine. Either the counselor had failed to meet the victim's initial request or the victim had no further need for counseling.
5. Advice: "What should I do?" The victims with this request explicitly ask for alternatives or ask what to do about certain legal, social, physical, or psychologic problems related to rape. They regard the counselor as a person who could suggest possible alternatives and call the counselor with their questions.

Lazare et al. (1972) described the varying therapeutic responses to be made to rape victims. If the victim asked for confirmation, she needed to know what the counselor was thinking and feeling in order to check out her own perceptions. The victim who requests ventilation wants an interested and respectful listener. The victim who requests advice should be provided with alternative ways of handling a situation. The victim who requests clarification wants definite feedback on her progress and some possible reasons for her reactions and feelings.

In the acute phase of rape trauma, most victims request ventilation or confirmation of concern. These requests change, however, and may shift to clarification. The findings of Lazare et al. (1972) indicate that there is progression when the counseling is heard and regression when the request is not heard.

RAPE CRISIS CENTERS

During the early 1970s, community rape crisis centers began to emerge in the United States (McCombie et al., 1976; Peters, 1977). Many of the women most active in establishing these centers are rape victims themselves or friends of rape victims. These centers are organized by nonprofessional and professional women with the stated purpose of providing support services to rape victims. Most centers establish a 24-hour hot line with immediate information regarding the medical examination, police interrogation, and court procedures to be faced by the rape victim. The volunteers make themselves available to accompany the rape victim to the health facility, the police department, or the courts.

Counseling services are usually immediate and short term through group effort and referral to an individual counselor with skills in rape crisis. Women at the center help the rape victim with her difficult feelings and decisions after rape. The emphasis of the counseling is to foster the rape victim's return to independent functioning and control.

Education is a second goal of rape crisis centers. These centers offer education and training to other members and to the community in physical self-defense, assertiveness training, and precautionary measures that protect against rape and reduce vulnerability to rape. They also prepare and distribute information about what to do if rape occurs.

Rape crisis centers have actively participated in the training of law enforcement, medical, nursing, and legal personnel to increase their understanding of rape and the needs of rape victims. Through their efforts, some hospitals and communities have established special interdisciplinary teams to treat and work with rape victims. Rape crisis centers have been influential in changing rape-related legislation and personal and community attitudes about rape.

Nurses should be aware of and familiar with rape crisis programs and centers. They should be responsive to the community's effort to provide understanding of, belief in, and compassion for the woman who has been subjected to rape.

THE MEDICAL CARE PROCESS AND THE NURSE

The first need of the rape victim may be medical care. The goals of medical care are: (1) immediate care of injury, (2) medical examination with possible documentation for law enforcement agencies, (3) prevention of sexually transmitted diseases, (4) prevention of pregnancy, and (5) emotional support to alleviate both short- and long-term psychologic effects (Massey, Garcia, & Emich, 1971). The manner in which these goals are achieved varies from agency to agency; however, the approaches are designed to support the client's need to regain feelings of safety, control, autonomy, trust, self-esteem, and integrity.

The rape victim should be considered a high-priority client, and psychologic support is begun at the first contact. An environment of reduced stimuli is provided, and the victim is listened to and continuously attended. The involved personnel acknowledge the trauma of the rape, communicate acceptance and understanding, and encourage the client to talk about the rape. The victim is given information about the subsequent treatments and the personnel to be encountered, a description of the procedures that will follow, the rationale for these procedures, the risks involved, and the choices she has. Providing information is part of making the environment predictable and safe and returns to the victim the right to make decisions and the power to exercise control and experience autonomy.

Medicolegal Considerations

An informed consent for the medical examination should be obtained in written form from the victim. Although most state laws require that physicians report the crime of rape, victims are not required to do so. The victim is informed of the physician's reporting responsibilities and informed of her rights regarding reporting and interacting with law enforcement personnel. Evidence collection (part of the physical examination) and release of evidence cannot be done without special and separate written consents. When photographs are taken, an additional written consent must be obtained. The victim who is uncertain about or unwilling to report is advised that she may consent to collect the evidence but withhold consent for its release until a later date (Abarbanel, 1979).

During the medicolegal examination and collection of evidence, the nurse's primary focus is on the physical and emotional well-being of the victim, not on the determination of whether the rape did or did not occur. Since the evidence obtained may be used in a criminal court to strengthen or weaken the victim's claim of rape, however, meticulous care must be used in collecting physical evidence and in preparing complete, accurate, and objective records (Burgess & Laszlo, 1977; Halbert & Jones, 1978).

Hospitals and law enforcement agencies have jointly developed detailed guidelines outlining procedures to be followed. Evidence-collection kits containing instructions and materials needed to collect, label, and preserve specimens are used. The specimens, such as saline wet smear for sperm, sample pubic hairs, and fingernail scrapings, are preserved in strict accordance with the guidelines established. Specimens are placed separately in paper, and wet specimens are allowed to dry before packaging. In order for the physical evidence to be admissible in court, the chain of custody is carefully documented and each person who handles the evidence signs and notes the time and the date (Halbert & Jones, 1977).

The record must contain concise and precise objective and subjective data about the physical and emotional status of the victim and include a complete and succinct account of the rape incident using as many of the victim's words as possible (Burgess & Laszlo, 1977). The nurse records objective data on the general appearance and physical and emotional status of the victim, physical and gynecologic trauma noted, physical evidence collected, photographs taken, and behavioral evidence of emotional trauma experienced. The subjective data, collected from the victim, includes the circumstances of the assault, number of assailants, types and amount of sexual contact, description of and conversation with assailants, physical and verbal threats made, presence and use of weapons or objects, statements describing the physical and emotional trauma experienced, activities after the assault that might alter or remove evidence (change of clothing, bathing, douching, urinating, defecating), and use of drugs or alcohol (see the Nursing Process section of this chapter) (Abarbanel, 1979; Kolodny, Masters, & Johnson, 1979).

History, Physical Examination, and Laboratory Tests

The purpose of the history, physical examination, and laboratory work is to gather data for diagnosis and treatment. The victim is given information about the purpose and process of the procedures and encouraged to make decisions about choices and treatment. The procedures are performed in such a way that the victim exercises judgment and exerts control over the starting and stopping of any procedure that might be uncomfortable or threatening to her.

The history should include information about the client's state of general health, chronic diseases, current illnesses, allergies, assessment of physical trauma, date of last menses, menstrual history, contraceptive use, previously diagnosed sexually transmitted diseases, and date and type of last sexual contact before the assault. The pelvic examination is performed to assess internal injury; samples should be obtained of vaginal fluid for presence of sperm and acid phosphatase (a component of seminal fluid that would be present even if the man had no sperm); cultures should be obtained from the cervix, urethra, and anus for detecting gonorrhea; and pregnancy should be determined (Kolodny, Masters, & Johnson, 1979).

Laboratory tests include baseline VDRL, urine pregnancy test, and throat culture for gonorrhea if oral–genital contact was part of the assault. Blood specimens for alcohol or other drug levels are taken only if they are clinically indicated or requested by law enforcement personnel (Abarbanel, 1979).

Treatment

The pregnancy test performed shortly after the rape will determine only if the victim was already pregnant when the rape occurred. If the victim is at risk for pregnancy, the options to prevent or terminate a problem pregnancy are presented to her. These options include the use of a postcoital contraceptive drug, menstrual extraction, and induced abortion if pregnancy occurs. The decision about pregnancy prevention or termination is the responsibility of the victim, and it is her decision that is implemented. The nurse emphasizes the need for follow-up examination and testing in six to eight weeks regardless of the treatment option chosen.

Serologic tests for syphilis and cultures for gonococci will determine only if the diseases were already present at the time of the rape. Most victims want and are given prophylactic treatment, however. The drug of choice is procaine penicillin G by intramuscular injection, with probenecid by mouth, for this is effective against gonorrhea and incubating syphilis simultaneously (Abarbanel, 1979). The nurse needs to emphasize that it is essential for the victim to have follow-up tests for gonorrhea and syphilis and receive treatment if positive.

RAPE COUNSELING AND THE NURSE

Rape is recognized as a situational crisis. The counseling of rape victims is based on principles of crisis intervention and concepts learned through the study and analysis of the victim's perceptions and reactions to the crime of rape. The concepts employed are the coping behaviors of the rape victim, the rape trauma syndrome, age-specific stresses, and crisis and counseling requests (Burgess & Huntington, 1978; Burgess & Holmstrom, 1974a, 1974b, 1974c, 1976; Notman & Nadelson, 1976).

The counseling of rape victims requires that the nurse view the rape victim not as a sick person but as a person in crisis. Rape counseling assumes the victim is a normal person who has adequately managed her life before the rape crisis. Rape counseling is not psychotherapy, and if such a need is identified or requested, a referral is discussed and initiated.

The goal of rape counseling is to restore the victim to her previous level of functioning as quickly as possible. Rape counseling recognizes that the essential need of the victim is emotional support from whomever she comes in contact with during the crisis. Rape counseling is intended to facilitate the working through of trauma and to diminish the likelihood of long-term harmful consequences. Rape counseling pays attention to the victim's family and significant others, for they may have need of emotional support also.

The nurse-counselor's ability to listen for and attend to the victim's requests and awareness of the course and content of the rape trauma syndrome is needed for assessment and planning with the victim. Information about the possible and expected sequelae of the rape can provide a framework for the victim to understand the experience and feel control. But the counselor's most significant responsibility is to be an available, accessible, and accepting listener time and time again as the victim grapples with and comes to psychologic terms with the crisis of rape. If the victim has decided to prosecute, the time before the court appearance may be difficult. The victim may experience feelings of worthlessness and be or feel alone. This may be the time the nurse-counselor is most helpful (Burgess & Huntington, 1978).

Support from husband, family, friends, and significant others is important for the victim's return to a normal life. For these people, the nurse-counselor can provide information about the nature of rape and the victim's anticipated psychologic reactions. The counselor can promote communication, clarify the emotional needs of the victim's significant others, and assist them in identifying their role in helping the victim. Providing information about community resources is a responsibility the nurse-counselor has to the victim and her significant others as well.

All recent reports agree that rape victims need immediate crisis counseling and that continued formal or informal counseling may be necessary for as long as twelve months. Hayman and Lanza (1971) reported a follow-up program in which rape victims were visited in their homes primarily by public health nurses and secondarily by mental health workers, especially in the first 90 days after the rape. Burgess and Holmstrom (1974c), through telephone contact, made themselves available for counseling on a weekly basis until there was evidence of stabilization.

The care of the rape victim requires acquiring knowledge about the crime of rape, developing special and specific medicolegal skills, focusing on crisis intervention, and attending to the acute and long-term counseling needs of these victim-clients.

NURSING PROCESS

Client: Amanda Humphreys, 26-year-old woman, walk-in client of emergency room of voluntary hospital in city of 35,000 people.

Nurse: Elaine Leininger-Bridges, nurse, trained to work with sexually assaulted people.

Assessment

Subjective Data

Circumstances of Assault

"I was just raped."
"It happened in the bushes right in front of my apartment house."
"I took the bus home from the Saturday night movies—must have been about 12:30 a.m."

Number of Assailants

"This man—he came up from behind me and grabbed me by the throat almost before I knew he was there."

Types and Amount of Sexual Contact

"He forced me to have sex with him."
"He put it in me—in the front."
"I don't know if he came. I just don't know."

Description of Assailant

"He seemed big—much taller than I—about six feet."
"He had dark, crazy-looking eyes."
"He had a heavy gold ring on his right hand, and a couple of them on the other."

"He wore blue jeans, a blue-jean jacket too, and a dirty gray sweatshirt."
"He was very suntanned."
"His hair was black and he had long sideburns."
"He ran down West Curry Street—that's all I know."

Conversation with Assailant

Assailant:
"Don't ask questions, just do as you are told."
"Take off your clothes. Take off your pants."
"Hurry up or I'll slap you some more."
"A couple more kicks should get you in line."
"I know you. I know where you work and where you live."
Victim:
"Who are you? What do you want?"
"You can have my money and my purse—take my rings and jewelry."
"Please don't hurt me."
"Please don't do this."

Physical and Verbal Threats Made

"Don't scream or I'll cut up on you."
"If you like living, you'll do as you're told."
"Hurry up or I'll kick you some more."
"If you tell anybody, I'll kill you."

Presence and Use of Weapons

"He had a pocket knife in his left hand."
"He slashed it against my forehead—my shoulder too."

Statements Describing Physical and Emotional Trauma

"He grabbed my neck and choked me. I couldn't scream, I could hardly
    breathe."
"He let go of my neck and grabbed my arm and twisted it."
"He shoved me into the bushes and kicked my back and legs and punched
    my chest and stomach."
"I fell down and he jumped on top of me."
"I struggled until I realized I couldn't stop him."
"He ripped off my underwear."
"I kept hoping somebody would pass by—or hear."
"I thought he was going to kill me."
"I can remember thinking 'Dear God, please let me live.'"
"I'm cut. I feel broken inside."

Activities after Assault

"I don't know how long I lay there."
"I felt myself crying and I saw my purse and underwear on the ground."
"I was afraid to go to my apartment."
"I picked up my things and walked here—six blocks, I think."

Crisis Requests

"I need a doctor—I'm cut."
"Is there a policeman here? Maybe I should talk to one."
"I want to call my grandmother and boyfriend, but what will I tell them?"

Objective Data

General Appearance

26-year-old woman dressed in green dress, left side of shirt and right
  sleeve torn. Hose have holes and runs at knees. Sitting in chair.
  Holding purse and torn underwear in lap.

Physical Status

T 99, P 90, R 25, B/P 130/80
Face—2-cm laceration on right side of forehead; ¼-cm laceration on left
  side of upper lip; multiple bruises with swelling and redness, espe-
  cially on left cheek and jaw
Shoulder—3-cm laceration on right shoulder
Neck—multiple bruises with redness and swelling prominent on right
  side of neck
Knees—abrasions with redness and swelling on both knees
Legs—multiple bruises on both calves
No signs of alcohol. No signs of recreational drugs.
Not on medication
LMP—10 days ago
Diaphragm used for contraception
Last intercourse 5 days before assault

Emotional Status

Volunteered information, answered questions, gave details.
Voice monotone, speech slow.
Crying when first seen. Crying stopped when police intervention sought.
Deep sighing as she talks. Clutching at handbag and underwear.
Expressed fear of bodily harm.
Expressed fear for life.

Psychosocial Information

Single, lives alone, has lived in city three years.
Speech and hearing therapist in local school system.
Parents killed in automobile accident two years ago.
Grandmother only family member in city.
Boyfriend on business trip, expected back in three days.

Nursing Diagnosis

Acute physical and emotional reaction due to trauma of sexual assault.

Planning

Emotional Support

Identify self as counselor of sexually assaulted people.
Listen attentively, attend constantly, and touch judiciously.
Provide atmosphere of acceptance, reduced stimuli, and limit people to be
    encountered.
Explain emergency service's protocol for sexually assaulted person.
Encourage expression of feelings.
Offer feedback of client's expressed feelings.
Recognize need for unique personal adjustment to stressful situation.
Identify and support client's coping behaviors.
Encourage questions.
Arrange situations that encourage client autonomy.
Encourage sharing of stressful situation with significant others.
Encourage mobilization of support systems.
Provide anticipatory guidance about commonly occurring physical, men-
    tal, and emotional reactions after sexual assault.
Provide information about community Rape Crisis Center.
Explain follow-up counseling of emergency service.
Offer counseling for significant others.
Identify and respond to counseling requests.
Arrange transportation to place of physical and emotional safety.

Medical Examination and Treatment

Arrange for medical support and treatment.
Provide information about medical history and examination.
Obtain written permission for medical examination.

Prevention of Sexually Transmitted Disease

Explain laboratory tests for sexually transmitted diseases.
Explain treatment for prevention of sexually transmitted diseases.
Emphasize need for follow-up examination.

Possible Problem Pregnancy

Explain laboratory tests for pregnancy.
Explain options available for pregnancy prevention or termination.
Emphasize need for follow-up examination.

Law Enforcement Intervention

Arrange for making report to police.
Explain collection and release of physical evidence and photography.
Obtain written permission for collection and release of physical evidence
    and photography.

Implementation

Emotional Support

Telephone Megan and Jim Merryman (sister and brother-in-law of boy-
    friend Don Ryder) for transportation home.
Telephone grandmother (Mrs. Billings) and ask for help and assistance.
Attempt to make telephone contact with Don Ryder (boyfriend) and ask
    him to return early from business trip.
Telephone principal at school and arrange sick leave.
Consider calling Rape Crisis Center.
Anticipate hearing from counselor in 48 hours.
Call counselor for support when needed.

Medical Examination and Treatment

Consent for medical examination signed.
2-cm laceration on right side of forehead sutured.

3-cm laceration on right shoulder sutured.
Darvon 65 mgm by mouth for generalized pain and discomfort taken.
    Prescription for medication received.
Medical history taken.
Medical examination done.
Consent for collection of physical evidence for law enforcement agency
    signed.
Physical evidence (vaginal smear and washing, sample pubic hair, pubic
    hair combings, fingernail scrapings) collected.
Consent for photography not signed.

Prevention of Sexually Transmitted Disease

Laboratory tests—GC cultures and serology—done.
4.8 million units of procaine penicillin I.M. with 1 gram probenecid
    by mouth received.
Follow-up examination scheduled.

Possible Problem Pregnancy

Pregnancy test done.
First dose of diethylstilbesterol 25 mgm BID for 5 days taken.
Follow-up examination scheduled.

Law Enforcement Intervention

Physical evidence collected during medical examination released directly
    to police.
Report of sexual assault made to police.

Evaluation

Telephone contact—48 hours postassault

"I was hoping you would call."
"Physical soreness still pretty bad."

"Eating a little and sleeping OK, but some bad dreams."

"Feeling some nausea from DES."

"Grandmother very good to me and here with me a lot."

"Megan and Jim have come to help and talk, that's good."

"Unable to make contact with Don, but he's expected home tomorrow."

"Principal was shocked, but he approved time off."

"Maybe when Don gets home, you'll talk to him too?"

"Do you think the women at the Crisis Center could help?"

"And the police—will there be much more with them?"

BIBLIOGRAPHY

Abarbanel, G. The sexual assault patient. In R. Green (Ed.), *Human sexuality: A health practitioner's text* (2nd ed.). Baltimore: Williams & Wilkins, 1979.

Abel, G. G., Barlow, D. H., Blanchard, E. D., & Guild, D. The components of rapist's sexual arousal. *Archives of General Psychiatry*, 1977, *34*, 895–903.

Amir, M. *Patterns of forcible rape.* Chicago: University of Chicago Press, 1971.

Bard, M., & Ellison, K. Crisis intervention and investigation of forcible rape. *The Police Chief*, 1974, *41*, 68–73.

Bohmer, C., & Blumberg, A. Twice traumatized—the rape victim and the court. *Judicature*, 1975, *58*, 391.

Brownmiller, S. *Against our will: Men, women and rape.* New York: Simon & Schuster, 1975.

Burgess, A. W., & Holmstrom, L. L. The rape victim in the emergency ward. *American Journal of Nursing*, 1973, *73*, 1741–1745.

Burgess, A. W., & Holmstrom, L. L. Crisis and counseling requests of rape victims. *Nursing Research*, 1974, *3*, 196–202. (a)

Burgess, A. W., & Holmstrom, L. L. Rape trauma syndrome. *American Journal of Psychiatry*, 1974, *131*, 981–986. (b)

Burgess, A. W., & Holmstrom, L. L. Coping behavior of the rape victim. *American Journal of Psychiatry*, 1976, *133*, 413–417.

Burgess, A. W., & Holmstrom, L. L. *Rape: Victims of crisis.* Bowee, Maryland: Robert J. Brady, 1974. (c)

Burgess, A. W., & Huntington, J. Rape counseling: Perspectives of victim and nurse. In M. V. Barnard, B. J. Clancy, & K. E. Krantz, *Human sexuality for health professionals.* Philadelphia: Saunders, 1978.

Burgess, A. W., & Laszlo, A. T. Courtroom use of hospital records in sexual assault cases. *American Journal of Nursing*, 1977, *77*, 64–68.

Campbell, C. *Nursing diagnosis and intervention in nursing practice.* New York: Wiley, 1978.

Center for Women Policy Studies. *Rape and its victims: A report for citizens, health facilities, and criminal justice agencies.* Washington, D.C.: Law Enforcement Assistance Administration, 1975.

Clark, T. P. Counseling victims of rape. *American Journal of Nursing*, 1976, *76*, 1964–1966.

Evrard, J. Rape: The medical, social and legal implications. *American Journal of Obstetrics and Gynecology*, 1971, *111*, 197–199.

Federal Bureau of Investigation. *Uniform crime reports of the United States.* Washington, D.C.: U.S. Government Printing Office, 1978.

Felice, M. Follow-up counseling of adolescent rape victims. *Medical Aspects of Human Sexuality*, 1980, *14*, 67–68.

Gates, M. J. The rape victim on trial. Paper presented at Special Session on Rape, American Psychiatric Association, Anaheim, California, 1975.

Giacinti, T. A., & Tjaden, C. *The crime of rape in Denver.* Denver, Colorado: Denver Anti-Crime Council, 1973.

Griffin, S. Rape: The all-American crime. *Ramparts,* 1971, *10*, 26–35.

Groth, A. N., & Burgess, A. W. Rape: A sexual deviation. *American Journal of Orthopsychiatry,* 1977, *47*, 400–406. (a)

Groth, A. N., & Burgess, A. W. Sexual dysfunction during rape. *New England Journal of Medicine*, 1977, *297*, 764–766. (b)

Groth, A. N., Burgess, A. W., & Holmstrom, L. L. Rape: Power, anger, and sexuality. *American Journal of Psychiatry*, 1977, *134*, 1239–1243.

Halbert, D. R., & Jones, D. E. Medical management of the sexually assaulted woman. *The Journal of Reproductive Medicine*, 1978, *20*, 265–274.

Hayman, C. R., & Lanza, C. Sexual assault on women and girls. *American Journal of Obstetrics and Gynecology*, 1971, *109*, 480–486.

Hibey, R. A. The trial of a rape case: An advocate's analysis of corroboration, consent, and character. In L. G. Schultz (Ed.), *Rape victimology.* Springfield, Ill.: Charles C Thomas, 1975.

Hilberman, E. Rape: "The ultimate violation of self." *American Journal of Psychiatry*, 1976, *133*, 436; 437. (a)

Hilberman, E. *The rape victim.* Washington, D.C.: American Psychiatric Association Committee on Women, 1976. (b)

Hilberman, E. The impact of rape. In M. T. Notman & C. C. Nadelson (Eds.), *Sexual and reproductive aspects of women's health care* (Vol. 1). New York: Plenum Press, 1978.

Holmstrom, L. L., & Burgess, A. W. Assessing trauma in the rape victim. *American Journal of Nursing*, 1975, *75*, 1288–1291.

Jones, C., & Aronson, E. Attribution of fault to a rape victim as a function of respectability of the victim. *Journal of Personality and Social Psychology*, 1973, *26*, 415–419.

Kalven, H., & Zeisel, H. *The American jury.* Chicago: The University of Chicago Press, 1971.

Kolodny, R. C., Masters, W. H., & Johnson, V. E. *Textbook of sexual medicine.* Boston: Little, Brown, 1979.

Lazare, A., Cohen, F., Jacobsen, A. M., Williams, M. W., Mignone, R. J., & Zisook, S. The walk-in patient as a "customer": A key dimension in evaluation and treatment. *American Journal of Orthopsychiatry*, 1972, *42,* 872–883.

McCartney, C. F. Counseling the husband and wife after the woman has been raped. *Medical Aspects of Human Sexuality*, 1980, *14*, 121–122.

McCombie, S. D., Bassuk, E., Saritz, R., & Pell, S. Development of a medical center rape crisis intervention program. *American Journal of Psychiatry*, 1976, *133*, 418–421.

MacNamara, D. E. J., & Sagarin, E. *Sex, crime, and the law.* New York: Free Press, 1977.

Massey, J. B., Carcia, C. R., & Emich, J. P. Management of sexually assaulted females. *Obstetrics and Gynecology*, 1971, *38*, 29–36.

Masters, W. H., & Johnson, V. E. *Human sexual inadequacy.* Boston: Little, Brown, 1970.

Medea, A., & Thompson, K. *Against rape: A survival manual for women.* New York: Farrar, Straus, & Giroux, 1974.

Metzger, D. It is always the woman who is raped. *American Journal of Psychiatry*, 1976, *133*, 405–408.

Nadelson, C. C. Rapist and victim. *New England Journal of Medicine*, 1977, *297*, 784–785.

Notman, M., & Nadelson, C. C. The rape victim: Psychodynamic considerations. *American Journal of Psychiatry*, 1976, *134*, 408–412.

Pepitone-Rockwell, F. Counseling women to be less vulnerable to rape. *Medical Aspects of Human Sexuality*, 1980, *14*, 150–151.

Peters, J. J. The Philadelphia rape victim project. In D. Chappell, R. Geis, & G. Geis (Eds.), *Forcible rape.* New York: Columbia University Press, 1977.

Plant, J., & Wood, E. Involvement grows in audit activities, rape treatment. *Hospitals*, 1977, *51*, 107–112.

Queen's Bench Foundation. *Rape: Prevention and resistance.* San Francisco: Queen's Bench Foundation, 1976.

Ryan, W. *Blaming the victim.* New York: Random House, 1971.

Schultz, L. G. (Ed.). *Rape victimology.* Springfield, Ill.: Charles C Thomas, 1975.

Silverman, D. First do no more harm: Female rape victims and the male counselor. *American Journal of Orthopsychiatry*, 1977, *47*, 91–96.

Slovenko, R. *Psychiatry and law.* Boston: Little, Brown, 1973.

Soules, M. R., Stewart, S. K., Brown, K. M., & Pollard, A. A. The spectrum of alleged rape. *Journal of Reproductive Medicine*, 1978, *20*, 33–39.

Sutherland, S., & Scherl, D. Patterns of response among victims of rape. *American Journal of Orthopsychiatry*, 1970, *40,* 503–511.

Symonds, M. The rape victim: Psychological patterns of response. *The American Journal of Psychoanalysis,* 1976, *36*, 27–34.

Symonds, M. Victims of violence: Psychological effects and aftereffects. *The American Journal of Psychoanalysis*, 1975, *35,* 19–26.

Tietze, C. Problems of pregnancy resulting from a single unprotected coitus. *Fertility and Sterility*, 1960, *11*, 485–488.

Voight, J. Sexual offenses in Copenhagen: A medical study. *Forensic Science*, 1972, *1*, 67–76.

Weiss, K. *What the rape victim should know about the "morning after" pill.* Houston, Texas: Advocates for Medical Information, 1975.

Weiss, K., & Borges, S. Victimology and rape: The case of the legitimate victim. *Issues in Criminology*, 1973, *8*, 71–115.

Wood, P. L. The victim in a forcible rape case: A feminist view. In L. G. Schultz (Ed.), *Rape victimology*. Springfield, Ill.: Charles C Thomas, 1975.

Woodling, B. A., Evans, J. R., & Brodbury, M. D. Sexual assault: Rape and molestation. *Clinical Obstetrics and Gynecology*, 1977, *20*, 509–530.

Woods, N. F. *Human sexuality in health and illness* (2nd ed.). St. Louis: Mosby, 1979.

Index

Abortion, 300. *See also* Induced
  abortion
Absolute infertility (sterility), 245.
  See also Infertility
Absolute primary orgasmic dysfunction, 216-217
Abstinence, 129
  aging, 152
Adolescent sexuality, 69-70
  contraceptive use, 79, 81, 86-87, 90,
    92
  decision-making process, 99-100
  homosexuality, 87-88, 243-244,
    248
  induced abortion, 315-318
  masturbation, 83
  nurse's role, 96-101
  nursing process, 101-104
  petting, 83-84
  pregnancy, 75, 81, 85-86, 90, 95-96
  premarital sex, 83-85, 89-90, 91
  psychosexual development, 72-73
    biologic gender, 73
    body image, 73-74
    cognitive development, 81
    factors affecting, 80-82
    gender identity, 74-75
    gender of partner preference, 75-
      78
    parents, 80-81, 100-101
    sexual identity, 79
    sexual self-concept, 80
    sexual value system, 78-79, 88-92,
      99
  puberty, 70-72
  sex education, 92-94
  sexual health history, 30
  sexually transmitted diseases, 349
  socioeconomic status, 94-96

values clarification, 67-68
Adult sexuality, 112
  climacteric, 121-123
  cohabitation, 132-133
  life cycle, 111
  masturbation, 120-121
  menopause, 121-122, 136-139
  nurse's role, 135-136
  nursing process, 136-139
  sexual fantasies, 123-124
  sexual outlet frequency, 124-125
  sexual response cycle, 112-114
    male and female differences in,
      116-117
    physiologic changes during, 114-
      116
  values clarification exercise, 109-110
  see also Aging; Intercourse; Marriage
Aging, sexuality and, 112, 144
  hormone replacement therapy, 155
  intercourse, 158, 161-163
  intervention for effective, 157-159
  masturbation, 149, 152, 154, 159
  nurse's role, 161
  nursing-home residents, 159-160
  nursing process, 161-163
  sexlessness, as myth, 145
  sexual behavior, 155-157
  sexual changes, 146
  sexual response cycle:
    men, 150-151, 152-155
    women, 146-152
  values clarification, 143-144
Alcohol consumption, sexual function,
  332-333
Ambisexuality, 182
Amniocentesis abortion, 302, 305, 320
Amphetamine, sexual function, 334
Amyl nitrate, sexual function, 333-334

485

Pediculosis pubis (pubic lice), *see* Sexually transmitted diseases
Pelvic examination, of women, 32-34
Pelvic surgery, *see* Hysterectomy; Oophorectomy
Penile prostheses, 384-385
  ostomy and, 410-411
Penile tumescence, nocturnal (NPT), 383
Penis:
  penectomy (removal), 413
  size of, 118
Perineum, physical examination of, 35
Permissiveness with/without affection, 129
Petting, 124
  adolescence, 83-84
Peyronie's disease, 218-219
Phenotype, 48
Phimosis, 218
Physical examination, 31-32
  breast and pelvic examination of women, 32-34
  genitorectal examination of men, 34-35
Planning, assessment, 25
Plateau phase, 112, 115, 116-117
  aging, 148, 149, 151, 153
  during pregnancy, 260
Postpartum sexuality, 278-281
  sexual response, 275, 278
Power rape, 452
Predatory rapists, 456
Pregnancy, sexuality, 259, 261-265, 266, 267
  adolescent, 75, 81, 85-86, 90, 95-96
  body image, 265, 268
  cesarean section, 281, 290-292
  childbirth education classes, 290
  cigarette smoking, 332
  closeness need, 268-269
  diabetes mellitus, 387
  effect of, 281
  gonorrhea, 351
  herpes progenitalis type II, 356
  husband's reactions, 284-286
  intercourse during, 263, 269-273, 289
  intrapartum sexuality, 275, 276-277
  masturbation during, 273
  nurse's role, 289-290
  nursing process, 290-292
  orgasm during, 260-261, 262-263, 273-274

postpartum sexuality, 275, 278-281
rape, 462
sexual history, 286-288
sexual response during, 259-261
spinal cord injury, 432-433
stoma, 411
values clarification, 257
venereal warts, 356-357
see also Breast-feeding; Induced abortion
Premarital intercourse:
  adolescence, 83-85, 89-90, 91
  adults, 129-130
Premature ejaculation, 206-209, 223-225
Prematurity, orgasm during pregnancy, 273-274
Prenatal sexual development, problems in, 48-49
Priapism, 218
Primary erectile dysfunction, 203
Primary general sexual dysfunction, 212-213
Primary orgasmic dysfunction, 214
  absolute, 216-217
Primary retarded ejaculation, 209
Problem pregnancy, 300. *See also* Induced abortion
Progesterone:
  in birth control pill, 235
  menopause and, 121
Prostate:
  female, 117
  physical examination for, 35
  prostatectomy, 413-415
Prostatectomy, sexuality, 413-415
Prostitutes, fetishism, 177
Psychogenic erection, spinal cord injury and, 430, 431, 434
Psychogenic impotence, 382-383
Psychosexual continuum, 52
Psychosexual development, adulthood, 111. *See also* Adolescent sexuality
Puberty, adolescent sexuality, 70-72
Pubic lice, *see* Sexually transmitted diseases
Pubococcygeus (PC) muscle, Kegel exercises for, 290

Quadriplegia, 430. *See also* Spinal cord injury